1 MONTH OF FREE READING

at

www.ForgottenBooks.com

By purchasing this book you are eligible for one month membership to ForgottenBooks.com, giving you unlimited access to our entire collection of over 1,000,000 titles via our web site and mobile apps.

To claim your free month visit:
www.forgottenbooks.com/free788384

* Offer is valid for 45 days from date of purchase. Terms and conditions apply.

ISBN 978-1-5282-8203-1
PIBN 10788384

This book is a reproduction of an important historical work. Forgotten Books uses state-of-the-art technology to digitally reconstruct the work, preserving the original format whilst repairing imperfections present in the aged copy. In rare cases, an imperfection in the original, such as a blemish or missing page, may be replicated in our edition. We do, however, repair the vast majority of imperfections successfully; any imperfections that remain are intentionally left to preserve the state of such historical works.

Forgotten Books is a registered trademark of FB &c Ltd.
Copyright © 2018 FB &c Ltd.
FB &c Ltd, Dalton House, 60 Windsor Avenue, London, SW19 2RR.
Company number 08720141. Registered in England and Wales.

For support please visit www.forgottenbooks.com

Breviary Offices

FROM LAUDS TO COMPLINE INCLUSIVE

Translated and arranged for use

FROM THE SARUM BOOK.

SECOND EDITION.

London:
J. T. HAYES, 17, HENRIETTA STREET, COVENT GARDEN.
MDCCCLXXX.

Ut obsequium servitutis nostrae rationabile facias:
Te rogamus, audi nos.

TABLE OF CONTENTS.

	Page
Preface	vii
General Rubrics	ix
Notes on the Kalendar	xxii
Prayers before and after Office	1

Psalter.

Lauds:	Sunday	3
	Monday	10
	Tuesday	14
	Wednesday	15
	Thursday	17
	Friday	19
	Saturday	21
Prime		25
Tierce		38
Sexts		41
Nones		44
Vespers:	Sunday	47
	Monday	51
	Tuesday	54
	Wednesday	55
	Thursday	57
	Friday	60
	Saturday	63
Compline		67

Proper of Seasons.

Advent	75
Christmas	89
Epiphany	112
Septuagesima	124
Lent	129
Passion-tide	149
Easter	162
Ascension-tide	178
Whitsun-tide	184
Trinity	191
Corpus Christi	193
Sundays after Trinity	197

Common of Saints.

	Page
Commemoration of B. V. M.	210
Common of Apostles in Easter-tide	212
Common of a Martyr or Confessor in Easter-tide	214
Common of Apostles through the year	214
Common of a Martyr through the year	217
Common of Many Martyrs through the year	219
Common of a Bishop and Confessor through the year	222
Common of an Abbot or Monk through the year	224
Common of a Virgin and Martyr	226
Common of a Virgin not Martyr	228
Common of a Matron	229
Dedication of a Church	230
Common Memorials of Saints	235

Proper of Saints.

S. Andrew	238
Conception of B. V. M.	240
S. Thomas	242
S. Agnes	244
Conversion of S. Paul	245
Purification of B. V. M.	248
S. Matthias	251
Annunciation of B. V. M.	253
S. Mark	256
SS. Philip and James	256
Invention of the Cross	258
S. John before the Latin Gate	260
S. Barnabas	262
S. John Baptist	263
SS. Peter and Paul	266
Commemoration of S. Paul	267
Octave of S. John Baptist	269
Visitation of B. V. M.	270
Octave of SS. Peter and Paul	272

CONTENTS.

	Page		Page
Octave of the Visitation	273	Holy Guardian Angels	296
S. Margaret	274	S. Luke	300
S. Mary Magdalene	274	SS. Simon and Jude	300
S. James	276	All Saints	301
S. Peter's Chains	277	All Souls	303
Transfiguration	278	Octave of All Saints	304
Holy Name of Jesus	281		
S. Laurence	284	**Occasional Offices.**	
Octave of the Holy Name	285	Preparation for Holy Communion	306
Repose of B. V. M.	286	Thanksgiving for Holy Communion	312
S. Bartholomew	288	Gradual Psalms and Litany	315
Beheading of S. John Baptist	289	Penitential Psalms	322
Nativity of B. V. M.	290	Commendatory Office	329
Exaltation of the Cross	291	Office of the Dead	334
S. Matthew	292	Itinerary	350
S. Michael and All Angels	294	Table of Moveable Feasts	353

ERRATA.

Kalendar. On September 1, *insert* 'S. Giles, Bp. and Conf.'

Page	col.	line	
162	1	2	*for* 'gave poisonous kisses' *read* 'drew nigh with feigned sweetness.'
208	1		under line 21 *insert* 'This R. serves till second Sunday in September.'
208	2	6	*dele* 'This R. serves till.'
208	2	34	
211	1	5	*for* 'femina' *read* 'fœmina.'
217	2	6	from bottom *for* 'Sanctorum meritis, p. 220,' *read* 'Martyr Dei qui Unicum, p. 289.'
239	2	11	from bottom, *for* 'All of the Common' *read* 'Memorial.'*
239	2	10	from bottom, *for* '224' *read* '236.'*
240	2	22	and 23 from top, *for* 'come over' *read* 'cover': *for* 'nation' *read* 'nations.'
243	2		*dele* lines 20, 21, 26, 39.
244	1	22	from bottom, *dele* *.
247	1		*dele* line 5 from bottom.
251	1		under line 6 *insert* 'in case of keeping this Feast.'
251	2		*dele* line 20 from bottom.
251	2	5	from bottom, *for* '8' *read* '7.'
252	2		*dele* lines 13, 14, 29 : line 10 from bottom, *dele* 'Both.'
253	1		*dele* lines 5, 6, 12.
255	1		*dele* bottom line and 6 from bottom.
255	2		*dele* lines 6, 20.
262	2	11	and 27, *dele* 'after Hymn.'
266	2	28	after 'eternity' } *insert* 'Amen.'
270	2	36	after 'tear'
271	2	41	after 'ever'
273	2	7	from bottom and in running title, *for* 'John Guaibert' *read* 'S. John Gualbert.'
276	2	22	from bottom, after 'MARY' *insert* '*.'
277	1		under line 23 *insert* 'This verse precedes.'
290	1		under line 12 *insert* { 'September 1. S. GILES, BISHOP AND CONFESSOR. Memorial of a Bishop and Confessor, p. 236.'
292	2	23	*for* 'times' *read* 'temples.'
293	1	6	
296	2	5	from bottom, *for* 'psaltimus' *read* 'psallimus.'
299	2	19	and 10 from bottom, *dele* 'after Hymn.'
300	1	9	after 'ABBESS' *insert* '*.'

* Corresponding corrections needed under the name of every Saint marked *.

PREFACE.

"THAT a community of women should offer to the English Church a new book of Offices, appears presumptuous as well as unnecessary, unless some explanation be given of the causes which led to the attempt. S. Margaret's Sisterhood, founded by the Rev. J. M. Neale, in 1854, was early provided with a MS. translation, abridged and simplified, of the shorter Sarum Hours, and with various other Offices, selected from Roman or Gallican uses, where Sarum was insufficient or apparently unsatisfactory. For although Dr. Neale considered the Sarum book as that of which the adoption was generally binding upon us, he preferred a degree of eclecticism to a servile following of the old English use, when better Offices were to be found elsewhere.

"Other persons, aware of our possessing many MSS., asked us to prepare a book which should supply Offices yet wanting in existing manuals, and provide abundance of materials for devotion from which they might select portions suitable for use. We have thus endeavoured to respond to their request, and the present volume is the careful, but very imperfect result of our labours, containing, besides much supplementary matter, the Breviary Offices from Prime to Compline inclusive, Matins being already in course of publication separately.

"In this compilation, our founder's plan has been retained: *i.e.* Sarum has been followed wherever possible. The Psalter, and Proper of Seasons exactly reproduce Sarum, with a few abbreviations and simplifications; except a few alterations mentioned below.*

"If it be asked why the Roman books would not suffice us, and why we should try to resuscitate a use long dead, we answer that the Gallican breviaries present us with rich and varied treasures of Scriptural applications and mystical interpretations, which might be sought vainly in the Roman forms; and that Sarum far surpasses Rome in the dignity and variety of its daily office; in its absence of unseemly haste (as when Rome continually replaces longer Psalms by Ps. cxvii.) and in its sedulous and hearty use of continual intercession for living and dead."

---

* The Christmas Eve Vesper Hymn is continued through the Octave, as in the York Breviary, instead of, as in Sarum, using *A solis ortus* both at Lauds and Vespers. The proper Office of S. Thomas of Canterbury is changed for the Common of a Martyr, the Antiphon, ℣. and ℟. to the Memorial, being all that are retained from the original. The Saturday Ants. after Trinity are from the Roman Breviary: because it was necessary to take the lectionary for Matins from that source, and those Ants. must agree with the lectionary of the current month. It should be added, that, also according to Dr. Neale's usage, in accordance with the present custom of the English Church, invocations of Saints and Angels are as a rule omitted, except when occurring in Psalms, Canticles, etc.

With such words the first edition of the Diurnal Breviary Offices was offered for the use of the Church. It proved acceptable beyond expectation, and a new impression was soon called for. Several men versed in the subject had now become interested in this book, and it was pointed out by them that certain alterations, bringing it into still closer accordance with the Sarum Breviary, would render it more valuable, trustworthy, and suitable for English use. The Offices for the Proper and Common of Saints had mostly been translated from French uses. Further study revealed merits in the equivalent Sarum Offices, which had previously been unperceived, and it was decided to remodel these portions of the book.* The preface to the concluding volume of the Night Hours (that volume having been arranged in accordance with these Diurnal Offices) contains a list of the divergencies from Sarum, still retained: which also may be clearly seen by comparison with the new Latin edition of the Great Breviary of 1531, now in course of publication at Cambridge. It should be added that the Office for the Dead is indicated for monthly recitation, according to the modern Roman practice, as its daily use after the old English manner would probably be deemed excessive; and that the Commendatory Office is Gallican and Benedictine.

The Prefatory Notes to the Kalendar explain the principle on which a number of new names have been added to it.

Owing to illness and absence, the original compiler was unable to finish her work. The publication of this edition has therefore been greatly delayed. We now once more send out our book, with many thanks to the kind and learned persons who have assisted us (particularly the Revs. H. G. Morse, A. T. Chapman, W. J. Blew, and G. Moultrie (the latter of whom has given most happy translations of several beautiful hymns); and with the humble prayer that our Lord may be pleased to let it contribute in its small measure to His honour and glory.

S. Margaret's, East Grinsted.
    Lent, 1880.

---

* An Antiphoner of 1519—20, in the British Museum, in admirable preservation and readily accessible, contains the whole of the Vesper music throughout the year, according to the use of Sarum.

GENERAL RUBRICS.

(SARUM.)

ADVENT.—If any Feast, not being a Principal or Greater Double, fall on any Sunday in Advent, it is transferred to Monday, and on Sunday are said first Vespers of the Feast, with Memorial of Sunday.[1] If on Monday, on Sunday are said first Vespers of the Feast. If on Saturday, Vespers are of the Feast, except the Saturday before Advent Sunday, when the first Vespers of Sunday are said, with Memorial of the Feast. Any Feast, which is the Feast of the place, falling on the first Sunday, is transferred to Monday, though on the other Sundays it is not transferred, but the whole office is said on its own day. On all Feasts in Advent a Memorial of the Feria is made at Lauds and both Vespers.

CANDLEMAS.—If Candlemas Day fall on Sunday, the whole Office is of the Feast, with Memorial of the Sunday. This applies to Septuagesima and Sexagesima. If on Monday, its first Vespers are said on Sunday. If on Saturday, the second Vespers of the Feast supersede the first Vespers of Sunday.

LENT.—On all Feasts kept in Lent, a Memorial of the Fast is made at Lauds and both Vespers. Lent Compline is not altered for any Feast, except that on the Annunciation the hymn takes the Christmas doxology.

From Ash Wednesday till Passion Sunday, Simple Feasts of the three first classes are observed with Memorial of the Feria. Simples of the fourth class are marked by a Memorial in place of first Vespers and Lauds, but are not otherwise noticed. Simples of the three first classes falling between Passion Sunday and Maundy Thursday may be transferred till the Octave of Easter.

From Passion Sunday till the morrow of Low Sunday no notice is taken of any Simple Feasts, but only of Doubles, and of these, only till Maundy Thursday. If any Double Feast fall on the Saturday before Passion or Palm Sunday, Vespers are to be of the Sunday, with solemn Memorial of the Feast.

If the Annunciation falls on any Sunday, including Palm Sunday, it is transferred to Monday, and in this case, and also when it falls on Monday, on Sunday are said first Vespers of the Feast. If it falls on Saturday, Vespers are of the Feast; except the Saturday before Passion or Palm Sunday, on which two days Vespers are of Sunday.

But if it be the Feast of the place, the whole Office is said on its own day, unless it be Passion or Palm Sunday, in which case it is transferred to Monday: the first Vespers being said on Sunday.

If it falls on Wednesday in Holy Week, the Office is of the Feast, but its second Vespers are superseded by first Vespers of Maundy Thursday.

On Tuesday in Holy Week the Office of the Dead is said throughout, unless prevented by a Double Feast, in which case it is said, if possible, on the day before. No Feasts are celebrated on or after Thursday in Holy Week; but Double Feasts and Simples of the three first classes are transferred to any convenient day after the Octave of Easter; Simple Feasts of the fourth class are omitted for that year.

(When the Feast of S. Edward (March 18) fell between Passion Sunday and

Easter Day it was omitted, not transferred; and the Translation of S. Edward (June 20) was kept for that year with two Vespers instead of one.)

EASTER-TIDE includes the season from Easter Day till Nones on Saturday in Whitsun Week inclusive. Feasts above the lowest class occurring in Easter Week, or on the three days preceding, are transferred to Tuesday after the Octave, or other convenient day, such that they can have both Vespers. Simple Feasts of the fourth class are omitted for that year. This same order serves for Whitsun Week. If a Double Feast occurs on Low Sunday it is transferred to Monday; if on Rogation Sunday, it is kept. Simple Feasts above the fourth rank occurring on either of these Sundays are transferred. If any Double Feast fall on the morrow of Low Sunday, or of Rogation Sunday, Vespers on Sunday are of the Feast, with solemn Memorial of the Sunday. No Memorials of Ferias are made in Easter-tide on any Double Feast, except when such falls on Rogation Monday or the Vigil of the Ascension, in which case Memorial is made of the Fast at Lauds only, before other Memorials. If a Simple Feast of the fourth class occurs on either of these days, it is observed only by a Memorial made at first Vespers and Lauds. The Memorials of the Resurrection are said on Sunday, whether the Office be of Sunday or of a Feast, except on the Invention of the Cross. Easter Compline does not change for Festivals, except that on the Annunciation the Hymn takes the Christmas Doxology as directed in the Rubric for Office of the Feast.

(When Low Sunday fell on the festival of S. George (April 23) the Feast was transferred to Monday, not Tuesday; and a Memorial was made of S. George at second Vespers of Sunday: Vespers of Monday being of S. George, with Memorial of first Vespers of S. Mark.)

If Low Sunday fall on SS. Philip and James (May 1) the Feast is transferred to Monday; but the second Vespers of Low Sunday are of SS. Philip and James, with Memorial of Low Sunday, and Vespers on Monday are of Invention of the Cross with Memorial of the Apostles.

If a Double Feast, or Simple above the lowest class, occur on the vigil of the Ascension, it is not transferred: but a Memorial of the vigil is made at Lauds. At first Vespers of the Ascension a Memorial is made of a Double, but not of a Simple Feast.

If a Double, or Simple of the three first classes, occur during the Octave of Ascension, it is kept, with Memorial of the Ascension, at both Vespers and at Lauds. If on Sunday, it is kept, with Memorial of the Sunday preceding that of the Ascension. If on the morrow of Ascension, Memorial of a Double Feast is made at second Vespers of Ascension Day. Simple Feasts of the fourth class are merely commemorated.

Simple Feasts of the three first classes occurring on the Octave of Ascension are transferred to the morrow. Simples of the lowest class are omitted. No Feast occurring on Whitsun Eve is to be observed or commemorated on that day. Doubles and Simples of the three first classes are transferred till after Trinity Sunday.

CORPUS CHRISTI.—Any Feast above the lowest class occurring on the Feast of Corpus Christi is transferred to the first vacant day in the Octave. The Office of the Feast is kept throughout the Octave with Rulers, including Sunday, unless any Feast of nine lessons intervene: in which case the Office is of that Feast, even if on Sunday; and Memorial and middle lessons are of the Octave, except on the Commemoration of S. Paul, when the whole service is of that Feast.

VIGILS.—Sarum Vigils noted in this book: Those of Christmas, Epiphany,

GENERAL RUBRICS.

Easter, Ascension, Whitsun, S. John Baptist, SS. Peter and Paul, S. James, S. Laurence, Repose of Blessed Virgin, S. Matthew, SS. Simon and Jude, All Saints', S. Andrew, S. Thomas. No proper Office was provided for Vigils of Saints' days: but the first Vespers of the Feast were said under that name, and in some cases, had a proper Collect.

OCTAVES.—The directions for keeping Octaves vary, according as the Feast is counted as having, or not having, Rulers of the choir. Octaves, according to Sarum, are:

1. All Principal Doubles; Corpus Christi, Visitation, Holy Name, S. Stephen, S. John Evang., Holy Innocents [S. Thomas of Canterbúry, and Nativity of B.V.M., which have not Octaves in this book]. (All the foregoing had Rulers throughout the Octave, except the Dedication of a Church, falling between Septuagesima and Easter, in which case it had Rulers on the Octave day only.)

2. Nativity of S. John Baptist, SS. Peter and Paul [SS. Laurence, Andrew, and Martin: not marked with Octaves in this book. S. Andrew's Octave was kept during the days before Advent; but in Advent a Memorial only of the day in Octave was said, until the Octave-day, which was kept with Memorial of the Advent Feria. The Octave-day of S. Martin was not kept when it fell on a Sunday.] This second division had no Rulers through the Octave; except that SS. Peter and Andrew had them on the Octave-days.

(All Saints, if kept with an Octave, should apparently be considered as having Rulers. It had no Octave in old English use.)

When a Feast is kept with an Octave, the Office of the Feast, beginning at Lauds, is said for the six following days, with these exceptions: At Lauds the five Psalms are said under the first Antiphon. The Antiphons to Benedictus, and to Magnificat at Vespers, are taken from among the Antiphons to Psalms at first Vespers, unless otherwise provided for. At Prime, Antiphon to *Quicunque* and Collect, as directed in Psalter for days in Octaves. At Vespers, the Psalms of the second Vespers of the day are said with the first Antiphon at Lauds, except when otherwise directed. The R̸. is not said.

On the Sunday falling within an Octave with Rulers, at first Vespers are said Psalms of second Vespers with the first Antiphon of Lauds; all the rest as at first Vespers of the Feast, except that the R̸. is not said. Lauds are said as through the Octave. Second Vespers are said as on the Feast, except that the R̸. is not said. Memorial of the Sunday, at Lauds and both Vespers.

But in an Octave without Rulers, on the Sunday within the Octave, the Offices are of the Sunday with Memorial of the Octave, unless a Double Feast or Simple of any of the three first classes fall on the Sunday, in which case the Offices are of that Feast, with Memorial, first of the Sunday, and next of the Octave.

On the Octave-day, all is said as on the first day, except that at first Vespers the Psalms (when not otherwise ordered) are all said under the first Antiphon, and no R̸. to the Chapter is said at either Vespers.

SIMPLE FEASTS.—It is necessary to understand that Simple Feasts in the old English and in the modern Roman use have little in common except the name. In the latter rite, Simple Feasts are all of one type: they begin after the chapter at first Vespers, have Ferial Psalms and three lessons at Matins, and end with Nones; never having second Vespers. So that a Feast of three or nine lessons means respectively a Simple or a Double or Semi-double. In the English use, Simple Feasts were of five classes, the lowest of which only was similar to the Roman. The first three had first and second Vespers, and the first two had nine lessons at Matins. If therefore anything like the ancient forms of keeping Feasts is to be maintained, it is necessary to mark these varieties, and this is here done in as plain a manner as could be devised. The Simples are divided into four sets, as follows:

First Class=Simples with Triple Invitatory.
Second Class=Simples of nine lessons with Double or Simple Invitatory.
Third Class=Simples of three lessons with Double or Simple Invitatory, but with Rulers of the Choir.
Fourth Class=Simples of three lessons without Rulers of Choir.

No Feast of only three lessons, without Rulers, has second Vespers, nor is any Memorial of it made instead of second Vespers. The Antiphons and Psalms at first Vespers are of the Feria, and the proper Office begins at the Chapter, continuing till Nones inclusive on the day following, with Ferial Psalms at Matins.

N.B.—These, as well as many others of the foregoing directions, are given here in case it be desired to keep any of these Feasts with their full Office; a case provided for, though not intended, in the Proper and Common of Saints.

COMMEMORATIONS.—These were Offices of devotion, used monthly, weekly, or at other intervals, and differing in different places, both as to their subject and their frequency. Of this nature is the monthly recitation of the Office of the Blessed Sacrament, and of the Holy Name, mentioned in Proper (but neither of these appears to have been so used in former times), and the Office of the Blessed Virgin as set down for use at Quinquagesima, before and after the Octave of Ascension, &c. This Office is set down in the Common of Saints. Commemorations never had second Vespers, nor any Memorial in lieu of second Vespers.

Commemorations are superseded by all Feasts with Rulers, by Octaves with Rulers, by Rogation Monday and Wednesday, Ember days, Vigils, and also weekdays of the third class.

MEMORIALS.—1. Memorials are appointed in the Breviary at Lauds and Vespers only. When the Office of any Feast which is not transferred, or of a Greater Feria, is superseded by that of a day of higher dignity, a Memorial is made of such superseded day, its proper Office being wholly omitted in case of Occurrence, or omitted at first or second Vespers, according to circumstances, in case of Concurrence. These especial Memorials are thus formed:

(1) At Lauds, Ant. to Ben.: at Vespers that to Mag., from the omitted Office.
(2) ℣. and ℟. following the hymn in the same Office.
(3) Collect of that Office, preceded by *Let us pray.*

2. It has been thought advisable to place in the Kalendar of this book, in order that it may form in some degree a chart of Church history, the names of many Saints connected with important events in the Church, and more especially in that of our own country. Although these names are marked in the Kalendar with their proper dignities, as set down in English or Roman books, this has been done only for the sake of supplying information to those who desire it, as the compilers of the present volume do not presume or wish to offer new Festivals for observance. These names are commemorated by Memorials set down in the Proper of Saints, as are also most of the black-letter days of the Prayer-book Kalendar. ALL DAYS MARKED * IN THE PROPER OF SAINTS ARE MEANT TO BE COMMEMORATED BY MEMORIALS ONLY. The only Festivals in the Proper of Saints intended to be kept with full Office, are those for which the Matin Offices are provided in the third volume of "Night Hours." These Memorials, as well as those referred to in paragraph 1, take precedence of those in the Psalter.

3. The number of Collects, including Memorials, said at any one Office, must not exceed seven: that being the number of petitions in the Lord's Prayer. The order of precedence in Memorials is as follows:
  (1) Memorial of any Feast-day of which the full Office is not kept.
  (2) Of Sunday.
  (3) Of day in Octave.
  (4) Of the Feria, in Advent and Lent.
  (5) Season Memorials, as, in Easter, of the Resurrection, etc.

The Memorials forbidden on certain days are those in this book. Such directions do not refer to the Memorials peculiar to any religious community.

ANTIPHONS.—The Antiphons to Benedictus, Magnificat, and Nunc Dimittis are sung before and after the Canticles on all Principal and Greater Doubles. At other times the first few words only are said before the Canticle, the whole being said after. In this latter way Antiphons to Psalms are always said, according to the use of Sarum. (The Roman use is also provided for in this book.) When the words of an Antiphon are taken from the beginning of the Psalm or Canticle, they are not repeated, but the Psalm is continued from the point where the Antiphon ceased.

COLLECTS.—If the Collect be addressed to the Father, it is concluded, *Through Jesus Christ our Lord*, etc. If to the Son: *Who livest and reignest*, etc. If in the beginning of the Collect the Son has been named: *Through the same*, etc.; if the mention of the Son occurs at the end: *Who liveth and reigneth with Thee and the Holy Ghost*, etc. If the Holy Ghost has been named, in the ending is said: *In the unity of the same Holy Ghost*.

When many Collects are said in the Litany, the first only shall end: *Through Jesus Christ*, etc., or otherwise, as above. The others shall be said without any ending at all, except the last; but every Collect shall have *Let us pray* before it.

But when Collects follow one another as Memorials, etc., the rule is different. The Collect for the day *always* (except on Good Friday and Easter Eve) ends with full ascription: the Collect of the Memorial last in order, likewise takes its full ending: the intermediate collects, if ending, *Through*, etc., close at the word *Lord*, without ascription; but if ending otherwise, they retain their full termination.

DIGNITY OF FEASTS.

ENGLISH.

. The English uses differed from each other considerably in dignity of Feasts: scarcely at all in form and order of service. The Sarum dignities are given here, and in the Kalendar of this book, except in cases of Saints not found in Sarum Kalendars, but only in York, Hereford, etc.

Principal Doubles.

Christmas Day, Epiphany, Easter Day, Ascension Day, Whitsun Day, Repose of Blessed Virgin Mary, Feast of the place, Dedication of Church.

Greater Doubles.

Purification, Trinity Sunday, Corpus Christi, Visitation, Holy Name, Nativity of Blessed Virgin, All Saints.

Lesser Doubles.

S. Stephen, S. John Ev., Holy Innocents, Circumcision, Annunciation; Easter Monday, Tuesday and Wednesday, and Whitsun Monday, Tuesday and Wednesday; Low Sunday, Invention of the Cross, Nativity of S. John Baptist, SS. Peter and Paul, Transfiguration, Exaltation of Holy Cross, Conception of Blessed Virgin.

Inferior Doubles.

SS. Andrew, Thomas, Thomas of Canterbury, Matthias, Gregory, Ambrose, George, Mark, SS. Philip and James, Augustine of England, James, Bartholomew, Augustine of Hippo, Matthew,

Michael and All Angels, Jerome, Translation of S. Edward, SS. Luke, Simon and Jude, All Souls.

All other Feasts are Simples: divided into four classes: see p. xi., and Kalendar.

Principal privileged Sundays.

First Sunday in Advent, Passion Sunday, Palm Sunday.

Greater Privileged Sundays.

Second, third, fourth in Advent; Septuagesima, and all after till Passion Sunday.

Lesser privileged Sundays.

Those on which a series of Matins lessons was begun: first Sunday after the Octave of Epiphany, Rogation Sunday, first Sunday after Trinity.

Inferior privileged Sundays.

All the rest, throughout the year.

Principal Ferias.

Ash-Wednesday, Maundy Thursday, Good Friday, Holy Saturday, Vigil of Whitsun Day.

Greater Ferias.

All week days from Passion Sunday to Maundy Thursday.

Lesser Ferias.

All week days from Ash-Wednesday to Passion Sunday, the first and third Rogation Days, the last nine days of Advent.

Inferior Ferias.

Week days in Advent before *O Sapientia.*

ROMAN.
Doubles of the First Class.

Christmas Day, Epiphany, Easter Day, Monday and Tuesday, Ascension Day, Whitsun Day, Monday and Tuesday, Corpus Christi, Nativity of S. John Baptist, of SS. Peter and Paul, Repose of Blessed Virgin Mary, All Saints, Dedication of Church, Patron or Title of Church.

Doubles of the Second Class.

Circumcision, Feasts of Holy Trinity, and of the Purification, Annunciation, Visitation, Nativity and Conception of the Blessed Virgin; Birthdays of Apostles, Feasts of Evangelists, S. Stephen, Holy Innocents; Invention of the Cross, Holy Name, SS. Joseph, Laurence, Michael.

Greater Doubles.

Transfiguration, Holy Cross Day, Conversion of S. Paul, S. John Port-Latin, S. Barnabas, Beheading of S. John Baptist, Lammas Day, S. Anne, Presentation of Blessed Virgin Mary, minor Patrons.

Semi-Doubles.*

Days within Octaves. The rest are set down in the Kalendar.

All other Feasts are Simples.

Greater Sundays of the First Class.

First Sunday in Advent, first in Lent, Passion Sunday, Palm Sunday, Easter Day, Low Sunday, Whitsun Day, Trinity Sunday.

Greater Sundays of the Second Class.

Second, third, and fourth Sundays in Advent, Septuagesima, Sexagesima, and Quinquagesima Sundays; second, third, and fourth Sundays in Lent.

Greater Ferias.

Ferias in Advent and Lent, Ember Days, Rogation Monday.

---

* The difference between Doubles and Semi-Doubles is that in the latter the Ants. to Psalms and Canticles at Lauds and Vespers are not doubled.

GENERAL NOTES (ROMAN USE).

Although this book endeavours carefully to represent the old English use, with as little alteration as possible, there are certain points regarding which some persons may give preference to the reformed Roman use; and, in order to accommodate all parties as far as possible, they are here set down: noting that *one use or the other must be wholly followed in these particulars*, as there are great discrepancies between the two; and also that the rubrics in the body of the book refer to English use alone, except when otherwise specified.

1. DIGNITY OF FEASTS.—See tables of Concurrence and Occurrence.
2. FEASTS IN HOLY WEEK.—All Doubles deferred till the first days unhindered after Low Sunday: all others wholly omitted.
3. OFFICE OF THE DEAD.—Said on the first day unhindered in every month, and on every Monday in Advent and Lent, except in Holy Week.
4. PRIME.—See rubric before the Office.
5. DOUBLING OF ANTS. TO PSALMS.—On all Double Feasts, these are doubled as well as those to the Canticles.
6. VESPERS.—Said in Octaves, &c. with the five Antiphons of Lauds: not with the first only.

TABLE I.

Occurrence (i.e. *when one Feast occurs on the same day as another Feast*).

A		Day in Octave without Rulers.	Octave-day without Rulers.	Day in Octave, *and* Octave-day, with Rulers.	Simple of the fourth class.	Simple of the three first classes.	Lesser *and* Inferior Double.	Principal *and* Greater Double.
	Principal Sunday	2	2	2	2	1	1	1
	Greater Sunday	2	2	2	2*	1	1	3
	Lesser Sunday	0	4	4	4	1	3	3
	Inferior Sunday	4	4	3	4	3	5†	5†
	Principal *and* Greater Double	2	2	4	2	1	1	6
	Lesser *and* Inferior Double	2	4	4	4	1	6	7
	Simple of the three first classes	4	4	4‡	4	6	7	7
	Simple of the fourth class	4	3	3	0	3	3	5
	Day in an Octave, *and* Octave-day, with Rulers	4	4	8	4	3‡	3	3
	Octave-day without Rulers	4	0	3	4	3	3	5
	Day in an Octave without Rulers	0	3	3	3	3	5	5
	Principal Feria	2	2	2	2	1	1	1
	Greater Feria	2	2	2	2*	1	3	3
	Lesser *and* Inferior Feria	4	4	3	2*	3	3	3

1. All of A, Translation of B.
2. All of A, nothing of B.
3. Service of B, Memorial of A.
4. Service of A, Memorial of B.
5. All of B, nothing of A.
6. All of the higher, Translation of the other.
7. All of B, Translation of A.
8. Service of the Octave-day, Memorial of the other.

* A Memorial is made of Feast at Lauds, but at no other Service.
† When a Double Feast falls on a Sunday in Easter-tide, a Memorial is made of the Sunday.
‡ A Simple Feast above the lowest class falling on the Octave-day of Ascension or Corpus Christi is translated.

Sarum.
TABLE II.

Concurrence (i.e. *when Second Vespers of one Feast falls on the same day as First Vespers of a Feast following*).

IF FIRST VESPERS OF B CONCUR WITH SECOND VESPERS OF A.

	Octave-day without Rulers.	Octave-day with Rulers.	Simple of the fourth class.	Simple of the three first classes.	Lesser *and* Inferior Double.	Greater Double.	Principal Double.	Lesser *and* Inferior Sunday.	Greater Sunday.	Principal Sunday.
Principal Sunday	0	3	4	3	1	1	1	0	0	0
Greater Sunday	0	1	3	1	1	1	2	0	0	0
Lesser *and* Inferior Sunday . . .	3	1	3	1	2	2	2	0	0	0
Principal Double	4	4	4	4	3	1	0	4	3	1
Greater Double	4	3	4	3	3	0	1	4	3	1
Lesser Double	4	3	4	3	1	1	1	4	3	1
Inferior Double	3	3	3	3	1	1	1	4	3	1
Simple of the three first classes . .	3	1	3	1	1	1	2	1	1	2
Simple of the fourth class . . .	2	2	2	2	2	2	2	2	2	2
Octave-day with Rulers	3	1*	3	1*	1*	2*	2*	1*	1*	1
Octave-day without Rulers . . .	0	1	3	1	2	2	2	1	1	2
Principal Feria	4	4	4	4	4	4	4	0	0	0

1. Service of B, Memorial of A.
2. All of B, nothing of A.
3. Service of A, Memorial of B.
4. All of A, nothing of B.

* The Octave-days which rank as Simples of the *first* class have their Second Vespers with a Memorial of the Feast following, unless such Feast is unable to have its own Second Vespers; viz. Octave-days of S. Andrew, Epiphany, Ascension, Corpus Christi, S. Peter, Visitation, Holy Name, Repose and Nativity of B. V. M.; also Octave-day of the Dedication, if not in Advent, or Septuagesima to Easter.

Roman.

TABLE I.

Occurrence (i.e. the falling of two Feasts on one day).

IF THERE OCCUR ON THE SAME DAY A

	Vigil.	Greater Feria.	Simple.	Semi-Double.	Day of Octave.	Day in Octave.	Double.	Double of the second class.	Double of the first class.	Ordinary Sunday.	Sunday of the second class.	Sunday of the first class.
Double of the first class	6	4	6	2	4	6	2	2	8	4	4	1
Double of the second class	4	4	4	2	4	6	2	8	1	4	1	1
Double	4	4	4	2	1	4	8	1	1	4	1	1
Day in Octave	4	4	4	3	3	7	3	5	5	3	3	3
Day of Octave	4	4	4	2	7	4	2	3	3	4	3	3
Semi-Double	4	4	4	8	1	4	1	1	1	1	1	1
Simple	3	3	0	3	3	3	3	3	5	3	3	3
Greater Feria	6	0	4	3	3	3	3	3	3	0	0	0
Vigil	0	5	4	3	3	3	3	3	5	0	0	0

1. Translation of the first, Office of the second.
2. Office of the first, Translation of the second.
3. Commemoration of the first, Office of the second.
4. Office of the first, Commemoration of the second.
5. Nothing of the first, Office of the second.
6. Office of the first, nothing of the second.
7. Office of the greater, Commemoration of the less.
8. Office of the greater, Translation of the less.

Roman.

TABLE II.

Concurrence (i.e. *when Second Vespers of a Feast fall on the same day as First Vespers of a Feast following*).

	Day within Octave.	Octave-day.	Simple.	Semi-Double.	Lesser Double.	Greater Double.	Patron or Title of the Church.	Double of the second class.	Double of the first class.	Any Sunday whatever.
Greater Sunday, or of first or second class	4	3	4	4	3	3	3	3	3	0
Lesser or Ordinary Sunday . . .	4	3	4	4	3	3	1	1	1	0
Double of the first class	2	4	2	4	4	4	0	4	6	4
Double of the second class . . .	4	4	4	4	4	4	3	6	3	4
Patron or Title of Church . . .	2	4	2	4	4	4	0	4	0	4
Greater Double	4	4	4	4	4	6	1	3	1	4
Lesser Double	4	5	4	4	5	3	1	3	1	4
Semi-Double	5	3	4	5	3	3	1	1	1	5
Octave-day	4	5	4	4	5	3	1	3	1	4
Day within Octave	0	3	4	5	3	3	1	1	1	5

1. All of the following, nothing of the preceding.
2. All of the preceding, nothing of the following.
3. All of the following, Commemoration of the preceding.
4. All of the preceding, Commemoration of the following.
5. Chapter of the following, Commemoration of the preceding.
6. All of the more worthy, Commemoration of the less worthy.

OF SAYING OFFICE.

THE Sarum manner of saying Office was not only elaborate, and complicated by varieties of Invitatories and Rulers, but probably, as elsewhere, received many modifications in process of time. The following notes attempt to combine correctness with as much simplicity as possible:—

The bell being rung for the commencement of the Office, all rise (except in Lent), and turn to the Altar, make the sign of the Cross, and say in silence the Lord's Prayer, and, if it be so ordered, the Angelic Salutation. The Officiant then begins aloud (signing himself with the Cross), ℣. "O God, make speed," etc., and the Office proceeds. (In Lent all kneel till the Officiant begins the ℣.) The Alleluia following the Gloria is said by all together. In Christmas- and Easter-tides the whole Office is said standing; but the choir kneels when the Priest gives the blessing. At other times, those not engaged in singing are permitted to sit during the Psalms; the Ferial Petitions and other Prayers are said kneeling, on Ferias when the Miserere is said, and the Priest, if present, alone stands when it is so noted in the Psalter; but at other times all stand. The three Gospel Canticles are recited, all standing. The Hymns are said or sung antiphonally, verse by verse. The Psalms are repeated antiphonally, whether said or sung, in this manner:—the first half of the first verse of each Psalm is said by the Precentor, the whole choir joins him in the second half; after which the even verses are said on one side, and the uneven on the other; or the first half of each verse is said by the Officiant, and the second by the choir. But when Psalms occur among the Petitions, they are not so said; the Officiant says the first half of each verse, and the congregation the other half; or the whole is said by all together. Antiphons are said in this manner:—1, Before the Psalm or Canticle, the Officiant or Precentor says or sings the first two or three words alone, and the Psalm is then begun. 2, Afterwards he again begins the Antiphon alone, and the choir joins in for the remainder. But when an Antiphon is doubled it is said or sung before the Psalm or Canticle, according to rule 2. After, the whole is said or sung by the choir.

On Wednesday in Holy Week there is no kneeling at Vespers or Compline. Nor on Maundy Thursday, except at Lauds. On Good Friday all kneel before the first Antiphon at every hour, and again for the Prayers after repetitions of the Antiphon, and so on Easter Eve.

The manner of saying the ℟. differs at Vespers and at the little hours. To put it briefly, at Vespers the Officiant or other person appointed says the first few words, and the choir take up the rest. At the little hours (*i.e.* Tierce, Sexts, Nones) the Officiant says the whole of the first sentence, and the choir repeats it all afterwards; except in Lent, when the rule is the same as at Vespers.

The exact manner in which the ℟. was recited at Salisbury was as follows:— 'At First Vespers on the Greater Feasts the ℟. is thus said: Two clerks only sing the three or four first words, the whole choir then joins in; the following versicles are sung by the two clerks only, and the repetition of the ℟. is sung by the whole choir. At Second Vespers (as also at First Vespers except on the

Greater Feasts), one boy begins the ℟. and sings the versicles, the choir taking up and singing the ℟. as above. At the little hours, except in Lent, and on three Sundays preceding, one clerk says the whole ℟. which is then repeated by the choir; the clerk sings the following versicles, the choir sings the repetition of the ℟., then the clerk sings the final versicle, and the choir answers with the final ℟.'

The manner of saying the Gradual in Easter Week was as follows:—'Two clerks sing the four first words; the choir joins in and sings till the beginning of the first ℣. which is sung by two clerks. Two seniors sing the ℟. "Alleluia": the whole choir repeats, "This is the day," etc. Two seniors sing the next ℣. and the choir takes it up at the last word, which it sings, and then sings "Alleluia."' A simpler manner of saying the Gradual is given in the body of the book, as so large a staff of clerks is not likely often to be available.

The Lord's Prayer and Apostles' Creed are said wholly in silence wherever they occur in Office.

The Confessions and Absolutions are said in a low voice.

The organ is not used during Lent, except on Sundays and on Maundy Thursday.

When two or more Offices are said by aggregation, that is, immediately following one another, the usual silent beginning is omitted in all but the first; and the Collect and Preces, if common to all, are said only in the last.

Space does not allow us here to dwell on the spiritual meaning which underlies the whole Office, and so richly repays investigation. We conclude in the words of the "Myrroure of our Ladye" "Though this be true after the spiritual meaning, yet after the letter the changing that is in God's service from one thing to another is ordained to let it drive away your dulness, that ye should not wax tedious and weary, but gladly and joyfully, not in vain joy, but in joy of spiritual devotion, continue in God's service. Therefore sometime ye sing, sometime ye read, sometime ye hear; now one alone, now twain together, now all. Sometime ye sit, sometime ye stand, sometime ye incline, sometime ye kneel, now toward the Altar, now toward the choir. And all to the praising of our Lord Jesus Christ; and so to exercise the body to the quickening of the soul, that all such bodily observances should not be found without cause of ghostly understanding. Now join to all this the fruit of that thing that is sung and read, and thereto the fellowship of the Angels among you in time of God's service, and most of all the marvellous and unspeakable presence of God Himself, from Whom our Lady is not far, and see whether it be not nigh another Heaven to serve and praise God in the choir."

NOTES ON THE KALENDAR.

The whole position of English Catholics is historical. The Kalendar is the chart of Church history, and, as set forth in the present attempt, more especially of English Church history.

The first conversion of England on the introduction of Christianity into the land was during the Roman occupation—of this, ALBAN the protomartyr is the representative. The Romans left the country, and the heathen Saxons drove the British into Cornwall, Wales, and Cumbria. DUBRITIUS and DAVID Abp. are among the greater Bishops of this Church. With these is associated GERMANUS of Auxerre, who helped them to conquer and root out Pelagianism. But the British Church was not missionary.

We turn to Ireland. Its people, the Gaelic Celts, had populated part of Scotland. They were, properly speaking, the Scots. The Picts of the east and of Strathclyde were probably Cymri. We have, first, independent missions, possibly from Rome. PATRICK, to Ireland, A.D. 460; NINIAN, to the Picts of Strathclyde, 432; PALLADIUS, to the Northern Picts, 430; TERNAN to the same district. This closes the second stage.

In the third, we must keep two lines in view: the Roman and the Celtic missions to this island.

At the opening we have COMGALL, the great Abbot of Bangor, near Belfast, the centre of life and civilization; and KENTIGERN (the little deserted child brought to Servan of Culross), afterwards Bishop of Glasgow and Strathclyde, and founder of S. Asaph monastery in North Wales, and friend of S. David in his old age. These two lived through the great period, though apparently independent of the chief actors. AUGUSTINE, 597, converted the Anglo-Saxons. PAULINUS went to York. Both missions seemed ready to perish. The Cymric Christians would have nothing to do with them. CADOC of Llancarvan, SAMPSON of Dol, GILDAS of Glastonbury, fled from the heathen Saxon.

About the same time COLUMBA, after his quarrel with Comgall, landed in Iona, and spread light all around. His disciple DROSTANE penetrated to Deer in Buchan. Columba died; but from his monastery came AYDAN to Northumbria, and, with OSWALD its king, converted the north of England. Aydan was succeeded by FINNAN, and he by COLMAN. England was subdued by Celtic missionaries; then came the clash with the Roman mission at Canterbury. There were COLMAN, CUTHBERT, HILDA, and BEGHA in the north among the Celts, and WILFRID in the south. Wilfrid prevailed, and Colman fled, carrying the remains of Aydan. Cuthbert submitted; and thenceforward the Church was one. The Celtic traditions were still preserved at Iona, till ADAMNAN, the historian of Columba, submitted to the now prevailing practices.

In the early Saxon period we have CHAD, JOHN OF BEVERLEY, BEDE, BOTOLPH, GUTHLAC, ALDHELM. At the same time, WINIFRED in North Wales, and Nathalan, a saint whose history is not absolutely certain, in Scotland. Thus closes what may be called the third period.

The fourth extends to the Norman invasion. We have SWITHIN the reformer; DUNSTAN, COLUMBANUS,* and BONIFACE, missionaries; ETHELDREDA, EDMUND and EDWARD, martyrs, and EDWARD the Confessor.

The fifth period is that of Norman civilization. In England, ANSELM. In Scotland, MARGARET, and afterwards DAVID. Then the contenders in England with royal power—THOMAS of CANTERBURY and EDMUND. Of more quiet persons, HUGH and THOMAS of HEREFORD.

Nearly all the local saints of this Kalendar have now been enumerated. BRIDGET was associated with Patrick. MAGNUS, a devout king of the Orkneys, 1102. OSMUND, the compiler of the Sarum rite. WULSTAN, the protector of the Saxons from the early Normans. GENOVEVA was connected with Germanus.

Their names are set down in the first of the following lists. The second gives the history of the Religious Life.

1. *First Christian Cenobites.*
PAUL, first hermit, 341. PACHOMIUS, 349. ANTONY, 356. HILARION, 372.

2. *Founders of Religious Orders.*
BASIL, founder of Eastern Monasticism, 379. BENEDICT, of Western, 543. PLACIDUS and MAUR, disciples of Benedict; his sister, SCHOLASTICA. COLUMBANUS, Celtic (COMGALL, COLUMBA, ADAMNAN, AYDAN).

3. *Revival of Monastic Life.*
ROMUALD, founder of Camaldunes, 1027. JOHN GUALBERT, of Vallombrosa, 1073. BRUNO, of Carthusians, 1101. NORBERT, of Premonstratensians, 1134. BERNARD, of Cistercians, 1153.

4. *Revival of Religious Life by Friars and Preaching Orders.*
DOMINIC, 1221. In his order, THOMAS AQUINAS, theologian, 1274. VINCENT FERRER, missionary, 1419.
FRANCIS, 1226. In his order, CLARA, foundress of female Order, 1253; BONAVENTURA, theologian, 1274; BERNARDINE, missionary, 1444; ELIZABETH, Q., tertiary, 1231.

5. *Period of Protestant Reform.*
FRANCIS DE PAULA, founder of Minims, 1507. IGNATIUS LOYOLA, of Jesuits, 1556; in that Order, FRANCIS XAVIER, missionary, 1552. PHILIP NERI, of Oratorians, 1595. PETER of ALCANTARA, 1562. THERESA, 1582, and JOHN of the CROSS, 1591, of reformed Carmelites. CHARLES BORROMEO, of Oblates, 1584. JANE FRANCES de Chantal, of Visitation, 1641. VINCENT de PAUL, of Lazarists and Sisters of Charity, 1660.

The names in the third list belong to Saints of the universal Church, and need no comment.

The fourth list gives the names of post-Reformation Saints. CHARLES BORROMEO, bishop of Milan; FRANCIS de SALES, of Geneva; and THOMAS of VILLANOVA, the saintly bishop of a very poor see.

No reference is made in this analysis to the black-letter Saints of the Prayerbook Kalendar, except in so far as they enter into this historical scheme. Many of the rest of them were retained in the Kalendar for no very apparent reason, unless the ancient connection between the English and Gallican Churches be counted sufficient cause.

---

* Soon after lived Benedict; not in this period. Their systems long were rivals.

NOTES ON THE KALENDAR.

List I.—*British, Irish, Scotch, and English Saints.*

Adamnan	Chad	Etheldred	Osmund
Alban	Colman	Frideswide	Oswald
Aldhelm	Columba	Germanus	Palladius
Alphege	Columbanus	Gilbert	Patrick
Anselm	Comgall	Gildas	Paulinus
Asaph	David, K.	Guthlac	Sampson
Augustine	David, B.	Hilda	Servan
Aydan	Drostane	Hugh	Swithin
Bede	Dubritius	John of Beverley	Ternah
Begha	Dunstan	Kentigern	Thomas of Cant.
Boniface	Edmund, K.	Magnus	Thomas of Hereford
Botolph	Edmund, B.	Margaret	Wilfrid
Bridget	Edward, K. M.	Ninian	Winifred
Cadoc	Edward, K. C.	Ode	Wolstan

List II.—*Founders of Orders or Great Religious.*

Anthony	Dominic	John Gualbert	Romuald
Benedict	Francis of Assisi	Maur	Scholastica
Bernard	Francis de Paula	Norbert	Theresa
Bernardine	Francis Xavier	Paul	Thomas Aquinas
Bonaventura	Hilarion	Peter of Alcantara	Vincent de Paul
Bruno	Ignatius Loyola	Philip Neri	Vincent Ferrer
Clara	Jane Frances	Placidus	

List III.—*Primitive Saints of Universal Church.*

Agatha	Forty MM. of Sebaste	Martin
Agnes	Gregory the Great	Mary, B. V. (6)
Ambrose	Gregory Nazianzen	Matthew, *Ap. Ev.*
Andrew, *Ap.*	Hilary	Matthias, *Ap.*
Anne	Holy Innocents	Maurice
Athanasius	Ignatius	Monica
Augustine	Irenæus	Nicolas
Barnabas, *Ap.*	James the Great, *Ap.*	Paul, *Ap.* (3)
Bartholomew, *Ap.*	Jerome	Perpetua
Basil	John Bapt. (2)	Peter, *Ap.* (2)
Blandina	John, *Ev.* (2)	Philip & James, *App.*
Cecilia	Joseph	Polycarp
Chrysostom	Justin Martyr	Pothinus
Clement	Katharine	Sebastian
Cosmas and Damian	Laurence	Simon & Jude, *App.*
Cyprian	Leo	Thomas, *Ap.*
Cyril of Jerusalem	Luke, *Ev.*	Timothy
Fabian	Margaret	Vincent
	Mark, *Ev.*	

List IV.—*Post-Reformation Saints.*

Charles Borromeo	Francis de Sales	Thomas of Villanova

The Kalendar.

JANUARY.

				DIGNITY	
				English.	Roman.
1	A	Kalendæ.	Circumcision.	L.D.	D.II. Cl.
2	b	iv. Non.	Oct. S. Stephen.	S. 3rd Cl.	D.
3	c	iii. Non.	Oct. S. John.	,,	D.
			Genoveva, V. at Paris, A.D. 512.		G.D.
4	d	Prid. Non.	Oct. Holy Innocents. [A.D. 1066.	,,	D.
5	e	Nonæ.	Eve of Epiphany. Edward, K.C.		
6	f	viii. Idus.	Epiphany.	P.D.	D.I. Cl.
7	g	vii. Id.	Of the Octave.		
8	A	vi. Id.	Lucian, Priest, M. A.D. 245.		
9	b	v. Id.	Of the Octave.		
10	c	iv. Id.	Of the Octave.		
11	d	iii. Id.	Of the Octave.		
12	e	Prid. Id.	Of the Octave.		
13	f	Idus.	Oct. Epiphany.	S. 1st Cl.	D.I. Cl.
			Mems. Hilary, Bp. of Poictiers, A.D. 368. Kentigern, Bp. Glasgow, A.D. 603 (fr. Nov. 13).		
14	g	xix. Kal. Feb.	(S. Hilary on this day, in Roman [use, from Jan. 13.)		D.
15	A	xviii. Kal.	Maur. D. Ab. A.D. 584.	S. 4th Cl.	D.
16	b	xvii. Kal.	[Paul, Hermit, A.D. 341.		
17	c	xvi. Kal.	Antony, Abbot, A.D. 356.	S. 4th Cl.	D.
18	d	xv. Kal.	Prisca, V.M. A.D. 270.	,,	Mem.
19	e	xiv. Kal.	Wulstan, Bp. A.D. 1095.	S. 2nd Cl.	D.
20	f	xiii. Kal.	Fabian, M, Bp. of Rome, A.D. 250, [Sebastian, M. A.D. 304.	,,	D.
21	g	xii. Kal.	Agnes, V.M. A.D. 304 or 301.	,,	D.
22	A	xi. Kal.	Vincent, Deacon, M. A.D. 304.	,,	S.D.
23	b	x. Kal.			
24	c	ix. Kal.	Timothy, Bp. of Ephesus, A.D. 97, Cadoc, Ab. of Llancarvan A.D.		D.
25	d	viii. Kal.	Conversion of S. Paul. [504.	S. 1st Cl.	G.D.
26	e	vii. Kal.	Polycarp, Bp. of Smyrna, A.D. 156, (fr. March 6.)		D.
27	f	vi. Kal.	John Chrysostom, Abp. of Constan[tinople, A.D. 407, (fr. Sept. 14.)		D.
28	g	v. Kal.			
29	A	iv. Kal.	Francis de Sales, Bp. of Geneva, A.D. 1622, (fr. Dec. 28,) Gildas, Abbot, A.D. 602.		D.
30	b	iii. Kal.	Charles, K.M. A.D. 1649.		
31	c	Prid. Kal.			

FEBRUARY.

				DIGNITY.	
				English.	Roman.
1	d	Kalendæ.	Bridget of Ireland, V. A.D. 525.	S. 4th Cl.	
			Ignatius, Bp. of Antioch, M. [A.D. 107, (fr. Dec. 20.)		S.D.
2	e	iv. Non.	Purification of B. V. Mary.	G.D.	D. II. Cl.
3	f	iii. Non.	Blasius, Bp. of Sebaste, A.D. 316.	S. 4th Cl.	S.
4	g	Prid. Non.			
5	A	Nonæ.	Agatha, V. M. of Catana in Sicily, [A.D. 251.	S. 2nd Cl.	D.
6	b	viii. Idus.			
7	c	vii. Id.	Romuald, Abbot. Founder of the [Camaldune Monks, A.D. 1027.		D.
8	d	vi. Id.			
9	e	v. Id.			
10	f	iv. Id.	Scholastica, V. Sister of S. Benedict, [A.D. 543.	S. 4th Cl.	D.
11	g	iii. Id.			
12	A	Prid. Id.			
13	b	Idus.			
14	c	xvi. Kal. Mart.	Valentine, Priest of Rome, M. [A.D. 270.	S. 4th Cl.	S.
15	d	xv. Kal.			
16	e	xiv. Kal.			
17	f	xiii. Kal.			
18	g	xii. Kal.	Colman, Bp. of Lindisfarne, A.D. 676, (fr. Aug. 8.) Simeon, Bp. of Jerusalem. M. A.D. 107.		S.
19	A	xi. Kal.			
20	b	x. Kal.			
21	c	ix. Kal.			
22	d	viii. Kal.			
23	e	vii. Kal.			
24	f	vi. Kal.	Matthias, Ap. M.	I.D.	D. II. Cl.
25	g	v. Kal.			
26	A	iv. Kal.			
27	b	iii. Kal.			
28	c	Prid. Kal.			
29	d				

MARCH.

				DIGNITY.	
				English.	Roman.
1	d	Kalendæ.	David, Bp. of Menevia, A.D. 544.	S.2nd Cl.	D.
2	e	vi. Non.	Chad, Bp. of Lichfield, A.D. 673.	,,	D.
3	f	v. Non.			
4	g	iv. Non.			
5	A	iii. Non.			
6	b	Prid. Non.	[204.		
7	c	Nonæ.	Perpetua and Felicitas, MM., A.D.	S. 4th Cl.	Mem.
			[A.D. 1274.		
			Thomas Aquinas, O.P. Conf. Doct.		D.
8	d	viii. Idus.			
9	e	vii. Id.			
10	f	vi. Id.	*Forty Martyrs at Sebaste*, A.D. 320.		S.D.
11	g	v. Id.	[*Conf. Doct.* A.D. 605.		
12	A	iv. Id.	Gregory the Great, Bp. of Rome,	I.D.	D.
13	b	iii. Id.			
14	c	Prid. Id.			
15	d	Idus.			
16	e	xvii. Kal. Apr.	[*Ireland, circ.* A.D. 460.		
17	f	xvi. Kal.	Patrick, Bp., Conf., Apostle of	S.2nd Cl.	D.
			[*of Jerusalem*, A.D. 386.		
18	g	xv. Kal.	Edward, K.M., A.D. 979 *Cyril, Bp.*	,,	
			[*Jesus Christ.*		
19	A	xiv. Kal.	*Joseph, Foster-father of our Lord*		D. II. Cl.
			[687.		
20	b	xiii. Kal.	Cuthbert, Bp. of Lindisfarne, A.D.	S.2nd Cl.	D.
21	c	xii. Kal.	Benedict, Abbot, A.D. 543.	S.2nd Cl.	D.
22	d	xi. Kal.			
23	e	x. Kal.			
24	f	ix. Kal.			
25	g	viii. Kal.	𝔄nnunciation of 𝔅. 𝔙. 𝔐ary.	L.D.	D. II. Cl.
26	A	vii. Kal.			
27	b	vi. Kal.			
28	c	v. Kal.			
29	d	iv. Kal.			
30	e	iii. Kal.			
31	f	Prid. Kal.			

APRIL.

				DIGNITY.	
				English.	Roman.
1	g	Kalendæ.	*Gilbert, Bp. of Caithness,* A.D. 1245.		
2	A	iv. Non.	[*Ord. Minim,* A.D. 1508. *Francis de Paula, Founder of the* [1253.		D.
3	b	iii. Non.	Richard, Bp. of Chichester, A.D.	S.2nd Cl.	D.
4	c	Prid. Non.	Ambrose, Bp. of Milan, A.D. 397.	I.D.	D.
5	d	Nonæ.	*Vincent Ferrer, O.P., C.,* A.D. 1419.		D.
6	e	viii: Idus.			
7	f	vii. Id.			
8	g	vi. Id.			
9	A	v. Id.			
10	b	iv. Id.			
11	c	iii. Id.	[461. *Guthlac, Hermit,* A.D. 714. Leo the Great, Bp. of Rome, A.D.		D.
12	d	Prid. Id.			
13	e	Idus.			
14	f	xviii.Kal.Maij.			
15	g	xvii. Kal.			
16	A	xvi. Kal.	*Magnus, K.M.,* A.D. 1110.		
17	b	xv. Kal.			
18	c	xiv. Kal.			
19	d	xiii. Kal.	[A.D. 1012. Alphege, Abp. of Canterbury, M.,	S. 4th Cl.	
20	e	xii. Kal.			
21	f	xi. Kal.	[A.D. 1109. *Anselm, Abp. of Canterbury, D.,*		D.
22	g	x. Kal.			
23	A	ix. Kal.	[circ. A.D. 303. George, M., Patron of England	I.D.	[w. Oct. D. I. Cl.,
24	b	viii. Kal.			
25	c	vii. Kal.	**Mark, Evangelist, M.**	I.D.	D. II. Cl.
26	d	vi. Kal.			
27	e	v. Kal.			
28	f	iv. Kal.			
29	g	iii. Kal.			
30	A	Prid. Kal.			

MAY.

				DIGNITY.	
				English.	Roman.
			[𝔐.𝔐.		
1	b	Kalendæ.	𝔓hilip and 𝔍ames the 𝔏ess, App.	I.D.	D. II. Cl.
2	c	vi. Non.	Athanasius, Abp. of Alexandria, Conf., Doct. A.D. 373. Asaph, Bp. A.D. 590.		D.
3	d	v. Non.	Invention of the Cross, A.D. 326.	L.D.	D. II. Cl.
			[Matron. A.D. 387.		
4	e	iv. Non.	Monica, Mother of S. Augustine,		D.
5	f	iii. Non.			
			[Gate, circ. A.D. 95.		
6	g	Prid. Non.	John, Ev. Ap., before the Latin	S. 1st Cl.	G.D.
			[A.D. 721.		
7	A	Nonæ.	John of Beverley, Bp. of York,	S. 3rd Cl.	D.
8	b	viii. Idus.			
			[stantinople, Doct. A.D. 391.		
9	c	vii. Id.	Gregory Nazianzen, Bp. of Con-		D.
10	d	vi. Id.			
11	e	v. Id.			
			[Ireland, A.D. 602.		
12	f	iv. Id.	Comgall, Abbot of Bangor, in Pancras, and his Companions, of		
13	g	iii. Id.	[Rome, MM. A.D. 304.	S. 3rd Cl.	S.D.
14	A	Prid. Id.	Pachomius, Abbot. A.D. 349.		
15	b	Idus. [Junü.			
16	c	xvii. Kal.			
17	d	xvi. Kal.			
18	e	xv. Kal.	[A.D. 988.		
19	f	xiv. Kal.	Dunstan, Abp. of Canterbury,	S. 2nd Cl.	D.
			[C. A.D. 1444.		
20	g	xiii. Kal.	Bernardine of Sienna, Ord. Min.		S.D.
21	A	xii. Kal.			D.
22	b	xi. Kal.			
23	c	x. Kal.			
24	d	ix. Kal.			
25	e	viii. Kal.	Aldhelm, Bp. of Sherborne, A.D. 709.	S.2nd Cl.	D.
			[Apostle of England, 605.		D. II. Cl.
26	f	vii. Kal.	Augustine, Abp. of Canterbury, Philip Neri, Founder of Congregation of the Oratory, A.D. 1595.	I.D.	[w. Oct. D.
27	g	vi. Kal.	Venerable Bede. A.D. 734.	S.4th. Cl.	D.
28	A	v. Kal			
29	b	iv. Kal.			
30	c	iii. Kal.			
31	d	Prid. Kal.			

JUNE.

				DIGNITY.	
				English.	Roman.
1	e	Kalendæ.	Nicomede of Rome, M. 1st cent.	S. 4th Cl.	S.
2	f	iv. Non.	*Pothinus, Bp., and Blandina, V. of*		
3	g	iii. Non.	*[Lyons, MM.* A.D. *177.*		
4	A	Prid. Non.	*[MM.* A.D. *755.*		
5	b	Nonæ.	Boniface, Bp., and his Companions,	S. 4th Cl.	D.
6	c	viii. Idus.	*Norbert, Bp. of Magdeburg. Founder of the Order of Prémonstré,* A.D. *1134.*		
7	d	vii. Id.			
8	e	vi. Id.	*[597.*		
9	f	v. Id.	*Columba, first Abbot of Iona,* A.D.		
10	g	iv. Id.			
11	A	iii. Id.	𝕭arnabas, 𝕬p. 𝕸.	S. 1st Cl.	G.D.
12	b	Prid. Id.	*Ternan, Bp. of the Picts,* A.D. *431.*		
13	c	Idus. [Julii.			
14	d	xviii. Kal.	Basil the Great, Bp. of Cæsarea, Conf. Doct. A.D. 379, (fr. Jan. 1.)	S. 4th Cl.	D.
15	e	xvii. Kal.			
16	f	xvi. Kal.			
17	g	xv. Kal.	Alban, Proto-martyr of England, (fr. June 22) 3rd cent. Botolph, Abbot, A.D. 655.	S. 2nd Cl.	G.D.
18	A	xiv. Kal.	*[Scotland,* A.D. *1093.*		
19	b	xiii. Kal.	*Translation of Margaret, Queen of*		
20	c	xii. Kal.	Translation of Edward, K.M.	S. 4th Cl.	
21	d	xi. Kal.			
22	e	x. Kal.			
23	f	ix. Kal.			
24	g	viii. Kal.	𝕹ativity of 𝕾. 𝕵ohn 𝕭aptist.	L.D. [w. Oct.	D.I.Cl. [w. Oct.
25	A	vii. Kal.	Of the Octave.		
26	b	vi. Kal.	Of the Octave.		
27	c	v. Kal.	Of the Octave.		
28	d	iv. Kal.	Of the Octave. Mem. Irenæus, Bp. *[of Lyons, circ.* A.D. *202.*		D.
29	e	iii. Kal.	𝕻eter and 𝕻aul, 𝕬pp. 𝕸𝕸.	L.D. [w. Oct.	D.I.Cl. [w. Oct.
30	f	Prid. Kal.	Commemoration of S. Paul.	S. 1st Cl.	

JULY.

				DIGNITY.	
				English.	Roman.
1	g	Kalendæ.	[Servan, Bp. C. circ. A.D. 430. Octave of S. John Baptist. Mem of	S. 4th Cl.	D. II. Cl.
2	A	vi. Non.	Visitation of B.V. Mary [Mem. of S. Peter.	G.D. [w. Oct.	D. II. Cl.
3	b	v. Non.	Of the Octave of the Visitation, with [Martin, Bp. of Tours.		
4	c	iv. Non.	Of the Octave. Translation of	S. 2nd Cl.	
5	d	iii. Non.	Of the Octave.		
6	e	Prid. Non.	Octave Day of SS. Peter and Paul. Mem. of Visitation. Palladius, Bp. Apostle of Scotland, A.D. 430.	S. 1st Cl.	D. I. Cl.
7	f	Nonæ.	Of the Octave of the Visitation. Translation of S. Thomas, M. Abp.		G.D.
8	g	viii. Id.	Of the Octave.		
9	A	vii. Id.	Octave of Visitation.	S. 1st Cl.	D. II. Cl.
10	b	vi. Id.			
11	c	v. Id.			
12	d	iv. Id.	John Gualbert, Founder of the Order		
13	e	iii. Id.	[of. Vallombrosa, A.D. 1073.		D.
14	f	Prid. Idus.	Bonaventura, Ord. Min. Bp. of Alba, Doct. A.D. 1274, (fr. 15.) [Winchester.		D.
15	g	Idus.	Translation of Swithun, Bp. of	S. 2nd Cl.	D.
16	A	xvii. Kal. Aug.	Translation of Osmund, Bp. of [Sarum.	S. 2nd Cl.	D.
17	b	xvi. Kal.			
18	c	xv. Kal.			
19	d	xiv. Kal.	Vincent de Paul, Founder of Con- greg. of Priests of Mission and of Sisters of Charity, A.D. 1660, (fr. Sept. 27th.)		D.
20	e	xiii. Kal.	Margaret of Antioch, V.M.	S. 2nd Cl.	S.
21	f	xii. Kal.			
22	g	xi. Kal.	Mary Magdalene. [A.D. 75.	S. 1st Cl.	
23	A	x. Kal.	Apollinaris, Bp. of Ravenna, M.	S. 4th Cl.	
24	b	ix. Kal.	Vigil of S. James.		
25	c	viii. Kal.	James the Great, Ap. M.	I. D.	D. II. Cl.
26	d	vii. Kal.	Anne, Mother of B.V. Mary.	S. 1st Cl.	G.D.
27	e	vi. Kal.			
28	f	v. Kal.	Sampson, Bp. of Dol. A.D. 465.	S. 4th Cl.	
29	g	iv. Kal.			
30	A	iii. Kal.			
31	b	Prid. Kal.	Germanus, Bp. of Auxerre, A.D. 448 or 444.	S. 4th Cl.	D.

AUGUST.

				DIGNITY.	
				English.	Roman.
1	c	Kalendæ.	Lammas Day. S. Peter's Chains.	S. 1st Cl.	G.D.
			[167.		
			The Holy Maccabees, MM., B.C.	Mem.	Mem.
2	d	iv. Non.			
3	e	iii. Non.			
			[*Preachers*, A.D. 1221, (*fr.* 6.)		
4	f	Prid. Non.	*Dominic, Founder of the Order of*		D.
5	g	Nonæ.	*Oswald, K.M.*, A.D. 642.	S. 4th Cl.	
6	A	viii. Id.	Transfiguration of our Lord.	L.D.	G.D.
7	b	vii. Id.	Holy Name of Jesus.	G.D.	G.D.
8	c	vi. Id.	Of the Octave.	[w. Oct.	
9	d	v. Id.	Of the Octave. Vigil.		
10	e	iv. Id.	Laurence, Deacon, M., A.D. 258.	S. 1st Cl.	D. II. Cl.
11	f	iii. Id.	Of the Octave.		
			[*V.*, A.D. 1253, (*fr.* 11.)		
12	g	Prid. Id.	*Clara, first of Sisters of Ord. Min.*,		D.
13	A	Idus.	Of the Octave.		
14	b	xix. Kal. Sept.	Octave of Holy Name. Vigil.	S. 1st Cl.	G.D.
15	c	xviii. Kal.	Repose of B.V. Mary, A.D. 63.	P.D.	D. I. Cl.
16	d	xvii. Kal.		[w. Oct.	[w. Oct.
17	e	xvi. Kal.			
18	f	xv. Kal.			
19	g	xiv. Kal.			
			[1153.		
20	A	xiii. Kal.	*Bernard, Abbot of Clairvaux*, A.D.		D.
21	b	xii. Kal.	*Jane Frances Fremiot de Chantal, Matron, Abbess, Foundress of Order of Visitation*, A.D. 1641, (*fr. Dec.* 13.)		D.
22	c	xi. Kal.			
23	d	x. Kal.	Vigil.		
24	e	ix. Kal.	𝔖. 𝔅artholomew, 𝔄p. 𝔐.	I.D.	D. II. Cl.
			[1270.		
25	f	viii. Kal.	*Louis IX., King of France*, A.D.		S.D.
			Hilda, V. Abbess, A.D. 680.	S. 4th Cl.	
26	g	vii. Kal.			
27	A	vi. Kal.			
			[Conf. A.D. 430.		
28	b	v. Kal.	Augustine, Bp. of Hippo, Doct.,	I.D.	D.
29	c	iv. Kal.	Beheading of S. John Baptist.	S. 1st Cl.	G.D.
30	d	iii. Kal.			
31	e	Prid. Kal.	Aydan, Bishop of Lindisfarne, Apostle of Northumbria, A.D. 651.		D.

SEPTEMBER.

				DIGNITY.	
				English.	Roman.
1	f	Kalendæ.			
2	g	iv. Non.			
3	A	iii. Non.			
4	b	Prid. Non.			
5	c	Nonæ.			
6	d	viii. Id.			
7	e	vii. Id.	Evurtius, Bp. of Orleans, [340. A.D.	S. 4th Cl.	S.
8	f	vi. Id.	Nativity of B. V. Mary.	[w. Oct. G.D.	[w. Oct. D. II. Cl.,
9	g	v. Id.			
10	A	iv. Id.			
11	b	iii. Id.			
12	c	Prid. Id.			
13	d	Idus.	[629.		
14	e	xviii. Kal.Oct.	Exaltation of the Holy Cross, A.D.	L.D.	G.D.
15	f	xvii. Kal.			
16	g	xvi. Kal.	[ern Picts, A.D. circ. 432. Ninian, Bp., Apostle of the South-		
17	A	xv. Kal.	[A.D. 709. Lambert, Bp. of Maestricht, M.,	S. 4th Cl.	S.
18	b	xiv. Kal.			
19	c	xiii. Kal.			
20	d	xii. Kal.	Vigil.		
21	e	xi. Kal.	𝕸𝖆𝖙𝖙𝖍𝖊𝖜, 𝕬𝖕., 𝕰𝖛., 𝕸.	I.D.	D. II. Cl.
22	f	x. Kal.	[Agaunum, MM., A.D. 286. Maurice and his Companions at	S.2nd Cl.	Mem.
23	g	ix. Kal.	[lentia, A.D. 1555, (fr. 8.) Thomas of Villanova, Bp. of Va-		D.
24	A	viii. Kal.	Adamnan, Bp. of Iona, A.D. 704.		
25	b	vii. Kal.			
26	c	vi. Kal.	[258, (fr. 14.) Cyprian, Abp. of Carthage, M., A.D.	S. 4th Cl.	S.D.
27	d	v. Kal.	[4th century. Cosmas and Damian, MM., 3rd or	S. 4th Cl.	S.D.
28	e	iv. Kal.			
29	f	iii. Kal.	𝕸𝖎𝖈𝖍𝖆𝖊𝖑 𝖆𝖓𝖉 𝕬𝖑𝖑 𝕬𝖓𝖌𝖊𝖑𝖘.	I.D.	D. II. Cl.
30	g	Prid. Kal.	[420. Jerome, Priest, Conf. Doct, A.D.	I.D.	D.

OCTOBER.

				DIGNITY.	
				English.	Roman.
1	A	Kalendæ.	Remigius, Bp. of Rheims, A.D. [533, (fr. Jan. 13.)	S. 2nd Cl.	S.D.
2	b	vi. Non.	Thomas, Bp. of Hereford, A.D. 1282.	S. 2nd Cl.	D.
			The Holy Guardian Angels.		D.
3	c	v. Non.			
4	d	iv. Non.	Francis of Assisi. Founder of [Ord. Minor., A.D. 1226.	S. 4th Cl.	D.
5	e	iii. Non.			S.
6	f	Prid. Non.	Faith, V.M.	S. 4th Cl.	
			[thusians, A.D. 1101.		D.
7	g	Nonæ.	Bruno, Founder of Order of Car-		
8	A	viii. Idus.			
			[panions, MM. 1st Century.		
9	b	vii. Id.	Denys, Bp. of Paris, and his Com-	S. 2nd Cl.	S.D.
10	c	vi. Id.	Paulinus, Bp. of York, C. A.D. 644.		D.
11	d	v. Id.			
12	e	iv. Id.	Wilfred, Bp. Conf. A.D. 709.		D.
13	f	iii. Id.	Translation of Edward, Confessor, [King of England.	I.D.	D. II. Cl. [w. Oct.
14	g	Prid. Id.			
15	A	Idus.	Theresa, Foundress of Order of Carmelites of stricter observance, V. A.D. 1582.		D.
16	b	xvii. Kal. Nov.			
17	c	xvi. Kal.	Translation of Etheldred, V.A.Q.	S. 2nd Cl.	
18	d	xv. Kal.	𝕷uke, 𝕰v.	I.D.	D. II. Cl.
19	e	xiv. Kal.	Peter of Alcantara, O.M. A.D. 1562 (fr. 18.) Frideswide, V. 8th Century.	S. 2nd Cl.	D.
20	f	xiii. Kal.			
			[372.		
21	g	xii. Kal.	Hilarion, Abbot in Palestine, A.D.		S.
22	A	xi. Kal.	[167.		
23	b	x. Kal.	Justin, Philosopher and M. A.D.		
24	c	ix. Kal.	[285.		
25	d	viii. Kal.	Crispin and Crispinian, MM. A.D.	S. 2nd Cl.	D.
26	e	vii. Kal.			
27	f	vi. Kal.	Vigil.		
28	g	v. Kal.	Simon and Jude, App. 𝕸.𝕸.	I.D.	D. II. Cl.
29	A	iv. Kal.			
30	b	iii. Kal.			
31	c	Prid. Kal.	Begha, V. circ., A.D. 660. Vigil.		

NOVEMBER.

				DIGNITY.	
				English.	Roman.
1	d	Kalendæ.	**All Saints' Day.**	G.D.	D. I. Cl.
					[w. Oct.
2	e	iv. Non.	*All Souls' Day.* [*Octave.*	I.D.	G.D.
3	f	iii. Non.	*Winifred, V.M., 7th cent. Of the*	S.2nd Cl.	D.
4	g	Prid. Non.	*Of the Octave. Mem. Charles Borromeo, Bp. of Milan and Conf.*, A.D. 1584.		D.
5	A	Nonæ.	*Of the Octave.*		
			[*Conf.*, A.D. 404.		
6	b	viii. Idus.	*Of the Octave. Mem. Leonard,*	S.2nd Cl.	
7	c	vii. Id.	*Of the Octave.*		
8	d	vi. Id.	*Octave of All Saints.*		
9	e	v. Id.			
10	f	iv. Id.			
11	g	iii. Id.	Martin, Bp. of Tours, A.D. 400.	S. 1st Cl.	D.
12	A	Prid. Id.			
13	b	Idus.	Britius, Bp. of Tours, A.D. 443.	S. 4th Cl.	
			[522.		
14	c	xviii.Kal.Dec.	*Dubritius, Bp. and Conf., circ.* A.D.		
15	d	xvii. Kal.	Machutus, Bp. of Alet, A.D. 565.	S. 4th Cl.	
			[A.D. 1242.		
16	e	xvi. Kal.	Edmund, Abp. of Canterbury, C.,	S. 1st Cl.	D.
17	f	xv. Kal.	Hugh, Bp. of Lincoln, A.D. 1200.	S.2nd Cl.	D.
18	g	xiv. Kal.			
			[*Matron*, A.D. 1231.		
19	A	xiii. Kal.	*Elizabeth of Hungary, Q. and*		D.
20	b	xii. Kal.	Edmund, K.M., A.D. 870.	S.2nd Cl.	G.D.
			[615.		
21	c	xi. Kal.	*Columbanus, Abbot of Luxeuil,* A.D.		
			[cent.		
22	d	x. Kal.	Cecilia of Rome, V.M., 3rd	S.2nd Cl.	D.
			[circ. 100.		
23	e	ix. Kal.	Clement, Bp. of Rome, M., A.D.	S. 2nd Cl.	D.
24	f	viii. Kal.	*John of the Cross, Founder of Order of Carmelites of Stricter Observance*, A.D. 1591, (*fr. Dec.* 14.)		D.
25	g	vii. Kal.	Katharine of Alexandria, V.M., 4th	S.2nd Cl.	D.
			[cent.		
26	A	vi. Kal.			
27	b	v. Kal.	*Ode of Scotland, V.*		
28	c	iv. Kal.			
29	d	iii. Kal.	*Vigil.*		
30	e	Prid. Kal.	**Andrew, Ap. M.**	I.D.	D. II. Cl.

DECEMBER.

				DIGNITY.	
				English.	Roman.
1	f	Kalendæ.			
2	g	iv. Non.			
			[*India*, A.D. 1552.		
3	A	iii. Non.	*Francis Xavier, S.J., Apostle of*		D.
4	b	Prid. Non.	*Drostane, Abbot of Deer in Buchan, circ.* A.D. *600, (fr. Dec. 13). Osmund, Bp. Sarum, 1109.*		
5	c	Nonæ.			
			[A.D. 330.		
6	d	viii. Idus.	Nicolas, Bp. of Myra in Lycia,	S. 1st Cl.	D.
7	e	vii. Id.			
8	f	vi. Id.	Conception of B.V. Mary.	L.D.	D. II. Cl.
9	g	v. Id.		[w. Oct.	[w. Oct.
10	A	iv. Id.			
11	b	iii. Id.			
12	c	Prid. Id.			
13	d	Idus.	Lucy, of Syracuse, V.M. A.D. 304.	S. 2nd Cl.	D.
14	e	xix. Kal. Jan.			
15	f	xviii. Kal.			
16	g	xvii. Kal.	Antiphon, O Sapientia, at Vespers.		
17	A	xvi. Kal.			
18	b	xv. Kal.			
19	c	xiv. Kal.			
20	d	xiii. Kal.	*Vigil.*		
21	e	xii. Kal.	𝕮𝖍𝖔𝖒𝖆𝖘, 𝕬𝖕. 𝕸.	I.D.	D. II. Cl.
22	f	xi. Kal.			
23	g	x. Kal.			
24	A	ix. Kal.			
25	b	viii. Kal.	𝕮𝖍𝖗𝖎𝖘𝖙𝖒𝖆𝖘 𝕯𝖆𝖞.	P.D.	D. I. Cl.
26	c	vii. Kal.	𝕾𝖙𝖊𝖕𝖍𝖊𝖓, 𝕻𝖗𝖔𝖙𝖔𝖒𝖆𝖗𝖙𝖞𝖗.	L.D.	D. II. Cl.
27	d	vi. Kal.	𝕵𝖔𝖍𝖓, 𝕰𝖛. 𝕬𝖕.	L.D.	D. II. Cl.
28	e	v. Kal.	𝕳𝖔𝖑𝖞 𝕴𝖓𝖓𝖔𝖈𝖊𝖓𝖙𝖘.	L.D.	D. II. Cl.
29	f	iv. Kal.	Thomas, Abp. of Canterbury, M.	L.D.	S.D.
30	g	iii. Kal.	[A.D. 1170.		
31	A	Prid. Kal.	Silvester, Bp. of Rome, A.D. 335.	S. 2nd Cl.	D.

✠

At Matins bound, at Prime reviled, condemned to death at Tierce;
Nailed to the Cross at Sexts; at Nones His blessed side they pierce;
They take Him down at Vesper-tide, in grave at Compline lay;
Who henceforth bids His Church observe these sevenfold hours alway.

Prayers that may be said privately before the Divine Office.

GRANT, O Lord, that what we sing with our lips, we may believe in our hearts, and practise in our lives; through Jesus Christ our Lord. Amen.

Prayer of the Venerable Bede.

GRANT, I entreat Thee, Almighty God, that speaking with understanding and good will, and in plainness, I may deserve to be heard by Thee: for I need Thy help in all things; so that by the gift of Thy grace I may be enabled not unworthily to sing the words of Thy Majesty; through Jesus Christ our Lord. Amen.

GRANT, I beseech Thee, Lord God, that by the melody of this holy salter, my soul may be refreshed; use me always to apply myself to hy praises, and joyfully to come to hy blessedness; who livest and reignst God, world without end. Amen.

At Matins.

LORD Jesu Christ, Son of the Living God, Who at this Matin Iour didst will to be born, to be betrayed, taken, beaten with stripes, buffeted, and spit upon for the salvation of mankind; make us, we beseech Thee, joyfully and patiently to endure injuries and reproaches for the glory of Thy Name; and so continually to keep in remembrance the memory of Thy most Sacred Passion, that we may be enabled happily to attain to the glory and fellowship of Thy Resurrection; Who livest and reignest with the Father and the Holy Ghost, God, world without end. Amen.

At Prime.

O LORD Jesu Christ, Son of the Living God, Who in the First Hour of the day wast brought before Pilate: Who, the Judge of all judges, didst yet endure the severest doom; we most devoutly beseech Thee that Thou in Thy judgment wouldest be lenient to us miserable sinners; that in the last eternal judgment we be not condemned to punishment, but may rather attain to the fellowship of Thy faithful ones in heavenly places; Who livest and reignest God, world without end. Amen.

At Tierce.

O LORD Jesu Christ, Son of the Living God, Who at the Third Hour of the day wast led forth to the pain of the Cross, for the salvation of the world; we humbly beseech Thee that by the virtue of Thy most Sacred Passion, Thou wouldest blot out all our sins, and mercifully bring us to the glory of Thy blessedness; Who livest and reignest God, world without end. Amen.

At Sexts.

O LORD Jesu Christ, Son of the Living God, Who at the Sixth Hour of the day in Golgotha with great tumult didst ascend the Cross of suffering, whereon, thirsting for our salvation, Thou didst permit gall and vinegar to be given Thee to drink; we, Thy suppliants, beseech Thee that, kindling and inflaming our hearts, Thou wouldest make us to thirst for the cup of Thy Passion, and continually to find delight in Thee only, our crucified Lord; Who livest and reignest God, world without end. Amen.

At Nones.

O LORD Jesu Christ, Son of the Living God, Who at the Ninth Hour of the day, with hands extended upon the Cross, and bowing the head, didst deliver up Thy spirit to God the Father, and with the key of death didst most meritoriously unlock the gate of Paradise; grant to us, Thy suppliants, that in the hour of death Thou wouldest mercifully cause our souls to attain unto Thee, Who art the true Paradise; Who livest and reignest God, world without end. Amen.

At Vespers.

O LORD Jesu Christ, Son of the Living God, Who at the Vesper Hour of the day, being now made subject unto death, didst will to be taken down from the Cross, and (as is piously believed) to be received into the arms of Thy Mother; mercifully grant that we, casting away the burthens of our sins, may be enabled to attain even unto the presence of Thy divine Majesty; Who livest and reignest God, world without end. Amen.

At Compline.

O LORD Jesu Christ, Son of the Living God, Who at the Compline Hour rested in the sepulchre, and wast bewailed and lamented by Thy most gentle Mother, and by the other women; make us, we beseech Thee, to abound in the sorrows of Thy Passion, and with entire devotion of heart to bewail that same Passion, and to keep it ever as it were fresh in the ardent affection of our hearts; Who livest and reignest God, world without end. Amen.

Prayers after the Divine Office.

PREVENT us, O Lord, in all our doings with Thy most gracious favour, and further us with Thy continual help; that in all our works begun, continued, and ended in Thee, we may glorify Thy holy Name, and finally by Thy mercy obtain everlasting life; through Jesus Christ our Lord. Amen.

TO Thee, O Lord, I commend the Service which I, an unworthy sinner, have offered up unto Thee. God be merciful to me a sinner; and after Thy good knowledge and will, have pity upon me; through Jesus Christ our Lord. Amen.

✠

THE PSALTER.

SUNDAY.
Lauds.

These Sunday Psalms are said at Lauds on every Sunday throughout the year, (except from Septuagesima to Easter, when certain Psalms are changed, as below) and on all Festivals.

Lauds, being said immediately after Matins, are not begun with the Invocation, &c., like the other Hours, but straightway with the Sacerdotal ℣. and ℟.

℣. The Lord is high above all heathen.

℟. And His glory above the heavens.

℣. O God, make speed to save us.

℟. O Lord, make haste to help us.

℣. Glory be to the Father, and to the Son, and to the Holy Ghost.

℟. As it was in the beginning, is now, and ever shall be, world without end. Amen.

Alleluia.

[*From Septuagesima till Wednesday in Holy Week, inclusive, instead of* Alleluia *is said:*]

Praise be to Thee, O Lord, King of eternal glory.]

The Antiphons are said entire both before and after each Psalm on Sundays of the first class, and on Double Feasts in the Roman use: at other times (and always in the Sarum use), the first words only are said before, and the whole Antiphon is said after each Psalm.

Ant. The Lord is King * and hath put on glorious apparel: He hath girded Himself with strength, and His seat is from everlasting.

Dominus regnavit. Psalm xciii.

THE Lord is King, and hath put on glorious apparel : the Lord hath put on His apparel, and girded Himself with strength.

2 He hath made the round world so sure : that it cannot be moved.

3 Ever since the world began hath Thy seat been prepared : Thou art from everlasting.

4 The floods are risen, O Lord, the floods have lift up their voice: the floods lift up their waves.

5 The waves of the sea are mighty, and rage horribly : but yet the Lord, who dwelleth on high, is mightier.

6 Thy testimonies, O Lord, are very sure: holiness becometh Thine house for ever.

Glory be, etc.

Ant. The Lord is King, and hath put on glorious apparel : He hath girded Himself with strength, and His seat is from everlasting.

[*Instead of* Psalm xciii. *is said, between Septuagesima and Easter, with Antiphon of the Season:*

Miserere mei, Deus. Psalm li.

HAVE mercy upon me, O God, after Thy great goodness : according to the multitude of Thy mercies do away mine offences.

2 Wash me throughly from my wickedness : and cleanse me from my sin.

3 For I acknowledge my faults : and my sin is ever before me.

4 Against Thee only have I sinned, and done this evil in Thy sight : that Thou mightest be justified in Thy saying, and clear when Thou art judged.

5 Behold, I was shapen in wickedness : and in sin hath my mother conceived me.

6 But lo, Thou requirest truth in the inward parts : and shalt make me to understand wisdom secretly.

7 Thou shalt purge me with hyssop, and I shall be clean : Thou shalt wash me, and I shall be whiter than snow.

8 Thou shalt make me hear of joy and gladness : that the bones which Thou hast broken may rejoice.

9 Turn Thy face from my sins : and put out all my misdeeds.

10 Make me a clean heart, O God : and renew a right spirit within me.

11 Cast me not away from Thy presence : and take not Thy Holy Spirit from me.

12 O give me the comfort of Thy help again : and stablish me with Thy free Spirit.

13 Then shall I teach Thy ways unto the wicked : and sinners shall be converted unto Thee.

14 Deliver me from blood-guiltiness, O God, Thou that art the God of my health : and my tongue shall sing of Thy righteousness.

15 Thou shalt open my lips, O Lord : and my mouth shall show Thy praise.

16 For Thou desirest no sacrifice, else would I give it Thee : but Thou delightest not in burnt-offerings.

17 The sacrifice of God is a troubled spirit : a broken and contrite heart, O God, shalt Thou not despise.

18 O be favourable and gracious unto Sion : build Thou the walls of Jerusalem.

19 Then shalt Thou be pleased with the sacrifice of righteousness, with the burnt-offerings and oblations : then shall they offer young bullocks upon Thine altar.

Glory be, etc.]

Ant. Let us all know * that the Lord He is God : in Him let us be joyful, and exalt and praise His Name for ever.

Jubilate Deo. Psalm c.

O BE joyful in the Lord, all ye lands : serve the Lord with gladness, and come before His presence with a song.

2 Be ye sure that the Lord He is God : it is He that hath made us, and not we ourselves ; we are His people, and the sheep of His pasture.

3 O go your way into His gates with thanksgiving, and into His courts with praise : be thankful unto Him, and speak good of His Name.

4 For the Lord is gracious, His mercy is everlasting : and His truth endureth from generation to generation.

Glory be, etc.

Ant. Let us all know that the Lord He is God : in Him let us be joyful, and exalt and praise His Name for ever.

[*Instead of* Ps. c. *is said, between Septuagesima and Easter, with Antiphon of the Season :*

Confitemini Domino. Psalm cxviii.

O GIVE thanks unto the Lord, for He is gracious : because His mercy endureth for ever.

2 Let Israel now confess that He is gracious : and that His mercy endureth for ever.

3 Let the house of Aaron now confess : that His mercy endureth for ever.

4 Yea, let them now that fear the Lord confess : that His mercy endureth for ever.

5 I called upon the Lord in trouble : and the Lord heard me at large.

6 The Lord is on my side : I will not fear what man doeth unto me.

7 The Lord taketh my part with them that help me : therefore shall I see my desire upon mine enemies.

8 It is better to trust in the Lord : than to put any confidence in man.

9 It is better to trust in the Lord : than to put any confidence in princes.

10 All nations compassed me round about : but in the Name of the Lord will I destroy them.

11 They kept me in on every side, they kept me in, I say, on every side : but in the Name of the Lord will I destroy them.

12 They came about me like bees, and are extinct even as the fire among the thorns : for in the Name of the Lord I will destroy them.

13 Thou hast thrust sore at me, that I might fall : but the Lord was my help.

14 The Lord is my strength, and my song : and is become my salvation.

15 The voice of joy and health is in the dwellings of the righteous : the right hand of the Lord bringeth mighty things to pass.

16 The right hand of the Lord hath the pre-eminence : the right hand of the Lord bringeth mighty things to pass.

17 I shall not die, but live : and declare the works of the Lord.

LAUDS: SUNDAY.

18 The Lord hath chastened and corrected me: but He hath not given me over unto death.
19 Open me the gates of righteousness: that I may go into them, and give thanks unto the Lord.
20 This is the gate of the Lord: the righteous shall enter into it.
21 I will thank Thee, for Thou hast heard me: and art become my salvation.
22 The same stone which the builders refused: is become the head-stone in the corner.
23 This is the Lord's doing: and it is marvellous in our eyes.
24 This is the day which the Lord hath made: we will rejoice and be glad in it.
25 Help me now, O Lord: O Lord, send us now prosperity.
26 Blessed be He that cometh in the Name of the Lord: we have wished you good luck, ye that are of the house of the Lord.
27 God is the Lord who hath shewed us light: bind the sacrifice with cords, yea, even unto the horns of the altar.
28 Thou art my God, and I will thank Thee: Thou art my God, and I will praise Thee.
29 O give thanks unto the Lord, for He is gracious: and His mercy endureth for ever.
Glory be, etc.]

Ant. As long as I live * will I magnify Thee: that I may behold Thy power and glory.

Deus, Deus meus. Psalm LXIII.

O GOD, Thou art my God: early will I seek Thee.
2 My soul thirsteth for Thee, my flesh also longeth after Thee: in a barren and dry land, where no water is.
3 Thus have I looked for Thee in holiness: that I might behold Thy power and glory.
4 For Thy loving-kindness is better than the life itself: my lips shall praise Thee.
5 As long as I live will I magnify Thee on this manner: and lift up my hands in Thy Name.
6 My soul shall be satisfied, even as it were with marrow and fatness: when my mouth praiseth Thee with joyful lips.
7 Have I not remembered Thee in my bed: and thought upon Thee when I was waking?

8 Because Thou hast been my helper: therefore under the shadow of Thy wings will I rejoice.
9 My soul hangeth upon Thee: Thy right hand hath upholden me.
10 These also that seek the hurt of my soul: they shall go under the earth.
11 Let them fall upon the edge of the sword: that they may be a portion for foxes.
12 But the King shall rejoice in God; all they also that swear by Him shall be commended: for the mouth of them that speak lies shall be stopped.

Here is not said Glory be, etc.

Deus misereatur. Psalm LXVII.

GOD be merciful unto us, and bless us: and show us the light of His countenance, and be merciful unto us;
2 That Thy way may be known upon earth: Thy saving health among all nations.
3 Let the people praise Thee, O God: yea, let all the people praise Thee.
4 O let the nations rejoice and be glad: for Thou shalt judge the folk righteously, and govern the nations upon earth.
5 Let the people praise Thee, O God: let all the people praise Thee.
6 Then shall the earth bring forth her increase: and God, even our own God, shall give us His blessing.
7 God shall bless us: and all the ends of the world shall fear Him.
Glory be, etc.

Ant. As long as I live will I magnify Thee: that I may behold Thy power and glory.

Ant. Let every creature * which is in heaven and on the earth bless the Lord: praise Him and magnify Him for ever.

Song of the Three Children.
Benedicite.

O ALL ye Works of the Lord, bless ye the Lord : praise Him, and magnify Him for ever.

2 O ye Angels of the Lord, bless ye the Lord : O ye Heavens, bless ye the Lord.

3 O ye Waters that be above the Firmament, bless ye the Lord : O all ye Powers of the Lord, bless ye the Lord.

4 O ye Sun and Moon, bless ye the Lord : O ye Stars of Heaven, bless ye the Lord.

5 O ye Showers and Dew, bless ye the Lord : O ye Winds of God, bless ye the Lord.

6 O ye Fire and Heat, bless ye the Lord : O ye Winter and Summer, bless ye the Lord.

7 O ye Dews and Frosts, bless ye the Lord : O ye Frost and Cold, bless ye the Lord.

8 O ye Ice and Snow, bless ye the Lord : O ye Nights and Days, bless ye the Lord.

9 O ye Light and Darkness, bless ye the Lord : O ye Lightnings and Clouds, bless ye the Lord.

10 O let the earth bless the Lord : yea, let it praise Him, and magnify Him for ever.

11 O ye Mountains and Hills, bless ye the Lord : O all ye Green Things upon the earth, bless ye the Lord.

12 O ye Wells, bless ye the Lord : O ye Seas and Floods, bless ye the Lord.

13 O ye Whales, and all that move in the waters, bless ye the Lord : O all ye Fowls of the air, bless ye the Lord.

14 O all ye Beasts and Cattle, bless ye the Lord : O ye Children of men, bless ye the Lord.

15 O let Israel bless the Lord : praise Him, and magnify Him for ever.

16 O ye Priests of the Lord, bless ye the Lord : O ye Servants of the Lord, bless ye the Lord.

17 O ye Spirits and Souls of the righteous, bless ye the Lord : O ye holy and humble Men of heart, bless ye the Lord.

18 O Ananias, Azarias, and Misael, bless ye the Lord : praise Him and magnify Him for ever.

Instead of Glory be, etc.

Let us bless the Father, the Son, and the Holy Ghost : let us praise and exalt Him above all for ever.

Blessed art Thou, O Lord, in the firmament of heaven : and above all to be praised and glorified for ever.

Ant. Let every creature which is in heaven, and on the earth, bless the Lord : praise Him and magnify Him for ever.

Ant. Let every thing that hath breath * praise the Lord : for He spake the word, and they were made; He commanded, and they were created.

Laudate Dominum. Psalm CXLVIII.

O PRAISE the Lord of heaven : praise Him in the height.

2 Praise Him, all ye angels of His : praise Him, all His host.

3 Praise Him, sun and moon : praise Him, all ye stars and light.

4 Praise Him, all ye heavens : and ye waters that are above the heavens.

5 Let them praise the Name of the Lord : for He spake the word, and they were made; He commanded, and they were created.

6 He hath made them fast for ever and ever : He hath given them a law which shall not be broken.

7 Praise the Lord upon earth : ye dragons, and all deeps;

8 Fire and hail, snow and vapours : wind and storm, fulfilling His word;

9 Mountains and all hills : fruitful trees and all cedars :
10 Beasts and all cattle : worms and feathered fowls;
11 Kings of the earth and all people: princes and all judges of the world;
12 Young men and maidens, old men and children, praise the Name of the Lord : for His Name only is excellent, and His praise above heaven and earth.
13 He shall exalt the horn of His people; all His saints shall praise Him : even the children of Israel, even the people that serveth Him.

Here is not said Glory be, etc.

Cantate Domino. Psalm CXLIX.

O SING unto the Lord a new song : let the congregation of saints praise Him.
2 Let Israel rejoice in Him that made him : and let the children of Sion be joyful in their King.
3 Let them praise His Name in the dance : let them sing praises unto Him with tabret and harp.
4 For the Lord hath pleasure in His people : and helpeth the meek-hearted.
5 Let the saints be joyful with glory : let them rejoice in their beds.
6 Let the praises of God be in their mouth : and a two-edged sword in their hands;
7 To be avenged of the heathen : and to rebuke the people;
8 To bind their kings in chains : and their nobles with links of iron.
9 That they may be avenged of them, as it is written : Such honour have all His saints.

Here is not said Glory be, etc.

Laudate Dominum. Psalm CL.

O PRAISE God in His holiness : praise Him in the firmament of His power.

2 Praise Him in His noble acts : praise Him according to His excellent greatness.
3 Praise Him in the sound of the trumpet : praise Him upon the lute and harp.
4 Praise Him in the cymbals and dances : praise Him upon the strings and pipe.
5 Praise Him upon the well-tuned cymbals : praise Him upon the loud cymbals.
6 Let every thing that hath breath : praise the Lord.

Glory be, etc.

Ant. Let every thing that hath breath praise the Lord : for He spake the word, and they were made; He commanded, and they were created.

[*These Antiphons are thus said except on lesser privileged Sundays : when all the Psalms are said under the first Antiphon.*]

From Epiphany to Septuagesima, and from Trinity to Advent :

CHAPTER. Rev. VII.

BLESSING, and glory, and wisdom, and thanksgiving, and honour, and power, and might, be unto our God for ever and ever. Amen.

℟. Thanks be to God.

[*For Chapter at other times, see Proper of Seasons.*]

After Trinity, on Sundays and all Ferias :

HYMN. *Ecce jam noctis.*

LO! now the melting shades of night are ending,
Flickers the golden gleam of dawning day,
Let us before the Lord of all, low bending,
   Suppliants pray;

That He would of the stain of guilt relieve us,
Grant our soul's health, of His most blessed love,
And of His pitying grace and mercy give us
   Heaven above.

Be this by Thy thrice holy Godhead granted,
Father, and Son, and Spirit ever blest,
Whose glory by the firmament is chanted,
   By all confest. Amen.

℣. The Lord is King.
℟. He hath put on glorious apparel. Alleluia.
[*For Hymns at other times, see Proper of Seasons.*]
Ant. to Ben. in Proper of Seasons.
[*Ferial Antiphons.*
Monday.—Blessed be: * the Lord God of Israel.
Tuesday.—And the Lord shall be to us * a mighty salvation: in the house of His servant David.
Wednesday.—That we should be saved * from our enemies, and from the hands of all that hate us: good Lord, deliver us.
Thursday.—Let us serve the Lord* in holiness : and He shall deliver us out of the hand of our enemies.
Friday.—Through the tender mercy * of our God : whereby the Dayspring from on high hath visited us.
Saturday.—Guide our feet, * O Lord: into the way of peace.]

Song of Zacharias.
Benedictus. S. Luke i.

BLESSED be the Lord God of Israel : for He hath visited and redeemed His people ;

2 And hath raised up a mighty salvation for us : in the house of His servant David ;

3 As He spake by the mouth of His holy prophets : which have been since the world began ;

4 That we should be saved from our enemies : and from the hands of all that hate us ;

5 To perform the mercy promised to our forefathers : and to remember His holy covenant.

6 To perform the oath which He sware to our forefather Abraham : that He would give us ;

7 That we being delivered out of the hand of our enemies : might serve Him without fear ;

8 In holiness and righteousness before Him : all the days of our life.

9 And thou, child, shalt be called the prophet of the Highest: for thou shalt go before the face of the Lord to prepare His ways ;

10 To give knowledge of salvation unto His people : for the remission of their sins,

11 Through the tender mercy of our God : whereby the day-spring from on high hath visited us ;

12 To give light to them that sit in darkness, and in the shadow of death : and to guide our feet into the way of peace.

Glory be, etc.

℣. The Lord be with you.
℟. And with thy spirit.

Let us pray.

Collect in Proper of Seasons.

The Sunday Collect is said at every hour on Sunday, and through the week, when the Office is of the Season ; except when otherwise ordered in the Proper of Seasons. For directions as to endings of Collects, see General Rubrics.

℣. The Lord be with you.
℟. And with thy spirit.
℣. Bless we the Lord.
℟. Thanks be to God.

Sunday Memorials,

which follow the Collect for the day, unless the Memorial of any Festival intervene, in which case the ordinary Memorials yield precedence.

[*For Memorials in other seasons than Trinity, see Proper.*]

From the Octave of Trinity till Advent,

MEMORIAL OF THE HOLY CROSS : *omitted on doubles and on days within Octaves.*

Ant. It behoveth us to glory: in the Cross of our Lord Jesus Christ.

℣. All the world shall worship Thee, and sing of Thee.
℟. And praise Thy Name.

Let us pray.

COLLECT.

O GOD, Who didst ascend Thy holy Cross to enlighten the darkness of the world; may it please Thee to enlighten our hearts and bodies, Thou Saviour of the world, Who livest and reignest with the Father and the Holy Ghost, ever one God, world without end. Amen.

MEMORIAL OF S. MARY:

said also on all Double Feasts; on every day of the week but Saturday, and on days within Octaves; but not on Feasts of S. Mary.

Ant. Lo, Mary hath brought forth the Saviour, of Whom when John saw Him, he said: Behold the Lamb of God, which taketh away the sins of the world.

℣. After child-bearing thou remainedst a Virgin.
℟. O Mother of God.

Let us pray.

COLLECT.

O GOD, Who through the fruitful virginity of the Blessed Virgin Mary, hast bestowed the rewards of eternal salvation on the human race; grant, we beseech Thee, that she may intercede for us, through whom we have received the Author of Life, Thy Son Jesus Christ our Lord. Amen.

℣. The Lord be with you.
℟. And with thy spirit.
℣. Bless we the Lord.
℟. Thanks be to God.

FOR THE PEACE OF THE CHURCH:

Said after Lauds daily throughout the year, except on Christmas Eve, and thence till first Sunday after Octave of Epiphany; after Wednesday before Easter till first Sunday after Trinity; on all Double Feasts, on All Souls' Day, and in the Octaves of Corpus Christi, Repose B.V.M., Holy Name, and Dedication.

Ad Te levavi oculos meos. Psalm CXXIII.

UNTO Thee lift I up mine eyes: O Thou that dwellest in the heavens.

2 Behold, even as the eyes of servants look unto the hand of their masters, and as the eyes of a maiden unto the hand of her mistress: even so our eyes wait upon the Lord our God, until He have mercy upon us.

3 Have mercy upon us, O Lord, have mercy upon us : for we are utterly despised.

4 Our soul is filled with the scornful reproof of the wealthy : and with the despitefulness of the proud.

Glory be, etc.

Lord, have mercy.
Christ, have mercy.
Lord, have mercy.

Our Father:

Said silently throughout. The Priest repeats aloud:

℣. And lead us not into temptation.
℟. But deliver us from evil.
℣. O Lord, arise, help us.
℟. And deliver us for Thy Name's sake.
℣. Turn us again, O Lord God of Hosts.
℟. Show the light of Thy countenance, and we shall be whole.
℣. Hear my prayer, O Lord.
℟. And let my crying come unto Thee.
℣. The Lord be with you.
℟. And with thy spirit.

Let us pray.

O LORD, we beseech Thee, mercifully to hear the prayers of Thy Church, and grant that we, being delivered from all adversities, may serve Thee with a quiet mind; and grant us Thy peace all the days of our life; through Jesus Christ our Lord, who liveth and reigneth with Thee and the Holy Ghost, ever One God, world without end. Amen.

MONDAY.
Lauds.

This ℣. and ℟. is said on all Ferias from Epiphany to Lent, and from Trinity to Advent, when the Office is of the Feria.

℣. Let Thy merciful kindness, O Lord, be upon us.

℟. As we do put our trust in Thee.

℣. O God, make speed to save us.

℟. O Lord, make haste to help us.

℣. Glory be to the Father, and to the Son: and to the Holy Ghost.

℟. As it was in the beginning, is now, and ever shall be: world without end. Amen.

Alleluia.

[*From Septuagesima to Wednesday in Holy Week:*

Praise be to Thee, O Lord, King of eternal glory.]

Ant. Have mercy.

(Antiphons are never doubled on Ferias.)

Miserere mei, Deus. Psalm LI.

HAVE mercy upon me, O God, after Thy great goodness: according to the multitude of Thy mercies, do away mine offences.

2 Wash me throughly from my wickedness: and cleanse me from my sin.

3 For I acknowledge my faults: and my sin is ever before me.

4 Against Thee only have I sinned, and done this evil in Thy sight: that Thou mightest be justified in Thy saying, and clear when Thou art judged.

5 Behold, I was shapen in wickedness: and in sin hath my mother conceived me.

6 But lo, Thou requirest truth in the inward parts: and shalt make me to understand wisdom secretly.

7 Thou shalt purge me with hyssop, and I shall be clean: Thou shalt wash me, and I shall be whiter than snow.

8 Thou shalt make me hear of joy and gladness: that the bones which Thou hast broken may rejoice.

9 Turn Thy face from my sins: and put out all my misdeeds.

10 Make me a clean heart, O God: and renew a right spirit within me.

11 Cast me not away from Thy presence: and take not Thy Holy Spirit from me.

12 O give me the comfort of Thy help again: and stablish me with Thy free Spirit.

13 Then shall I teach Thy ways unto the wicked: and sinners shall be converted unto Thee.

14 Deliver me from blood-guiltiness, O God, Thou that art the God of my health: and my tongue shall sing of Thy righteousness.

15 Thou shalt open my lips, O Lord: and my mouth shall show Thy praise.

16 For Thou desirest no sacrifice, else would I give it Thee: but Thou delightest not in burnt-offerings.

17 The sacrifice of God is a troubled spirit: a broken and contrite heart, O God, shalt Thou not despise.

18 O be favourable and gracious unto Sion: build Thou the walls of Jerusalem.

19 Then shalt Thou be pleased with the sacrifice of righteousness, with the burnt-offerings and oblations : then shall they offer young bullocks upon Thine altar.
Glory be, etc.

Ant. Have mercy : upon me, O God.

Ant. Consider.
Verba mea auribus. Psalm v.

PONDER my words, O Lord : consider my meditation.
2 O hearken Thou unto the voice of my calling, my King and my God: for unto Thee will I make my prayer.
3 My voice shalt Thou hear betimes, O Lord : early in the morning will I direct my prayer unto Thee, and will look up.
4 For Thou art the God that hast no pleasure in wickedness : neither shall any evil dwell with Thee.
5 Such as be foolish shall not stand in Thy sight : for Thou hatest all them that work vanity.
6 Thou shalt destroy them that speak leasing : the Lord will abhor both the blood-thirsty and deceitful man.
7 But as for me, I will come into Thine house, even upon the multitude of Thy mercy : and in Thy fear will I worship toward Thy holy temple.
8 Lead me, O Lord, in Thy righteousness, because of mine enemies : make Thy way plain before my face.
9 For there is no faithfulness in his mouth : their inward parts are very wickedness.
10 Their throat is an open sepulchre : they flatter with their tongue.
11 Destroy Thou them, O God; let them perish through their own imaginations : cast them out in the multitude of their ungodliness; for they have rebelled against Thee.
12 And let all them that put their trust in Thee rejoice : they shall ever be giving of thanks, because Thou defendest them; they that love Thy Name shall be joyful in Thee.
13 For Thou, Lord, wilt give Thy blessing unto the righteous : and with Thy favourable kindness wilt Thou defend him as with a shield.
Glory be, etc.

Ant. Consider my meditation : O Lord.

Ant. O God.
Deus, Deus meus. Psalm LXIII.
Deus misereatur. Psalm LXVII., p. 5.

Ant. O God, Thou art my God : early will I seek Thee.

Ant. Thine anger is turned away.
SONG OF ISAIAH.
Confitebor Tibi. Is. XII.

O LORD, I will praise Thee : though Thou wast angry with me, Thine anger is turned away, and Thou comfortedst me.
2 Behold, God is my salvation; I will trust, and not be afraid : for the Lord Jehovah is my strength and my song; He also is become my salvation.
3 Therefore with joy shall ye draw water: out of the wells of salvation.
4 Praise the Lord, call upon His Name : declare His doings among the people, make mention that His Name is exalted.
5 Sing unto the Lord; for He hath done excellent things : this is known in all the earth.
6 Cry out and shout, thou inhabitant of Sion : for great is the Holy One of Israel in the midst of thee.
Glory be, etc.

Ant. Thine anger is turned away, O Lord : and Thou comfortedst me.

Ant. O praise.
Laudate Dominum. Psalm CXLVIII.
Cantate Domino. Psalm CXLIX.
Laudate Dominum. Psalm CL., p. 6.

Ant. O praise: the Lord of heaven.

From Epiphany to Lent, and from Trinity to Advent :

CHAPTER. 1 Cor. XVI.

WATCH ye, stand fast in the faith, quit you like men, be strong. Let all your things be done with charity.

℟. Thanks be to God.

From Trinity to Advent :
HYMN. *Ecce jam noctis,* p. 7.

℣. Have I not thought upon Thee when I was waking?
℟. Because Thou hast been my helper.

[*For Chapters and Hymns at other times, see Proper of Seasons.*]

Ferial Antiphons and Benedictus, p. 8.

PETITIONS.

(These are not said in Christmas or Easter tides. Lauds then end as on Sunday.)

Lord, have mercy [iii].
Christ, have mercy [iii].
Lord, have mercy [iii].
Our Father :

Said silently throughout. The Priest repeats aloud :

℣. And lead us not into temptation.
℟. But deliver us from evil.
℣. I said, Lord, be merciful unto me.
℟. Heal my soul, for I have sinned against Thee.
℣. Turn Thee again, O Lord, at the last.
℟. And be gracious unto Thy servants.

℣. Let Thy merciful kindness, O Lord, be upon us.
℟. As we do put our trust in Thee.
℣. Let Thy priests be clothed with righteousness.
℟. And Thy saints sing with joyfulness.
℣. O Lord, save the Queen.
℟. And mercifully hear us when we call upon Thee.
℣. O Lord, save Thy servants and handmaidens.
℟. Which put their trust in Thee.
℣. O Lord, save Thy people, and bless Thine inheritance.
℟. Govern them, and lift them up for ever.
℣. Peace be within Thy walls.
℟. And plenteousness within Thy palaces.
℣. Let us pray for the faithful departed.
℟. Eternal rest grant unto them, O Lord, and light perpetual shine upon them.
℣. Hearken unto my voice, O Lord, when I cry unto Thee.
℟. Have mercy upon me, and hear me.

Miserere mei, Deus. Psalm LI., p. 10. *with* Glory be, etc.

[*Here follows in Lent :*

Domine, ne in furore. Psalm VI.

O LORD, rebuke me not in Thine indignation : neither chasten me in Thy displeasure.

2 Have mercy upon me, O Lord, for I am weak : O Lord, heal me, for my bones are vexed.

3 My soul also is sore troubled : but, Lord, how long wilt Thou punish me?

4 Turn Thee, O Lord, and deliver my soul : O save me for Thy mercy's sake.

5 For in death no man remembereth Thee : and who will give Thee thanks in the pit?

6 I am weary of my groaning ; every night wash I my bed : and water my couch with my tears.

7 My beauty is gone for very trouble : and worn away because of all mine enemies.

8 Away from me, all ye that work vanity :

LAUDS : MONDAY.

for the Lord hath heard the voice of my weeping.
9 The Lord hath heard my petition : the Lord will receive my prayer.
10 All mine enemies shall be confounded, and sore vexed : they shall be turned back, and put to shame suddenly.
Glory be, etc.]

(Here the reader, if a Priest, rising, stands at the step of the Sanctuary.)

℣. O Lord, arise, help us.
℟. And deliver us for Thy Name's sake.
℣. Turn us again, O Lord God of Hosts.
℟. Show the light of Thy countenance, and we shall be whole.
℣. Hear my prayer, O Lord.
℟. And let my crying come unto Thee.
℣. The Lord be with you.
℟. And with thy spirit.

Let us pray.
Collect.

℣. The Lord be with you.
℟. And with thy spirit.
℣. Bless we the Lord.
℟. Thanks be to God.

Ferial Memorials :

Said on all Ferias and Simple Feasts, according to the rubric before Sunday Memorials, p. 8.

[*For Memorials in other seasons than Trinity, see Proper.*]

From the Octave of Trinity till Advent:

MEMORIAL OF THE HOLY CROSS.

Ant. Save us, O Christ our Saviour, by the virtue of the Holy Cross : as Thou savedst Peter in the sea; and have mercy upon us.

℣. All the world shall worship Thee, and sing of Thee.
℟. And praise Thy Name.

Let us pray.
COLLECT.

KEEP, we beseech Thee, O Lord, in perpetual peace, those whom Thou hast vouchsafed to redeem by the wood of the Holy Cross, O Saviour of the world, Who livest and reignest with the Father and the Holy Ghost, ever one God, world without end. Amen.

MEMORIAL OF S. MARY.

Ant. The Root of Jesse hath budded; a Star hath risen out of Jacob ; a Virgin hath brought forth the Saviour: We praise Thee, O our God.

℣. After child-bearing thou remainedst a Virgin.
℟. O Mother of God.

Let us pray.
COLLECT.

O GOD, Who through the fruitful virginity of the Blessed Virgin Mary hast bestowed the rewards of eternal salvation on the human race; grant, we pray Thee, that she may intercede for us, through whom we have received the Author of Life, Thy Son Jesus Christ our Lord. Amen.

MEMORIAL OF ALL SAINTS.

Ant. Let the Saints be joyful with glory : they shall rejoice in their beds.
℣. The souls of the righteous are in the hand of God.
℟. And there shall no torment touch them.

Let us pray.
COLLECT.

WE pray Thee, O Lord, let the intercession of all Thy Saints be acceptable unto Thee ; and grant us forgiveness of our sins and the remedies of eternal life, through Jesus Christ our Lord. Amen.

℣. The Lord be with you.
℟. And with thy spirit.
℣. Bless we the Lord.
℟. Thanks be to God.

FOR THE PEACE OF THE CHURCH
As at Sunday Lauds, p. 9.

TUESDAY.

Lauds.

℣. Let Thy merciful kindness, O Lord, be upon us.
℟. As we do put our trust in Thee.
℣. O God, make speed to save us.
℟. O Lord, make haste to help us.
℣. Glory be to the Father, and to the Son : and to the Holy Ghost.
℟. As it was in the beginning, is now, and ever shall be : world without end. Amen.
Alleluia.

[*From Septuagesima to Wednesday in Holy Week :*

Praise be to Thee, O Lord, King of eternal glory.]

Ant. According to the multitude.

Miserere mei. Psalm LI., p. 10.

Ant. According to the multitude of Thy mercies : have mercy upon me, O God.

Ant. The help of my countenance.

Judica me, Deus. Psalm XLIII.

GIVE sentence with me, O God, and defend my cause against the ungodly people : O deliver me from the deceitful and wicked man.

2 For Thou art the God of my strength, why hast Thou put me from Thee: and why go I so heavily, while the enemy oppresseth me?

3 O send out Thy light and Thy truth, that they may lead me : and bring me unto Thy holy hill, and to Thy dwelling.

4 And that I may go unto the altar of God, even unto the God of my joy and gladness : and upon the harp will I give thanks unto Thee, O God, my God.

5 Why art thou so heavy, O my soul : and why art thou so disquieted within me?

6 O put thy trust in God : for I will yet give Him thanks, which is the help of my countenance, and my God.

Glory be, etc.

Ant. The help of my countenance : and my God.

Ant. Early.

Deus, Deus meus. Psalm LXIII.
Deus misereatur. Psalm LXVII., p. 5.

Ant. Early : will I seek Thee.

Ant. All the days of my life.

SONG OF HEZEKIAH.

Ego dixi. Isaiah XXXVIII.

I SAID, in the cutting off of my days : I shall go to the gates of the grave.

2 I am deprived of the residue of my years : I said, I shall not see the Lord, even the Lord in the land of the living.

3 I shall behold man no more : with the inhabitants of the world.

4 Mine age is departed : and is removed from me as a shepherd's tent.

5 I have cut off like a weaver my

life : He will cut me off with pining sickness.

6 From day even to night, wilt Thou make an end of me : I reckoned till morning that, as a lion, so will He break all my bones.

7 From day even to night wilt Thou make an end of me : like a crane or a swallow, so did I chatter; I did mourn as a dove.

8 Mine eyes fail : with looking upward.

9 O Lord, I am oppressed; undertake for me : what shall I say? He hath both spoken unto me, and Himself hath done it.

10 I shall go softly all my years: in the bitterness of my soul.

11 O Lord, by these things men live, and in all these things is the life of my spirit: so wilt Thou recover me, and make me to live; behold, for peace I had great bitterness.

12 But Thou hast in love to my soul delivered it from the pit of corruption : for Thou hast cast all my sins behind Thy back.

13 For the grave cannot praise Thee, death cannot celebrate Thee : they that go down into the pit cannot hope for Thy truth.

14 The living, the living, he shall praise Thee, as I do this day : the father to the children shall make known Thy truth.

15 The Lord was ready to save me : therefore we will sing my songs to the stringed instruments all the days of our life in the house of the Lord.

Glory be, etc.

Ant. All the days of my life : the Lord was ready to save me.

Ant. Praise Him.

Laudate Dominum. Psalm CXLVIII.
Cantate Domino. Psalm CXLIX.
Laudate Dominum. Psalm CL., p. 6.

Ant. Praise Him : in the firmament of His power.

From Epiphany to Lent, and from Trinity to Advent:

CHAPTER. 1 Cor. XVI.

WATCH ye, stand fast in the faith, quit you like men, be strong. Let all your things be done with charity.

℟. Thanks be to God.

From Trinity to Advent, all the rest as pp. 12, 13.

WEDNESDAY.
Lauds.

℣. Let Thy merciful kindness, O Lord, be upon us.
℟. As we do put our trust in Thee.
℣. O God, make speed to save us.
℟. O Lord, make haste to help us.
℣. Glory be to the Father, and to the Son : and to the Holy Ghost.
℟. As it was in the beginning, is now, and ever shall be : world without end. Amen.

[*From Septuagesima to Wednesday in Holy Week:*

Praise be to Thee, O Lord, King of eternal glory.]

Ant. Wash me throughly.

Miserere mei. Psalm LI., p. 10.

Ant. Wash me throughly : from my wickedness, O God.

Ant. Thou, O God.

Te decet hymnus. Psalm LXV.

THOU, O God, art praised in Sion: and unto Thee shall the vow be performed in Jerusalem.

2 Thou that hearest the prayer: unto Thee shall all flesh come.

3 My misdeeds prevail against me: O be Thou merciful unto our sins.

4 Blessed is the man, whom Thou choosest, and receivest unto Thee: he shall dwell in Thy court, and shall be satisfied with the pleasures of Thy house, even of Thy holy temple.

5 Thou shalt show us wonderful things in Thy righteousness, O God of our salvation: Thou that art the hope of all the ends of the earth, and of them that remain in the broad sea.

6 Who in His strength setteth fast the mountains: and is girded about with power.

7 Who stilleth the raging of the sea: and the noise of his waves, and the madness of the people.

8 They also that dwell in the uttermost parts of the earth shall be afraid at Thy tokens: Thou that makest the outgoings of the morning and evening to praise Thee.

9 Thou visitest the earth, and blessest it: Thou makest it very plenteous.

10 The river of God is full of water: Thou preparest their corn, for so Thou providest for the earth.

11 Thou waterest her furrows, Thou sendest rain into the little valleys thereof: Thou makest it soft with the drops of rain, and blessest the increase of it.

12 Thou crownest the year with Thy goodness: and Thy clouds drop fatness.

13 They shall drop upon the dwellings of the wilderness: and the little hills shall rejoice on every side.

14 The folds shall be full of sheep: the valleys also shall stand so thick with corn, that they shall laugh and sing.

Glory be, etc.

Ant. Thou, O God: art praised in Sion.

Ant. My lips shall praise Thee.
Deus, Deus meus. Psalm LXIII.
Deus misereatur. Psalm LXVII., p. 5.

Ant. My lips shall praise Thee: as long as I live.

Ant. The Lord shall judge.

SONG OF HANNAH.
Exultavit cor meum. 1 Sam. II.

MY heart rejoiceth in the Lord: mine horn is exalted in the Lord.

2 My mouth is enlarged over mine enemies: because I rejoice in Thy salvation.

3 There is none holy as the Lord: for there is none beside Thee: neither is there any rock like our God.

4 Talk no more: so exceeding proudly.

5 Let not arrogancy come out of your mouth: for the Lord is a God of knowledge, and by Him actions are weighed.

6 The bows of the mighty men are broken: and they that stumbled are girded with strength.

7 They that were full have hired out themselves for bread: and they that were hungry ceased.

8 So that the barren hath born seven: and she that hath many children is waxed feeble.

9 The Lord killeth, and maketh alive: He bringeth down to the grave, and bringeth up.

10 The Lord maketh poor, and maketh rich: He bringeth low, and lifteth up.

11 He raiseth up the poor out of the dust: and lifteth up the beggar from the dunghill.

12 To set them among princes: and to make them inherit the throne of glory.

13 For the pillars of the earth are the Lord's : and He hath set the world upon them.

14 He will keep the feet of His saints, and the wicked shall be silent in darkness : for by strength shall no man prevail.

15 The adversaries of the Lord shall be broken to pieces : out of heaven shall He thunder upon them.

16 The Lord shall judge the ends of the earth : and He shall give strength unto His king, and exalt the horn of His anointed.

Glory be, etc.

Ant. The Lord shall judge : the ends of the earth.

Ant. O praise God.

Laudate Dominum. Psalm CXLVIII.
Cantate Domino. Psalm CXLIX.
Laudate Dominum. Psalm CL. p. 6.

Ant. O praise God : all ye heavens.

From Epiphany to Lent and from Trinity to Advent:

CHAPTER. 1 Cor. XVI.

WATCH ye, stand fast in the faith, quit you like men, be strong. Let all your things be done with charity.

℟. Thanks be to God.

From Trinity to Advent, all the rest as pp. 12, 13.

THURSDAY.
Lauds.

℣. Let Thy merciful kindness, O Lord, be upon us.

℟. As we do put our trust in Thee.

℣. O God, make speed to save us.

℟. O Lord, make haste to help us.

℣. Glory be to the Father, and to the Son : and to the Holy Ghost.

℟. As it was in the beginning, is now, and ever shall be : world without end. Amen.

Alleluia.

[*From Septuagesima till Wednesday in Holy Week:*

Praise be to Thee, O Lord, King of eternal glory.]

Ant. Against Thee only.

Miserere mei. Psalm LI., p. 10.

Ant. Against Thee only have I sinned : have mercy upon me, O God.

Ant. Lord, Thou hast been.

Domine refugium. Psalm XC.

LORD, Thou hast been our refuge : from one generation to another.

2 Before the mountains were brought forth, or ever the earth and the world were made : Thou art God from everlasting, and world without end.

3 Thou turnest man to destruction : again Thou sayest, Come again, ye children of men.

4 For a thousand years in Thy sight are but as yesterday : seeing that is past as a watch in the night.

5 As soon as Thou scatterest them they are even as a sleep : and fade away suddenly like the grass.

6 In the morning it is green, and groweth up : but in the evening it is cut down, dried up, and withered.

7 For we consume away in Thy displeasure : and are afraid at Thy wrathful indignation.

8 Thou hast set our misdeeds before Thee : and our secret sins in the light of Thy countenance.

9 For when Thou art angry all our days are gone : we bring our

years to an end, as it were a tale that is told.

10 The days of our age are threescore years and ten; and though men be so strong that they come to fourscore years : yet is their strength then but labour and sorrow ; so soon passeth it away, and we are gone.

11 But who regardeth the power of Thy wrath : for even thereafter as a man feareth, so is Thy displeasure.

12 So teach us to number our days : that we may apply our hearts unto wisdom.

13 Turn Thee again, O Lord, at the last : and be gracious unto Thy servants.

14 O satisfy us with Thy mercy, and that soon : so shall we rejoice and be glad all the days of our life.

15 Comfort us again now after the time that Thou hast plagued us : and for the years wherein we have suffered adversity.

16 Show Thy servants Thy work : and their children Thy glory.

17 And the glorious Majesty of the Lord our God be upon us : prosper Thou the work of our hands upon us, O prosper Thou our handy-work.

Glory be, etc.

Ant. O Lord : Thou hast been our refuge.

Ant. Have I not thought?

Deus, Deus meus. Psalm LXIII.
Deus misereatur. Psalm LXVII., p. 5.

Ant. Have I not thought upon Thee : when I was waking?

Ant. The Lord shall reign.

Song of Moses.

Cantemus Domino. Exodus xv.

I WILL sing unto the Lord, for He hath triumphed gloriously : the horse and his rider hath He thrown into the sea.

2 The Lord is my strength and song : and is become my salvation.

3 He is my God, and I will prepare Him an habitation : my father's God, and I will exalt Him.

4 The Lord is a man of war; the Lord is His Name: Pharaoh's chariots and his host hath He cast into the sea.

5 His chosen captains also are drowned in the Red sea : the depths have covered them; they sank into the bottom as a stone.

6 Thy right hand, O Lord, is become glorious in power ; Thy right hand, O Lord, hath dashed in pieces the enemy : and in the greatness of Thine excellency Thou hast overthrown them that rose up against Thee.

7 Thou sentest forth Thy wrath, which consumed them as stubble : and with the blast of Thy nostrils the waters were gathered together.

8 The floods stood upright as an heap : and the depths were congealed in the heart of the sea.

9 The enemy said, I will pursue, I will overtake, I will divide the spoil : my lust shall be satisfied upon them.

10 I will draw my sword : my hand shall destroy them.

11 Thou didst blow with Thy wind, the sea covered them : they sank as lead in the mighty waters.

12 Who is like unto Thee, O Lord, among the gods : who is like unto Thee, glorious in holiness, fearful in praises, doing wonders?

13 Thou stretchedst out Thy right hand : the earth swallowed them.

14 Thou in Thy mercy : hast led forth the people which Thou hast redeemed.

15 Thou hast guided them in Thy strength : unto Thy holy habitation.

16 The people shall hear, and be afraid : sorrow shall take hold on the inhabitants of Palestina.

17 Then the dukes of Edom shall be amazed; the mighty men of Moab, trembling shall take hold upon them : all the inhabitants of Canaan shall melt away.

18 Fear and dread shall fall upon them : by the greatness of Thine arm.

19 They shall be as still as a stone: till Thy people pass over, O Lord, till the people pass over, which Thou hast purchased.

20 Thou shalt bring them in, and plant them in the mountain of Thine inheritance : in the place, O Lord, which Thou hast made for Thee to dwell in.

21 In the sanctuary, O Lord, which Thy hands have established : the Lord shall reign for ever and ever.

22 For the horse of Pharaoh went in with his chariots and with his horsemen into the sea : and the Lord brought again the waters of the sea upon them.

23 But the children of Israel went on dry land : in the midst of the sea.

Glory be, etc.

Ant. The Lord shall reign : for ever and ever.

Ant. O praise.

Laudate Dominum. Psalm CXLVIII.
Cantate Domino. Psalm CXLIX.
Laudate Dominum. Psalm CL., p. 6.

Ant. O praise : the Lord of heaven.

From Epiphany to Lent, and from Trinity to Advent :

CHAPTER. 1 Cor. XVI.

WATCH ye, stand fast in the faith, quit you like men, be strong.

Let all your things be done with charity.

℞. Thanks be to God.

From Trinity to Advent, all the rest as pp. 12, 13.

FRIDAY.

Lauds.

℣. Let Thy merciful kindness, O Lord, be upon us.

℞. As we do put our trust in Thee.

℣. O God, make speed to save us.

℞. O Lord, make haste to help us.

℣. Glory be to the Father, and to the Son : and to the Holy Ghost.

℞. As it was in the beginning, is now, and ever shall be : world without end. Amen.

Alleluia.

[*From Septuagesima to Wednesday in Holy Week :*

Praise be to Thee, O Lord, King of eternal glory.]

Ant. O stablish me.

Miserere mei, Deus. Psalm LI., p. 10.

Ant. O stablish me : with Thy free Spirit.

Ant. Hearken unto me.

Domine, exaudi. Psalm CXLIII.

HEAR my prayer, O Lord, and consider my desire: hearken unto me for Thy truth and righteousness' sake.

2 And enter not into judgment with Thy servant : for in Thy sight shall no man living be justified.

3 For the enemy hath persecuted my soul; he hath smitten my life down to the ground : he hath laid me in the darkness, as the men that have been long dead.

4 Therefore is my spirit vexed within me : and my heart within me is desolate.

5 Yet do I remember the time past; I muse upon all Thy works: yea, I exercise myself in the works of Thy hands.

6 I stretch forth my hands unto Thee : my soul gaspeth unto Thee as a thirsty land.

7 Hear me, O Lord, and that soon, for my spirit waxeth faint : hide not Thy face from me, lest I be like unto them that go down into the pit.

8 O let me hear Thy loving-kindness betimes in the morning, for in Thee is my trust : show Thou me the way that I should walk in, for I lift up my soul unto Thee.

9 Deliver me, O Lord, from mine enemies : for I flee unto Thee to hide me.

10 Teach me to do the thing that pleaseth Thee, for Thou art my God : let Thy loving Spirit lead me forth into the land of righteousness.

11 Quicken me, O Lord, for Thy Name's sake : and for Thy righteousness' sake bring my soul out of trouble.

12 And of Thy goodness slay mine enemies : and destroy all them that vex my soul; for I am Thy servant.

Glory be, etc.

Ant. Hearken unto me : for Thy truth and righteousness' sake.

Ant. God shew us.
Deus, Deus meus. Psalm LXIII.
Deus misereatur. Psalm LXVII., p. 5.

Ant. God shew us : the light of His countenance.

Ant. O Lord, I have heard.

SONG OF HABAKKUK.
Domine audivi. Habakkuk III.

O LORD, I have heard Thy speech: and was afraid.

2 O Lord, revive Thy work : in the midst of the years.

3 In the midst of the years make known : in wrath remember mercy.

4 God came from Teman : and the Holy One from Mount Paran.

5 His glory covered the heavens : and the earth was full of His praise.

6 And His brightness was as the light : He had horns coming out of His hand.

7 And there was the hiding of His power : before Him went the pestilence.

8 And burning coals went forth at His feet : He stood and measured the earth.

9 He beheld and drove asunder the nations : and the everlasting mountains were scattered.

10 The perpetual hills did bow : His ways are everlasting.

11 I saw the tents of Cushan in affliction : and the curtains of the land of Midian did tremble.

12 Was the Lord displeased against the rivers? was Thine anger against the rivers : was Thy wrath against the sea;

13 That Thou didst ride upon Thine horses : and Thy chariots of salvation?

14 Thy bow was made quite naked : according to the oaths of the tribes, even Thy word.

15 Thou didst cleave the earth with rivers : the mountains saw Thee, and they trembled.

16 The overflowing of the water : passed by.

17 The deep uttered his voice : and lifted up his hands on high.

18 The sun and moon stood still in their habitation : at the light of Thine arrows they went, and at the shining of Thy glittering spear.

19 Thou didst march through the

land in indignation : Thou didst thresh the heathen in anger.

20 Thou wentest forth for the salvation of Thy people : even for salvation with Thine Anointed.

21 Thou woundedst the head out of the house of the wicked : by discovering the foundation unto the neck.

22 Thou didst strike through with his staves the head of his villages : they came out as a whirlwind to scatter me.

23 Their rejoicing : was as to devour the poor secretly.

24 Thou didst walk through the sea with Thine horses : through the heap of great waters.

25 When I heard, my belly trembled : my lips quivered at the voice.

26 Rottenness entered into my bones : and I trembled in myself, that I might rest in the day of trouble.

27 When He cometh up unto the people : He will invade them with His troops.

28 Although the fig-tree shall not blossom : neither shall fruit be on the vines;

29 The labour of the olives shall fail : and the fields shall yield no meat;

30 The flock shall be cut off from the fold : and there shall be no herd in the stalls;

31 Yet I will rejoice in the Lord : I will joy in the God of my salvation.

32 The Lord God is my strength : and He will make my feet like hinds' feet.

33 And He will make me to walk : upon mine high places.

Glory be, etc.

Ant. O Lord, I have heard Thy speech : and was afraid.

Ant. Praise Him in the cymbals.
Laudate Dominum. Psalm CXLVIII.
Cantate Domino. Psalm CXLIX.
Laudate Dominum. Psalm CL., p. 6.

Ant. Praise Him in the cymbals and dances : praise Him upon the strings and pipe.

From Epiphany to Lent, and from Trinity to Advent:

CHAPTER. 1 Cor. XVI.

WATCH ye, stand fast in the faith, quit you like men, be strong. Let all your things be done with charity.

℟. Thanks be to God.

From Trinity to Advent, all the rest as pp. 12, 13.

SATURDAY.

Lauds.

℣. Let Thy merciful kindness, O Lord, be upon us.
℟. As we do put our trust in Thee.
℣. O God, make speed to save us.
℟. O Lord, make haste to help us.
℣. Glory be to the Father, and to the Son : and to the Holy Ghost.
℟. As it was in the beginning, is now, and ever shall be : world without end. Amen.

Alleluia.

[*From Septuagesima to Wednesday in Holy Week:*

Praise be to Thee, O Lord, King of eternal glory.]

Ant. O be favourable.
Miserere mei, Deus. Psalm LI., p. 10.

Ant. O be favourable : and gracious unto Sion.

Ant. It is a good thing.

Bonum est confiteri. Psalm xcii.

IT is a good thing to give thanks unto the Lord : and to sing praises unto Thy Name, O most Highest.

2 To tell of Thy loving-kindness early in the morning : and of Thy truth in the night-season.

3 Upon an instrument of ten strings, and upon the lute : upon a loud instrument, and upon the harp.

4 For Thou, Lord, hast made me glad through Thy works : and I will rejoice in giving praise for the operations of Thy hands.

5 O Lord, how glorious are Thy works : Thy thoughts are very deep.

6 An unwise man doth not well consider this : and a fool doth not understand it.

7 When the ungodly are green as the grass, and when all the workers of wickedness do flourish : then shall they be destroyed for ever; but Thou, Lord, art the most Highest for evermore.

8 For lo, Thine enemies, O Lord, lo, Thine enemies shall perish : and all the workers of wickedness shall be destroyed.

9 But mine horn shall be exalted like the horn of an unicorn : for I am anointed with fresh oil.

10 Mine eye also shall see his lust of mine enemies : and mine ear shall hear his desire of the wicked that arise up against me.

11 The righteous shall flourish like a palm-tree : and shall spread abroad like a cedar in Libanus.

12 Such as are planted in the house of the Lord : shall flourish in the courts of the house of our God.

13 They also shall bring forth more fruit in their age : and shall be fat and well-liking.

14 That they may show how true the Lord my strength is : and that there is no unrighteousness in Him.

Glory be, etc.

Ant. It is a good thing : to give thanks unto the Lord.

Ant. All the ends of the world.

Deus, Deus meus. Psalm lxiii.
Deus misereatur. Psalm lxvii., p. 5.

Ant. All the ends of the world : shall fear Him.

Ant. The Lord shall repent.

Song of Moses.

Audite cæli. Deut. xxxii.

GIVE ear, O ye heavens, and I will speak : and hear, O earth, the words of my mouth.

2 My doctrine shall drop as the rain : my speech shall distil as the dew.

3 As the small rain upon the tender herb : and as the showers upon the grass.

4 Because I will publish : the Name of the Lord.

5 Ascribe ye greatness : unto our God.

6 He is the Rock, His work is perfect : for all His ways are judgment.

7 A God of truth and without iniquity : just and right is He.

8 They have corrupted themselves : their spot is not the spot of His children.

9 They are a perverse : and crooked generation.

10 Do ye thus requite the Lord : O foolish people and unwise?

11 Is not He thy Father that hath bought thee : hath He not made thee, and established thee?

12 Remember the days of old : consider the years of many generations.

13 Ask thy father, and he will show thee : thy elders, and they will tell thee.

14 When the Most High divided to the nations their inheritance : when He separated the sons of Adam;

15 He set the bounds of the people : according to the number of the children of Israel.

16 For the Lord's portion is His people : Jacob is the lot of His inheritance.

17 He found him in a desert land : and in the waste howling wilderness.

18 He led him about, He instructed him : He kept him as the apple of His eye.

19 As an eagle stirreth up her nest, fluttereth over her young : spreadeth abroad her wings, taketh them, beareth them on her wings;

20 So the Lord alone did lead him : and there was no strange God with him.

21 He made him ride on the high places of the earth : that he might eat the increase of the fields.

22 And He made him suck honey out of the rock : and oil out of the flinty rock.

23 Butter of kine, and milk of sheep, with fat of lambs and rams of the breed of Bashan : and goats with the fat of the kidneys of wheat, and thou didst drink the pure blood of the grape.

24 But Jeshurun waxed fat, and kicked : thou art waxen fat, thou art grown thick, thou art covered with fatness.

25 Then he forsook God Which made him : and lightly esteemed the Rock of his salvation.

26 They provoked Him to jealousy with strange gods : with abominations provoked they Him to anger.

27 They sacrificed unto devils, not to God : to gods whom they knew not;

28 To new gods that came newly up : whom your fathers feared not.

29 Of the Rock that begat thee, thou art unmindful : and hast forgotten God that formed thee.

30 And when the Lord saw it He abhorred them : because of the provoking of His sons and of His daughters.

31 And He said, I will hide My face from them : I will see what their end shall be.

32 For they are a very froward generation : children in whom is no faith.

33 They have moved Me to jealousy with that which is not God : they have provoked Me to anger with their vanities;

34 And I will move them to jealousy with those which are not a people : I will provoke them to anger with a foolish nation.

35 For a fire is kindled in Mine anger : and shall burn unto the lowest hell;

36 And shall consume the earth with her increase : and set on fire the foundations of the mountains.

37 I will heap mischiefs upon them : I will spend Mine arrows upon them.

38 They shall be burnt with hunger : and devoured with burning heat, and with bitter destruction.

39 I will also send the teeth of beasts upon them : with the poison of serpents of the dust.

40 The sword without and terror within shall destroy both the young man and the virgin : the suckling also, with the man of grey hairs.

41 I said, I would scatter them into corners : I would make the remembrance of them to cease from among men.

42 Were it not that I feared the wrath of the enemy : lest their adversaries should behave themselves strangely;

43 And lest they should say : Our hand is high, and the Lord hath not done all this.

44 For they are a nation void of counsel : neither is there any understanding in them.

45 O that they were wise, that they understood this : that they would consider their latter end!

46 How should one chase a thousand : and two put ten thousand to flight?

47 Except their Rock had sold them : and the Lord had shut them up.

48 For their rock is not as our Rock : even our enemies themselves being judges.

49 For their vine is of the vine of Sodom : and of the fields of Gomorrah.

50 Their grapes are grapes of gall : their clusters are bitter.

51 Their wine is the poison of dragons : and the cruel venom of asps.

52 Is not this laid up in store with Me : and sealed up among My treasures?

53 To Me belongeth vengeance : and recompense.

54 Their foot shall slide : in due time.

55 For the day of their calamity is at hand : and the things that shall come upon them make haste.

56 For the Lord shall judge His people : and repent Himself for His servants;

57 When He seeth that their power is gone : and there is none shut up, or left.

58 And He shall say, Where are their gods : their rock in whom they trusted?

59 Which did eat the fat of their sacrifices : and drank the wine of their drink-offerings?

60 Let them rise up and help you : and be your protection.

61 See now that I, even I, am He : and there is no god with Me.

62 I kill, and I make alive; I wound, and I heal : neither is there any that can deliver out of My hand.

63 For I lift up My hand to heaven : and say, I live for ever.

64 If I whet My glittering sword : and Mine hand take hold on judgment;

65 I will render vengeance to Mine enemies : and will reward them that hate Me.

66 I will make Mine arrows drunk with blood : and My sword shall devour flesh.

67 And that with the blood of the slain, and of the captives : from the beginning of revenges upon the enemy.

68 Rejoice, O ye nations, with His people : for He will avenge the blood of His servants.

69 And will render vengeance to His adversaries : and will be merciful unto His land, and to His people.

Glory be, etc.

Ant. The Lord shall repent Himself : for His servants.

Ant. Praise Him.

Laudate Dominum.   Psalm CXLVIII.
Cantate Domino.   Psalm CXLIX.
Laudate Dominum.   Psalm CL., p. 6.

Ant. Praise Him : on the well-tuned cymbals.

From Epiphany to Lent, and from Trinity to Advent :

PRIME. 25

CHAPTER. 1 Cor. XVI.

WATCH ye, stand fast in the faith, quit you like men, be strong. Let all your things be done with charity.
℟. Thanks be to God.

From Trinity to Advent, all the rest as pp. 12, 13.

Prime.

Prime, and every other hour except Lauds, begins as follows, in silence:

✠ In the Name of the Father, and of the Son, and of the Holy Ghost. Amen.

Our Father, etc.

Then aloud:

✠ ℣. O God, make speed to save us.
℟. O Lord, make haste to help us.
℣. Glory be to the Father, and to the Son : and to the Holy Ghost.
℟. As it was in the beginning, is now, and ever shall be : world without end. Amen.
Alleluia.

[From Septuagesima to Wednesday in Holy Week :
Praise be to Thee, O Lord, King of eternal glory.]

HYMN. *Jam lucis orto sidere.*

NOW that the daylight fills the sky,
We lift our hearts to God on high,
That He, in all we do or say,
Would keep us free from harm to-day :

Would guard our hearts and tongues from strife ;
From anger's din would hide our life ;
From all ill sights would turn our eyes ;
Would close our ears from vanities ;

Would keep our inmost conscience pure ;
Our souls from folly would secure ;
Would bid us check the pride of sense
With due and holy abstinence.

So we, when this new day is gone,
And night in turn is drawing on,
With conscience by the world unstain'd
Shall praise His Name for victory gain'd.

All laud to God the Father be ;
All laud, Eternal Son, to Thee ;
All laud for ever, as is meet,
To God the Holy Paraclete. Amen.

[*The foregoing verse forms the doxology to the Office Hymn after Candlemas till Wednesday in Holy Week inclusive ; and from Trinity till Christmas : except through the octaves of Corpus Christi and of the Holy Name, and on all feasts of the Blessed Virgin, and through their Octaves, when the following verse is substituted :*

All honour, laud, and glory be,
O Jesu, Virgin-born, to Thee !
All glory, as is ever meet,
To Father and to Paraclete. Amen.

This last verse is also used from Christmas Day to Candlemas, inclusive.

From Low Sunday to Ascension :

We pray Thee, King, with glory deck'd,
In this our Paschal joy, protect,
From all that death would fain effect,
Thy ransom'd flock, Thine own elect.

To Thee Who, dead, again dost live,
All glory, Lord, Thy people give ;
All glory, as is ever meet,
To Father and to Paraclete. Amen.

From Ascension to Whitsun Day :

Be Thou our Joy and Thou our Guard,
Who art to be our great Reward :
Our glory and our boast in Thee,
For ever and for ever be !

All glory, Lord, to Thee we pay,
Ascending o'er the stars to-day ;
All glory, as is ever meet,
To Father and to Paraclete. Amen.

From Whitsun Day to Trinity :

Thou once in every holy breast
Didst bid indwelling grace to rest :
This day our sins, we pray, release,
And in our time, O Lord, give peace.

To God the Father, God the Son,
And God the Spirit, praise be done ;
And Christ the Lord upon us pour,
The Spirit's gift for evermore. Amen.

And the like rule is observed at all the Hours.]

[*All the Psalms which follow were used in the Sarum Office on Sundays, except at Christmas and Easter tides.*

On Ferias, *Deus, in nomine,* Psalm LIV. *Beati immaculati,* and *Retribue,* Psalm CXIX.

For those who prefer it, the modern Roman use is here subjoined. And before each Psalm is indicated the day on which it is so used.

In this latter use, Glory be *is said after each Psalm : in the former, after every alternate Psalm, as marked below.*

ROMAN USE.

Sunday. 1. *Deus in nomine,* Psalm LIV. 2. *Confitemini Domino,* Psalm CXVIII. (changed in Lent to *Dominus regnavit,* Psalm XCIII.) 3. *Beati immaculati,* and *Retribue servo tuo,* Psalm CXIX. 4. *Quicunque vult.*

Daily. 1. *Deus in nomine,* Psalm LIV. 3. *Beati immaculati,* and *Retribue servo tuo,* Psalm CXIX.

After Psalm LIV. *is said :*

Monday. 2. *Domini est terra.* Psalm XXIV.
Tuesday. 2. *Ad te, Domine, levavi.* Psalm XXV.
Wednesday. 2. *Judica me Domine.* Psalm XXVI.
Thursday. 2. *Dominus regit me.* Psalm XXIII.
Friday. 2. *Deus, Deus meus.* Psalm XXII.

On Saturdays and Festivals no intermediate Psalms, but only :

1. *Deus in nomine,* Psalm LIV., and 2. *Beati immaculati,* and *Retribue servo tuo,* Psalm CXIX.]

On ordinary Sundays.
Ant. The Lord is my Shepherd.

[*For other Antiphons, see Proper of Seasons.*]

[Or Friday only.]
Deus, Deus meus. Psalm XXII.

MY God, my God, look upon me; why hast Thou forsaken me and art so far from my health, and from the words of my complaint?

2 O my God, I cry in the daytime, but Thou hearest not : and in the night-season also I take no rest.

3 And Thou continuest holy : O Thou worship of Israel.

4 Our fathers hoped in Thee : they trusted in Thee, and Thou didst deliver them.

5 They called upon Thee, and were holpen : they put their trust in Thee, and were not confounded.

6 But as for me, I am a worm, and no man : a very scorn of men, and the outcast of the people.

7 All they that see me laugh me to scorn : they shoot out their lips, and shake their heads, saying,

8 He trusted in God, that He would deliver Him : let Him deliver Him, if He will have Him.

9 But Thou art He that took me out of my mother's womb : Thou wast my hope, when I hanged yet upon my mother's breasts.

10 I have been left unto Thee ever since I was born : Thou art my God even from my mother's womb.

11 O go not from me; for trouble is hard at hand : and there is none to help me.

12 Many oxen are come about me : fat bulls of Basan close me in on every side.

13 They gape upon me with their mouths : as it were a ramping and a roaring lion.

14 I am poured out like water, and all my bones are out of joint : my heart also in the midst of my body is even like melting wax.

15 My strength is dried up like a

potsherd, and my tongue cleaveth to my gums : and Thou shalt bring me into the dust of death.

16 For many dogs are come about me : and the counsel of the wicked layeth siege against me.

17 They pierced my hands and my feet; I may tell all my bones : they stand staring and looking upon me.

18 They part my garments among them : and cast lots upon my vesture.

19 But be not Thou far from me, O Lord : Thou art my succour, haste Thee to help me.

20 Deliver my soul from the sword : my darling from the power of the dog.

21 Save me from the lion's mouth : Thou hast heard me also from among the horns of the unicorns.

22 I will declare Thy Name unto my brethren : in the midst of the congregation will I praise Thee.

23 O praise the Lord, ye that fear Him : magnify Him, all ye of the seed of Jacob, and fear Him, all ye seed of Israel;

24 For He hath not despised, nor abhorred, the low estate of the poor : He hath not hid His face from him, but when he called unto Him He heard him.

25 My praise is of Thee in the great congregation : my vows will I perform in the sight of them that fear Him.

26 The poor shall eat, and be satisfied : they that seek after the Lord shall praise Him; your heart shall live for ever.

27 All the ends of the world shall remember themselves, and be turned unto the Lord : and all the kindreds of the nations shall worship before Him.

28 For the kingdom is the Lord's : and He is the Governour among the people.

29 All such as be fat upon earth : have eaten, and worshipped.

30 All they that go down into the dust shall kneel before Him : and no man hath quickened his own soul.

31 My seed shall serve Him : they shall be counted unto the Lord for a generation.

32 They shall come, and the heavens shall declare His righteousness : unto a people that shall be born, whom the Lord hath made.

[Or Thursday only.]

Dominus regit me. Psalm XXIII.

THE Lord is my Shepherd : therefore can I lack nothing.

2 He shall feed me in a green pasture : and lead me forth beside the waters of comfort.

3 He shall convert my soul : and bring me forth in the paths of righteousness, for His Name's sake.

4 Yea, though I walk through the valley of the shadow of death, I will fear no evil : for Thou art with me; Thy rod and Thy staff comfort me.

5 Thou shalt prepare a table before me against them that trouble me : Thou hast anointed my head with oil, and my cup shall be full.

6 But Thy loving-kindness and mercy shall follow me all the days of my life : and I will dwell in the house of the Lord for ever.

Glory be, etc.

[Or Monday only.]

Domini est terra. Psalm XXIV.

THE earth is the Lord's and all that therein is : the compass of the world, and they that dwell therein.

2 For He hath founded it upon

the seas : and prepared it upon the floods.

3 Who shall ascend into the hill of the Lord : or who shall rise up in His holy place?

4 Even he that hath clean hands, and a pure heart : and that hath not lift up his mind unto vanity, nor sworn to deceive his neighbour.

5 He shall receive the blessing from the Lord : and righteousness from the God of his salvation.

6 This is the generation of them that seek Him : even of them that seek thy face, O Jacob.

7 Lift up your heads, O ye gates, and be ye lift up, ye everlasting doors : and the King of Glory shall come in.

8 Who is the King of Glory : it is the Lord strong and mighty, even the Lord mighty in battle.

9 Lift up your heads, O ye gates, and be ye lift up, ye everlasting doors : and the King of Glory shall come in.

10 Who is the King of Glory : even the Lord of hosts, He is the King of Glory.

[Or Tuesday only.]

Ad te, Domine, levavi. Psalm xxv.

UNTO Thee, O Lord, will I lift up my soul; my God, I have put my trust in Thee : O let me not be confounded, neither let mine enemies triumph over me.

2 For all they that hope in Thee shall not be ashamed : but such as transgress without a cause shall be put to confusion.

3 Show me Thy ways, O Lord : and teach me Thy paths.

4 Lead me forth in Thy truth, and learn me : for Thou art the God of my salvation; in Thee hath been my hope all the day long.

5 Call to remembrance, O Lord, Thy tender mercies : and Thy loving-kindnesses, which have been ever of old.

6 O remember not the sins and offences of my youth : but according to Thy mercy think Thou upon me, O Lord, for Thy goodness.

7 Gracious and righteous is the Lord : therefore will He teach sinners in the way.

8 Them that are meek shall He guide in judgment : and such as are gentle, them shall He learn His way.

9 All the paths of the Lord are mercy and truth : unto such as keep His covenant, and His testimonies.

10 For Thy Name's sake, O Lord : be merciful unto my sin, for it is great.

11 What man is he, that feareth the Lord : him shall He teach in the way that He shall choose.

12 His soul shall dwell 'at ease : and his seed shall inherit the land.

13 The secret of the Lord is among them that fear Him : and He will show them His covenant.

14 Mine eyes are ever looking unto the Lord : for He shall pluck my feet out of the net.

15 Turn Thee unto me, and have mercy upon me : for I am desolate, and in misery.

16 The sorrows of my heart are enlarged : O bring Thou me out of my troubles.

17 Look upon my adversity and misery : and forgive me all my sin.

18 Consider mine enemies, how many they are : and they bear a tyrannous hate against me.

19 O keep my soul, and deliver me : let me not be confounded, for I have put my trust in Thee.

20 Let perfectness and righteous

dealing wait upon me : for my hope hath been in Thee.

21 Deliver Israel, O God : out of all his troubles.

Glory be, etc.

[Or Wednesday only.]
Judica me, Domine. Psalm XXVI.

BE Thou my Judge, O Lord, for I have walked innocently : my trust have been also in the Lord, therefore shall I not fall.

2 Examine me, O Lord, and prove me : try out my reins and my heart.

3 For Thy loving-kindness is ever before mine eyes : and I will walk in Thy truth.

4 I have not dwelt with vain persons : neither will I have fellowship with the deceitful.

5 I have hated the congregation of the wicked : and will not sit among the ungodly.

6 I will wash my hands in innocency, O Lord : and so will I go to Thine Altar :

7 That I may show the voice of thanksgiving : and tell of all Thy wondrous works.

8 Lord, I have loved the habitation of Thy house : and the place where Thine honour dwelleth.

9 O shut not up my soul with the sinners : nor my life with the bloodthirsty;

10 In whose hands is wickedness : and their right hand is full of gifts.

11 But as for me, I will walk innocently : O deliver me, and be merciful unto me.

12 My foot standeth right : I will praise the Lord in the congregations.

On ordinary Ferias.

Ant. Hear my prayer, O God.

On Ferias in Advent.

Ant. Come and deliver us.

[Daily.]
Deus, in nomine. Psalm LIV.

SAVE me, O God, for Thy Name's sake : and avenge me in Thy strength.

2 Hear my prayer, O God : and hearken unto the words of my mouth.

3 For strangers are risen up against me : and tyrants, which have not God before their eyes, seek after my soul.

4 Behold, God is my Helper : the Lord is with them that uphold my soul.

5 He shall reward evil unto mine enemies : destroy Thou them in Thy truth.

6 An offering of a free heart will I give Thee, and praise Thy Name, O Lord : because it is so comfortable.

7 For He hath delivered me out of all my trouble : and mine eye hath seen His desire upon mine enemies.

Glory be, etc.

[Sunday only.]
Confitemini Domino. Psalm CXVIII.

O GIVE thanks unto the Lord, for He is gracious : because His mercy endureth for ever.

2 Let Israel now confess, that He is gracious : and that His mercy endureth for ever.

3 Let the house of Aaron now confess : that His mercy endureth for ever.

4 Yea, let them now that fear the Lord confess : that His mercy endureth for ever.

5 I called upon the Lord in trouble : and the Lord heard me at large.

6 The Lord is on my side : I will not fear what man doeth unto me.

7 The Lord taketh my part with them that help me : therefore shall I see my desire upon my enemies.

8 It is better to trust in the Lord : than to put any confidence in man.

9 It is better to trust in the Lord : than to put any confidence in princes.

10 All nations compassed me round about : but in the Name of the Lord will I destroy them.

11 They kept me in on every side, they kept me in, I say, on every side : but in the Name of the Lord will I destroy them.

12 They came about me like bees, and are extinct even as the fire among the thorns : for in the Name of the Lord I will destroy them.

13 Thou hast thrust sore at me, that I might fall : but the Lord was my help.

14 The Lord is my strength and my song : and is become my salvation.

15 The voice of joy and health is in the dwellings of the righteous : the right hand of the Lord bringeth mighty things to pass.

16 The right hand of the Lord hath the pre-eminence : the right hand of the Lord bringeth mighty things to pass.

17 I shall not die, but live : and declare the works of the Lord.

18 The Lord hath chastened and corrected me : but He hath not given me over unto death.

19 Open me the gates of righteousness : that I may go into them, and give thanks unto the Lord.

20 This is the gate of the Lord : the righteous shall enter into it.

21 I will thank Thee, for Thou hast heard me : and art become my salvation.

22 The same stone which the builders refused : is become the headstone in the corner.

23 This is the Lord's doing : and it is marvellous in our eyes.

24 This is the day which the Lord hath made : we will rejoice and be glad in it.

25 Help me now, O Lord : O Lord, send us now prosperity.

26 Blessed be He that cometh in the Name of the Lord : we have wished you good luck, ye that are of the house of the Lord.

27 God is the Lord who hath showed us light : bind the sacrifice with cords, yea, even unto the horns of the altar.

28 Thou art my God, and I will thank Thee : Thou art my God, and I will praise Thee.

29 O give thanks unto the Lord, for He is gracious : and His mercy endureth for ever.

[*From Septuagesima till Easter*, *instead of* Confitemini Domino, Psalm cxviii., *is said Dominus regnavit*, Psalm xciii.

Dominus regnavit. Psalm xciii.

THE Lord is King, and hath put on glorious apparel : the Lord hath put on His apparel, and girded Himself with strength.

2 He hath made the round world so sure : that it cannot be moved.

3 Ever since the world began hath Thy seat been prepared : Thou art from everlasting.

4 The floods are risen, O Lord, the floods have lift up their voice : the floods lift up their waves.

5 The waves of the sea are mighty, and rage horribly : but yet the Lord, Who dwelleth on high, is mightier.

6 Thy testimonies, O Lord, are very sure : holiness becometh Thine house for ever.]

[Daily.]

Beati immaculati. Psalm cxix.

BLESSED are those that are undefiled in the way : and walk in the law of the Lord.

2 Blessed are they that keep His testimonies : and seek Him with their whole heart.

3 For they who do no wickedness : walk in His ways.

4 Thou hast charged : that we shall diligently keep Thy commandments.

5 O that my ways were made so direct : that I might keep Thy statutes!
6 So shall I not be confounded : while I have respect unto all Thy commandments.
7 I will thank Thee with an unfeigned heart : when I shall have learned the judgments of Thy righteousness.
8 I will keep Thy ceremonies : O forsake me not utterly.
9 Wherewithal shall a young man cleanse his way : even by ruling himself after Thy Word.
10 With my whole heart have I sought Thee : O let me not go wrong out of Thy commandments.
11 Thy words have I hid within my heart : that I should not sin against Thee.
12 Blessed art Thou, O Lord : O teach me Thy statutes.
13 With my lips have I been telling : of all the judgments of Thy mouth.
14 I have had as great delight in the way of Thy testimonies : as in all manner of riches.
15 I will talk of Thy commandments : and have respect unto Thy ways.
16 My delight shall be in Thy statutes : and I will not forget Thy Word.

Glory be, etc.

[Daily.]

Retribue servo tuo.

O DO well unto Thy servant : that I may live, and keep Thy word.
18 Open Thou mine eyes : that I may see the wondrous things of Thy law.
19 I am a stranger upon earth : O hide not Thy commandments from me.
20 My soul breaketh out for the very fervent desire : that it hath alway unto Thy judgments.
21 Thou hast rebuked the proud : and cursed are they that do err from Thy commandments.
22 O turn from me shame and rebuke : for I have kept Thy testimonies.
23 Princes also did sit and speak against me : but Thy servant is occupied in Thy statutes.
24 For Thy testimonies are my delight : and my counsellors.
25 My soul cleaveth to the dust : O quicken Thou me, according to Thy Word.
26 I have acknowledged my ways, and Thou heardest me : O teach me Thy statutes.
27 Make me to understand the way of Thy commandments : and so shall I talk of Thy wondrous works.
28 My soul melteth away for very heaviness : comfort Thou me according unto Thy Word.
29 Take from me the way of lying : and cause Thou me to make much of Thy law.
30 I have chosen the way of truth : and Thy judgments have I laid before me.
31 I have stuck unto Thy testimonies : O Lord, confound me not.
32 I will run the way of Thy commandments : when Thou hast set my heart at liberty.

Glory be, etc.

On ordinary Sundays.

Ant. The Lord is my Shepherd : therefore can I lack nothing.

On ordinary Ferias.

Ant. Hear my prayer, O God : and hearken unto the words of my mouth.

On Ferias in Advent.
Ant. Come and deliver us : O our God.

CREED OF S. ATHANASIUS,
Said daily, except at Christmas and Easter [but in Roman use, on Sunday only.]

ANTIPHONS.
On Sundays, when the Passion Psalms are said:

Thee, God the Father unbegotten, Thee, God the Son only-begotten, Thee, Holy Ghost, Paraclete, Holy and undivided Trinity : * with our whole heart and our lips we confess, praise and bless; to Thee be glory for ever.

In Easter tide is added, Alleluia.

On other Sundays, and simple feasts whose office is kept, in octaves, and in commemorations of S. Mary, and the patron of the place : except within the octave of Trinity :

Thee duly praise and adore : * Thee all Thy creatures glorify, O Blessed Trinity.

In Easter tide is added, Alleluia.

On Double Feasts, except in the week following Trinity Sunday :

Thanks be to Thee, O God, thanks be to Thee, One Very Trinity : * One and Supreme Deity, and One and Holy Unity.

In Easter tide is added, Alleluia.

On all Ferias, Vigils, and Ember days, except in Whitsun and Trinity weeks:

Glory to Thee, Equal Trinity, One Deity : * both before all ages, and now, and for ever.

In Easter tide is added, Alleluia.

Through the week of the Holy Trinity, whatever may be the office:

O Beatific and Blessed and Glorious Trinity : * Father, and Son, and Holy Ghost.

Quicunque vult.

WHOSOEVER will be saved : before all things it is necessary that he hold the Catholick Faith.

2 Which Faith except every one do keep whole and undefiled : without doubt he shall perish everlastingly.

3 And the Catholick Faith is this : That we worship one God in Trinity, and Trinity in Unity ;

4 Neither confounding the Persons : nor dividing the Substance.

5 For there is one Person of the Father, another of the Son : and another of the Holy Ghost.

6 But the Godhead of the Father, of the Son, and of the Holy Ghost, is all one : the Glory equal, the Majesty co-eternal.

7 Such as the Father is, such is the Son : and such is the Holy Ghost.

8 The Father uncreate, the Son uncreate : and the Holy Ghost uncreate.

9 The Father incomprehensible, the Son incomprehensible : and the Holy Ghost incomprehensible.

10 The Father eternal, the Son eternal : and the Holy Ghost eternal.

11 And yet they are not three eternals : but one eternal.

12 As also there are not three incomprehensibles, nor three uncreated : but one uncreated, and one incomprehensible.

13 So likewise the Father is Almighty, the Son Almighty : and the Holy Ghost Almighty.

14 And yet they are not three Almighties : but one Almighty.

15 So the Father is God, the Son is God : and the Holy Ghost is God.

16 And yet they are not three Gods : but one God.

17 So likewise the Father is Lord,

the Son Lord : and the Holy Ghost Lord.

18 And yet not three Lords : but one Lord.

19 For like as we are compelled by the Christian verity : to acknowledge every Person by Himself to be God and Lord;

20 So are we forbidden by the Catholick Religion : to say, There be three Gods, or three Lords.

21 The Father is made of none : neither created, nor begotten.

22 The Son is of the Father alone : not made, nor created, but begotten.

23 The Holy Ghost is of the Father and of the Son : neither made, nor created, nor begotten, but proceeding.

24 So there is one Father, not three Fathers; one Son, not three Sons : one Holy Ghost, not three Holy Ghosts.

25 And in this Trinity none is afore, or after other : none is greater, or less than another.

26 But the whole three Persons are co-eternal together : and co-equal.

27 So that in all things, as is aforesaid : the Unity in Trinity, and the Trinity in Unity is to be worshipped.

28 He therefore that will be saved : must thus think of the Trinity.

29 Furthermore, it is necessary to everlasting salvation : that he also believe rightly the Incarnation of our Lord Jesus Christ.

30 For the right faith is, that we believe and confess : that our Lord Jesus Christ, the Son of God, is God and Man.

31 God, of the Substance of the Father, begotten before the worlds : and Man, of the substance of His Mother, born in the world;

32 Perfect God, and perfect Man : of a reasonable soul and human flesh subsisting;

33 Equal to the Father, as touching His Godhead : and inferior to the Father, as touching His Manhood.

34 Who although He be God and Man : yet He is not two, but one Christ.

35 One; not by conversion of the Godhead into flesh : but by taking of the manhood into God;

36 One altogether; not by confusion of Substance : but by unity of Person.

37 For as the reasonable soul and flesh is one man : so God and Man is one Christ;

38 Who suffered for our salvation : descended into hell, rose again the third day from the dead.

39 He ascended into heaven, He sitteth on the right hand of the Father, God Almighty : from whence He shall come to judge the quick and the dead.

40 At Whose coming all men shall rise again with their bodies : and shall give account for their own works.

41 And they that have done good shall go into life everlasting : and they that have done evil into everlasting fire.

42 This is the Catholick Faith : which except a man believe faithfully, he cannot be saved.

Glory be, etc.

Chapter.

On Sundays and Doubles:

1 Tim. I.

NOW unto the King Eternal, Immortal, Invisible, the only wise God, be honour and glory for ever and ever. Amen.

On all other Feasts : on Ferias from Low Sunday till the Octave of Whitsun Day : in Octaves : on the eves of Ascension,

Whitsun Day, Christmas, and Epiphany:

Is. XXXIII.

O LORD, be gracious unto us, we have waited for Thee : be Thou their arm every morning, our salvation also in the time of trouble.

On Ferias throughout the year :

Zech. VIII.

LOVE the truth and peace, saith the Lord of hosts.

Responsory, used daily, except when otherwise marked in the Proper.

℟. Jesu Christ, Son of the living God, have mercy upon us. ℣. Thou that sittest at the right hand of the Father. ℟. Have mercy upon us. ℣. Glory be to the Father, and to the Son, and to the Holy Ghost. ℟. Jesu Christ, Son of the living God, have mercy upon us.

℣. O Lord, arise, help us.
℟. And deliver us for Thy Name's sake.

PETITIONS.

Said daily, except as hereafter noted.

Lord, have mercy [iii].
Christ, have mercy [iii].
Lord, have mercy [iii].

Our Father :

Said silently throughout. The Priest repeats aloud :

℣. And lead us not into temptation.
℟. But deliver us from evil.
℣. O let my soul live, and it shall praise Thee.
℟. And Thy judgments shall help me.
℣. I have gone astray like a sheep that is lost.
℟. O seek Thy servant, for I do not forget Thy commandments.

I believe :

Said silently throughout. The Priest repeats aloud :

℣. The resurrection of the body.
℟. And the life everlasting.
℣. O let my mouth be filled with Thy praise.
℟. That I may sing of Thy glory and honour all the day long.
℣. Turn Thy face from my sins.
℟. And put out all my misdeeds.
℣. Make me a clean heart, O God.
℟. And renew a right spirit within me.
℣. Cast me not away from Thy presence.
℟. And take not Thy Holy Spirit from me.
℣. O give me the comfort of Thy help again.
℟. And stablish me with Thy free Spirit.
℣. Deliver me, O Lord, from the evil man.
℟. And preserve me from the wicked man.
℣. Deliver me from mine enemies, O God.
℟. Defend me from them that rise up against me.
℣. Deliver me from the wicked doers.
℟. And save me from the bloodthirsty men.
℣. So will I alway sing praise unto Thy Name.
℟. That I may daily perform my vows.
℣. Hear us, O God of our salvation.
℟. Thou that art the hope of all the ends of the earth, and of them that remain in the broad sea.
℣. O God, make speed to save us.
℟. O Lord, make haste to help us.
℣. Holy God, Holy and Mighty, Holy and Immortal.
℟. O Lamb of God, that takest away the sins of the world, have mercy upon us.

℣. Praise the Lord, O my soul.
℟. And forget not all His benefits.
℣. Who forgiveth all thy sin.
℟. And healeth all thine infirmities.
℣. Who saveth thy life from destruction.
℟. And crowneth thee with mercy and loving-kindness.
℣. Who satisfieth thy mouth with good things.
℟. Making thee young and lusty as an eagle.

Confession and Absolution, said in a low voice.

The Officiant:

I CONFESS to God Almighty, the Father, the Son, and the Holy Ghost, in the sight of the whole company of heaven, and to you, my *brethren*, that I have sinned exceedingly in thought, word, and deed, by my fault; therefore I pray God to have mercy upon me, and you, my *brethren*, to pray for me.

The Choir replies:

ALMIGHTY God have mercy upon thee, pardon and deliver thee from all thy sins, confirm and strengthen thee in all goodness, and bring thee to everlasting life. ℟. Amen.

The Choir.

I CONFESS to God Almighty, the Father, the Son, and the Holy Ghost, in the sight of the whole company of heaven, [and to thee, *father*,] that I have sinned exceedingly in thought, word, and deed, of my fault; therefore I pray God to have mercy upon me, [and thee, *father*, to pray for me.]

The Officiant:

ALMIGHTY God have mercy upon you, pardon and deliver you from all your sins, confirm and strengthen you in all goodness, and bring you to everlasting life. ℟. Amen.

[If a Priest:

THE Almighty and merciful Lord grant you absolution and remission of all your sins, time for true repentance, amendment of life, and the grace and comfort of the Holy Spirit. ℟. Amen.

℣. Wilt Thou not turn again and quicken us, O Lord?
℟. That Thy people may rejoice in Thee.
℣. Shew us Thy mercy, O Lord.
℟. And grant us Thy salvation.
℣. Vouchsafe, O Lord.
℟. To keep us this day without sin.
℣. O Lord, have mercy upon us.
℟. Have mercy upon us.
℣. O Lord, let Thy mercy lighten upon us.
℟. As our trust is in Thee.

The foregoing Petitions are said daily throughout the year (except from Maundy Thursday till Low Sunday, and on All Souls' Day); then follows

[ON SUNDAYS AND FESTIVALS:

℣. Turn us again, O Lord God of Hosts.
℟. Shew the light of Thy countenance, and we shall be whole.
℣. Hear my prayer, O Lord.
℟. And let my crying come unto Thee.
℣. The Lord be with you.
℟. And with thy spirit.

Let us pray.

COLLECT.

On ordinary Sundays and all Simple Feasts:

O LORD, our heavenly Father, Almighty and everlasting God,

Who hast safely brought us to the beginning of this day; defend us in the same with Thy mighty power; and grant that this day we fall into no sin, neither run into any kind of danger; but that all our doings may be ordered by Thy governance, to do always that is righteous in Thy sight; through Jesus Christ our Lord : Who liveth. Amen.

COLLECT.

On Double Feasts, except in Easter week:

IN this hour of this day, fill us, O Lord, with Thy mercy; that going forth in Thy strength, we may make our boast of Thee all the day long; through Jesus Christ our Lord : Who liveth. Amen.

℣. The Lord be with you.
℟. And with thy spirit.
℣. Bless we the Lord.
℟. Thanks be to God.]

ON FERIAS

Through the year, except in Christmas and Easter tides:

℣. Hearken unto my voice, O Lord, when I cry unto Thee.
℟. Have mercy upon me, and hear me.

Miserere mei, Deus. Psalm LI., p. 10.

[*Here follows in Lent :*

Beati, quorum. Psalm XXXII.

BLESSED is he whose unrighteousness is forgiven : and whose sin is covered.
2 Blessed is the man unto whom the Lord imputeth no sin : and in whose spirit there is no guile.
3 For while I held my tongue : my bones consumed away through my daily complaining.
4 For Thy hand is heavy upon me day and night : and my moisture is like the drought in summer.
5 I will acknowledge my sin unto Thee : and mine unrighteousness have I not hid.
6 I said, I will confess my sins unto the Lord : and so Thou forgavest the wickedness of my sin.

7 For this shall every one that is godly make his prayer unto Thee, in a time when Thou mayest be found : but in the great water-floods they shall not come nigh him.
8 Thou art a place to hide me in, Thou shalt preserve me from trouble : Thou shalt compass me about with songs of deliverance.
9 I will inform thee, and teach thee in the way wherein thou shalt go : and I will guide thee with Mine eye.
10 Be ye not like to horse and mule, which have no understanding : whose mouths must be held with bit and bridle, lest they fall upon thee.
11 Great plagues remain for the ungodly : but whoso putteth his trust in the Lord, mercy embraceth him on every side.
12 Be glad, O ye righteous, and rejoice in the Lord : and be joyful, all ye that are true of heart.
Glory be, etc.]

[*Here the reader, if a Priest, rising, stands at the step of the Sanctuary.*]

℣. O Lord, arise, help us.
℟. And deliver us for Thy Name's sake.
℣. Turn us again, O Lord God of Hosts.
℟. Shew the light of Thy countenance, and we shall be whole.
℣. Hear my prayer, O Lord.
℟. And let my crying come unto Thee.
℣. The Lord be with you.
℟. And with thy spirit.

Let us pray.

COLLECT.

O LORD, our heavenly Father, Almighty and everlasting God, Who hast safely brought us to the beginning of this day : defend us in the same with Thy mighty power; and grant that this day we fall into no sin, neither run into any kind of danger; but that all our doings may be ordered by Thy governance, to do always that is righteous in Thy sight; through Jesus Christ our Lord : Who liveth. Amen.

℣. The Lord be with you.
℟. And with thy spirit.
℣. Bless we the Lord.
℟. Thanks be to God.

Office of Chapter.

(If the Martyrology is used, here is read the portion for the day, the reader ending with,

℣. But Thou, O Lord, have mercy upon us.

℞. Thanks be to God.)

℣. Right-dear in the sight of the Lord;

℞. Is the death of His Saints.

(Benediction. The Lord Almighty bless us with His grace.

℞. Amen.)

℣. O God, make speed to save us.

℞. O Lord, make haste to help us.

[*The above ℣ and ℞ are here said thrice.*]

℣. Glory be to the Father, and to the Son : and to the Holy Ghost.

℞. As it was in the beginning, is now, and ever shall be : world without end. Amen.

Lord, have mercy.
Christ, have mercy.
Lord, have mercy.

Our Father :

Said silently throughout. The Priest repeats aloud :

℣. And lead us not into temptation.

℞. But deliver us from evil.

℣. And let Thy loving mercy come also unto me, O Lord.

℞. Even Thy salvation, according unto Thy word.

℣. And shew Thy servants Thy work.

℞. And their children Thy glory.

℣. And the glorious Majesty of the Lord our God be upon us.

℞. And prosper Thou the work of our hands upon us : O .prosper Thou our handywork.

[*On Double Feasts, Sundays* (*Simples of the first three classes, if their office be kept*), *and in Octaves, except in Easter week :*

Let us pray.

Collect.

ALMIGHTY and everlasting God, direct our actions according to Thy good pleasure; that through the Name of Thy beloved Son we may be found worthy to abound in good works : Who liveth. In the unity. Amen.

℣. The Lord be with you.

℞. And with thy spirit.

℣. Bless we the Lord.

℞. Thanks be to God.]

On simple Feasts of the fourth class, and Ferias :

Let us pray.

Collect.

O ALMIGHTY Lord and everlasting God, vouchsafe, we beseech Thee, to direct, sanctify, and govern both our hearts and bodies, in the ways of Thy laws, and in the works of Thy commandments; that through Thy most mighty protection, both here and ever, we may be governed and preserved in body and soul; through Jesus Christ our Lord : Who liveth. Amen.

℣. The Lord be with you.

℞. And with thy spirit.

℣. Bless we the Lord.

℞. Thanks be to God.

Then, after reading the list of persons to be prayed for, is said what follows on all days when the prayers for the Peace of the Church are said at Lauds.

Levavi oculos. Psalm cxxi.

I WILL lift up mine eyes unto the hills : from whence cometh my help.

2 My help cometh even from the Lord : Who hath made heaven and earth.

3 He will not suffer thy foot to be moved : and He that keepeth thee will not sleep.

4 Behold, He that keepeth Israel : shall neither slumber nor sleep.

5 The Lord Himself is thy keeper : the Lord is thy defence upon thy right hand.

6 So that the sun shall not burn thee by day : neither the moon by night.

7 The Lord shall preserve thee from all evil : yea, it is even He that shall keep thy soul.

8 The Lord shall preserve thy going out, and thy coming in : from this time forth for evermore.

Glory be, etc.

Lord, have mercy.
Christ, have mercy.
Lord, have mercy.
Our Father :

Said silently throughout. The Priest repeats aloud :

℣. And lead us not into temptation.
℞. But deliver us from evil.
℣. O Lord, shew Thy mercy upon us.
℞. And grant us Thy salvation.
℣. O God, save Thy servants and handmaidens.
℞. Which put their trust in Thee.
℣. Send them help from the sanctuary.
℞. And strengthen them out of Sion.
℣. Be unto them, O Lord, a tower of strength.
℞. From the face of the enemy.
℣. Let the enemy have no advantage over them.
℞. Neither the son of wickedness approach to hurt them.
℣. Hear my prayer, O Lord.
℞. And let my crying come unto Thee.
℣. The Lord be with you.
℞. And with thy spirit.

Let us pray.
COLLECTS.

ASSIST us mercifully, O Lord, in these our supplications and prayers, and dispose the way of Thy servants towards the attainment of everlasting salvation; that, among all the changes and chances of this mortal life, they may ever be defended by Thy most gracious and ready help; through Jesus Christ our Lord. Amen.

Let us pray.

ALMIGHTY and everlasting God, the eternal salvation of them that believe, hear us in behalf of Thy servants for whom we entreat the help of Thy compassion: that, their health being restored to them, they may return to Thee the offering of thanks in Thy Church; through Jesus Christ our Lord, Who liveth. Amen.

℣. Pray for a blessing.
℞. The Lord bless us.

Each person signing himself [and the Priest, if present, making the sign of the Cross over those present],

✠ In the Name of the Father, and of the Son, and of the Holy Ghost.
℞. Amen.

Tierce.

✠ ℣. O God, make speed to save us.
℞. O Lord, make haste to help us.
℣. Glory be to the Father, and to the Son : and to the Holy Ghost.
℞. As it was in the beginning, is now, and ever shall be : world without end. Amen.

Alleluia.

[*From Septuagesima to Wednesday in Holy Week :*

Praise be to Thee, O Lord, King of eternal glory.]

HYMN. *Nunc Sancte nobis Spiritus.*

COME, Holy Ghost, with God the Son,
And God the Father, ever One ;
Shed forth Thy grace within our breast,
And dwell with us, a ready guest.

By every power, by heart and tongue,
By act and deed, Thy praise be sung;
Inflame with perfect love each sense,
That others' souls may kindle thence.

O Father, that we ask be done,
Through Jesus Christ, Thine only Son,
Who, with the Holy Ghost, and Thee,
Shall live and reign eternally. Amen.

Ant. SUNDAY. Praise and everlasting glory.

Ant. FERIAL. O let Thy loving mercies.

Legem pone. Psalm cxix.

TEACH me, O Lord, the way of Thy statutes: and I shall keep it unto the end.

34 Give me understanding, and I shall keep Thy law: yea, I shall keep it with my whole heart.

35 Make me to go in the path of Thy commandments: for therein is my desire.

36 Incline my heart unto Thy testimonies: and not to covetousness.

37 O turn away mine eyes, lest they behold vanity: and quicken Thou me in Thy way.

38 O stablish Thy word in Thy servant: that I may fear Thee.

39 Take away the rebuke that I am afraid of: for Thy judgments are good.

40 Behold, my delight is in Thy commandments: O quicken me in Thy righteousness.

41 Let Thy loving mercy come also unto me, O Lord: even Thy salvation, according unto Thy word.

42 So shall I make answer unto my blasphemers: for my trust is in Thy word.

43 O take not the word of Thy truth utterly out of my mouth: for my hope is in Thy judgments.

44 So shall I alway keep Thy law: yea, for ever and ever.

45 And I will walk at liberty: for I seek Thy commandments.

46 I will speak of Thy testimonies also, even before kings: and will not be ashamed.

47 And my delight shall be in Thy commandments: which I have loved.

48 My hands also will I lift up unto Thy commandments, which I have loved: and my study shall be in Thy statutes.

Glory be, etc.

Memor esto servi tui.

O THINK upon Thy servant, as concerning Thy word: wherein Thou hast caused me to put my trust.

50 The same is my comfort in my trouble: for Thy word hath quickened me.

51 The proud have had me exceedingly in derision: yet have I not shrinked from Thy law.

52 For I remembered Thine everlasting judgments, O Lord: and received comfort.

53 I am horribly afraid: for the ungodly that forsake Thy law.

54 Thy statutes have been my songs: in the house of my pilgrimage.

55 I have thought upon Thy Name, O Lord, in the night-season: and have kept Thy law.

56 This I had: because I kept Thy commandments.

57 Thou art my portion, O Lord: I have promised to keep Thy law.

58 I made my humble petition in Thy presence with my whole heart: O be merciful unto me, according to Thy word.

59 I called mine own ways to remembrance: and turned my feet unto Thy testimonies.

60 I made haste, and prolonged not the time: to keep Thy commandments.

61 The congregations of the ungodly have robbed me: but I have not forgotten Thy law.

62 At midnight I will rise to give thanks unto Thee : because of Thy righteous judgments.

63 I am a companion of all them that fear Thee : and keep Thy commandments.

64 The earth, O Lord, is full of Thy mercy : O teach me Thy statutes. Glory be, etc.

Bonitatem fecisti.

O LORD, Thou hast dealt graciously with Thy servant : according unto Thy word.

66 O learn me true understanding and knowledge : for I have believed Thy commandments.

67 Before I was troubled, I went wrong : but now have I kept Thy word.

68 Thou art good and gracious : O teach me Thy statutes.

69 The proud have imagined a lie against me : but I will keep Thy commandments with my whole heart.

70 Their heart is as fat as brawn : but my delight hath been in Thy law.

71 It is good for me that I have been in trouble : that I may learn Thy statutes.

72 The law of Thy mouth is dearer unto me : than thousands of gold and silver.

73 Thy hands have made me and fashioned me : O give me understanding, that I may learn Thy commandments.

74 They that fear Thee will be glad when they see me : because I have put my trust in Thy word.

75 I know, O Lord, that Thy judgments are right : and that Thou of very faithfulness hast caused me to be troubled.

76 O let Thy merciful kindness be my comfort : according to Thy word unto Thy servant.

77 O let Thy loving mercies come unto me, that I may live : for Thy law is my delight.

78 Let the proud be confounded, for they go wickedly about to destroy me : but I will be occupied in Thy commandments.

79 Let such as fear Thee, and have known Thy testimonies : be turned unto me.

80 O let my heart be sound in Thy statutes : that I be not ashamed. Glory be, etc.

[*Sunday :*

Ant. Praise and everlasting glory be to God the Father, and the Son : with the Holy Paraclete, to ages of ages.

CHAPTER. 2 Cor. XIII.

THE grace of the Lord Jesus Christ, and the love of God, and the communion of the Holy Ghost, be with us all.

℟. Incline my heart, O God : unto Thy testimonies. ℣. Turn away mine eyes, lest they behold vanity, and quicken Thou me in Thy way. ℟. Unto Thy testimonies. ℣. Glory be to the Father, and to the Son : and to the Holy Ghost. ℟. Incline my heart, O God : unto Thy testimonies.

℣. I said, Lord, be merciful unto me.

℟. Heal my soul, for I have sinned against Thee.

℣. The Lord be with you.

℟. And with thy spirit.

Collect of the day.

℣. The Lord be with you.
℟. And with thy spirit.
℣. Bless we the Lord.
℟. Thanks be to God.]

Ferial :

Ant. O let Thy loving mercies come unto me : that I may live.

CHAPTER. Jer. XVII.

HEAL me, O Lord, and I shall be healed; save me, and I shall be saved; for Thou art my praise.

℟. Heal my soul : for I have sinned against Thee. ℣. I said, Lord, be merciful unto me. ℟. For I have sinned against Thee. ℣. Glory be to the Father, and to the Son : and to the Holy Ghost. ℟. Heal my soul : for I have sinned against Thee.

℣. Thou hast been my succour.

℟. Leave me not, neither forsake me, O God of my salvation.

Petitions as at Monday Lauds, p. 12.

[*In Lent, after* Miserere, Ps. LI., *is said*

Domine, ne in furore. Psalm XXXVIII.

PUT me not to rebuke, O Lord, in Thine anger : neither chasten me in Thy heavy displeasure.

2 For Thine arrows stick fast in me : and Thy hand presseth me sore.

3 There is no health in my flesh, because of Thy displeasure : neither is there any rest in my bones, by reason of my sin.

4 For my wickednesses are gone over my head : and are like a sore burden, too heavy for me to bear.

5 My wounds stink, and are corrupt : through my foolishness.

6 I am brought into so great trouble and misery : that I go mourning all the day long.

7 For my loins are filled with a sore disease : and there is no whole part in my body.

8 I am feeble and sore smitten : I have roared for the very disquietness of my heart.

9 Lord, Thou knowest all my desire : and my groaning is not hid from Thee.

10 My heart panteth, my strength hath failed me : and the sight of mine eyes is gone from me.

11 My lovers and my neighbours did stand looking upon my trouble : and my kinsmen stood afar off.

12 They also that sought after my life laid snares for me : and they that went about to do me evil talked of wickedness, and imagined deceit all the day long.

13 As for me, I was like a deaf man, and heard not : and as one that is dumb, who doth not open his mouth.

14 I became even as a man that beareth not : and in whose mouth are no reproofs.

15 For in Thee, O Lord, have I put my trust : Thou shalt answer for me, O Lord my God.

16 I have required that they, even mine enemies, should not triumph over me : for when my foot slipped, they rejoiced greatly against me.

17 And I, truly, am set in the plague : and my heaviness is ever in my sight.

18 For I will confess my wickedness : and be sorry for my sin.

19 But mine enemies live, and are mighty : and they that hate me wrongfully are many in number.

20 They also that reward evil for good are against me : because I follow the thing that good is.

21 Forsake me not, O Lord my God : be not Thou far from me.

22 Haste Thee to help me : O Lord God of my salvation.

Glory be, etc.]

Sexts.

✠ ℣. O God, make speed to save us.

℟. O Lord, make haste to help us.

℣. Glory be to the Father, and to the Son : and to the Holy Ghost.

℟. As it was in the beginning, is now, and ever shall be : world without end. Amen.

Alleluia.

[*From Septuagesima till Wednesday in Holy Week :*

Praise be to Thee, O Lord, King of eternal glory.] . . .

HYMN. *Rector potens, verax Deus.*

O GOD of truth, O Lord of might,
Who ord'rest time and change aright,
And send'st the early morning ray,
And light'st the glow of perfect day :

Extinguish Thou each sinful fire,
And banish every ill desire ;
And while Thou keep'st the body whole,
Shed forth Thy peace upon the soul.

O Father, that we ask be done,
Through Jesus Christ, Thine only Son ;
Who, with the Holy Ghost and Thee,
Shall live and reign eternally. Amen.

Ant. SUNDAY. Let the glory of praise.

Ant. FERIAL. Let me not.

Defecit anima mea. Psalm CXIX.

MY soul hath longed for Thy salvation : and I have a good hope because of Thy word.

82 Mine eyes long sore for Thy

word : saying, O when wilt Thou comfort me?

83 For I am become like a bottle in the smoke : yet do I not forget Thy statutes.

84 How many are the days of Thy servant : when wilt Thou be avenged of them that persecute me?

85 The proud have digged pits for me : which are not after Thy law.

86 All Thy commandments are true : they persecute me falsely; O be Thou my help.

87 They had almost made an end of me upon earth : but I forsook not Thy commandments.

88 O quicken me after Thy lovingkindness : and so shall I keep the testimonies of Thy mouth.

89 O Lord, Thy word : endureth for ever in heaven.

90 Thy truth also remaineth from one generation to another : Thou hast laid the foundation of the earth, and it abideth.

91 They continue this day according to Thine ordinance : for all things serve Thee.

92 If my delight had not been in Thy law : I should have perished in my trouble.

93 I will never forget Thy commandments : for with them Thou hast quickened me.

94 I am Thine, O save me : for I have sought Thy commandments.

95 The ungodly laid wait for me to destroy me : but I will consider Thy testimonies.

96 I see that all things come to an end : but Thy commandment is exceeding broad.

Glory be, etc.

Quomodo dilexi!

LORD, what love have I unto Thy law : all the day long is my study in it.

98 Thou through Thy commandments hast made me wiser than mine enemies : for they are ever with me.

99 I have more understanding than my teachers : for Thy testimonies are my study.

100 I am wiser than the aged : because I keep Thy commandments.

101 I have refrained my feet from every evil way : that I may keep Thy word.

102 I have not shrunk from Thy judgments : for Thou teachest me.

103 O how sweet are Thy words unto my throat : yea, sweeter than honey unto my mouth.

104 Through Thy commandments I get understanding : therefore I hate all evil ways.

105 Thy word is a lantern unto my feet : and a light unto my paths.

106 I have sworn, and am stedfastly purposed : to keep Thy righteous judgments.

107 I am troubled above measure : quicken me, O Lord, according to Thy word.

108 Let the free-will offerings of my mouth please Thee, O Lord : and teach me Thy judgments.

109 My soul is alway in my hand : yet do I not forget Thy law.

110 The ungodly have laid a snare for me : but yet I swerved not from Thy commandments.

111 Thy testimonies have I claimed as mine heritage for ever : and why? they are the very joy of my heart.

112 I have applied my heart to fulfil Thy statutes alway : even unto the end.

Glory be, etc.

Iniquos odio habui.

I HATE them that imagine evil things : but Thy law do I love.

114 Thou art my defence and shield : and my trust is in Thy word.

115 Away from me, ye wicked : I will keep the commandments of my God.

116 O stablish me according to Thy word, that I may live : and let me not be disappointed of my hope.

117 Hold Thou me up, and I shall be safe : yea, my delight shall be ever in Thy statutes.

118 Thou hast trodden down all them that depart from Thy statutes : for they imagine but deceit.

119 Thou puttest away all the ungodly of the earth like dross : therefore I love Thy testimonies.

120 My flesh trembleth for fear of Thee : and I am afraid of Thy judgments.

121 I deal with the thing that is lawful and right : O give me not over unto mine oppressors.

122 Make Thou Thy servant to delight in that which is good : that the proud do me no wrong.

123 Mine eyes are wasted away with looking for Thy health : and for the word of Thy righteousness.

124 O deal with Thy servant according unto Thy loving mercy : and teach me Thy statutes.

125 I am Thy servant, O grant me understanding : that I may know Thy testimonies.

126 It is time for Thee, Lord, to lay to Thine hand : for they have destroyed Thy law.

127 For I love Thy commandments : above gold and precious stone.

128 Therefore hold I straight all Thy commandments : and all false ways I utterly abhor.

Glory be, etc.

[*Sunday :*

Ant. Let the glory of praise resound from the lips of all to the Father, and the Only-begotten Son : to the Holy Spirit let like praise be paid for ever.

CHAPTER. 1 St. John v.

THERE are Three that bear record in heaven, the Father, the Word, and the Holy Ghost : and these Three are One.

℟. O Lord, Thy word endureth : for ever in heaven. ℣. Thy truth also remaineth from one generation to another. ℟. For ever in heaven. ℣. Glory be to the Father, and to the Son : and to the Holy Ghost. ℟. O Lord, Thy word endureth : for ever in heaven.

℣. The Lord is my Shepherd, therefore can I lack nothing.

℟. He shall feed me in a green pasture.

℣. The Lord be with you.
℟. And with thy spirit.

Collect of the day.

℣. The Lord be with you.
℟. And with thy spirit.
℣. Bless we the Lord.
℟. Thanks be to God.]

Ferial :

Ant. Let me not : be disappointed of my hope.

CHAPTER. 1 Thess. v.

PROVE all things ; hold fast that which is good. Abstain from all appearance of evil.

℟. I will alway give : thanks unto the Lord. ℣. His praise shall ever be in my mouth. ℟. Thanks unto the Lord. ℣. Glory be to the Father, and to the Son : and to the Holy Ghost. ℟. I will alway give : thanks unto the Lord.

℣. The Lord is my Shepherd, therefore shall I lack nothing.

℟. He shall feed me in a green pasture.

Petitions as at Monday Lauds, p. 12.

[*In Lent, instead of* Miserere, *Psalm* LI., *is said*

Deus misereatur. Psalm LXVII.

GOD be merciful unto us, and bless us : and shew us the light of His countenance, and be merciful unto us ;

2 That Thy way may be known upon earth : Thy saving health among all nations.

3 Let the people praise Thee, O God : yea, let all the people praise Thee.

4 O let the nations rejoice and be glad : for Thou shalt judge the folk righteously, and govern the nations upon earth.

5 Let the people praise Thee, O God : let all the people praise Thee.

6 Then shall the earth bring forth her increase : and God, even our own God, shall give us His blessing.

7 God shall bless us : and all the ends of the world shall fear Him.

Glory be, etc.]

Nones.

✠ ℣. O God, make speed to save us.

℟. O Lord, make haste to help us.

℣. Glory be to the Father, and to the Son : and to the Holy Ghost.

℟. As it was in the beginning, is now, and ever shall be : world without end. Amen.

Alleluia.

[*From Septuagesima to Wednesday in Holy Week:*

Praise be to Thee, O Lord, King of eternal glory.]

HYMN. *Rerum Deus tenax vigor.*

O GOD, creation's secret force,
Thyself unmov'd, all motion's source,
Who from the morn till evening's ray,
Through all its changes guid'st the day :

Grant us, when this short life is past,
The glorious evening that shall last :
That by a holy death attain'd,
Eternal glory may be gain'd.

O Father, that we ask be done,
Through Jesus Christ, Thine only Son ;
Who, with the Holy Ghost and Thee,
Shall live and reign eternally. Amen.

Ant. SUNDAY. Of Whom and through Whom.

Ant. FERIAL. Give me understanding.

Mirabilia. Psalm CXIX.

THY testimonies are wonderful : therefore doth my soul keep them.

130 When Thy word goeth forth : it giveth light and understanding unto the simple.

131 I opened my mouth, and drew in my breath : for my delight was in Thy commandments.

132 O look Thou upon me, and be merciful unto me : as Thou usest to do unto those that love Thy Name.

133 Order my steps in Thy word : and so shall no wickedness have dominion over me.

134 O deliver me from the wrongful dealings of men : and so shall I keep Thy commandments.

135 Shew the light of Thy countenance upon Thy servant : and teach me Thy statutes.

136 Mine eyes gush out with water : because men keep not Thy law.

137 Righteous art Thou, O Lord : and true is Thy judgment.

138 The testimonies that Thou hast commanded : are exceeding righteous and true.

139 My zeal hath even consumed me : because mine enemies have forgotten Thy words.

140 Thy word is tried to the uttermost : and Thy servant loveth it.

141 I am small, and of no reputation : yet do I not forget Thy commandments.

142 Thy righteousness is an everlasting righteousness : and Thy law is the truth.

143 Trouble and heaviness have taken hold upon me : yet is my delight in Thy commandments.

144 The righteousness of Thy testimonies is everlasting : O grant me understanding, and I shall live.

Glory be, etc.

Clamavi in toto corde meo.

I CALL with my whole heart : hear me, O Lord, I will keep Thy statutes.

146 Yea, even unto Thee do I call : help me, and I shall keep Thy testimonies.

147 Early in the morning do I cry unto Thee : for in Thy word is my trust.

148 Mine eyes prevent the night-watches : that I might be occupied in Thy words.

149 Hear my voice, O Lord, according unto Thy loving-kindness: quicken me, according as Thou art wont.

150 They draw nigh that of malice persecute me : and are far from Thy law.

151 Be Thou nigh at hand, O Lord : for all Thy commandments are true.

152 As concerning Thy testimonies, I have known long since : that Thou hast grounded them for ever.

153 O consider mine adversity, and deliver me : for I do not forget Thy law.

154 Avenge Thou my cause, and deliver me : quicken me, according to Thy word.

155 Health is far from the ungodly : for they regard not Thy statutes.

156 Great is Thy mercy, O Lord : quicken me, as Thou art wont.

157 Many there are that trouble me, and persecute me : yet do I not swerve from Thy testimonies.

158 It grieveth me when I see the transgressors : because they keep not Thy law.

159 Consider, O Lord, how I love Thy commandments : O quicken me, according to Thy loving-kindness.

160 Thy word is true from everlasting : all the judgments of Thy righteousness endure for evermore.

Glory be, etc.

Principes persecuti sunt.

PRINCES have persecuted me without a cause : but my heart standeth in awe of Thy word.

162 I am as glad of Thy word : as one that findeth great spoils.

163 As for lies, I hate and abhor them : but Thy law do I love.

164 Seven times a day do I praise Thee : because of Thy righteous judgments.

165 Great is the peace that they have who love Thy law : and they are not offended at it.

166 Lord, I have looked for Thy saving health : and done after Thy commandments.

167 My soul hath kept Thy testimonies : and loved them exceedingly.

168 I have kept Thy commandments and testimonies : for all my ways are before Thee.

169 Let my complaint come before Thee, O Lord : give me understanding, according to Thy word.

170 Let my supplication come before Thee : deliver me, according to Thy word.

171 My lips shall speak of Thy praise : when Thou hast taught me Thy statutes.

172 Yea, my tongue shall sing of Thy word : for all Thy commandments are righteous.

173 Let Thine hand help me : for I have chosen Thy commandments.

174 I have longed for Thy saving health, O Lord : and in Thy law is my delight.

175 O let my soul live, and it shall praise Thee : and Thy judgments shall help me.

176 I have gone astray like a sheep that is lost : O seek Thy servant, for I do not forget Thy commandments.

Glory be, etc.

[*Sunday.*]

Ant. Of Whom, and through Whom, and to Whom, are all things: to Him be glory for ever.

CHAPTER. Eph. IV.

ONE Lord, one faith, one baptism, one God and Father of all, Who is above all, and through all, and in you all, Who is blessed for ever.

R︎. I call with my whole heart : hear me, O Lord. V︎. I will keep Thy statutes. R︎. Hear me, O Lord.
V︎. Glory be to the Father, and to the Son : and to the Holy Ghost. R︎. I call with my whole heart : hear me, O Lord.

V︎. O cleanse Thou me from my secret faults.
R︎. Keep Thy servant also from presumptuous sins.
V︎. The Lord be with you.
R︎. And with thy spirit.

Collect of the day.

V︎. The Lord be with you.
R︎. And with thy spirit.
V︎. Bless we the Lord.
R︎. Thanks be to God.]

Ferial.

Ant. Give me understanding : according to Thy word.

CHAPTER. Gal. VI.

BEAR ye one another's burdens, and so fulfil the law of Christ.

R︎. O deliver me : and be merciful unto me. V︎. My foot standeth right : I will praise the Lord in the congregations. R︎. And be merciful unto me. V︎. Glory be to the Father, and to the Son : and to the Holy Ghost. R︎. O deliver me : and be merciful unto me.

V︎. O cleanse Thou me from my secret faults.
R︎. Keep Thy servant also from presumptuous sins.

Petitions as at Monday Lauds, p. 12.

[*In Lent, after Miserere,* Ps. LI., *is said* Domine, exaudi. Psalm CII.

HEAR my prayer, O Lord : and let my crying come unto Thee.
2 Hide not Thy face from me in the time of my trouble : incline Thine ear unto me when I call; O hear me, and that right soon.
3 For my days are consumed away like smoke : and my bones are burnt up as it were a fire-brand.
4 My heart is smitten down, and withered like grass : so that I forget to eat my bread.
5 For the voice of my groaning : my bones will scarce cleave to my flesh.
6 I am become like a pelican in the wilderness : and like an owl that is in the desert.
7 I have watched, and am even as it were a sparrow : that sitteth alone upon the house-top.
8 Mine enemies revile me all the day long : and they that are mad upon me are sworn together against me.
9 For I have eaten ashes as it were bread : and mingled my drink with weeping ;
10 And that because of Thine indignation and wrath : for Thou hast taken me up, and cast me down.
11 My days are gone like a shadow : and I am withered like grass.
12 But Thou, O Lord, shalt endure for ever : and Thy remembrance throughout all generations.
13 Thou shalt arise, and have mercy upon Sion : for it is time that Thou have mercy upon her, yea, the time is come.
14 And why ? Thy servants think upon her stones : and it pitieth them to see her in the dust.
15 The heathen shall fear Thy Name, O Lord : and all the kings of the earth Thy majesty ;
16 When the Lord shall build up Sion : and when His glory shall appear ;
17 When He turneth Him unto the prayer of the poor destitute : and despiseth not their desire.
18 This shall be written for those that come after : and the people which shall be born shall praise the Lord.
19 For He hath looked down from His sanctuary : out of the heaven did the Lord behold the earth ;
20 That He might hear the mournings of such as are in captivity : and deliver the children appointed unto death ;
21 That they may declare the Name of the Lord in Sion : and His worship at Jerusalem ;
22 When the people are gathered together : and the kingdoms also, to serve the Lord.
23 He brought down my strength in my journey : and shortened my days.
24 But I said, O my God, take me not away in the midst of mine age : as for Thy years, they endure throughout all generations.

25 Thou, Lord, in the beginning hast laid the foundation of the earth : and the heavens are the work of Thy hands.
26 They shall perish, but Thou shalt endure : they all shall wax old as doth a garment ;
27 And as a vesture shalt Thou change them, and they shall be changed : but Thou art the same, and Thy years shall not fail.
28 The children of Thy servants shall continue : and their seed shall stand fast in Thy sight.
Glory be, etc.]

Vespers.
SUNDAY.

✠ ℣. O God, make speed to save us.
℟. O Lord, make haste to help us.
℣. Glory be to the Father, and to the Son : and to the Holy Ghost.
℟. As it was in the beginning, is now, and ever shall be : world without end. Amen.
Alleluia.

[*From Septuagesima to Wednesday in Holy Week :*
Praise be to Thee, O Lord, King of eternal glory.]

Ant. Sit Thou * on My right hand : said the Lord my God.

Dixit Dominus. Psalm cx.

THE Lord said unto my Lord : Sit Thou on My right hand, until I make Thine enemies Thy footstool.
2 The Lord shall send the rod of Thy power out of Sion : be Thou ruler, even in the midst among Thine enemies.
3 In the day of Thy power shall the people offer Thee free-will offerings with an holy worship : the dew of Thy birth is of the womb of the morning.
4 The Lord sware, and will not repent : Thou art a Priest for ever after the order of Melchisedech.
5 The Lord upon Thy right hand : shall wound even kings in the day of His wrath.
6 He shall judge among the heathen ; He shall fill the places with the dead bodies : and smite in sunder the heads over divers countries.
7 He shall drink of the brook in the way : therefore shall He lift up His head.
Glory be, etc.

Ant. Sit Thou on My right hand : said the Lord my God.

Ant. All His commandments * are true : they stand fast for ever and ever.

Confitebor tibi. Psalm cxi.

I WILL give thanks unto the Lord with my whole heart : secretly among the faithful, and in the congregation.
2 The works of the Lord are great : sought out of all them that have pleasure therein.
3 His work is worthy to be praised, and had in honour : and His righteousness endureth for ever.
4 The merciful and gracious Lord hath so done His marvellous works : that they ought to be had in remembrance.
5 He hath given meat unto them that fear Him : He shall ever be mindful of His covenant.
6 He hath shewed His people the power of His works : that He may give them the heritage of the heathen.
7 The works of His hands are verity and judgment : all His commandments are true.
8 They stand fast for ever and ever : and are done in truth and equity.
9 He sent redemption unto His people : He hath commanded His covenant for ever ; holy and reverend is His Name.

10 The fear of the Lord is the beginning of wisdom : a good understanding have all they that do thereafter; the praise of it endureth for ever.

Glory be, etc.

Ant. All His commandments are true : they stand fast for ever and ever.

Ant. He hath great delight * in His commandments.

Beatus vir. Psalm cxii.

BLESSED is the man that feareth the Lord : he hath great delight in His commandments.

2 His seed shall be mighty upon earth : the generation of the faithful shall be blessed.

3 Riches and plenteousness shall be in his house : and his righteousness endureth for ever.

4 Unto the godly there ariseth up light in the darkness : he is merciful, loving and righteous.

5 A good man is merciful, and lendeth : and will guide his words with discretion.

6 For he shall never be moved : and the righteous shall be had in everlasting remembrance.

7 He will not be afraid of any evil tidings : for his heart standeth fast, and believeth in the Lord.

8 His heart is established, and will not shrink : until he see his desire upon his enemies.

9 He hath dispersed abroad, and given to the poor : and his righteousness remaineth for ever; his horn shall be exalted with honour.

10 The ungodly shall see it, and it shall grieve him : he shall gnash with his teeth, and consume away; the desire of the ungodly shall perish.

Glory be, etc.

Ant. He hath great delight : in His commandments.

Ant. Blessed be the Name * of the Lord : from this time forth for evermore.

Laudate, pueri. Psalm cxiii.

PRAISE the Lord, ye servants : O praise the Name of the Lord.

2 Blessed be the Name of the Lord : from this time forth for evermore.

3 The Lord's Name is praised : from the rising up of the sun unto the going down of the same.

4 The Lord is high above all heathen : and His glory above the heavens.

5 Who is like unto the Lord our God, that hath His dwelling so high : and yet humbleth Himself to behold the things that are in heaven and earth?

6 He taketh up the simple out of the dust : and lifteth the poor out of the mire ;

7 That He may set him with the princes : even with the princes of His people.

8 He maketh the barren woman to keep house : and to be a joyful mother of children.

Glory be, etc.

Ant. Blessed be the Name of the Lord : from this time forth for evermore.

Ant. But we who live * will praise the Lord.

In exitu Israel. Psalm cxiv.

WHEN Israel came out of Egypt: and the house of Jacob from among the strange people;

2 Judah was His sanctuary : and Israel His dominion.

3 The sea saw that, and fled : Jordan was driven back.

4 The mountains skipped like rams: and the little hills like young sheep.
5 What aileth thee, O thou sea, that thou fleddest : and thou Jordan, that thou wast driven back?
6 Ye mountains, that ye skipped like rams : and ye little hills, like young sheep?
7 Tremble, thou earth, at the presence of the Lord : at the presence of the God of Jacob;
8 Who turned the hard rock into a standing water : and the flint stone into a springing well.

Here is not said, Glory be, etc.

Non nobis, Domine. Psalm cxv.

NOT unto us, O Lord, not unto us, but unto Thy Name give the praise : for Thy loving mercy, and for Thy truth's sake.
2 Wherefore shall the heathen say : Where is now their God?
3 As for our God, He is in heaven : He hath done whatsoever pleased Him.
4 Their idols are silver and gold : even the work of men's hands.
5 They have mouths, and speak not : eyes have they, and see not.
6 They have ears, and hear not : noses have they, and smell not.
7 They have hands, and handle not; feet have they, and walk not : neither speak they through their throat.
8 They that make them are like unto them : and so are all such as put their trust in them.
9 But thou, house of Israel, trust thou in the Lord : He is their succour and defence.
10 Ye house of Aaron, put your trust in the Lord : He is their helper and defender.
11 Ye that fear the Lord, put your trust in the Lord : He is their helper and defender.
12 The Lord hath been mindful of us, and He shall bless us : even He shall bless the house of Israel, He shall bless the house of Aaron.
13 He shall bless them that fear the Lord : both small and great.
14 The Lord shall increase you more and more : you and your children.
15 Ye are the blessed of the Lord : Who made heaven and earth.
16 All the whole heavens are the Lord's : the earth hath He given to the children of men.
17 The dead praise not Thee, O Lord : neither all they that go down into silence.
18 But we will praise the Lord : from this time forth for evermore. Praise the Lord.

Glory be, etc.

Ant. But we who live : will praise the Lord.

Daily from Epiphany to Septuagesima, on all Ferias from Septuagesima till the first Sunday in Lent, and daily from Trinity to Advent, Saturday always excepted:

CHAPTER. 2 Thess. III.

THE Lord direct your hearts into the love of God, and into the patient waiting for Christ.

R̃. Thanks be to God.

On Sundays from Epiphany to Lent, and daily from Trinity to Advent,

HYMN. *Lucis Creator optime.*

O BLEST Creator of the light,
Who mak'st the day with radiance bright,
And o'er the forming world didst call
The light from chaos first of all ;

Whose wisdom joined in meet array
The morn and eve, and named them day :
Night comes with all its darkling fears,
Regard Thy people's prayers and tears.

Lest, sunk in sin, and whelmed with strife,
They lose the gift of endless life;
While thinking but the thoughts of time,
They weave new chains of woe and crime.

But grant them grace that they may strain
The heavenly gate, and prize to gain;
Each harmful lure aside to cast,
And purge away each error past.

O Father, that we ask be done,
Through Jesus Christ, Thine only Son;
Who, with the Holy Ghost, and Thee,
Shall live and reign eternally. Amen.

℣. Lord, let my prayer be set forth.
℟. In Thy sight as the incense.

Ant. to Magnificat, in Proper of Seasons.

[*Ferial Antiphons.*

Monday. My soul shall magnify Thee *: for ever, O my God.
Tuesday. My spirit hath rejoiced :* in God my Saviour.
Wednesday. O Lord my God : * Thou hast regarded my lowliness.
Thursday. He hath put down * the mighty from their seat : and hath exalted the humble and meek that confess His Christ.
Friday. God hath holpen * His servant Israel, as He promised Abraham and his seed : and He hath exalted the humble for ever.]

THE SONG OF THE BLESSED VIRGIN.

Magnificat. S. Luke i.

MY soul doth magnify the Lord : and my spirit hath rejoiced in God my Saviour.

2 For He hath regarded : the lowliness of His handmaiden.

3 For behold, from henceforth : all generations shall call me blessed.

4 For He that is mighty hath magnified me : and holy is His Name.

5 And His mercy is on them that fear Him : throughout all generations.

6 He hath shewed strength with His arm : He hath scattered the proud in the imagination of their hearts.

7 He hath put down the mighty from their seat : and hath exalted the humble and meek.

8 He hath filled the hungry with good things : and the rich He hath sent empty away.

9 He remembering His mercy hath holpen His servant Israel : as He promised to our forefathers, Abraham and his seed for ever.

Glory be, etc.

℣. The Lord be with you.
℟. And with thy spirit.

Let us pray.

COLLECT.

℣. The Lord be with you.
℟. And with thy spirit.
℣. Bless we the Lord.
℟. Thanks be to God.

Memorials
For Sundays, Festivals, and Ferias,

which immediately follow the Collect for the day, unless the Memorial of any Festival intervene, in which case the ordinary Memorials yield precedence.

[*For Memorials for other Seasons than after Trinity, see Proper of Seasons.*]

MEMORIAL OF THE HOLY CROSS,
Omitted on Doubles, and on Days within Octaves.

Ant. Save us, O Christ our Saviour, by the virtue of the Holy Cross : as Thou savedst Peter in the sea; and have mercy upon us.

℣. All the world shall worship Thee, and sing of Thee.
℟. And praise Thy name.

Let us pray.

COLLECT.

KEEP, we beseech Thee, O Lord, in perpetual peace, those whom Thou hast vouchsafed to redeem by the wood of the Holy Cross, O Saviour of the world, Who livest and reignest with the Father and the Holy Ghost, ever one God, world without end. Amen.

MEMORIAL OF S. MARY,

Omitted only on Feasts of S. Mary.

Ant. In the Bush which Moses saw unconsumed : we recognize thy glorious virginity, O Mother of God.

℣. Thou art fairer than the children of men.

℟. Full of grace are thy lips.

Let us pray.

ALMIGHTY, everlasting God, by the right hand of Thy power defend Thy servants from all perils; and, blessed Mary ever-virgin gloriously interceding, grant us prosperity both now and hereafter; through Jesus Christ our Lord. Who. Amen.

MEMORIAL OF ALL SAINTS,

Said on Ferias only, and not on days within Octaves.

Ant. O how glorious is the kingdom where all the Saints rejoice with Christ : they are clothed with white robes and follow the Lamb whithersoever He goeth.

℣. Let the Saints be joyful with glory.

℟. Let them rejoice in their beds.

Let us pray.

GRANT, we beseech Thee, O Lord, that all Thy Saints may always pray for us; and vouchsafe always to hear their prayers; through Jesus Christ our Lord. Who. Amen.

℣. The Lord be with you.
℟. And with thy spirit.
℣. Bless we the Lord.
℟. Thanks be to God.

It is to be noted that these ℣℣. and ℟℟. are always said after the Collect for the day, and again after the last Memorial.

MONDAY.

Vespers.

✠ ℣. O God, make speed to save us.
℟. O Lord, make haste to help us.
℣. Glory be to the Father, and to the Son : and to the Holy Ghost.
℟. As it was in the beginning, is now, and ever shall be : world without end. Amen.
Alleluia.

[*From Septuagesima to Wednesday in Holy Week :*

Praise be to Thee, O Lord, King of eternal glory.]

Ant. The Lord hath inclined.

Dilexi, quoniam. Psalm cxvi.

I AM well pleased : that the Lord hath heard the voice of my prayer.

2 That He hath inclined His ear unto me : therefore will I call upon Him as long as I live.

3 The snares of death compassed me round about : and the pains of hell gat hold upon me.

4 I shall find trouble and heaviness, and I will call upon the Name of the Lord : O Lord, I beseech Thee, deliver my soul.

5 Gracious is the Lord, and righteous : yea, our God is merciful.

6 The Lord preserveth the simple : I was in misery, and He helped me.

7 Turn again then unto thy rest, O my soul : for the Lord hath rewarded thee.

8 And why? Thou hast delivered my soul from death : mine eyes from tears, and my feet from falling.

9 I will walk before the Lord : in the land of the living.

Glory be, etc.

Ant. The Lord hath inclined : His ear unto me.

Ant. I believed.

Credidi. Psalm cxvi. 10.

I BELIEVED, and therefore will I speak; but I was sore troubled : I said in my haste, All men are liars.

11 What reward shall I give unto the Lord : for all the benefits that He hath done unto me?

12 I will receive the cup of salvation : and call upon the Name of the Lord.

13 I will pay my vows now in the presence of all His people : right dear in the sight of the Lord is the death of His Saints.

14 Behold, O Lord, how that I am Thy servant : I am Thy servant, and the son of Thine handmaid; Thou hast broken my bonds in sunder.

15 I will offer to Thee the sacrifice of thanksgiving : and will call upon the Name of the Lord.

16 I will pay my vows unto the Lord, in the sight of all His people : in the courts of the Lord's house, even in the midst of thee, O Jerusalem. Praise the Lord.

Glory be, etc.

Ant. I believed : and therefore will I speak.

Ant. O praise the Lord.

Laudate Dominum. Psalm cxvii.

O PRAISE the Lord, all ye heathen : praise Him, all ye nations.

2 For His merciful kindness is ever more and more towards us : and the truth of the Lord endureth for ever. Praise the Lord.

Glory be, etc.

Ant. O praise the Lord : all ye heathen.

Ant. I called.

Ad Dominum. Psalm cxx.

WHEN I was in trouble I called upon the Lord : and He heard me.

2 Deliver my soul, O Lord, from lying lips : and from a deceitful tongue.

3 What reward shall be given or done unto thee, thou false tongue : even mighty and sharp arrows, with hot burning coals.

4 Wo is me, that I am constrained to dwell with Mesech : and to have my habitation among the tents of Kedar.

5 My soul hath long dwelt among them : that are enemies unto peace.

6 I labour for peace, but when I speak unto them thereof : they make them ready to battle.

Glory be, etc.

Ant. I called : and He heard me.

Ant. My help.

Levavi oculos. Psalm cxxi.

I WILL lift up mine eyes unto the hills : from whence cometh my help.

2 My help cometh even from the Lord : Who hath made heaven and earth.

3 He will not suffer thy foot to be moved : and He that keepeth thee will not sleep.

4 Behold, He that keepeth Israel : shall neither slumber nor sleep.

5 The Lord Himself is thy keeper : the Lord is thy defence upon thy right hand.

6 So that the sun shall not burn thee by day : neither the moon by night.

7 The Lord shall preserve thee from all evil : yea, it is even He that shall keep thy soul.

8 The Lord shall preserve thy going out, and thy coming in : from this time forth for evermore.

Glory be, etc.

Ant. My help : cometh even from the Lord.

From Epiphany to Septuagesima ; from Septuagesima to First Friday in Lent, inclusive; and from Trinity to Advent,

VESPERS: MONDAY.

CHAPTER. 2 Thess. III., p. 49.
From Trinity to Advent,
HYMN. *Lucis Creator optime,*
℣. and ℟. *p.* 49.
Ferial Antiphons and Magnificat, p. 50.
[*For Chapters, Hymns, and Antiphons at other times, see Proper of Seasons.*]

PETITIONS.
These are not said in Christmas or Easter tides.

Lord, have mercy [iii].
Christ, have mercy [iii].
Lord, have mercy [iii].
Our Father:
Said silently throughout. The Priest repeats aloud:
℣. And lead us not into temptation.
℟. But deliver us from evil.
℣. I said, Lord, be merciful unto me.
℟. Heal my soul, for I have sinned against Thee.
℣. Turn Thee again, O Lord, at the last.
℟. And be gracious unto Thy servants.
℣. Let Thy merciful kindness, O Lord, be upon us.
℟. As we do put our trust in Thee.
℣. Let Thy priests be clothed with righteousness.
℟. And Thy Saints sing with joyfulness.
℣. O Lord, save the Queen.
℟. And mercifully hear us when we call upon Thee.
℣. O God, save Thy servants and handmaidens.
℟. Which put their trust in Thee.
℣. O Lord, save Thy people, and bless Thine inheritance.
℟. Govern them, and lift them up for ever.
℣. Peace be within Thy walls.
℟. And plenteousness within Thy palaces.
℣. Let us pray for the faithful departed.
℟. Eternal rest grant unto them, O Lord, and light perpetual shine upon them.
℣. Hearken unto my voice, O Lord, when I cry unto Thee.
℟. Have mercy upon me, and hear me.

Miserere mei, Deus. Psalm LI., p. 10.
[*Here follows in Lent:*
De profundis. Psalm CXXX.
OUT of the deep have I called unto Thee, O Lord : Lord, hear my voice.
2 O let Thine ears consider well : the voice of my complaint.
3 If Thou, Lord, wilt be extreme to mark what is done amiss : O Lord, who may abide it?
4 For there is mercy with Thee : therefore shalt Thou be feared.
5 I look for the Lord; my soul doth wait for Him : in His word is my trust.
6 My soul fleeth unto the Lord : before the morning watch, I say, before the morning watch.
7 O Israel, trust in the Lord, for with the Lord there is mercy : and with Him is plenteous redemption.
8 And He shall redeem Israel : from all his sins.
Glory be, etc.

[*Here the reader, if a Priest, rising, stands at the step of the Sanctuary.*]

℣. O Lord, arise, help us.
℟. And deliver us for Thy Name's sake.
℣. Turn us again, O Lord God of Hosts.
℟. Shew the light of Thy countenance and we shall be whole.
℣. Hear my prayer, O Lord.
℟. And let my crying come unto Thee.
℣. The Lord be with you.
℟. And with thy spirit.

Let us pray.

COLLECT AND MEMORIALS.
For Memorials after Trinity, see p. 50 : for other Seasons, see Proper.

℣. The Lord be with you.
℟. And with thy spirit.
℣. Bless we the Lord.
℟. Thanks be to God.

TUESDAY.
Vespers.

✠ ℣. O God, make speed to save us.
℟. O Lord, make haste to help us.
℣. Glory be to the Father, and to the Son : and to the Holy Ghost.
℟. As it was in the beginning, is now, and ever shall be : world without end. Amen.
Alleluia.

[*From Septuagesima to Wednesday in Holy Week :*
Praise be to Thee, O Lord, King of eternal glory.]

Ant. We will go.

Lætatus sum. Psalm cxxii.

I WAS glad when they said unto me : We will go into the house of the Lord.

2 Our feet shall stand in thy gates : O Jerusalem.

3 Jerusalem is built as a city : that is at unity in itself.

4 For thither the tribes go up, even the tribes of the Lord : to testify unto Israel, to give thanks unto the Name of the Lord.

5 For there is the seat of judgment : even the seat of the house of David.

6 O pray for the peace of Jerusalem : they shall prosper that love thee.

7 Peace be within thy walls : and plenteousness within thy palaces.

8 For my brethren and companions' sakes : I will wish thee prosperity.

9 Yea, because of the house of the Lord our God : I will seek to do thee good.
Glory be, etc.

Ant. We will go gladly : into the house of the Lord.

Ant. O Thou that dwellest.

Ad te levavi oculos meos. Ps. cxxiii.

UNTO Thee lift I up mine eyes : O Thou that dwellest in the heavens.

2 Behold, even as the eyes of servants look unto the hand of their masters, and as the eyes of a maiden unto the hand of her mistress : even so our eyes wait upon the Lord our God, until He have mercy upon us.

3 Have mercy upon us, O Lord, have mercy upon us : for we are utterly despised.

4 Our soul is filled with the scornful reproof of the wealthy : and with the despitefulness of the proud.
Glory be, etc.

Ant. O Thou that dwellest in the heavens : have mercy upon us.

Ant. Our help.

Nisi quia Dominus. Psalm cxxiv.

IF the Lord Himself had not been on our side, now may Israel say : if the Lord Himself had not been, on our side, when men rose up against us ;

2 They had swallowed us up quick : when they were so wrathfully displeased at us.

3 Yea, the waters had drowned us : and the stream had gone over our soul.

4 The deep waters of the proud : had gone even over our soul.

5 But praised be the Lord : Who hath not given us over for a prey unto their teeth.

6 Our soul is escaped even as a

bird out of the snare of the fowler : the snare is broken, and we are delivered.

7 Our help standeth in the Name of the Lord : Who hath made heaven and earth.

Glory be, etc.

Ant. Our help standeth : in the Name of the Lord.

Ant. Do well.

Qui confidunt. Psalm cxxv.

THEY that put their trust in the Lord shall be even as the mount Sion : which may not be removed, but standeth fast for ever.

2 The hills stand about Jerusalem : even so standeth the Lord round about His people, from this time forth for evermore.

3 For the rod of the ungodly cometh not into the lot of the righteous : lest the righteous put their hand unto wickedness.

4 Do well, O Lord : unto those that are good and true of heart.

5 As for such as turn back unto their own wickedness : the Lord shall lead them forth with the evil doers; but peace shall be upon Israel.

Glory be, etc.

Ant. Do well, O Lord : unto those that are good and true of heart.

Ant. Then were we like.

In convertendo. Psalm cxxvi.

WHEN the Lord turned again the captivity of Sion : then were we like unto them that dream.

2 Then was our mouth filled with laughter : and our tongue with joy.

3 Then said they among the heathen : The Lord hath done great things for them.

4 Yea, the Lord hath done great things for us already : whereof we rejoice.

5 Turn our captivity, O Lord : as the rivers in the south.

6 They that sow in tears : shall reap in joy.

7 He that now goeth on his way weeping, and beareth forth good seed : shall doubtless come again with joy, and bring his sheaves with him.

Glory be, etc.

Ant. Then were we like : unto them that dream.

From Epiphany to Septuagesima; from Septuagesima to First Friday in Lent inclusive, and from Trinity to Advent,

CHAPTER. 2 Thess. III., p. 49.

From Trinity to Advent,

HYMN. *Lucis Creator optime,*
℣. and ℟. p. 49.

Ferial Antiphons and Magnificat, p. 50.

[*For Chapters, Hymns, and Antiphons at other times, see Proper of Seasons.*]

PETITIONS *and the rest,* p. 53.

WEDNESDAY.

Vespers.

✠ ℣. O God, make speed to save us.

℟. O Lord, make haste to help us.

℣. Glory be to the Father, and to the Son : and to the Holy Ghost.

℟. As it was in the beginning, is now, and ever shall be : world without end. Amen.

Alleluia.

[*From Septuagesima till Wednesday in Holy Week:*

Praise be to Thee, O Lord, King of eternal glory.]

Ant. Happy is the man.

Nisi Dominus. Psalm cxxvii.

EXCEPT the Lord build the house : their labour is but lost that build it.

2 Except the Lord keep the city : the watchman waketh but in vain.

3 It is but lost labour that ye haste to rise up early, and so late take rest, and eat the bread of carefulness : for so He giveth His beloved sleep.

4 Lo, children and the fruit of the womb : are an heritage and gift that cometh of the Lord.

5 Like as the arrows in the hand of the giant : even so are the young children.

6 Happy is the man that hath his quiver full of them : they shall not be ashamed when they speak with their enemies in the gate.

Glory be, etc.

Ant. Happy is the man : that hath his quiver full.

Ant. Blessed are all they.

Beati omnes. Psalm cxxviii.

BLESSED are all they that fear the Lord : and walk in His ways.

2 For thou shalt eat the labours of thine hands : O well is thee, and happy shalt thou be.

3 Thy wife shall be as the fruitful vine : upon the walls of thine house.

4 Thy children like the olive-branches : round about thy table.

5 Lo, thus shall the man be blessed : that feareth the Lord.

6 The Lord from out of Sion shall so bless thee : that thou shalt see Jerusalem in prosperity all thy life long.

7 Yea, that thou shalt see thy children's children : and peace upon Israel.

Glory be, etc.

Ant. Blessed are all they : that fear the Lord.

Ant. We wish you good luck.

Sæpe expugnaverunt. Psalm cxxix.

MANY a time have they fought against me from my youth up : may Israel now say.

2 Yea, many a time have they vexed me from my youth up : but they have not prevailed against me.

3 The plowers plowed upon my back : and made long furrows.

4 But the righteous Lord : hath hewn the snares of the ungodly in pieces.

5 Let them be confounded and turned backward : as many as have evil will at Sion.

6 Let them be even as the grass growing upon the house-tops : which withereth afore it be plucked up;

7 Whereof the mower filleth not his hand : neither he that bindeth up the sheaves his bosom.

8 So that they who go by say not so much as, The Lord prosper you : we wish you good luck in the Name of the Lord.

Glory be, etc.

Ant. We wish you good luck : in the Name of the Lord.

Ant. Out of the deep.

De profundis. Psalm cxxx.

OUT of the deep have I called unto Thee, O Lord : Lord, hear my voice.

2 O let Thine ears consider well : the voice of my complaint.

3 If Thou, Lord, wilt be extreme to mark what is done amiss : O Lord, who may abide it?

4 For there is mercy with Thee : therefore shalt Thou be feared.

5 I look for the Lord; my soul doth wait for Him : in His word is my trust.

6 My soul fleeth unto the Lord : before the morning watch, I say, before the morning watch.

7 O Israel, trust in the Lord, for with the Lord there is mercy : and with Him is plenteous redemption.
8 And He shall redeem Israel : from all his sins.
Glory be, etc.

Ant. Out of the deep : have I called unto Thee, O Lord.

Ant. O Israel.

Domine, non est. Psalm cxxxi.

LORD, I am not high-minded : I have no proud looks.
2 I do not exercise myself in great matters : which are too high for me.
3 But I refrain my soul, and keep it low, like as a child that is weaned from his mother : yea, my soul is even as a weaned child.
4 O Israel, trust in the Lord : from this time forth for evermore.
Glory be, etc.

Ant. O Israel : trust in the Lord.

From Epiphany to Septuagesima ; from Septuagesima to First Friday in Lent inclusive ; and from Trinity to Advent,
CHAPTER. 2 Thess. III., p. 49.

From Trinity to Advent,
HYMN. *Lucis Creator optime,*
℣. and ℟. p. 49.

Ferial Antiphons and Magnificat, p. 50.

[*For Chapters, Hymns, and Antiphons at other times, see Proper of Seasons.*]

PETITIONS, *and the rest,* p. 53.

THURSDAY.
Vespers.

✠ ℣. O God, make speed to save us.
℟. O Lord, make haste to help us.
℣. Glory be to the Father, and to the Son : and to the Holy Ghost.

℟. As it was in the beginning, is now, and ever shall be : world without end. Amen.
Alleluia.

[*From Septuagesima till Wednesday in Holy Week:*
Praise be to Thee, O Lord, King of eternal glory.]

Ant. And all.

Memento, Domine. Psalm cxxxii.

LORD, remember David : and all his trouble ;
2 How he sware unto the Lord : and vowed a vow unto the Almighty God of Jacob.
3 I will not come within the tabernacle of mine house : nor climb up into my bed ;
4 I will not suffer mine eyes to sleep, nor mine eyelids to slumber : neither the temples of my head to take any rest ;
5 Until I find out a place for the temple of the Lord : an habitation for the mighty God of Jacob.
6 Lo, we heard of the same at Ephrata : and found it in the wood.
7 We will go into His tabernacle : and fall low on our knees before His footstool.
8 Arise, O Lord, into Thy resting-place : Thou, and the ark of Thy strength.
9 Let Thy priests be clothed with righteousness : and let Thy saints sing with joyfulness.
10 For Thy servant David's sake : turn not away the presence of Thine Anointed.
11 The Lord hath made a faithful oath unto David : and He shall not shrink from it.
12 Of the fruit of thy body : shall I set upon thy seat.
13 If thy children will keep My covenant, and My testimonies that I

shall learn them : their children also shall sit upon thy seat for evermore.

14 For the Lord hath chosen Sion to be an habitation for Himself : He hath longed for her.

15 This shall be My rest for ever : here will I dwell, for I have a delight therein.

16 I will bless her victuals with increase : and will satisfy her poor with bread.

17 I will deck her priests with health : and her saints shall rejoice and sing.

18 There shall I make the horn of David to flourish : I have ordained a lantern for Mine anointed.

19 As for his enemies, I shall clothe them with shame : but upon himself shall his crown flourish.

Glory be, etc.

Ant. And all : his trouble.

Ant. Behold, how good.

Ecce, quam bonum. Psalm cxxxiii.

BEHOLD, how good and joyful a thing it is : brethren, to dwell together in unity!

2 It is like the precious ointment upon the head, that ran down unto the beard : even unto Aaron's beard, and went down to the skirts of his clothing.

3 Like as the dew of Hermon : which fell upon the hill of Sion.

4 For there the Lord promised His blessing : and life for evermore.

Glory be, etc.

Ant. Behold : how good and joyful.

Ant. Whatsoever.

Laudate nomen. Psalm cxxxv.

O PRAISE the Lord, laud ye the Name of the Lord : praise it, O ye servants of the Lord ;

2 Ye that stand in the house of the Lord : in the courts of the house of our God.

3 O praise the Lord, for the Lord is gracious : O sing praises unto His Name, for it is lovely.

4 For why? the Lord hath chosen Jacob unto Himself : and Israel for His own possession.

5 For I know that the Lord is great : and that our Lord is above all gods.

6 Whatsoever the Lord pleased, that did He in heaven, and in earth : and in the sea, and in all deep places.

7 He bringeth forth the clouds from the ends of the world : and sendeth forth lightnings with the rain, bringing the winds out of His treasures.

8 He smote the first-born of Egypt : both of man and beast.

9 He hath sent tokens and wonders into the midst of thee, O thou land of Egypt : upon Pharaoh, and all his servants.

10 He smote divers nations : and slew mighty kings ;

11 Sehon king of the Amorites, and Og the king of Basan : and all the kingdoms of Canaan ;

12 And gave their land to be an heritage : even an heritage unto Israel His people.

13 Thy Name, O Lord, endureth for ever : so doth Thy memorial, O Lord, from one generation to another.

14 For the Lord will avenge His people : and be gracious unto His servants.

15 As for the images of the heathen, they are but silver and gold : the work of men's hands.

16 They have mouths, and speak not : eyes have they, but they see not.

17 They have ears, and yet they hear not : neither is there any breath in their mouths.

18 They that make them are like unto them : and so are all they that put their trust in them.
19 Praise the Lord, ye house of Israel : praise the Lord, ye house of Aaron.
20 Praise the Lord, ye house of Levi : ye that fear the Lord, praise the Lord.
21 Praised be the Lord out of Sion : who dwelleth at Jerusalem.
Glory be, etc.

Ant. Whatsoever : the Lord pleased, that did He.

Ant. For His mercy.

Confitemini Domino. Psalm cxxxvi.

O GIVE thanks unto the Lord, for He is gracious : and His mercy endureth for ever.
2 O give thanks unto the God of all gods : for His mercy endureth for ever.
3 O thank the Lord of all lords : for His mercy endureth for ever.
4 Who only doeth great wonders : for His mercy endureth for ever.
5 Who by His excellent wisdom made the heavens : for His mercy endureth for ever.
6 Who laid out the earth above the waters : for His mercy endureth for ever.
7 Who hath made great lights : for His mercy endureth for ever.
8 The sun to rule the day : for His mercy endureth for ever.
9 The moon and the stars to govern the night : for His mercy endureth for ever.
10 Who smote Egypt with their first-born : for His mercy endureth for ever.
11 And brought out Israel from among them : for His mercy endureth for ever.
12 With a mighty hand, and stretched out arm : for His mercy endureth for ever.
13 Who divided the Red Sea in two parts : for His mercy endureth for ever.
14 And made Israel to go through the midst of it : for His mercy endureth for ever.
15 But as for Pharaoh and his host, He overthrew them in the Red Sea : for His mercy endureth for ever.
16 Who led His people through the wilderness : for His mercy endureth for ever.
17 Who smote great kings : for His mercy endureth for ever.
18 Yea, and slew mighty kings : for His mercy endureth for ever.
19 Sehon king of the Amorites : for His mercy endureth for ever.
20 And Og the king of Basan : for His mercy endureth for ever.
21 And gave away their land for an heritage : for His mercy endureth for ever.
22 Even for an heritage unto Israel His servant : for His mercy endureth for ever.
23 Who remembered us when we were in trouble : for His mercy endureth for ever.
24 And hath delivered us from our enemies : for His mercy endureth for ever.
25 Who giveth food to all flesh : for His mercy endureth for ever.
26 O give thanks unto the God of heaven : for His mercy endureth for ever.
27 O give thanks unto the Lord of lords : for His mercy endureth for ever.
Glory be, etc.

Ant. For His mercy : endureth for ever.

Ant. Sing us.

Super flumina. Psalm CXXXVII.

BY the waters of Babylon we sat down and wept : when we remembered thee, O Sion.

2 As for our harps, we hanged them up : upon the trees that are therein.

3 For they that led us away captive required of us then a song, and melody, in our heaviness : Sing us one of the songs of Sion.

4 How shall we sing the Lord's song : in a strange land?

5 If I forget thee, O Jerusalem : let my right hand forget her cunning.

6 If I do not remember thee, let my tongue cleave to the roof of my mouth : yea, if I prefer not Jerusalem in my mirth.

7 Remember the children of Edom, O Lord, in the day of Jerusalem : how they said, Down with it, down with it, even to the ground.

8 O daughter of Babylon, wasted with misery : yea, happy shall he be that rewardeth thee, as thou hast served us.

9 Blessed shall he be that taketh thy children : and throweth them against the stones.

Glory be, etc.

Ant. Sing us : one of the songs of Sion.

From Epiphany to Septuagesima; from Septuagesima to First Friday in Lent inclusive; and from Trinity to Advent,

CHAPTER. 2 Thess. III., p. 49.

From Trinity to Advent,

HYMN. *Lucis Creator optime,*
℣. and ℟. p. 49.

Ferial Antiphons and Magnificat, p. 50.

[*For Chapters, Hymns, and Antiphons at other times, see Proper of Seasons.*]

PETITIONS, *and the rest,* p. 53.

FRIDAY.
Vespers.

✠ ℣. O God, make speed to save us.

℟. O Lord, make haste to help us.

℣. Glory be to the Father, and to the Son : and to the Holy Ghost.

℟. As it was in the beginning, is now, and ever shall be : world without end. Amen.

Alleluia.

[*From Septuagesima to Wednesday in Holy Week:*

Praise be to Thee, O Lord, King of eternal glory.]

Ant. Before the gods.

Confitebor tibi. Psalm CXXXVIII.

I WILL give thanks unto Thee, O Lord, with my whole heart : even before the gods will I sing praise unto Thee.

2 I will worship toward Thy holy temple, and praise Thy Name, because of Thy loving-kindness and truth : for Thou hast magnified Thy Name, and Thy Word, above all things.

3 When I called upon Thee, Thou heardest me : and enduedst my soul with much strength.

4 All the kings of the earth shall praise Thee, O Lord : for they have heard the words of Thy mouth.

5 Yea, they shall sing in the ways of the Lord : that great is the glory of the Lord.

6 For though the Lord be high, yet hath He respect unto the lowly : as for the proud, He beholdeth them afar off.

7 Though I walk in the midst of trouble, yet shalt Thou refresh me : Thou shalt stretch forth Thy hand upon the furiousness of mine enemies, and Thy right hand shall save me.

8 The Lord shall make good His loving kindness toward me : yea, Thy mercy, O Lord, endureth for ever ; despise not then the works of Thine own hands.

Glory be, etc.

Ant. Before the gods : will I sing praise unto Thee, my God.

Ant. O Lord, Thou hast searched.

Domine, probasti.   Psalm cxxxix.

O LORD, Thou hast searched me out, and known me : Thou knowest my down-sitting, and mine up-rising; Thou understandest my thoughts long before.

2 Thou art about my path, and about my bed : and spiest out all my ways.

3 For lo, there is not a word in my tongue : but Thou, O Lord, knowest it altogether.

4 Thou hast fashioned me behind and before : and laid Thine hand upon me.

5 Such knowledge is too wonderful and excellent for me : I cannot attain unto it.

6 Whither shall I go then from Thy Spirit : or whither shall I go then from Thy presence?

7 If I climb up into heaven, Thou art there : if I go down to hell, Thou art there also.

8 If I take the wings of the morning : and remain in the uttermost parts of the sea;

9 Even there also shall Thy hand lead me : and Thy right hand shall hold me.

10 If I say, Peradventure the darkness shall cover me : then shall my night be turned to day.

11 Yea, the darkness is no darkness with Thee, but the night is as clear as the day : the darkness and light to Thee are both alike.

12 For my reins are Thine : Thou hast covered me in my mother's womb.

13 I will give thanks unto Thee, for I am fearfully and wonderfully made : marvellous are Thy works, and that my soul knoweth right well.

14 My bones are not hid from Thee : though I be made secretly, and fashioned beneath in the earth.

15 Thine eyes did see my substance, yet being imperfect : and in Thy book were all my members written ;

16 Which day by day were fashioned : when as yet there was none of them.

17 How dear are Thy counsels unto me, O God : O how great is the sum of them !

18 If I tell them, they are more in number than the sand : when I wake up I am present with Thee.

19 Wilt Thou not slay the wicked, O God? : depart from me, ye blood-thirsty men.

20 For they speak unrighteously against Thee : and Thine enemies take Thy Name in vain.

21 Do not I hate them, O Lord, that hate Thee : and am not I grieved with those that rise up against Thee?

22 Yea, I hate them right sore : even as though they were mine enemies.

23 Try me, O God, and seek the ground of my heart : prove me, and examine my thoughts.

24 Look well if there be any way of wickedness in me : and lead me in the way everlasting.

Glory be, etc.

Ant. O Lord, Thou hast searched me out : and known me.

Ant. Preserve me.

Eripe me, Domine. Psalm CXL.

DELIVER me, O Lord, from the evil man : and preserve me from the wicked man.

2 Who imagine mischief in their hearts : and stir up strife all the day long.

3 They have sharpened their tongues like a serpent : adder's poison is under their lips.

4 Keep me, O Lord, from the hands of the ungodly : preserve me from the wicked men, who are purposed to overthrow my goings.

5 The proud have laid a snare for me, and spread a net abroad with cords : yea, and set traps in my way.

6 I said unto the Lord, Thou art my God : hear the voice of my prayers, O Lord.

7 O Lord God, Thou strength of my health : Thou hast covered my head in the day of battle.

8 Let not the ungodly have his desire, O Lord : let not his mischievous imagination prosper, lest they be too proud.

9 Let the mischief of their own lips fall upon the head of them : that compass me about.

10 Let hot burning coals fall upon them : let them be cast into the fire, and into the pit, that they never rise up again.

11 A man full of words shall not prosper upon the earth : evil shall hunt the wicked person to overthrow him.

12 Sure I am that the Lord will avenge the poor : and maintain the cause of the helpless.

13 The righteous also shall give thanks unto Thy Name : and the just shall continue in Thy sight.

Glory be, etc.

Ant. Preserve me : from the wicked man.

Ant. Lord, I call.

Domine, clamavi. Psalm CXLI.

LORD, I call upon Thee, haste Thee unto me : and consider my voice when I cry unto Thee.

2 Let my prayer be set forth in Thy sight as the incense : and let the lifting up of my hands be an evening sacrifice.

3 Set a watch, O Lord, before my mouth : and keep the door of my lips.

4 O let not mine heart be inclined to any evil thing : let me not be occupied in ungodly works with the men that work wickedness, lest I eat of such things as please them.

5 Let the righteous rather smite me friendly : and reprove me.

6 But let not their precious balms break my head : yea, I will pray yet against their wickedness.

7 Let their judges be overthrown in stony places : that they may hear my words, for they are sweet.

8 Our bones lie scattered before the pit : like as when one breaketh and heweth wood upon the earth.

9 But mine eyes look unto Thee, O Lord God : in Thee is my trust, O cast not out my soul.

10 Keep me from the snare that they have laid for me : and from the traps of the wicked doers.

11 Let the ungodly fall into their own nets together : and let me ever escape them.

Glory be, etc.

Ant. Lord, I call upon Thee : haste Thee unto me.

Ant. Thou art my portion.

Voce mea ad Dominum. Psalm CXLII.

I CRIED unto the Lord with my voice : yea, even unto the Lord did I make my supplication.

2 I poured out my complaints

before Him : and shewed Him of my trouble.

3 When my spirit was in heaviness Thou knewest my path : in the way wherein I walked have they privily laid a snare for me.

4 I looked also upon my right hand : and saw there was no man that would know me.

5 I had no place to flee unto : and no man cared for my soul.

6 I cried unto Thee, O Lord, and said : Thou art my hope and my portion in the land of the living.

7 Consider my complaint : for I am brought very low!

8 O deliver me from my persecutors : for they are too strong for me.

9 Bring my soul out of prison, that I may give thanks unto Thy Name : which thing if Thou wilt grant me, then shall the righteous resort unto my company.

Glory be, etc.

Ant. Thou art my portion : in the land of the living. p.53. Patriti

From Epiphany to Septuagesima; from Septuagesima to First Friday in Lent, inclusive; and from Trinity to Advent,

CHAPTER. 2 Thess. III., p. 49.

From Trinity to Advent,

HYMN. *Lucis Creator optime,* ℣. and ℟. p. 49.

Ferial Antiphons and Magnificat, p. 50.

[*For Chapters, Hymns, and Antiphons at other times, see Proper of Seasons.*]

PETITIONS *and the rest,* p. 53.

SATURDAY.

First Vespers of Sunday.

✠ ℣. O God, make speed to save us.

℟. O Lord, make haste to help us.

℣. Glory be to the Father, and to the Son : and to the Holy Ghost.

℟. As it was in the beginning, is now, and ever shall be : world without end. Amen.

Alleluia.

[*From Septuagesima to Wednesday in Holy Week :*

Praise be to Thee, O Lord, King of eternal glory.]

Ant. Blessed be ✱ : the Lord my strength.

Benedictus Dominus. Psalm CXLIV.

BLESSED be the Lord my strength : Who teacheth my hands to war, and my fingers to fight ;

2 My hope and my fortress, my castle and deliverer, my defender in Whom I trust : Who subdueth my people that is under me.

3 Lord, what is man, that Thou hast such respect unto him : or the son of man, that Thou so regardest him ?

4 Man is like a thing of nought : his time passeth away like a shadow.

5 Bow Thy heavens, O Lord, and come down : touch the mountains, and they shall smoke.

6 Cast forth Thy lightning, and tear them : shoot out Thine arrows, and consume them.

7 Send down Thine hand from above : deliver me, and take me out of the great waters, from the hand of strange children ;

8 Whose mouth talketh of vanity : and their right hand is a right hand of wickedness.

9 I will sing a new song unto Thee, O God : and sing praises unto Thee upon a ten-stringed lute.

10 Thou hast given victory unto kings : and hast delivered David Thy servant from the peril of the sword.

11 Save me, and deliver me from the hand of strange children : whose mouth talketh of vanity, and their right hand is a right hand of iniquity.

12 That our sons may grow up as the young plants : and that our daughters may be as the polished corners of the temple.

13 That our garners may be full and plenteous with all manner of store : that our sheep may bring forth thousands and ten thousands in our streets.

14 That our oxen may be strong to labour, that there be no decay : no leading into captivity, and no complaining in our streets.

15 Happy are the people that are in such a case : yea, blessed are the people who have the Lord for their God.

Glory be, etc.

Ant. Blessed be : the Lord my strength.

Ant. For ever * : and ever.

Exaltabo te, Deus. Psalm CXLV.

I WILL magnify Thee, O God, my King : and I will praise Thy Name for ever and ever.

2 Every day will I give thanks unto Thee : and praise Thy Name for ever and ever.

3 Great is the Lord, and marvellous, worthy to be praised : there is no end of His greatness.

4 One generation shall praise Thy works unto another : and declare Thy power.

5 As for me, I will be talking of Thy worship : Thy glory, Thy praise, and wondrous works ;

6 So that men shall speak of the might of Thy marvellous acts : and I will also tell of Thy greatness.

7 The memorial of Thine abundant kindness shall be shewed : and men shall sing of Thy righteousness.

8 The Lord is gracious, and merciful : long-suffering, and of great goodness.

9 The Lord is loving unto every man : and His mercy is over all His works.

10 All Thy works praise Thee, O Lord : and Thy saints give thanks unto Thee.

11 They shew the glory of Thy kingdom : and talk of Thy power ;

12 That Thy power, Thy glory, and mightiness of Thy kingdom : might be known unto men.

13 Thy kingdom is an everlasting kingdom : and Thy dominion endureth throughout all ages.

14 The Lord upholdeth all such as fall : and lifteth up all those that are down.

15 The eyes of all wait upon Thee, O Lord : and Thou givest them their meat in due season.

16 Thou openest Thine hand : and fillest all things living with plenteousness.

17 The Lord is righteous in all His ways : and holy in all His works.

18 The Lord is nigh unto all them that call upon Him : yea, all such as call upon Him faithfully.

19 He will fulfil the desire of them that fear Him : He also will hear their cry, and will help them.

20 The Lord preserveth all them that love Him : but scattereth abroad all the ungodly.

21 My mouth shall speak the praise of the Lord : and let all flesh give thanks unto His holy Name for ever and ever.

Glory be, etc.

Ant. For ever : and ever.

Ant. While I live * : will I praise the Lord.

VESPERS: SATURDAY.

Lauda anima mea. Psalm CXLVI.

PRAISE the Lord, O my soul; while I live will I praise the Lord : yea, as long as I have any being, I will sing praises unto my God.

2 O put not your trust in princes, nor in any child of man : for there is no help in them.

3 For when the breath of man goeth forth he shall turn again to his earth : and then all his thoughts perish.

4 Blessed is he that hath the God of Jacob for his help : and whose hope is in the Lord his God;

5 Who made heaven and earth, the sea, and all that therein is : Who keepeth His promise for ever;

6 Who helpeth them to right that suffer wrong : Who feedeth the hungry.

7 The Lord looseth men out of prison : the Lord giveth sight to the blind.

8 The Lord helpeth them that are fallen : the Lord careth for the righteous.

9 The Lord careth for the strangers; He defendeth the fatherless and widow : as for the way of the ungodly, He turneth it upside down.

10 The Lord thy God, O Sion, shall be King for evermore : and throughout all generations.

Glory be, etc.

Ant. While I live : will I praise the Lord.

Ant. Yea, a joyful and pleasant thing : * it is to be thankful.

Laudate Dominum. Psalm CXLVII.

O PRAISE the Lord, for it is a good thing to sing praises unto our God : yea, a joyful and pleasant thing it is to be thankful.

2 The Lord doth build up Jerusalem : and gather together the outcasts of Israel.

3 He healeth those that are broken in heart : and giveth medicine to heal their sickness.

4 He telleth the number of the stars : and calleth them all by their names.

5 Great is our Lord, and great is His power : yea, and His wisdom is infinite.

6 The Lord setteth up the meek : and bringeth the ungodly down to the ground.

7 O sing unto the Lord with thanksgiving : sing praises upon the harp unto our God;

8 Who covereth the heaven with clouds, and prepareth rain for the earth : and maketh the grass to grow upon the mountains, and herb for the use of men;

9 Who giveth fodder unto the cattle : and feedeth the young ravens that call upon Him.

10 He hath no pleasure in the strength of an horse : neither delighteth He in any man's legs.

11 But the Lord's delight is in them that fear Him : and put their trust in His mercy.

Glory be, etc.

Ant. Yea, a joyful and pleasant thing : it is to be thankful.

Ant. Praise the Lord : * O Jerusalem.

Lauda Hierusalem. Psalm CXLVII. 12.

PRAISE the Lord, O Jerusalem : praise thy God, O Sion.

13 For He hath made fast the bars of thy gates : and hath blessed thy children within thee.

14 He maketh peace in thy borders : and filleth thee with the flour of wheat.

15 He sendeth forth His com-

mandment upon earth : and His word runneth very swiftly.

16 He giveth snow like wool : and scattereth the hoar-frost like ashes.

17 He casteth forth His ice like morsels : who is able to abide His frost?

18 He sendeth out His word, and melteth them : He bloweth with His wind, and the waters flow.

19 He sheweth His word unto Jacob : His statutes and ordinances unto Israel.

20 He hath not dealt so with any nation : neither have the heathen knowledge of His laws.

Glory be, etc.

Ant. Praise the Lord : O Jerusalem.

From the Octave of Epiphany to Septuagesima, and from Trinity to Advent,

CHAPTER. 2 Cor. i.

BLESSED be God, even the Father of our Lord Jesus Christ, the Father of mercies, and the God of all comfort; Who comforteth us in all our tribulation.

℟. Thanks be to God.

From Trinity to Advent,

HYMN. *O lux beata Trinitas.*

O TRINITY of blessed light,
O Unity of princely might,
The fiery sun now goes his way :
Shed Thou within our hearts Thy ray.

To Thee our morning song of praise,
To Thee our evening prayer we raise;
Thy glory suppliant we adore
For ever and for evermore.

[All laud to God the Father be;
All laud, Eternal Son, to Thee;
All laud, as is for ever meet,
To God the blessed Paraclete.] Amen.

℣. Let our evening prayer come up before Thee, O Lord.

℟. And let Thy mercy come down on us.

For Chapters and Hymns at other times, and Ants. to Magnificat, see Proper of Seasons.

Magnificat, p. 50.

℣. The Lord be with you.
℟. And with thy spirit.

Let us pray.

COLLECT.

℣. The Lord be with you.
℟. And with thy spirit.
℣. Bless we the Lord.
℟. Thanks be to God.

From the Octave of Trinity till Advent, when the Office is of Sunday, or memorial of Sunday is made, are said these Memorials; those of the Cross and of S. Mary being omitted on Double Feasts.

MEMORIAL OF THE HOLY TRINITY.

Ant. Thou art our hope, our salvation, our honour : O blessed Trinity.

℣. Let us bless the Father, the Son, and the Holy Ghost.

℟. Let us praise and exalt Him for ever.

Let us pray.

COLLECT.

ALMIGHTY and everlasting God, Who hast given unto us Thy servants grace by the confession of a true faith to acknowledge the glory of the eternal Trinity, and in the power of the Divine Majesty to worship the Unity; grant that by stedfastness in this faith we may be evermore defended from all adversities : Who livest and reignest, one God, world without end. Amen.

MEMORIAL OF THE HOLY CROSS.

Ant. O glorious Cross, O adorable Cross, O precious wood, O admirable sign : whereby the devil hath been conquered, and the world redeemed with the Blood of Christ. Alleluia.

℣. We adore Thee, O Christ, and bless Thee.

℟. For by Thy Cross Thou hast redeemed the world.

Let us pray.

COLLECT.

O GOD, Who by the precious and life-giving Blood of Thy only-begotten Son our Lord Jesus Christ, hast willed to consecrate the standard of the Cross; grant, we pray Thee, that they who rejoice in the honour of the holy Cross, may also rejoice everywhere in Thy protection; through the same Thy Son Jesus Christ our Lord. Amen.

MEMORIAL OF S. MARY.

Ant. Thou art become fair and pleasant, O holy Mother of God, in the delights of virginity : when the daughters of Sion saw thee among the roses and lilies they blessed thee, and queens praised thee.

℣. After child-bearing thou remainedst a Virgin.

℟. O Mother of God.

Let us pray.

COLLECT.

ALMIGHTY, everlasting God, by the right hand of Thy power defend Thy servants from all perils; and, blessed Mary, ever-Virgin, gloriously interceding, grant us prosperity both now and hereafter; through.

℣. The Lord be with you.
℟. And with thy spirit.
℣. Bless we the Lord.
℟. Thanks be to God.

Compline.

✠ ℣. Turn us, O God our Saviour.
℟. And let Thine anger cease from us.
℣. O God, make speed to save us.
℟. O Lord, make haste to help us.
℣. Glory be to the Father, and to the Son : and to the Holy Ghost.

℟. As it was in the beginning, is now, and ever shall be : world without end. Amen.

Alleluia.

[*From Septuagesima to Wednesday in Holy Week,*

Praise be to Thee, O Lord, King of eternal glory.]

Ant. Have mercy.

Cum invocarem. Psalm IV.

HEAR me when I call, O God of my righteousness : Thou hast set me at liberty when I was in trouble; have mercy upon me, and hearken unto my prayer.

2 O ye sons of men, how long will ye blaspheme Mine honour : and have such pleasure in vanity, and seek after leasing?

3 Know this also, that the Lord hath chosen to Himself the man that is godly : when I call upon the Lord, He will hear me.

4 Stand in awe, and sin not : commune with your own heart, and in your chamber, and be still.

5 Offer the sacrifice of righteousness : and put your trust in the Lord.

6 There be many that say : Who will shew us any good?

7 Lord, lift Thou up : the light of Thy countenance upon us.

8 Thou hast put gladness in my heart : since the time that their corn, and wine, and oil, increased.

9 I will lay me down in peace, and take my rest : for it is Thou, Lord, only, that makest me dwell in safety.

Glory be, etc.

In Te, Domine, speravi. Psalm XXXI.

IN Thee, O Lord, have I put my trust : let me never be put to confusion, deliver me in Thy righteousness.

2 Bow down Thine ear to me : make haste to deliver me.

3 And be Thou my strong rock, and house of defence : that Thou mayest save me.

4 For Thou art my strong rock, and my castle : be Thou also my guide, and lead me for Thy Name's sake.

5 Draw me out of the net that they have laid privily for me : for Thou art my strength.

6 Into Thy hands I commend my spirit : for Thou hast redeemed me, O Lord, Thou God of truth.

Glory be, etc.

Qui habitat. Psalm xci.

WHOSO dwelleth under the defence of the most High : shall abide under the shadow of the Almighty.

2 I will say unto the Lord, Thou art my hope, and my strong hold : my God, in Him will I trust.

3 For He shall deliver thee from the snare of the hunter : and from the noisome pestilence.

4 He shall defend thee under His wings, and thou shall be safe under His feathers : His faithfulness and truth shall be thy shield and buckler.

5 Thou shalt not be afraid for any terror by night : nor for the arrow that flieth by day;

6 For the pestilence that walketh in darkness : nor for the sickness that destroyeth in the noon-day.

7 A thousand shall fall beside thee, and ten thousand at thy right hand : but it shall not come nigh thee.

8 Yea, with thine eyes shalt thou behold : and see the reward of the ungodly.

9 For Thou, Lord, art my hope : Thou hast set Thine house of defence very high.

10 There shall no evil happen unto thee : neither shall any plague come nigh thy dwelling.

11 For He shall give His angels charge over thee : to keep thee in all thy ways.

12 They shall bear thee in their hands : that thou hurt not thy foot against a stone.

13 Thou shalt go upon the lion and adder : the young lion and the dragon shalt thou tread under thy feet.

14 Because he hath set his love upon Me, therefore will I deliver him : I will set him up, because he hath known My Name.

15 He shall call upon Me, and I will hear him : yea, I am with him in trouble ; I will deliver him, and bring him to honour.

16 With long life will I satisfy him : and shew him My salvation.

Glory be, etc.

Ecce nunc. Psalm cxxxiv.

BEHOLD now, praise the Lord : all ye servants of the Lord;

2 Ye that by night stand in the house of the Lord : even in the courts of the house of our God.

3 Lift up your hands in the sanctuary : and praise the Lord.

4 The Lord that made heaven and earth : give thee blessing out of Sion.

Glory be, etc.

Ant. Have mercy upon me, O Lord : and hearken unto my prayer.

This Ant. is always said, unless some other be appointed in Proper of Seasons.

CHAPTER. Jer. xiv.

THOU, O Lord, art in the midst of us, and we are called by Thy Name; leave us not, O Lord our God.

℟. Thanks be to God.

This Chapter is always said, except from Maundy Thursday to Low Sunday, inclusive.

HYMN. *Te lucis ante terminum.*

BEFORE the ending of the day,
   Creator of the world, we pray
That with Thy wonted favour, Thou
Wouldst be our Guard and Keeper now.

From all ill dreams defend our eyes,
From nightly fears and fantasies;
Tread under foot our ghostly foe,
That no pollution we may know.

O Father, that we ask be done,
Through Jesus Christ, Thine only Son;
Who, with the Holy Ghost and Thee,
Shall live and reign eternally. Amen.

℣. Keep us, O Lord.

℟. As the apple of an eye : hide us under the shadow of Thy wings.

This Hymn, ℣. and ℟. are said on ordinary Sundays, Simple Feasts, Days within Octaves (except as noted below) and Ferias, from Epiphany to Lent, and from Trinity to Christmas.

[HYMN. *Salvator mundi Domine.*

SAVIOUR of man, and Lord alone,
   Who through this day hast led Thine own,
Protect us through the coming night,
And ever keep us by Thy might.

Be with us, Lord, in mercy nigh,
And spare Thy servants when they cry;
Blot out our every past offence,
And lighten Thou our darkened sense.

O let not sleep oppress the soul,
Nor Satan with his spirits foul;
Our flesh keep chaste, that it may be
An holy temple unto Thee.

To Thee, Who makest souls anew,
With heartfelt vows we humbly sue;
That pure in heart, and free from stain,
We from our beds may rise again.

All laud to God the Father be;
All laud, Eternal Son, to Thee;
All laud, as is for ever meet,
To God the blessed Paraclete. Amen.

℣. Keep us, O Lord.

℟. As the apple of an eye : hide us under the shadow of Thy wings.

This Hymn, ℣. and ℟. are said from Christmas to the First Sunday after Octave of Epiphany; on Whitsun Eve, and on Thursday, Friday, and Saturday in Whitsun Week; on all Double Feasts from Epiphany to First Sunday in Lent, and from First Sunday after Trinity to Christmas, except the Feast of the Holy Name, and during the Octaves of Corpus Christi, Repose of S. Mary, and Dedication.

Festival Ant. said except in Eastertide, and when otherwise signified in the Proper.

Lord, grant us Thy light : * that being rid of the darkness of our hearts, we may come to the true Light, which is Christ.]

Ferial. Ant. Save us waking,* O Lord, and guard us sleeping : that awake we may be with Christ, and may sleep in peace.

Nunc Dimittis.

LORD, now lettest Thou Thy servant depart in peace : according to Thy word.

2 For mine eyes have seen : Thy salvation.

3 Which Thou hast prepared : before the face of all people.

4 To be a light to lighten the Gentiles : and to be the glory of Thy people Israel.

Glory be, etc.

PETITIONS.

Lord, have mercy [iii].
Christ, have mercy [iii].
Lord, have mercy [iii].

Our Father :

Said silently throughout. The Priest repeats aloud :

℣. And lead us not into temptation.
℟. But deliver us from evil.
℣. I will lay me down in peace.
℟. And take my rest.

I believe :

Said silently throughout. The Priest repeats aloud :

℣. The resurrection of the body.
℟. And the life everlasting.
℣. Let us bless the Father, the Son, and the Holy Ghost.
℟. Let us praise and exalt Him above all for ever.
℣. Blessed art Thou, O Lord, in the firmament of heaven.

℟. And above all to be praised and glorified for ever.
℣. May the Almighty and most merciful Lord bless us and keep us.
℟. Amen.

Confession and Absolution, said in a low voice.

The Officiant:

I CONFESS to God Almighty, the Father, the Son, and the Holy Ghost, in the sight of the whole company of heaven, and to you, my *brethren*, that I have sinned exceedingly in thought, word, and deed, by my fault; therefore I pray God to have mercy upon me, and you, my *brethren*, to pray for me.

The Choir replies:

ALMIGHTY God have mercy upon thee, pardon and deliver thee from all thy sins, confirm and strengthen thee in all goodness, and bring thee to everlasting life. ℟. Amen.

The Choir.

I CONFESS to God Almighty, the Father, the Son, and the Holy Ghost, in the sight of the whole company of heaven, [and to thee, *father*,] that I have sinned exceedingly in thought, word, and deed, by my fault; therefore I pray God to have mercy upon me, [and thee, *father*, to pray for me.]

The Officiant:

ALMIGHTY God have mercy upon you, pardon and deliver you from all your sins, confirm and strengthen you in all goodness, and bring you to everlasting life. ℟. Amen.

[*Then let the Officiant, if a Priest, add:*
THE Almighty and merciful Lord grant you absolution and remission of all your sins, time for true repentance, amendment of life, and the grace and comfort of the Holy Ghost. ℟. Amen.]
℣. Wilt Thou not turn again and quicken us, O Lord?
℟. That Thy people may rejoice in Thee.
℣. Shew us Thy mercy, O Lord.
℟. And grant us Thy salvation.
℣. Vouchsafe, O Lord.
℟. To keep us this day without sin.
℣. O Lord, have mercy upon us.
℟. Have mercy upon us.
℣. O Lord, let Thy mercy lighten upon us.
℟. As our trust is in Thee.

The foregoing Petitions are said daily through the year (except from Maundy Thursday till Low Sunday, and on All Souls' Day): then follows

[ON SUNDAYS AND ALL FESTIVALS:
℣. Turn us again, O Lord God of Hosts.
℟. Shew the light of Thy countenance, and we shall be whole.
℣. Hear my prayer, O Lord.
℟. And let my crying come unto Thee.
℣. The Lord be with you.
℟. And with thy spirit.

Let us pray.

LIGHTEN our darkness, we beseech Thee, O Lord: and by Thy great mercy defend us from all perils and dangers of this night; for the love of Thy only Son, our Saviour, Jesus Christ : Who liveth. Amen.
℣. The Lord be with you.
℟. And with thy spirit.
℣. Bless we the Lord.
℟. Thanks be to God.]

ON FERIAS

Through the year, except in Christmas and Easter tides:

℣. Hearken unto my voice, O Lord, when I cry unto Thee.

℟. Have mercy upon me, and hear me.
Miserere. Psalm LI., p. 10.

[*Here follows in Lent:*
Domine, exaudi. Psalm CXLIII.

HEAR my prayer, O Lord, and consider my desire : hearken unto me for Thy truth and righteousness' sake.

2 And enter not into judgment with Thy servant : for in Thy sight shall no man living be justified.

3 For the enemy hath persecuted my soul; he hath smitten my life down to the ground; he hath laid me in the darkness, as the men that have been long dead.

4 Therefore is my spirit vexed within me : and my heart within me is desolate.

5 Yet do I remember the time past; I muse upon all Thy works : yea, I exercise myself in the works of Thy hands.

6 I stretch forth my hands unto Thee : my soul gaspeth unto Thee as a thirsty land.

7 Hear me, O Lord, and that soon, for my spirit waxeth faint : hide not Thy face from me, lest I be like unto them that go down into the pit.

8 O let me hear Thy loving kindness betimes in the morning, for in Thee is my trust: shew Thou me the way that I should walk in, for I lift up my soul unto Thee.

9 Deliver me, O Lord, from mine enemies: for I flee unto Thee to hide me.

10 Teach me to do the thing that pleaseth Thee, for Thou art my God : let Thy loving Spirit lead me forth into the land of righteousness.

11 Quicken me, O Lord, for Thy Name's sake : and for Thy righteousness' sake bring my soul out of prison.

12 And of Thy goodness slay mine enemies: and destroy all them that vex my soul; for I am Thy servant.

Glory be, etc.]

[*Here the reader, if a Priest, rises, and stands at the step of the Sanctuary*].

℣. O Lord, arise, help us.
℟. And deliver us for Thy Name's sake.
℣. Turn us again, O Lord God of Hosts.
℟. Shew the light of Thy countenance, and we shall be whole.
℣. Hear my prayer, O Lord.
℟. And let my crying come unto Thee.
℣. The Lord be with you.
℟. And with thy spirit.

Let us pray.

LIGHTEN our darkness, we beseech Thee, O Lord, and by Thy great mercy defend us from all perils and dangers of this night, for the love of Thy only Son, our Saviour Jesus Christ : Who liveth. Amen.

℣. The Lord be with you.
℟. And with thy spirit.
℣. Bless we the Lord.
℟. Thanks be to God.

FOR THE PEACE OF THE CHURCH.

Said daily throughout the year, all kneeling, except on Christmas Eve, and thence till First Sunday after Octave of Epiphany; from Wednesday before Easter till First Sunday after Trinity; on all Double Feasts, on All Souls' Day, and in the Octaves of Corpus Christi. Repose B. V. M., Holy Name, and Dedication.

Ad Te levavi oculos meos. Psalm CXXIII.

UNTO Thee lift I up mine eyes :
O Thou that dwellest in the heavens.

2 Behold, even as the eyes of servants look unto the hand of their masters, and as the eyes of a maiden unto the hand of her mistress : even so our eyes wait upon the Lord our God, until He have mercy upon us.

3 Have mercy upon us, O Lord, have mercy upon us : for we are utterly despised.

4 Our soul is filled with the scornful reproof of the wealthy : and with the despitefulness of the proud.

Glory be, etc.

Lord, have mercy.
Christ, have mercy.
Lord, have mercy.

Our Father :
Said silently throughout. The Priest repeats aloud :

℣. And lead us not into temptation.
℟. But deliver us from evil.
℣. O Lord, arise, help us.

℞. And deliver us for Thy Name's sake.
℣. Turn us again, O Lord God of Hosts.
℞. Shew the light of Thy countenance, and we shall be whole.
℣. Hear my prayer, O Lord.
℞. And let my crying come unto Thee.
℣. The Lord be with you.
℞. And with thy spirit.

Let us pray.

O LORD, we beseech Thee, mercifully to hear the prayers of Thy Church, and grant that we, being delivered from all adversities, may serve Thee with a quiet mind; and grant us Thy peace all the days of our life; through Jesus Christ our Lord, Who liveth and reigneth with Thee and the Holy Ghost, ever one God, world without end. Amen.

℣. The Lord be with you.
℞. And with thy spirit.
℣. Bless we the Lord.
℞. Thanks be to God.

MAY the souls of the faithful, through the mercy of God, rest in peace. Amen.

This prayer, May the souls, etc., *is said at Compline only.*

✠

Proper of Seasons.

ENDINGS OF COLLECTS.

Through (the same) Jesus Christ our Lord, Who liveth and reigneth with Thee and the Holy Ghost, one God, world without end. Amen.

Who, with Thee and the Holy Ghost, liveth and reigneth, ever one God, world without end. Amen.

Who livest and reignest with the Father and the Holy Ghost, one God, world without end. Amen.

Who liveth. In the Unity. Who liveth and reigneth with Thee in the Unity of the Holy Ghost, one God, world without end. Amen.

SARUM USE.

The first and last Collect in each office is said with full ending; and so are the intermediate Collects, unless they close with Through, *or* Through the same, *etc., in which case the ending is* Through, *or* Through the same Jesus Christ our Lord. Amen.

(ROMAN USE.

The last Collect only has full ending. The rest have neither ascription nor Amen.)

In this book the Collects of the English Common Prayer Book are always set down in the first place, when they differ from those of the more ancient use (which then, with a few exceptions, follow within brackets), and are reproduced exactly from the Prayer Book, although, strictly speaking, they should all end with full doxology when said in the office of the day.

✠

PROPER OF SEASONS.

ALL IS SAID THROUGHOUT AS IN THE PSALTER, EXCEPT WHEN HERE OTHERWISE NOTED.

FIRST SUNDAY IN ADVENT.
First Vespers.

CHAPTER. Is. II.

AND it shall come to pass in the last days, that the mountain of the Lord's house shall be established in the top of the mountains, and shall be exalted above the hills; and all nations shall flow unto it.

℟. Thanks be to God.

This ℟., Thanks be to God, is always said at all Hours, immediately after the Chapter.

℟. Behold, the days come, saith the Lord, that I will raise unto David a righteous branch, and a King shall reign and prosper, and shall execute judgment and justice in the earth : And this is His Name whereby He shall be called : The Lord our Righteousness. ℣. In His days Judah shall be saved, and Israel shall dwell safely. ℟. And this is His Name whereby He shall be called : the Lord our Righteousness. ℣. Glory be to the Father, and to the Son : and to the Holy Ghost. ℟. The Lord our Righteousness.

HYMN. *Conditor alme siderum.*

CREATOR of the stars of night,
Thy people's everlasting light,
Jesu, Redeemer, save us all,
And hear Thy servants when they call.

Thou, grieving that the ancient curse
Should doom to death an universe,
Hast found the med'cine, full of grace,
To save and heal a ruin'd race.

Thou cam'st, the Bridegroom of the Bride,
As drew the world to evening tide, -
Proceeding from a virgin shrine,
The spotless Victim all divine.

At Whose dread Name, majestic now,
All knees must bend, all hearts must bow;
And things celestial Thee shall own,
And things terrestrial, Lord alone.

O Thou Whose coming is with dread,
To judge and doom the quick and dead,
Preserve us, while we dwell below,
From ev'ry insult of the foe,

To Him Who comes the world to free,
To God the Son, all glory be :
To God the Father, as is meet,
To God the blessed Paraclete. Amen.

℣. Drop down, ye heavens, from above. ℟. And let the skies pour down righteousness : let the earth open, and let them bring forth salvation.

Ant. to Mag. Behold, the Name of the Lord cometh from far : for His glory filleth the whole earth.

COLLECT. (*English.* 1549.)

ALMIGHTY God, give us grace that we may cast away the works of darkness, and put upon us the armour of light, now in the time of this mortal life, in which Thy Son Jesus Christ came to visit us in great humility; that in the last day, when He shall come again in His glorious

Majesty to judge both the quick and dead, we may rise to the life immortal, through Him Who liveth and reigneth with Thee and the Holy Ghost, now and ever. Amen.

[*Or this,*

RAISE up, we pray Thee, O Lord, Thy power, and come : that from the dangers which hang over us by reason of our sins, we may be shielded by Thy protection, and delivered by Thy salvation. Who livest.]

On this day no Memorial is said except that of S. Mary.

MEMORIAL OF S. MARY.

Ant. Hail, Mary, full of grace, the Lord is with thee : blessed art thou among women. Alleluia.

℣. There shall come forth a rod out of the stem of Jesse.

℟. And a branch shall grow out of his roots.

Let us pray.

COLLECT.

O GOD, Who didst will that Thy Word should take flesh in the womb of Blessed Mary, ever-virgin; grant to Thy suppliants, that we, who believe her to be indeed the Mother of God, may be helped by her intercession before Thee; through the same.

[*At Lauds the* MEMORIAL OF S. MARY *is said with the same* ℣., ℟., *and Collect, but with this*

Ant. The Angel Gabriel was sent to Mary : a virgin espoused to Joseph.

At Second Vespers, with this

Ant. Blessed art thou, Mary, that hast believed : for there shall be a performance of those things which were told thee from the Lord. Alleluia.]

These Memorials are said on all Sundays and Festivals of nine lessons until Christ-
mas Eve, except on the Feast of the Conception. *But when the Ant.,* Blessed art thou, *is said to* Magnificat, *the Ant. of the Memorial is as on Ferias :*

Ant. Fear not, Mary; thou hast found favour with God : behold, thou shalt conceive and bring forth a Son. Alleluia.

[*If* O Sapientia *is begun on a Sunday, the Memorial of S. Mary at the second Vespers is the same as at the first Vespers :* Hail, Mary.]

℣. The Lord be with you.
℟. And with thy spirit.
℣. Bless we the Lord.
℟. Thanks be to God.

Compline.

Ant. to Nunc Dim. Come, O Lord, and visit us in peace : that we may rejoice before Thee with a perfect heart.

This Ant. is said daily through Advent.

Lauds.

Daily until Christmas Eve is said this ℣. *and* ℟.

℣. Send, O Lord, the Lamb, the Ruler of the land.

℟. From the rock of the wilderness, unto the mount of the daughter of Sion.

℣. O God, make speed, etc.

Psalms of Sunday, p. 3.

Ant. 1. In that day the mountains shall drop down new wine : and the hills shall flow with milk and honey. Alleluia.

Ant. 2. Rejoice greatly, O daughter of Sion : shout, O daughter of Jerusalem. Alleluia.

Ant. 3. Behold, the Lord shall come, and all His Saints with Him : and there shall be in that day a great light. Alleluia.

Ant. 4. Ho, every one that thirsteth, come ye to the waters: seek ye the Lord, while He may be found. Alleluia.

Ant. 5. Behold, a great Prophet cometh: and He shall renew Jerusalem. Alleluia.

CHAPTER. Rom. XIII.

NOW it is high time to awake out of sleep: for now is our salvation nearer than when we believed.

℞. Thanks be to God.

HYMN. *Vox clara ecce intonat.*

A THRILLING voice by Jordan rings,
Rebuking guilt and darksome things:
Vain dreams of sin and visions fly;
Christ in His might shines forth on high.

Now let each torpid soul arise,
That sunk in guilt and wounded lies;
See! the new Star's refulgent ray
Shall chase disease and sin away!

The Lamb descends from Heaven above,
To pardon sin with freest love;
For such indulgent mercy shewn,
With tearful joy our thanks we own:

That when again He shines revealed,
And trembling worlds to terror yield,
He give not sin its just reward,
But in His love protect and guard.

To Him, Who comes the world to free,
To God the Son, all glory be:
To God the Father, as is meet,
To God the blessed Paraclete. Amen.

℣. A voice crying in the wilderness.

℞. Prepare ye the way of the Lord: make straight a highway for our God.

Ant. to Ben. The Holy Ghost shall come down upon thee, Mary, fear not: who hast in thy womb the Son of God. Alleluia.

Collect as at First Vespers, p. 75.

MEMORIAL OF S. MARY, p. 76.

Prime.

(The Antiphons at the little Hours are never doubled.)

Ant. In that day * the mountains shall drop down new wine: and the hills shall flow with milk and honey. Alleluia.

Ant. to Quicunque. Thee, God the Father, p. 32.

Tierce.

Ant. Rejoice greatly,* O daughter of Sion: shout, O daughter of Jerusalem. Alleluia.

CHAPTER. Rom. XIII.

NOW it is high time to awake out of sleep: for now is our salvation nearer than when we believed.

Thanks be to God.

The Clerk says ℞. Come and save us, * O Lord God of Hosts. *The Choir repeats the same. The Clerk says* ℣. Shew the light of Thy countenance, and we shall be whole. *Choir.* O Lord God of Hosts. *Clerk.* Glory be to the Father, and to the Son: and to the Holy Ghost. *Choir.* Come and save us, O Lord God of Hosts.

The Clerk says ℣. The heathen shall fear Thy Name, O Lord.

The Choir answers: ℞. And all the kings of the earth Thy majesty.

This order is to be observed in all ℣/℞. at the little Hours throughout the year, out of Lent, except on Septuagesima, Sexagesima, and Quinquagesima Sundays. Then the Reader says the Collect of the day, preceded by

℣. The Lord be with you.
℞. And with thy spirit.

Let us pray.

Collect as at Lauds.

This Collect is said at every Hour through this day, and during the week, when the Office is of the season. And this rule is to be observed throughout the year, whether the Office be of the season, or of any Saint: the Collect said at Lauds is repeated at Tierce, Sexts, Nones, and Second Vespers, except on certain days, as hereafter noted.

Sexts.

Ant. Behold, the Lord shall come,* and all His Saints with Him:

and there shall be in that day a great light. Alleluia.

CHAPTER. Rom. XIII.

THE night is far spent, the day is at hand; let us therefore cast off the works of darkness, and let us put on the armour of light.

℟. O Lord, shew: Thy mercy upon us. ℣. And grant us Thy salvation. ℟. Thy mercy upon us. ℣. Glory be to the Father, and to the Son: and to the Holy Ghost. ℟. O Lord, shew Thy mercy upon us.

℣. Remember me, O Lord, according to the favour that Thou bearest unto Thy people.

℟. O visit me with Thy salvation.

Nones.

Ant. Behold, a great Prophet cometh: and He shall renew Jerusalem. Alleluia.

CHAPTER. Rom. XIII.

LET us walk honestly as in the day; not in rioting and drunkenness, not in chambering and wantonness, not in strife and envying. But put ye on the Lord Jesus Christ.

℟. The Lord shall arise upon thee: O Jerusalem. ℣. And His glory shall be seen upon thee. ℟. O Jerusalem. ℣. Glory be to the Father, and to the Son: and to the Holy Ghost. ℟. The Lord shall arise upon thee, O Jerusalem.

℣. Turn us again, O Lord God of Hosts.

℟. Shew the light of Thy countenance, and we shall be whole.

Second Vespers.

CHAPTER. Rom. XIII.

NOW it is high time to awake out of sleep: for now is our salvation nearer than when we believed.

℟. Thanks be to God.

One Clerk begins this ℟. Thou shalt arise, O Lord,* *The Choir continues:* ℟. And have mercy upon Sion. *The Clerk:* ℣. For it is time that Thou have mercy upon her, yea, the time is come. ℟. And have mercy upon Sion. ℣. Glory be, etc. ℟. Thou shalt arise, O Lord, and have mercy upon Sion.

This ℟. *is said daily till* O Sapientia. *The* ℟. *at Vespers is always said in the above order, though at times two Clerks begin together.*

HYMN. *Conditor alme siderum,* ℣. and ℟., p. 75.

Ant. to Mag. Fear not, Mary; thou hast found favour with God: behold, thou shalt conceive, and bring forth a Son. Alleluia.

COLLECT.

MEMORIAL OF S. MARY, p. 76.

MONDAY.

Lauds.

℣. Send, O Lord, the Lamb, the Ruler of the land. ℟. From the rock of the wilderness, unto the mount of the daughter of Sion.

CHAPTER. Jer. XXIII.

BEHOLD, the days come, saith the Lord, that I will raise unto David a righteous branch, and a King shall reign and prosper, and shall execute judgment and justice in the earth.

HYMN. *Vox clara ecce intonat,* ℣. and ℟., p. 77.

Ant. to Ben. The Angel of the Lord brought tidings unto Mary: and she conceived of the Holy Ghost. Alleluia.

Ferial Memorials.

MEMORIAL OF S. MARY.

Ant. The Holy Ghost shall come down upon thee, Mary, fear not:

FIRST SUNDAY IN ADVENT.

who hast in thy womb the Son of God. Alleluia.

℣. ℟. *and Collect, as at Vespers,* p. 80.

MEMORIAL OF ALL SAINTS.

Ant. As at Vespers, p. 80.

These Memorials of S. Mary and of All Saints are said at Lauds and Vespers on all Ferias until Christmas Eve, except that the Memorial of All Saints is not said on O Sapientia.

Prime.

Ant. to Psalms. Come and deliver us : * O our God. *Deus in nomine.* Ps. LIV. *Beati* and *Retribue.* Ps. CXIX.

Ant. to Quicunque. Glory to Thee, p. 32.

Tierce.

At Tierce, Sexts and Nones throughout Advent, Ant. and Chap. as in the Psalter. (An optional use is however given below :

Ant. O Lord, raise up Thy power : * and come and save us.

CHAPTER. Heb. X.

FOR yet a little while, and He that shall come will come, and will not tarry.)

℟. Come and save us : O Lord God of Hosts. ℣. Shew the light of Thy countenance, and we shall be whole. ℟. O Lord God of Hosts. ℣. Glory be to the Father, and to the Son : and to the Holy Ghost. ℟. Come and save us, O Lord God of Hosts.

℣. The heathen shall fear Thy Name, O Lord.

℟. And all the kings of the earth Thy Majesty.

Sexts.

(*Ant.* When Thou comest : * deliver us, O Lord.

CHAPTER. Is. XIII., XIV.

HER time is near to come, and her days shall not be prolonged. For the Lord will have mercy on Jacob, and will yet choose Israel.)

℟. O Lord, shew : Thy mercy upon us. ℣. And grant us Thy salvation. ℟. Thy mercy upon us. ℣. Glory be to the Father, and to the Son : and to the Holy Ghost. ℟. O Lord, shew Thy mercy upon us.

℣. Remember me, O Lord, according to the favour that Thou bearest unto Thy people.

℟. O visit me with Thy salvation.

Nones.

(*Ant.* Come, O Lord, * and tarry not : do away the offences of Thy people Israel.

CHAPTER. Micah IV.

COME, and let us go up to the mountain of the Lord, and to the house of the God of Jacob; and He will teach us of His ways, and we will walk in His paths : for the law shall go forth of Sion, and the word of the Lord from Jerusalem.)

℟. The Lord shall arise upon thee : O Jerusalem. ℣. And His glory shall be seen upon thee. ℟. O Jerusalem. ℣. Glory be to the Father, and to the Son : and to the Holy Ghost. ℟. The Lord shall arise upon thee, O Jerusalem.

℣. Turn us again, O Lord God of Hosts.

℟. Shew the light of Thy countenance, and we shall be whole.

Vespers.

CHAPTER. Jer. XXIII.

IN His days Judah shall be saved, and Israel shall dwell safely : and this is His Name whereby He shall be called, The Lord our Righteousness.

One Clerk: ℟. Thou shalt arise, O Lord,* *Choir.* And have mercy upon Sion. ℣. For it is time that Thou have mercy upon her, yea, the time is come. ℟. And have mercy upon Sion. ℣. Glory be to the Father, and to the Son: and to the Holy Ghost. ℟. Thou shalt arise, O Lord, and have mercy upon Sion.

This ℟. *is changed at* O Sapientia, p. 84.

Hymn. *Conditor alme siderum,* ℣. *and* ℟., p. 75.

Ant. to Mag. O Jerusalem, look about thee toward the east: and behold. Alleluia.

Ferial Memorials.

Memorial of S. Mary.

Ant. Fear not, Mary; thou hast found favour with God : behold, thou shalt conceive and bring forth a Son. Alleluia.

℣. And there shall come forth a rod out of the stem of Jesse.

℟. And a branch shall grow out of his roots.

Collect.

O GOD, Who didst will that Thy Word should take flesh in the womb of Blessed Mary ever-virgin; grant to Thy suppliants, that we, who believe her to be indeed the Mother of God, may be helped by her intercession before Thee; through the same Thy Son Jesus Christ our Lord: Who liveth.

Memorial of All Saints.

Ant. Behold, the Lord shall come, and all His Saints with Him : and there shall be in that day a great light. Alleluia.

℣. Behold, the Lord shall appear on a white cloud.

℟. And with Him ten thousands of His Saints.

Collect.

VISIT, we beseech Thee, O Lord, and cleanse our consciences, that Thy Son our Lord Jesus Christ, when He cometh with all His Saints, may find in us a mansion prepared for Himself; Who liveth.

The office is thus said on Ferias through Advent, except the Ants. to Benedictus *and* Magnificat, *which change as below.*

TUESDAY.

Ant. to Ben. Lift up thine eyes, O Jerusalem, and behold the power of the King : Lo, the Saviour comes to loose thee from thy chain.

Ant. to Mag. Seek ye the Lord while He may be found : call ye upon Him while He is near. Alleluia.

WEDNESDAY.

Ant. to Ben. The law shall go forth of Sion : and the word of the Lord from Jerusalem.

Ant. to Mag. One cometh after me mightier than I : the latchet of Whose shoes I am not worthy to unloose.

THURSDAY.

Ant. to Ben. Blessed art thou among women : and blessed is the fruit of thy womb.

Ant. to Mag. I will wait for the God of my salvation : and I will look for Him, which He is near. Alleluia.

FRIDAY.

Ant. to Ben. Behold, God and Man shall come forth from the house of David : to sit on the throne. Alleluia.

Ant. to Mag. Out of Egypt have I called My Son : He shall come to save His people.

SATURDAY.

Ant. to Ben. Fear not, O Sion : behold, thy God cometh. Alleluia.

SECOND SUNDAY IN ADVENT.
First Vespers.
CHAPTER. Is. IV.

IN that day shall the branch of the Lord be y beautiful and glorious, and the fruit of the earth shall be excellent and comely, for them that are escaped of Israel.

℟. The Lord will teach us of His ways, and we will walk in His paths: For the law shall go forth of Sion, and the word of the Lord from Jerusalem. ℣. Come ye, and let us go up to the mountain of the Lord, to the house of the God of Jacob. ℟. For the law shall go forth of Sion, and the word of the Lord from Jerusalem. ℣. Glory be to the Father, and to the Son: and to the Holy Ghost. ℟. And the word of the Lord from Jerusalem.

HYMN. *Conditor alme siderum*, ℣. and ℟., p. 75.

Ant. to Mag. The Saviour of the world shall arise as the sun: and come down into the Virgin's womb, as the showers upon the grass. Alleluia.

COLLECT. (*English.* 1549.)

BLESSED Lord, Who hast caused all holy Scriptures to be written for our learning; grant that we may in such wise hear them, read, mark, learn, and inwardly digest them, that by patience and comfort of Thy holy word, we may embrace and ever hold fast the blessed hope of everlasting life, which Thou hast given us in our Saviour Jesus Christ: Who. Amen.

[*Or this*,

QUICKEN our hearts, O Lord, to make ready the way of Thine only-begotten Son; that through His Advent we may attain to serve Thee with pure hearts: through the same Jesus Christ our Lord: Who.]

Lauds.
Psalms of Sunday.

Ant. 1. Behold, the Lord shall come in the clouds of heaven: with great power. Alleluia.

Ant. 2. The city of our strength, our Sion, is the Saviour, He shall be for walls and bulwarks: open ye the gates, for God is with us. Alleluia.

Ant. 3. Behold, the Lord will appear, and will not lie: though He tarry, wait for Him, because He will surely come, He will not tarry. Alleluia.

Ant. 4. The mountains and the hills shall break forth before God into singing: and all the trees of the field shall clap their hands, for the Lord the Ruler shall come unto His everlasting kingdom. Alleluia. Alleluia.

Ant. 5. Behold, our Lord shall come with power: to enlighten the eyes of His servants. Alleluia.

CHAPTER. Rom. xv.

WHATSOEVER things were written aforetime were written for our learning, that we through patience and comfort of the scriptures might have hope.

℟. Thanks be to God.

HYMN. *Vox clara ecce intonat*, ℣. and ℟., p. 77.

Ant. to Ben. Upon the throne of David, and upon his kingdom: shall He sit for ever. Alleluia.

Collect as at First Vespers.

Prime.
Ant. to Psalms. Behold, the Lord shall come in the clouds of heaven: with great power. Alleluia.

Tierce.
Ant. The city of our strength, our Sion, is the Saviour, He shall be for

walls and bulwarks : open ye the gates, for God is with us. Alleluia.

CHAPTER. Rom. xv.

WHATSOEVER things were written aforetime were written for our learning, that we through patience and comfort of the scriptures might have hope.

℟. Come and save us. p. 77.

Sexts.

Ant. Behold the Lord will appear, and will not lie : though He tarry, wait for Him, because He will surely come, He will not tarry. Alleluia.

CHAPTER. Rom. xv.

NOW the God of patience and consolation grant you to be likeminded one toward another according to Christ Jesus : that ye may with one mind and one mouth glorify God, even the Father of our Lord Jesus Christ.

℟. O Lord, shew Thy mercy. p. 78.

Nones.

Ant. Behold, our Lord shall come with power : to enlighten the eyes of His servants. Alleluia.

CHAPTER. Rom. xv.

NOW the God of hope fill you with all joy and peace in believing, that ye may abound in hope, through the power of the Holy Ghost.

℟. The Lord shall arise. p. 78.

Second Vespers.

CHAPTER. Rom. xv.

WHATSOEVER things were written aforetime were written for our learning, that we through patience and comfort of the scriptures might have hope.

℟. Thou shalt arise. p. 78.

HYMN. *Conditor alme siderum*, ℣. and ℟., p. 75.

Ant. to Mag. Blessed art thou, Mary, who believed : there shall be a performance of those things which were told thee from the Lord. Alleluia.

MONDAY.

Ant. to Ben. From heaven shall come the Lord the Ruler : and in His hand are honour and power.

Ant. to Mag. Behold, the Ruler of the earth shall come : and He shall take away the yoke of our captivity.

TUESDAY.

Ant. to Ben. The Lord shall arise upon thee, O Jerusalem : and His glory shall be seen upon thee.

Ant. to Mag. The voice of one crying in the wilderness ; Prepare ye the way of the Lord : make straight a highway for our God.

WEDNESDAY.

Ant. to Ben. Behold, I send My Messenger : which shall prepare Thy way before Thee.

Ant. to Mag. O Sion, thou shalt be renewed : and shalt see thy Holy One, Which is to come unto thee.

THURSDAY.

Ant. to Ben. Thou art He that should come, O Lord : for Whom we look to save Thy people.

Ant. to Mag. He that cometh after me is preferred before me : the latchet of Whose shoes I am not worthy to unloose.

FRIDAY.

Ant. to Ben. Say to them that are of a fearful heart, be strong : behold, the Lord your God will come.

Ant. to Mag. Sing unto the Lord a new song : and His praise from the end of the earth.

SATURDAY.

Ant. to Ben. The Lord shall set up an ensign for the nations : and shall assemble the outcasts of Israel.

THIRD SUNDAY IN ADVENT.

First Vespers.

CHAPTER. Gen. XLIX.

THE sceptre shall not depart from Judah, nor a lawgiver from between his feet, until Shiloh come; and unto Him shall the gathering of the people be.

R7. He that shall come, will come, and will not tarry. Now shall there be no more fear in our borders : For He is our Saviour. V. He will subdue our iniquities : and cast our sins into the depths of the sea. R7. For He is our Saviour. V. Glory be to the Father, and to the Son : and to the Holy Ghost. R7. For He is our Saviour.

HYMN. *Conditor alme siderum,* V. and R7., p. 75.

Ant. to Mag. (*if not* O Sapientia.) Before Me there was no God formed, neither shall there be after Me: for to Me every knee shall bow, and Me every tongue confess.

COLLECT. (*English.* 1661.)

O LORD Jesu Christ, Who at Thy first coming didst send Thy messenger to prepare Thy way before Thee; grant that the ministers and stewards of Thy mysteries may likewise so prepare and make ready Thy way, by turning the hearts of the disobedient to the wisdom of the just, that, at Thy second coming to judge the world, we may be found an acceptable people in Thy sight, Who livest and reignest with the Father and the Holy Spirit, ever one God, world without end. Amen.

[*Or this,*

BOW down Thine ear to our prayers, O Lord; we beseech Thee; and lighten the darkness of our souls by the grace of Thy visitation; Who livest.]

Lauds.

Ant. 1. The Lord will surely come, He will not tarry : and will bring to light the hidden things of darkness, and reveal Himself to all people. Alleluia.

Ant. 2. Rejoice, O Jerusalem, with great joy : for the Saviour shall come to thee. Alleluia.

Ant. 3. I will place salvation in Sion : for Israel My glory. Alleluia.

Ant. 4. Every mountain and hill shall be made low, and the crooked shall be made straight : and the rough places plain. Come, O Lord, and tarry not. Alleluia.

Ant. 5. Let us live soberly, righteously, and godly : looking for that blessed hope, and the coming of the Lord.

CHAPTER. 1 Cor. IV.

LET a man so account of us, as of the ministers of Christ, and stewards of the mysteries of God. Moreover, it is required in stewards, that a man be found faithful.

R7. Thanks be to God.

HYMN. *Vox clara ecce intonat,* V. and R7., p. 77.

Ant. to Ben. When John had heard in the prison the works of Christ, he sent two of his disciples : and said unto Him, Art Thou He that should come, or do we look for another?

Collect as at First Vespers.

Prime.

Ant. to Psalms. The Lord will surely come, He will not tarry : and

Tierce.

Ant. Rejoice, O Jerusalem, with great joy : for the Saviour shall come to thee. Alleluia.

CHAPTER. 1 Cor. iv.

LET a man so account of us, as of the ministers of Christ, and stewards of the mysteries of God. Moreover, it is required in stewards, that a man be found faithful.

℟. Come and save us. p. 77.

Sexts.

Ant. I will place salvation in Sion : for Israel My glory. Alleluia.

CHAPTER. 1 Cor. iv.

BUT with me it is a very small thing that I should be judged of you, or of man's judgment : yea, I judge not mine own self.

℟. O Lord, shew Thy mercy. p. 78.

Nones.

Ant. Let us live soberly, righteously, and godly : looking for that blessed hope, and the coming of the Lord.

CHAPTER. 1 Cor. iv.

THEREFORE judge nothing before the time, until the Lord come, who both will bring to light the hidden things of darkness, and will make manifest the counsels of the hearts : and then shall every man have praise of God.

℟. The Lord shall arise. p. 78.

Second Vespers.

Chapter as at Tierce.

℟. Thou shalt arise. p. 78.

Unless on, or after O Sapientia, *in which case is said,*

℟. Make haste, O Lord, tarry not : * and deliver Thy people. ℣. Come, O Lord, tarry not, do away the offences of Thy people Israel. ℟. And deliver Thy people. ℣. Glory be to the Father, and to the Son : and to the Holy Ghost. ℟. Make haste, O Lord, tarry not : and deliver Thy people.

HYMN. *Conditor alme siderum,* ℣. *and* ℟., *p. 75.*

Ant. to Mag. (if not one of the Great Ant^s.*)* Go and shew John again those things which ye do hear and see : the blind receive their sight, and the lame walk, the lepers are cleansed, and the deaf hear.

The ℟. *of the Third Sunday in Advent,* Make haste, O Lord, *is said daily before the Great Ant*^{s}., *except at the first Vespers of the Fourth Sunday in Advent. On, but not after* O Sapientia, *the Memorial of All Saints is omitted : thenceforth no petitions are said at Vespers; but at Compline and the other Hours they are said as usual.*

THE GREAT ANTIPHONS,
Each of which is said at Vespers on its own day.

DECEMBER 16. *O Sapientia.*

O WISDOM, Which camest forth out of the mouth of the Most High, and reachest from one end to the other, mightily and sweetly ordering all things : Come and teach us the way of prudence.

DECEMBER 17. *O Adonai.*

O LORD and Ruler of the house of Israel, Who appearedst unto Moses in a flame of fire in the bush, and gavest unto him the law in Sinai : Come and redeem us with an outstretched arm.

DECEMBER 18. *O Radix Jesse.*

O ROOT of Jesse, Who standest for an ensign of the people, at Whom

THIRD SUNDAY IN ADVENT.

kings shall shut their mouths, unto Whom the Gentiles shall pray: Come and deliver us, and tarry not.

DECEMBER 19. *O Clavis David.*

O KEY of David, the Sceptre of the house of Israel, Thou that openest, and no man shutteth, and shuttest, and no man openeth: Come, and loose the prisoner from the prison-house, and him that sitteth in darkness from the shadow of death.

DECEMBER 20. *O Oriens.*

O ORIENT, Brightness of the eternal light, and Sun of righteousness: Come and lighten them that sit in darkness, and in the shadow of death.

DECEMBER 21. *O Rex Gentium.*

O KING of the Gentiles, and their desire, the Corner-stone, Who madest both one: Come and save man, whom Thou hast made out of the dust of the earth.

DECEMBER 22. *O Emmanuel.*

O EMMANUEL, our King and Lawgiver, the Desire of all nations, and their Saviour: Come and save us, O Lord our God.

DECEMBER 23. *O Virgo Virginum.*

O VIRGIN of virgins, how shall this be? For neither before thee was any like thee, nor shall there be after: Daughters of Jerusalem, why marvel ye at me? The thing which ye behold is a divine mystery.

MONDAY.

Lauds.

On the remaining Ferias in Advent, each Psalm at Lauds has a proper Ant.

Psalms of the Feria.

Ant. 1. Behold, the Lord shall come, the Prince of the kings of the earth: blessed are they that are ready to go out to meet Him.

Ant. 2. When the Son of man cometh: shall He find faith on the earth?

Ant. 3. Behold, the fulness of the time is come: wherein God hath sent forth His Son into the world.

Ant. 4. With joy shall ye draw water: out of the wells of salvation.

Ant. 5. The Lord shall come forth from His holy place: He shall come to save His people.

Ant. to Ben. There shall come forth a rod out of the stem of Jesse: and all the earth shall be filled with the glory of the Lord; and all flesh shall see the salvation of God.

Vespers.

Ant. to Mag. (*if not a Great Ant.*) Awake, awake: stand up, O Jerusalem; loose thyself from the bands of thy neck, O captive daughter of Sion.

TUESDAY.

Lauds.

Ant. 1. Behold, our Lord shall come with power: and Himself shall break the yoke of our captivity.

Ant. 2. Send, O Lord, the Lamb, the Ruler of the land: from the rock of the wilderness unto the mount of the daughter of Sion.

Ant. 3. That Thy way, O Lord, may be known upon earth: Thy saving health among all nations.

Ant. 4. Reward them, O Lord, that wait for Thee: and let Thy prophets be found faithful.

Ant. 5. The law was given by Moses: but grace and truth came by Jesus Christ.

Ant. to Ben. And thou, Bethlehem, in the land of Judah, art not the least among the princes of Judah : for out of thee shall come a Governour, that shall rule My people Israel.

Vespers.

Ant. to Mag. (if not a Great Ant.) Let the mountains break forth with joy, and the hills with righteousness : for the Lord, the Light of the world, cometh with power.

EMBER WEDNESDAY.
Lauds.

Ant. 1. Drop down, ye heavens, from above, and let the skies pour down righteousness : let the earth open, and let them bring forth salvation.

Ant. 2. The prophets did foretell : that the Saviour should be born of the Virgin Mary.

Ant. 3. The spirit of the Lord is upon Me : He hath anointed Me to preach the gospel to the poor.

Ant. 4. Behold, the Lord shall come : that He may sit among princes, and inherit the throne of His glory.

Ant. 5. Tell it out among the nations and say ye : Behold, God our Saviour shall come.

Ant. to Ben. The Angel Gabriel was sent to Mary : a virgin espoused to Joseph.

The petitions are not said at Lauds on the three Ember Days, but are said at all the other Hours (except Vespers, if after O Sapientia).

[COLLECT.

GRANT, we beseech Thee, Almighty God, that the coming solemnity of our redemption may bestow on us all things needful to this life, and the rewards of eternal blessedness; through Jesus Christ our Lord : Who.

This Collect is said at Lauds only. At all the other Hours is said the Collect of Sunday.]

Vespers.

Ant. to Mag. (if not a Great Ant.) How shall this be, O Angel of God, seeing I know not a man? : Hearken, Mary, Virgin of Christ, the Holy Ghost shall come upon thee, and the power of the Highest shall overshadow thee.

THURSDAY.
Lauds.

Ant. 1. Out of Sion shall come forth the Lord Almighty : to save His people.

Ant. 2. Turn Thee again, O Lord, a little : and delay not to come unto Thy servants.

Ant. 3. Out of Sion shall the Lord come to reign : great is His Name, Emmanuel.

Ant. 4. Behold, this is our God ; and I will prepare Him an habitation : my father's God, and I will exalt Him.

Ant. 5. The Lord our Lawgiver ; the Lord our King : Himself will come and save us.

Ant. to Ben. The Lord our God is at hand : watch ye therefore in your hearts.

Vespers.

Ant. to Mag. (if not a Great Ant.) Rejoice ye with Jerusalem : and be glad with her, all ye that love her for ever.

EMBER FRIDAY.
Lauds.

Ant. 1. Stand ye still : and see the salvation of the Lord with you.

Ant. 2. Unto Thee, O Lord, have I lift up my soul : come and deliver me, O Lord, for unto Thee have I fled.

Ant. 3. Come, O Lord, and tarry not : do away the offences of Thy people Israel.

Ant. 4. God shall come from Libanus : His brightness shall be as the light.

Ant. 5. Therefore will I look unto the Lord : I will wait for the God of my salvation.

Ant. to Ben. As soon as the voice of thy salutation sounded in mine ears : the babe leaped in my womb for joy. Alleluia.

[COLLECT.]

RAISE up, we pray Thee, O Lord, Thy power, and come : that they who trust in Thy loving-kindness may speedily be delivered from all adversity : Who livest.

This Collect is said at Lauds only. At all the other Hours is said the Collect of Sunday.]

Vespers.

Ant. to Magnificat. *A Great Ant., according to the day of the month, and so on till Christmas.*

EMBER SATURDAY.
Lauds.

Ant. 1. The Lord shall come with great power : and all flesh shall see Him, and He shall save us.

Ant. 2. Consider how great this Man is : Who entereth in to save His people.

Ant. 3. Thy Angel shall come again, O Lord : and shall teach us Thy ways.

Ant. 4. The word of the Lord shall be looked for as rain : and our God shall come down upon us as the dew.

Ant. 5. Prepare to meet thy God, O Israel : for He cometh.

Ant. to Ben. Every valley shall be exalted, and every mountain and hill shall be made low : and all flesh shall see the salvation of God.

[COLLECT.]

O GOD, who seest that we grieve by reason of our sinfulness, mercifully grant that by Thy visitation we may be consoled : Who livest.

This Collect is said at Lauds only. At all the other Hours is said the Collect of Sunday.]

FOURTH SUNDAY IN ADVENT.

If Christmas Eve fall on this day, the Office is of Sunday till Lauds, and thenceforth of the Vigil, with memorial of Sunday at Lauds.

First Vespers.

CHAPTER. Is. XXVIII. Rom. IX.

BEHOLD I lay in Sion for a foundation a Stone, a tried Stone, a precious Corner-stone, a sure foundtion : and whosoever believeth on Him shall not be ashamed.

℟. The sceptre shall not depart from Judah, nor a lawgiver from between his feet : until Shiloh come* and unto Him shall the gathering of the people be. ℣. His eyes shall be fairer than wine, and His teeth whiter than milk. ℟. And unto Him shall the gathering of the people be. ℣. Glory be to the Father, and to the Son, and to the Holy Ghost. ℟. And unto Him shall the gathering of the people be.

HYMN. *Conditor alme siderum,*
℣. and ℟. p. 75.
Great Antiphon.

COLLECT.
(Altered from Gelasian. 5th cent.)

O LORD, raise up, we pray Thee, Thy power, and come among us, and with great might succour us ;

that whereas, through our sins and wickedness, we are sore let and hindered in running the race that is set before us, Thy bountiful grace and mercy may speedily help and deliver us; through the satisfaction of Thy Son our Lord, to Whom with Thee and the Holy Ghost be honour and glory, world without end. Amen.

[*Or this,*

RAISE up, we beseech Thee, O Lord, Thy power, and come, and with great might succour us; that whereas, through our sins and wickedness we are sore let and hindered, Thy mercy may speedily deliver us; Who livest.]

Lauds.

Ant. 1. Blow ye the trumpet in Sion : for the day of the Lord is nigh at hand, behold, He cometh to save us. Alleluia. Alleluia.

Ant. 2. Behold, the Desire of all nations shall come : and the house of the Lord shall be filled with glory. Alleluia.

Ant. 3. The crooked shall be made straight, and the rough places plain : come, O Lord, and tarry not. Alleluia.

Ant. 4. The Lord cometh ; go ye out to meet Him, saying, Great is His dominion, and of His kingdom there shall be no end : the mighty God, the everlasting Father, the Prince of peace. Alleluia. Alleluia.

Ant. 5. Thine Almighty Word, O Lord, leapeth down from Heaven : out of Thy royal throne. Alleluia.

CHAPTER. Phil. IV.

REJOICE in the Lord alway, and again I say, Rejoice. Let your moderation be known unto all men. The Lord is at hand.

HYMN. *Vox clara ecce intonat,*
℣. and ℟. p. 77.

Ant. to Ben. I am the voice of one crying in the wilderness : Make straight the way of the Lord, as said the prophet Esaias.

Collect as at First Vespers.

Prime.

Ant. Blow ye the trumpet in Sion, for the day of the Lord is nigh at hand : behold, He cometh to save us. Alleluia.

Tierce.

Ant. Behold, the Desire of all nations shall come : and the house of the Lord shall be filled with glory. Alleluia. Alleluia.

Chapter as at Lauds.

℟. Come and save us. p. 77.

Sexts.

Ant. The crooked shall be made straight, and the rough places plain : Come, O Lord, and tarry not. Alleluia.

CHAPTER. Phil. IV.

BE careful for nothing : but in everything by prayer and supplication with thanksgiving, let your requests be made known unto God.

℟. O Lord, shew Thy mercy. p. 78.

Nones.

Ant. Thine Almighty Word, O Lord, leapeth down from Heaven : out of Thy royal throne. Alleluia.

CHAPTER. Phil. IV.

AND the peace of God, which passeth all understanding, shall keep your hearts and minds.

℟. The Lord shall arise. p. 78.

Second Vespers.

Chapter as at Lauds.

℟. Make haste, O Lord. p. 84.

HYMN. *Conditor alme siderum,*
℣. and ℟. p. 75.
Great Antiphon.

MONDAY.
If not Christmas Eve,
Lauds.
Ants. to Psalms as on Third Monday in Advent, p. 85.

Ant. to Ben. The Lord saith, Repent ye : for the kingdom of heaven is at hand. Alleluia.

TUESDAY.
If not Christmas Eve,
Lauds.
Ants. to Psalms as on Third Tuesday in Advent, p. 85.

Ant. to Ben. Awake, awake, put on strength : O arm of the Lord.

WEDNESDAY.
If not Christmas Eve,
Lauds.
Ants. to Psalms as on Third Wednesday in Advent, p. 86.

Ant. to Ben. Let them give glory unto the Lord, and declare His praise in the islands : for behold, He shall come, and shall not tarry.

THURSDAY.
If not Christmas Eve,
Lauds.
Ants. to Psalms as on Third Thursday in Advent, p. 86.

Ant. to Ben. Comfort ye, comfort ye My people : saith the Lord our God.

FRIDAY.
If not Christmas Eve,
Lauds.
Ants. to Psalms as on Third Friday in Advent, p. 86.

Ant. to Ben. The day of the Lord shall come as a thief in the night : be ye therefore also ready, for at such an hour as ye think not, the Son of man cometh.

CHRISTMAS EVE.
Lauds.
℣. To-morrow shall the wickedness of the earth be done away.

℟. And the Saviour of the world shall be King over us.

Psalms of the Feria, or of Sunday, if the Eve fall on a Sunday.

Ant. 1. O Judah and Jerusalem, fear not, to-morrow go ye forth : and the Lord will be with you.

Ant. 2. Ye shall know this day that the Lord will come : and in the morning shall ye see His glory.

Ant. 3. To-morrow shall the wickedness of the earth be done away : and the Saviour of the world shall be King over us.

Ant. 4. The word of the Lord shall be looked for as rain : and our God shall come down upon us as the dew.

Ant. 5. To-morrow ye shall have help : saith the Lord God of Hosts.

CHAPTER. Is. LXII.

FOR Sion's sake will I not hold my peace, and for Jerusalem's sake I will not rest, until the righteousness thereof go forth as brightness, and the salvation thereof as a lamp that burneth.

HYMN. *Vox clara ecce intonat,* p. 77.

℣. Ye shall know this day that the Lord will come.

℟. And in the morning shall ye see His glory.

Ant. to Ben. When Mary the

Mother of Jesus was espoused unto Joseph, before they came together she was found with child: for That which was conceived in her was of the Holy Ghost. Alleluia.

[COLLECT.

O GOD, Who makest us glad with the yearly expectation of our redemption : grant that we, who with joy receive Thine only-begotten Son as our Redeemer, may, without fear, behold Him when He shall come to be our Judge, even Thy Son our Lord Jesus Christ; Who liveth.

℣. The Lord be with you.
℟. And with thy spirit.
℣. Bless we the Lord.
℟. Thanks be to God.

This Collect is said at every Hour of Christmas Eve.] No Memorial is said on this day but that of All Saints (except it be Sunday, when the Memorial of Sunday is said before that of All Saints).
From henceforth till after the Octave of Epiphany, the Ferial petitions are not said. Ps. cxxiii., Ad Te levavi, with the prayers following, at Prime and Compline is omitted till the Sunday after the Octave of Epiphany.

Prime.

Ant. O Judah and Jerusalem, fear not, nor be dismayed; to-morrow go ye forth : for the Lord will be with you.

℟. Jesu Christ, Son of the living God : have mercy upon us. Alleluia. Alleluia. ℣. Thou that sittest at the right hand of the Father. Alleluia. ℟. Have mercy upon us. Alleluia. Alleluia. ℣. Glory be to the Father, and to the Son : and to the Holy Ghost. ℟. Jesu Christ, Son of the living God, have mercy upon us. Alleluia. Alleluia.

Tierce.

Ant. Ye shall know this day that the Lord will come : and in the morning shall ye see His glory.

CHAPTER. Is. LXII.

FOR Sion's sake will I not hold my peace, and for Jerusalem's sake I will not rest, until the righteousness thereof go forth as brightness, and the salvation thereof as a lamp that burneth.

℟. Stand ye still : Alleluia. Alleluia. ℣. And see the salvation of the Lord with you. ℟. Alleluia. Alleluia. ℣. Glory be to the Father, and to the Son : and to the Holy Ghost. ℟. Stand ye still. Alleluia. Alleluia.

℣. To-morrow ye shall have help.
℟. Saith the Lord God of Hosts.

Sexts.

Ant. To-morrow shall the wickedness of the earth be done away : and the Saviour of the world shall be King over us.

CHAPTER. Is. LXII.

THE Gentiles shall see thy righteousness, and all kings thy glory : and thou shalt be called by a new name, which the mouth of the Lord shall name.

℟. To-morrow ye shall have help : Alleluia. Alleluia. ℣. Saith the Lord God of Hosts. ℟. Alleluia. Alleluia. ℣. Glory be to the Father, and to the Son : and to the Holy Ghost. ℟. To-morrow ye shall have help. Alleluia. Alleluia.

℣. Ye shall know this day that the Lord will come.
℟. And in the morning shall ye see His glory.

Nones.

Ant. To-morrow ye shall have help : saith the Lord God of Hosts.

Chapter. Is. LXII.

THOU shalt no more be termed forsaken : neither shall thy land any more be termed desolate : but thou shalt be called Hephzi-bah, and thy land Beulah : for the Lord delighteth in thee, and thy land shall be married.

℟. Ye shall know this day that the Lord will come : Alleluia. Alleluia. ℣. And in the morning shall ye see His glory. ℟. Alleluia. Alleluia. ℣. Glory be to the Father, and to the Son : and to the Holy Ghost. ℟. Ye shall know this day that the Lord will come. Alleluia. Alleluia.

℣. Stand ye still.

℟. And see the salvation of the Lord with you.

CHRISTMAS DAY.

First Vespers.

Ant. 1. The King of peace * is exalted : Whom the whole earth seeketh.

Laudate, pueri. Psalm CXIII.

PRAISE the Lord, ye servants : O praise the Name of the Lord.

2 Blessed be the Name of the Lord : from this time forth for evermore.

3 The Lord's Name is praised : from the rising up of the sun unto the going down of the same.

4 The Lord is high above all heathen : and His glory above the heavens.

5 Who is like unto the Lord our God, that hath His dwelling so high : and yet humbleth Himself to behold the things that are in heaven and earth?

6 He taketh up the simple out the dust : and lifteth the poor out of the mire ;

7 That He may set him with the princes : even with the princes of His people.

8 He maketh the barren woman to keep house : and to be a joyful mother of children.

Glory be, etc.

Ant. 2. The King of peace * is exalted : higher than all the kings of the earth.

Laudate Dominum. Psalm CXVII.

O PRAISE the Lord, all ye heathen : praise Him, all ye nations.

2 For His merciful kindness is ever more and more towards us : and the truth of the Lord endureth for ever. Praise the Lord.

Glory be, etc.

Ant. 3. Know ye * that the kingdom of God is nigh at hand : Verily I say unto you, it shall not tarry.

Lauda anima mea. Psalm CXLVI.

PRAISE the Lord, O my soul ; while I live will I praise the Lord : yea, as long as I have any being, I will sing praises unto my God.

2 O put not your trust in princes, nor in any child of man : for there is no help in them.

3 For when the breath of man goeth forth he shall turn again to his earth : and then all his thoughts perish.

4 Blessed is he that hath the God of Jacob for his help : and whose hope is in the Lord his God ;

5 Who made heaven and earth, the sea, and all that therein is : Who keepeth His promise for ever ;

6 Who helpeth them to right that suffer wrong : Who feedeth the hungry.

7 The Lord looseth men out of prison : the Lord giveth sight to the blind.

8 The Lord helpeth them that are fallen : the Lord careth for the righteous.

9 The Lord careth for the strangers; He defendeth the fatherless and widow : as for the way of the ungodly, He turneth it upside down.

10 The Lord thy God, O Sion, shall be King for evermore : and throughout all generations.

Glory be, etc.

Ant. 4. Lift up * your heads : for your redemption draweth nigh.

Laudate Dominum. Psalm CXLVII.

O PRAISE the Lord, for it is a good thing to sing praises unto our God : yea, a joyful and pleasant thing it is to be thankful.

2 The Lord doth build up Jerusalem : and gather together the outcasts of Israel.

3 He healeth those that are broken in heart : and giveth medicine to heal their sickness.

4 He telleth the number of the stars : and calleth them all by their names.

5 Great is our Lord, and great is His power : yea, and His wisdom is infinite.

6 The Lord setteth up the meek : and bringeth the ungodly down to the ground.

7 O sing unto the Lord with thanksgiving : sing praises upon the harp unto our God;

8 Who covereth the heaven with clouds; and prepareth rain for the earth : and maketh the grass to grow upon the mountains, and herb for the use of men;

9 Who giveth fodder unto the cattle : and feedeth the young ravens that call upon Him.

10 He hath no pleasure in the strength of an horse : neither delighteth He in any man's legs.

11 But the Lord's delight is in them that fear Him : and put their trust in His mercy.

Glory be, etc.

Ant. 5. The days of Mary * were accomplished : that she should bring forth her first-born Son.

Lauda Hierusalem. Psalm CXLVII. 12.

PRAISE the Lord, O Jerusalem : praise thy God, O Sion.

13 For He hath made fast the bars of thy gates : and hath blessed thy children within thee.

14 He maketh peace in thy borders : and filleth thee with the flour of wheat.

15 He sendeth forth His commandment upon earth : and His word runneth very swiftly.

16 He giveth snow like wool : and scattereth the hoar-frost like ashes.

17 He casteth forth His ice like morsels : who is able to abide His frost?

18 He sendeth out His word, and melteth them : He bloweth with His wind, and the waters flow.

19 He sheweth His word unto Jacob : His statutes and ordinances unto Israel.

20 He hath not dealt so with any nation : neither have the heathen knowledge of His laws.

Glory be, etc.

CHAPTER. Is. IX.

THE people that walked in darkness have seen a great light : they that dwell in the land of the shadow of death, upon them hath the light shined.

℟. O Judah and Jerusalem, fear not : to-morrow go ye forth : and the Lord will be with you. ℣. Stand ye still, and see the salvation of the Lord with you. ℟. To-morrow go ye forth : and the Lord will be with you. ℣. Glory be to the Father, and to the Son : and to the Holy Ghost. ℟. And the Lord will be with you.

HYMN. *Veni Redemptor gentium.*

COME, Thou Redeemer of the earth,
Come, testify Thy Virgin birth :
All lands admire,—all times applaud ;
Such is the birth that fits a God.

Begotten of no human will,
But of the Spirit, mystic still,
The Word of God, in flesh arrayed,
The promised fruit to man displayed.

The Virgin womb that burden gained,
With Virgin honour all unstained ;
The banners there of virtue glow :
God in His temple dwells below.

Proceeding from His chamber free,
The royal hall of chastity,
Giant of twofold substance, straight
His destined way He runs elate.

From God the Father He proceeds :
To God the Father back He speeds :
Proceeds,—as far as very hell ;
Speeds back, to light ineffable.

O Equal to Thy Father, Thou,
Gird on Thy fleshly mantle now ;
The weakness of our mortal state
With deathless might invigorate.

Thy cradle here shall glitter bright,
And darkness breathe a newer light :
Where endless faith shall shine serene,
And twilight never intervene.

[*At these Vespers only, this Doxology:*
All laud to God the Father be,
All laud, eternal Son, to Thee ;
All laud, as is for ever meet,
To God the blessed Paraclete. Amen.]

But through Christmas tide the following :
All honour, laud, and glory be,
O Jesu, Virgin-born, to Thee !
All glory, as is ever meet,
To Father and to Paraclete. Amen.

This doxology is said to all Hymns of this metre, except A solis ortus cardine, *till the morrow of the Purification (except on the Feast, and through the Octave of Epiphany).*

℣. As a bridegroom.
℟. The Lord coming forth out of His chamber.
Ant. to Mag. At sunrise ye shall behold the King of kings from heaven: as a bridegroom out of his chamber, coming forth from God the Father.

COLLECT. (*English.* 1549.)

ALMIGHTY God, Who hast given us Thy only-begotten Son to take our nature upon Him, and as at this time to be born of a pure Virgin : grant that we, being regenerate, and made Thy children by adoption and grace, may daily be renewed by Thy Holy Spirit ; through the same our Lord Jesus Christ. Who liveth. Amen.

[*Or Collect for Christmas Eve*, p. 90.]

These Vespers end with Bless we the Lord, etc., *without* Alleluia.

Compline.

Ant. to Psalms. Be ye ready, like unto men that wait for their lord : when he shall return from the wedding.

HYMN. *Salvator mundi Domine,* ℣. *and* ℟. *p.* 69, *with Doxology as there given.*

Ant. to Nunc Dim. Let all men watch and pray : for ye know not when the time is : Watch therefore, for ye know not when the Master of the house cometh : at even, or at midnight, or at the cock-crowing, or in the morning : lest coming suddenly He find you sleeping.

Lauds.

℣. The Word was made flesh.
℟. And dwelt among us. Alleluia.

Psalms of Sunday.

Ant. 1. Whom saw ye, O shepherds ? Speak, Tell us, who hath appeared on earth : We beheld the Child, the Saviour, the Lord, in the choir of Angels. Alleluia. Alleluia.

Ant. 2. A maiden hath borne the King Whose name is everlasting : she hath the joy of a mother, and likewise the honour of virginity; none hath been seen like unto her, neither shall there be any such. Alleluia.

Ant. 3. The Angel said unto the shepherds: Behold, I bring you good tidings of great joy; for unto you is born this day the Saviour of the world. Alleluia.

Ant. 4. There was with the Angel a multitude of the heavenly host, praising God, and saying : Glory to God in the highest, and on earth peace, good will towards men. Alleluia.

Ant. 5. Unto us a Child is born this day : and His name shall be called the mighty God. Alleluia. Alleluia.

CHAPTER. Titus II.

THE grace of God that bringeth salvation hath appeared to all men, teaching us that, denying ungodliness and worldly lusts, we should live soberly, righteously, and godly in this present world.

HYMN. *A solis ortus cardine.*

FROM lands that see the sun arise,
To earth's remotest boundaries,
The Virgin-born to-day we sing,
The Son of Mary, Christ the King.

Blest Author of this earthly frame,
To take a servant's form He came,
That liberating flesh by flesh,
Whom He had made might live afresh.

In that chaste parent's holy womb
Celestial grace hath found its home :
And she, as earthly bride unknown,
Yet calls that Offspring blest her own.

The mansion of the modest breast
Becomes a shrine where God shall rest :
The pure and undefiled one
Conceived in her womb the Son.

That Son, that royal Son she bore,
Whom Gabriel's voice had told afore;
Whom, in his mother yet conceal'd,
The infant Baptist had reveal'd.

The manger and the straw He bore,
The cradle did He not abhor :
A little milk His infant fare
Who feedeth ev'n each fowl of air.

The heavenly chorus filled the sky,
The angels sang to God on high,
What time to shepherds, watching lone,
They made creation's Shepherd known.

For that Thine Advent glory be,
O Jesu, Virgin-born, to Thee !
With Father, and with Holy Ghost,
From men and from the heavenly host.
Amen.

℣. Blessed be He that cometh in the Name of the Lord.

℟. God is the Lord Who hath shewed us light.

Ant. to Ben. Glory to God in the highest : and on earth peace, good will towards men. Alleluia. Alleluia.

Collect as at First Vespers.

[*Or this*,

GRANT, we beseech Thee, Almighty God, that the new birth of Thine only-begotten Son may deliver us, who by old bondage are held under the yoke of sin. Through the same.]

MEMORIAL OF S. MARY,

At the full consummation of the mystery of the Incarnation.

Ant. Behold, all things are fulfilled : which were spoken by the angel concerning the Virgin Mary.

℣. After child-bearing thou remainedst a Virgin.

℟. O Mother of God.

Let us pray.

COLLECT.

O GOD, Who through the fruitful virginity of the Blessed Virgin Mary hast bestowed the rewards of eternal salvation on the human race : grant, we beseech Thee, that she may

CHRISTMAS DAY.

intercede for us, through whom we have received the Author of Life, Thy Son Jesus Christ our Lord: Who.
℣. Bless we the Lord.
℟. Thanks be to God.
Bless we the Lord *is not said with* Alleluia *except at Easter.*

Prime.

Ant. to Psalms. Whom saw ye, O shepherds? Speak, Tell us, who hath appeared upon earth : We beheld the Child, the Saviour, the Lord, in the choir of Angels. Alleluia. Alleluia. *Deus in nomine*, Psalm LIV. *Beati* and *Retribue*, Psalm CXIX.

CHAPTER. 1 Tim. I.

NOW unto the King eternal, immortal, invisible, the only wise God, be honour and glory, for ever and ever. Amen.
℟. Jesu Christ, Son of the living God : have mercy upon us. Alleluia. Alleluia. ℣. Thou that didst vouchsafe to be born of a Virgin. ℟. Have mercy upon us. Alleluia. Alleluia. ℣. Glory be to the Father, and to the Son : and to the Holy Ghost. ℟. Jesu Christ, Son of the living God, have mercy upon us. Alleluia. Alleluia.
℣. O Lord, arise, help us.
℟. And deliver us for Thy Name's sake.

This ℟. is said at Prime daily till the morrow of the Purification, except on the Feast, and through the Octave, of Epiphany.

Tierce.

Ant. A maiden hath borne the King, Whose name is everlasting : She hath the joy of a mother, and likewise the honour of virginity; none hath been seen like unto her, neither shall there be any such. Alleluia.

Chapter as at Lauds.
℟. The Word was made flesh : Alleluia. Alleluia. ℣. And dwelt among us. ℟. Alleluia. Alleluia. ℣. Glory be to the Father, and to the Son : and to the Holy Ghost. ℟. The Word was made flesh. Alleluia. Alleluia.
℣. He shall call Me.
℟. Thou art my Father.

Sexts.

Ant. The Angel said unto the shepherds : Behold, I bring you good tidings of great joy ; for unto you is born this day the Saviour of the world. Alleluia.

CHAPTER. Titus III.

AFTER that the kindness and love of God our Saviour towards man appeared, not by works of righteousness which we have done, but according to His mercy He saved us.
℟. He shall call Me : Alleluia. Alleluia. ℣. Thou art my Father. ℟. Alleluia. Alleluia. ℣. Glory be to the Father, and to the Son : and to the Holy Ghost. ℟. He shall call Me. Alleluia. Alleluia.
℣. The Lord declared.
℟. His salvation.

Nones.

Ant. Unto us a Child is born this day : and His Name shall be called the mighty God. Alleluia. Alleluia.

CHAPTER. Heb. I.

GOD, Who at sundry times and in divers manners spake in time past unto the fathers by the prophets, hath in these last days spoken unto us by His Son.
℟. The Lord declared : Alleluia. Alleluia. ℣. His salvation. ℟. Alleluia. Alleluia. ℣. Glory be to the Father, and to the Son : and to the Holy Ghost. ℟. The Lord declared. Alleluia. Alleluia.

℣. Blessed be He that cometh in the Name of the Lord.
℟. God is the Lord Who hath shewed us light.

Second Vespers.

Ant. 1. In the day of Thy power * shall the people offer Thee free-will offerings with an holy worship : the dew of Thy birth is of the womb of the morning.

Dixit Dominus. Psalm cx.

THE Lord said unto my Lord : Sit Thou on My right hand, until I make Thine enemies Thy footstool.
2 The Lord shall send the rod of Thy power out of Sion : be Thou ruler, even in the midst among Thine enemies.
3 In the day of Thy power shall the people offer Thee free-will offerings with an holy worship : the dew of Thy birth is of the womb of the morning.
4 The Lord sware, and will not repent : Thou art a Priest for ever after the order of Melchisdech.
5 The Lord upon Thy right hand : shall wound even kings in the day of His wrath.
6 He shall judge among the heathen ; He shall fill the places with the dead bodies : and smite in sunder the heads over divers countries.
7 He shall drink of the brook in the way : therefore shall He lift up His head.
Glory be, etc.

Ant. 2. He sent redemption * unto His people : He hath commanded His covenant for ever.

Confitebor tibi. Psalm cxi.

I WILL give thanks unto the Lord with my whole heart : secretly among the faithful, and in the congregation.
2 The works of the Lord are great : sought out of all them that have pleasure therein.
3 His work is worthy to be praised, and had in honour : and His righteousness endureth for ever.
4 The merciful and gracious Lord hath so done His marvellous works : that they ought to be had in remembrance.
5 He hath given meat unto them that fear Him : He shall ever be mindful of His covenant.
6 He hath shewed His people the power of His works : that He may give them the heritage of the heathen.
7 The works of His hands are verity and judgment : all His commandments are true.
8 They stand fast for ever and ever : and are done in truth and equity.
9 He sent redemption unto His people : He hath commanded His covenant for ever; holy and reverend is His Name.
10 The fear of the Lord is the beginning of wisdom : a good understanding have all they that do thereafter; the praise of it endureth for ever.
Glory be, etc.

Ant. 3. Unto the godly * there ariseth up light in the darkness : the Lord is merciful, loving, and righteous.

Beatus vir. Psalm cxii.

BLESSED is the man that feareth the Lord : he hath great delight in His commandments.
2 His seed shall be mighty upon earth : the generation of the faithful shall be blessed.
3 Riches and plenteousness shall be in his house : and his righteousness endureth for ever.
4 Unto the godly there ariseth up

light in the darkness : he is merciful, **loving, and righteous.**

5 A **good man** is merciful, and lendeth : and will guide his words **with discretion.**

6 For he shall never be moved : and the righteous shall be had in everlasting remembrance.

7 He will not be afraid of any evil tidings : for his heart standeth fast, and believeth in the Lord.

8 His heart is established, and **will not shrink** : until he see his desire upon his enemies.

9 He hath dispersed abroad, and given to the poor : and his righteous**ness remaineth for ever**; his horn shall be exalted with honour.

10 The ungodly shall see it, and it shall grieve him : he shall gnash with his teeth, and consume away ; the desire of the ungodly shall perish.

Glory be, etc.

Ant. 4. With the Lord * there is mercy : and with Him is plenteous **redemption.**

De profundis. Psalm cxxx.

OUT of the deep have I called unto Thee, O Lord : Lord, hear my voice.

2 O let Thine ears consider well : the voice of my complaint.

3 If Thou, Lord, wilt be extreme to mark what is done amiss : O Lord, **who may abide it ?**

4 For there is mercy with Thee : therefore shalt Thou be feared.

5 I look for the Lord ; my soul doth wait for Him : in His word is **my trust.**

6 **My soul fleeth unto the Lord** : before the morning watch, I say, before the morning watch.

7 O Israel, trust in the Lord, for with the Lord there is mercy : and with Him is plenteous redemption.

8 And He shall redeem Israel : from all his sins.

Glory be, etc.

*Ant.*5. Of the fruit * of thy body : shall I set upon thy seat.

Memento, Domine. Psalm cxxxii.

LORD, remember David : and all his trouble;

2 How he sware unto the Lord : and vowed a vow unto the Almighty God of Jacob.

3 I will not come within the tabernacle of mine house : nor climb up into my bed ;

4 I will not suffer mine eyes to sleep, nor mine eyelids to slumber : neither the temples of my head to take any rest ;

5 Until I find out a place for the temple of the Lord : an habitation for the mighty God of Jacob.

6 Lo, we heard of the same at Ephrata : and found it in the wood.

7 **We will go into His tabernacle** : and fall low on our knees before His footstool.

8 Arise, O Lord, into Thy restingplace : Thou, and the ark of Thy strength.

9 Let Thy priests be clothed with righteousness : and let Thy saints sing with joyfulness.

10 For Thy servant David's sake : turn not away the presence of Thine Anointed.

11 The Lord hath made a faithful oath unto David : and He shall not shrink from it.

12 Of the fruit of thy body : shall I set upon thy seat.

13 If thy children will keep My covenant, and My testimonies that I shall learn them : their children also shall sit upon thy seat for evermore.

14 For the Lord hath chosen Sion

to be an habitation for Himself: He hath longed for her.

15 This shall be My rest for ever: here will I dwell, for I have a delight therein.

16 I will bless her victuals with increase: and will satisfy her poor with bread.

17 I will deck her priests with health: and her saints shall rejoice and sing.

18 There shall I make the horn of David to flourish: I have ordained a lantern for Mine Anointed.

19 As for His enemies, I shall clothe them with shame: but upon Himself shall His crown flourish.

Glory be, etc.

These Antiphons and Psalms are said daily till the Octave of Epiphany, inclusive.

CHAPTER. Heb. i.

GOD, Who at sundry times and in divers manners spake in time past unto the fathers by the prophets, hath in these last days spoken unto us by His Son.

℟. The Word was made flesh, and dwelt among us: and we beheld His glory, the glory as of the Only-Begotten of the Father: full of grace and truth. ℣. In the beginning was the Word, and the Word was with God, and the Word was God. ℟. And we beheld His glory, the glory as of the Only-Begotten of the Father, full of grace and truth. ℣. Glory be to the Father, and to the Son: and to the Holy Ghost. ℟. Full of grace and truth.

HYMN. *Veni Redemptor gentium,* ℣. and ℟. p. 93.

Ant. to Mag. To-day Christ is born, to-day our Saviour appeared; to-day Angels sing upon earth, and Archangels rejoice: to-day the righteous are merry and say, Glory be to God on high. Alleluia.

Collect as at First Vespers [or Lauds].

MEMORIAL OF S. STEPHEN.

Ant. Thou art chief in the choirs of martyrs, like unto an Angel: who didst pray to God for them that stoned thee.

℣. Thou hast crowned him with glory and worship.

℟. Thou makest him to have dominion of the works of Thy hands.

COLLECT.

As at Lauds on S. Stephen's Day.

At these Vespers, and henceforth until the morrow of the Circumcision, no Memorial is made of S. Mary, at Lauds or Vespers. No Memorial is made of All Saints.

Compline.

Ant. to Psalms. Unto us is born this day in the city of David: a Saviour, which is Christ the Lord.

HYMN. *Salvator mundi Domine, with Christmas Doxology.*

Ant. to Nunc Dim. Alleluia. The Word was made flesh; Alleluia: and dwelt among us. Alleluia. Alleluia.

Compline is thus said till the Feast of the Circumcision.

FESTIVAL OF S. STEPHEN.

Lauds.

℣. The righteous shall flourish like a palm-tree.

℟. And shall spread abroad like a cedar in Libanus.

℣. O God, make speed, etc.

Psalms of Sunday.

Ant. 1. And they stoned Stephen, calling upon God, saying: Lord, lay not this sin to their charge.

Ant. 2. The stones of the brook were sweet unto him: him doth every soul of the righteous follow.

Ant. 3. My soul hangeth upon Thee, O God: for Thy sake hath my body been stoned.

Ant. 4. Stephen saw the heavens opened; he saw and entered in: blessed is he to whom the heavens shall be opened.

Ant. 5. Behold, I see the heavens opened: and Jesus standing on the right hand of God.

CHAPTER. Acts VI.

AND Stephen, full of faith and power, did great wonders and miracles among the people.

HYMN. *Sancte Dei pretiose.*

SAINT of God, elect and precious,
Protomartyr Stephen, bright
With thy love, of amplest measure,
Shining round thee like a light,
Who to God commendedst, dying,
Them that did thee all despite:

Glitters now the crown above thee,
Figured in thy sacred name:
Oh! that we, who truly love thee,
May have portion in the same;
In the dreadful day of judgment
Fearing neither sin nor shame.

Laud to God, and might and honour,
Who with flowers of rosy dye
Crowned thy forehead, and hath placed thee
In the starry throne on high:
He direct us, He protect us
From death's sting eternally. Amen.

℣. The righteous shall blossom as a lily.

℟. He shall flourish for ever before the Lord.

Ant. to Ben. The wicked laid charge against him to give him over unto death, but he joyfully endured the stones: that he might be accounted worthy to receive the crown of glory. Alleluia.

COLLECT.

GRANT, O Lord, that, in all our sufferings here upon earth for the testimony of Thy truth, we may stedfastly look up to heaven, and by faith behold the glory that shall be revealed; and, being filled with the Holy Ghost, may learn to love and bless our persecutors by the example of Thy first martyr Saint Stephen, who prayed for his murderers to Thee, O blessed Jesus, Who standest at the right hand of God to succour all those that suffer for Thee, our only Mediator and Advocate. Amen.

MEMORIAL OF THE NATIVITY.

Ant. To-day a faithful Virgin hath brought forth the Incarnate Word; and yet after child-bearing abideth a virgin: in whose praise let us all say, Blessed art thou among women.

℣. Blessed is He that cometh in the Name of the Lord.

℟. God is the Lord Who hath shewed us light.

Collect, p. 94.

Prime.

Ant. And they stoned Stephen, calling upon God, saying: Lord, lay not this sin to their charge.

Tierce.

Ant. The stones of the brook were sweet unto him: him doth every soul of the righteous follow.

CHAPTER. Acts VI.

AND Stephen, full of faith and power, did great wonders and miracles among the people.

℟. Thou hast crowned him with glory and worship: Alleluia. Alleluia.
℣. Thou makest him to have dominion of the works of Thy hands.
℟. Alleluia. Alleluia. ℣. Glory be to the Father, and to the Son: and to the Holy Ghost. ℟. Thou hast crowned him with glory and worship. Alleluia. Alleluia.

℣. Thou hast set upon his head, O Lord.

℟. A crown of pure gold.

The ℣/℟. *are said with* Alleluia *daily till the morrow of the Octave of the Epiphany.*

Sexts.

Ant. My soul hangeth upon Thee, O God : for Thy sake hath my body been stoned.

CHAPTER. Acts VII.

STEPHEN, being full of the Holy Ghost, looked up stedfastly into heaven, and saw the glory of God, and Jesus standing on the right hand of God, and said, Behold, I see the heavens opened, and the Son of man standing on the right hand of God.

℟. Thou hast set upon his head, O Lord : Alleluia. Alleluia. ℣. A crown of pure gold. ℟. Alleluia. Alleluia. ℣. Glory be to the Father, and to the Son : and to the Holy Ghost. ℟. Thou hast set upon his head, O Lord. Alleluia. Alleluia.

℣. The righteous shall flourish like a palm-tree.

℟. And shall spread abroad like a cedar in Libanus.

Nones.

Ant. Behold, I see the heavens opened : and Jesus standing on the right hand of God.

CHAPTER. Acts VII.

AND he kneeled down and cried with a loud voice, Lord, lay not this sin to their charge. And when he had said this, he fell asleep.

℟. The righteous shall flourish like a palm-tree : Alleluia. Alleluia. ℣. And shall spread abroad like a cedar in Libanus. ℟. Alleluia. Alleluia. ℣. Glory be to the Father, and to the Son : and to the Holy Ghost. ℟. The righteous shall flourish like a palm-tree. Alleluia. Alleluia.

℣. The righteous shall blossom as a lily.

℟. He shall flourish for ever before the Lord.

Vespers.

Ants. and Psalms, p. 96.

CHAPTER. Acts VI.

AND Stephen, full of faith and power, did great wonders and miracles among the people.

℟. They ran upon him with one accord, and cast him out of the city, praying, and saying : * Lord, receive my spirit. ℣. Stephen was full of the grace of God ; he did great wonders among the people ; he beheld the heavens opened ; he saw Jesus standing at the right hand of God : and he said. ℟. Lord, receive my spirit. ℣. Glory be to the Father, God most High, and to the King His only Son, and to the Holy Ghost, from both proceeding : as it was in the beginning, is now, and ever shall be. ℟. Lord, receive my spirit.

HYMN. *Sancte Dei pretiose,*
℣. and ℟. p. 99.

Ant. to Mag. The doors of heaven are laid open to Christ's martyr, blessed Stephen : who was first to be numbered among the saints, and is therefore triumphantly crowned in heaven. Alleluia.

Collect, p. 99.

MEMORIAL OF S. JOHN THE EVANGELIST.

Ant. Greatly is blessed John to be had in honour : for he leaned on the Lord's bosom at Supper.

℣. Thou shalt make them princes in all lands.

℟. They shall remember Thy Name, O Lord.

FESTIVAL OF S. JOHN THE EVANGELIST.

Collect as at Lauds on S. John's Day.

MEMORIAL OF THE NATIVITY.

Ant. Light is risen upon us : because to-day the Saviour hath been born. Alleluia.

℣. The Word was made flesh.

℟. And dwelt among us. Alleluia.

Collect, p. 94.

FESTIVAL OF S. JOHN THE EVANGELIST.

Lauds.

℣. Greatly to be had in honour is blessed John.

℟. For he leaned on the Lord's bosom at Supper.

Psalms of Sunday.

Ant. 1. This is the disciple which did testify: and we know that his testimony is true.

Ant. 2. This is My disciple : so I will that he tarry till I come.

Ant. 3. Behold Mine elect servant, whom I have chosen : I have put My Spirit upon him.

Ant. 4. There be some of them standing here, which shall not taste of death : till they see the Son of man in His kingdom.

Ant. 5. So I will that he tarry till I come : follow thou Me.

CHAPTER. Ecclus. xv.

HE that feareth the Lord will do good; and he that hath knowledge of the law shall obtain wisdom. And as a mother shall she meet him.

HYMN. *Exultet cælum laudibus,* ℣. *and* ℟. *as in Common of Apostles.*

Ant. to Ben. This is John who leaned on the Lord's bosom at Supper: blessed Apostle to whom were made known the secrets of heaven.

COLLECT.

MERCIFUL Lord, we beseech Thee to cast Thy bright beams of light upon Thy church, that it being enlightened by the doctrine of Thy blessed Apostle and Evangelist Saint John, may so walk in the light of Thy truth, that it may at length attain to the light of everlasting life; through Jesus Christ our Lord. Amen.

MEMORIAL OF THE NATIVITY.

Ant. To-day a spotless Virgin hath brought forth God, clothed in our flesh : let us all worship Him Who came to save us.

℣. Blessed be He that cometh in the Name of the Lord.

℟. God is the Lord Who hath shewed us light.

Collect, p. 94.

MEMORIAL OF S. STEPHEN.

Ant. Devout men carried Stephen to his burial : and made great lamentation over him.

℣. The righteous shall blossom as a lily.

℟. He shall flourish for ever before the Lord.

Collect of S. Stephen, p. 99.

Prime.

Ant. to Psalms. This is the disciple which did testify : and we know that his testimony is true.

Tierce.

Ant. This is My disciple : so I will that he tarry till I come.

Chapter as at Lauds.

℟. Their sound is gone out into all lands : Alleluia. Alleluia. ℣. And their words into the ends of the world. ℟. Alleluia. Alleluia. ℣. Glory be to the Father, and to the Son : and to the Holy Ghost. ℟. Their sound is gone out into all lands: Alleluia. Alleluia.

℣. Thou shalt make them princes in all lands.

℟. They shall remember Thy Name, O Lord.

Sexts.

Ant. Behold Mine elect servant, whom I have chosen : I have put My spirit upon him.

CHAPTER. Ecclus. xv.

WITH the bread of understanding hath she fed him, and given him the water of wisdom to drink. He shall be stayed upon her, and shall not be moved; and shall rely upon her, and shall not be confounded. She shall exalt him above his neighbours.

℟. Thou shalt make them princes in all lands : Alleluia. Alleluia. ℣. They shall remember Thy name, O Lord. ℟. Alleluia. Alleluia. ℣. Glory be to the Father, and to the Son : and to the Holy Ghost. ℟. Thou shalt make them princes in all lands. Alleluia. Alleluia.

℣. Exceedingly honoured are Thy friends, O Lord.

℟. Surely established in their pre-eminence.

Nones.

Ant. So I will that he tarry till I come : follow thou Me.

CHAPTER. Ecclus. xv.

IN the midst of the congregation shall she open his mouth; he shall find joy and a crown of gladness, and she shall cause him to inherit an everlasting name.

℟. Exceedingly honoured : are Thy friends, O Lord. Alleluia. Alleluia. ℣. Surely established in their pre-eminence. ℟. Alleluia. Alleluia. ℣. Glory be to the Father, and to the Son : and to the Holy Ghost. ℟. Exceedingly honoured are Thy friends, O Lord. Alleluia. Alleluia.

Vespers.

Ants. and Psalms, p. 96.
Chapter as at Lauds.

℟. This is John who leaned on the Lord's bosom at Supper : blessed Apostle, to whom were made known the secrets of heaven. ℣. John the Divine, filled with the heavenly Spirit, as an eagle flying from heaven, made manifest to mortals that Christ the Son of Mary is God the Word of God. ℟. Blessed Apostle, to whom were made known the secrets of heaven. ℣. Glory be to the Almighty Father Unbegotten, to His Only-begotten Son : and to the Spirit the Comforter. ℟. Blessed Apostle, to whom were made known the secrets of heaven.

HYMN. *Exultet cœlum laudibus*, ℣. *and* ℟., *as in Common of Apostles.*

Ant. to Mag. In the midst of the Church he opened his lips : and the Lord filled him with the spirit of wisdom and understanding. He put upon him a robe of glory. Alleluia, Alleluia.

COLLECT.

MERCIFUL Lord, we beseech Thee to cast Thy bright beams of light upon Thy Church, that it being enlightened by the doctrine of Thy blessed Apostle and Evangelist Saint John, may so walk in the light of Thy truth, that it may at length attain to the light of everlasting life; through Jesus Christ our Lord. Amen.

MEMORIAL OF THE HOLY INNOCENTS.

Ant. Innocent children by cruel

Herod were slain for Christ, even children at the breast : They follow the Lamb without spot, and say alway, Glory be to Thee, O Lord.

℣. Be glad, O ye righteous, and rejoice in the Lord.

℟. And be joyful, all ye that are true of heart.

Collect.

O ALMIGHTY God, Who out of the mouth of babes and sucklings hast ordained strength, and madest infants to glorify Thee by their deaths; mortify and kill all vices in us, and so strengthen us by Thy grace, that by the innocency of our lives and constancy of our faith even unto death, we may glorify Thy holy Name; through Jesus Christ our Lord. Amen.

Memorial of the Nativity.

Ant. Let the faithful be glad; our Saviour is born into the world; to-day hath He gone forth, offspring of a noble race : and virginal purity is preserved.

℣. The Word was made flesh.
℟. And dwelt among us. Alleluia.

Collect.

GRANT, we beseech Thee, Almighty God, that the new birth of Thine Only-begotten may deliver us, who by old bondage are held under the yoke of sin. Through the Same : Who.

Memorial of S. Stephen.

Ant. And they stoned Stephen, calling upon God : saying, Lord, lay not this sin to their charge.

℣. Thou hast crowned him with glory and honour.
℟. Thou hast put all things in subjection under his feet.

Collect.

GRANT, O Lord, that, in all our sufferings here upon earth for the testimony of Thy truth, we may steadfastly look up to heaven, and by faith behold the glory that shall be revealed; and, being filled with the Holy Ghost, may learn to love and bless our persecutors by the example of Thy first Martyr Saint Stephen, who prayed for his murderers to Thee, O blessed Jesus, Who standest at the right hand of God to succour all those that suffer for Thee, our only Mediator and Advocate. Amen.

FESTIVAL OF THE HOLY INNOCENTS.

Lauds.

℣. The righteous live for evermore.
℟. Their reward also is with the Lord.

Psalms of Sunday.

Ant. 1. Wrathful Herod slew many children : in Bethlehem of Judea, the city of David.

Ant. 2. From two years old and under : did Herod slay many children for the Lord's sake.

Ant. 3. A voice was heard in Ramah, lamentation and bitter weeping : Rachel weeping for her children.

Ant. 4. From under the throne of God the Saints cry out : Avenge our blood, O our God.

Ant. 5. Let children praise Thee, O Lord of Hosts : for, through the victory wrought by Thee the Innocents rejoice.

Chapter. Rev. xiv.

I LOOKED, and lo, a Lamb stood on the Mount Sion, and with Him an hundred forty and four thousand, having His Father's Name written in their foreheads.

℟. Thanks be to God.

HYMN. *Rex gloriose Martyrum.*

ALL-GLORIOUS King of Martyrs Thou,
  Crown of Confessors here below;
Whom, casting earthly joys away,
Thou guidest to celestial day.

O quickly bend a gracious ear,
To this our suppliant voice of prayer,
As we their sacred triumphs chant,
Forgiveness to our errors grant.

In Martyrs, victory is Thine,
In Thy Confessors, mercies shine,
Then conquer, Lord, our wickedness,
And us with loving pardon bless.

All honour, laud, and glory be,
O Jesu, Virgin-born, to Thee!
All glory, as is ever meet,
To Father and to Paraclete. Amen.

℣. Wonderful art Thou in Thy Saints, O God.

℟. And glorious in Thy Majesty.

Ant. to Ben. These are they which were not defiled with women : for they are virgins, and follow the Lamb whithersoever He goeth.

Collect of the Day, p. 103.

Throughout the Octave all the Collects to Memorials are as on S. John's Day.

MEMORIAL OF THE NATIVITY.

Ant. The Virgin Mother, knowing no man, painlessly brought forth the Saviour of the world : the holy Virgin, filled with heaven, gave nourishment to the King of Angels.

℣. Blessed be He that cometh in the Name of the Lord.

℟. God is the Lord Who hath shewed us light.

Collect, p. 103.

MEMORIAL OF S. STEPHEN.

Ant. The stones of the brook were sweet unto him : him doth every soul of the righteous follow.

℣. The righteous shall blossom as a lily.

℟. He shall flourish for ever before the Lord.

Collect for S. Stephen's Day, p. 99.

MEMORIAL OF S. JOHN.

Ant. This is the disciple which did testify : and we know that his testimony is true.

℣. Greatly is blessed John to be had in honour.

℟. For he leaned on the Lord's bosom at Supper.

Collect for S. John's Day, p. 101.

Prime.

Ant. Wrathful Herod slew many children : in Bethlehem of Judea, the city of David.

Tierce.

Ant. From two years old and under : did Herod slay many children for the Lord's sake.

Chapter as at Lauds.

℟. Be glad, O ye righteous, and rejoice in the Lord : Alleluia. Alleluia. ℣. And be joyful, all ye that are true of heart. ℟. Alleluia. Alleluia. ℣. Glory be to the Father, and to the Son : and to the Holy Ghost. ℟. Be glad, O ye righteous, and rejoice in the Lord : Alleluia. Alleluia.

℣. Let the righteous be glad, and rejoice before God.

℟. Let them also be merry and joyful.

Sexts.

Ant. A voice was heard in Ramah, lamentation and bitter weeping : Rachel weeping for her children.

CHAPTER. Rev. XIV.

THESE are they which were not defiled with women; for they are virgins.

℟. Let the righteous be glad, and rejoice before God : Alleluia. Alleluia. ℣. Let them also be merry and joyful. ℟. Alleluia. Alleluia. ℣. Glory be to the Father, and to the Son :

and to the Holy Ghost. ℟. Let the righteous be glad, and rejoice before God : Alleluia. Alleluia.

℣. The souls of the righteous are in the hand of God.

℟. And there shall no torment touch them.

Nones.

Ant. From under the throne of God the Saints cry out : Avenge our blood, O our God.

Chapter. Rev. xiv.

THESE were redeemed from among men, being the first-fruits unto God, and to the Lamb. And in their mouth was found no guile.

℟. The souls of the righteous are in the hand of God : Alleluia. Alleluia. ℣. And there shall no torment touch them. ℟. Alleluia. Alleluia. ℣. Glory be to the Father, and to the Son : and to the Holy Ghost. ℟. The souls of the righteous are in the hand of God : Alleluia. Alleluia.

℣. Wonderful art Thou in Thy saints, O God.

℟. And glorious in Thy majesty.

Vespers.

Ants. and Psalms as on Christmas Day, p. 96.

Chapter as at Lauds.

℟. The hundred and forty and four thousand which were redeemed from the earth : these are they which were not defiled with women, for they are virgins.* Thus they reign with God : and the Lamb of God with them. ℣. These were redeemed from among men, first fruits to God and the Lamb, and in their mouth was found no guile. ℟. Thus they reign with God : and the Lamb of God with them. ℣. Glory be to the Father, and to the Son : and to the Holy Ghost. ℟. Thus they reign with God : and the Lamb of God with them.

Hymn. *Rex gloriose Martyrum,* ℣. and ℟. p. 104.

Ant. to Mag. I looked, and lo, a Lamb stood on the Mount Sion : and with Him an hundred forty and four thousand, having His Father's Name written in their foreheads.

Memorial of S. Thomas of Canterbury.

Ant. The keeper of the vine fell in the vineyard : the leader in the camp, the husbandman in the field.

℣. As corn purged in the threshing-floor.

℟. He was carried to the heavenly garner.

Collect.

ALMIGHTY and eternal God, Who didst kindle the flame of Thy love in the heart of Thy holy Martyr and Bishop Thomas; give to our minds the same strength of faith, and charity, that as we rejoice in his triumph, so we may profit by his example; Through.

Memorial of the Nativity.

Ant. A Virgin at the word conceived, a Virgin she abode : a Virgin, she brought forth the King of all kings.

℣. The Word was made flesh.

℟. And dwelt among us. Alleluia.

Collect, p. 103.

Memorial of S. Stephen.

Ant. My soul hangeth upon Thee, O God : for Thy sake hath my body been stoned.

℣. Thou hast crowned him with glory and worship.

℟. Thou makest him to have dominion of the works of Thy hands.

Collect for S. Stephen's Day, p. 99.

Memorial of S. John.

Ant. This is My disciple : so I will that he tarry till I come.

℣. Greatly to be had in honour is blessed John.
℟. For he leaned on the Lord's bosom at Supper.
Collect for S. John's Day, p. 101.

FESTIVAL OF S. THOMAS OF CANTERBURY.

All of the Common of one Martyr Bishop, except Ants. and Psalms at Vespers, with Memorials as below.

If this office be not kept, all as on Dec. 30, with Common Memorial of a Martyr Bishop. The Memorial of the Nativity is omitted, and its Ants. are used for Mag. and Ben.

Lauds.

MEMORIAL OF THE NATIVITY.

Ant. Blessed is the womb that bare Thee, O Christ : and the paps which gave suck to the Lord and Saviour of the world. Alleluia.
℣. Blessed be He that cometh in the Name of the Lord.
℟. God is the Lord Who hath shewed us light.
Collect, p. 103.

MEMORIAL OF S. STEPHEN.

Ant. Stephen saw the heavens opened; he saw and entered in : blessed is he, to whom the heavens shall be opened.
℣. Thou hast set upon his head, O Lord.
℟. A crown of pure gold.
Collect for S. Stephen's Day, p. 99.

MEMORIAL OF S. JOHN.

Ant. Behold Mine elect servant, whom I have chosen : I have put My Spirit upon him.
℣. Greatly to be had in honour is blessed John.
℟. For he leaned on the Lord's bosom at Supper.

Collect for S. John's Day, p. 101.

MEMORIAL OF THE HOLY INNOCENTS.

Ant. They have washed their robes : and made them white in the blood of the Lamb.
℣. Wonderful art Thou in Thy Saints, O God.
℟. And glorious in Thy majesty.
Collect for Holy Innocents, p. 103.

Vespers.

MEMORIAL OF THE NATIVITY.

Ant. O Virgin Mother of God : Him Whom the whole world cannot contain, thou didst contain in thy womb.
℣. The Word was made flesh.
℟. And dwell among us. Alleluia.
Collect, p. 103.

MEMORIAL OF S. STEPHEN.

Ant. Behold, I see the heavens opened : and Jesus standing on the right hand of God.
℣. Thou hast crowned him with glory and worship.
℟. Thou makest him to have dominion of the works of Thy hands.
Collect for S. Stephen's Day, p. 99.

MEMORIAL OF S. JOHN.

Ant. There be some of them standing here which shall not taste of death : till they see the Son of man in His kingdom.
℣. Greatly to be had in honour is blessed John.
℟. For he leaned on the Lord's bosom at Supper.
Collect for S. John's Day, p. 101.

MEMORIAL OF THE HOLY INNOCENTS.

Ant. They shall walk with Me in white : for they are worthy.

℣. Be glad, O ye righteous, and rejoice in the Lord.
℞. And be joyful, all ye that are true of heart.
Collect for Holy Innocents, p. 103.

SIXTH DAY AFTER THE NATIVITY.
(*Dec.* 30.)

Lauds.

℣. The Word was made flesh.
R. And dwelt among us. Alleluia.
Psalms of Sunday, all said under this

Ant. Whom saw ye, O shepherds? Speak. Tell us who hath appeared upon earth : We beheld the Child, the Saviour, the Lord, in the choir of Angels. Alleluia.

CHAPTER. Gal. iv.

NOW I say that the heir, as long as he is a child, differeth nothing from a servant, though he be lord of all; but is under tutors and governors until the time appointed of the father.
℞. Thanks be to God.

HYMN. *A solis ortus cardine,*
℣. *and* ℞. p. 94.

Ant. to Ben. While all things were in quiet silence, and that night was in the midst of her swift course: Thy Almighty Word leaped down from heaven out of Thy royal throne. Alleluia.

Collect for Christmas Day, p. 93.

[*Or this,*

ALMIGHTY, Everlasting God, direct our ways according to Thy good pleasure ; that in the Name of Thy beloved Son we may be worthy to abound in good works. Who liveth.
This Collect is said at Lauds only; at the other Hours is said the Collect for Christmas Day.]

MEMORIAL OF THE NATIVITY.

Ant. O Shepherds, tell us what ye have seen, and make known the birth of Christ : We have seen the Child wrapped in swaddling clothes, and choirs of Angels praising the Saviour.
℣. He shall call Me.
℞. Thou art My Father. Alleluia.
Collect, p. 103.

MEMORIAL OF S. STEPHEN.

Ant. Blessed Stephen, strengthened by constant meditation in the law of God : like a tree bearing fruit, planted beside living waters, brought forth the first-fruit of martyrdom in due season.
℣. The righteous shall blossom as a lily.
℞. He shall flourish for ever before the Lord.
Collect for S. Stephen's day, p. 99.

MEMORIAL OF S. JOHN.

Ant. So I will that he tarry till I come : follow thou Me.
℣. Greatly to be had in honour is blessed John.
℞. For he leaned on the Lord's bosom at Supper.
Collect for S. John's Day, p. 101.

MEMORIAL OF
THE HOLY INNOCENTS.

Ant. They sung as it were a new song : before the throne.
℣. Wonderful art Thou in Thy Saints, O God.
℞. And glorious in Thy majesty.
Collect for the Holy Innocents, p. 103.

Prime, Tierce, Sexts, and Nones, as on Christmas Day.
No special Office of Sunday is to be said on any day within the Octave of Christmas except on Dec. 30, on which day it is noticed at Matins, but at no other Hour.

This rubric holds good also of Dec. 29, if the Feast of S. Thomas be not kept.

Vespers.

Ants. and Psalms as on Christmas Day.

Ant. to Mag. To-day a faithful Virgin hath brought forth the Incarnate Word: and yet after child-bearing she abideth a Virgin; in whose praise let us all say, Blessed art thou among women.

MEMORIAL OF S. SILVESTER,
As in Common Memorials of Saints.

MEMORIAL OF S. STEPHEN.

Ant. Ordained by God a preacher of His commandments, in holy fear he studied to serve Him : and having filled the office with fidelity was counted worthy to ascend into His holy hill.

℣. Thou hast crowned him with glory and worship.

℟. Thou makest him to have dominion of the works of Thy hands.

Collect for S. Stephen's Day, p. 99.

MEMORIAL OF S. JOHN.

Ant. John the Apostle and Evangelist was chosen by the Lord, being a virgin : and was loved above the rest.

℣. Greatly to be had in honour is blessed John.

℟. For he leaned on the Lord's bosom at Supper.

Collect for S. John's Day, p. 101.

MEMORIAL OF
THE HOLY INNOCENTS.

Ant. Wrathful Herod slew many children : in Bethlehem of Judea, the city of David.

℣. Be glad, O ye righteous, and rejoice in the Lord.

℟. And be joyful, all ye that are true of heart.

Collect for the Holy Innocents, p. 103.

DECEMBER 31.
All as on Dec. 30, except

Lauds.

Ant. to Ben. To-day a spotless Virgin hath brought forth God, clothed in our flesh : let us all worship Him Who came to save us.

MEMORIAL OF S. SILVESTER,
As in Common Memorial of Saints.

MEMORIAL OF NATIVITY,
As Dec. 30.

MEMORIAL OF S. STEPHEN.

Ant. A shower of stones overwhelmed him, a multitude surrounded him, but he feared not : for he saw Jesus his deliverer, ready to bring him to heaven in safety.

℣. The righteous shall blossom as a lily.

℟. He shall flourish for ever before the Lord.

Collect for S. Stephen's Day, p. 99.

MEMORIAL OF S. JOHN.

Ant. As he leaned on the bosom of the Lord Jesus : he drank of the waters of the Gospel at that hallowed source.

℣. Greatly to be had in honour is blessed John.

℟. For he leaned on the Lord's bosom at Supper.

Collect for S. John's Day, p. 101.

MEMORIAL OF
THE HOLY INNOCENTS.

Ant. From two years old and under : did Herod slay many children for the Lord's sake.

℣. Wonderful art Thou in Thy Saints, O God.

℟. And glorious in Thy majesty.

Collect for the Holy Innocents, p. 103.

FESTIVAL OF THE CIRCUMCISION.

First Vespers.

Ants. and Psalms as on Christmas Day,
p. 96.

CHAPTER. Titus II.

THE grace of God that bringeth salvation hath appeared to all men, teaching us that, denying ungodliness and worldly lusts, we should live soberly, righteously, and godly in this present world.

℟. *As on Christmas Day.*

HYMN. *Veni Redemptor gentium,* p. 93.

℣. As a bridegroom.

℟. The Lord coming out of His chamber.

Ant. to Mag. He that is of the earth speaketh of the earth : He that cometh from heaven is above all, and what He hath seen and heard, that He testifieth, and no man receiveth His testimony, but he that hath received His testimony hath set to his seal that God is true.

COLLECT. (1549.)

ALMIGHTY God, Who madest Thy blessed Son to be circumcised, and obedient to the law for man; grant us the true circumcision of the Spirit, that, our hearts and all our members, being mortified from all worldly and carnal lusts, we may in all things obey Thy blessed will; through the same. Amen.

[*Or this,*

O GOD Who grantest us to celebrate the Octave of our Saviour's birth; grant, we beseech Thee, that as we are renewed by the communion of His Flesh, so we may ever be defended by His Divinity; Who liveth.]

No Memorial is said at these Vespers.

Compline.

Ant. to Psalms. When the Lord was born, the choirs of Angels sang, saying : Salvation to our God, which sitteth upon the throne, and unto the Lamb.

HYMN. *Salvator mundi Domine,* ℣. and ℟., p. 69.

Ant. to Nunc Dim. Alleluia. The Word was made flesh, Alleluia : and dwelt among us. Alleluia, Alleluia.

Compline is thus said till the Feast of the Epiphany.

Lauds.

℣. The Word was made flesh.

℟. And dwelt among us. Alleluia.

Psalms of Sunday.

Ant 1. O wonderful exchange! The Creator of mankind taking to Himself a living body, vouchsafed to be born of a Virgin : and, proceeding forth as man, made us co-heirs of His Godhead.

Ant. 2. When Thou wast born ineffably of a Virgin, then was the Scripture fulfilled : He shall come down like the rain into a fleece of wool, to save mankind. We praise Thee, O our God.

Ant. 3. In the burning bush which Moses saw unconsumed : we recognise the preservation of thy glorious virginity, O Mother of God.

Ant. 4. The Root of Jesse hath budded; a Star hath risen out of Jacob : a Virgin hath brought forth the Saviour. We praise Thee, O our God.

Ant. 5. Lo, Mary hath brought forth the Saviour, of Whom, when John saw Him, he said : Behold the Lamb of God, which taketh away the sins of the world. Alleluia.

CHAPTER. Titus II.

THE grace of God that bringeth salvation hath appeared to all men, teaching us that, denying ungodliness and worldly lusts, we should live soberly, righteously, and godly in this present world.

℟. Thanks be to God.

HYMN. *A solis ortus cardine*, ℣. and ℟., p. 94.

Ant. to Ben. A wonderful mystery is made known to-day, nature does a new thing, God is made Man : that which was, still abideth, and that which was not, He assumed, suffering no confusion nor divison.

Collect as at First Vespers.

No Memorial is said at these Lauds.

Prime.

All as on Christmas Day, except the

Ant. O wonderful exchange! The Creator of mankind taking to Himself a living body, vouchsafed to be born of a Virgin : and proceeding forth as man made us co-heirs of His Godhead.

At Tierce, Sexts, and Nones, all as on Christmas Day, except the Antiphons; and the Collect, which is that of the Circumcision.

Tierce.

Ant. When Thou wast born ineffably of a Virgin, then was the Scripture fulfilled : He shall come down like the rain into a fleece of wool, to save mankind. We praise Thee, O our God.

Sexts.

Ant. In the burning bush which Moses saw unconsumed : we recognise the preservation of thy glorious virginity, O Mother of God.

Nones.

Ant. The Root of Jesse hath budded; a Star hath risen out of Jacob : a Virgin hath brought forth the Saviour. We praise Thee, O our God.

Second Vespers.

Ants. and Psalms as on Christmas Day, p. 96.

CHAPTER. Titus II.

THE grace of God that bringeth salvation hath appeared to all men, teaching us that, denying ungodliness and worldly lusts, we should live soberly, righteously, and godly in this present world.

℟. Established is the heart of the Virgin who, receiving divine mysteries, at the word of the angel conceived Him that is fairer than the children of men.* And she, who is blessed for ever, brought forth God and man for us. ℣. The mansion of the modest breast becomes a shrine where God shall rest : the undefiled who knows not man, at angel's word, conceives a Son. ℟. And she, who is blessed for ever, brought forth God and man for us. ℣. Glory be to the Father and to the Son : and to the Holy Ghost. ℟. And she, who is blessed for ever, brought forth God and man for us.

HYMN. *Veni Redemptor gentium*, ℣. and ℟. p. 93.

Ant. to Mag. O marvellous mystery! The womb of a Virgin who knew not man is become the unspotted temple of God : of her He taketh flesh, and to Him shall all nations come, saying, Glory be to Thee, O Lord.

MEMORIAL OF S. STEPHEN, *As on Christmas Day*, p. 98.

OCTAVE OF S. STEPHEN.

Lauds.

℣. Thou hast set upon his head, O Lord.

℟. A crown of pure gold.

Psalms of Sunday, all said under one Ant., unless the day fall on Sunday, in which case the Ants. are said as on the festival. This rule applies also to the two days following.

Ant. And they stoned Stephen, calling upon God, and saying: Lord, lay not this sin to their charge.

The rest of the Office at Lauds and all the Hours as on S. Stephen's Day, except that the ℟. is not said at Vespers, and that these Memorials are said:

Lauds.

Memorial of S. John.

Ant. As one of the streams of Paradise : the Evangelist John shed the grace of the Word of God throughout the whole world.

℣. Greatly to be had in honour is blessed John.

℟. For he leaned on the Lord's bosom at Supper.

Collect for S. John's Day, p. 101.

Memorial of The Holy Innocents.

Ant. A voice was heard in Ramah; lamentation and bitter weeping : Rachel weeping for her children.

℣. Wonderful art Thou in Thy Saints, O God.

℟. And glorious in Thy majesty.

Collect for the Holy Innocents, p. 103.

Memorial of S. Mary.

Ant. Lo, Mary hath brought forth the Saviour, of Whom when John saw Him, he said : Behold the Lamb of God, which taketh away the sins of the world.

℣. After child-bearing thou remainedst a virgin.

℟. O Mother of God.

Collect as in Memorial at Vespers, infra. From this day till Candlemas, a Memorial of S. Mary is made daily at Vespers and Lauds, whatever be the service, except on the eve and day of Epiphany.

Vespers.

Memorial of S. John.

Ant. Greatly to be had in honour is blessed John : for he leaned on the Lord's bosom at Supper.

℣. Thou shalt make them princes in all lands.

℟. They shall remember Thy Name, O Lord.

Collect for S. John's Day, p. 101.

Memorial of The Holy Innocents.

Ant. Under the throne of God the Saints cry out : Avenge our blood, O our God.

℣. Be glad, O ye righteous, and rejoice in the Lord.

℟. And be joyful, all ye that are true of heart.

Collect for the Holy Innocents, p. 103.

Memorial of S. Mary.

Ant. When Thou wast born ineffably of a Virgin, then was the Scripture fulfilled : He shall come down like the rain into a fleece of wool to save mankind. We praise Thee, O our God.

℣. Thou art fairer than the children of men.

℟. Full of grace are Thy lips.

Collect.

O GOD, Who through the fruitful virginity of the blessed Virgin Mary, hast bestowed the rewards of eternal salvation on the human race; grant, we beseech Thee, that she may intercede for us, through whom we have received the Author of Life, Thy Son Jesus Christ our Lord. Amen.

OCTAVE OF
S. JOHN THE EVANGELIST.

All as on S. John's Day, except that which follows:

Lauds.

Ant. to Psalms. This is the disciple which did testify : and we know that his testimony is true.

MEMORIAL OF
THE HOLY INNOCENTS.

Ant. Let children praise Thee, O Lord of Hosts : for through the triumph wrought by Thee the Innocents rejoice.

℣. Wonderful art Thou in Thy Saints, O God.
℟. And glorious in Thy majesty.
Collect, p. 103.

MEMORIAL OF S. MARY,
As on Octave of S. Stephen, p. 111.

Vespers.

The ℟. is not said.

MEMORIAL OF THE HOLY INNOCENTS.

Ant. Innocent children by cruel Herod were slain for Christ, even children at the breast : they follow the Lamb without spot, and say alway, Glory be to Thee, O Lord.

℣. Be glad, O ye righteous, and rejoice in the Lord.
℟. And be joyful, all ye that are true of heart.

Collect for the Holy Innocents, p. 103.

Memorial of S. Mary as at p. 111.

The Memorial of S. Mary is said as at Lauds and Vespers to-day, on Sundays and Feasts of Nine Lessons; and on and in Octaves and during Octaves; from henceforth till Candlemas.

OCTAVE OF
THE HOLY INNOCENTS.

All as on Holy Innocents' Day, except that which follows:

Lauds.

Ant. to Psalms. Wrathful Herod slew many children : in Bethlehem of Judea, the city of David.

Memorial of S. Mary as on Octave of S. Stephen, p. 111.

Vespers.

The ℟. is not said.

MEMORIAL OF S. EDWARD, KING AND CONFESSOR.

Ant. I will liken him unto a wise man : which built his house upon a rock.

℣. The Lord loved him, and beautified him with comely ornaments.
℟. He clothed him with a robe of glory.

COLLECT.

O GOD, Who hast vouchsafed unto the blessed King Edward Thy Confessor a crown of heavenly glory; grant that we who commemorate him here on earth, may hereafter reign with him in heaven; through.

VIGIL OF THE EPIPHANY.

Lauds.

℣. The Word was made flesh.
℟. And dwelt among us. Alleluia.

Sunday Psalms, all said under one Ant. whether the day be Sunday or not.

Ant. to Psalms. O wonderful exchange! The Creator of mankind taking to Himself a living body, vouchsafed to be born of a Virgin : and, proceeding forth as man, made us co-heirs of His Godhead.

Chapter, Hymn, A solis ortus cardine, ℣. *and* ℟., p. 94.

Ant. to Ben. Blessed is the womb that bare Thee, O Christ : and the paps which Thou hast sucked.

VIGIL OF THE EPIPHANY.

Collect.

LIGHTEN our hearts, we beseech Thee, O Lord, by this coming Festival: that being rid of the darkness of this world, we may come to the light of the eternal Country; through.

Memorial of S. Edward, King and Confessor.

Ant. Well done, thou good and faithful servant: enter thou into the joy of thy Lord.

℣. The righteous shall flourish like a palm-tree.

℟. And spread abroad like a cedar in Libanus.

Collect as in Memorial at Vespers.

Memorial of All Saints.

Ant. The Saints shall be joyful with glory: they shall rejoice in their beds.

℣. Wonderful art Thou in Thy Saints, O God.

℟. And glorious in Thy majesty.

Collect.

WE pray Thee, O Lord, let the intercession of all Thy Saints be acceptable unto Thee; and grant to us forgiveness of our sins, and the remedies of eternal life: through.

No Memorial is made of S. Mary. If this Vigil falls on a Sunday, no Memorial is made of All Saints.

All at the other Hours as on the Circumcision, except the Chapter at Prime, p. 32, and the Collect, which is the same as at Lauds.

THE EPIPHANY.

First Vespers.

Ants. and Psalms as at the Second Vespers of Christmas Day, p. 96.

Chapter. Is. lx.

ARISE, shine; for thy light is come, and the glory of the Lord is risen upon thee.

℟. The kings of Tharsis and of the isles shall give presents, the kings of Arabia and Saba shall bring gifts to the Lord God. ℣. All kings shall fall down before Him: all nations shall do Him service. ℟. The kings of Arabia and Saba shall bring gifts to the Lord God. ℣. Glory be to the Father, and to the Son: and to the Holy Ghost. ℟. Shall bring gifts to the Lord God.

Hymn. *Hostis Herodes impie.*

WHY impious Herod, vainly fear,
That Christ the Saviour cometh here?
He takes not earthly realms away,
Who gives the crown that lasts for aye.

To greet His birth the wise men went,
Led by the star before them sent:
Called on by light, towards Light they press'd,
And by their gifts their God confess'd.

In holy Jordan's purest wave
The heav'nly Lamb vouchsafed to lave;
That He, to Whom was sin unknown,
Might cleanse His people from their own.

New miracle of power divine!
The water reddens into wine:
He spake the word; and pour'd the wave
In other streams than nature gave.

All glory, Lord, to Thee we pay,
For Thine Epiphany to-day:
All glory, as is ever meet,
To Father and to Paraclete. Amen.

This Doxology is said throughout the Octave to hymns of this metre.

℣. All they from Sheba shall come.

℟. They shall bring gold and incense, and they shall shew forth the praises of the Lord.

Ant. to Mag. When the wise men saw the star, they said one to another: This is the sign of the great King, come let us seek Him and present unto Him gifts; gold and incense and myrrh.

Collect.

O GOD, Who by the leading of a star didst manifest Thy Only-begotten Son to the Gentiles; mercifully grant that we, which know Thee now by faith, may after this life have the fruition of Thy glorious Godhead; through Jesus Christ our Lord. Amen.

Compline.

Ant. to Psalms. Thou hast appeared, O Christ, Light of Light: to Whom the wise men present gifts. Alleluia, Alleluia, Alleluia.

HYMN. *Salvator mundi Domine,*
℣. and ℟. p. 69.

Ant. to Nunc Dim. Alleluia. All they from Sheba shall come. Alleluia: They shall bring gold and incense. Alleluia, Alleluia.

This Compline is said daily throughout the Octave.

Lauds.

℣. All they from Sheba shall come.
℟. They shall bring gold and incense, and they shall shew forth the praises of the Lord.

Psalms of Sunday.

Ant. 1. The Lord our Saviour, begotten before the morning star, and before all ages: to-day appeared to the world.

Ant. 2. Thy light, O Jerusalem, is come; and the glory of the Lord is risen upon thee: and the Gentiles shall come to thy light. Alleluia.

Ant. 3. When they had opened their treasures, they presented unto Him gifts: gold, and frankincense, and myrrh. Alleluia.

Ant. 4. O ye seas and floods, bless ye the Lord: O ye wells, bless ye the Lord. Alleluia.

Ant. 5. Three are the gifts which the wise men presented unto the Lord: gold, and incense, and myrrh, to the Son of God, the Mighty King. Alleluia.

CHAPTER. Is. LX.

ARISE, shine, for thy light is come, and the glory of the Lord is risen upon thee.
℟. Thanks be to God.

HYMN. *A Patre Unigenitus.*

FROM God the Father, Virgin-born
To us the only Son came down;
By death the font to consecrate,
The faithful to regenerate.

From highest heaven His course began,
He took the form of mortal man;
Creation by His death restored,
And shed new joys of life abroad.

Glide on, Thou glorious Sun, and bring
The gift of healing on Thy wing;
The clearness of Thy light dispense
Unto Thy people's every sense.

Abide with us, O Lord, we pray,
The gloom of night remove away;
Thy work of healing, Lord, begin,
And do away the stain of sin.

We know that Thou didst come of yore;
Thou, we believe, shalt come once more:
Thy guardian shield o'er us extend,
Thine own dear sheepfold to defend.

All glory, Lord, to Thee, we pay,
For thine Epiphany to-day;
All glory, as is ever meet,
To Father and to Paraclete. Amen.

℣. It is the Lord that commandeth the waters.
℟. It is the glorious God that maketh the thunder. It is the Lord that ruleth the sea.

Ant. to Ben. To-day is the Church joined to her heavenly Bridegroom; for in Jordan Christ hath washed away her sins: the wise men hasten with gifts to the royal nuptials; and by water made wine are the guests rejoiced. Alleluia.

Collect as at First Vespers.

Prime.

Ant. The Lord our Saviour, begotten before the morning star, and before all ages: to-day appeared to the world.

Ant. to Quicunque. Thanks be to Thee. p. 32.

CHAPTER. 1 Tim. I.

NOW unto the King eternal, immortal, invisible, the only wise God, be honour and glory, for ever and ever. Amen.

℟. Jesu Christ, Son of the living God : have mercy upon us. Alleluia. Alleluia. ℣. Thou Who to-day didst appear to the world. ℟. Have mercy upon us. Alleluia. Alleluia. ℣. Glory be to the Father, and to the Son : and to the Holy Ghost. ℟. Jesu Christ, Son of the living God, have mercy upon us. Alleluia. Alleluia.

℣. O Lord, arise, help us.
℟. And deliver us for Thy Name's sake.

Tierce.

Ant. Thy light, O Jerusalem, is come; and the glory of the Lord is risen upon thee : and the Gentiles shall come to thy light. Alleluia.

Chapter as at Lauds.

℟. All they from Sheba shall come: Alleluia. Alleluia. ℣. They shall bring gold and incense, and they shall shew forth the praises of the Lord. ℟. Alleluia. Alleluia. ℣. Glory be to the Father, and to the Son : and to the Holy Ghost. ℟. All they from Sheba shall come. Alleluia. Alleluia.

℣. The kings of Tharsis and of the isles shall give presents.
℟. The kings of Arabia and Saba shall bring gifts.

Sexts.

Ant. When they had opened their treasures, they presented unto Him gifts : gold, and frankincense, and myrrh. Alleluia.

CHAPTER. Is. LX.

THE Lord shall arise upon thee, and His glory shall be seen upon thee. And the Gentiles shall come to thy light, and kings to the brightness of thy rising.

℟. The kings of Tharsis and of the isles shall give presents : Alleluia. Alleluia. ℣. The kings of Arabia and Saba shall bring gifts. ℟. Alleluia. Alleluia. ℣. Glory be to the Father, and to the Son : and to the Holy Ghost. ℟. The kings of Tharsis and of the isles shall give presents. Alleluia. Alleluia.

℣. O worship the Lord.
℟. In the beauty of holiness.

Nones.

Ant. Three are the gifts which the wise men presented unto the Lord : gold, and incense, and myrrh, to the Son of God, the Mighty King. Alleluia.

CHAPTER. Is. LX.

ALL they from Sheba shall come; they shall bring gold and incense, and they shall shew forth the praises of the Lord.

℟. O worship the Lord : Alleluia. Alleluia. ℣. In the beauty of holiness. ℟. Alleluia. Alleluia. ℣. Glory be to the Father, and to the Son: and to the Holy Ghost. ℟. O worship the Lord. Alleluia. Alleluia.

℣. Worship the Lord.
℟. All ye angels of His.

Second Vespers.

Ants. and Psalms of Christmas Day, p. 96.

CHAPTER. Is. LX.

ARISE, shine, for thy light is come. and the glory of the Lord is risen upon thee.

℟. Three are the gifts of mystic meaning which the wise men presented to-day, by gold is signified the power of the King, incense proclaims the Great High Priest, and myrrh, the burial of the Lord. ℣. The wise men worshipped the Author of our salvation in the cradle, and of their treasures they offered Him mystical gifts. ℟. By gold is signified the power of the King, incense proclaims the Great High Priest, and myrrh, the burial of the Lord. ℣. Glory be to the Father, and to the Son : and to the Holy Ghost. ℟. By gold is signified the power of the King, incense proclaims the Great High Priest, and myrrh, the burial of the Lord.

HYMN. *Hostis Herodes impie,* ℣. *and* ℟. *as at First Vespers,* p. 113.

Ant. to Mag. There came wise men from the East to Bethlehem, to worship the Lord, and when they had opened their treasures, they presented unto Him precious gifts : gold as to the great King, incense as to the true God, and myrrh for His burial. Alleluia.

FROM THE FEAST OF THE EPIPHANY TILL THE OCTAVE.

All as on the Festival except that which follows :

The Psalms at Lauds are all said under this

Ant. The Lord our Saviour, begotten before the morning star, and before all ages : to-day appeared to the world.

At Vespers the ℟. *is omitted.*

The following Antiphons are said at Lauds and Vespers to Benedictus *and* Magnificat, *except on Sunday* :

Ant. 1. The star shines like a flame, and points out God, the King of kings : wise men saw it, and brought gifts to Christ the King.

Ant. 2. When the wise men saw the star, they rejoiced with exceeding great joy : and when they were come into the house, they presented unto Him gifts ; gold, and incense, and myrrh.

Ant. 3. A voice sounded from heaven, and the voice of the Father was heard, saying : This is My beloved Son, in Whom I am well pleased ; hear Him.

Ant. 4. The wise men, being warned of God in a dream : departed into their own country another way.

The Office is thus said until the day of the Octave, except on Sunday.

SUNDAY IN THE OCTAVE.

All as on the Feast of the Epiphany, except that which follows : at both Vespers all as on the Second Vespers of the Feast ; except that the ℟. *to the Chapter is omitted.*

First Vespers.

MEMORIAL OF SUNDAY.

Ant. And the Child Jesus tarried behind in Jerusalem : and Joseph and His mother knew not of it.

℣. Let our evening prayer come up before Thee, O Lord.

℟. And let Thy mercy come down upon us.

COLLECT.

O LORD, we beseech Thee, mercifully to receive the prayers of Thy people which call upon Thee ; and grant that they may both perceive and know what things they ought to do, and also may have grace and power faithfully to fulfil the same ; through Jesus Christ our Lord. Amen.

After the Octave, this Collect is said at every Hour till the next Sunday.

MEMORIAL OF S. MARY, *As on Octave of S. Stephen,* p. 111.

Lauds.

Memorial of Sunday.

Ant. But they, supposing Him to have been in the company, went a day's journey : and they sought Him among their kinsfolk and acquaintance.

℣. The Lord is King.

℟. He hath put on glorious apparel. Alleluia.

Collect as above.

Memorial of S. Mary,

As on Octave of S. Stephen, p. 111.
At Prime, Ant. to Quicunque, Thee duly, &c. p. 32.

Second Vespers.

Memorial of Sunday.

Ant. Son, why hast Thou thus dealt with us? behold, Thy father and I have sought Thee sorrowing : And He said unto them, How is it that ye sought Me? wist ye not that I must be about My Father's business?

℣. Lord, let my prayer be set forth.

℟. In Thy sight as the incense.

Collect as above.

Memorial of S. Mary.

As on p. 111.

OCTAVE OF THE EPIPHANY.

If the Octave of the Epiphany fall on Sunday, the Office is of the Octave, with Memorial of Sunday.

First Vespers.

Ants. and Psalms as on Christmas Day, p. 96.

CHAPTER. Is. xxv.

O LORD, Thou art my God; I will exalt Thee, I will praise Thy Name; for Thou hast done wonderful things; Thy counsels of old are faithfulness and truth.

℟. In the form of a dove the Holy Spirit was seen. The voice of the Father was heard, This is My Beloved Son, in Whom I am well pleased, hear ye Him. ℣. It is the Lord that commandeth the waters, it is the glorious God that maketh the thunder. It is the Lord that ruleth the sea. ℟. The voice of the Father was heard, This is My beloved Son, in Whom I am well pleased, hear ye Him. ℣. Glory be to the Father, and to the Son : and to the Holy Ghost. ℟. Hear ye Him.

HYMN. *Hostis Herodes impie,*
℣. and ℟., p. 113.

Ant. to Mag. The soldier baptizes the King, the servant his Lord, John the Saviour : the water of Jordan was astonished, the Dove bore witness, and the voice of the Father was heard, This is My beloved Son.

Collect of the Epiphany, p. 114.

Memorial of S. Mary.

As on the Octave of S. Stephen, p. 111.

Lauds.

℣. All they from Sheba shall come.

℟. They shall bring gold and incense, and they shall shew forth the praises of the Lord.

Psalms of Sunday.

Ant. 1. The Saviour came to be baptised that by water He might restore fallen nature : and renew the old man and clothe us with a garment of grace.

Ant. 2. Thee, O God our Saviour, we all glorify : Who by the Holy Ghost and by fire dost purify human corruption.

Ant. 3. The Baptist trembles, and

dares not touch the holy head of God: but cries with fear, Sanctify me, O my Saviour.

Ant. 4. The Saviour breaks the head of the dragon in the waters of Jordan : delivering all men from his power.

Ant. 5. To-day is declared a great mystery : for the Creator of all things hath purged our sins in Jordan.

CHAPTER. IS. XXV.

O LORD, Thou art my God; I will exalt Thee, I will praise Thy Name : for Thou hast done wonderful things; Thy counsels of old are faithfulness and truth.

HYMN. *A Patre Unigenitus,*
V̄. and R̄. p. 114.

Ant. to Ben. John the forerunner was glad, and all the world made joyful when the Lord was baptised in Jordan : water was hallowed and a fountain opened for sins. To the same Lord let all men cry, Have mercy upon us.

MEMORIAL OF S. MARY.
As on the Octave of S. Stephen, p. 111.

Prime.

Ant. The Saviour came to be baptised, that by water He might restore fallen nature : and renew the old man and clothe us with a garment of grace.

Tierce.

Ant. Thee, O God our Saviour, we all glorify : Who by the Holy Ghost and by fire, dost purify human corruption.

Chapter as at Lauds.
R̄R̄. *at all the Hours as on the Epiphany.*

Sexts.

Ant. The Baptist trembles, and dares not touch the holy head of God: but cries with fear, Sanctify me, O my Saviour.

CHAPTER. IS. XXVI. XXVIII.

O LORD, Thy hand is lifted up. The Lord of Hosts shall be for a crown of glory.

Nones.

Ant. To-day is declared a great mystery : for the Creator of all things hath purged our sins in Jordan.

CHAPTER. IS. XII.

WITH joy shall ye draw water out of the wells of salvation : and in that day shall ye say, Praise the Lord, call upon His Name.

Second Vespers.

Sunday Psalms, with Ants. of Lauds.

CHAPTER, HYMN, V̄. and R̄.,
as at First Vespers.

Ant. to Mag. Water was hallowed when the glory of Christ appeared : may the whole world draw water out of the wells of salvation, for now is every creature sanctified through Christ our God.

Collect of the Epiphany, p. 114.

MEMORIAL OF S. MARY.
As p. 111.

If the Octave of the Epiphany falls on Saturday, the Second Vespers are of the Octave, and a Memorial is made of Sunday.

The day after the Octave of the Epiphany, everything as in the Psalter, except that which follows.

These Hymns are said from the Octave of the Epiphany till the First Vespers of the First Sunday in Lent, exclusive.

SATURDAY.

Vespers.

HYMN. *Deus Creator omnium.*

O BLEST Creator, God most high,
Great Ruler of the starry sky,
Who, robing day with beauteous light,
Hast clothed in soft repose the night :

That sleep may wearied limbs restore,
And fit for toil and use once more;
May gently soothe the careworn breast,
And lull our anxious griefs to rest;

We thank Thee for the day now gone;
We pray Thee while the night comes on,
Help us, poor sinners, as we raise
Our wonted offering of praise.

To Thee our hearts their music bring,
Thee our united voices sing;
To Thee our pure affections soar,
Thee may our chastened souls adore.

So when the deepening shades prevail,
And night o'er day hath dropped her veil,
Faith may no wildering darkness know,
But night with faith's own radiance glow.

From every wrongful passion free,
Our inmost hearts make sleep in Thee,
Nor let the fiend with envious snare
Our rest with sinful terrors scare.

Christ, with the Father ever one:
Spirit, of Father and of Son;
God over all, of mighty sway,
Shield us, great Trinity, we pray. Amen.

℣. Let our evening prayer come up before Thee, O Lord.

℟. And let Thy mercy come down on us.

SUNDAY.
Lauds.

HYMN. *Æterne rerum Conditor.*

DREAD Framer of the earth and sky,
　Who dost the circling seasons give,
And all the cheerful change supply
　Of alternating morn and eve:

Light of our darksome journey here,
　With days dividing night from night:
Loud crows the dawn's shrill harbinger,
　And wakens up the sunbeams bright.

Forthwith at this, the darkness chill
　Retreats before the star of morn:
And from their busy schemes of ill,
　The vagrant crews of night return.

Fresh hope, at this, the sailor cheers,
　The waves their stormy strife allay;
The Church's Rock at this, in tears,
　Hastens to wash his guilt away.

Arise ye, then, with one accord:
　Nor longer wrapt in slumber lie;
The cock rebukes all who their Lord
　By sloth neglect, by sin deny.

At his clear cry joy springs afresh,
　Health courses through the sick man's veins,
The dagger glides into its sheath,
　The fallen soul her faith regains.

Jesu! look on us when we fall;—
　One momentary glance of Thine
Can from her guilt the soul recall
　To tears of penitence divine.

Awake us from false sleep profound,
　And through our senses pour Thy light;
Be Thy blest Name the first we sound
　At early dawn, the last at night.

Doxology till Candlemas:

All honour, laud, and glory be,
O Jesu, Virgin-born, to Thee!
All glory, as is ever meet,
To Father and to Paraclete. Amen.

And the Doxology is thus said in all Hymns, except Deus Creator omnium, *during this season.*

After Candlemas:

All laud to God the Father be;
All laud, etérnal Son, to Thee;
All laud, as is for ever meet,
To God the Holy Paraclete. Amen.

℣. *and* ℟. *to Hymns at Sunday Lauds: Till Septuagesima:*

℣. The Lord is King.

℟. He hath put on glorious apparel. Alleluia.

From Septuagesima till Lent:

℣. Lord, Thou hast been our refuge.

℟. From one generation to another.

Vespers.

HYMN. *Lucis Creator optime,*
℣. and ℟. p. 49.

MONDAY.
Lauds.

HYMN. *Splendor Paternæ Gloriæ.*

THOU brightness of the Father's ray,
　True Light of light and Day of day;
Light's fountain and eternal spring:
Thou Morn the morn illumining!

Glide in, Thou very Sun divine;
With everlasting brightness shine:
And shed abroad on every sense
The Spirit's light and influence.

Thee, Father, let us seek aright:
The Father of perpetual light:
The Father of almighty grace:
Each wile of sin away to chase.

Our acts with courage do Thou fill:
Blunt Thou the tempter's tooth of ill:
Misfortune into good convert,
Or give us grace to bear unhurt.

Our spirits, whatsoe'er betide,
In chaste and loyal bodies guide;
Let faith, with fervour unalloy'd,
The bane of falsehood still avoid;

And Christ our daily food be nigh,
And faith our daily cup supply;
So may we quaff, to calm and bless,
The Spirit's rapturous holiness.

Now let the day in joy pass on:
Our modesty like early dawn,
Our faith like noontide splendour glow,
Our souls the twilight never know.

Doxology till Candlemas:

All honour, laud, and glory be,
O Jesu, Virgin-born, to Thee!
All glory, as is ever meet,
To Father and to Paraclete. Amen.

℣. Have I not thought upon Thee when I was waking?
℞. Because Thou hast been my helper.

After Candlemas:

All laud to God the Father be;
All laud, eternal Son, to Thee;
All laud, as is for ever meet,
To God the Holy Paraclete. Amen.

℣. and ℞. *as before Candlemas.*

Vespers.

HYMN. *Immense cœli Conditor.*

O GREAT Creator of the sky,
Who wouldest not the floods on high
With earthly waters to confound,
But mad'st the firmament their bound;

The floods above Thou didst ordain;
The floods below Thou didst restrain:
That moisture might attemper heat,
Lest the parch'd earth should ruin meet.

Upon our souls, good Lord, bestow
The gift of grace in endless flow:
Lest some renewed deceit or wile
Of former sin should us beguile.

Let faith discover heavenly light;
So shall its rays direct us right:
And let this faith each error chase;
And never give to falsehood place.

Doxology till Candlemas:

All honour, laud, and glory be,
O Jesu, Virgin-born, to Thee!
All glory, as is ever meet,
To Father and to Paraclete. Amen.

℣. Lord, let my prayer be set forth.
℞. In Thy sight as the incense.

After Candlemas:

O Father, that we ask be done,
Through Jesus Christ, Thine only Son;
Who, with the Holy Ghost, and Thee,
Shall live and reign eternally. Amen.

℣. and ℞. *as before Candlemas.*

TUESDAY.
Lauds.

HYMN. *Ales diei nuntius.*

THE wingèd herald of the day
Proclaims the morn's approaching ray:
And Christ the Lord our souls excites,
And so to endless life invites.

Take up thy bed, to each He cries,
Who sick, or wrapped in slumber lies:
And chaste, and just, and sober stand,
And watch: My coming is at hand.

With earnest cry, with tearful care,
Call we the Lord to hear our prayer,
While supplication, pure and deep,
Forbids each chastened heart to sleep.

Do Thou, O Christ, our slumbers wake;
Do Thou the chains of darkness break;
Purge Thou our former sins away,
And in our souls new light display.

Doxology, ℣. and ℞., according to Rubric, p. 120.

Vespers.

HYMN. *Telluris ingens Conditor.*

EARTH'S mighty Maker, Whose command
Rais'd from the sea the solid land;
And drove each billowy heap away,
And bade the earth stand firm for aye:

That so with flowers of golden hue,
The seeds of each it might renew;
And fruit-trees bearing fruit might yield,—
And pleasant pasture of the field:

Our spirit's rankling wounds efface
With dewy freshness of Thy grace:
That grief may cleanse each deed of ill,
And o'er each lust may triumph still.

Let every soul Thy law obey,
And keep from every evil way;
Rejoice each promis'd good to win,
And flee from every mortal sin.

Doxology, ℣. and ℞., according to Rubric, p. 120.

WEDNESDAY.
Lauds.

HYMN. *Nox et tenebræ et nubila.*

HENCE, night and clouds that night-time brings,
Confus'd and dark and troubled things:
The dawn is here; the sky grows white;
Christ is at hand: depart from sight!

Earth's dusky veil is torn away,
Pierc'd by the sparkling beams of day:
The world resumes its hues apace,
Soon as the day-star shews its face.

But Thee, O Christ, alone we seek,
With conscience pure and temper meek :
With tears and chants we humbly pray
That Thou would'st guide us through the day.

For many a shade obscures each sense,
Which needs Thy beams to purge it thence :
Light of the morning star, illume,
Serenely shining, all our gloom !

Doxology, ℣. and ℟., according to Rubric,
p. 120.

Vespers.

HYMN. *Cœli Deus sanctissime.*

O GOD, Whose hand hath spread the sky
And all its shining hosts on high,
And painting it with fiery light,
Made it so beauteous and so bright :

Thou, when the Wednesday was begun,
Didst frame the circle of the sun,
And set the moon for ordered change,
And planets for their wider range :

To night and day, by certain line,
Their varying bounds Thou didst assign ;
And gav'st a signal known and meet,
For months begun and months complete.

Enlighten Thou the hearts of men ;
Polluted souls make pure again ;
Unloose the bands of guilt within ;
Remove the burden of our sin.

Doxology, ℣. and ℟., according to Rubric,
p. 120.

THURSDAY.
Lauds.

HYMN. *Lux ecce surgit aurea.*

BEHOLD the golden dawn arise ;
The paling night forsakes the skies :
Those shades that hid the world from view,
And us to dangerous error drew.

May this new day be calmly past,
May we keep pure while it shall last ;
Nor let our lips from truth depart,
Nor dark designs engage the heart.

So may the day speed on ; the tongue
No falsehood know, the hands no wrong :
Our eyes from wanton gaze refrain ;
No guilt our guarded bodies stain.

For God All-seeing from on high
Surveys us with a watchful eye ;
Each day our ev'ry act He knows,
From early dawn to evening's close.

Doxology, ℣. and ℟., according to Rubric,
p. 120.

Vespers.

HYMN. *Magnæ Deus potentiæ.*

ALMIGHTY God, Who from the flood
Didst bring to light a twofold brood ;
Part in the firmament to fly,
And part in ocean depths to lie :

Appointing fishes in the sea,
And fowls in open air to be ;
That each, by origin the same,
Its separate dwelling-place might claim :

Grant that Thy servants, by the tide
Of blood and water purified,
No guilty fall from Thee may know,
Nor death eternal undergo.

Let none despair through sin's distress ;
Be none puffed up with boastfulness ;
That contrite hearts be not dismayed,
Nor haughty souls in ruin laid.

Doxology, ℣. and ℟., according to Rubric,
p. 120.

FRIDAY.
Lauds.

HYMN. *Æterna cæli gloria.*

ETERNAL glory of the sky,
Blest hope of frail humanity,
The Father's sole-begotten One,
Yet born a spotless Virgin's Son :

Uplift us with Thine arm of might,
And let our hearts rise pure and bright ;
And ardent in God's praises, pay
The thanks we owe Him every day.

The day-star's rays are glittering clear,
And tells that day itself is near ;
The shadows of the night depart ;
Thou, Holy Light, illume the heart !

Within our senses ever dwell,
And worldly darkness thence expel :
Long as the days of life endure,
Preserve our souls devout and pure.

The faith that first must be possessed,
Root deep within our inmost breast :
And joyous hope in second place ;
Then charity, Thy greatest grace.

Doxology, ℣. and ℟., according to Rubric,
p. 120.

Vespers.

HYMN. *Plasmator hominis Deus.*

MAKER of men ! from heaven Thy throne
Who orderest all things, God alone ;
By Whose decree the teeming earth
To reptile and to beast gave birth :

The mighty forms that fill the land,
Instinct with life at Thy command,
Thou gav'st subdued to humankind
For service in their rank assigned.

From all Thy servants chase away
Whate'er of thought impure to-day
Hath mingled with the heart's intent,
Or with the actions hath been blent.

In heaven Thine endless joys bestow,
But grant Thy gifts of grace below:
From chains of strife our souls release;
Bind fast the gentle bands of peace.

Doxology, ℣. *and* ℟. *according to Rubric,*
p. 120.

SATURDAY.
Lauds.

HYMN. *Aurora jam spargit polum.*

DAWN sprinkles all the east with light;
Day o'er the earth is gliding bright;
Morn's glittering rays their course begin;
Farewell to darkness and to sin.

Each phantom of the night depart,
Each thought of guilt forsake the heart:
Let every ill that darkness brought
Beneath its shade now come to nought.

So that last morning, dread and great,
Which we with trembling hope await,
With blessed light for us shall glow,
Who chant the song we sang below.

Doxology, ℣. *and* ℟. *according to Rubric,*
p. 120.

Ferial Memorials.
Lauds.
MEMORIAL OF S. MARY.

Said on Ferias and Simple Feasts till Candlemas.

Ant. The Root of Jesse hath budded; a Star hath risen out of Jacob: a Virgin hath brought forth the Saviour. We praise Thee, O our God.

℣. After child-bearing thou remainedst a Virgin.

℟. O Mother of God.

Collect as at Vespers.

MEMORIAL OF ALL SAINTS.

Said on Ferias and Simple Feasts till Ash Wednesday.

Ant. Let the Saints be joyful with glory: let them rejoice in their beds.

℣. Wonderful art Thou in Thy Saints, O God.

℟. And glorious in Thy Majesty.

Collect as at Vespers.

Vespers.
MEMORIAL OF S. MARY.

Ant. In the burning bush which Moses saw unconsumed: we recognise the preservation of thy glorious virginity, O Mother of God.

℣. Thou art become fair and pleasant.

℟. In thy delights, O holy Mother of God.

Let us pray.
COLLECT.

O GOD, Who through the fruitful virginity of the blessed Virgin Mary hast bestowed the rewards of eternal salvation on the human race: grant, we pray Thee, that she may intercede for us, through whom we have received the Author of Life, Thy Son Jesus Christ our Lord. Amen.

MEMORIAL OF ALL SAINTS.

Ant. O how glorious is the kingdom where all the Saints rejoice with Christ: they are clothed with white robes, and follow the Lamb whithersoever He goeth.

℣. Be glad, O ye righteous, and rejoice in the Lord.

℟. And be joyful, all ye that are true of heart.

Let us pray.
COLLECT.

WE pray Thee, O Lord, let the intercession of all Thy Saints be acceptable unto Thee; and grant to us forgiveness of our sins, and the remedies of eternal life; through Jesus Christ our Lord; Who.

On Sundays till Septuagesima, and Feasts of Nine Lessons, Memorial of S. Mary as on Octave of S. Stephen, p. 111.

SECOND SUNDAY AFTER THE EPIPHANY.

First Vespers.

Ant. to Mag. My sins, O Lord, are stuck fast in me like arrows : but do Thou heal me by the remedies of penitence, before the wounds become corrupt.

COLLECT.

ALMIGHTY and everlasting God, Who dost govern all things in heaven and earth; mercifully hear the supplications of Thy people, and grant us Thy peace all the days of our life; through Jesus Christ our Lord. Amen.

Lauds.

Ant. to Ben. There was a marriage in Cana of Galilee : and the Mother of Jesus was there. And Jesus also was called.

Second Vespers.

Ant. to Mag. And when they wanted wine, Jesus saith unto them : Fill the waterpots with water; and it was made wine. Alleluia.

THIRD SUNDAY AFTER THE EPIPHANY.

First Vespers.

Ant. to Mag. as on Second Sunday after Epiphany.

COLLECT.

ALMIGHTY and everlasting God, mercifully look upon our infirmities, and in all our dangers and necessities stretch forth Thy right hand to help and defend us; through Jesus Christ our Lord. Amen.

Lauds.

Ant. to Ben. When He was come down from the mountain, great multitudes followed Him. And behold, there came a leper and worshipped Him, saying : Lord, if Thou wilt, Thou canst make me clean. And Jesus put forth His hand, and touched him, saying, I will; be thou clean.

Second Vespers.

Ant. to Mag. Lord, my servant lieth at home sick of the palsy, grievously tormented : and Jesus saith unto him, I will come and heal him.

FOURTH SUNDAY AFTER THE EPIPHANY.

First Vespers.

Ant. to Mag. as on Second Sunday after Epiphany.

COLLECT.

O GOD, Who knowest us to be set in the midst of so many and great dangers, that by reason of the frailty of our nature we cannot always stand upright : grant to us such strength and protection, as may support us in all dangers, and carry us through all temptations; through Jesus Christ our Lord. Amen.

Lauds.

Ant. to Ben. And when He was entered into a ship, His disciples followed Him. And behold, there arose a great tempest in the sea, insomuch that the ship was covered with the waves : but He was asleep. And His disciples came to Him, and awoke Him, saying, Lord, save us, we perish.

Second Vespers.

Ant. to Mag. He arose, and rebuked the winds and the sea : and there was a great calm.

FIFTH SUNDAY AFTER THE EPIPHANY.
First Vespers.
Ant. to Mag. as on Second Sunday after Epiphany.

COLLECT.
O LORD, we beseech Thee to keep Thy Church and household continually in Thy true religion : that they who do lean only upon the hope of Thy heavenly grace, may evermore be defended by Thy mighty power; through Jesus Christ our Lord. Amen.

Lauds.
Ant. to Ben. Sir, didst not thou sow good seed in thy field? from whence then hath it tares? : He said unto them, An enemy hath done this.

Second Vespers.
Ant. to Mag. Gather ye together first the tares, and bind them in bundles to burn them : but gather the wheat into my barn.

SIXTH SUNDAY AFTER THE EPIPHANY.
First Vespers.
Ant. to Mag. as on Second Sunday after Epiphany.

COLLECT. *(English, 1661.)*
O GOD, Whose blessed Son was manifested that He might destroy the works of the devil, and make us the sons of God, and heirs of eternal life; grant us, we beseech Thee, that, having this hope, we may purify ourselves, even as He is pure; that, when He shall appear again with power and great glory, we may be made like unto Him in His eternal and glorious kingdom; where with Thee, O Father, and Thee, O Holy Ghost, He liveth and reigneth, ever one God, world without end. Amen.

Lauds.
Ant. to Ben. Immediately after the tribulation of those days shall the sun be darkened, and the moon shall not give her light : and the stars shall fall from heaven, and the powers of the heavens shall be shaken.

Second Vespers.
Ant. to Mag. Then shall appear the sign of the Son of Man in heaven: and then shall all the tribes of the earth mourn.

SEPTUAGESIMA SUNDAY.
From henceforth till Easter, Alleluia *is not said. In its place at the beginning of each Hour is said :*

Praise be to Thee, O Lord, King of eternal glory.

First Vespers.
CHAPTER. 1 Cor. XI.
KNOW ye not, that they which run in a race run all, but one receiveth the prize? So run that ye may obtain.

℟. Thus the heavens and the earth were finished, and all the host of them : and on the seventh day God ended His work which He had made, and He rested from all His work which He had made. ℣. And God saw every thing that He had made, and behold, it was very good. ℟. And He rested from all His work which He had made. ℣. Glory be to the Father, and to the Son : and to the Holy Ghost. ℟. And He rested from all His work which He had made.

HYMN. *Deus Creator omnium*, p.118.

Ant. to Mag. And the Lord God planted a garden eastward in Eden: and there He put the man whom He had formed.

COLLECT.

O LORD, we beseech Thee favourably to hear the prayers of Thy people; that we, who are justly punished for our offences, may be mercifully delivered by Thy goodness, for the glory of Thy Name; through Jesus Christ our Saviour, Who liveth and reigneth with Thee and the Holy Ghost, ever one God, world without end. Amen.

From Septuagesima till Passiontide no Memorial is to be said on Saturday or Sunday, except a Feast falls on one of those days and except in the case of Septuagesima falling before Candlemas, in which latter case the Memorial of S. Mary, p. 111, is said at both Vespers, and at Lauds, omitting Alleluia.

Lauds.

Psalms of Sunday, as follows:

Ant. 1. Have mercy upon me, O God: wash me throughly from my wickedness, for against Thee only have I sinned.

Miserere mei, Deus. Psalm li.

Ant. 2. I will thank Thee: for Thou hast heard me.

Confitemini Domini. Psalm cxviii.

Ant. 3. O God, my God, early will I seek Thee: because Thou hast been my helper.

Deus, Deus meus, Psalm lxiii. and *Deus misereatur,* Psalm LXVII.

Ant. 4. Blessed art Thou, O God, in the firmament of heaven: and above all to be praised and glorified for ever.

Benedicite, omnia opera.

Ant. 5. O praise: the Lord of heaven.

Laudate Dominum. Psalm cxlvii.

These are the Sunday Psalms from henceforth till Easter.

CHAPTER. 1 Cor. IX.

KNOW ye not, that they which run in a race run all, but one receiveth the prize? So run that ye may obtain.

℟. Thanks be to God.

HYMN. *Æterne rerum Conditor,* ℣. and ℟. p. 119.

Ant. to Ben. The kingdom of heaven is like unto a man that is an householder: which went out early in the morning to hire labourers into his vineyard, saith the Lord.

Prime.

Ant. And when he had agreed with the labourers for a penny a-day: he sent them into his vineyard.

Dominus regnavit, Psalm xciii., *is said at Prime from henceforth till Easter, instead of* Confitemini Domino, Psalm cxviii.

Tierce.

Ant. And he went out about the third hour, and saw others standing idle in the market-place, and said unto them: Go ye also into the vineyard, and whatsoever is right I will give you.

CHAPTER. 1 Cor. XI.

KNOW ye not, that they which run in a race run all, but one receiveth the prize? So run that ye may obtain.

℟. Thou hast been* [*the Choir continues*] my succour; O Lord, leave me not. ℣. Neither forsake me, O God of my salvation. ℟. Leave me not. ℣. Glory be to the Father, and to the Son: and to the Holy Ghost.

℞. Thou hast been my succour, O Lord, leave me not.
℣. I said, Lord, be merciful unto me.
℞. Heal my soul, for I have sinned against Thee.

The ℞. is thus said at the Hours on Sunday from this day till the end of Lent: and on all Ferias in Lent, between the first Sunday and Maundy Thursday.

Sexts.

Ant. Why stand ye here all the day idle? : They say unto him, Because no man hath hired us.

CHAPTER. 1 Cor. ix.

AND every man that striveth for the mastery is temperate in all things : now they do it to obtain a corruptible crown, but we an incorruptible.

℞. Thou, O Lord,* art my hope even from my youth. ℣. Through Thee have I been holden up ever since I was born, Thou art He that took me out of my mother's womb. ℞. My hope even from my youth. ℣. Glory be to the Father, and to the Son : and to the Holy Ghost. ℞. Thou, O Lord, art my hope even from my youth.

℣. The Lord is my Shepherd, therefore can I lack nothing.
℞. He shall feed me in a green pasture.

Nones.

Ant. The householder said to his labourers : Why stand ye here all the day idle? They say unto him, Because no man hath hired us. He saith unto them, Go ye also into the vineyard; and whatsoever is right, that shall ye receive.

CHAPTER. 1 Cor. x.

MOREOVER, brethren, I would not that ye should be ignorant, how that all our fathers were under the cloud, and all passed through the sea; and were all baptized unto Moses in the cloud and in the sea.

℞. O cleanse * Thou me from my secret faults. ℣. Keep Thy servant also from presumptuous sins. ℞. From my secret faults. ℣. Glory be to the Father, and to the Son : and to the Holy Ghost. ℞. O cleanse Thou me from my secret faults.

℣. Thou hast been my succour.
℞. Leave me not, neither forsake me, O God of my salvation.

Second Vespers.

CHAPTER. 1 Cor. ix.

KNOW ye not, that they which run in a race run all, but one receiveth the prize? So run, that ye may obtain.

℞. Thanks be to God.

HYMN. *Lucis Creator optime,*
℣. and ℞., p. 49.

Ant. to Mag. So when even was come, the lord of the vineyard saith unto his steward : Call the labourers, and give them their hire.

Ants. to Benedictus and Magnificat for the current week when the Office is of the feria.

Ant. 1. Call the labourers : and give them their hire, saith the Lord.

Ant. 2. But the lord of the vineyard answered one of them, and said, Friend, I do thee no wrong : didst thou not agree with me for a penny? Take that thine is, and go thy way.

Ant. 3. Friend, I do thee no wrong: didst not thou agree with me for a penny? Take that thine is, and go thy way.

Ant. 4. Take that thine is, and go thy way : for I am just, saith the Lord.

Ant. 5. Is it not lawful for me to

do what I will with mine own? : Is thine eye evil, because I am good? saith the Lord.

Ant. 6. The first shall be last, and the last first : for many are called, but few chosen, saith the Lord.

Ant. 7. So the last shall be first, and the first last : for many are called, but few chosen, saith the Lord.

SEXAGESIMA SUNDAY.
First Vespers.
CHAPTER. 2 Cor. XI.

YE suffer fools gladly, seeing ye yourselves are wise. For ye suffer if a man bring you into bondage, if a man devour you, if a man take of you, if a man exalt himself, if a man smite you on the face.

R⁷. Noah sent forth a dove, to see if the waters were abated, and lo, in her mouth was an olive leaf when she returned to him into the ark. V. The dove, bearing in her mouth the sign of God's mercy. R⁷. Returned to him into the ark. V. Glory be to the Father, and to the Son : and to the Holy Ghost. R⁷. She returned to him into the ark.

HYMN. *Deus Creator omnium,* V. and R⁷., p. 118.

Ant. to Mag. And God said unto Noah : I do set My bow in the cloud, and it shall be for a token of a covenant between Me and the earth.

COLLECT.

O LORD God, Who seest that we put not our trust in any thing that we do; mercifully grant that by Thy power we may be defended against all adversity : through Jesus Christ our Lord. Amen.

Lauds.

Psalms as on Septuagesima Sunday.

Ant. 1. According to the multitude of Thy mercies : do away mine offences.

Ant. 2. Thou art my God, and I will thank Thee : Thou art my God, and I will praise Thee.

Ant. 3. Early will I seek Thee : that I might behold Thy power.

Ant. 4. Praise Him : and magnify Him for ever.

Ant. 5. O praise the Lord of heaven : praise Him, all ye angels of His.

Chapter as at First Vespers.

R⁷. Thanks be to God.

HYMN. *Æterne rerum Conditor,* V. and R⁷., p. 119.

Ant. to Ben. When much people were gathered together, and were come to Him out of every city, He spake by a parable : A sower went out to sow his seed.

Prime.

Ant. And other fell on good ground, and sprang up, and bare fruit an hundred-fold : and other some sixty-fold.

Tierce.

Ant. The seed fell on good ground : and brought forth fruit with patience.

CHAPTER. 2 Cor. XI.

YE suffer fools gladly, seeing ye yourselves are wise. For ye suffer if a man bring you into bondage, if a man devour you, if a man take of you, if a man exalt himself, if a man smite you on the face.

R⁷. Thou hast been. p. 125.

Sexts.

Ant. When Jesus had said these things, He cried : He that hath ears to hear, let him hear.

CHAPTER. 2 Cor. XII.

I KNEW a man in Christ, above fourteen years ago (whether in the body I cannot tell; or whether out of the body I cannot tell : God knoweth;) such an one caught up to the third heaven.

℞. Thou, O Lord, art my hope. p. 126.

Nones.

Ant. Unto you it is given to know the mysteries of the kingdom of God: but to others in parables, saith Jesus to His disciples.

CHAPTER. 2 Cor. XII.

AND I knew such a man, (whether in the body or out of the body I cannot tell : God knoweth :) how that he was caught up into paradise, and heard unspeakable words, which it is not lawful for a man to utter.

℞. O cleanse Thou me. p. 126.

Second Vespers.

Chapter as at First Vespers.

℞. Thanks be to God.

HYMN. *Lucis Creator optime,*
℣. and ℞., p. 49.

Ant. to Mag. They, which in an honest and good heart keep the word of God : bring forth fruit with patience.

Ants. to Benedictus *and* Magnificat *for the week, when the Office is of the Feria.*

Ant. 1. The seed is the word of God, but the Sower is Christ : he that heareth Him abideth for ever.

Ant. 2. But that on the good ground are they, which in an honest and good heart : having heard the word, keep it, and bring forth fruit with patience.

Ant. 3. If ye desire to be truly rich : love the true riches.

Ant. 4. If ye seek the height of true honour : hasten with all speed to the heavenly country.

QUINQUAGESIMA SUNDAY.
First Vespers.

CHAPTER. 1 Cor. XIII.

THOUGH I speak with the tongues of men and of angels, and have not charity, I am become as sounding brass, or a tinkling cymbal.

℞. When Abraham returned from the slaughter of the four kings, there met him Melchisedec, king of Salem, bringing forth bread and wine, and he was the priest of the most high God, and he blessed him. ℣. Blessed be Abraham of the most high God, Who created heaven and earth. ℞. And he was the priest of the most high God, and he blessed him. ℣. Glory be to the Father, and to the Son : and to the Holy Ghost. ℞. And he blessed him.

HYMN. *Deus Creator omnium,*
℣. and ℞., p. 118.

Ant. to Mag. When Abraham abode in the plain of Mamre, he saw three youths coming down by the way: he beheld three, but adored One.

COLLECT.

O LORD, Who hast taught us that all our doings without charity are nothing worth : send Thy Holy Ghost, and pour into our hearts that most excellent gift of charity, the very bond of peace and of all virtues, without which whosoever liveth is counted dead before Thee; grant this for Thine only Son Jesus Christ's sake. Amen.

[*Or this,*

WE beseech Thee, O Lord, mercifully to hear our prayers : that we, being loosed from the chains of our sins, may be preserved from all adversities; through Jesus Christ our Lord. Amen.]

Lauds.

Psalms as on Septuagesima Sunday.

Ant. 1. Turn Thy face, O Lord,

ASH-WEDNESDAY.

from my sins : and put out all my misdeeds.

Ant. 2. The Lord is my strength, and my song : and is become my salvation.

Ant. 3. Have I not thought upon Thee, when I was waking ? : because Thou hast been my helper.

Ant. 4. Let us ever bless the Father, the Son : and the Holy Ghost.

Ant. 5. Young men and maidens, old men and children : shall praise the Name of the Lord.

CHAPTER. 1 Cor. XIII.

THOUGH I speak with the tongues of men and of angels, and have not charity, I am become as sounding brass, or a tinkling cymbal.

℟. Thanks be to God.

HYMN. *Æterne rerum Conditor,* ℣. and ℟., p. 119.

Ant. to Ben. Behold, we go up to Jerusalem : and all things that are written by the prophets concerning the Son of Man shall be accomplished.

Prime.

Ant. to Psalms. As Jesus was come nigh unto Jericho : the blind man cried to Him that he might receive his sight.

Tierce.

Ant. As the Lord passed by, the blind man cried unto Him : Thou Son of David, have mercy upon me.

Chapter as at Lauds.

℟. Thou hast been. p. 125.

Sexts.

Ant. The blind man sat by the way, and cried : Have mercy upon me, Thou Son of David.

CHAPTER. 1 Cor. XIII.

CHARITY suffereth long, and is kind; charity envieth not : charity vaunteth not itself, is not puffed up, doth not behave itself unseemly, seeketh not her own.

℟. Thou, O Lord, art my hope. p. 126.

Nones.

Ant. The blind man cried so much the more : that the Lord would give him light.

CHAPTER. 1 Cor. XIII.

CHARITY is not easily provoked, thinketh no evil; rejoiceth not in iniquity, but rejoiceth in the truth.

℟. O cleanse Thou me. p. 126.

Second Vespers.

Chapter as at Lauds.

℟. Thanks be to God.

HYMN. *Lucis Creator optime,* ℣. and ℟., p. 49.

Ant. to Mag. And Jesus stood, and commanded him to be brought unto Him, and asked him, saying, What wilt thou that I should do unto thee ? And he said, Lord, that I may receive my sight : and Jesus said unto him, Receive thy sight ; thy faith hath saved thee. And immediately he received his sight, and followed Him, glorifying God.

On this following Monday is to be said the (Commemoration) Office of the Blessed Virgin : if this be not done, the Ants. for Tuesday must be used on both days.

TUESDAY.

Ant. to Ben. What wilt thou : that I should do unto thee ?

Ant. to Mag. All the people, when they saw it : gave praise unto God.

ASH-WEDNESDAY,
THE HEAD OF THE FAST.

Lauds.

Ants., Psalms and Hymn of the Feria.

CHAPTER. Joel II.

TURN ye even unto Me, saith the Lord, with all your heart, and with fasting, and with weeping, and with mourning: and rend your heart, and not your garments, saith the Lord Almighty.

This Chapter is said daily, at Ferial Lauds, till Passion Sunday.

Ant. to Ben. When ye fast, be not as the hypocrites, of a sad countenance.

COLLECT. (1549.)

ALMIGHTY and everlasting God, Who hatest nothing that Thou hast made, and dost forgive the sins of all them that are penitent; create and make in us new and contrite hearts, that we worthily lamenting our sins, and acknowledging our wretchedness, may obtain of Thee, the God of all mercy, perfect remission and forgiveness; through Jesus Christ our Lord. Amen.

[*Or this,*

GRANT, we beseech Thee, O Lord, to Thy faithful people, that the holy solemnities of the fast may be begun with due reverence, and continued with sure devotion; through.]

The same Collect is said at every Hour of this day.

MEMORIAL OF PENITENTS.

Ant. Turn ye even unto Me, saith the Lord, with all your heart, and with fasting, and with weeping, and with mourning.

℣. We have sinned with our fathers.

℟. We have done amiss, and dealt wickedly.

Collect as at Vespers.

Prime and the other Hours as usual.

The Hours are thus said till the First Sunday in Lent, except that the Collect and Ants. to Benedictus *and* Magnificat *are changed.*

Vespers.

Ants., Psalms, Chapter and Hymn of the Feria.

Ant. to Mag. Lay up for yourselves treasures in heaven : where neither moth nor rust doth corrupt.

[COLLECT.

WE beseech Thee, O Lord, mercifully to hear the prayers of them that bow before Thy Majesty : that being refreshed with Divine gifts, they may ever be supported by heavenly aid; through.]

MEMORIAL OF PENITENTS.

Ant. Who knoweth if the Lord will return and repent : and leave a blessing behind Him?

℣. O Lord, deal not with us after our sins.

℟. Neither reward us after our iniquities.

COLLECT.

O LORD, we beseech Thee, mercifully hear our prayers, and spare all those who confess their sins unto Thee; that they, whose consciences by sin are accused, by Thy merciful pardon may be absolved; through Christ our Lord. Amen.

The Office for this day is not to be changed for any Feast whatever.

The Memorial of Penitents is said as on this day at Lauds and Vespers, when the Office is of the Feria (not on Sundays), till Wednesday in Holy Week.

THURSDAY.

Lauds.

All of the Feria except that which follows.

Chapter as on Wednesday.

Ant. to Ben. Lord, my servant

lieth at home sick of the palsy, grievously tormented : Verily, I say unto thee, I will come and heal him.

[COLLECT.]

GOD, Who art offended by sin, and appeased by penitence; mercifully regard the prayers of Thy suppliant people, and turn away the scourges of Thy wrath, which by our sins we have justly deserved; through.]

Vespers.

All of the Feria except that which follows.

Ant. to Mag. Lord, I am not worthy that Thou shouldest come under my roof : but speak the word only, and my servant shall be healed.

[COLLECT.]

SPARE, O Lord, spare Thy people; that they, worthily chastised by Thy scourges, may be relieved by Thy tender mercy; through.]

FRIDAY.
Lauds.

Ant. to Ben. When thou doest alms : let not thy left hand know what thy right hand doeth.

[COLLECT.]

WE beseech Thee, O Lord, of Thy loving favour, that we may persevere in the fast now begun, and, as we outwardly set forth its observance, so we may perform it inwardly with pure hearts; through.]

Vespers.

Ant. to Mag. But thou, when thou prayest, enter into thy closet : and when thou hast shut thy door, pray to thy Father.

[COLLECT.]

DEFEND Thy people, O Lord, and graciously purify them from all sin; forasmuch as no adversity may harm, if no wickedness have dominion over them; through.]

SATURDAY.
Lauds.

Ant. to Ben. Wherefore have we fasted, and Thou seest not ? : wherefore have we afflicted our soul, and Thou takest no knowledge ?

[COLLECT.]

ASSIST us mercifully, O Lord, in these our supplications; and grant us grace devoutly to celebrate this holy fast, fitly ordained for the healing of our souls and bodies; through.]

FIRST SUNDAY IN LENT.
First Vespers.

CHAPTER. 2 Cor. VI.

WE then beseech you also that ye receive not the grace of God in vain. For He saith, I have heard thee in a time accepted, and in the day of salvation have I succoured thee.

℟. Let us amend * those things wherein we have ignorantly sinned; lest, suddenly prevented by the day of death, we seek place of repentance, and find it not. Hear, Lord, and have mercy, for we have sinned against Thee. ℣. We have sinned with our fathers, we have done amiss, and dealt wickedly. ℟. Hear, Lord, and have mercy, for we have sinned against Thee. ℣. Glory be to the Father, and to the Son : and to the Holy Ghost. ℟. Hear, Lord, and have mercy, for we have sinned against Thee.

HYMN. *Ex more docti mystico.*

THE fast, as taught by holy lore,
We keep in solemn course once more :
The fast to all men known, and bound
In forty days of yearly round.

The law and seers that were of old
In divers ways this Lent foretold,
Which Christ, all seasons' King and Guide,
In after ages sanctified.

More sparing therefore let us make
The words we speak, the food we take,
Our sleep and mirth—and closer barred
Be every sense in holy guard.

In prayer together let us fall,
And cry for mercy, one and all,
And weep before the Judge's feet,
And His avenging wrath entreat.

Thy grace have we offended sore
By sins, O God, which we deplore;
But pour upon us from on high,
O pardoning One, Thy clemency.

Remember Thou, though frail we be,
That yet Thine handiwork are we;
Nor let the honour of Thy Name
Be by another put to shame.

Forgive the sin that we have wrought;
Increase the good that we have sought;
That we at length, our wanderings o'er,
May please Thee here and evermore.

Grant, O Thou blessed Trinity,
Grant, O Essential Unity,
That this our fast of forty days
May work our profit and Thy praise. Amen.

℣. He shall give His angels charge over thee.

℟. To keep thee in all thy ways.

This Hymn, ℣. and ℟. are said at Vespers daily, till the Third Sunday in Lent.

Ant. to Mag. Behold, now is the accepted time; behold, now is the day of salvation : let us then in all things approve ourselves as the servants of God, in much patience, in watchings, in fastings; by love unfeigned.

COLLECT. (1549.)

O LORD, Who for our sake didst fast forty days and forty nights; give us grace to use such abstinence, that our flesh being subdued to the Spirit, we may ever obey Thy godly motions, in righteousness and true holiness, to Thy honour and glory, Who livest and reignest with the Father and the Holy Ghost, One God, world without end. Amen.

[*Or*,

O GOD, Who dost purify Thy Church by the yearly observance of Lent : grant to Thy family, that those things which by abstinence they seek to obtain of Thee, by good works they may ensue; through.]

Compline.

Ant. to Psalms. Lord, lift Thou up : the light of Thy countenance upon us.

CHAPTER. Jer. XIV.

THOU, O Lord, art in the midst of us, and we are called by Thy Name; leave us not, O our God.

℟. I will lay me down : *The Choir continue* : in peace and take my rest. ℣. If I shall have suffered mine eyes to sleep, or mine eyelids to slumber. ℟. In peace and take my rest. ℣. Glory be to the Father, and to the Son : and to the Holy Ghost. ℟. I will lay me down in peace and take my rest.

HYMN. *Christe qui lux es et dies.*

O CHRIST, Who art the Light and Day,
Who driv'st the clouds of night away;
The very Light of Light art Thou,
Preaching glad tidings here below.

We pray Thee, holy Lord, our Light,
Defend us in this coming night;
Grant us a perfect rest in Thee,
A quiet night from perils free.

Let not dull slumber quell the soul,
Nor Satan with his spirits foul;
Nor let our flesh consent begin
To make us in Thy presence sin.

Grant that our eyes due sleep may take,
Our hearts to Thee be e'er awake;
May Thy right hand defend and guide
Thy servants who in Thee confide.

Look down, O Lord, our strong defence,
Repress our foes' proud insolence;
Direct Thy people in all good,
The purchase of Thy precious Blood.

Remember us, O Lord, we pray,
Pent in this cumb'ring frame of clay;
Thou Who dost e'er our souls defend,
Be with us, our eternal Friend.

All laud to God the Father be;
All laud, eternal Son to Thee;
All laud, as is for ever meet,
To God the blessed Paraclete. Amen.

℣. Keep us, O Lord.

℟. As the apple of an eye, hide us under the shadow of Thy wings.

Ant. to Nunc Dim. When thou seest the naked, cover thou him : and hide not thyself from thine own flesh. Then shall thy light break forth as the morning, and the glory of the Lord shall be thy rereward.

Here follow the prayers, p. 69.

On all Ferias is said after Psalm LI., Domine exaudi, Psalm CXLIII.

This Compline is said daily till the Third Sunday in Lent.

Lauds.

℣. He shall deliver thee from the snare of the hunter.

℟. And from the noisome pestilence.

Psalms as on Septuagesima Sunday.

Ant. 1. Make me a clean heart, O God : and renew a right spirit within me.

Ant. 2. Help me now, O Lord : O Lord, send us now prosperity.

Ant. 3. As long as I live will I magnify Thee on this manner : and lift up my hands in Thy Name.

Ant. 4. In the spirit of humility and with contrite heart may we be accepted of Thee, O Lord : and may our sacrifice be so offered in Thy sight as to be accepted of Thee this day, and be well pleasing to Thee, O Lord God.

Ant. 5. Praise Him, all ye heavens : and ye waters that are above the heavens.

CHAPTER.   2 Cor. VI.

WE then beseech you also that ye receive not the grace of God in vain. For He saith, I have heard thee in a time accepted, and in the day of salvation have I succoured thee.

HYMN. *Audi benigne Conditor.*

O MAKER of the world, give ear!
  Accept the prayer, and own the tear,
Towards Thy seat of mercy sent,
In this most holy fast of Lent.

Each heart is manifest to Thee :
Thou knowest our infirmity :
Forgive Thou then each soul that fain
Would seek to Thee, and turn again.

Our sins are manifold and sore ;
But pardon them that sin deplore ;
And, for Thy Name's sake, make each soul,
That feels and owns its languor, whole.

So mortify we every sense
By grace of outward abstinence,
That from each stain and spot of sin
The soul may keep her fast within.

Grant, O Thou blessed Trinity,
Grant, O Essential Unity,
That this our fast of forty days
May work our profit and Thy praise. Amen.

℣. His faithfulness and truth shall be thy shield and buckler.

℟. Thou shalt not be afraid for any terror by night.

This Hymn, ℣. and ℟. are said at Lauds daily, till the Third Sunday in Lent.

Ant. to Ben. Then was Jesus led up of the Spirit into the wilderness to be tempted of the devil : and when He had fasted forty days and forty nights, He was afterwards an hungered.

Collect as at First Vespers.

Prime.

Ant. to Psalms. And when Jesus had fasted forty days and forty nights: He was afterwards an hungered.

Tierce.

Ant. Man shall not live by bread alone : but by every word that proceedeth out of the mouth of God.

CHAPTER.   2 Cor. VI.

WE then beseech you also that ye receive not the grace of God in vain. For He saith, I have heard thee in a time accepted, and in the day of salvation have I succoured thee.

℟. Make me : *The Choir continue :* a companion of all them that fear Thee and keep Thy commandments. ℣. O look Thou upon me, and be merciful unto me, as Thou usest to do unto those that love Thy Name. ℟. And keep Thy commandments. ℣. Glory be to the Father, and to the Son : and to the Holy Ghost. ℟. Make me a companion of all them that fear Thee, and keep Thy commandments.

℣. I will say unto the Lord, Thou art my hope and my strong hold. ℟. My God, in Him will I trust.

Sexts.

Ant. Then the devil taketh Him up into the holy city, and setteth Him on a pinnacle of the temple, and saith unto Him : If Thou be the Son of God, cast Thyself down.

CHAPTER. 2 Cor. VI.

BEHOLD, now is the accepted time; behold, now is the day of salvation. Giving no offence in anything, that the ministry be not blamed.

℟. Refrain : *The Choir continue* : my feet from every evil way, that I may keep Thy word, O Lord. ℣. I have not shrunk from Thy judgments, for Thou teachest me. ℟. That I may keep Thy word, O Lord. ℣. Glory be to the Father, and to the Son : and to the Holy Ghost. ℟. Refrain my feet from every evil way, that I may keep Thy word, O Lord.

℣. He shall deliver thee from the snare of the hunter. ℟. And from the noisome pestilence.

Nones.

Ant. Get thee hence, Satan : thou shalt not tempt the Lord thy God.

CHAPTER. 2 Cor. VI.

IN all things approving ourselves as the ministers of God : in much patience.

℟. Shew us : *The Choir continue :* Thy mercy, O Lord. ℣. When Thy word goeth forth, it giveth understanding. ℟. Thy mercy, O Lord. ℣. Glory be to the Father, and to the Son : and to the Holy Ghost. ℟. Shew us Thy mercy, O Lord.

℣. He shall defend thee under His wings. ℟. And thou shalt be safe under His feathers.

Second Vespers.

CHAPTER. 2 Cor. VI.

WE then beseech you also that ye receive not the grace of God in vain. For He saith, I have heard thee in a time accepted, and in the day of salvation have I succoured thee.

℟. Be thou to us : *The Choir continue :* O Lord, a strong tower. ℣. Against the face of the enemy. ℟. A strong tower. ℣. Glory be to the Father, and to the Son : and to the Holy Ghost. ℟. Be Thou to us, O Lord, a strong tower.

HYMN. *Ex more docti mystico,* ℣. and ℟., p. 131.

Ant. to Mag. Then the devil leaveth Him : and behold, angels came and ministered unto Him.

MONDAY.

Lauds.

℣. He shall deliver thee from the snare of the hunter. ℟. And from the noisome pestilence.

This ℣. and ℟. is said daily at Ferial Lauds.

Ants. and Psalms of the Feria.

CHAPTER. Joel II.

TURN ye even unto Me, saith the Lord, with all your heart, and with fasting, and with weeping, and with mourning. And rend your heart, and not your garments, and turn unto the Lord your God.

℟. Thanks be to God.

HYMN. *Audi benigne Conditor*, ℣. and ℟., p. 133.

Ant. to Ben. Come, ye blessed of My father : inherit the kingdom prepared for you from the foundation of the world.

Then are said the Ferial Petitions; and Domine, ne in furore, Psalm VI., *is said after* Miserere, Psalm LI. *After every hour in Lent, in Sarum use, when the Office is of the Feria, one of the seven Penitential Psalms is said, according to order, after* Psalm LI., *except at Sexts, when* Deus misereatur, Psalm LXVII., *is said alone, instead of* Psalm LI. *And if a Double Feast follow on the morrow, then at Nones the three last Penitential Psalms shall be said. And so in like manner on Saturdays.*

[COLLECT.]

TURN us, O God of our salvation; and, that the Lenten fast may profit us, instruct our souls with heavenly discipline; through.]

Prime.

Ant. As I live, saith the Lord, I have no pleasure in the death of a sinner : but rather that he be converted and live.

After Psalm LI. *is said* Beati quorum, Psalm XXXII.

Tierce.

Ant. Let us chasten ourselves : in much patience, by the armour of the righteousness of God.

CHAPTER. Joel II.

TURN unto the Lord your God; for He is gracious and merciful; slow to anger, and of great kindness, and repenteth Him of the evil.

℟. Make me * a companion of all them that fear Thee : and keep Thy commandments. ℣. O look Thou upon me, and be merciful unto me, as Thou usest to do unto those that love Thy Name. ℟. And keep Thy commandments. ℣. Glory be to the Father, and to the Son : and to the Holy Ghost. ℟. Make me a companion of all them that fear Thee, and keep Thy commandments.

℣. I will say unto the Lord, Thou art my hope, and my strong hold.

℟. My God, in Him will I trust.

After Psalm LI. *is said* Domine ne in furore, Psalm XXXVIII.

From this day till the Wednesday before Easter inclusive, in Sarum use, when the Office is of the Feria, are said, after Tierce, the fifteen Gradual Psalms, for all the people of God, with Litany, as in Occasional Offices.

Sexts.

Ant. Let us chasten ourselves : in much patience and fastings, by the armour of righteousness.

CHAPTER. Is. IV.

LET the wicked forsake his way, and the unrighteous man his thoughts : and let him return unto the Lord, and He will have mercy upon him, and to our God, for He will abundantly pardon.

℟. Refrain * my feet from every evil way, that I may keep Thy word, O Lord. ℣. I have not shrunk from Thy judgments, for Thou teachest me me. ℟. That I may keep Thy word, O Lord. ℣. Glory be to the Father, and to the Son : and to the Holy Ghost. ℟. Refrain my feet from every evil way, that I may keep Thy word, O Lord.

℣. He shall deliver thee from the snare of the hunter.

℟. And from the noisome pestilence.

Instead of Psalm LI. *is said* Deus misereatur, Psalm LXVII.

Nones.

Ant. The days of penitence are come to us : for the redemption of sins, and the salvation of souls.

Chapter. Is. LVIII.

DEAL thy bread to the hungry, and bring the poor that are cast out to thy house : when thou seest the naked, cover thou him ; and hide not thyself from thine own flesh, saith the Lord Almighty.

℟. Shew us * Thy mercy, O Lord. ℣. When Thy word goeth forth, it giveth understanding. ℟. Thy mercy, O Lord. ℣. Glory be to the Father, and to the Son : and to the Holy Ghost. ℟. Shew us Thy mercy, O Lord.

℣. He shall defend thee under His wings.

℟. And thou shalt be safe under His feathers.

After Psalm LI. *is said* Domine exaudi, Psalm CII.

Vespers.

Ants. and Psalms of the Feria.

Chapter. Ezekiel XVIII.

THE soul that sinneth, it shall die. The son shall not bear the iniquity of the father, neither shall the father bear the iniquity of the son, saith the Lord Almighty.

℟. Be Thou to us : *The Choir continue :* O Lord, a strong tower. ℣. Against the face of the enemy. ℟. A strong tower. ℣. Glory be to the Father, and to the Son : and to the Holy Ghost. ℟. Be Thou to us, O Lord, a strong tower.

Hymn. *Ex more docti mystico,* ℣. and ℟., p. 131.

Ant. to Mag. Inasmuch as ye have done it unto one of the least of these My brethren : ye have done it unto Me, saith the Lord.

After Psalm LI. *is said* De profundis, Psalm CXXX.

[Collect.

LOOSE, we beseech Thee, O Lord, the bands of all our sins ; and graciously turn from us those things which by reason thereof we have deserved; through.]

The Ferial Office is thus said till the Third Sunday in Lent, except the daily change of Collect, and Ants. to Benedictus *and* Magnificat.

TUESDAY.
Lauds.

Ant. to Ben. And Jesus went into the temple, and began to cast out them that sold and bought in the temple : and overthrew the tables of the money-changers, and the seats of them that sold doves.

[Collect.

LOOK down, O Lord, upon Thy family, and grant that our hearts, chastened by bodily mortification, may be radiant in Thy sight, by reason of their desire for Thee ; through.]

Vespers.

Ant. to Mag. Jesus went out of the city to Bethany : and there He taught them the things concerning the kingdom of God.

[Collect.

LET our prayers come up before Thee, O Lord ; and vouchsafe to drive all iniquity from Thy Church; through.]

EMBER WEDNESDAY.
Lauds.

Ant. to Ben. An evil and adulterous generation seeketh after a sign : and there shall no sign be given to it, but the sign of the prophet Jonas.

SECOND SUNDAY IN LENT.

[COLLECT.

WE beseech Thee, O Lord, mercifully hear our prayers; and stretch forth the right hand of Thy Majesty to be our defence against all our enemies; through.]

Vespers.

Ant. to Mag. For as Jonas was three days and three nights in the whale's belly : so shall the Son of man be three days and three nights in the heart of the earth.

[COLLECT.

ENLIGHTEN our souls, we beseech Thee, O Lord, with the brightness of Thy glory; that we may perceive what things we ought to do, and may be enabled to perform such as are righteous in Thy sight; through.]

THURSDAY.
Lauds.

Ant. to Ben. If ye continue in My word, then are ye My disciples indeed : and ye shall know the truth, and the truth shall make you free.

[COLLECT.

ALMIGHTY, Everlasting God, Who hast appointed fasting and almsgiving as the seal of our repentance; grant us ever to be devoted to Thee in body and soul; through.]

Vespers.

Ant. to Mag. I proceeded forth and came from God : neither came I of Myself, but He sent Me.

[COLLECT.

GRANT, we beseech Thee, O Lord, to Thy Christian people, that those things which they set forth outwardly, they may experience inwardly, and may love the heavenly gift which they are wont to receive; through.]

EMBER FRIDAY.
Lauds.

Ant. to Ben. An angel went down at a certain season into the pool : and troubled the water, and healed one.

[COLLECT.

BE favourable to Thy people, O Lord; and with Thy tender care graciously comfort those whom Thou dost fill with devotion unto Thee; through.]

Vespers.

Ant. to Mag. He that made me whole, the Same said unto me : Take up thy bed, and walk in peace.

[COLLECT.

HEAR us, O merciful God, and shed the light of Thy grace on our hearts; through.]

EMBER SATURDAY.
Lauds.

Ant. to Ben. Jesus took His disciples, and went up into a mountain : and was transfigured before them.

[COLLECT.

WE beseech Thee, O Lord, to look favourably on Thy people, and mercifully turn from them the scourges of Thy wrath; through.]

SECOND SUNDAY IN LENT.
First Vespers.

CHAPTER. 1 Thess. IV.

WE beseech you, brethren, and exhort you by the Lord Jesus, that as ye have received of us how ye ought to walk, and to please God, so ye would abound more and more.

℟. God give thee * of the dew of heaven, and the fatness of the earth. Let people and nations serve thee : be lord over thy brethren. ℣. And let thy mother's sons bow down to thee. ℟. Be lord over thy brethren. ℣. Glory be to the Father, and to the Son : and to the Holy Ghost. ℟. Be lord over thy brethren.

HYMN. *Ex more docti mystico,* ℣. and ℟., p. 131.

Ant. to Mag. Lord, it is good for us to be here : if Thou wilt, let us make here three tabernacles; one for Thee, and one for Moses, and one for Elias.

COLLECT.

ALMIGHTY God, Who seest that we have no power of ourselves to help ourselves; keep us both outwardly in our bodies, and inwardly in our souls; that we may be defended from all adversities which may happen to the body, and from all evil thoughts which may assault and hurt the soul; through Jesus Christ our Lord. Amen.

Lauds.

℣. He shall deliver thee from the snare of the hunter.

℟. And from the noisome pestilence.

Ant. 1. Thou shalt open my lips, O Lord : and my mouth shall shew Thy praise.

Ant. 2. The right hand of the Lord hath the pre-eminence : the right hand of the Lord bringeth mighty things to pass.

Ant. 3. My God, Thou hast been : my helper.

Ant. 4. Let us sing the song of the three children : which they sang in the fiery furnace, giving thanks unto the Lord.

Ant. 5. He hath made them fast for ever and ever : He hath given them a law which shall not be broken.

CHAPTER. 1 Thess. IV.

WE beseech you, brethren, and exhort you by the Lord Jesus, that as ye have received of us how ye ought to walk, and to please God, so ye would abound more and more.

℟. Thanks be to God.

HYMN. *Audi benigne Conditor,* ℣. and ℟., p. 133.

Ant. to Ben. Jesus went thence, and departed into the coasts of Tyre and Sidon : And behold, a woman of Canaan came out of the same coasts, and cried unto Him, saying, Have mercy on me, O Lord, Thou Son of David.

Collect as at First Vespers.

Prime.

Ant. And His disciples came and besought Him, saying : Send her away; for she crieth after us.

Tierce.

Ant. I am not sent but unto the lost sheep of the house of Israel : saith the Lord.

CHAPTER. 1 Thess. IV.

WE beseech you, brethren, and exhort you by the Lord Jesus, that as ye have received of us how ye ought to walk, and to please God, so ye would abound more and more.

℟. Make me. p. 135.

Sexts.

Ant. O woman, great is thy faith; be it unto thee even as thou wilt.

CHAPTER. 1 Thess. IV.

FOR this is the will of God, even your sanctification, that ye should abstain from fornication; that every one of you should know how to possess his vessel in sanctification and honour.

℟. Refrain my feet. p. 135.

Nones.

Ant. Said I not unto thee, that if

thou wouldest believe : thou shouldest see greater things than these?

CHAPTER. 1 Thess. iv.

THIS is the will of God : that no man go beyond and defraud his brother in any matter; because that the Lord is the avenger of all such, as we have also forewarned you, and testified.

℞. Shew us Thy mercy. p. 136.

Second Vespers.

CHAPTER. 1 Thess. IV.

WE beseech you, brethren, and exhort you by the Lord Jesus, that as ye have received of us how ye ought to walk, and to please God, so ye would abound more and more.

℞. Be Thou to us. p. 136.

HYMN. *Ex more docti mystico,* ℣. and ℞., p. 131.

Ant. to Mag. Jesus said unto the woman of Canaan, It is not meet to take the children's bread, and to cast it to dogs. And she said, Truth, Lord : yet the dogs eat of the crumbs which fall from their master's table. Then Jesus answered and said unto her, O woman, great is thy faith : be it unto thee even as thou wilt.

Collect as at First Vespers.

MONDAY.
Lauds.

Ant. to Ben. I am the Beginning : even I that speak unto you.

[COLLECT.

GRANT, we beseech Thee, Almighty God, that Thy family, which chastens itself and abstains from food, may follow after righteousness and fast from sin; through.]

Vespers.

Ant. to Mag. He that sent Me is with Me : and hath not left Me alone; for I do always those things that please Him.

[COLLECT.

ASSIST us mercifully, O God Almighty, in these our supplications, and let the fruit of Thy wonted mercy be shewn forth on them to whom Thou dost grant confidence in Thy lovingkindness; through.]

TUESDAY.
Lauds.

Ant. to Ben. One is your Master : Which is in heaven, saith the Lord.

[COLLECT.

GRANT to us, Lord, we beseech Thee, the full blessing of this holy season; that as by Thy guidance we have learned what things we ought to do, so by Thy operation we may fulfil the same; through.]

Vespers.

Ant. to Mag. He that is greatest among you shall be your servant : for whosoever exalteth himself shall be abased, saith the Lord.

[COLLECT.

ASSIST us mercifully, O Lord, we beseech Thee, in these our supplications, and heal the sickness of our souls : that, having received pardon, we may alway rejoice in Thy blessing; through.]

WEDNESDAY.
Lauds.

Ant. to Ben. Behold we go up to Jerusalem : and the Son of Man shall be betrayed to be crucified.

[COLLECT.

WE beseech Thee, O Lord, favourably behold Thy people; and as Thou biddest us cease from carnal food, so grant us likewise to cease from sin; through.]

Vespers.

Ant. to Mag. To sit with Me is not Mine to give : save to those for whom it is prepared of My Father.

[COLLECT.

O GOD, Restorer and Lover of innocence, direct the hearts of Thy servants unto Thee; that kindled with the fervour of Thy spirit, we may be found strong in faith and zealous in works; through.]

THURSDAY.
Lauds.

Ant. to Ben. I receive not testimony from man : but these things I say, that ye might be saved.

[COLLECT.

GRANT us, we beseech Thee, O Lord, the help of Thy grace; that, duly intent on fasting and prayer, we may be delivered from our ghostly and bodily enemies; through.]

Vespers.

Ant. to Mag. The works that I do, bear witness of Me : that the Father hath sent Me.

[COLLECT.

BE present, O Lord, with Thy servants : and to them that call on Thee grant perpetual mercy, that to them which acknowledge Thee their Author and Governour, Thy blessings may be restored and preserved; through.]

FRIDAY.
Lauds.

Ant. to Ben. He will miserably destroy those wicked men : and will let out His vineyard to other husbandmen, which shall render Him the fruits in their seasons.

[COLLECT.

GRANT, we beseech Thee, Almighty God, that, cleansed by the sacred fast, we may come with pure hearts to the holy feast which lies before us; through.]

Vespers.

Ant. to Mag. When they sought to lay hands on Him : they feared the multitude, because they took Him for a Prophet.

[COLLECT.

GRANT, we beseech Thee, O Lord, to Thy people health both of body and mind : that, holding fast to good works, they may ever be defended by the protection of Thy might; through.]

SATURDAY.
Lauds.

Ant. to Ben. I will go to my father, and will say unto him : make me as one of thy hired servants.

[COLLECT.

O LORD, we beseech Thee, give good effect to our fasts, that the chastening bestowed upon the flesh may avail to the growth of the spirit; through.]

THIRD SUNDAY IN LENT.
First Vespers.
CHAPTER. Eph. v.

BE ye therefore followers of God, as dear children; and walk in love, as Christ also hath loved us, and hath given Himself for us, an offering and a sacrifice to God for a sweet-smelling savour.

℟. And Joseph * was brought down to Egypt, and the Lord was with him : and he was a prosperous man. ℣. God shewed him mercy, and that which he did, the Lord made it to prosper. ℟. And he was a prosperous

THIRD SUNDAY IN LENT.

man. ℣. Glory be to the Father, and to the Son: and to the Holy Ghost. ℟. And he was a prosperous man.

HYMN. *Ecce tempus idoneum.*

LO! now is our accepted day,
The med'cine, purging sin away;
Where'er our lives have wrought offence,
By thought and word, by deed and sense.

For God, the merciful and true,
Hath spared His people hitherto;
Nor us and ours, with searching eyes,
Destroyed for our iniquities.

Him therefore now, with earnest care,
And contrite fast, and tear and prayer,
And works of mercy and of love,
We pray for pardon from above:

That from pollution making whole,
With virtues He may deck each soul,
And join us, in the heavenly place,
To angel cohorts by His grace.

O Father, that we ask be done,
Through Jesus Christ, Thine only Son;
Who, with the Holy Ghost and Thee,
Shall live and reign eternally. Amen.

℣. He shall give His angels charge over thee.

℟. To keep thee in all thy ways.

This Hymn, ℣. and ℟. are said at Vespers daily till Passion Sunday.

Ant. to Mag. The father gave to his penitent son the best robe, and a ring; and putting shoes on his feet, made a great feast: we receive in baptism the best robe, and, for a ring, the sign of the faith.

COLLECT.

WE beseech Thee, Almighty God, look upon the hearty desires of Thy humble servants, and stretch forth the right hand of Thy Majesty to be our defence against all our enemies; through Jesus Christ our Lord. Amen.

Compline.

All as p. 132, till

Ant. to Nunc Dim. In the midst of life we are in death; of whom may we seek for succour but of Thee, O Lord, Who for our sins art justly displeased: Holy God, Holy and Mighty, Holy and Merciful Saviour, deliver us not into the bitter pains of eternal death.

Compline is thus said till Passion Sunday.

On Saturdays and Sundays, and at both Complines of Double Feasts, after Nunc Dimittis *and its Antiphon, is added,*

℣. Cast us not away in the time of age: forsake us not when our strength faileth us, O Lord.

℟. Holy God, Holy and Mighty, Holy and Merciful Saviour, deliver us not into the bitter pains of eternal death.

℣. Shut not Thy merciful ears to our prayer.

℟. Holy God, Holy and Mighty, Holy and Merciful Saviour, deliver us not into the bitter pains of eternal death.

℣. Thou that knowest, Lord, the secrets of our hearts; be merciful unto our sins.

℟. Holy God, Holy and Mighty, Holy and Merciful Saviour, deliver us not into the bitter pains of eternal death.

Lauds.

℣. He shall deliver thee from the snare of the hunter.

℟. And from the noisome pestilence.

Ant. 1. O be favourable and gracious unto Sion: build Thou the walls of Jerusalem.

Ant. 2. The Lord is on my side: I will not fear what man doeth unto me.

Ant. 3. God be merciful unto us: and bless us.

Ant. 4. The fire forgat his own virtue: that Thy servants might be delivered unhurt.

Ant. 5. Praise Him, sun and moon: for His Name only is excellent.

CHAPTER. Eph. v.

BE ye therefore followers of God, as dear children : and walk in love, as Christ also hath loved us, and hath given Himself for us, an offering and a sacrifice to God for a sweet-smelling savour.

℞. Thanks be to God.

HYMN. *Jesu quadrigenariæ.*

JESU, the Law and Pattern, whence
  Our forty days of abstinence,
Who souls to save, that else had died,
This sacred fast hast ratified ;

That so to Paradise once more
Might abstinence preserv'd restore
Them that had lost its fields of light
Through crafty wiles of appetite

Be present now, be present here,
And mark Thy Church's falling tear,
And own the grief that fills her eyes
In mourning her iniquities.

Oh by Thy grace be pardon won
For sins that former years have done ;
And let Thy mercy guard us still
From crimes that threaten future ill.

That by the fast we offer here,
Our annual sacrifice sincere,
To Paschal gladness at the end,
Set free from guilt our souls may tend.

O Father, that we ask be done,
Through Jesus Christ, Thine only Son ;
Who, with the Holy Ghost and Thee,
Shall live and reign eternally. Amen.

℣. His faithfulness and truth shall be thy shield and buckler.

℞. Thou shalt not be afraid for any terror by night.

This Hymn, ℣. and ℞. are said at Lauds till Passion Sunday.

Ant. to Ben. Jesus was casting out a devil, and it was dumb ; and it came to pass, when the devil was gone out, the dumb spake : and the people wondered.

Collect as at First Vespers.

Prime.

Ant. If I, by the finger of God, cast out devils : no doubt the kingdom of God is come upon you.

Tierce.

Ant. When a strong man armed keepeth his palace : his goods are in peace.

CHAPTER. Eph. v.

BE ye therefore followers of God, as dear children : and walk in love, as Christ also hath loved us, and hath given Himself for us, an offering and a sacrifice to God for a sweet-smelling savour.

℞. It is good for me, O Lord, *The Choir continue :* that I have been in trouble : the law of Thy mouth is dearer unto me than thousands of gold and silver. ℣. Thy hands have made me, and fashioned me : O give me understanding, that I may learn Thy commandments. ℞. The law of Thy mouth is dearer unto me than thousands of gold and silver. ℣. Glory be to the Father, and to the Son : and to the Holy Ghost. ℞. The law of Thy mouth is dearer unto me than thousands of gold and silver.

℣. I will say unto the Lord, Thou art my hope, and my strong hold.

℞. My God, in Him will I trust.

Sexts.

Ant. He that is not with Me is against Me : and He that gathereth not with Me scattereth.

CHAPTER. Eph. v.

BUT fornication, and all unclean-ness or covetousness, let it not be once named amongst you, as becometh saints.

℞. I am * Thy servant, grant me understanding, O Lord. ℣. That I may know Thy testimonies. ℞. Grant me understanding, O Lord. ℣. Glory be to the Father, and to the Son : and to the Holy Ghost. ℞. I am Thy servant, grant me understanding, O Lord.

℣. He shall deliver thee from the snare of the hunter.

℞. And from the noisome pestilence.

Nones.

Ant. When the unclean spirit is gone out of a man : he walketh through dry places, seeking rest and finding none.

CHAPTER. Eph. v.

FOR this ye know, that no whoremonger, nor unclean person, nor covetous man, who is an idolater, hath any inheritance in the kingdom of Christ, and of God.

℞. Seven times a day * do I praise Thee, O Lord. My God, cast me not away. ℣. I have gone astray like a sheep that is lost : O seek Thy servant, for I do not forget Thy commandments. ℞. My God, cast me not away. ℣. Glory be to the Father, and to the Son : and to the Holy Ghost. ℞. Seven times a day do I praise Thee, O Lord. My God, cast me not away.

℣. He shall defend thee under His wings.

℞. And thou shalt be safe under His feathers.

Second Vespers.

CHAPTER. Eph. v.

BE ye therefore followers of God, as dear children; and walk in love, as Christ also hath loved us, and hath given Himself for us, an offering and a sacrifice to God for a sweet-smelling savour.

℞. Bring my soul * out of prison : that I may give thanks unto Thy Name, O Lord. ℣. I had no place to flee unto, and no man cared for my soul. ℞. That I may give thanks unto Thy Name, O Lord. ℣. Glory be to the Father, and to the Son : and to the Holy Ghost. ℞. Bring my soul out of prison : that I may give thanks unto Thy Name, O Lord.

HYMN. *Ecce tempus idoneum,*
℣. and ℞., p. 141.

Ant. to Mag. A certain woman of the company lifted up her voice, and said unto Him, Blessed is the womb that bare Thee, and the paps which Thou hast sucked : but He said, Yea, rather, blessed are they that hear the word of God, and keep it.

MONDAY.

Lauds.

℣. He shall deliver thee from the snare of the hunter.

℞. And from the noisome pestilence.

CHAPTER. Joel II.

TURN ye even unto Me, saith the Lord, with all your heart, and with fasting, and with weeping, and with mourning. And rend your heart, and not your garments, and turn unto the Lord your God.

℞. Thanks be to God.

HYMN. *Jesu quadrigenariæ,*
℣. and ℞., p. 142.

Ant. to Ben. Verily I say unto you : no prophet is accepted in his own country.

[COLLECT.

WE beseech Thee, O Lord, mercifully to pour Thy grace into our hearts : that as we abstain from bodily food, so likewise we may restrain our senses from evil excesses ; through.]

Prime.

Ant. As I live, saith the Lord, I have no pleasure in the death of a sinner : but rather that he be converted and live.

Tierce.

Ant. Let us chasten ourselves : in much patience, by the armour of the righteousness of God.

Chapter. Is. i.

WASH you, make you clean : put away the evil of your doings from before Mine eyes : cease to do evil; learn to do well.

℞. It is good for me, O Lord,* that I have been in trouble : the law of Thy mouth is dearer unto me than thousands of gold and silver. ℣. Thy hands have made me and fashioned me : O give me understanding, that I may learn Thy commandments. ℞. The law of Thy mouth is dearer unto me than thousands of gold and silver. ℣. Glory be to the Father, and to the Son, and to the Holy Ghost. ℞. The law of Thy mouth is dearer unto me than thousands of gold and silver.

℣. I will say unto the Lord, Thou art my hope and my strong hold.

℞. My God, in Him will I trust.

Sexts.

Ant. Let us chasten ourselves : in much patience and fastings, by the armour of righteousness.

Chapter. Is. i.

SEEK judgment, relieve the oppressed, judge the fatherless, plead for the widow. Come now, and let us reason together, saith the Lord.

℞. I am * Thy servant, grant me understanding, O Lord. ℣. That I may know Thy testimonies. ℞. Grant me understanding, O Lord. ℣. Glory be to the Father and to the Son : and to the Holy Ghost. ℞. I am Thy servant, grant me understanding, O Lord.

℣. He shall deliver thee from the snare of the hunter.

℞. And from the noisome pestilence.

Nones.

Ant. The days of penitence are come to us : for the redemption of sins, and the salvation of souls.

Chapter. Is. i.

THOUGH your sins be as scarlet, they shall be as white as snow; though they be red like crimson, they shall be as wool.

℞. Seven times a day * do I praise Thee, O Lord. My God, cast me not away. ℣. I have gone astray like a sheep that is lost : O seek Thy servant, for I do not forget Thy commandments. ℞. My God, cast me not away. ℣. Glory be to the Father, and to the Son : and to the Holy Ghost. ℞. Seven times a day do I praise Thee, O Lord. My God, cast me not away.

℣. He shall defend thee under His wings.

℞. And thou shalt be safe under His feathers.

Vespers.

Chapter. Ezek. xviii.

THE soul that sinneth, it shall die. The son shall not bear the iniquity of the father, neither shall the father bear the iniquity of the son, saith the Lord Almighty.

℞. Bring my soul * out of prison: that I may give thanks unto Thy Name, O Lord. ℣. I had no place to flee unto, and no man cared for my soul. ℞. That I may give thanks unto Thy Name, O Lord. ℣. Glory be to the Father, and to the Son : and to the Holy Ghost. ℞. Bring my soul out of prison : that I may give thanks unto Thy Name, O Lord.

Hymn. *Ecce tempus idoneum,*
℣. and ℞., p. 141.

Ant. to Mag. But Jesus, passing through the midst of them : went His way.

[COLLECT.

LET Thy mercy lighten upon us, we beseech Thee, O Lord; that whereas we are in sore danger by reason of our sins, Thy care may rescue, Thy deliverance save us. Through.]

The Ferial Hours are thus said till Passion Sunday, except the daily changes of Collects and Antiphons to Benedictus *and* Magnificat; *and the Responsary at Vespers, which changes after the fourth Sunday.*

TUESDAY.

Lauds.

Ant. to Ben. If two of you shall agree on earth as touching anything that they shall ask : it shall be done for them of My Father, Which is in heaven, saith the Lord.

[COLLECT.

HEAR us, Almighty and gracious God, and mercifully bestow upon us the gift of healthful temperance. Through.]

Vespers.

Ant. to Mag. Where two or three are gathered together in My Name : there am I in the midst of them, saith the Lord.

[COLLECT.

DEFEND us, O Lord, by Thy protection, and evermore preserve us from all sin. Through.]

WEDNESDAY.

Lauds.

Ant. to Ben. Hear and understand the traditions : which the Lord hath given unto you.

[COLLECT.

GRANT us, we beseech Thee, O Lord, that taught by healthful fasts, and abstaining from noxious vices, we may more readily obtain Thy favour. Through.]

Vespers.

Ant. to Mag. To eat with unwashen hands : defileth not a man.

[COLLECT.

GRANT, we beseech Thee, Almighty God, that we who seek the grace of Thy protection, may be delivered from all evils, and serve Thee with a quiet mind. Through.]

THURSDAY.

Lauds.

Ant. to Ben. Labour not for the meat which perisheth : but for that meat which endureth unto everlasting life.

[COLLECT.

GRANT, we beseech Thee, Almighty God, that the holy devotion of our fasts may make us pure and well pleasing in the sight of Thy Divine Majesty. Through.]

Vespers.

Ant. to Mag. The Bread of God is He which cometh down from heaven : and giveth life unto the world.

[COLLECT.

LET Thy heavenly favour, we beseech Thee, O Lord, multiply Thy people that is under Thee, and make them ever to cleave to Thy commandments. Through.]

FRIDAY.

Lauds.

Ant. to Ben. Sir, I perceive that Thou art a Prophet : Our fathers worshipped in this mountain.

[COLLECT.]

LET Thy gracious favour, we beseech Thee, O Lord, accompany our fast, that, as outwardly we abstain from food, so inwardly we may fast from evil. Through.]

Vespers.

Ant. to Mag. True worshippers shall worship the Father : in spirit and in truth.

[COLLECT.]

GRANT, we beseech Thee, Almighty God, that we who trust in Thy protection, may by Thy help overcome all things adverse. Through.]

SATURDAY.
Lauds.

Ant. to Ben. Jesus stooped down and wrote on the ground : He that is without sin among you, let him first cast a stone at her.

[COLLECT.]

GRANT, we beseech Thee, Almighty God, that we, who afflict the flesh by abstinence from food, may, following after righteousness, fast from sin. Through.]

FOURTH SUNDAY IN LENT.
First Vespers.

CHAPTER. Gal. IV.

IT is written, that Abraham had two sons, the one by a bond-maid, the other by a free-woman. But he who was of the bond-woman was born after the flesh ; but he of the free-woman was by promise.

℟. Hear, O Israel,* the commandments of the Lord, and write them in thy heart as in a book : and I will give thee the land that floweth with milk and honey. ℣. Beware, therefore, and hearken unto My voice, and I will be an enemy unto thine enemies. ℟. And I will give thee the land that floweth with milk and honey. ℣. Glory be to the Father, and to the Son : and to the Holy Ghost. ℟. And I will give thee the land that floweth with milk and honey.

HYMN. *Ecce tempus idoneum,*
℣. and ℟., p. 141.

Ant. to Mag. Woman, hath no man condemned thee ? No man, Lord : neither do I condemn thee ; go, and sin no more.

COLLECT.

GRANT, we beseech Thee, Almighty God, that we, who for our evil deeds do worthily deserve to be punished, by the comfort of Thy grace may mercifully be relieved ; through our Lord and Saviour Jesus Christ. Amen.

Lauds.

℣. He shall deliver thee from the snare of the hunter.

℟. And from the noisome pestilence.

Ant. 1. Then shalt Thou be pleased with the sacrifice of righteousness : if Thou wilt turn Thy face from my sins.

Ant. 2. It is better to trust in the Lord : than to put any confidence in princes.

Ant. 3. God, even our own God, shall give us His blessing : God shall bless us.

Ant. 4. Thou art mighty, O Lord, to save us from the hand of death : deliver us, O our God.

Ant. 5. Kings of the earth and all people : praise the Name of the Lord.

CHAPTER. Gal. IV.

IT is written, that Abraham had two sons, the one by a bond-maid, the other by a free-woman. But he

who was of the bond-woman was born after the flesh; but he of the free-woman was by promise.
℟. Thanks be to God.

HYMN. *Jesu quadrigenariæ*,
℣. and ℟., p. 142.

Ant. to Ben. Jesus went over the sea of Galilee. And a great multitude followed Him: because they saw His miracles which He did. And the passover, a feast of the Jews, was nigh.

Prime.

Ant. And Jesus went up into a mountain, and there He sat with His disciples: And the passover, a feast of the Jews, was nigh.

Tierce.

Ant. And Jesus took the loaves, and when He had given thanks, He distributed to the disciples: and the disciples to them that were set down; and likewise of the fishes as much as they would.

CHAPTER. Gal. IV.

IT is written, that Abraham had two sons, the one by a bond-maid, the other by a free-woman. But he who was of the bond-woman was born after the flesh; but he of the free-woman was by promise.
℟. It is good for me. p. 142.

Sexts.

Ant. With five loaves and two fishes: the Lord fed men in number about five thousand.

CHAPTER. Gal. IV.

REJOICE, thou barren that bearest not; break forth and cry, thou that travailest not: for the desolate hath many more children than she which hath an husband.
℟. I am Thy servant. p. 142.

Nones.

Ant. The Lord fed five thousand men: with five loaves and two fishes.

CHAPTER. Gal. IV.

NOW we, brethren, as Isaac was, are the children of promise. But as then he that was born after the flesh persecuted him that was born after the Spirit; even so it is now. Nevertheless, what saith the Scripture? Cast out the bond-woman and her son.
℟. Seven times a day. p. 143.

Second Vespers.

CHAPTER. Gal. IV.

IT is written, that Abraham had two sons, the one by a bond-maid, the other by a free-woman. But he who was of the bond-woman was born after the flesh; but he of the free-woman was by promise.
℟. The Lord did lead them * with great power; He fed them with the increase of the fields; He made them to suck honey out of the rock, and oil out of the flinty rock. ℣. He fed them also with the finest wheat-flour: and with honey out of the stony rock did He satisfy them. ℟. He made them to suck honey out of the rock, and oil out of the flinty rock. ℣. Glory be to the Father, and to the Son: and to the Holy Ghost. ℟. The Lord did lead them with great power; He fed them with the increase of the fields; He made them to suck honey out of the rock, and oil out of the flinty rock.

HYMN. *Ecce tempus idoneum*,
℣. and ℟., p. 141.

Ant. to Mag. Then those men, when they had seen the miracle that Jesus did, said: This is of a truth that Prophet that should come into the world.

MONDAY.

Lauds.

Ant. to Ben. Take these things hence, saith the Lord : make not My Father's House an house of merchandise.

[COLLECT.

GRANT, we beseech Thee, Almighty God, that we, yearly observing holy seasons with true devotion, may please Thee both in body and soul. Through.]

Vespers.

CHAPTER. Ezek. XVIII.

THE soul that sinneth, it shall die. The son shall not bear the iniquity of the father, neither shall the father bear the iniquity of the son, saith the Lord Almighty.

℟. The Lord did lead them. p. 147.

This ℟. is used on Ferias till Passion Sunday.

Ant. to Mag. Destroy this temple, saith the Lord; and in three days I will raise it up : but He spake of the temple of His body.

[COLLECT.

WE beseech Thee, O Lord, mercifully hear our supplications, and grant that we, to whom Thou hast given an hearty desire to pray, may obtain the help of Thy protection. Through.]

TUESDAY.

Lauds.

Ant. to Ben. Ye seek to kill Me : a Man that hath told you the truth.

[COLLECT.

GRANT, we beseech Thee, O Lord, that the observance of the holy fasts may avail to the increase of holiness, and the continual assistance of Thy loving-kindness. Through.]

Vespers.

Ant. to Mag. I have done a work, and ye all marvel : because I have made a man every whit whole on the Sabbath-day.

[COLLECT.

HAVE mercy on Thy people, we beseech Thee, O Lord; and to them that labour under continual tribulations grant a little breathing-space. Through.]

WEDNESDAY.

Lauds.

Ant. to Ben. Master, who did sin, this man, or his parents, that he was born blind ? : Jesus answered, Neither hath this man sinned, nor his parents; but that the works of God should be made manifest in him.

[COLLECT.

GOD, Who by means of fasting dost reward the righteous, and pardon the sinful, have mercy on Thy suppliants, and let the confession of our guilt obtain remission of our sins. Through.]

Vespers.

Ant. to Mag. A Man that is called Jesus put clay upon mine eyes : and I washed, and do see.

[COLLECT.

LET Thy merciful ears, O Lord, be open to the prayers of Thy humble servants, and that they may obtain their petitions, make them to ask such things as shall please Thee. Through.]

THURSDAY.

Lauds.

Ant. to Ben. The Father loveth the Son : and sheweth Him all things that Himself doeth.

[COLLECT.]

GRANT, we beseech Thee, Almighty God, that they who are chastened by fasting may be gladdened by holy fervour, so that the love of earthly things being tempered, they may more readily attain to things heavenly. Through.]

Vespers.

Ant. to Mag. As the Father raiseth up the dead and quickeneth them: even so the Son quickeneth whom He will.

[COLLECT.]

O GOD, the Teacher and Governour of Thy people, cast out those sins whereby they are assaulted; that they may ever be well-pleasing in Thy sight, and secure under Thy protection. Through.]

FRIDAY.
Lauds.

Ant. to Ben. Our friend Lazarus sleepeth: but I go, that I may awake him out of sleep.

[COLLECT.]

O GOD, Who dost renew the world by ineffable Sacraments, grant, we beseech Thee, that they may avail to the eternal welfare of Thy Church, and that in this present life it be not left destitute of assistance. Through.]

Vespers.

Ant. to Mag. Lord, if Thou hadst been here, Lazarus had not died: by this time he stinketh, for he hath been dead four days.

[COLLECT.]

GRANT, we beseech Thee, Almighty God, that we, who, owning our weakness, put our trust in Thy strength, may ever rejoice in Thy protection. Through.]

SATURDAY.
Lauds.

Ant. to Ben. I am the Light of the world: he that followeth Me shall not walk in darkness, but shall have the light of life, saith the Lord.

[COLLECT.]

WE beseech Thee, O Lord, by Thy grace, let our devout affections bring forth fruit, for then shall our fasts profit us, when they are pleasing in the eyes of Thy mercy. Through.]

PASSION SUNDAY.
First Vespers.

CHAPTER. Lament. III.

O LORD, Thou hast pleaded the causes of my soul; Thou hast redeemed my life.

℟. The ungodly * compassed me about, and scourged me without a cause : but Thou, O Lord, my Defender, avenge Thou me. ℣. For trouble is hard at hand, and there is none to help me. ℟. But Thou, O Lord, my Defender, avenge Thou me. *Here is not said* Glory be, *etc. but the* ℟. *is repeated.* The ungodly compassed me about, and scourged me without a cause : * but Thou, O Lord, my Defender, avenge Thou me.

The Reader repeats this ℟. *as far as the * alone : the Choir then joins in, and finishes it. And this order is observed in all* ℟℟. *in Passion-tide.*

At the verse in the following Hymn, O Cross, our one reliance, hail : *the Choir turns to the Altar, and so continues till the beginning of* Magnificat.

HYMN. *Vexilla Regis prodeunt.*

THE Royal Banners forward go;
The Cross shines forth in mystic glow;
Where He in flesh, our flesh Who made,
Our sentence bore, our ransom paid :

Where deep, for us the spear was dy'd,
Life's torrent rushing from His side,
To wash us in that precious flood
Where mingled Water flow'd, and Blood.

Fulfill'd is all that David told
In true prophetic song of old;
Amidst the nations, God, saith he,
Hath reign'd and triumph'd from the Tree.

O Tree of beauty, Tree of light!
O Tree with royal purple dight!
Elect on whose triumphal breast
Those holy limbs should find their rest:

On whose dear arms, so widely flung,
The weight of this world's ransom hung:
The price of human kind to pay,
And spoil the spoiler of his prey:

O Cross, our one reliance, hail!
This holy Passion-tide avail
To give fresh merit to the saint,
And pardon to the penitent.

To Thee, eternal Three in One,
Let homage meet by all be done:
Whom by the Cross Thou dost restore,
Preserve and govern evermore! Amen.

℣. They gave me gall to eat.
℟. And when I was thirsty they gave me vinegar to drink.

This Hymn, ℣. and ℟. are said at Vespers daily, till Wednesday in Holy Week inclusive.

Ant. to Mag. I am One that bear witness of Myself: and the Father that sent Me beareth witness of Me.

Collect.

WE beseech Thee, Almighty God, mercifully to look upon Thy people; that by Thy great goodness they may be governed and preserved evermore, both in body and soul; through Jesus Christ our Lord. Amen.

Compline.

Ant. to Psalms. Have mercy upon me: and hearken unto my prayer.

Chapter. Jer. xiv.

THOU, O Lord, art in the midst of us, and we are called by Thy Name; leave us not, O our God. ℟. Into Thy hands: *the Choir continue:* O Lord, I commend my spirit. ℣. For Thou hast redeemed me, O Lord, Thou God of Truth. ℟. I commend my spirit. ℟. Into Thy hands, * O Lord, I commend my spirit.

Hymn. *Cultor Dei memento.*

SERVANT of Christ; remember
The font's Baptismal dew;
Remember thy renewal
In Confirmation too.

When at the call of slumber
Thou seekest needful rest,
Let then the Cross's symbol
Sign both Thy heart and breast.

The Cross repels all evil,
The Cross makes darkness flee,
A mind by this sign hallowed,
Unstable cannot be.

Away, ye wandering phantoms,
Away, all evil dreams,
Away, thou arch deceiver,
With all thy subtle schemes.

And thou, O crafty serpent,
Who seek'st by many an art,
And many a guileful winding,
To vex the quiet heart:

Depart, for Christ is present;
Since Christ is here, give place;
And let the sign thou ownest
Thy ghostly legions chase.

And though awhile the body
In sleep may lie reclin'd,
Yet Christ, in very slumber,
Shall fill the Christian mind.

All laud to God the Father,
All laud to God the Son;
To God the Holy Spirit
Be equal honour done. Amen.

℣. Keep us, O Lord.
℟. As the apple of an eye, hide us under the shadow of Thy wings.

Ant. to Nunc Dim. O King, glorious among Thy Saints, Who art ever to be praised, and yet art ineffable; Thou, Lord, art in the midst of us, and we are called by Thy Name; leave us not, O our God: and in the day of judgment vouchsafe to number us with Thy Saints, O blessed King. ℣. O blessed King, govern Thy servants in the right way. ℟. With Thy Saints, O blessed King.

℣. By holy fasts to amend our sinful lives.
℟. O blessed King.
℣. And duly keep Thy Paschal Feast.
℟. With Thy Saints, O blessed King.

Compline is said thus till Maundy Thursday, except that the ℣℣. and ℟℟: after the Ant. are not said on Ferias.

Petitions as p. 69.

Lauds.

℣. Draw nigh unto my soul and save it.
℟. O deliver me because of mine enemies.

This ℣. and ℟. is said daily at Lauds till Wednesday in Holy Week inclusive.

Ant. 1. O Lord, behold my affliction : for the enemy hath magnified himself.
Ant. 2. I called upon the Lord in trouble : and the Lord heard me at large.
Ant. 3. O Lord, Thou hast pleaded the causes of my soul : Thou hast redeemed my life, O Lord my God.
Ant. 4. O my people, what have I done unto thee? and wherein have I wearied thee? : testify against me.
Ant. 5. Shall evil be recompensed for good? : for they have digged a pit for my soul.

CHAPTER. Heb. IX.

CHRIST being come an High-Priest of good things to come, by a greater and more perfect tabernacle, not made with hands, that is to say, not of this building; neither by the blood of goats and calves, but by His own blood He entered in once into the holy place, having obtained eternal redemption for us.
℟. Thanks be to God.

HYMN. *Lustra sex qui jam peracta.*

THIRTY years among us dwelling,
　His appointed time fulfill'd,
Born for this, He meets His Passion,
　For that this He freely will'd :
On the Cross the Lamb is lifted,
　Where His life-blood shall be spill'd.

He endur'd the nails, the spitting,
　Vinegar, and spear, and reed ;
From that holy Body broken
　Blood and water forth proceed :
Earth, and stars, and sky, and ocean,
　By that flood from stain are freed.

Faithful Cross! above all other,
　One and only noble Tree ;
None in foliage, none in blossom,
　None in fruit thy peers may be ;
Sweetest wood, and sweetest iron!
　Sweetest weight is hung on thee.

Bend thy boughs, O Tree of glory!
　Thy relaxing sinews bend
For awhile the ancient rigour,
　That Thy birth bestow'd, suspend :
And the King of Heavenly beauty
　On thy bosom gently tend.

Thou alone wast counted worthy,
　This world's ransom to uphold ;
For a shipwreck'd race preparing
　Harbour, like the ark of old :
With the sacred Blood anointed
　From the smitten Lamb that roll'd.

To the Trinity be glory
　Everlasting, as is meet ;
Equal to the Father, equal
　To the Son and Paraclete ;
Trinal Unity, Whose praises
　All created things repeat. Amen.

℣. Deliver me from mine enemies, O God.
℟. Defend me from them that rise up against me.

Ant. to Ben. Which of you convinceth Me of sin? and if I say the truth, why do ye not believe Me? : He that is of God heareth God's words ; ye therefore hear them not, because ye are not of God.

Collect as at First Vespers.

Prime.

Ant. I have not a devil : but I honour My Father, saith the Lord.

Till Wednesday in Holy Week, instead of ℟. to the Chapter at Prime, is said,

℣. O Lord, arise, help us.

℞. And deliver us for Thy mercy's sake.

Tierce.

Ant. I seek not Mine own glory: there is One that seeketh and judgeth.

Chapter. Heb. ix.

CHRIST being come an High-Priest of good things to come, by a greater and more perfect tabernacle, not made with hands, that is to say, not of this building; neither by the blood of goats and calves, but by His own blood He entered in once into the holy place, having obtained eternal redemption for us.

℞. Deliver * my soul, O God, from the sword, and my darling from the power of the dog. ℣. Deliver me, O Lord, from the evil man: and preserve me from the wicked man. ℞. And my darling from the power of the dog. ℞. Deliver my soul from the sword * my darling from the power of the dog.

℣. Save me from the lion's mouth. ℞. And my lowliness from the horns of the unicorns.

Sexts.

Ant. Verily, verily, I say unto you: If a man keep My saying, he shall never see death.

Chapter. Heb. ix.

FOR if the blood of bulls and of goats, and the ashes of an heifer sprinkling the unclean, sanctifieth to the purifying of the flesh; how much more shall the blood of Christ, Who, through the eternal Spirit, offered Himself without spot to God, purge your conscience from dead works to serve the living God?

℞. Save me * from the lion's mouth: and my lowliness from the horns of the unicorns. ℣. Deliver my soul from the sword, my darling from the power of the dog. ℞. And my lowliness from the horns of the unicorns. ℞. Save me from the lion's mouth,* and my lowliness from the horns of the unicorns.

℣. O shut not up my soul with the sinners.

℞. Nor my life with the bloodthirsty.

Nones.

Ant. Your father Abraham rejoiced to see My day: and he saw it, and was glad.

Chapter. Heb. ix.

AND for this cause He is the Mediator of the new testament, that by means of death, for the redemption of the transgressions that were under the first testament, they which are called might receive the promise of eternal inheritance.

℞. Princes * have persecuted me without a cause, but my heart standeth in awe of Thy word. I am glad of Thy word. ℣. As one that findeth great spoils. ℞. I am glad of Thy word. ℞. Princes have persecuted me without a cause, but my heart standeth in awe of Thy word.* I am glad of Thy word.

℣. Deliver me, O Lord, from the evil man.

℞. And preserve me from the wicked man.

Second Vespers.

Chapter. Heb. ix.

CHRIST being come an High Priest of good things to come, by a greater and more perfect tabernacle, not made with hands, that is to say, not of this building; neither by the blood of goats and calves, but by His own blood He entered in once into the holy place, having obtained eternal redemption for us.

℞. How long * shall mine enemies triumph over me? consider and hear me, O Lord my God. ℣. For if I be cast down, they that trouble me will rejoice at it. But I have hoped in Thy mercy. ℞. Consider and hear me, O Lord my God. ℞. How long shall mine enemies triumph over me?* consider and hear me, O Lord my God.

HYMN. *Vexilla Regis prodeunt*, ℣. and ℞., p. 149.

Ant. to Mag. Verily, verily, I say unto you, Before Abraham was, I am: Then the Jews took up stones to cast at Jesus; but Jesus hid Himself and went out of the temple.

MONDAY.
Lauds.

℣. Draw nigh unto my soul, and save it.
℞. O deliver me, because of mine enemies.

Ants. and Psalms of the Feria.

CHAPTER. Jer. XI.

THE Lord hath given me knowledge of it, and I know it: then Thou shewedst me their doings. But I was like a lamb or an ox that is brought to the slaughter.
℞. Thanks be to God.

HYMN. *Lustra sex qui jam peracta*, ℣. and ℞., p. 151.

Ant. to Ben. In the last day, that great day of the feast, Jesus stood and cried, saying: If any man thirst, let him come unto Me and drink.

[COLLECT.

SANCTIFY, we beseech Thee, O Lord, our fasts, and mercifully grant us forgiveness of all our sins. Through.]

Prime.

Ant. to Psalms. The ungodly are minded to do me some mischief: and my heart is disquieted within me.

Tierce.

Ant. O Lord, Thou hast pleaded the causes of my soul: Thou hast redeemed my life.

CHAPTER. Is. L.

I HID not my face from shame and spitting. For the Lord God will help me: therefore shall I not be confounded.
℞. Deliver my soul. p. 152.

Sexts.

Ant. O my people, what have I done unto thee?: and wherein have I wearied thee? testify against me.

CHAPTER. Is. L.

FOR the Lord God will help me; therefore shall I not be confounded: therefore have I set my face like a flint, and I know that I shall not be ashamed.
℞. Save me. p. 152.

Nones.

Ant. Shall evil be recompensed for good?: for they have digged a pit for my soul.

CHAPTER. Jer. XVII.

LET them be confounded that persecute me, but let not me be confounded; let them be dismayed, but let not me be dismayed: bring upon them the day of evil, and destroy them with double destruction, O Lord our God.
℞. Princes have persecuted. p. 152.

Vespers.

Ants. and Psalms of the Feria.

CHAPTER. Lament. III.

O LORD, Thou hast pleaded the causes of my soul: Thou hast redeemed my life.

℟. How long * shall mine enemies triumph over me? consider and hear me, O Lord my God. ℣. For if I be cast down, they that trouble me will rejoice at it. But I have hoped in Thy mercy. ℟. Consider and hear me, O Lord my God. ℟. How long shall mine enemies triumph over me? * consider and hear me, O Lord, my God.

HYMN. *Vexilla Regis prodeunt,* ℣. and ℟., p. 149.

Ant. to Mag. If any man thirst, let him come unto Me, and drink: and out of his belly shall flow rivers of living water.

[COLLECT.]

GRANT, we beseech Thee, O Lord, to Thy people the spirit of truth and peace; that with all their heart they may acknowledge Thee, and may reverently fulfil those things which are pleasing unto Thee. Through.]

The Hours are said thus throughout the week, except the changes of Collects, and of Ants. to Benedictus and Magnificat.

TUESDAY.
Lauds.

Ant. to Ben. My time is not yet come: but your time is alway ready.

[COLLECT.]

LET our fasts, we beseech Thee, O Lord, be pleasing in Thy sight, that being cleansed thereby, we may become worthy of Thy favour: and may attain to everlasting salvation. Through.]

Vespers.

Ant. to Mag. Go ye up unto this feast: I go not up yet, for My time is not yet full come.

[COLLECT.]

GRANT, we beseech Thee, O Lord, that the company of Thy servants may persevere in the performance of Thy will, so that, both in multitude and holiness, Thy kingdom may increase upon the earth in our days. Through.]

WEDNESDAY.
Lauds.

Ant. to Ben. My sheep hear My voice: and I know them.

[COLLECT.]

O GOD, we beseech Thee, as Thou hast hallowed this fast, so in Thy mercy lighten the hearts of Thy faithful people; and as Thou hast given them an hearty desire to pray, so graciously hear their supplications. Through.]

Vespers.

Ant. to Mag. Many good works have I shewed you: for which of these works do ye stone Me.

[COLLECT.]

O LORD, in Whom is all our hope, let Thy mercy lighten upon Thy suppliant servants, and of Thy heavenly bounty grant them to ask such things as be right, and also to obtain that which they desire. Through.]

THURSDAY.
Lauds.

Ant. to Ben. Why trouble ye the woman?: for she hath wrought a good work upon Me.

[COLLECT.]

GRANT, we beseech Thee, Almighty God, that the dignity of human nature being wounded by excess, may be restored by healthful abstinence. Through.]

Vespers.

Ant. to Mag. In that she hath

poured this ointment on My body: she did it for My burial.

[COLLECT.]

BE favourable, we beseech Thee, O Lord, to Thy people, so that, eschewing those things which are displeasing unto Thee, they may be filled more exceedingly with the delights which pertain to Thy commandments. Through.]

FRIDAY.

Lauds.

Ant. to Ben. Now the feast-day drew nigh, and the chief priests and scribes sought how they might kill Jesus: but they feared the people.

[COLLECT.]

WE beseech Thee, O Lord, mercifully to pour the help of Thy grace into our hearts; that, subduing our sins by voluntary chastening, we may choose suffering in this life rather than eternal punishment in the world to come. Through.]

Vespers.

Ant. to Mag. The chief priests and the scribes sought how they might take Him by craft, and put Him to death: but they said, Not on the feast-day, lest there be an uproar of the people.

[COLLECT.]

GRANT us, we beseech Thee, O Lord, pardon of sins and increase of piety; and, that Thou mayest multiply Thy gifts upon us, make us more ready to the fulfilment of Thy will. Through.]

SATURDAY.

Lauds.

Ant. to Ben. With desire have I desired: to eat this Passover with you before I suffer.

[COLLECT.]

LET Thy consecrated people, O Lord, increase in the spirit of devotion; that, being exercised in holy acts, we may become so much the more pleasing to Thy majesty, and be filled the more abundantly with Thy gifts. Through.]

PALM SUNDAY.

First Vespers.

Ants. and Psalms as in the Psalter.

CHAPTER. Phil. ii.

LET this mind be in you, which was also in Christ Jesus: Who, being in the form of God, thought it not robbery to be equal with God: but made Himself of no reputation, and took upon Him the form of a servant.

R⁊. The ungodly. p. 149.

HYMN. *Vexilla Regis prodeunt*, V̌. and R⁊., p. 149.

Ant. to Mag. And now, O Father, glorify Thou Me with Thine own self: with the glory which I had with Thee before the world was.

COLLECT.

ALMIGHTY and everlasting God, Who, of Thy tender love towards mankind, hast sent Thy Son, our Saviour Jesus Christ, to take upon Him our flesh, and to suffer death upon the Cross, that all mankind should follow the example of His great humility; mercifully grant, that we may both follow the example of His patience, and also be made partakers of His resurrection; through the same Jesus Christ our Lord. Amen.

Lauds.

V̌. Draw nigh unto my soul, and save it.

℟. O deliver me because of mine enemies.

Ant. 1. The Lord God will help me : therefore shall I not be confounded.

Ant. 2. They kept me in on every side, they kept me in, I say, on every side : but in the Name of the Lord will I destroy them.

Ant. 3. Give sentence with me, O God : for Thou, Lord, art mighty.

Ant. 4. Let them be confounded that persecute me : but let not me be confounded, O Lord God.

Ant. 5. With angels and children may the faithful be found : singing to the Conqueror of death, Hosanna in the highest.

CHAPTER. Phil. II.

LET this mind be in you, which was also in Christ Jesus : Who, being in the form of God, thought it not robbery to be equal with God; but made Himself of no reputation, and took upon Him the form of a servant.

℟. Thanks be to God.

HYMN. *Lustra sex qui jam peracta,* ℣. and ℟., p. 151.

Ant. to Ben. And the great multitude that came together to the feast day, cried unto the Lord : Blessed is He that cometh in the Name of the Lord; Hosanna in the highest.

Collect as at Vespers.

Prime.

Ant. to Psalms. Hosanna to the Son of David. Blessed is the King of Israel : that cometh in the Name of the Lord; Hosanna in the highest.

Tierce.

Ant. The children of the Hebrews cast their garments in the way, and cried, saying : Hosanna to the Son of David; blessed is He that cometh in the Name of the Lord.

CHAPTER. Phil. II.

LET this mind be in you, which was also in Christ Jesus : Who, being in the form of God, thought it not robbery to be equal with God; but made Himself of no reputation, and took upon Him the form of a servant.

℟. He hath put * my brethren far from me, and mine acquaintance are verily estranged from me. ℣. My friends and my neighbours. ℟. And mine acquaintance, are verily estranged from me. ℟. He hath put my brethren far from me, * and mine acquaintance are verily estranged from me.

℣. Deliver my soul from the sword.

℟. My darling from the power of the dog.

Sexts.

Ant. The children of the Hebrews, bearing palms, went forth to meet the Lord, crying out and saying : Hosanna in the highest.

CHAPTER. Phil. II.

HE humbled Himself, and became obedient unto death, even the death of the Cross.

℟. Give heed * to me, O Lord, and hearken to the voice of them that contend with me : Shall evil be recompensed for good? for they have digged a pit for my soul. ℣. Remember that I stood before Thee to speak good for them, and to turn away Thy wrath from them. ℟. Shall evil be recompensed for good? for they have digged a pit for my soul. ℟. Give heed to me, O Lord, and hearken to the voice of them that contend with me : * Shall evil be recompensed for good? for they have digged a pit for my soul.

MONDAY IN HOLY WEEK.

℣. Save me from the lion's mouth. ℟. And my lowliness from the horns of the unicorns.

Nones.

Ant. All men greatly praise Thy Name and say, Blessed is He that cometh in the Name of the Lord: Hosanna in the highest.

CHAPTER. Phil. II.

WHEREFORE God also hath highly exalted Him, and given Him a Name which is above every name; that at the Name of Jesus every knee should bow, of things in heaven, and things in earth, and things under the earth.

℟. Save me, * O God, for the waters are come in, even unto my soul. And hide not Thy face from Thy servant: for I am in trouble. Hear me, O my God. ℣. Draw nigh unto my soul, and save it: O deliver me because of mine enemies. ℟. For I am in trouble. Hear me, O my God. ℟. Save me, O God, for the waters are come in, even unto my soul. And hide not Thy face from Thy servant: * for I am in trouble. Hear me, O my God.

℣. O shut not up my soul with the sinners. ℟. Nor my life with the blood-thirsty.

Second Vespers.

Ants. and Psalms as in the Psalter.

CHAPTER. Phil. II.

LET this mind be in you, which was also in Christ Jesus: Who, being in the form of God, thought it not robbery to be equal with God; but made Himself of no reputation, and took upon Him the form of a servant.

℟. The chief priests * consulted that they might put Lazarus also to death: because that by reason of him many of the Jews went away, and believed on Jesus. ℣. The people therefore that was with Him when He called Lazarus out of his grave, and raised him from the dead, bare record. ℟. Because that by reason of him many of the Jews went away, and believed on Jesus. ℟. The chief priests consulted that they might put Lazarus also to death: * because that by reason of him many of the Jews went away, and believed on Jesus.

HYMN. *Vexilla Regis prodeunt*, ℣. and ℟., p. 149.

Ant. to Mag. Multitudes go forth with palms and flowers to meet the Redeemer, and render due homage to the Son of God triumphing gloriously: The nations utter their voice and to the praise of Christ re-echoes through the sky, Hosanna.

Collect as at First Vespers.

MONDAY IN HOLY WEEK.

Lauds.

Psalms of the Feria.

Ant. 1. I hid not my face: from shame and spitting.

Ant. 2. Awake, O sword: against them that disperse the flock.

Ant. 3. So they weighed for my price thirty pieces of silver: that I was prised at of them.

Ant. 4. Waters flowed over mine head: then I said, I am cut off. I will call upon Thy Name, O Lord.

Ant. 5. Behold, O Lord, the lips of them that rise up against me: and their devices.

CHAPTER. Jer. XI.

THE Lord hath given me knowledge of it and I know it: then Thou shewedst me their doings. I was like a lamb or an ox that is brought to the slaughter.

℟. Thanks be to God.

HYMN. *Lustra sex qui jam peracta*, ℣. and ℟., p. 151.

Ant. to Ben. Thou couldest have no power at all against Me : except it were given thee from above.

[COLLECT.]

GRANT, we beseech Thee, Almighty God, that whereas by reason of our infirmity we faint in adversity, the Passion of Thine Only-begotten Son may plead for us and refresh us. Through the same.]

Prime.

Ant. The ungodly are minded to do me some mischief : and my heart is disquieted within me.

Tierce.

Ant. O Lord, Thou hast pleaded the causes of my soul : Thou hast redeemed my life.

CHAPTER. Is. L.

I GAVE my back to the smiters, and my cheeks to them that plucked off the hair : I hid not my face from shame and spitting. For the Lord God will help me; therefore shall I not be confounded.

℟. He hath put. p. 156.

Sexts.

Ant. O my people, what have I done unto Thee? : and wherein have I wearied thee? testify against me.

CHAPTER. Is. L.

FOR the Lord God will help me; therefore shall I not be confounded : therefore have I set my face like a flint, and I know that I shall not be ashamed.

℟. Give heed. p. 156.

Nones.

Ant. Shall evil be recompensed for good : for they have digged a pit for my soul.

CHAPTER. Jer. XVII.

LET them be confounded that persecute me, but let not me be confounded ; let them be dismayed, but let not me be dismayed : bring upon them the day of evil, and destroy them with double destruction.

℟. Save me. p. 157.

Vespers.

Ants. and Psalms of the Feria.

CHAPTER. Lament. III.

O LORD, Thou hast pleaded the causes of my soul : Thou hast redeemed my life.

℟. The chief priests. p. 157.

HYMN. *Vexilla Regis prodeunt*, ℣. and ℟., p. 149.

Ant. to Mag. I have power to lay down My life : and I have power to take it again.

[COLLECT.]

HELP us, O God of our salvation, and whereas Thou hast vouchsafed to restore us by Thy marvellous bounty, grant us to come joyfully to the commemoration of the same. Through.]

The Hours are thus said till Wednesday inclusive, Collects and Antiphons being changed as usual.

TUESDAY IN HOLY WEEK.
Lauds.

Psalms of the Feria.

Ant. 1. Hide not Thy face from me, for I am in trouble : O haste Thee, and hear me.

Ant. 2. Defend my cause against

the ungodly people : O deliver me from the deceitful and wicked man.

Ant. 3. I cried by reason of mine affliction to the Lord : and He heard me out of the belly of hell.

Ant. 4. O Lord, I am oppressed ; undertake for me : for I know not what I shall say to mine enemies.

Ant. 5. The wicked said, Let us oppress the poor righteous man : because he is clean contrary to our doings.

Ant. to Ben. No man taketh My life from Me : but I lay down My life, that I may take it again.

[COLLECT.

ALMIGHTY, everlasting God, grant us so to celebrate the mysteries of the Lord's Passion, that we may attain to receive mercy. Through the same.]

Vespers.

Ant. to Mag. I sat daily with you teaching in the temple, and ye laid no hold on Me : and now, being scourged, ye lead Me to be crucified.

[COLLECT.

LET Thy mercy, O Lord, cleanse us from all corruption of our old nature, and enable us to walk in newness of life. Through.]

WEDNESDAY IN HOLY WEEK.
Lauds.

Psalms of the Feria.

Ant. 1. Deliver me from blood-guiltiness, O Lord, Thou that art the God of my health : and my tongue shall sing of Thy righteousness.

Ant. 2. I have suffered shame and terror at their hands : but the Lord is with me as a mighty Man of war.

Ant. 3. These also that seek the hurt of my soul : they shall go under the earth.

Ant. 4. All mine enemies heard of my trouble : they have been made glad, for it was Thy doing.

Ant. 5. Bind, O Lord, the nations of the heathen in chains : and their kings with fetters.

Ant. to Ben. Simon, sleepest thou : couldest thou not watch with Me one hour?

[COLLECT.

GRANT, we beseech Thee, Almighty God, that we, who by reason of our trespasses, are continually afflicted by the Passion of Thine Only-begotten Son, may be delivered. Who liveth.]

Vespers.

CHAPTER. Is. LIII.

ALL we like sheep have gone astray; we have turned every one to his own way; and the Lord hath laid on Him the iniquity of us all. He was oppressed, and He was afflicted, yet He opened not His mouth.

℟. The ungodly. p. 149.

Ant. to Mag. I sat daily with you teaching in the temple, and ye laid no hold on Me : and now, being scourged, ye lead Me to be crucified.

COLLECT.

ALMIGHTY God, we beseech Thee graciously to behold this Thy family, for which our Lord Jesus Christ was contented to be betrayed, and given up into the hands of wicked men, and to suffer death upon the Cross; Who now liveth and reigneth with Thee and the Holy Ghost, ever One God, world without end. Amen.

At these Vespers no Petitions are said, neither is the Altar censed, nor are any Memorials said, except when a Double Feast has been kept on this day.

Compline is said as p. 150, *the Petitions being said, as on Sundays, without* Psalm LI. *From this day till the First Sunday after Trinity inclusive,* Psalm CXXIII. *is not said after Compline.*

MAUNDY THURSDAY.
Lauds.
Psalms of the Feria.

The ℣. and ℟. are omitted, and the first Antiphon is begun at once, and so on the two nights following. The Psalms are said without Glory be, etc., from this time till the First Vespers of Easter.

Ant. 1. Thou wilt be justified in Thy saying, O Lord: and clear when Thou art judged.

Ant. 2. The Lord was brought as a lamb to the slaughter : and He opened not His mouth.

Ant. 3. Mine heart within me is broken : all my bones shake.

Ant. 4. Thou art made strong in Thine own strength : and in Thy holy comfort, O Lord.

Ant. 5. Because He so willed it He was made an offering : and His own Self bare our sins.

Ant. to Ben. Now he that betrayed Him gave them a sign, saying : Whomsoever I shall kiss, that same is He, hold Him fast.

After the repetition of the Ant.:

Lord, have mercy.
Lord, have mercy.
Lord, have mercy.

℟. Lord, have mercy : *The Choir continue :* Christ the Lord became obedient unto death.

Christ, have mercy.

℣. Who didst come to suffer for us.

Christ, have mercy.

℣. Who stretching forth Thy hands upon the Cross didst draw all men unto Thee.

Christ, have mercy.

℣. Who by Thy prophet didst say, O death I will be thy death.

℟. Lord, have mercy, *The Choir continue :* Christ the Lord became obedient unto death.

Christ, have mercy.
Christ, have mercy.
Christ, have mercy.

℟. Lord, have mercy upon us, *The Choir continue :* Christ the Lord became obedient unto death.

℣. Even the death of the Cross.

All kneel at once and say the Lord's Prayer in silence, after which Miserere, *Psalm* LI., *shall be said in a low voice, without* Glory be, etc., *and followed immediately by the Collect as at previous Vespers, without* The Lord be with you, *but with* Let us pray. *Nor is anything further said after the Collect, but all rise.*

The Petitions, etc. are not said from henceforth till after Trinity. No Memorials till after Low Sunday.

At Prime, and at the other Hours on this and the two days following, the ℣℣., *℟℟., and Hymns are omitted at the beginning of Office, and immediately after the Lord's Prayer is begun the Ant. to Psalms.*

Prime.

Ant. Christ became obedient unto death for us : even the death of the Cross.

Deus in nomine tuo, Psalm LIV.

Beati immaculati and *Retribue servo tuo,* Psalm CXIX.

℣. The Lord be with you.
℟. And with thy spirit.
Let us pray.

Collect as at Wednesday Vespers.

℣. The Lord be with you.
℟. And with thy spirit.
℣. Bless we the Lord.
℟. Thanks be to God.

Prime thus ends, and Tierce, Sexts, and Nones are said in like manner with their own Psalms.

Chapter is said on this day ending after the prayer, May the souls, etc., *with* The Lord be with you, *and* Bless we

GOOD FRIDAY.

the Lord ; *and so Chapter ends daily till Low Sunday, except on Good Friday and Easter Eve, when it is wholly omitted.*

Vespers.

On this day Vespers shall be sung festively in Choir ; but without the ℣℣. and ℟℟. at the commencement of Office, and without Glory be, etc.

Ant. 1. I will receive the cup of salvation : and call upon the Name of the Lord.

Credidi. Psalm CXVI. 10. p. 52.

Ant. 2. I labour for peace, but when I speak unto them thereof : they make them ready to battle.

Ad Dominum. Psalm CXX. p. 52.

Ant. 3. Preserve me from the wicked man : O Lord.

Eripe me Domine. Psalm CXL. p. 62.

Ant. 4. Keep me from the snare that they have laid for me : and from the traps of the wicked doers.

Domine clamavi. Psalm CXLI. p. 62.

Ant. 5. I looked also upon my right hand : and saw there was no man that would know me.

Voce mea. Psalm CXLII. p. 62.

Ant. to Mag. As they were eating, Jesus took bread : and blessed it, and brake it, and gave it to the disciples.

℣. The Lord be with you.
℟. And with thy spirit.

Collect as on Wednesday.

[*Or,*

WE beseech Thee, O Lord our God, that we who are refreshed with the life-giving Food may, in Thy gift of immortality, attain that which now in the time of our mortal life we earnestly desire. Through.]

℣. The Lord be with you.
℟. And with thy spirit.
℣. Bless we the Lord.
℟. Thanks be to God.

Compline.

Ant. Christ became obedient unto death for us : even the death of the Cross.

Cum invocarem. Psalm IV.
In te, Domine. Psalm XXXI.
Ecce nunc. Psalm CXXXIV.
Nunc Dimittis.

(*All without* Glory be, *etc., and all said under one Ant.*)

℣. The Lord be with you.
℟. And with thy spirit.

Let us pray.

Collect as at Wednesday Vespers.

℣. The Lord be with you.
℟. And with thy spirit.
℣. Bless we the Lord.
℟. Thanks be to God.

GOOD FRIDAY.
Lauds.

Psalms of the Feria.

Ant. 1. God spared not His own Son : but delivered Him up for us all.

Ant. 2. My spirit is vexed within me : and my heart within me is desolate.

Ant. 3. Thief answered to thief, saying, we receive the due reward of our deeds : but what hath this Man done? Lord, remember me when Thou comest into Thy kingdom.

Ant. 4. When my soul is sore troubled : Thou wilt remember mercy, O Lord.

Ant. 5. Lord, remember me : when Thou comest into Thy kingdom.

Ant. to Ben. And they set up over His head, His accusation written : Jesus of Nazareth, the King of the Jews.

The rest as at Lauds on Maundy Thursday, except that in place of the three ℣℣. there given after the Benedictus *the three following are said with Kyries and ℟℟. as before.*

℣. Gentle Lamb to Whom the wolf gave poisonous kisses.
℣. Life suffers death on the Tree; but death and hell are despoiled.
℣. Thou hast suffered the bonds Thyself; and so hast snatched us from the bonds of death.

The Collect at every Hour ends without Who now liveth, etc.

Prime, Tierce, Sexts, and Nones are said as on Maundy Thursday, except that all kneel till the middle of the first Ant. and after its repetition at the end of the Psalms.

After the repetition of the Ant. is said, all kneeling, the Lord's Prayer *and the Collect as at Lauds, without* The Lord be with you, *or,* Let us pray. *And so each Office ends.*

Chapter is not said on this and the following day.

Vespers.

Vespers are not sung on this day, but are said in a low voice before the Altar.

All is as on Maundy Thursday, till

Ant. to Mag. Now there stood by the Cross of Jesus : His Mother.

After the repetition of the Ant. to Magnificat is said the Lord's Prayer *and* Psalm LI., Miserere, *without* Glory be, *etc. Then the Priest says the Collect audibly, as at the other Hours, and so Vespers end.*

Compline.

All as on Maundy Thursday.

After the repetition of the Antiphon is said, all kneeling, the Lord's Prayer, *and* Psalm LI., Miserere, *without* Glory be, *etc.*

Collect as at Wednesday Vespers.

All the ℣℣. *and* ℞℞. *are omitted.*

EASTER EVE.
Lauds.

Psalms of the Feria, except the Canticle, which is the Song of Hezekiah, Ego dixi, *p. 13.*

Ant. 1. O death, I will be thy death : O grave, I will be thy destruction.
Ant. 2. Give heed, all ye people : and behold my sorrow.
Ant. 3. All ye that pass by, behold and see : if there be any sorrow like unto my sorrow.
Ant. 4. From the gates of hell : deliver my soul, O Lord.
Ant. 5. They shall mourn for Him, as one mourneth for his only son : because the innocent Lord is slain.
Ant. to Ben. Women sitting by the sepulchre : mourned and wept for the Lord.

The rest as at Lauds on Maundy Thursday, except the

COLLECT. (1661.)

GRANT, O Lord, that as we are baptised into the death of Thy blessed Son our Saviour Jesus Christ, so by continual mortifying our corrupt affections we may be buried with Him: and that through the grave and gate of death, we may pass to our joyful resurrection; for His merits, Who died, and was buried, and rose again for us, Thy Son Jesus Christ our Lord. Amen.

[*Or else the Collect of Wednesday, ending without* Who now liveth, *etc.*]

The Hours are said in a low voice, and as on Good Friday.

EASTER DAY.
First Vespers.

Vespers begin at once, with

Ant. Alleluia. Alleluia. Alleluia. Alleluia.

Laudate Dominum. Psalm CXVII.

O PRAISE the Lord, all ye heathen : praise Him, all ye nations.

2 For His merciful kindness is ever more and more towards us : and

the truth of the Lord endureth for ever. Praise the Lord.
Glory be, etc.
Ant. Alleluia. Alleluia. Alleluia. Alleluia.
Ant. to Mag. In the end of the Sabbath, as it began to dawn toward the first day of the week : came Mary Magdalene and the other Mary to see the sepulchre. Alleluia.
℣. The Lord be with you.
℟. And with thy spirit.

Let us pray.
Collect as at Lauds.

[*Or,*

POUR into our hearts, O Lord, the spirit of Thy love; that we, whom Thou hast satisfied with Paschal sacraments, may of Thy mercy be made one in heart. Through. Who liveth. In the unity.]
℣. The Lord be with you.
℟. And with thy spirit.
℣. Bless we the Lord.
℟. Thanks be to God.

So end all Hours till Low Sunday.

Compline.

The usual Invocation is made in silence : the Office begins thus :
℣. O God, make speed to save us.
℟. O Lord, make haste to help us.
℣. Glory be to the Father, etc.
℟. As it was, etc.
Alleluia.

Ant. to Psalms. Alleluia. Alleluia. Alleluia. Alleluia.

Cum invocarem. Psalm IV.
In te, Domine. Psalm XXXI.
Ecce nunc. Psalm CXXXIV.
Nunc Dimittis.

(*Each with* Glory be, etc., *and all said under one Ant.*)

[*After, but not on, this day, throughout the week, after the repetition of the Ant., a Cantor immediately commences*
Gradual. This is the day, *Choir*
join in : which the Lord hath made : we will rejoice and be glad in it.
Reader. ℣. In Thy Resurrection, O Christ.
Choir. ℟. Let heaven and earth rejoice.]

℣. The Lord be with you.
℟. And with thy spirit.

Let us pray.
COLLECT.

ALMIGHTY God, Who through Thine Only-begotten Son Jesus Christ hast overcome death, and opened unto us the gate of everlasting life : we humbly beseech Thee, that as by Thy special grace preventing us, Thou dost put into our minds good desires, so by Thy continual help we may bring the same to good effect; through Jesus Christ our Lord, Who liveth and reigneth with Thee and the Holy Ghost, ever one God, world without end. Amen.

℣. The Lord be with you.
℟. And with thy spirit.
℣. Bless we the Lord.
℟. Thanks be to God.

Compline is thus said throughout the week, without change of Collect.

Lauds.

℣. In Thy Resurrection, O Christ.
℟. Let heaven and earth rejoice. Alleluia.

This ℣. and ℟. is said every day at Lauds till Ascension Day.

℣. O God, make speed to save us.
℟. O Lord, make haste to help us.
℣. Glory be to the Father, etc.
℟. As it was, etc.
Alleluia.

Psalms of Sunday.

Ant. 1. The Angel of the Lord descended from heaven : and rolled back the stone from the door, and sat upon it. Alleluia. Alleluia.

Ant. 2. Behold, there was a great earthquake : for the Angel of the Lord descended from heaven. Alleluia.

Ant. 3. His countenance was like lightning : and his raiment white as snow. Alleluia. Alleluia.

Ant. 4. For fear of him the keepers did shake : and became as dead men. Alleluia.

Ant. 5. And the Angel answered and said unto the women, Fear not ye : for I know that ye seek Jesus. Alleluia.

Then immediately, without Hymn or Chapter :

℣. The Lord is risen from the tomb.
℟. Who for our sakes hung upon the tree. Alleluia.

Ant. to Ben. And very early in the morning, the first day of the week : they came unto the sepulchre at the rising of the sun. Alleluia.

COLLECT.

ALMIGHTY God, Who through Thy Only-begotten Son Jesus Christ hast overcome death, and opened unto us the gate of everlasting life; we humbly beseech Thee, that, as by Thy special grace preventing us Thou dost put into our minds good desires, so by Thy continual help we may bring the same to good effect; through Jesus Christ our Lord, Who liveth and reigneth with Thee and the Holy Ghost, ever one God, world without end. Amen.

℣. Bless we the Lord. Alleluia.
℟. Thanks be to God. Alleluia.

Alleluia *is said with this* ℣. *and* ℟. *till Trinity.*

Prime.

The Offices, except Vespers, now begin as usual, but no Hymns are said till the First Vespers of Low Sunday.

Ant. to Psalms. The Angel of the Lord descended from heaven : and came and rolled back the stone from the door, and sat upon it. Alleluia. Alleluia.

Deus in nomine tuo. Psalm LIV.
Confitemini. Psalm CXVIII.
Beati immaculati and *Retribue servo tuo.* Psalm CXIX.

After, the repetition of the Ant. immediately follows the

Gradual. This is the day * which the Lord hath made : we will rejoice and be glad in it.
℣. The Lord is risen.
℟. As He said unto you. Alleluia.
℣. The Lord be with you.
℟. And with thy spirit.

Let us pray.

Collect as at Lauds.

℣. The Lord be with you.
℟. And with thy spirit.
℣. Bless we the Lord.
℟. Thanks be to God.

Prime is thus said till Low Sunday, except that, throughout the week, Psalm CXVIII. *is omitted.*
Chapter is said, ending after : ℟. Is the death of His Saints, *and following Collect, with* The Lord be, *etc. and* Bless we, *etc.*

Tierce.

Ant. Behold, there was a great earthquake : for the Angel of the Lord descended from heaven. Alleluia.

Gradual. This is the day * which the Lord hath made : we will rejoice and be glad in it.
℣. The Lord is risen indeed.
℟. And hath appeared to Simon. Alleluia.

Collect as at Lauds.

Sexts.

Ant. His countenance was like lightning : and his raiment white as snow. Alleluia.

Gradual. This is the day * which the Lord hath made : we will rejoice and be glad in it.
℣. The Lord is risen from the tomb.
℟. Who for our sakes hung upon the tree. Alleluia.

Nones.

Ant. For fear of him the keepers did shake : and became as dead men. Alleluia.

Gradual. This is the day * which the Lord hath made : we will rejoice and be glad in it.
℣. In Thy Resurrection, O Christ.
℟. Let heaven and earth rejoice. Alleluia.

Tierce, Sexts, and Nones, are thus said throughout the week, with change of Collect, according to the day.

Second Vespers.

Vespers begin thus :
℣. Lord, have mercy [iii].
℟. Christ, have mercy [iii].
℣. Lord, have mercy [iii].
Ant. Alleluia. Alleluia. Alleluia. Alleluia.

Psalms of Sunday.

After repetition of the Antiphon :
Gradual. This is the day : *Choir join in* : which the Lord hath made : we will rejoice and be glad in it.
℣. O give thanks unto the Lord, for He is gracious : because His mercy endureth for ever.
℟. Alleluia. *Choir join in* : This is the day which the Lord hath made : we will rejoice and be glad in it.
℣. Let us keep the feast with the unleavened bread of sincerity and : *Choir continue* : truth. Alleluia.
℣. The Lord is risen.
℟. As He said unto you. Alleluia.
Ant. to Mag. And when they looked, they saw that the stone was rolled away : for it was very great. Alleluia.

Collect as at Lauds.
[*Or*,
GRANT, we beseech Thee, Almighty God, that as we celebrate the solemnities of the Lord's Resurrection, so by the invocation of Thy Spirit our souls may rise from death. Through the same.]

Memorial of S. Mary.

Ant. I went down into the garden of nuts to see the fruits of the valley, and to see whether the vines flourished, and the pomegranates budded : return, return, O Shulamite ; return, return, that we may look upon thee. Alleluia.
℣. Thou art the holy Mother of God.
℟. O Ever Virgin Mary. Alleluia.

Collect.

WE beseech Thee, O Lord, pour Thy grace into our hearts ; that as we have known the Incarnation of Thy Son Jesus Christ by the message of an Angel, so by His Cross and Passion we may be brought unto the glory of His Resurrection ; through the same Jesus Christ our Lord. Amen.

This Memorial is said daily at Vespers throughout the week.

℣. Bless we the Lord. Alleluia.
℟. Thanks be to God. Alleluia.

Vespers are thus said throughout the week, except the Graduals, Ants. to Magnificat, and Collects.

EASTER MONDAY.

Lauds.

℣. In Thy Resurrection, O Christ.
℟. Let heaven and earth rejoice. Alleluia.

On this day, and throughout the week, the Sunday Psalms are said under this one

Ant. The Angel of the Lord descended from heaven : and rolled back the stone from the door, and sat upon it. Alleluia.

Ant. to Ben. What manner of communications are these that ye have one with another, as ye walk, and are sad? Alleluia : And the one of them, whose name was Cleophas, answering, said unto Him, Art Thou only a stranger in Jerusalem, and hast not known the things which are come to pass there in these days? Alleluia. And He said unto them, What things? And they said unto Him, Concerning Jesus of Nazareth, Who was a Prophet mighty in deed and word, before God and all the people. Alleluia.

Collect of Sunday.

[*Or,*

GOD, Who by the Paschal solemnity hast bestowed healing on the world, continue, we beseech Thee, to shed forth upon Thy people Thy heavenly gifts; that they may attain to perfect freedom, and advance to life eternal. Through.]

Memorial of S. Mary.

Ant. My soul failed when He spake; I sought Him, but I could not find Him; I called Him, but He gave me no answer; The watchmen that went about the city found me, they wounded me : the keepers of the walls took away my veil from me. Alleluia.

℣., ℟., *and Collect as at Sunday Vespers.*
This Memorial is said daily at Lauds throughout the week.
Lauds are thus said thoughout the week, except the changes of Collects and Ants. to Benedictus.
No notice is taken of any ⸸*feast or* ⸸*fast during this week, because all Saints arose in Christ, and the Feast of Christ's Resurrection is common to all Saints. A Double Feast so occurring is trans-* ⸸*ferred to the first vacant day after the Octave. And this order holds good during the Octave of Whitsun Day.*

No Petitions are said at any Hour, except Prime and Compline, till Trinity. On and after Low Sunday they are said at those two Hours.

Vespers.

As on Sunday, except that which ⸸*follows:*

Gradual. This is the day * which the Lord hath made : we will rejoice and be glad in it.

℣. Let Israel now confess that He is gracious, and that His mercy endureth for ever.

℟. Alleluia. * This is the day which, etc.

℣. Did not our heart burn within us concerning Jesus : while He talked with us by the way?

℟. Alleluia.

℣. The Lord is risen.

℟. As He said unto you. Alleluia.

Ant. to Mag. Did not our heart burn within us concerning Jesus : while He talked with us by the way? Alleluia.

Collect of Sunday.

[*Or,*

GRANT, we beseech Thee, Almighty God, that as we are bowed down under the weight of our sins, so by this Paschal feast we may be delivered from all evils that beset us. Through.]

EASTER TUESDAY.

Lauds.

Ant. to Ben. Jesus Himself stood in the midst of them, and saith unto them : Peace be unto you. Alleluia. Alleluia.

Collect of Sunday.

[*Or,*

GOD, Who dost ever increase Thy Church with new offspring; grant to Thy servants that they hold fast in their lives that which in faith they accepted. Through.]

Vespers.

Gradual. This is the day * which the Lord hath made : we will rejoice, and be glad in it.

℣. Let them give thanks whom the Lord hath redeemed, and delivered from the hand of the enemy; and gathered them out of the lands.

℟. Alleluia. * This is the day, etc.

℣. The Lord Jesus arose and stood in the midst of His disciples, and said unto them, Peace be unto you.

℟. Alleluia.

℣. The Lord is risen.

℟. As He said unto you. Alleluia.

Ant. to Mag. Behold My hands and My feet : that it is I Myself. Alleluia. Alleluia.

Collect of Sunday.
[*Or*,

GRANT, we beseech Thee, Almighty God, that we who keep the solemnity of the Paschal feast, may ever abide in the grace of holiness. Through.]

WEDNESDAY.
Lauds.

Ant. to Ben. Cast the net on the right side of the ship : and ye shall find. Alleluia.

Collect of Sunday.
[*Or*,

GOD, Who makest us glad with the yearly solemnity of our Lord's Resurrection; mercifully grant that through our temporal feasts we may attain to eternal joys. Through.]

Vespers.

Gradual. This is the day * which the Lord hath made: we will rejoice, and be glad in it.

℣. The right hand of the Lord bringeth mighty things to pass : the right hand of the Lord hath the pre-eminence.

℟. Alleluia. * This is the day, etc.

℣. The Lord arose, and met the women, saying, All hail; and they came and held Him by the feet.

℟. Alleluia.

℣. The Lord is risen.

℟. As He said unto you. Alleluia.

Ant. to Mag. This is now the third time that Jesus shewed Himself : after that He was risen from the dead. Alleluia.

Collect of Sunday.
[*Or*,

GRANT, we beseech Thee, Almighty God, that the marvellous mystery of this Paschal festivity may bring us peace in this world, and in the world to come eternal life. Through.]

THURSDAY.
Lauds.

Ant. to Ben. Mary stood without at the sepulchre weeping : and seeth two angels in white sitting, the one at the head, the other at the feet, where the body of Jesus had lain. Alleluia.

Collect of Sunday.
[*Or*,

GOD, Who hast gathered together divers nations in the confession of Thy Name; grant that they who are regenerate by baptism may be one in inward faith, and in outward devotion. Through.]

Vespers.

Gradual. This is the day * which the Lord hath made : we will rejoice, and be glad in it.

℣. The same stone which the builders refused : is become the headstone in the corner. This is the Lord's doing : and it is marvellous in our eyes.

℟. Alleluia. * This is the day, etc.

℣. In the day of My resurrection,

saith the Lord, I will go before you into Galilee.
℞. Alleluia.
℣. The Lord is risen.
℞. As He said unto you. Alleluia.
Ant. to Mag. They have taken away my Lord, and I know not where they have laid Him : If thou hast borne Him hence, tell me. Alleluia. And I will take Him away. Alleluia.

Collect of Sunday.
[*Or*,
GOD, who hast granted us to celebrate the Paschal mystery with free hearts; teach us to fear that which displeaseth Thee, and to love that which Thou dost command. Through.]

FRIDAY.
Lauds.

Ant. to Ben. The eleven disciples saw the Lord in Galilee: and worshipped Him. Alleluia.

Collect of Sunday.
[*Or*,
ALMIGHTY, everlasting God, Who hast ordained the Paschal mystery for the reconciliation of the human race; grant to our souls, that what we profess with our lips we may shew forth with our lives. Through.]

Vespers.

Gradual. This is the day * which the Lord hath made : we will rejoice, and be glad in it.
℣. Blessed be He that cometh in the Name of the Lord : God is the Lord Who hath shewed us light.
℞. Alleluia. * This is the day, etc.
℣. Tell it out among the heathen that the Lord hath reigned from the tree.
℞. Alleluia.
℣. The Lord is risen.
℞. As He said unto you. Alleluia.

Ant. to Mag. All power is given unto Me : in heaven and earth. Alleluia.

Collect of Sunday.
[*Or*,
O GOD, by Whom cometh redemption, and adoption is bestowed; grant to the works of Thy hands, that being born anew in Christ, they may attain to their eternal heritage and to true liberty. Through.]

SATURDAY.
Lauds.

Ant. to Ben. So they ran both together : and the other disciple did outrun Peter, and came first to the sepulchre. Alleluia.

Collect of Sunday.
[*Or*,
GRANT, we beseech Thee, Almighty God, that we, who have reverently passed through the Paschal feast, may through the same attain to eternal joys. Through.]

On this day, at every Hour, Alleluia *is said before and after the words*, This is the day, *etc.*

LOW SUNDAY.
First Vespers.

℣. O God, make speed, etc.
Ant. Alleluia. Alleluia. Alleluia. Alleluia.

Psalms of the Feria.

CHAPTER. Rom. VI.
CHRIST being raised from the dead, dieth no more; death hath no more dominion over Him. For in that He liveth, He liveth unto God.
℞. Thanks be to God.

HYMN. *Chorus novæ Hierusalem.*

YE Choirs of New Jerusalem!
To sweet new strains attune your theme;
The while we keep, from care released,
With sober joy our Paschal feast.

When Christ, unconquered Lion, first
The Dragon's chains by rising burst :
And while with living voice·He cries,·
The dead of other ages rise.

Engorged in former years, their prey
Must death and hell restore to-day :
And many a captive soul, set free,
With Jesus leaves captivity.

Right gloriously He triumphs now,
Worthy to Whom should all things bow :
And joining heaven and earth again
Links in one commonweal the twain.

And we, as these His deeds we sing,
His suppliant soldiers, pray our King,
That in His palace, bright and vast,
We may keep watch and ward at last.

Long as unending ages run,
To God the Father laud be done,
To God the Son our equal praise,
And God the Holy Ghost, we raise. Amen.

℣. Abide with us.

℟. For it is toward evening, and the day is far spent. Alleluia.

Ant. to Mag. Now when Jesus was risen early the first day of the week : He appeared first unto Mary Magdalene, out of whom He had cast seven devils. Alleluia.

COLLECT. (1549.)

ALMIGHTY Father, Who hast given Thine only Son to die for our sins, and to rise again for our justification; grant us so to put away the leaven of malice and wickedness, that we may alway serve Thee in pureness of living and truth; through the merits of the same Thy Son Jesus Christ our Lord. Amen.

[*Or*,

GRANT, we beseech Thee, Almighty God, that as we have passed through the Paschal feast, so by Thy grace our hearts and lives may ever be conformed thereto. Through.]

MEMORIAL OF S. MARY. p. 165.

This Memorial is said at First Vespers of Sunday till the Ascension.

The First Vespers of Sunday are thus said till the Ascension, except the changes of Collect and Ant. to Magnificat.

Compline.

Compline begins as usual with

℣. Turn us, etc.
Ant. to Psalms. Alleluia. Alleluia. Alleluia. Alleluia.

Cum invocarem. Psalm IV.
In te, Domine. Psalm XXXI.
Qui habitat. Psalm XCI.
Ecce nunc. Psalm CXXXIV.

CHAPTER. Jer. XIV., *as in Psalter.*

℟. Thanks be to God.

HYMN. *Jesu Salvator seculi.*

JESU, Who brought'st redemption nigh,
Word of the Father, God most High;
O Light of Light, to man unknown,
And watchful Guardian of Thine own;

Thy hand Creation made and guides;
Thy wisdom time from time divides :
By this world's cares and toils opprest,
O give our weary bodies rest.

That while in frames of sin and pain
A little longer we remain,
Our flesh may here in such wise sleep
That watch with Christ our souls may keep.

O free us, while we dwell below,
From insults of our ghostly foe,
That he may ne'er victorious be
O'er them that are redeemed by Thee.

We pray Thee, King with glory decked,
In this our Paschal joy, protect,
From all that death would fain effect,
Thy ransomed flock, Thine own elect.

To Thee Who, dead, again dost live,
All glory, Lord, Thy people give ;
All glory, as is ever meet,
To Father and to Paraclete. Amen.

These two last verses are said at the end of all Hymns of this metre, till Ascension, except at Saturday Vespers.

℣. Keep us, O Lord.

℟. As the apple of an eye, hide us under the shadow of Thy wings.

Ant. to Nunc Dim. Alleluia. The Lord is risen. Alleluia : As He said. Alleluia. Alleluia.

Petitions, p. 69.

Compline is thus said till the Ascension, except that the Christmas Doxology is used on any Feast of the Blessed Virgin.

Lauds.

℣. and ℟., *Ants. and Psalms,* p. 163.

CHAPTER. 1 St. John v.

WHATSOEVER is born of God overcometh the world; and this is the victory that overcometh the world, even our faith.

℟. Thanks be to God.

HYMN. *Sermone blando Angelus.*

WITH gentle voice the Angel gave
    The women tidings at the grave;
"Forthwith your Master shall ye see:
He goes before to Galilee."

And while with fear and joy they pressed
To tell these tidings to the rest,
Their Lord, their living Lord, they meet,
And see His form, and kiss His feet.

Th' eleven, when they hear, with speed
To Galilee forthwith proceed;
That there they may behold once more
The Lord's dear face, as oft before.

In this our bright and Paschal day
The sun shines out with purer ray:
When Christ, to earthly sight made plain,
The glad Apostles see again.

The wounds, the riven wounds, He shews
Of that His flesh with light that glows,
In loud accord, both far and nigh,
The Lord's arising testify.

O Christ, the King, Who lov'st to bless,
Do Thou our hearts and souls possess;
To Thee our praise that we may pay,
To Whom our laud is due, for aye.

We pray Thee, King with glory decked,
In this our Paschal joy protect,
From all that death would fain effect,
Thy ransomed flock, Thine own elect.

To Thee Who, dead, again dost live,
All glory, Lord, Thy people give;
All glory, as is ever meet,
To Father and to Paraclete. Amen.

℣. The Lord is risen from the tomb.

℟. Who for our sakes hung upon the tree. Alleluia.

Ant. to Ben. Then the same day at evening, being the first day of the week, when the doors were shut where the disciples were assembled: Jesus stood in the midst, and saith unto them, Peace be unto you. Alleluia.

MEMORIAL OF THE RESURRECTION.

Ant. And very early in the morning, the first day of the week: they came unto the sepulchre at the rising of the sun. Alleluia.

℣. The Lord is risen indeed.

℟. And hath appeared to Simon. Alleluia.

Collect as in Memorial at Second Vespers.
This Memorial is said at Lauds on Sunday till the Ascension.
A Double Feast occurring on Low Sunday is to be transferred to the next day.
If a Double Feast be kept on the Monday, Second Vespers on Sunday shall be of the Feast, with Memorials of the Sunday and the Resurrection.

Prime.

HYMN. *Jam lucis orto sidere, with Easter Doxology.*

Ant. to Psalms. The Angel of the Lord descended from heaven: and came and rolled back the stone from the door, and sat upon it. Alleluia.

Deus in nomine tuo. Psalm LIV.
Beati immaculati and *Retribue servo tuo.* Psalm CXIX.

Ant. Thanks be to Thee, O God; One Very Trinity: One Supreme Deity, One Holy Unity, thanks be to Thee. Alleluia.

Quicunque vult.

CHAPTER. 1 Tim. I.

NOW unto the King Eternal, Immortal, Invisible, the only wise God, be honour and glory for ever and ever. Amen.

℟. Jesu Christ, Son of the living God, have mercy upon us. Alleluia. Alleluia. ℣. Thou Who hast risen from the dead. Alleluia. ℟. Have mercy upon us. Alleluia. Alleluia. ℣. Glory be to the Father, and to the Son: and to the Holy Ghost. ℟. Jesu Christ, Son of the living

God, have mercy upon us. Alleluia. Alleluia.

This ℟. *is used daily till the Ascension.*

℣. O Lord, arise, help us.

℟. And deliver us for Thy Name's sake.

Petitions, p. 33.

Tierce.

HYMN. *Nunc sancte nobis Spiritus, with Easter Doxology.*

Ant. And, behold, there was a great earthquake : for the Angel of the Lord descended from heaven. Alleluia.

CHAPTER. 1 S. John v.

WHATSOEVER is born of God overcometh the world; and this is the victory that overcometh the world, even our faith.

℟. The Lord is risen. Alleluia. Alleluia. ℣. As He said. ℟. Alleluia. Alleluia. ℣. Glory be to the Father, and to the Son : and to the Holy Ghost. ℟. The Lord is risen. Alleluia. Alleluia.

℣. The Lord is risen indeed.

℟. And hath appeared to Simon. Alleluia.

Collect as at First Vespers.

Sexts.

HYMN. *Rector potens verax Deus, with Easter Doxology.*

Ant. His countenance was like lightning : and his raiment white as snow. Alleluia.

CHAPTER. 1 S. John v.

WHO is he that overcometh the world, but he that believeth that Jesus is the Son of God? This is He that came by water and blood, even Jesus Christ.

℟. The Lord is risen indeed. Alleluia. Alleluia. ℣. And hath appeared to Simon. ℟. Alleluia. Alleluia. ℣.

Glory be to the Father, and to the Son : and to the Holy Ghost. ℟. The Lord is risen indeed. Alleluia. Alleluia.

℣. The Lord is risen from the tomb.

℟. Who for our sakes hung upon the tree. Alleluia.

Nones.

HYMN. *Rerum Deus tenax vigor, with Easter Doxology.*

Ant. And for fear of him the keepers did shake : and became as dead men. Alleluia.

CHAPTER. 1 S. John v.

AND there are three that bear witness in earth, the spirit, and the water, and the blood : and these three agree in one.

℟. The Lord is risen from the tomb. Alleluia. Alleluia. ℣. Who for our sakes hung upon the tree. ℟. Alleluia. Alleluia. ℣. Glory be to the Father and to the Son : and to the Holy Ghost. ℟. The Lord is risen from the tomb. Alleluia. Alleluia.

℣. In Thy Resurrection, O Christ.

℟. Let heaven and earth rejoice. Alleluia.

Second Vespers.

Ant. Alleluia. Alleluia. Alleluia. Alleluia.

CHAPTER. 1 S. John v.

WHATSOEVER is born of God overcometh the world : and this is the victory that overcometh the world, even our faith.

℟. Thanks be to God.

HYMN. *Ad Cœnam Agni providi.*

THE Lamb's high banquet we await,
In snow-white robes of royal state :
And now, the Red Sea's channel past,
To Christ our Prince we sing at last.

Upon the Altar of the Cross,
His body hath redeemed our loss :
And tasting of His roseate blood,
Our life is hid with Him in God.

That Paschal eve God's arm was bared:
The devastating Angel spared:
By strength of hand our hosts went free
From Pharaoh's ruthless tyranny.

Now Christ, our Paschal Lamb, is slain,
The Lamb of God that knows no stain,
The true Oblation offered here,
Our own unleavened Bread sincere.

O Thou, from Whom hell's monarch flies,
O great, O very Sacrifice,
Thy captive people are set free,
And endless life restored in Thee.

For Christ, arising from the dead,
From conquered hell victorious sped:
And thrust the tyrant down to chains,
And Paradise for man regains.

We pray Thee, King with glory decked,
In this our Paschal joy protect,
From all that death would fain effect,
Thy ransomed flock, Thine own elect.

To Thee Who, dead, again dost live,
All glory, Lord, Thy people give;
All glory, as is ever meet,
To Father and to Paraclete. Amen.

℣. Abide with us.
℟. For it is toward evening, and the day is far spent. Alleluia.

Ant. to Mag. And after eight days came Jesus, the doors being shut, and stood in the midst, and said: Peace be unto you. Alleluia. Alleluia.

MEMORIAL OF THE RESURRECTION.

Ant. And when they looked, they saw that the stone was rolled away: for it was very great. Alleluia.
℣. The Lord is risen.
℟. As He said unto you. Alleluia.

COLLECT.

ALMIGHTY God, Who through Thy Only-begotten Son Jesus Christ hast overcome death, and opened unto us the gate of everlasting life; we humbly beseech Thee, that, as by Thy special grace preventing us Thou dost put into our minds good desires, so by Thy continual help we may bring the same to good effect. Through.

This Memorial is said at Second Vespers of Sunday till Ascension, whether the Office be of the Sunday or of a Feast, except in the case of the Invention of the Cross.

Until Ascension the Hours are said as on Low Sunday, with these exceptions: the Vesper Psalms change according to the Feria, though the Lauds Psalms continue to be those of Sunday. The Psalms at all Offices are said under this Ant., Alleluia. Alleluia. Alleluia. Alleluia. *The Ants. to* Benedictus *and* Magnificat *change daily. The Chapter and Collect at each Office, except Prime, change weekly.*

Prime is said with the usual Petitions, the Psalms, and Responsary as on Sunday, Quicunque vult *being said (according to Sarum) on the Ferias, with Ant.* Glory to Thee, p. 31, *and Chapter,* O Lord, be gracious, p. 33.

Ants. to Benedictus *and* Magnificat *for the week:*

1. Thomas, because thou hast seen Me, thou hast believed: blessed are they that have not seen and yet have believed. Alleluia.

2. And many other signs truly did Jesus in the presence of His disciples; Alleluia: which are not written in this book. Alleluia.

3. But these are written that ye might believe that Jesus is the Christ, the Son of God: and that believing ye might have life through His Name. Alleluia.

Ferial Memorials,
From this time till Ascension.

At Lauds.

MEMORIAL OF THE HOLY CROSS.

Ant. The Crucified hath risen from the dead: He hath redeemed us. Alleluia. Alleluia.
℣., ℟., *and Collect as at Vespers.*

MEMORIAL OF S. MARY.
As at Vespers.

MEMORIAL OF ALL SAINTS.

Ant. Thy Saints, O Lord, shall

flourish as a lily; Alleluia : And they shall be as the odour of balsam before Thee. Alleluia.

℣., ℞., and Collect, as at Vespers.

At Vespers,
On Ferias and simple feasts.

MEMORIAL OF THE HOLY CROSS.

Ant. He hath endured the holy Cross Who burst the bars of hell : He is girded with power. He rose on the third day. Alleluia.

℣. Tell it out among the heathen.
℞. That the Lord reigneth from the tree. Alleluia.

Let us pray.

COLLECT.

GOD, Who for our sake didst will that Thy Son should undergo the suffering of the Cross to drive away from us the power of the enemy; grant to us Thy servants that we may ever live in the joys of His Resurrection; through the same Jesus Christ our Lord. Amen.

MEMORIAL OF S. MARY.

Ant. The gate of Paradise was closed to all by Eve : and by Mary it is again set open. Alleluia.

℣. After child-bearing thou remainedst a Virgin.
℞. O Mother of God. Alleluia.

Let us pray.

COLLECT.

WE beseech Thee, O Lord, pour Thy grace into our hearts; that as we have known the Incarnation of Thy Son Jesus Christ by the message of an Angel, so by His Cross and Passion we may be brought to the glory of His Resurrection; through the same Thy Son Jesus Christ our Lord. Amen.

MEMORIAL OF ALL SAINTS.

Ant. In the kingdom of heaven is the dwelling place of the Saints. Alleluia : And their rest in eternity. Alleluia:

℣. The voice of joy and health.
℞. Is in the dwellings of the righteous. Alleluia.

Let us pray.

COLLECT.

GRANT, we beseech Thee, Almighty God, that in the Resurrection of Thy Son our Lord Jesus Christ with all the Saints we may truly receive a portion; Who liveth and reigneth with Thee and the Holy Ghost, ever one God, world without end. Amen.

Festival Memorials,

Used till Ascension-tide at both Vespers and at Lauds on all Double Feasts, except the Invention of the Cross, which fall on Ferias.

Vespers.

MEMORIAL OF THE RESURRECTION.

Ant. Go quickly, and tell His disciples : that He is risen from the dead. Alleluia.
℣. The Lord is risen indeed.
℞. And hath appeared to Simon. Alleluia.

Collect, p. 172.

Lauds.

Ant. The Lord is risen from the tomb: Who for our sakes hung upon the tree. Alleluia.
℣. The Lord is risen.
℞. As He said unto you. Alleluia.

Collect, p. 172.

No Memorial of the Feria is made on festivals except on Rogation Monday and Ascension Eve, and then only at Lauds.

SECOND SUNDAY AFTER EASTER.

First Vespers.

As p. 168, *till*

Ant. to Mag. Thou art worthy, O Lord, to receive glory, and honour, and power, for Thou hast created all things, and for Thy pleasure they are, and were created : Salvation to our God, Which sitteth upon the throne, and unto the Lamb. Alleluia.

COLLECT. (1549.)

ALMIGHTY God, Who hast given Thine only Son to be unto us both a sacrifice for sin, and also an ensample of godly life; give us grace that we may always most thankfully receive that His inestimable benefit, and also daily endeavour ourselves to follow the blessed steps of His most holy life; through the same Jesus Christ our Lord. Amen.

[*Or,*

O GOD, Who by the humiliation of Thy Son didst raise a fallen world, grant perpetual joy to Thy faithful people; that those whom Thou hast delivered from the danger of eternal death, may be made partakers of eternal joys. Through the same.]

Lauds.

Ant. The Angel of the Lord descended from heaven : and came and rolled back the stone from the door, and sat upon it. Alleluia. Alleluia.
The Psalms are all said under this Ant.

CHAPTER. 1 S. Pet. II.

CHRIST also suffered for us, leaving us an example, that ye should follow His steps : Who did no sin, neither was guile found in His mouth.

℟. Thanks be to God.

HYMN. *Sermone blando Angelus,* ℣. *and* ℟., p. 170.

Ant. to Ben. I am the good Shepherd Who feed My sheep : I lay down My life for My sheep. Alleluia. Alleluia.

Prime.

As p. 170., *except Ant to Quicunque.* Thee duly praise, p. 31, *which is said on all Sundays till Ascension when the Office is of Sunday.*

Tierce.

As p. 171, *except*
Chapter as at Lauds.

Sexts.

As p. 171, *except*
CHAPTER. 1 S. Pet. II.

BUT He committed Himself to Him that judgeth righteously: Who His own self bare our sins in His own body on the tree: by Whose stripes ye were healed.

Nones.

As p. 171, *except*
CHAPTER. 1 S. Pet. II.

FOR ye were as sheep going astray : but are now returned to the Shepherd and Bishop of your souls.

Second Vespers.

As p. 171, *except*
Chapter as at Lauds.

Ant. to Mag. I am the Shepherd of the sheep. I am the Way and the Truth : I am the good Shepherd, and know My sheep, and am known of Mine. Alleluia. Alleluia.

Ants. to Benedictus *and* Magnificat *for the week :*

1. The good Shepherd : giveth His life for the sheep. Alleluia.
2. As the Father knoweth Me, even so know I the Father : and I lay down My life for the sheep. Alleluia.

3. But the hireling, whose own the sheep are not, seeth the wolf coming, and leaveth the sheep and fleeth : and the wolf catcheth them, and scattereth the sheep. Alleluia.

4. And other sheep I have, which are not of this fold : them also I must bring, and they shall hear My voice; and there shall be one fold and one Shepherd. Alleluia.

THIRD SUNDAY AFTER EASTER.

First Vespers.

As p. 168, except

Ant. to Mag. I am Alpha and Omega, the First and the Last : I am the Root and Offspring of David, and the bright and morning Star. Alleluia.

COLLECT.

ALMIGHTY God, Who shewest to them that be in error the light of Thy truth, to the intent that they may return into the way of righteousness; grant unto all them that are admitted into the fellowship of Christ's religion, that they may eschew those things that are contrary to their profession, and follow all such things as are agreeable to the same; through our Lord Jesus Christ. Amen.

Lauds.

Ant to Psalms, p. 174.

CHAPTER. 1 S. Pet. II.

DEARLY beloved, I beseech you as strangers and pilgrims, abstain from fleshly lusts, which war against the soul.

R/. Thanks be to God.

Ant. to Ben. Jesus said to His disciples, A little while and ye shall not see Me : and again a little while and ye shall see Me, because I go to the Father. Alleluia. Alleluia.

Prime.

As p. 170, *except Ant. to Quicunque.*

Tierce.

Chapter as at Lauds.

Sexts.

CHAPTER. 1 S. Pet. II.

SUBMIT yourselves to every ordinance of man for the Lord's sake : whether it be to the king, as supreme; or unto governours, as unto them that are sent by him, for the punishment of evil doers, and for the praise of them that do well.

Nones.

CHAPTER. 1 S. Pet. II.

FOR so is the will of God, that with well-doing ye may put to silence the ignorance of foolish men.

Second Vespers.

Chapter as at Lauds.

Ant. to Mag. What is this that He saith, A little while? Alleluia : We cannot tell what He saith. Alleluia.

Ants. to Benedictus *and* Magnificat *for the week :*

1. Verily, verily, I say unto you, that ye shall weep and lament. Alleluia. But the world shall rejoice : and ye shall be sorrowful, but your sorrow shall be turned into joy. Alleluia.

2. Sorrow hath filled your hearts : but your joy no man taketh from you. Alleluia. Alleluia.

3. I will see you again, and your heart shall rejoice : and your joy no man taketh from you. Alleluia.

FOURTH SUNDAY AFTER EASTER.

First Vespers.
As p. 168, *except*

Ant. to Mag. Great and marvellous are Thy works, Lord God Almighty; just and true are Thy ways, Thou King of Saints : Who shall not fear Thee, O Lord, and glorify Thy Name? for Thou only art holy; for all nations shall come and worship before Thee ; for Thy judgments are made manifest. Alleluia.

Collect.

O ALMIGHTY God, Who alone canst order the unruly wills and affections of sinful men ; grant unto Thy people, that they may love the thing which Thou commandest, and desire that which Thou dost promise; that so, among the sundry and manifold changes of the world, our hearts may surely there be fixed, where true joys are to be found; through Jesus Christ our Lord. Amen.

Lauds.

Ant. to Psalms, p. 174.

Chapter. S. James i.

EVERY good gift and every perfect gift is from above, and cometh down from the Father of lights, with Whom is no variableness, neither shadow of turning.

℟. Thanks be to God.

Ant. to Ben. I go My way to Him that sent Me : But, because I have said these things unto you, sorrow hath filled your heart. Alleluia.

Prime.
As p. 170, *except Ant. to Quicunque.*

Tierce.
Chapter as at Lauds.

Sexts.
Chapter. S. James i.

LET every man be swift to hear, slow to speak, slow to wrath.

Nones.
Chapter. S. James i.

WHEREFORE lay apart all filthiness and superfluity of naughtiness, and receive with meekness the engrafted word, which is able to save your souls.

Second Vespers.
Chapter as at Lauds.

Ant. to Mag. I tell you the truth; it is expedient for you that I go away : for if I go not away, the Comforter will not come unto you. Alleluia.

Ants. to Benedictus *and* Magnificat *for the week :*

1. I have yet many things to say unto you, but ye cannot bear them now : Howbeit, when He, the Spirit of truth, is come, He will guide you into all truth. Alleluia.

2. When He, the Spirit of truth, is come, He will guide you into all truth : and He will shew you things to come. Alleluia.

3. He shall glorify Me : for He shall receive of Mine, and shall shew it unto you. Alleluia.

ROGATION SUNDAY.

First Vespers.
As p. 168, *except*

Ant. to Mag. Great and marvellous are Thy works, Lord God Almighty; just and true are Thy ways, Thou King of Saints : Who shall not fear Thee, O Lord, and glorify Thy Name? for Thou only art holy; for all nations shall come and worship Thee, for Thy judgments are made manifest. Alleluia.

COLLECT.

O LORD, from Whom all good things do come; grant to us Thy humble servants, that by Thy holy inspiration we may think those things that be good, and by Thy merciful guiding may perform the same; through our Lord Jesus Christ. Amen.

Lauds.

Ant. 1. The Angel of the Lord descended from heaven : and rolled back the stone from the door, and sat upon it. Alleluia. Alleluia.

Ant. 2. And, behold, there was a great earthquake : for the Angel of the Lord descended from heaven. Alleluia.

Ant. 3. His countenance was like lightning : and his raiment white as snow. Alleluia. Alleluia.

Ant. 4. And for fear of him the keepers did shake : and became as dead men. Alleluia.

Ant. 5. And the Angel answered and said unto the women, Fear not ye : for I know that ye seek Jesus. Alleluia.

CHAPTER. S. James I.

BE ye doers of the word, and not hearers only, deceiving your own selves. For if any be a hearer of the word, and not a doer, he is like unto a man beholding his natural face in a glass.

Ant. to Ben. Hitherto have ye asked nothing in My Name : ask, and ye shall receive. Alleluia.

Prime.

All as p. 170, *except Ant. to Quicunque.*

Tierce.

Chapter as at Lauds.

Sexts.

CHAPTER. S. James I.

BUT whoso looketh into the perfect law of liberty, and continueth therein, he being not a forgetful hearer, but a doer of the work, this man shall be blessed in his deed.

Nones.

CHAPTER. S. James I.

PURE religion and undefiled before God and the Father is this, To visit the fatherless and widows in their affliction, and to keep himself unspotted from the world.

Second Vespers.

Chapter as at Lauds.

Ant. to Mag. Ask, and ye shall receive, that your joy may be full : for the Father Himself loveth you, because ye have loved Me, and have believed. Alleluia.

ROGATION MONDAY.

Lauds.

CHAPTER. S. James v.

CONFESS your faults one to another, and pray one for another, that ye may be healed. The effectual fervent prayer of a righteous man availeth much.

Ant. to Ben. Ask, and it shall be given you; seek, and ye shall find : knock, and it shall be opened unto you. Alleluia.

Collect of Sunday.

[*Or*,

GRANT, we beseech Thee, Almighty God, that we who in our afflictions trust to Thy mercy, may by Thy protection be guarded from all adversities. Through.]

At all the other Hours are said the Chapter and Collect of Rogation Sunday. If a Feast above the lowest class occurs on this or the following day, the Feast is kept, with memorial of the Fast at Lauds only. On this day are to be said Vespers of the Blessed Virgin, with full service on the morrow, to Nones, inclusive, except a Double Feast occur: no memorial of the Fast or of any Saint, but only of the Resurrection. If this be not observed, let the Ant. to Magnificat *on both days be as here set down for Tuesday, and the rest of the Tuesday Office as on Monday. If a Double Feast occur on Tuesday, the Office of the Blessed Virgin is wholly omitted.*

ROGATION TUESDAY.
Vespers.

Ant. to Mag. Lo, now speakest Thou plainly, and speakest no proverb : Now are we sure that Thou knowest all things, and needest not that any man should ask Thee. Alleluia.

Collect of Sunday.

VIGIL OF THE ASCENSION.
Lauds.

CHAPTER. Acts IV.

AND the multitude of them that believed were of one heart and of one soul: neither said any of them that ought of the things which he possessed was his own; but they had all things common.

Ant. to Ben. And now, O Father, glorify Thou Me with Thine own self: with the glory which I had with Thee before the world was. Alleluia.

[COLLECT.]

GRANT, we beseech Thee, Almighty God, that the intention of our hearts may ever tend to that place whither Thine Only-begotten Son our Lord, the Author of this coming solemnity, hath entered in; and as we press on thereunto by faith, so grant us to attain to the same by holy conversation. Through the same.]

This Collect is said at every Hour on this day.

Memorial of S. MARY *and of* ALL SAINTS, p. 172.

No Memorial of the CROSS *is made till after the First Sunday after Trinity.*

Tierce.

Chapter as at Lauds.

Sexts.

CHAPTER. Acts IV.

AND with great power gave the apostles witness of the resurrection of the Lord Jesus: and great grace was upon them all.

Nones.

CHAPTER. Acts IV.

AS many as were possessors of lands or houses sold them, and brought the prices of the things that were sold, and laid them down at the Apostles' feet: and distribution was made unto every man according as he had need.

THE ASCENSION OF OUR LORD JESUS CHRIST.
First Vespers.

Ant. I will not leave you comfortless. Alleluia : I go, but I will come to you. Alleluia. And your heart shall rejoice. Alleluia. Alleluia.

Psalms of the Feria.

CHAPTER. Acts I.

THE former treatise have I made, O Theophilus, of all that Jesus began both to do and teach, until the day in which He was taken up,

THE ASCENSION.

after that He through the Holy Ghost had given commandments unto the Apostles whom He had chosen.

℟. Let not your heart be troubled; I go to the Father, and when I am taken up from you, I will send you; Alleluia : the Spirit of truth, and your heart shall rejoice. Alleluia. ℣. I will pray the Father, and He shall give you another Comforter. ℟. The Spirit of truth, and your heart shall rejoice. Alleluia. ℣. Glory be to the Father, and to the Son : and to the Holy Ghost. ℟. Alleluia. Alleluia. Alleluia.

HYMN. *Æterne Rex altissime.*

ETERNAL Monarch, King most high,
Whose blood hath brought redemption nigh,
By Whom the death of death was wrought,
And conqu'ring grace's battle fought :

Ascending to the Throne of might,
And seated at the Father's right,
All power in heaven is Jesu's own,
That here His Manhood had not known.

That so, in Nature's triple frame,
Each heavenly and each earthly name,
And things in hell's abyss abhorred,
May bend the knee and own Him Lord.

Yea, angels tremble when they see
How changed is our humanity,
That flesh hath purged what flesh had stained,
And God, the flesh of God, hath reigned.

Be Thou our Joy and Thou our Guard,
Who art to be our great Reward :
Our glory and our boast in Thee,
For ever and for ever be !

All glory, Lord, to Thee we pay,
Ascending o'er the stars to-day ;
All glory, as is ever meet,
To Father and to Paraclete. Amen.

These two last verses are said at the end of all Hymns of this metre till Whitsuntide, except at Vespers of the Invention of the Cross, and on Commemorations of the Blessed Virgin.

℣. Christ going up on high.
℟. Led captivity captive. Alleluia.
This Hymn is said daily till Whitsun Eve.

Ant. to Mag. Father, I have manifested Thy Name unto the men which Thou gavest Me : I pray for them, I pray not for the world. And now come I to Thee. Alleluia.

Collect as at the following Lauds [or of the Vigil].

Compline.

Ant. to Psalms. Alleluia. Alleluia. Alleluia. Alleluia.

HYMN. *Jesu nostra Redemptio.*

JESU, Redemption all divine,
Whom here we love, for Whom we pine,
God, working out creation's plan,
And, in the latter time, made Man ;

What love of Thine was that, which led
To take our woes upon Thy head,
And pangs and cruel death to bear,
To ransom us from death's despair !

To Thee hell's gate gave ready way,
Demanding there his captive prey :
And now, in pomp and victor's pride,
Thou sittest at the Father's side.

Let very mercy force Thee still
To spare us, conquering all our ill ;
And, granting that we ask, on high
With Thine own face to satisfy.

Be Thou our Joy and Thou our Guard,
Who art to be our great Reward :
Our glory and our boast in Thee,
For ever and for ever be !

All glory, Lord, to Thee we pay,
Ascending o'er the stars to-day ;
All glory, as is ever meet,
To Father and to Paraclete. Amen.

℣. Keep us, O Lord.
℟. As the apple of an eye, hide us under the shadow of Thy wings.

Ant. to Nunc Dim. Alleluia. Christ going up on high. Alleluia : Led captivity captive. Alleluia. Alleluia.

Lauds.

℣. I ascend to My Father, and your Father.
℟. To My God, and your God. Alleluia.

Psalms of Sunday.

Ant. 1. Ye men of Galilee, why stand ye gazing up into heaven? : This same Jesus, Which is taken up from you into heaven, shall so come. Alleluia.

Ant. 2. And while they looked steadfastly toward heaven as He went up : they said, Alleluia.

Ant. 3. While He blessed them, He was parted from them : and carried up into heaven. Alleluia.

Ant. 4. Exalt ye the King of kings : and sing praises to God. Alleluia.

Ant. 5. While they beheld, He was taken up : and in the sky a cloud received Him. Alleluia.

CHAPTER. Acts I.

THE former treatise have I made, O Theophilus, of all that Jesus began both to do and teach, until the day in which He was taken up, after that He through the Holy Ghost had given commandments unto the Apostles whom He had chosen.

HYMN.
Tu Christe nostrum gaudium.

THOU, Christ, Who art our joy alone,
Abiding on the heavenly throne,
Throughout the earth Thy sway extends,
And earth-born joys Thy victory ends.

Therefore we pray Thee, of Thy grace,
From all our sins to turn Thy face :
And lift our hearts by Thy dear love
To rest with Thee in realms above.

That when before our dazzled sight
Thy judgment cloud glows red and bright,
Our sins' award be done away,
And our lost crowns restored for aye.

Be Thou our Joy and Thou our Guard,
Who art to be our great Reward :
Our glory and our boast in Thee
For ever and for ever be!

All glory, Lord, to Thee we pay,
Ascending o'er the stars to-day;
All glory, as is ever meet,
To Father and to Paraclete. Amen.

℣. God is gone up with a merry noise.

℟. And the Lord with the sound of the trump. Alleluia.

Ant. to Ben. I ascend unto My Father, and your Father : to My God, and your God. Alleluia.

COLLECT.

GRANT, we beseech Thee, Almighty God, that like as we do believe Thy Only-begotten Son our Lord Jesus Christ to have ascended into the heavens : so we may also in heart and mind thither ascend, and with Him continually dwell, Who liveth and reigneth with Thee and the Holy Ghost, one God, world without end. Amen.

Prime.

Ant. Ye men of Galilee, why stand ye gazing up into heaven ? : This same Jesus, Which is taken up from you into heaven, shall so come. Alleluia.

Deus in nomine. Psalm liv.
Beati immaculati and *Retribuo servo Tuo.* Psalm cxix.

Ant. to Quicunque. Thanks be to Thee, p. 31.

℟. Jesu Christ, Son of the living God, have mercy upon us. Alleluia. Alleluia. ℣. Thou that sittest at the right hand of God the Father. Alleluia. Alleluia. ℟. Have mercy upon us. Alleluia. Alleluia. ℣. Glory be to the Father, and to the Son : and to the Holy Ghost. ℟. Jesu Christ, Son of the living God, have mercy upon us. Alleluia. Alleluia.

℣. O Lord, arise, help us.
℟. And deliver us for Thy Name's sake.

Tierce.

Ant. And while they looked steadfastly toward heaven as He went up : they said, Alleluia.

Chapter as at Lauds.

℟. Thou hast set Thy glory. Alleluia. Alleluia. ℣. Above the heavens, O Lord. ℟. Alleluia. Alleluia. ℣. Glory be to the Father, and to the Son : and to the Holy Ghost.

℟. Thou hast set Thy glory. Alleluia. Alleluia.
℣. God is gone up with a merry noise.
℟. And the Lord with the sound of the trump. Alleluia.

Sexts.

Ant. While He blessed them, He was parted from them : and carried up into heaven. Alleluia.

CHAPTER. Acts I.

HE being assembled together with them, commanded them that they should not depart from Jerusalem, but wait for the promise of the Father, which, saith He, ye have heard of Me.

℟. God is gone up with a merry noise. Alleluia. Alleluia. ℣. And the Lord with the sound of the trump. ℟. Alleluia. Alleluia. ℣. Glory be to the Father, and to the Son : and to the Holy Ghost. ℟. God is gone up with a merry noise. Alleluia. Alleluia.
℣. Christ going up on high.
℟. Led captivity captive. Alleluia.

Nones.

Ant. While they beheld, He was taken up : and in the sky a cloud received Him. Alleluia.

CHAPTER. Acts I.

FOR John truly baptized with water; but ye shall be baptized with the Holy Ghost not many days hence.

℟. Christ going up on high. Alleluia. Alleluia. ℣. Led captivity captive. ℟. Alleluia. Alleluia. ℣. Glory be to the Father, and to the Son : and to the Holy Ghost. ℟. Christ going up on high. Alleluia. Alleluia.

℣. I ascend to My Father, and your Father.
℟. To My God, and your God. Alleluia.

Second Vespers.

Ant. Ye men of Galilee, why stand ye gazing up into heaven? : This same Jesus, Which is taken up from you into heaven, shall so come. Alleluia. Alleluia.

Psalms of Sunday.

CHAPTER. Acts I.

THE former treatise have I made, O Theophilus, of all that Jesus began both to do and teach, until the day in which He was taken up, after that He through the Holy Ghost had given commandments unto the Apostles whom He had chosen.

℟. Go ye into all the world and preach, saying; Alleluia : He that believeth and is baptized shall be saved. Alleluia. Alleluia. Alleluia. ℣. But the Comforter, Which is the Holy Ghost, Whom the Father will send in My Name, He shall teach you all things, and bring all things to your remembrance, whatsoever I have said unto you. ℟. He that believeth and is baptized shall be saved. Alleluia. Alleluia. Alleluia. ℣. Glory be to the Father, and to the Son : and to the Holy Ghost. ℟. Alleluia. Alleluia. Alleluia.

HYMN. *Æterne Rex altissime,*
℣. and ℟., p. 179.

Ant. to Mag. O King of glory, Lord of Hosts, Who, triumphing to-day, hast ascended above all heavens : leave us not comfortless, but send us the promise of the Father, the Spirit of truth. Alleluia.

Collect as at Lauds.

No Memorial is made of any Feast, except its Office be kept on the morrow.

The Hours are thus said, except on Sunday, till the Octave, except that the Ants. to Benedictus *and* Magnificat *change daily, and that the Psalms at Lauds are said under one Ant., as below. The* R̃. *at Vespers is omitted, and at Prime the Ant. to* Quicunque is Thee duly praise, p. 31, *and Chapter,* O Lord, be gracious, p. 33.

FRIDAY.
Lauds.

Ant. to Psalms. Ye men of Galilee, why stand ye gazing up into heaven ? : This same Jesus, Which is taken up from you into heaven, shall so come. Alleluia.

Ant. to Ben. Go ye into all the world, and preach the Gospel to every creature. Alleluia : He that believeth and is baptized shall be saved. Alleluia. But he that believeth not shall be damned. Alleluia.

Collect of Ascension Day.

Vespers.

Ant. to Mag. I will pray the Father : and He shall give you another Comforter. Alleluia.

No Memorials of the Cross, *of* S. Mary, *or of* All Saints *are said throughout this Octave.*

SATURDAY.
Lauds.

Ant. to Ben. If I go not away, the Comforter will not come unto you : but if I depart, I will send Him unto you. Alleluia.

SUNDAY AFTER THE ASCENSION.
First Vespers.

Nothing of the Sunday, not even Memorial, all as on Second Vespers of Ascension Day, except

Ant. to Mag. After the Lord had spoken unto them, He was received up into heaven : and sat on the right hand of God. Alleluia.

Collect of Ascension Day, except the Collect for following Lauds be deemed preferable.

Lauds.

Psalms of Sunday, under this one

Ant. Ye men of Galilee, why stand ye gazing up into heaven ? : This same Jesus, Which is taken up from you into heaven, shall so come. Alleluia. Alleluia.

Chapter. 1 S. Pet. iv.

BE ye therefore sober, and watch unto prayer. And above all things have fervent charity among yourselves : for charity shall cover the multitude of sins.

R̃. Thanks be to God.

Ant. to Ben. When the Comforter is come, Whom I will send unto you from the Father : even the Spirit of truth, Which proceedeth from the Father, He shall testify of Me. Alleluia.

Collect.

O GOD the King of glory, Who hast exalted Thine only Son Jesus Christ with great triumph unto Thy kingdom in heaven ; we beseech Thee, leave us not comfortless ; but send to us Thine Holy Ghost to comfort us, and exalt us unto the same place whither our Saviour Christ is gone before, Who liveth and reigneth with Thee and the Holy Ghost, one God, world without end. Amen.

[*Or,*

ALMIGHTY, everlasting God, grant that our wills may alway be devoted to Thee, and that we may alway serve Thy Majesty with a pure heart. Through.]

Memorial of the Ascension.

Ant. I ascend to My Father, and your Father : to My God, and your God. Alleluia.

℣. Christ going up on high.

℟. Led captivity captive. Alleluia.

Collect of Ascension Day.

All at Prime, except Ant. to Quicunque, *Thee duly praise, p. 31, Tierce, Sexts, and Nones, as on Ascension Day, except these Chapters and the Collect.*

Tierce.

Chapter as at Lauds.

Sexts.

CHAPTER. 1 S. Pet. IV.

USE hospitality one to another without grudging. As every man hath received the gift, even so minister the same one to another, as good stewards of the manifold grace of God.

Nones.

CHAPTER. 1 S. Pet. IV.

IF any man minister, let him do it as of the ability which God giveth : that God in all things may be glorified through Jesus Christ.

Second Vespers.

As at Second Vespers of Ascension, except

CHAPTER. 1 S. Pet. IV.

BE ye therefore sober, and watch unto prayer. And above all things have fervent charity among yourselves : for charity shall cover the multitude of sins.

Ant. to Mag. But these things have I told you : that when the time shall come, ye may remember that I told you of them. Alleluia.

Collect as at Lauds.

Memorial of the Ascension.

Ant. O King of glory, Lord of Hosts, Who, triumphing to-day, hast ascended above all heavens : leave us not comfortless, but send us the promise of the Father, the Spirit of truth. Alleluia.

℣. God is gone up with a merry noise.

℟. And the Lord with the sound of the trump. Alleluia.

Collect of Ascension Day.

MONDAY.
Lauds.

Ant. to Ben. And they went forth, and preached everywhere : the Lord working with them, and confirming the word with signs following. Alleluia. Alleluia.

Collect of Ascension Day, and so till the Octave, inclusive.

Vespers.

Ant. to Mag. Go ye into all the world, and preach the gospel to every creature. Alleluia : He that believeth and is baptized shall be saved. Alleluia. But he that believeth not shall be damned. Alleluia.

TUESDAY.
Lauds.

Ant. to Ben. I will pray the Father : and He shall give you another Comforter. Alleluia.

Vespers.

Ant. to Mag. If I go not away, the Comforter will not come unto you : but if I depart, I will send Him unto you. Alleluia.

WEDNESDAY.

Ant. to Benedictus *as on Monday.*

OCTAVE OF THE ASCENSION.

At First and Second Vespers all as at First and Second Vespers of Ascension Day respectively, except that the R̺. *after the Chapter is not said at Second Vespers. The other Hours all as on Ascension Day.*

FRIDAY.

If a vacant day, Commemoration Office of the Blessed Virgin till Nones, inclusive, Memorial of the same being made at Vespers; but if this be not used:

Lauds.

(*Ant. to Psalms.* Alleluia. Alleluia. Alleluia. Alleluia.

This Ant. is used at every Hour. All else as on the previous Sunday, with Sunday Collect, and so at all the Hours.)

Vespers.

As on the previous Sunday. Memorials of S. MARY *and of* ALL SAINTS, p. 172, *are said at Lauds and Vespers.*

WHITSUN EVE.

Lauds.

V̺. I ascend to My Father, and your Father.

R̺. To My God, and your God. Alleluia.

Ant. Alleluia. Alleluia. Alleluia. Alleluia.

Psalms of Sunday.

CHAPTER. Acts XIX.

AND it came to pass, that, while Apollos was at Corinth, Paul having passed through the upper coasts came to Ephesus: and finding certain disciples, he said unto them, Have ye received the Holy Ghost since ye believed? And they said unto him, We have not so much as heard whether there be any Holy Ghost.

HYMN. *Tu Christe nostrum gaudium,*
V̺. and R̺., p. 180.

Ant. to Ben. If ye love Me, keep My commandments: Alleluia. Alleluia. Alleluia.

[COLLECT.

GRANT, we beseech Thee, Almighty God, that the brightness of Thy glory may shine upon us, and cause the illumination of the Holy Spirit to shed the light of Thy light upon them that are born again by Thy grace. Through. Who liveth. In the unity.]

This Collect is said at every Hour of this day. Memorials of S. MARY *and of* ALL SAINTS, *as p. 172. At all the Hours are said Easter Alleluias (four Alleluias) as Ants. to Psalms, with* R̺R̺. *and* V̺V̺. *of Ascension Day.*

Tierce.

Chapter as at Lauds.

Sexts.

CHAPTER. Acts XIX.

JOHN verily baptized with the baptism of repentance, saying unto the people, that they should believe on Him which should come after him, that is, on Christ Jesus.

Nones.

CHAPTER. Acts XIX.

PAUL went into the synagogue, and spake boldly for the space of three months, disputing and persuading the things concerning the kingdom of God.

If any Feast occur on this day, its Office is wholly omitted, but if it be above the lowest class it is translated to a day after Trinity Sunday, on which it can be kept with both Vespers.

WHITSUN DAY.
First Vespers.

Ant. to Psalms. Come, Holy Ghost, fill the hearts of Thy faithful people, and kindle in them the fire of Thy love : Who, through diversity of many tongues, hast gathered the Gentiles into the unity of the faith. Alleluia. Alleluia. Alleluia.

Psalms of the Feria.

CHAPTER. Acts II.

WHEN the day of Pentecost was fully come, they were all with one accord in one place.

℟. The Apostles did speak with other tongues. Alleluia : The wonderful works of God. Alleluia. ℣. They were all filled with the Holy Ghost, and began to speak. ℟. The wonderful works of God. Alleluia. ℣. Glory be to the Father, and to the Son : and to the Holy Ghost. ℟. Alleluia. Alleluia.

HYMN.
Jam Christus astra ascenderat.

NOW Christ, ascending whence He came,
Had mounted o'er the starry frame;
The Holy Ghost on man to pour,
As God the Father's promise bore.

The solemn time was drawing nigh,
Replete with heavenly mystery,
On seven days' sevenfold circles borne,
That first and blessed Whitsun-morn.

When the third hour shone all around,
There came a rushing mighty sound,
And told the Apostles, while in prayer,
That, as 'twas promised, God was there.

Forth from the Father's light it came,
That beautiful and kindly flame :
To fill, with fervour of His word,
The spirits faithful to their Lord.

Thou once in every holy breast
Didst bid indwelling grace to rest :
This day our sins, we pray, release,
And in our time, O Lord, give peace.

To God the Father, God the Son,
And God the Spirit, praise be done ;
And Christ the Lord upon us pour
The Spirit's gift for evermore. Amen.

These two last verses are said at the end of all Hymns of this metre till Trinity, except Veni Creator, *which takes the last verse only.*

℣. The Spirit of the Lord filleth the world.
℟. And That which containeth all things hath knowledge of the voice. Alleluia.

Ant. to Mag. If a man love Me, he will keep My words, and My Father will love him : and We will come unto him, and make Our abode with him. Alleluia.

Collect of Whitsun Eve, or as at the following Lauds.

Compline.

Ant. to Psalms. Alleluia. Alleluia. Alleluia. Alleluia.

CHAPTER. Jer. XIV., p. 68.

HYMN. *Salvator mundi Domine,* ℣. *and* ℟., p. 69.

On the four days following is said instead,

Alma Chorus Domini.

CHOIR of the Lord our God, now sing the
Names of the Highest ;
Saviour of men, Messias, Lord God of Hosts, Adonai,
Only-begotten Son, Emmanuel, Way for the weary,
Life of the fainting soul, strong Hand of the Lord, of one substance,
First-born of all Creation, Beginning, Wisdom, and Virtue :
Alpha, the First, we name Thee, then Omega, last of the cycle,
Fountain and source of good, Holy Comforter, blest Mediator,
Lamb, and Sheep of the Altar, meek Heifer, Serpent uplifted,
Ram of the mystic page, Judah's Lion, Worm of abasement,
Mouth of the Word, God's splendour, bright Sun of glory, His Image,
Light of His Light, Thou Bread of Life, sweet Flower of the valley,
Vine of the vineyard, Mountain uncut, firm Gate of the sheepfold,
Rock, and Angel, and Bridegroom, and Shepherd, God's Prophet and High Priest :
Lord, Everlasting God, Great King of the Universe, Jesus,
Hear and save us, we pray, to Whom be glory for ever. Amen.

[Or,

HYMN. *Veni sancte Spiritus.*

COME, Thou holy Paraclete,
And from Thy celestial seat,
Send Thy light and brilliancy:

Father of the poor, draw near,
Giver of all gifts, be here:
Come, the soul's true radiancy:

Come, of Comforters the best,
Of the soul the sweetest guest,
Come in toil refreshingly:

Thou in labour rest most sweet,
Thou art shadow from the heat,
Comfort in adversity.

O Thou Light, most pure and blest,
Shine within the inmost breast
Of Thy faithful company.

Where Thou art not, man hath nought;
Every holy deed and thought
Comes from Thy divinity.

What is soiled, make Thou pure;
What is wounded, work its cure;
What is parched, fructify;

What is rigid, gently bend;
What is frozen, warmly tend;
Strengthen what goes erringly.

Fill Thy faithful who confide
In Thy power to guard and guide,
With Thy sevenfold mystery.

Here Thy grace and virtue send;
Grant salvation in the end,
And in heaven felicity. Amen.]

Ant. to Nunc Dim. Alleluia. The Spirit the Comforter. Alleluia: shall teach you all things. Alleluia. Alleluia.

Lauds.

℣. When Thou lettest Thy breath go forth, they shall be made.

℟. And Thou shalt renew the face of the earth. Alleluia.

Psalms of Sunday.

Ant. 1. When the day of Pentecost was fully come: they were all with one accord in one place. Alleluia.

Ant. 2. The Spirit of the Lord: filleth the world. Alleluia.

Ant. 3. They were all filled with the Holy Ghost: and began to speak. Alleluia.

Ant. 4. O ye wells and all that move in the waters: say unto God, Alleluia.

Ant. 5. The Apostles did speak with other tongues: the wonderful works of God. Alleluia. Alleluia. Alleluia.

CHAPTER. Acts II.

WHEN the day of Pentecost was fully come, they were all with one accord in one place.

℟. Thanks be to God.

HYMN. *Impleta gaudent viscera.*

BREATHED on by God the Holy Ghost,
The breasts, which He hath filled, rejoice,
And of His wondrous deeds they boast
In languages of diverse voice.

And to the men of every race,
Barbarian, Latin, and the Greek,
While wondering eyes upon them gaze,
In each one's dialect they speak.

Then Jewry, trusting not the sign,
And by malicious hate enticed,
Reproaches, as but full of wine,
The holy messengers of Christ.

But Peter hastes with mighty deeds,
Of power miraculous to teach,
And with the words of Joel pleads
Against the falsehood of their speech.

Thou once in every holy breast
Didst bid indwelling grace to rest:
This day our sins, we pray, release,
And in our time, O Lord, give peace.

To God the Father, and the Son,
And God the Spirit, praise be done;
And Christ the Lord upon us pour
The Spirit's gift for evermore. Amen.

℣. The Apostles did speak with other tongues.

℟. The wonderful works of God. Alleluia.

Ant. to Ben. Receive ye the Holy Ghost: whosesoever sins ye remit, they are remitted unto them. Alleluia.

COLLECT.

GOD, Who as at this time didst teach the hearts of Thy faithful people, by the sending to them the light of Thy Holy Spirit: grant us by the same Spirit to have a right judgment in all things, and ever-

WHITSUN DAY.

more to rejoice in His holy comfort; through the merits of Christ Jesus our Saviour, Who liveth and reigneth with Thee, in the unity of the same Spirit, one God, world without end. Amen.

Prime.

Ant. When the day of Pentecost was fully come : they were all with one accord in one place. Alleluia.

The rest as on Ascension Day.

Tierce.

HYMN. *Veni Creator Spiritus.*

COME, Holy Ghost, our souls inspire,
And lighten with celestial fire :
Thou the anointing Spirit art,
Who dost Thy sevenfold gifts impart.

Thy blessed unction from above
Is comfort, life, and fire of love :
Enable with perpetual light
The dulness of our blinded sight.

Anoint and cheer our soiled face,
With the abundance of Thy grace ;
Keep far our foes, give peace at home :
Where Thou art Guide, no ill can come.

Teach us to know the Father, Son,
And Thee, of both, to be but One ;
That through the ages all along,
This may be our endless song :

To God the Father, God the Son,
And God the Spirit, praise be done ;
And Christ the Lord upon us pour
The Spirit's gift for evermore. Amen.

(*A fuller version of the above Hymn, for optional use.*)

COME, Holy Ghos our souls inspire,
And lighten with celestial fire ;
With grace divine our spirits fill,
Thyself into our hearts instil.

O Comforter of man, draw nigh,
Consoling gift of God most High ;
Thou living fount of fire and love,
Thou heavenly unction from above.

Thou the anointing Spirit art,
Who dost Thy sevenfold gifts impart ;
The Father's promise, hope of rest,
The still, small Voice within the breast.

Enable with perpetual light
The dulness of our blinded sight ;
Thy love bestow, Thy healing give,
And bid the wounded spirit live.

Do Thou repel the deadly foe,
Grant Thou the soul Thy peace to know :

If Thou be Guardian, Thou be Guide,
No fear may turn our steps aside.

Teach us the Father's love to see,
To know the only Son through Thee,
Thyself of both the Spirit blest,
Giver of life, of peace, of rest.

To God the Father be the praise ;
To God the Son our voice we raise ;
To Thee, O Holy Ghost above,
The fire of purity and love. Amen.

This Hymn is also said instead of Nunc sancte nobis, on Monday, Tuesday, and Wednesday, in this week, but on the other days the latter Hymn is said as usual.

Ant. The Spirit of the Lord : filleth the world. Alleluia.

CHAPTER. Acts II.

WHEN the day of Pentecost was fully come, they were all with one accord in one place.

R⁄. They were all filled with the Holy Ghost. Alleluia. Alleluia. V⁄. And began to speak. R⁄. Alleluia. Alleluia V⁄. Glory be to the Father, and to the Son : and to the Holy Ghost. R⁄. They were all filled with the Holy Ghost. Alleluia. Alleluia.

V⁄. The Apostles did speak with other tongues.

R⁄. The wonderful works of God. Alleluia.

Sexts.

Ant. They were all filled with the Holy Ghost : and began to speak. Alleluia.

CHAPTER. Acts II.

AND suddenly there came a sound from heaven, as of a rushing mighty wind, and it filled all the house where they were sitting.

R⁄. The Apostles did speak with other tongues. Alleluia. Alleluia. V⁄. Alleluia. Alleluia. V⁄. Glory be to the Father, and to the Son : and to the Holy Ghost. R⁄. The Apostles did speak with other tongues. Alleluia. Alleluia.

℣. The Spirit of the Lord filleth the world.

℟. And That which containeth all things hath knowledge of the voice. Alleluia.

Nones.

Ant. The Apostles did speak with other tongues : the wonderful works of God. Alleluia.

CHAPTER. Acts II.

AND there appeared unto them cloven tongues, like as of fire, and It sat upon each of them.

℟. The Spirit of the Lord filleth the world. Alleluia. Alleluia. ℣. And That which containeth all things hath knowledge of the voice. ℟. Alleluia. Alleluia. ℣. Glory be to the Father, and to the Son : and to the Holy Ghost. ℟. The Spirit of the Lord filleth the world. Alleluia. Alleluia.

℣. When Thou lettest Thy breath go forth they shall be made.

℟. And Thou shalt renew the face of the earth. Alleluia.

Second Vespers.

Ant. When the day of Pentecost was fully come : they were all with one accord in one place. Alleluia.

Psalms of Sunday.

CHAPTER. Acts II.

THE multitude came together, and were confounded, because that every man heard them speak in his own language.

℟. The Holy Ghost proceeded from the throne; unseen He entered the hearts of the Apostles; earnest of sanctification, token that in their lips should every tongue be born. Alleluia. ℣. The fire of God came upon them, not burning, but enlightening; and bestowed on them the gifts of grace. ℟. That in their lips should every tongue be born. Alleluia. ℣. Glory be to the Father, and to the Son : and to the Holy Ghost. ℟. Alleluia. Alleluia.

HYMN. *Beata nobis gaudia.*

BLEST joys for mighty wonders wrought
The year's revolving orb has brought,
What time the Holy Ghost in flame
Upon the Lord's disciples came.

The quivering fire their heads bedewed,
In cloven tongues' similitude,
That eloquent their words might be,
And fervid all their charity.

In varying tongues the Lord they praised,
The gathering people stood amazed;
And whom the Comforter Divine
Inspired, they mocked as full of wine.

These things were done in type to-day,
When Easter-tide had worn away,
The number told which once set free
The captive at the jubilee.

Thy servants, falling on their face,
Beseech Thy mercy, God of grace,
To send us from Thy heavenly seat
The blessings of the Paraclete.

Thou once in every holy breast
Didst bid indwelling grace to rest :
This day our sins, we pray, release,
And in our time, O Lord, give peace.

To God the Father, God the Son,
And God the Spirit, praise be done;
And Christ the Lord upon us pour
The Spirit's gift for evermore. Amen.

℣. The Spirit of the Lord filleth the world.

℟. And That which containeth all things hath knowledge of the voice. Alleluia.

This Hymn, ℣., and ℟., are said daily till the First Vespers of Trinity Sunday.

Ant. to Mag. To-day is the day of Pentecost fully come, Alleluia; to-day the Holy Ghost appeared in fire to the disciples, and bestowed on them the gifts of grace : He sent them into all the world to preach and to testify; he that believeth and is baptized shall be saved. Alleluia.

Collect as at Lauds.

WHITSUN MONDAY.
Lauds.

Ant. When the day of Pentecost was fully come : they were all with one accord in one place. Alleluia.

Psalms of Sunday.

CHAPTER. Acts II.

AND suddenly there came a sound from heaven as of a rushing mighty wind, and it filled all the house where they were sitting.

R͑. Thanks be to God.

HYMN. *Impleta gaudent viscera,* V͑. and R͑., p. 186.

Ant. to Ben. God so loved the world, that He gave His Only-begotten Son : that whosoever believeth in Him should not perish, but have everlasting life. Alleluia.

Ant. to Benedictus *changes daily [also the Collect].*

Collect for Whitsun Day.

[*Or,*

GOD, Who didst bestow the Holy Spirit on Thine Apostles : grant to Thy people the fruit of their devout petitions, that they to whom Thou hast given faith may also receive peace ; Through. Who liveth. In the unity.

This Collect is said at every Hour on this day only;] the Ants., R͑R͑., *and* V͑V͑., *as on Whitsun Day : and this order is observed through the week, each day having its own Collect and Ants. to* Benedictus *and* Magnificat : *the Chapters at the Little Hours being said as on this day. The* R͑. *is omitted at Vespers.*

Prime.

Ant. to Quicunque, Thee duly praise, p. 31, *and Chapter,* O Lord, be gracious, p. 33.

Tierce.

CHAPTER. Acts II.

AND suddenly there came a sound from heaven as of a rushing mighty wind, and it filled all the house where they were sitting.

Sexts.

CHAPTER. Acts II.

AND there appeared unto them cloven tongues, like as of fire, and It sat upon each of them.

Nones.

CHAPTER. Acts II.

AND they were all filled with the Holy Ghost, and began to speak with other tongues, as the Spirit gave them utterance.

Vespers.

Psalms of Sunday.

Ant. to Mag. For God sent not His Son into the world to condemn the world : but that the world through Him might be saved. Alleluia.

Collect as at Lauds.

WHITSUN TUESDAY.
Lauds.

Ant. to Ben. Verily, verily, I say unto you, He that entereth not by the door into the sheep-fold, but climbeth up some other way, the same is a thief and a robber : but he that entereth in by the door is the shepherd of the sheep. Alleluia.

[COLLECT.

LET the might of Thy Holy Spirit be present with us, we beseech Thee, O Lord, that it may mercifully purge our hearts, and guard us from all adversities. Through. Who liveth. In the unity.]

Vespers.

Ant. to Mag. I am the Door, saith the Lord : by Me if any man enter in, he shall be saved, and shall go in and out, and find pasture. Alleluia.

Collect as at Lauds.

WEDNESDAY.
Lauds.

Ant. to Ben. Verily, verily, I say unto you: He that believeth on Me hath everlasting life. Alleluia. Alleluia.

[COLLECT.]

WE beseech Thee, O Lord, let the Comforter Which proceedeth from Thee lighten our hearts, and lead us into all truth, according to the promise of Thy Son, Who liveth. In the unity.]

Vespers.

Ant. to Mag. I am the living Bread which came down from heaven : if any man eat of this Bread he shall live for ever; and the Bread that I will give is My Flesh, which I will give for the life of the world. Alleluia. Alleluia.

Collect as at Lauds.

THURSDAY.
Lauds.

Ant. to Ben. Jesus called His twelve disciples together, and gave them power and authority over all devils, and to cure diseases : and He sent them to preach the kingdom of God, and to heal the sick. Alleluia. Alleluia.

[COLLECT.]

GRANT, we beseech Thee, Almighty and merciful God, that Thy Holy Spirit, coming into our hearts, may make them fit temples for His glory to inhabit. Through. Who liveth. In the unity.]

Vespers.

Ant. to Mag. The twelve departed, and went through the towns : preaching the gospel, and healing everywhere. Alleluia. Alleluia.

Collect as at Lauds.

FRIDAY.
Lauds.

Ant. to Ben. It came to pass on a certain day, as Jesus was teaching, that there were Pharisees and doctors of the law sitting by, which had come out of every town of Galilee, and Judea, and Jerusalem : and the power of the Lord was present to heal them. Alleluia. Alleluia.

[COLLECT.]

GRANT to Thy Church, we beseech Thee, O merciful God, that being gathered together in the Holy Spirit, it may be vexed by no incursions of the enemy. Through. Who liveth. In the unity.]

Vespers.

Ant. to Mag. And the sick of the palsy took up that whereon he lay, glorifying God : and all the people when they saw it, gave praise unto God. Alleluia.

Collect as at Lauds.

SATURDAY.
Lauds.

Ant. to Ben. Now when the sun was setting, all they that had any sick with divers diseases brought them unto Jesus : and He laid His hands on every one of them, and healed them. Alleluia.

[COLLECT.]

WE beseech Thee, O Lord, mercifully to pour Thy Spirit into our hearts; that, as we are created by His wisdom, so we may be governed by His providence. Through. Who liveth. In the unity.]

When the septiform Feast of Pentecost has been completed in seven days, on the eighth day, that is, the first Sunday after Whitsun Day, shall be held full service of the Holy Trinity.

TRINITY SUNDAY.
First Vespers.

Ant. 1. Glory to Thee, co-equal Trinity, One Deity : before all worlds, and now and for ever.

Psalms as at First Vespers of Christmas Day, p. 91.

Ant. 2. Praise and ceaseless glory be to God, the Father, the Son, and the Holy Ghost : world without end.

Ant. 3. Glory and praise resound from the lips of all to the Father, and the Only-begotten Son : and like praise for ever to the Holy Ghost.

Ant. 4. For ever from all lips let praise resound to God the Father, and the Only-begotten Son : and Thee, O Holy Ghost.

Ant. 5. Of Whom, and through Whom, and in Whom, are all things : to Him be glory for ever.

CHAPTER. 2 Cor. XIII.

THE grace of our Lord Jesus Christ, and the love of God, and the communion of the Holy Ghost, be with you all.

℟. Honour and might, dominion and power, be to the Trinity in Unity, and to the Unity in Trinity, through everlasting ages. ℣. To the Trinity be constant praise, unceasing glory to the Unity. ℟. Through everlasting ages. ℣. Glory be to the Father, and to the Son : and to the Holy Ghost. ℣. Through everlasting ages.

HYMN. *Adesto Sancta Trinitas.*

BE present, Holy Trinity;
Like splendour, and one Deity:
Of things above, and things below,
Beginning that no end shall know.

Thee all the armies of the sky
Adore, and laud, and magnify :
While Nature, in her triple frame,
For ever sanctifies Thy Name.

And we, too, thanks and homage pay,
Thine own adoring flock to-day;
O join to that celestial song
The praises of our suppliant throng!

Light, sole and one, we Thee confess,
With triple praise we rightly bless;
Alpha and Omega we own,
With every spirit round Thy throne.

To Thee, O Unbegotten One,
And Thee, O Sole-begotten Son,
And Thee, O Holy Ghost, we raise
Our equal and eternal praise. : Amen.

℣. Let us bless the Father, the Son, and the Holy Ghost.

℟. Let us praise and exalt Him above all for ever.

Ant. to Mag. Thanks be to Thee, O God ; thanks be to Thee, One Very Trinity : One Supreme Deity, One Holy Unity.

COLLECT.

ALMIGHTY and Everlasting God, Who hast given unto us Thy servants grace by the confession of a true faith to acknowledge the glory of the Eternal Trinity, and in the power of the Divine Majesty to worship the Unity; we beseech Thee, that Thou wouldest keep us stedfast in this faith, and evermore defend us from all adversities, Who livest and reignest, One God, world without end. Amen.

Compline.

As on Festivals in Trinity season, p. 69.

Compline is thus said for this and the three following days, and till after the Octave of Corpus Christi.

Lauds.

℣. Blessed art Thou, O Lord, in the firmament of heaven.

℟. And above all to be praised and glorified for ever.

Psalms of Sunday.

Immediately on the conclusion of each Psalm, the ℣. is begun by the reader, and continued by the Choir, before the resuming of the Antiphon.

Ant. 1. O Holy, blessed, glorious Trinity : Father, and Son, and Holy Ghost. ℣. To Thee be praise, glory, and thanksgiving.

Ant. 2. O Holy, blessed, glorious Trinity : Father, and Son, and Holy Ghost. ℣. Have mercy, have mercy, have mercy upon us.

Ant. 3. O very and eternal Trinity, supreme : Father, and Son, and Holy Ghost. ℣. To Thee be praise, glory, and thanksgiving.

Ant. 4. O very and eternal Trinity, supreme : Father, and Son, and Holy Ghost. ℣. Have mercy, have mercy, have mercy upon us.

Ant. 5. Justly, O Blessed Trinity, do all Thy creatures : praise Thee and worship Thee, and glorify Thee. ℣. To Thee be praise, glory, and thanksgiving.

CHAPTER. Rom. XI.

O THE depth of the riches both of the wisdom and knowledge of God! For of Him, and through Him, and to Him, are all things : to Whom be glory for ever. Amen.

HYMN.
O Pater sancte, mitis atque pie.

O HOLY Father, merciful and loving;
   O Jesu Christ, the only Son Eternal;
O Spirit blest, our spirits sweetly moving,
   One God supernal.

O Trine, thrice hallowed, Unity unshaken,
   Godhead most mighty; good, all goodness giving,
Light of the Angels, health of the forsaken,
   Hope of all living.

Thee, all things worship, which Thou hast created :
All Thy creation, Lord, in Thee rejoices,
We too, will worship Thee with hearts elated;
   O hear our voices.

Glory to Thee, Whose might all might excelleth,
One in Three Persons, Thee Whom nought can sever,
Thee, song beseemeth, Thee, with Whom praise dwelleth,
   Ever and ever. Amen.

℣. Blessed be the Name of the Lord.

℞. From this time forth for evermore.

Ant. to Ben. Blessed be the Creator and Preserver of all things, the Holy and Undivided Trinity : now and ever, and to ages of ages.

Prime.

Ant. O Holy, blessed, glorious Trinity : Father, and Son, and Holy Ghost.

Deus in nomine, Ps. liv., Beati *and* Retribue, Ps. cxix., *and* Quicunque, *all said under this Ant.* ℞. *with Alleluia.*

Tierce.

Ant. O Holy, blessed, glorious Trinity : Father, and Son, and Holy Ghost.

Chapter as at Lauds.

℞. Let us bless the Father, the Son, and the Holy Ghost. Alleluia. Alleluia. ℣. Let us praise and exalt Him above all for ever. ℞. Alleluia. Alleluia. ℣. Glory be to the Father, and to the Son : and to the Holy Ghost. ℞. Let us bless the Father, the Son, and the Holy Ghost. Alleluia. Alleluia.

℣. Blessed art Thou, O Lord, in the firmament of heaven.

℞. And above all to be praised and glorified for ever.

Sexts.

Ant. O very and eternal Trinity, supreme : Father, and Son, and Holy Ghost.

CHAPTER. 1 S. John V.

THERE are Three that bear record in heaven, the Father, the Word, and the Holy Ghost : and these Three are One.

℞. Blessed art Thou, O Lord, in the firmament of heaven. Alleluia. Alleluia. ℣. And above all to be praised and glorified for ever. ℞. Alleluia. Alleluia. ℣. Glory be to the Father, and to the Son : and to the Holy Ghost. ℞. Blessed art

Thou, O Lord, in the firmament of heaven. Alleluia. Alleluia.

℣. By the Word of the Lord were the heavens made.

℞. And all the hosts of them by the Breath of His mouth.

Nones.

Ant. Justly, O Blessed Trinity, do all Thy creatures : praise Thee, and worship Thee, and glorify Thee.

CHAPTER. Eph. IV.

THERE is one Lord, one faith, one baptism, one God and Father of all, Who is above all, and through all, and in you all.

℞. By the Word of the Lord were the heavens made. Alleluia. Alleluia. ℣. And all the hosts of them by the Breath of His mouth. ℞. Alleluia. Alleluia. ℣. Glory be to the Father, and to the Son : and to the Holy Ghost. ℞. By the Word of the Lord were the heavens made. Alleluia. Alleluia.

℣. Blessed be the Name of the Lord.

℞. From this time forth for evermore.

Second Vespers.

Ant. O holy, blessed, glorious Trinity: Father, Son and Holy Ghost.

Psalms of Sunday.

CHAPTER. Rom. XI.

O THE depth of the riches both of the wisdom and knowledge of God! For of Him, and through Him, and to Him are all things : to Whom be glory for ever.

℞. Let us bless the Father, the Son, and the Holy Ghost. Alleluia. Alleluia. ℣. Let us praise and exalt Him above all for ever. ℞. Alleluia. Alleluia. ℣. Glory be to the Father, and to the Son : and to the Holy Ghost. ℞. Let us bless the Father, the Son, and the Holy Ghost. Alleluia. Alleluia.

HYMN. *Adesto Sancta Trinitas,* ℣. and ℞., p. 191.

Ant. to Mag. Thee O Father unbegotten, Thee O Son Only-begotten, Thee O Holy Ghost the Comforter, O Holy and undivided Trinity : with our whole heart and with our lips we acknowledge Thee, we praise Thee, we bless Thee, to Thee be glory for ever.

Collect as at First Vespers.

Memorial is made at these Vespers of any Feast above the lowest class.

If this be the Feast of the place, the Octave services are kept for the next three days, as in rubric for Octave of the Visitation, except a Feast above the lowest class, or S. John's Eve occur: (but when this is not the case) Commemoration Offices may be used on these days.

WEDNESDAY.
First Vespers
OF THE
FESTIVAL OF CORPUS CHRISTI.

If any Feast above the lowest class occur on this Wednesday, a Memorial of it is made at the First Vespers of Corpus Christi: if any such occur on the Feast itself, it is transferred to the first day in the Octave not similarly occupied. The Office of Corpus Christi is said throughout the Octave, even on Sunday, except a Feast above the lowest class occur, in which case the Feast is kept, with Memorial of Corpus Christi. A simple Feast, above the lowest class, occurring on the Octave Day, is transferred.

This Office may be used on any Thursday in the year, if unhindered by a Vigil or Double Feast, except in Advent and Lent. Alleluia is omitted in the ℞℞. of the Little Hours, etc., except in the Octave of Corpus Christi, and in Eastertide.

First Vespers.

Ant. 1. Christ the Lord, a Priest for ever after the order of Melchisedec : offered bread and wine.

Psalm cx. *Dixit Dominus*, p. 47.

Ant. 2. The merciful Lord hath given meat to them that fear Him : in remembrance of His marvellous works.

Psalm cxi. *Confitebor tibi*, p. 47.

Ant. 3. I will receive the cup of salvation : and offer the sacrifice of thanksgiving.

Psalm cxvi. 10. *Credidi*, p. 52.

Ant. 4. May the children of the church be like the olive-branches : round about the table of the Lord.

Psalm cxxviii. *Beati omnes*, p. 56.

Ant. 5. The Lord Who maketh peace in the borders of the church : filleth us with the flour of wheat.

Psalm cxlvii. 12. *Lauda Hierusalem*, p. 65.

Chapter. 1 Cor. xi.

THE Lord Jesus the same night in which He was betrayed, took bread, and when He had given thanks, He brake it, and said, Take, eat : This is My Body, which is broken for you.

℟. A certain man made a great supper, and sent his servants at supper-time to say to them that were bidden, Come, for all things are now ready. ℣. Come, eat of my bread, and drink of the wine which I have mingled for you. ℟. For all things are now ready. ℣. Glory be to the Father, and to the Son : and to the Holy Ghost. ℟. For all things are now ready.

Hymn. *Sacris Solemniis.*

LET this our solemn feast
  With holy joys be crowned,
And from each loving breast
  The voice of gladness sound ;
Let ancient things depart,
  And all be new around,
In every act and voice and heart.

Remember we that eve,
  That Supper last and dread,
When Christ, as we believe,
  The Lamb and leavenless Bread
Unto His brethren brought ;
  And thus the law obeyed,
Of old time to the fathers taught.

But when the law's repast
  Was o'er, the type complete,
To His disciples last
  The Lord His Flesh to eat,
The whole to all, no less
  The whole to each, doth mete,
With His own hand, as we confess.

He gave the weak and frail,
  His Body for their food,
The sad for their regale
  The Chalice of His Blood,
And said—Take ye of this,
  My Cup, with life imbued ;
O drink ye all this draught of bliss !

He ordered in this wise
  Our Holy Offering,
To be the Sacrifice
  Which Priests alone should bring :
For whom is meet and fit
  That they should eat of it,
And in their turn to others give.

Lo ! Angels' Bread is made
  The Bread of mortal man ;
Shews forth this heavenly Bread
  The ends which types began ;
O wondrous boon indeed !
  Upon his Lord now can
A poor and humble servant feed !

Thee, Deity Triune
  Yet One, we meekly pray
O visit us right soon,
  As we our homage pay ;
And in Thy footsteps bright,
  Conduct us on our way,
To where Thou dwell'st in cloudless light.
Amen.

℣. Thou gavest them Bread from heaven.

℟. Containing in Itself all sweetness. [Alleluia.]

And so throughout the Octave of Corpus Christi is added Alleluia *to all the proper versicles of the Blessed Sacrament. At the other versicles it is not added, except in Eastertide.*

Ant. to Mag. O how sweet is Thy Spirit, O Lord, Who, that thou mightest shew Thy kindness unto Thy children : giving them most sweet Bread from heaven, fillest the hungry with good things, and sendest the scornful and rich empty away. [Alleluia.]

Collect.

O GOD, Who in this wonderful Sacrament hast left unto us a memorial of Thy Passion; grant to us, we beseech Thee, so to venerate the sacred mysteries of Thy Body and Blood, that we may always perceive in ourselves the fruit of Thy redemption, Who livest and reignest with the Father in the unity of the Holy Ghost, one God, world without end. Amen.

No Memorial is said on this day unless any Double Feast have been celebrated on it, in which case Memorial shall be made of such Feast.

Compline.

As in the Psalter on Festivals, except the Ant. to Nunc Dimittis. *The Hymn* Salvator mundi Domine, *is said with proper doxology, as at Prime, below.*

Ant. to Nunc Dim. [Alleluia.] The Bread that I will give [Alleluia]: is My Flesh, which I will give for the life of the world. [Alleluia. Alleluia.]

This Ant. is said throughout the Octave of Corpus Christi, even on the Feasts of Saints.

Lauds.

℣. Thou gavest them Bread from heaven.
℟. Containing in Itself all sweetness. [Alleluia.]

Psalms of Sunday.

Ant. 1. Wisdom hath builded her house, she hath mingled her wine: she hath also furnished her table. [Alleluia.]

Ant. 2. Thou feddest Thine own people with Angels' food : and didst send them Bread from heaven. [Alleluia.]

Ant. 3. The Bread of Christ is fat: yielding royal dainties. [Alleluia. Alleluia. Alleluia.]

Ant. 4. Consecrated priests offer incense : and Bread unto the Lord. [Alleluia.]

Ant. 5. To him that overcometh will I give the hidden manna : and a new name. [Alleluia.]

Chapter as at Vespers.

Hymn. *Verbum supernum prodiens.*

THE Word of God proceeding forth,
  Yet leaving not the Father's side,
And going to His work on earth,
  Had reached at length life's eventide.

By a disciple to be given
  To rivals, for His Blood athirst :
Himself, the very Bread of heaven,
  He gave to His disciples first.

He gave Himself in either kind,
  His precious Flesh ; His precious Blood ;
Of flesh and blood is man combined,
  And He of man would be the Food.

In birth, man's fellow man was He ;
  His Meat, while sitting at the board ;
He died, his Ransomer to be ;
  He reigns, to be his great Reward.

O saving Victim, slain to bless,
  Who op'st the heavenly gate to all
The attacks of many a foe oppress ;
  Give strength in strife, and help in fall.

To God, the Three in One, ascend
  All thanks and praise for evermore ;
He grant the life that shall not end,
  Upon the heavenly country's shore. Amen.

℣. He maketh peace in thy borders.
℟. And filleth thee with the flour of wheat. [Alleluia.]

Ant. to Ben. I am the Living Bread which came down from heaven : if any man eat of this Bread he shall live for ever. [Alleluia.]

Collect as at First Vespers.

Prime.

The Hymn ends with this Doxology (as all Hymns of the same metre, throughout the Office, except the Hymn, Verbum supernum*) :*

All honour, laud, and glory be,
  O Jesu, Virgin-born to Thee,
All glory as is ever meet,
  To Father, and to Paraclete. Amen.

Ant. to Psalms. Wisdom hath builded her house, she hath mingled her wine : she hath also furnished her table. [Alleluia.]

Ant. to Quicunque. O Beatific, &c., p. 32.

R℣. to Chapter.

R℣. Jesu Christ, Son of the Living God : have mercy upon us. Alleluia. ℣. Thou Who wast born of the Virgin Mary. Alleluia. Alleluia. Alleluia. R℣. Have mercy upon us. Alleluia. Alleluia. ℣. Glory be to the Father, and to the Son : and to the Holy Ghost. R℣. Jesu Christ, Son of the Living God, have mercy upon us. Alleluia.

Tierce.

Ant. Thou feddest Thine own people with Angels' food : and didst send them Bread from heaven. [Alleluia.]

Chapter as at Vespers.

R℣. He gave them * Bread from heaven. [Alleluia. Alleluia.] ℣. So man did eat Angels' food. R℣. [Alleluia. Alleluia.] ℣. Glory be to the Father, and to the Son : and to the Holy Ghost. R℣. He gave them Bread from heaven. [Alleluia. Alleluia.]

℣. He fed them with the finest wheat flour.

R℣. And with honey out of the stony rock did He satisfy them. [Alleluia.]

*When Alleluia is omitted, the repetition of the R℣. at the Hours begins at *.*

Sexts.

Ant. The Bread of Christ is fat : yielding royal dainties. [Alleluia. Alleluia. Alleluia.]

CHAPTER. 1 Cor. XI.

AS often as ye eat this Bread and drink this Cup, ye do shew the Lord's death till He come.

R℣. He fed them * with the finest wheat-flour. [Alleluia. Alleluia.] ℣. And with honey out of the stony rock did He satisfy them. R℣. [Alleluia. Alleluia.] ℣. Glory be to the Father, and to the Son : and to the Holy Ghost. R℣. He fed them with the finest wheat-flour. [Alleluia. Alleluia.]

℣. Thou bringest Bread out of the earth.

R℣. And Wine that maketh glad the heart of man. [Alleluia.]

Nones.

Ant. To him that overcometh will I give the hidden manna : and a new name. [Alleluia.]

CHAPTER. 1 Cor. XI.

WHOSOEVER shall eat this Bread, and drink this Cup of the Lord unworthily, shall be guilty of the Body and Blood of the Lord.

R℣. Thou bringest Bread * out of the earth. [Alleluia. Alleluia.] ℣. And Wine that maketh glad the heart of man. R℣. [Alleluia. Alleluia.] ℣. Glory be to the Father, and to the Son : and to the Holy Ghost. R℣. Thou bringest Bread out of the earth. [Alleluia. Alleluia.]

℣. He maketh peace in thy borders.

R℣. And filleth thee with the flour of wheat. [Alleluia.]

Second Vespers.

Ant. to Psalms. Wisdom hath builded her house, she hath mingled her wine: she hath also furnished her table. [Alleluia.]

Psalms as at First Vespers.

These Psalms are said under the above Antiphon throughout the Octave, including Sunday, when the Office is of the Octave.

Chapter as at First Vespers.

℟. And Elijah looked, and behold, there was a cake baken on the coals, and he arose and did eat and drink, and in the strength of that meat he went unto the mount of God. ℣. If any man eat of this Bread, he shall live for ever. ℟. And in the strength of that meat he went unto the mount of God. ℣. Glory be to the Father, and to the Son : and to the Holy Ghost. ℟. He went unto the mount of God.

HYMN. *Sacris Solemniis,* ℣. *and* ℟. *as at First Vespers.*

Ant. to Mag. O Sacred Banquet, wherein Christ is received, the memory of His Passion renewed : the soul filled with grace, and a pledge of future glory given unto us. [Alleluia.]

Throughout the Octave, the Sunday Psalms are said at Lauds under the first Ant. Wisdom, &c. *The Ants. to Ben. and Mag. are taken from those to Psalms at First Vespers, except on Sunday, and on the Octave Day. And these are used in making Memorial of Corpus Christi, if any Festival be kept in the Octave. At Prime, Tierce, Sexts, Nones, and Compline as on the day : the Ant. to Quicunque being,* O beatific, &c., p. 32.

On Sunday, the Office at First Vespers is as on the other days of the Octave, except that the Ant. to Mag. is, O how sweet, &c., *and Memorial is made of Saints, if any (or their Octave), of Sunday, the Holy Trinity, and the Cross. At the Hours all as on the first day, except that the Psalms at Lauds are said under the first Ant. and the Ant. to Quicunque is, on this day, and henceforth throughout the Octave,* Thee duly, &c., p. 31. *At Second Vespers, all as on the first day, except the* ℟., *which is omitted.*

On the Octave Day, the Psalms are said under the first Ant., Christ the Lord, &c. *All the rest, including* ℟., *as at First Vespers on the first day. Ant. to Quicunque,* Thee duly, &c., p. 31. *At Vespers, all as on Second Vespers of the day, except the* ℟., *which is omitted.*

FIRST SUNDAY AFTER TRINITY.

(SUNDAY IN THE OCTAVE OF CORPUS CHRISTI.)

The Office is wholly of Corpus Christi, with Memorial of Sunday at both Vespers and at Lauds.

First Vespers.

Ant. Speak, Lord : for Thy servant heareth.

℣. Let our evening prayer come up before Thee, O Lord.

℟. And let Thy mercy come down on us.

COLLECT.

O GOD, the Strength of all them that put their trust in Thee; mercifully accept our prayers ; and because through the weakness of our mortal nature we can do no good thing without Thee, grant us the help of Thy grace, that in keeping of Thy commandments we may please Thee, both in will and deed; through Jesus Christ our Lord. Amen.

Lauds.

Ant. Father Abraham, have mercy on me : and send Lazarus that he may dip the tip of his finger in water, and cool my tongue.

℣. The Lord is King.

℟. He hath put on glorious apparel. Alleluia.

Collect as at First Vespers.

Second Vespers.

Ant. Son, remember that thou in thy lifetime receivedst thy good things : and likewise Lazarus evil things.

℣. Lord, let my prayer be set forth.

℟. In Thy sight as the incense.
Collect as at First Vespers.
After the Octave of Corpus Christi, all as in the Psalter at every Hour.

SECOND SUNDAY AFTER TRINITY.
First Vespers.

[*The Ants. to the* Magnificat *for First Vespers are not Sarum. For the Sarum arrangement see* p 207.]

Ant. to Mag. And all Israel from Dan even unto Beersheba knew: that Samuel was established to be a prophet of the Lord.

Collect.

O LORD, Who never failest to help and govern them whom Thou dost bring up in Thy stedfast fear and love; keep us, we beseech Thee, under the protection of Thy good providence, and made us to have a perpetual fear and love of Thy holy Name; through Jesus Christ our Lord. Amen.

Lauds.

Ant. to Ben. A certain man made a great supper, and bade many: and sent his servants at supper-time to say to them that were bidden, Come, for all things are now ready. Alleluia.

Second Vespers.

Ant. to Mag. Go out quickly into the streets and lanes of the city: and bring in hither the poor, and the maimed, and the halt, and the blind, that my house may be filled. Alleluia.

THIRD SUNDAY AFTER TRINITY.
First Vespers.

Ant. to Mag. So David prevailed over the Philistine with a sling and with a stone: in the Name of the Lord.

Collect.

O LORD, we beseech Thee, mercifully to hear us; and grant that we, to whom Thou hast given an hearty desire to pray, may by Thy mighty aid be defended and comforted in all dangers and adversities; through Jesus Christ our Lord. Amen.

Lauds.

Ant. to Ben. What man of you having an hundred sheep, if he lose one of them: doth not leave the ninety and nine in the wilderness, and go after that which is lost, until he find it? Alleluia.

Second Vespers.

Ant. to Mag. What woman having ten pieces of silver, if she lose one piece: doth not light a candle, and sweep the house, and seek diligently till she find it? Alleluia.

FOURTH SUNDAY AFTER TRINITY.
First Vespers.

Ant. to Mag. Ye mountains of Gilboa, let there be no dew, neither let there be rain upon you; for there the shield of the mighty is vilely cast away, the shield of Saul, as though he had not been anointed with oil: How are the mighty fallen in the midst of the battle! O Jonathan, thou wast slain in thine high places. Saul and Jonathan were lovely and pleasant in their lives, and in their deaths they were not divided.

Collect.

O GOD, the protector of all that trust in Thee, without Whom nothing is strong, nothing is holy; increase and multiply upon us Thy mercy; that, Thou being our ruler and guide, we may so pass through things temporal, that we finally lose not the things eternal; grant this, O heavenly Father, for Jesus Christ's sake our Lord. Amen.

Lauds.

Ant. to Ben. Be ye therefore merciful : as your Father also is merciful, saith the Lord.

Second Vespers.

Ant. to Mag. Judge not, and ye shall not be judged : for with the same measure that ye mete withal, it shall be measured to you again.

FIFTH SUNDAY AFTER TRINITY.
First Vespers.

Ant. to Mag. I beseech Thee, O Lord, do away the iniquity of Thy servant : for I have done very foolishly.

Collect.

GRANT, O Lord, we beseech Thee, that the course of this world may be so peaceably ordered by Thy governance, that Thy Church may joyfully serve Thee in all godly quietness; through Jesus Christ our Lord. Amen.

Lauds.

Ant. to Ben. And Jesus entered into one of the ships : and sat down, and taught the people. Alleluia.

Second Vespers.

Ant. to Mag. Master, we have toiled all the night, and have taken nothing : nevertheless, at Thy word I will let down the net.

SIXTH SUNDAY AFTER TRINITY.
First Vespers.

Ant. to Mag. Zadok the priest and Nathan the prophet, anointed Solomon king in Gihon : and all the people came up and rejoiced, and said, God save king Solomon.

Collect.

O GOD, Who hast prepared for them that love Thee such good things as pass man's understanding; pour into our hearts such love towards Thee, that we, loving Thee above all things, may obtain Thy promises, which exceed all that we can desire : through Jesus Christ our Lord. Amen.

Lauds.

Ant. to Ben. Ye have heard that it was said by them of old time, Thou shalt not kill : and whosoever shall kill, shall be in danger of the judgment.

Second Vespers.

Ant. to Mag. If thou bring thy gift to the altar, and there rememberest that thy brother hath ought against thee : leave there thy gift before the altar, and go thy way, first be reconciled to thy brother, and then come and offer thy gift. Alleluia.

SEVENTH SUNDAY AFTER TRINITY.
First Vespers.

Ant. to Mag. When the Lord would take up Elijah into heaven by a whirlwind, Elisha cried : My father, my father, the chariot of Israel and the horsemen thereof.

Collect.

LORD of all power and might, Who art the author and giver of all good things; graft in our hearts the love of Thy Name, increase in us true religion, nourish us with all goodness, and of Thy great mercy keep us in the same; through Jesus Christ our Lord. Amen.

Lauds.

Ant. to Ben. I have compassion on the multitude, because they have now been with Me three days, and have nothing to eat : and if I send them away fasting to their own houses, they will faint by the way. Alleluia.

Second Vespers.

Ant. to Mag. And Jesus took the seven loaves, and gave thanks, and brake, and gave to His disciples to set before them : and they did set them before the people. Alleluia.

EIGHTH SUNDAY AFTER TRINITY.

First Vespers.

Ant. to Mag. And Jehoash did that which was right in the sight of the Lord : all his days, wherein Jehoiada the priest instructed him.

Collect.

O GOD, Whose never-failing providence ordereth all things both in heaven and earth; we humbly beseech Thee to put away from us all hurtful things, and to give us those things which be profitable for us; through Jesus Christ our Lord. Amen.

Lauds.

Ant. to Ben. Beware of false prophets, which come to you in sheep's clothing but inwardly they are ravening wolves. Ye shall know them by their fruits.

Second Vespers.

Ant. to Mag. Not every one that saith unto Me, Lord, Lord, shall enter into the kingdom of heaven : but he that doeth the will of My Father Which is in heaven. Alleluia.

NINTH SUNDAY AFTER TRINITY.

First Vespers.

Ant. to Mag. I beseech Thee, O Lord, remember now, how I have walked before Thee in truth and with a perfect heart : and have done that which is good in Thy sight.

Collect.

GRANT to us, Lord, we beseech Thee, the spirit to think and do always such things as be rightful; that we, who cannot do any thing that is good without Thee, may by Thee be enabled to live according to Thy will; through Jesus Christ our Lord. Amen.

Lauds.

Ant. to Ben. And his lord called him, and said unto him, How is it that I hear this of thee? : Give an account of thy stewardship. Alleluia.

Second Vespers.

Ant. to Mag. What shall I do? for my lord taketh away from me the stewardship: I cannot dig, to beg I am ashamed ; I am resolved what to do, that, when I am put out of the stewardship, they may receive me into their houses.

TENTH SUNDAY AFTER TRINITY.

First Vespers.

Ant. to Mag. Wisdom hath builded

her house, she hath hewn out her seven pillars: she hath sent forth her maidens, she crieth upon the highest places of the city.

Collect.

LET Thy merciful ears, O Lord, be open to the prayers of Thy humble servants; and that they may obtain their petitions, make them to ask such things as shall please Thee; through Jesus Christ our Lord. Amen.

Lauds.

Ant. to Ben. And when He was come near, He beheld the city, and wept over it, saying, If thou hadst known!: For the days shall come upon thee, that thine enemies shall cast a trench about thee, and compass thee round, and keep thee in on every side, and shall lay thee even with the ground, because thou knewest not the time of thy visitation. Alleluia.

Second Vespers.

Ant. to Mag. It is written, My house is the house of prayer: but ye have made it a den of thieves. And He taught daily in the temple.

ELEVENTH SUNDAY AFTER TRINITY.

First Vespers.

Ant. to Mag. I dwell in high places: and My throne is in a cloudy pillar.

Collect.

O GOD, Who declarest Thy almighty power most chiefly in shewing mercy and pity; mercifully grant unto us such a measure of Thy grace, that we, running the way of Thy commandments, may obtain Thy gracious promises, and be made partakers of Thy heavenly treasure; through Jesus Christ our Lord. Amen.

Lauds.

Ant. to Ben. Two men went up into the temple to pray; the one a Pharisee, and the other a publican: This man went down to his house justified rather than the other. Alleluia.

Second Vespers.

Ant. to Mag. And the publican, standing afar off, would not lift up so much as his eyes unto heaven, but smote upon his breast, saying: God be merciful to me a sinner.

TWELFTH SUNDAY AFTER TRINITY.

First Vespers.

Ant. to Mag. All wisdom cometh from the Lord: and is with Him for ever.

Collect.

ALMIGHTY and everlasting God, Who art always more ready to hear than we to pray, and art wont to give more than either we desire or deserve: pour down upon us the abundance of Thy mercy; forgiving us those things whereof our conscience is afraid, and giving us those good things which we are not worthy to ask, but through the merits and mediation of Jesus Christ, Thy Son, our Lord. Amen.

Lauds.

Ant. to Ben. Jesus, departing from the coasts of Tyre and Sidon, came unto the sea of Galilee: through the midst of the coasts of Decapolis. Alleluia.

Second Vespers.

Ant. to Mag. He hath done all things well : He maketh both the deaf to hear and the dumb to speak.

THIRTEENTH SUNDAY AFTER TRINITY.
First Vespers.

Ant. to Mag. My son, keep thy father's commandment, and forsake not the law of thy mother : bind them continually upon thy heart.

Collect.

ALMIGHTY and merciful God, of Whose only gift it cometh that Thy faithful people do unto Thee true and laudable service; grant, we beseech Thee, that we may so faithfully serve Thee in this life, that we fail not finally to attain Thy heavenly promises; through the merits of Jesus Christ our Lord. Amen.

Lauds.

Ant. to Ben. A certain man went down from Jerusalem to Jericho, and fell among thieves : which stripped him of his raiment, and wounded him, and departed, leaving him half dead.

Second Vespers.

Ant. to Mag. Which now of these three, thinkest thou, was neighbour unto him that fell among the thieves? : And he said, He that shewed mercy on him. Go, and do thou likewise. Alleluia.

FOURTEENTH SUNDAY AFTER TRINITY.
First Vespers.

Ant. to Mag. In all this, Job sinned not with his lips : nor charged God foolishly.

Collect.

ALMIGHTY and everlasting God, give unto us the increase of faith, hope, and charity; and, that we may obtain that which Thou dost promise, make us to love that which Thou dost command; through Jesus Christ our Lord. Amen.

Lauds.

Ant. to Ben. And as He entered into a certain village, there met Him ten men that were lepers, which stood afar off : and they lifted up their voices, and said, Jesus, Master, have mercy on us.

Second Vespers.

Ant. to Mag. Were there not ten cleansed? but where are the nine? There are not found that returned to give glory to God, save this stranger : Arise, go thy way, thy faith hath made thee whole. Alleluia.

FIFTEENTH SUNDAY AFTER TRINITY.
First Vespers.

Ant. to Mag. Remember not, Lord, our offences, nor the offences of our forefathers : neither take Thou vengeance on our sins.

Collect.

KEEP, we beseech Thee, O Lord, Thy Church with Thy perpetual mercy; and, because the frailty of man without Thee cannot but fall, keep us ever by Thy help from all things hurtful, and lead us to all things profitable to our salvation; through Jesus Christ our Lord. Amen.

Lauds.

Ant. to Ben. Take no thought,

saying, What shall we eat? or what shall we drink? : for your heavenly Father knoweth that ye have need of all these things. Alleluia.

Second Vespers.

Ant. to Mag. Seek ye first the kingdom of God, and His righteousness : and all these things shall be added unto you. Alleluia.

SIXTEENTH SUNDAY AFTER TRINITY.

First Vespers.

Ant. to Mag. But the Almighty Lord hath disappointed them : by the hand of a woman.

COLLECT.

O LORD, we beseech Thee, let Thy continual pity cleanse and defend Thy Church; and, because it cannot continue in safety without Thy succour, preserve it evermore by Thy help and goodness; through Jesus Christ our Lord. Amen.

Lauds.

Ant. to Ben. Jesus went into a city called Nain : and behold, there was a dead man carried out, the only son of his mother.

Second Vespers.

Ant. to Mag. And there came a fear on all, and they glorified God, saying : That a great prophet is risen up among us, and that God hath visited His people.

SEVENTEENTH SUNDAY AFTER TRINITY.

First Vespers.

Ant. to Mag. O Lord, Lord, the King Almighty, the whole world is in Thy power : and there is none that can gainsay Thee.

COLLECT.

LORD, we pray Thee, that Thy grace may always prevent and follow us, and make us continually to be given to all good works; through Jesus Christ our Lord. Amen.

Lauds.

Ant. to Ben. And Jesus spake unto the lawyers and Pharisees, saying, Is it lawful to heal on the Sabbath-day? : And they held their peace. And He took him, and healed him, and let him go.

Second Vespers.

Ant. to Mag. When thou art bidden to a wedding; go and sit down in the lowest room; that, when he that bade thee cometh, he may say unto thee, Friend, go up higher : then shalt thou have worship in the presence of them that sit at meat with thee. Alleluia.

EIGHTEENTH SUNDAY AFTER TRINITY.

First Vespers.

Ant. to Mag. God open your hearts in His law and commandments : and send you peace.

COLLECT.

LORD, we beseech Thee, grant Thy people grace to withstand the temptations of the world, the flesh, and the devil, and with pure hearts and minds to follow Thee, the only God; through Jesus Christ our Lord. Amen.

Lauds.

Ant. to Ben. Master, which is the

great commandment in the law? : Jesus said unto him, Thou shalt love the Lord thy God with all thy heart. Alleluia.

Second Vespers.

Ant. to Mag. What think ye of Christ? whose Son is He? They say unto Him, The Son of David : He saith unto them, How then doth David in spirit call Him Lord, saying, The Lord said unto my Lord, Sit Thou on My right hand?

NINETEENTH SUNDAY AFTER TRINITY.

First Vespers.

Ant. to Mag. When the sun shone upon the shields of gold : the mountains glistered therewith.

COLLECT.

O GOD, forasmuch as without Thee we are not able to please Thee; mercifully grant, that Thy Holy Spirit may in all things direct and rule our hearts; through Jesus Christ our Lord. Amen.

Lauds.

Ant. to Ben. Jesus said unto the sick of the palsy : Son, be of good cheer, thy sins be forgiven thee.

Second Vespers.

Ant. to Mag. But when the multitude saw it, they marvelled, and glorified God : Who had given such power unto men.

TWENTIETH SUNDAY AFTER TRINITY.

First Vespers.

Ant. to Mag. And all Israel made great lamentation for Judas, saying : How is the valiant man fallen, that delivered Israel!

COLLECT.

O ALMIGHTY and most merciful God, of Thy bountiful goodness keep us, we beseech Thee, from all things that may hurt us; that we, being ready both in body and soul, may cheerfully accomplish those things that Thou wouldest have done; through Jesus Christ our Lord. Amen.

Lauds.

Ant. to Ben. Tell them which are bidden, Behold, I have prepared my dinner : come unto the marriage. Alleluia.

Second Vespers.

Ant. to Mag. The wedding is ready, but they who were bidden were not worthy : go ye therefore into the highways, and as many as ye shall find, bid to the marriage. Alleluia.

TWENTY-FIRST SUNDAY AFTER TRINITY.

First Vespers.

Ant. to Mag. The Lord hear your prayers, and be at one with you : and never forsake you in time of trouble.

COLLECT.

GRANT, we beseech Thee, merciful Lord, to Thy faithful people pardon and peace, that they may be cleansed from all their sins, and serve Thee with a quiet mind; through Jesus Christ our Lord. Amen.

Lauds.

Ant. to Ben. There was a certain nobleman, whose son was sick at

Capernaum: when he heard that Jesus was come out of Judea into Galilee, he besought Him that He would come down and heal his son.

Second Vespers.

Ant. to Mag. So the father knew that it was at the same hour, in the which Jesus said unto him: Thy son liveth; and himself believed, and his whole house.

TWENTY-SECOND SUNDAY AFTER TRINITY.

First Vespers.

Ant. to Mag. O Lord, Lord God, fearful and strong, the only and gracious King, the only giver of all things: preserve Thine own portion and sanctify it.

Collect.

LORD, we beseech Thee to keep Thy household the Church in continual godliness; that through Thy protection it may be free from all adversities, and devoutly given to serve Thee in good works, to the glory of Thy Name; through Jesus Christ our Lord. Amen.

Lauds.

Ant. to Ben. And the lord commanded payment to be made. The servant therefore fell down and worshipped him, saying: Lord, have patience with me, and I will pay thee all.

Second Vespers.

Ant. to Mag. O thou wicked servant, I forgave thee all that debt, because thou desiredst me: shouldest not thou also have had compassion on thy fellow-servant, even as I had pity on thee? Alleluia.

TWENTY-THIRD SUNDAY AFTER TRINITY.

First Vespers.

Ant. to Mag. I saw the Lord sitting upon a throne high and lifted up: and His train filled the temple; the whole earth was full of His glory.

Collect.

O GOD, our refuge and strength, Who art the author of all godliness; be ready, we beseech Thee, to hear the devout prayers of Thy Church; and grant that those things which we ask faithfully we may obtain effectually; through Jesus Christ our Lord. Amen.

Lauds.

Ant. to Ben. Master, we know that Thou art true: and teachest the way of God in truth. Alleluia.

Second Vespers.

Ant. to Mag. Render therefore unto Cæsar the things which are Cæsar's: and unto God the things that are God's. Alleluia.

TWENTY-FOURTH SUNDAY AFTER TRINITY.

First Vespers.

Ant. to Mag. How doth the city sit solitary that was full of people? she that was great among the nations: and there is none to comfort her, but only Thou, O God.

Collect.

O LORD, we beseech Thee, absolve Thy people from their offences; that through Thy bountiful goodness we may all be delivered from the bands of those sins, which by our frailty we have committed; grant this, O heavenly Father, for Jesus Christ's sake, our blessed Lord and Saviour. Amen.

Lauds.

Ant. to Ben. While Jesus spake these things unto John's disciples, behold, there came a certain ruler, and worshipped Him, saying : My daughter is even now dead ; but come and lay Thy hand upon her, and she shall live.

Second Vespers.

Ant. to Mag. Daughter, be of good comfort, thy faith hath made thee whole : and the woman was made whole from that hour.

TWENTY-FIFTH SUNDAY AFTER TRINITY.

First Vespers.

Ant. to Mag. I have set watchmen upon thy walls, O Jerusalem : which shall never hold their peace day nor night.

COLLECT.

STIR up, we beseech Thee, O Lord, the wills of Thy faithful people ; that they, plenteously bringing forth the fruit of good works, may of Thee be plenteously rewarded ; through Jesus Christ our Lord. Amen.

Lauds.

Ant. to Ben. When Jesus then lift up His eyes, and saw a great company come unto Him, He saith unto Philip, Whence shall we buy bread that these may eat ? : (And this He said to prove him ; for He Himself knew what he would do.)

Second Vespers.

Ant. to Mag. Then those men, when they had seen the miracle that Jesus did, said : This is of a truth that Prophet that should come into the world.

If there be any more Sundays before Advent Sunday, the Service of some of those Sundays that were omitted after the Epiphany shall be taken in to supply so many as are here wanting. And if there be fewer, the overplus may be omitted : provided that this last Collect, with the Antiphons to Benedictus and Magnificat, shall always be used upon the Sunday next before Advent. But if a Double Feast occur on the last Sunday before Advent, the Office is of the Feast, with the above Ants. and Collect, as Memorials of the Sunday.

EMBER-TIDE IN SEPTEMBER.

WEDNESDAY.

Lauds.

Ant. to Ben. This kind goeth not out : save by prayer and fasting.

Ferial Petitions, p. 11.

COLLECT.

WE beseech Thee, O Lord, let the remedies of Thy mercy strengthen our frailty ; that, wheresoever it hath decayed, by Thy clemency it may be restored ; through our Lord Jesus Christ. Amen.

This Collect is said at every Hour of this day only, till Vespers. At Vespers, if the Office is of the Feria, the Ferial Petitions are said with the Sunday Collect.

FRIDAY.

Lauds.

Ant. to Ben. A woman, in the city, which was a sinner, stood at the feet of the Lord behind Him : and began to wash His feet with tears, and did wipe them with the hairs of her head, and kissed His feet, and anointed them with the ointment.

Ferial Petitions, p. 11.

COLLECT.

GRANT, we beseech Thee, Almighty God, that by the holy observance of this yearly devotion, we may please Thee in body and mind; through our Lord Jesus Christ. Amen.

This Collect is said till Vespers of this day only. At Vespers, if the Office is of the Feria, the Ferial Petitions are said, with the Sunday Collect.

SATURDAY.

Lauds.

Ant. to Ben. Lighten, O Lord, them that sit in darkness : and guide our feet into the way of peace, O God of Israel.

Ferial Petitions, p. 11.

COLLECT.

ALMIGHTY, everlasting God, Who by healthful continence dost restore both body and soul; we humbly entreat Thy Majesty, that being well pleased by the deprecation of our devout fasting, Thou wouldst grant us present and future help; through our Lord Jesus Christ. Amen.

This Collect is said till Vespers of this day only.

The following is the Sarum arrangement of ℟. *to Chapters and Ants. to Magnificat.*

℟. *to Chapter.* Fear God and keep His commandments,* for this is the whole duty of man. ℣. They that fear the Lord shall lack nothing, neither they that love Him in truth.

This ℟. *is said at First Vespers of Sunday till the First Sunday in August.*

Ants. until First Sunday in August.

1. And all Israel from Dan even to Beersheba : knew that Samuel was established to be a prophet of the Lord.

2. So David prevailed over the Philistines with a sling and with a stone : in the name of the Lord.

3. Is not this David of whom they sung one to another in dances, saying: Saul hath slain his thousands, and David his ten thousands?

4. King Saul was very wroth and said : They have ascribed unto David ten thousands, and to me they have ascribed but thousands.

5. And who is so faithful among all thy servants as David : which is the king's son in law, and goeth at thy bidding, and is honourable in thine house?

6. Ye mountains of Gilboa, let there be no dew, neither let there be rain upon you : for there the shield of the mighty is vilely cast away, the shield of Saul, as though he had not been anointed with oil. How are the mighty fallen in the midst of the battle! O Jonathan, thou wast slain in thine high places : Saul and Jonathan were lovely and pleasant in their lives, and in their death they were not divided.

7. I am distressed for thee, my brother Jonathan; very pleasant hast thou been unto me : thy love to me was wonderful, passing the love of women. From the blood of the slain, from the fat of the mighty, the bow of Jonathan turned not back, and the sword of Saul returned not empty.

8. And David spake unto the Lord when he saw the angel that smote the people, and said, Lo, I have sinned and I have done wickedly : but these sheep, what have they done?

9. And the king was much moved, and went up to the chamber over the gate, and wept : saying, O my

son Absalom, my son, my son Absalom! would God I had died for thee, O Absalom, my son, my son!

℟.℟. *for the First Vespers of Sunday in and after August.*

First Sunday in August.
(*i.e. the Sunday nearest, before or after, to the first day of the month.*)

℟. I alone compassed the circuit of the heaven; and walked upon the waves of the sea, and in every people and nation I got a possession : and I trod upon the necks of the mighty in Mine own strength. ℣. I dwelt in high places, and My throne is in a cloudy pillar. ℟. And I trod upon the necks of the mighty in Mine own strength. ℣. Glory be to the Father and to the Son : and to the Holy Ghost. ℟. And I trod upon the necks of the mighty in Mine own strength.

When the time is long then all the preceding Antiphons are said in their order, but when it is short, that is, eight Sundays or less, the Antiphon Ye mountains, &c., *shall always be said in the last place, and the Antiphon* King Saul, &c., *and others preceding shall be omitted that year.*

August.
(When the books of Solomon begin.)
Ants. to Mag.

Wisdom hath builded her house, she hath hewn out her seven pillars : she hath subjected nations to herself and hath trodden down the proud and mighty by her own strength.

Wisdom crieth in the streets. If any love wisdom let him turn unto me, and he shall find her : and when he hath found her, blessed is he if he hold her fast.

The Lord possessed me in the beginning of his way, before his works of old. When there were no depths, I was brought forth; When he prepared the heavens, I was there : Then I was by him, as one brought up by him. I dwelt in high places, and my throne is in a cloudy pillar.

This ℟. serves till

Second Sunday in September.

℟. My sighing cometh before I eat; and my roarings are poured out like the waters; for the thing which I greatly feared is come upon me, and that which I was afraid of is come unto me. I was not in saefty, neither had I rest, neither was I quiet : yet trouble came. ℣. If I speak of strength, lo, He is strong; and if of judgment, who shall set me a time to plead ? ℟. I was not in safety, neither had I rest, neither was I quiet : yet trouble came. ℣. Glory be to the Father, and to the Son : and to the Holy Ghost. ℟. I was not in safety, neither had I rest, neither was I quiet : yet trouble came.

September. Job.
Ant. to Mag.

When Job heard the words of the messengers he endured patiently, and said : Shall we receive good at the hand of God, and shall we not receive evil ? In all this did not Job sin with his lips, nor charged God foolishly.

This ℟. serves till

Third Sunday in September.

℟. Bless the Lord thy God alway, and desire of Him that thy ways may be directed; and that all thy paths and counsels may prosper. ℣. Fear not, my son, that we are made poor : for thou hast much wealth, if thou fear God. ℟. And that all thy paths and counsels may prosper. ℣. Glory be to the Father, and to the Son : and to the Holy Ghost. ℟.

And that all thy paths and counsels may prosper.

1st Sunday after the 3rd of the Ides of September. Tobit.
(Omitted altogether in the A.V.)

Ant. to Mag. Remember not, Lord, our offences, nor the offences of our forefathers : neither take Thou vengeance of our sins.

FOURTH SUNDAY IN SEPTEMBER.

℟. O Lord, Lord, the King Almighty; the whole world is in Thy power, and there is no man that can resist Thee : Deliver us for Thy Name's sake. ℣. Hear our prayer, and turn our sorrow into joy. ℟. Deliver us for Thy Name's sake. ℣. Glory be to the Father, and to the Son : and to the Holy Ghost. ℟. Deliver us for Thy Name's sake.

This ℟. serves till
FIRST SUNDAY IN OCTOBER.

℟. Thine, O Lord, is the power : Thine is the kingdom, O Lord, and Thou art exalted as head above all : Give peace in our time, O Lord. ℣. O Lord, Lord God, Creator of all things, Who art fearful and strong, and righteous and merciful. ℟. Give peace in our time, O Lord. ℣. Glory be to the Father, and to the Son : and to the Holy Ghost. ℟. Give peace in our time, O Lord.

This ℟. serves till
FIRST SUNDAY IN NOVEMBER.
After the 4th of the Kalends of October.

Ant. to Mag. O Lord, Thou art great and glorious, Who gavest salvation by the hand of a woman : hear the prayers of Thy servants.

1st Sunday after the 5th of the Kalends of October.
Ants. to Mag.

The Lord open your hearts in his law and commandments: and send you peace.

Give peace in our time, O Lord: because there is none other that fighteth for us, but only Thou, O our God.

Thine, O Lord, is the power ; Thine is the kingdom, O Lord : Thou art exalted as head above all. Give peace in our time, O Lord. Alleluia.

Arm yourselves, and be valiant men, and see that ye be in readiness to fight: for it is better for us to die in battle, than to behold the calamities of our people and our sanctuary. Nevertheless, as the will of God is in heaven, so let him do.

The Lord hear your prayers, and be at one with you: and never forsake you in time of trouble.

FIRST SUNDAY IN NOVEMBER.

℟. Look down, O Lord, from Thy holy habitation, and think upon us : Lord, bow down Thine ear, and hear ; open Thine eyes, O Lord, and see our tribulation. ℣. Look down from heaven, and behold from the habitation of Thy holiness and of Thy glory. ℟. Open Thine eyes, O Lord, and see our tribulation. ℣. Glory be to the Father, and to the Son : and to the Holy Ghost. ℟. Open Thine eyes, O Lord, and see our tribulation.

1st Sunday after the Kalends of November.
Ants. to Mag.

I saw also the Lord sitting upon a throne, high and lifted up, and the whole earth was full of his glory: and the skirts thereof filled the temple.

With thine invincible wall surround us, O Lord: and with the arms of thy power protect us always, O our God.

We looked for peace, and there is no good: and for the time of healing, and behold trouble! We acknowledge, O Lord, our wickedness, and the iniquity of our fathers: for we have sinned against thee. Do not abhor us for ever, O God of Israel.

✠

COMMON OF SAINTS.

Commemoration of the Blessed Virgin Mary,
Through the year, except in Advent.

Vespers.

Ant. to Psalms. Thou art all fair, My love : there is no spot in thee.

Psalms of the Feria.

Chapter. S. Luke i.

BLESSED is she that believed : for there shall be a performance of those things which were told her from the Lord.

℟. Thanks be to God.

Hymn. *Ave, maris Stella.*

AVE, star of ocean !
God's dear Mother holy ;
Portal of salvation,
Virgin pure and lowly.

Gabriel's word was Ave,
Eva's name reversing ;
Be true peace our portion,
Ghostly foes dispersing.

Now the chain is shattered,
Light on darkness beaming ;
Ills are chased ; all blessings
Follow our redeeming.

Weak our hearts and cold : yet
May our Lord and Brother
Teach us, as He loves thee,
So to love His Mother.

Virgin of all virgins !
Meek and passing holy,
Freed from guilt, may we be
Tender, strong, and lowly.

Pure and brave, life's journey,
May it falter never,
Till, beholding Jesus,
We rejoice together.

Sing we equal glory,
Equal praise and blessing ;
Father, Son and Spirit,
God Triune, confessing. Amen.

℣. Thou art the holy Mother of God.

℟. O Mary, ever Virgin.

Ant. to Mag. Thy lips drop as the honeycomb : honey and milk are under thy tongue.

Collect.

WE beseech Thee, O merciful God, grant succour to our frailty : that we who commemorate the holy Virgin Mary, Mother of God, assisted by her pleading, may rise anew from our iniquities. Through.

Compline is said according to the season ; but with Christmas Doxology to the Hymn, and Ant. to Nunc Dimittis as on the Purification.

Lauds.

℣. Thou art the holy Mother of God.

℟. O Mary, ever Virgin.

Ant. to Psalms. O wonderful exchange ! The Creator of mankind taking to Himself a living body, vouchsafed to be born of a Virgin : and, proceeding forth as man, made us co-heirs of His Godhead.

Chapter. Ecclus. xxiv.

WITH all these I sought rest : and in whose inheritance shall I abide ? So the Creator of all things gave me a commandment, and he that made me caused my tabernacle to rest, and said, Let thy dwelling be in Jacob, and thine inheritance in Israel.

Hymn. *O gloriosa femina.*

O GLORIOUS Virgin, throned in rest,
  Amidst the starry host above,
Who gavest nurture from thy breast
  To God, with pure maternal love.

What we had lost, through sinful Eve,
  The Blossom sprung from thee restores;
And granting bliss to souls that grieve,
  Unbars the everlasting doors.

O gate, through which hath passed the King;
  O hall, whence light shone through the gloom;
The ransomed nations praise and sing
  Life given from the Virgin womb.

All honour, laud, and glory be,
  O Jesu, Virgin-born, to Thee;
All glory, as is ever meet,
  To Father and to Paraclete. Amen.

℣. God is in the midst of her.

℟. Therefore shall she not be removed.

Ant. to Ben. Who is this that goeth forth as the morning: fair as the moon, clear as the sun, terrible as an army with banners?

Prime.

Ant. to Psalms as at Lauds. Psalms liv. and cxix. *Ant. to Quicunque.* Thee duly, p. 31. ℟. As at Christmas.

Tierce.

Ant. When Thou wast born ineffably of a Virgin, then was the Scripture fulfilled: He shall come down like the rain into a fleece of wool, to save mankind. We praise Thee, O our God.

Chapter as at Lauds.

℟. at Tierce, Sexts, and Nones, as on the Annunciation.

Sexts.

Ant. In the burning bush which Moses saw unconsumed: we recognise the preservation of thy glorious virginity, O Mother of God.

Chapter. Ecclus. xxiv.

IN the holy tabernacle I served before him: and so was I established in Sion.

Nones.

Ant. The Root of Jesse hath budded; a Star hath risen out of Jacob: a Virgin hath brought forth the Saviour. We praise Thee, O our God.

Chapter. Ecclus. xxiv.

AND I took root in an honourable people, even in the portion of the Lord's inheritance.

In Advent these variations.

Vespers.

Ant. to Psalms. The prophets did tell: that the Saviour should be born of the Virgin Mary.

Chapter. Is. vii.

BEHOLD, a Virgin shall conceive, and bear a Son, and shall call His name Emmanuel; butter and honey shall He eat, that He may know to refuse the evil and choose the good.

After Hymn. ℣. Full of grace are thy lips.

℟. Because God hath blessed thee for ever.

Ant. to Mag: Fear not, Mary, thou hast found favour with God: behold, thou shalt conceive and bring forth a Son. Alleluia.

Collect.

O GOD, Who didst will that at the word of an Angel Thy word should take flesh in the womb of blessed Mary, ever-Virgin: grant to Thy suppliants, that we, who believe her to be the Mother of God, may be helped by her pleading before Thee; through the same Thy Son, Jesus Christ our Lord. Who liveth.

Lauds.

Ant. to Psalms and Chapter as at Vespers.

COMMON OF SAINTS.

Ant. to Ben. The Holy Ghost shall come down upon thee, Mary: fear not, thou who hast in thy womb the Son of God. Alleluia.
  Collect as at Vespers.

Prime.
Ant. to Psalms as at Vespers.

Tierce.
Ant. The Angel Gabriel was sent to Mary, a Virgin : espoused to Joseph.
Chapter as at Vespers.

Sexts.
Ant. The Angel of the Lord brought tidings unto Mary : and she conceived of the Holy Ghost. Alleluia.

CHAPTER. Is. XI.

HE shalt smite the earth with the rod of His mouth, and with the breath of His lips shall He slay the wicked. And righteousness shall be the girdle of His loins, and faithfulness the girdle of His reins.

Nones.
Ant. Hail, Mary, full of grace, the Lord is with thee : blessed art thou among women. Alleluia.

CHAPTER. Is. VII.

THE Lord spake unto Ahaz, saying, ask thee a sign of the Lord thy God : ask it either in the depth or in the height above. But Ahaz said, I will not ask, neither will I tempt the Lord.

OF ONE OR MORE APOSTLES OR EVANGELISTS IN EASTER TIDE
(*That is to say, from* LOW SUNDAY *to* TRINITY SUNDAY, *exclusive*).

First Vespers.
Ant. to Psalms. Light perpetual shall shine upon Thy Saints : and an eternity of ages. Alleluia.
Psalms of the Feria.
The Chapter at the First Vespers, and those at all the Hours, are of the Proper, if there be any ; if not, of the Common of Apostles through the year.

℟. Her Nazarites were made white. Alleluia. To the glory of God they shone forth. Alleluia : They were compacted as milk. Alleluia. Alleluia. ℣. Their sound is gone out into all lands, and their words into the end of the world. ℟. They were compacted as milk. Alleluia. Alleluia. ℣. Glory be to the Father, and to the Son : and to the Holy Ghost. ℟. Alleluia. Alleluia.

HYMN. *Tristes erant Apostoli.*

TH' Apostles' hearts were full of pain,
  For their dear Lord so lately slain,
That Lord His servants' wicked train
With bitter scorn had dared arraign.

We pray Thee, King with glory decked,
In this our Paschal joy protect
From all that death would fain effect,
Thy ransomed flock, Thine own elect.

To Thee Who, dead, again dost live,
All glory, Lord, Thy people give ;
All glory, as is ever meet,
To Father and to Paraclete. Amen.

From the Ascension to Whitsun-eve instead of the last two verses are said :

Be Thou our Joy, and Thou our Guard,
Who art to be our great Reward :
Our glory and our boast in Thee,
For ever and for ever be !

All glory, Lord, to thee we pay,
Ascending o'er the stars to-day ;
All glory, as is ever meet,
To Father and to Paraclete. Amen.

℣. Then were the disciples glad.
℟. When they saw the Lord. Alleluia.

Ant. to Mag. Daughters of Jerusalem, come and behold the Martyr with the crown : wherewith the Lord crowned Him, on the day of solemnity and gladness. Alleluia. Alleluia.

This Ant. is to be said in Easter-tide for one or many Martyrs or Confessors,

OF ONE OR MORE APOSTLES OR EVANGELISTS.   213

not changing the word Martyr *to the plural, because it refers to Christ.*
Collect of the Proper.
Memorial of the Resurrection, p. 173.
(*Easter Compline is not changed.*)

Lauds.

℣. The voice of joy and health.
℟. Is in the dwellings of the righteous. Alleluia.

Psalms of Sunday.

Ant. 1. Thy Saints, O Lord, shall flourish as a lily. Alleluia : as the odour of balsam shall they be before Thee. Alleluia.

Ant. 2. O ye holy and righteous, rejoice in the Lord. Alleluia : God hath chosen you to be His inheritance. Alleluia.

Ant. 3. Within the veil, O Lord, Thy Saints cry : Alleluia. Alleluia. Alleluia.

Ant. 4. O ye spirits and souls of the righteous : bless ye the Lord. Alleluia. Alleluia.

Ant. 5. In the kingdom of heaven is the habitation of the Saints. Alleluia : and their rest in eternity. Alleluia.

Chapter according to direction at First Vespers, p. 212.

HYMN. *Claro Paschali gaudio.*

IN this our bright and Paschal day
The sun shines out with purer ray;
When Christ, to earthly sight made plain,
The glad Apostles see again.

The wounds, the riven wounds He shows
In that His flesh with light that glows,
In loud accord both far and nigh
The Lord's arising testify.

O Christ, the King, Who lov'st to bless,
Do Thou our hearts and souls possess;
To Thee our praise that we may pay,
To Whom our laud is due for aye.

We pray Thee, King with glory decked,
In this our Paschal joy protect,
From all that death would fain effect,
Thy ransomed flock, Thine own elect.

To Thee Who, dead, again dost live,
All glory, Lord, Thy people give :
All glory, as is ever meet,
To Father and to Paraclete. Amen.

From the Ascension to Whitsun-eve the Doxology is altered as at Vespers, p. 212.

℣. Rejoice in the Lord, ye righteous.
℟. For it becometh well the just to be thankful. Alleluia.

Ant. to Ben. Light perpetual shall shine upon Thy Saints, O Lord, Alleluia : and an eternity of ages. Alleluia. Alleluia. Alleluia.

Prime.

Ant. Thy Saints, O Lord, shall flourish as a lily. Alleluia : as the odour of balsam shall they be before Thee. Alleluia.

Tierce.

Ant. O ye holy and righteous, rejoice in the Lord. Alleluia : God hath chosen you to be His inheritance. Alleluia.

Chapter according as directed, p. 212.

℟. Your sorrow : Alleluia. Alleluia. ℣. Shall be turned into joy. ℟. Alleluia. Alleluia. ℣. Glory be to the Father, and to the Son : and to the Holy Ghost. ℟. Your sorrow : Alleluia. Alleluia.

℣. Right dear in the sight of the Lord.
℟. Is the death of His Saints. Alleluia.

Sexts.

Ant. Within the veil, O Lord, Thy Saints cry : Alleluia. Alleluia. Alleluia.

Chapter according as directed, p. 212.

℟. Right dear in the sight of the Lord : Alleluia. Alleluia. ℣. Is the death of His Saints. ℟. Alleluia. Alleluia. ℣. Glory be to the Father, and to the Son : and to the Holy Ghost. ℟. Right dear in the sight of the Lord. Alleluia. Alleluia.

℣. Rejoice in the Lord, ye righteous.

℟. For it becometh well the just to be thankful. Alleluia.

Nones.

Ant. In the kingdom of heaven is the habitation of the Saints. Alleluia : and their rest in eternity. Alleluia.

Chapter according as directed, p. 212.

℟. Rejoice in the Lord, ye righteous : Alleluia. Alleluia. ℣. For it becometh well the just to be thankful. ℟. Alleluia. Alleluia. ℣. Glory be to the Father, and to the Son : and to the Holy Ghost. ℟. Rejoice in the Lord, ye righteous : Alleluia. Alleluia.

℣. The voice of joy and health.
℟. Is in the dwellings of the righteous. Alleluia.

Second Vespers.

Ants. of Lauds, with Psalms of the Second Vespers of Common of Apostles, p. 216.
Chapter and ℟. *as at First Vespers of this Office,* p. 212.
Hymn, Claro paschali gaudio, ℣. *and* ℟., p. 213.
Ant. to Mag. as at First Vespers.

Of a Martyr or Confessor in Easter tide.

First Vespers.

Ant. to Psalms. Light perpetual shall shine upon Thy Saints : and an eternity of ages. Alleluia.

Psalms of the Feria.

Chapter of the Proper, if any : if not, of the Common : and so at every Hour.

℟. Daughters of Jerusalem, come and behold the Martyr with the crown wherewith the Lord crowned Him : on the day of solemnity and gladness. Alleluia. ℣. For He hath made fast the bars of thy gates, and hath blessed thy children within thee.

℟. On the day of solemnity and gladness. Alleluia. ℣. Glory be to the Father, and to the Son : and to the Holy Ghost. ℟. Alleluia.

Hymns at Vespers and Lauds of the Common throughout the year with Doxology of the season.

After the Hymn (at First Vespers) :
℣. Your sorrow.
℟. Shall be turned into joy. Alleluia.
Ant. to Mag. as for Apostles, p. 212.

Lauds.

℣. *and* ℟. *and Ants. to Psalms, as for Apostles,* p. 213.
After the Hymn :
℣. Rejoice in the Lord, ye righteous.
℟. For it becometh well the just to be thankful. Alleluia.

Ant. to Ben. as for Apostles.
At Prime and the other Hours, Ants. ℣℣. *and* ℟℟. *as for Apostles.*

Second Vespers.

First Ant. of Lauds with Psalms of the Feria.
If a Sarum Double, ℟. Daughters of Jerusalem, *as at First Vespers.*
℣. ℟. *and Ant. to Mag. as at First Vespers.*

Of one or more Apostles or Evangelists through the year, except in Easter tide.

First Vespers.

Psalms of the Feria.

Ant. Be ye strong in battle, and fight with the old serpent : so shall ye receive an eternal kingdom. Alleluia.

After Septuagesima, at the end of this Antiphon, instead of Alleluia, *is said,* Saith the Lord. *But at the end of other Antiphons, usually ending with* Alleluia, *is said,* For evermore.

OF ONE OR MORE APOSTLES OR EVANGELISTS.   215

CHAPTER. Eph. II.

NOW therefore ye are no more strangers and foreigners, but fellow-citizens with the saints, and of the household of God; and are built upon the foundation of the apostles and prophets.

℟. Who are these that fly as a cloud : and as the doves to their windows ? ℣. They were purer than snow, they were whiter than milk, they were more ruddy in body than rubies. ℟. And as the doves to their windows. ℣. Glory be to the Father, and to the Son : and to the Holy Ghost. ℟. And as the doves to their windows.

HYMN. *Annue Christe.*

O CHRIST, Thou Lord of worlds!
Thine ear to hear us bow
On this the festival
Of Thine Apostle [*or*, Apostles] now :
That all the weary load
Of many a foul offence
May, by his [their] glorious prayers,
Be lost in penitence.

Redeemer! save Thy work,
Thy noble work of grace,
Sealed with the holy light
That beameth from Thy face :
Nor suffer them to fall
To Satan's wiles a prey,
For whom Thou didst on earth
Death's costly ransom pay.

Pity Thy flock, enthralled
By sin's captivity;
Forgive each guilty soul,
And set the bondmen free;
And those Thou hast redeemed
With Thine Own precious Blood,
Grant to rejoice with Thee,
Thou Monarch kind and good.

O Jesu, Saviour blest
And gracious Lord, to Thee,
All glory, virtue, power,
And laud and empire be :
The Father with like praise,
And Spirit we adore;
With Whom Thou reignest God,
For ages evermore. Amen.

℣. Their sound is gone out into all lands.

℟. And their words into the ends of the world.

Ant. to Mag. (*if none Proper*).
Blessed are ye, when men shall hate you, and when they shall separate you from their company, and shall reproach you, and cast out your name as evil, for the Son of man's sake : Rejoice ye in that day, and leap for joy; for, behold, your reward is great in heaven.

Collect of the Vigil, if any; if not, that of the Feast.

Lauds.

℣. Thou hast given an heritage.
℟. Unto those that fear Thy Name, O Lord.

Psalms of Sunday.

Ant. 1. This is My commandment, that ye love one another : as I have loved you.

Ant. 2. Greater love hath no man than this : that a man lay down his life for his friends.

Ant. 3. Ye are My friends : if ye do whatsoever I command you, saith the Lord.

Ant. 4. Blessed are the pure in heart : for they shall see God.

Ant. 5. In your patience : possess ye your souls.

Chapter as at First Vespers.

HYMN. *Exultet cælum laudibus.*

LET the round world with songs rejoice,
Let heaven return the joyful voice;
All, mindful of the Apostles' fame,
Earth, sky, their Sovereign's praise proclaim !

Thou, at Whose word they bore the light
Of gospel truth o'er heathen night,
Still unto us that light impart,
To glad our eyes and cheer our heart.

Thou, at Whose will to them was given
The key that shuts and opens heaven,
Our chains unbind, our loss repair,
And grant us grace to enter there.

Thou, at Whose will they preached the word
Which cured disease, which health conferred,
To us its healing power prolong,
The weak support, confirm the strong.

That when Thy Son again shall come,
And speak the world's unerring doom,
He may with them pronounce us blest,
And place us in Thy endless rest.

All laud to God the Father be;
All laud, Eternal Son, to Thee;
All laud, as is for ever meet,
To God the Holy Paraclete. Amen.

℣. And all men that see it shall say, This hath God done.

℟. For they shall perceive that it is His work.

Ant. to Ben. (*if none Proper*). They will deliver you up to the councils, and they will scourge you in their synagogues : and ye shall be brought before governors and kings for My sake, for a testimony against them and the Gentiles.

Collect of the Proper.

Prime.

Ant. This is My commandment : that ye love one another, as I have loved you.

Tierce.

Ant. Greater love hath no man than this : that a man lay down his life for his friends.

Chapter as at First Vespers.

℟. Their sound is gone out : into all lands. ℣. And their words into the ends of the world. ℟. Into all lands. ℣. Glory be to the Father, and to the Son : and to the Holy Ghost. ℟. Their sound is gone out : into all lands.

℣. Thou shalt make them princes in all lands.

℟. They shall remember Thy Name, O Lord.

Sexts.

Ant. Ye are My friends : if ye do whatsoever I command you, saith the Lord.

CHAPTER. Acts v.

BY the hands of the apostles were many signs and wonders wrought among the people : but the people magnified them.

℟. Thou shalt make them princes : in all lands. ℣. They shall remember Thy Name, O Lord. ℟. In all lands. ℣. Glory be to the Father, and to the Son : and to the Holy Ghost. ℟. Thou shalt make them princes : in all lands.

℣. Exceedingly honoured are Thy friends, O Lord.

℟. Surely established in their pre-eminence.

Nones.

Ant. In your patience : possess ye your souls.

CHAPTER. Acts v.

AND they departed from the presence of the council, rejoicing that they were counted worthy to suffer shame for His Name.

℟. Exceedingly honoured : are Thy friends, O Lord. ℣. Surely established in their pre-eminence. ℟. Are Thy friends, O Lord. ℣. Glory be to the Father, and to the Son : and to the Holy Ghost. ℟. Exceedingly honoured : are Thy friends, O Lord.

℣. All men that see it shall say, This hath God done.

℟. For they shall perceive that it is His work.

Second Vespers.

Ant. 1. The Lord sware, and will not repent : thou art a priest for ever.

Psalm cx. *Dixit Dominus*, p. 47.

Ant. 2. That He may set him with

the princes : even with the princes of His people.

Psalm cxiii. *Laudate pueri*, p. 48.

Ant. 3. Thou hast broken my bonds in sunder : I will offer to Thee the sacrifice of thanksgiving.

Psalm cxvi. 10. *Credidi*, p. 52.

Ant. 4. He that goeth on his way weeping : sowing good seed.

Psalm cxxvi. *In convertendo*, p. 55.

Ant. 5. Exceedingly honoured are Thy friends, O Lord : surely established in their pre-eminence.

Psalm cxxxix. *Domine probasti*, p. 61.

CHAPTER. Eph. II.

NOW therefore ye are no more strangers and foreigners, but fellow-citizens with the saints, and of the household of God; and are built upon the foundation of the apostles and prophets.

℟. *If a Sarum Double.* Fellow-citizens with the Apostles, of the household of God, have come to-day : bringing peace and showing light to our land, to give peace to the nations and to set free the people of the Lord. ℣. Hear the prayers of suppliants who ask the rewards of eternal life, ye who to-day have come again with joy bearing the sheaves of righteousness in your hands. ℟. Bringing peace and showing light to our land, to give peace to the nations, and to set free the people of the Lord. ℣. Glory be to the Father, and to the Son : and to the Holy Ghost. ℟. And to set free the people of the Lor .

HYMN. *Exultet cælum*, ℣. and ℟., p. 215.

Ant. to Mag. In the regeneration when the Son of Man shall sit in the throne of His glory : ye also shall sit upon twelve thrones judging the twelve tribes of Israel, saith the Lord.

OF A MARTYR THROUGH THE YEAR.

First Vespers.

Ant. to Psalms. Blessed is the man that endureth temptation : for when he is tried, he shall receive the crown of life, which the Lord hath promised to them that love Him.

Psalms of the Feria.

CHAPTER. Ecclus. XIV.

BLESSED is the man that doth meditate good things in wisdom, and that reasoneth of holy things by his understanding.

If a Bishop :

CHAPTER. Heb. V.

FOR every high priest taken from among men is ordained for men in things pertaining to God, that he may offer both gifts and sacrifices for sins.

℟. *Not said on Simples of the lowest class.* Thou hast prevented him, O Lord, with the blessings of goodness : Thou hast set a crown of pure gold upon his head. ℣. He asked life of Thee, and Thou gavest him a long life, O Lord. ℟. Thou hast set a crown of pure gold upon his head. ℣. Glory be to the Father, and to the Son :yand to the Holy Ghost. ℟. Thou hast set a crown of pure gold upon his head.

HYMN. *Sanctorum meritis*, p. 220.

℣. Thou hast crowned him, O Lord, with glory and worship.

℟. Thou makest him to have dominion of the works of Thy hands.

Ant. to Mag. This is in truth a

Martyr who poured forth his blood for the name of Christ : who feared not the terrors of judgment, nor sought for the glory of earthly dignity, but with joy attained to the heavenly kingdom.

If no Proper :
COLLECT.

WE beseech Thee, O Lord (blessed *N.*, Thy Martyr, interceding), grant us constancy in Thy faith and truth ; that being grounded in Divine love, we may be moved from its perfection by no temptations. Through.

If a Bishop :
COLLECT.

O GOD, whose grace elected blessed *N.*, Thy Bishop, to the Priesthood, Whose learning instructed him in preaching, Whose power strengthened him in perseverance : grant us, after his pattern, to instruct Thy people by our lives, and to strengthen them by our patience. Through.

If a Priest not a Bishop :
COLLECT.

O GOD, from Whom cometh constant faith, and Whose strength is made perfect in weakness; grant, we beseech Thee, that (by the pattern and the prayers of blessed *N.*, Thy Priest and Martyr) the horrors of persecution, and the terrors of death, may be overcome through the confession of Thy Name. Through.

Lauds.

℣. Thou hast crowned him, O Lord.
℟. With glory and worship.

Psalms of Sunday.

Ant. 1. Whosoever therefore shall confess Me before men : him will I confess also before My Father.

Ant. 2. He that followeth Me shall not walk in darkness : but shall have the light of life, saith the Lord.

Ant. 3. If any man serve Me, him will My Father honour : which is in heaven, saith the Lord.

Ant. 4. If any man serve Me, let him follow Me : and where I am, there shall also My servant be.

Ant. 5. Father, I will that where I am : there shall also My servant be.

Chapter as at First Vespers.

HYMN. *Deus tuorum militum.*

O GOD, Thy soldiers' Crown and Guard,
And their exceeding great reward,
From all transgressions set us free,
Who sing Thy Martyr's victory.

The pleasures of the world he spurned,
From sin's pernicious lures he turned ;
He knew their joys imbued with gall,
And thus he reached Thy heavenly hall.

For Thee through many a woe he ran,
In many a fight he played the man ;
For Thee his blood he dared to pour,
And thence hath joy for evermore.

We therefore pray Thee, full of love,
Regard us from Thy throne above :
On this Thy Martyr's triumph-day,
Wash every stain of sin away.

O Father, that we ask be done,
Through Jesus Christ, Thine only Son :
Who, with the Holy Ghost, and Thee,
Shall live and reign eternally. Amen.

℣. The righteous shall blossom as a lily.
℟. He shall flourish for ever before the Lord.

Ant. to Ben. Except a corn of wheat fall into the ground and die : it abideth alone.

Prime.

Ant. Whosoever therefore shall confess Me before men : him will I confess also before My Father.

Tierce.

Ant. He that followeth Me shall not walk in darkness : but shall have the light of life, saith the Lord.

Chapter as at First Vespers.

℟. With glory and worship : Thou hast crowned him, O Lord. ℣. Thou makest him to have dominion of the works of Thy hands. ℟. Thou hast crowned him, O Lord. ℣. Glory be to the Father, and to the Son : and to the Holy Ghost. ℟. With glory and worship Thou hast crowned him, O Lord.

℣. Thou hast set upon his head, O Lord.

℟. A crown of pure gold.

Sexts.

Ant. If any man serve Me, let him follow Me : and where I am, there shall also My servant be.

CHAPTER. Ecclus. XLV.

HE made him like to the glorious saints, and shewed him part of His glory. He made him to hear His voice, and gave him commandments before His face.

If a Bishop :
Heb. v.

AND no man taketh this honour unto himself, but he that is called of God, as was Aaron. As He saith also in another place, Thou art a priest for ever, after the order of Melchisedec.

℟. Thou hast set : upon his head, O Lord. ℣. A crown of pure gold. ℟. Upon his head, O Lord. ℣. Glory be to the Father, and to the Son : and to the Holy Ghost. ℟. Thou hast set upon his head, O Lord.

℣. The righteous shall flourish like a palm-tree.

℟. And shall spread abroad like a cedar in Libanus.

Nones.

Ant. Father, I will that where I am : there shall also My servant be.

CHAPTER. Ecclus. XLV.

THE Lord clothed him with a robe of glory, He put upon him perfect glory.

If a Bishop :
Ecclus. XV.

WISDOM shall exalt him above his neighbours, and in the midst of the congregation shall she open his mouth. He shall find joy and a crown of gladness, and she shall cause him to inherit an everlasting name.

℟. The righteous shall flourish like a palm-tree : in the house of the Lord. ℣. And shall spread abroad like a cedar in Libanus. ℟. In the house of the Lord. ℣. Glory be to the Father, and to the Son : and to the Holy Ghost. ℟. The righteous shall flourish like a palm-tree.

℣. The righteous shall blossom as a lily.

℟. He shall flourish for ever before the Lord.

Second Vespers.

First Ant. of Lauds with Psalms of the Feria.

Chapter as at First Vespers (and ℟. *if said).*

Hymn, Deus tuorum militum, ℣. *and* ℟. *as at Lauds,* p. 218.

Ant. to Mag. He made him like to the glorious saints, and shewed him part of His glory : He made him to hear His voice, and gave him commandments before His face.

OF MANY MARTYRS
THROUGHOUT THE YEAR.

First Vespers.

Ant. The Saints through faith subdued kingdoms, wrought righteousness : obtained promises.

Psalms of the Feria.

CHAPTER. Wisd. III.

THE souls of the righteous are in the hand of God, and there shall no torment touch them. In the sight of the unwise they seemed to die : but they are in peace.

℟. Round about Thee, O Lord, is never-failing light : where Thou hast built most bright mansions; there rest the souls of the Saints. ℣. Light perpetual shall shine upon Thy Saints, O Lord, and an eternity of ages. ℟. Where Thou hast built most bright mansions; there rest the souls of the Saints. ℣. Glory be to the Father, and to the Son : and to the Holy Ghost. ℟. There rest the souls of the Saints.

HYMN. *Sanctorum meritis.*

THE merits of the Saints,
  Blessed for evermore,
Their love that never faints,
  The toils they bravely bore—
For these the Church to-day
Pours forth her joyous lay—
These victors win the noblest bay.

They, whom this world of ill,
  While it yet held, abhorred :
Is withering flowers that still
  They spurned with one accord :
They knew them short-lived all,
And followed at Thy call,
King Jesu, to Thy heavenly hall.

For Thee all pangs they bare,
  Fury and mortal hate,
The cruel scourge to tear,
  The hook to lacerate ;
But vain their foes' intent :
For, every torment spent,
Their valiant spirits stood unbent.

Like sheep their blood they poured :
  And without groan or tear,
They bent before the sword
  For that their King most dear :
Their souls, serenely blest,
In patience they possessed,
And looked in hope towards their rest.

What tongue may here declare,
  Fancy or thought descry,
The joys Thou dost prepare
  For these Thy Saints on high !
Empurpled in the flood
Of their victorious blood,
They won the laurel from their God.

To Thee, O Lord, Most High,
  One in Three Persons still,
To pardon us we cry,
  And to preserve from ill :
Here give Thy servants peace ;
Hereafter glad release,
And pleasures that shall never cease.
                Amen.

℣. Be glad, O ye righteous, and rejoice in the Lord.

℟. And be joyful, all ye that are true of heart.

Ant. to Mag. In heaven rejoice the souls of the Saints, who followed the footsteps of Christ : and because for His love they shed their blood, therefore with Christ they shall reign for ever.

COLLECT. *(Sarum.)*

ALMIGHTY, everlasting God, grant us worthily to venerate Thy holy Martyrs, *M.* and *N.*, that so we may be delivered from the dangers of this world, and be made worthy of eternal joys. Through.

For many Martyrs, being Bishops or Priests :

COLLECT. *(Sarum.)*

ALMIGHTY, everlasting God, Who didst kindle the fire of Thy love in the hearts of Thy holy Martyrs and Bishops (*or* Priests) *M.* and *N.* : give to our hearts the strength of the same faith and charity, that we may profit by the example of those in whose triumphs we rejoice. Through.

Lauds.

℣. But the righteous live for evermore.

℟. Their reward also is with the Lord.

Psalms of Sunday.

Ant. 1. But the souls of the righteous are in the hand of God : and there shall no torment touch them.

Ant. 2. With the palm the Saints attained the kingdom : they received a beautiful crown from the Lord's hand.

Ant. 3. The bodies of the Saints are buried in peace : but their name liveth for evermore.

Ant. 4. O ye Martyrs of the Lord : bless ye the Lord for ever.

Ant. 5. Let the Saints be joyful

with glory : let them rejoice in their beds.

Chapter as at First Vespers.

HYMN. *Rex gloriose Martyrum.*

ALL-GLORIOUS King of Martyrs Thou,
Crown of Confessors here below;
Whom, casting earthly joys away,
Thou guidest to celestial day.

O quickly bend a gracious ear,
To this our suppliant voice of prayer,
As we their sacred triumphs chant,
Forgiveness to our errors grant.

In Martyrs, victory is Thine,
In Thy Confessors, mercies shine,
Then conquer, Lord, our wickedness,
And us with loving pardon bless.

All laud to God the Father be;
All laud, eternal Son, to Thee!
All laud, as is for ever meet,
To God the Holy Paraclete. Amen.

℣. Wonderful art Thou in Thy Saints, O God.
℟. And glorious in Thy majesty.

Ant. to Ben. Theirs is the kingdom of heaven who despised the life of this world : they have gained the rewards of the kingdom, and have washed their robes in the Blood of the Lamb.

Prime.

Ant. But the souls of the righteous are in the hand of God : and there shall no torment touch them.

Tierce.

Ant. With the palm the Saints attained the kingdom : they received a beautiful crown from the Lord's hand.

Chapter as at First Vespers.

℟. Be glad, O ye righteous : and rejoice in the Lord. ℣. And be joyful all ye that are true of heart. ℟. And rejoice in the Lord. ℣. Glory be to the Father, and to the Son : and to the Holy Ghost. ℟. Be glad, O ye righteous, and rejoice in the Lord.
℣. Let the righteous be glad, and rejoice before God.
℟. Let them also be merry and joyful.

Sexts.

Ant. The bodies of the Saints are buried in peace : but their name liveth for evermore.

CHAPTER. Wisd. x.

FOR though they be punished in the sight of men, yet is their hope full of immortality.

℟. Let the righteous be glad : and rejoice before God. ℣. Let them also be merry and joyful. ℟. And rejoice before God. ℣. Glory be to the Father, and to the Son : and to the Holy Ghost. ℟. Let the righteous be glad and rejoice before God.
℣. The souls of the righteous are in the hand of God.
℟. And there shall no torment touch them.

Nones.

Ant. Let the Saints be joyful with glory : let them rejoice in their beds.

CHAPTER. Wisd. III.

AND having been a little chastised, they shall be greatly rewarded : for God proved them, and found them worthy for Himself.

℟. The souls of the righteous are : in the hand of God. ℣. And there shall no torment touch them. ℟. In the hand of God. ℣. Glory be to the Father and to the Son : and to the Holy Ghost. ℟. The souls of the righteous are in the hand of God.
℣. Wonderful art Thou in Thy Saints, O God.
℟. And glorious in Thy Majesty.

Second Vespers.

First Ant. of Lauds with Psalms of the Feria.

Chapter (and ℟. if it be said) as at First Vespers.

Hymn, Rex gloriose Martyrum, ℣. *and* ℟. *as at Lauds.*

COMMON OF SAINTS.

Ant. to Mag. God shall wipe away all tears from the eyes of the Saints: and there shall be no more sorrow, nor crying; neither shall there be any more pain, for the former things are passed away.

OF A BISHOP AND CONFESSOR
THROUGHOUT THE YEAR.

First Vespers.

Ant. Wisdom guided the righteous man in right paths, shewed him the kingdom of God, and gave him knowledge of holy things: made him rich in his travails, and multiplied the fruit of his labours.

Psalms of the Feria.

CHAPTER. Ecclus. XLV.

HE stood up with good courage of heart, and made reconciliation for Israel. Therefore was there a covenant of peace made with him, that he should be the chief of the sanctuary and of his people.

℟. Well done, thou good and faithful servant; thou hast been faithful over a few things, I will make thee ruler over many things: enter thou into the joy of thy Lord. ℣. Lord, Thou deliveredst unto me five talents; behold, I have gained besides them five talents more. ℟. Enter thou into the joy of Thy Lord. ℣. Glory be to the Father, and to the Son: and to the Holy Ghost. ℟. Enter thou into the joy of thy Lord.

HYMN. *Iste Confessor.*

HE, the Confessor of the Lord, with triumph,
Whom through the wide world celebrate
the faithful,
He on this festal merited to enter
Heavenly mansions.

Pious and prudent, continent and humble,
Sober he was, and gentle of behaviour,
While in his frame dwelt, animate with action,
Earthly existence.

Wherefore our choir, with willing hymns and anthems,
Here, on his feast day, doth him fitting honour;
That in his glory we may have our portion,
Ever and ever.

Glory and virtue, honour and salvation,
Be unto Him that, sitting in the highest,
Ordereth meetly earth, and sky, and ocean,
Onely and Trinal. Amen.

℣. The Lord loved him, and beautified him with comely ornaments.

℟. He clothed him with a robe of glory.

Ant. to Mag. I will liken him to a wise man: which built his house upon a rock.

COLLECT.

GRANT, we beseech Thee, Almighty God, that as we venerate the solemnity of blessed *N.*, Thy Confessor [and Bishop], so it may avail to increase in us true devotion, and strengthen us in the way that leadeth to everlasting life. Through.

Lauds.

℣. The righteous shall flourish like a palm-tree.

℟. And spread abroad like a cedar in Libanus.

Psalms of Sunday.

Ant. 1. Behold a great priest, who in his days pleased God: and was found righteous.

Ant. 2. In glory was there none like unto him: who kept the law of the most High.

Ant. 3. A faithful and wise steward: whom his Lord shall make ruler over His household.

Ant. 4. Blessed is that servant: whom the Lord when He cometh shall find watching.

Ant. 5. Good and faithful servant: enter thou into the joy of thy Lord.

CHAPTER. Ecclus. XXXIX.

HE will give his heart to resort early to the Lord that made him, and will pray before the Most High.

OF A BISHOP AND CONFESSOR THROUGHOUT THE YEAR. 223

HYMN. *Jesu Redemptor omnium.*

JESU, the world's Redeemer, hear!
Thy *Bishop's* fadeless crown, draw near!
Accept with gentler love to-day
The prayers and praises that we pay!

The day that crowned with deathless fame
This meek Confessor of Thy Name,
Whose yearly feast, in solemn state,
Thy faithful people celebrate.

The world, and all its boasted good,
As vain and passing, he eschewed;
And therefore, with angelic bands,
In endless joys for ever stands.

Grant then that we, O gracious God,
May follow in the steps he trod;
And freed from every stain of sin,
As he hath won, may also win.

To Thee, O Christ, our loving King,
All glory, praise, and thanks we bring:
All glory, as is ever meet,
To Father and to Paraclete. Amen.

(*For a Confessor not a Bishop, substitute in the first verse,* Servant's *for* Bishop's.)

℣. The righteous shall blossom as a lily.

℟. He shall flourish for ever before the Lord.

Ant. to Ben. Well done, good and faithful servant : thou hast been faithful over a few things, I will make thee ruler over many things, saith the Lord.

Prime.

Ant. Behold a great priest, who in his days pleased God : and was found righteous.

Tierce.

Ant. In glory was there none like unto him : who kept the law of the most High.

Chapter as at Lauds.

℟. The Lord loved him : and beautified him with comely ornaments. ℣. He clothed him with a robe of glory. ℟. And beautified him with comely ornaments. ℣. Glory be to the Father, and to the Son : and to the Holy Ghost. ℟. The Lord loved him, and beautified him with comely ornaments.

℣. The Lord guided the righteous man in right paths.

℟. And shewed him the kingdom of God.

Sexts.

Ant. A faithful and wise steward : whom his Lord shall make ruler over His household.

CHAPTER. Ecclus. xxxix.

WHEN the great Lord will, he shall be filled with the spirit of understanding : he shall pour out wise sentences, and give thanks unto the Lord in his prayer.

℟. The Lord guided the righteous man : in right paths. ℣. And shewed him the kingdom of God. ℟. In right paths. ℣. Glory be to the Father, and to the Son : and to the Holy Ghost. ℟. The Lord guided the righteous man in right paths.

℣. The righteous shall flourish like a palm tree.

℟. And spread abroad like a cedar in Libanus.

Nones.

Ant. Good and faithful servant : enter thou into the joy of thy Lord.

CHAPTER. Ecclus. xxxix.

THE Lord shall direct his counsel and knowledge, and he shall glory in the law of the covenant of the Lord.

℟. The righteous shall flourish like a palm-tree : in the house of the Lord. ℣. And shall spread abroad like a cedar in Libanus. ℟. In the house of the Lord. ℣. Glory be to the Father, and to the Son : and to the Holy Ghost. ℟. The righteous shall flourish like a palm-tree.

℣. The righteous shall blossom as a lily.

℟. He shall flourish for ever before the Lord.

Second Vespers.

First Ant. of Lauds with Psalms of the Feria.
Chapter as at Lauds. ℟., if any, as at First Vespers.

HYMN. *Jesu Redemptor omnium,*
 ℣. *and* ℟., *p. 223.*

Ant. to Mag. In all his works he praised the Holy One most high : with words of glory.

FOR A CONFESSOR NOT A BISHOP.

All as for a Confessor Bishop, except at First Vespers :

Ant. to Psalms. The Lord loved him, and beautified him with comely ornaments : He clothed him with a robe of glory, and at the gates of Paradise He crowned him.
Psalms of the Feria.
Chapter as at Lauds.

Lauds.

Ant. 1. He led the righteous man by right ways : and shewed him the kingdom of God.

The other Ants. of a Confessor Bishop.

Prime.

Ant. as first at Lauds.
(This is the Sarum Office for Abbots; that which follows is Gallican.)

OF AN ABBOT OR MONK.

First Vespers.

Ant. to Psalms. Escape for thy life : look not behind thee, escape lest thou be consumed.
Psalms of the Feria.

CHAPTER. 2 Cor. VI.

WHEREFORE come out from among them, and be ye separate, saith the Lord, and touch not the unclean thing; and I will receive you, and will be a Father unto you, and ye shall be My sons and daughters, saith the Lord Almighty.

℟. Thou art my defence and shield, and my trust is in Thy word : Away from me, ye wicked, I will keep the commandments of my God. ℣. Master, I will follow Thee whithersoever Thou goest. ℟. Away from me, ye wicked, I will keep the commandments of my God. ℣. Glory be to the Father, and to the Son : and to the Holy Ghost. ℟. Thou art my defence and shield, and my trust is in Thy word : Away from me, ye wicked, I will keep the commandments of my God.

HYMN. *Iste Confessor, p. 222.*

If an Abbot :

℣. His seed shall be mighty upon earth.
℟. The generation of the faithful shall be blessed.

Ant. to Mag. Get thee out of thy country, and from thy kindred : and come into the land which I shall shew thee.

COLLECT. *(Paris.)*

O GOD, Who didst grant to blessed N., the Abbot, to imitate Christ in His poverty, and with humble heart to follow Him to the end; grant to all who have entered on the path of Thy commandments, neither to look back nor to err in the way, but hasting to Thee without stumbling, to attain eternal life, through the same Thy Son Jesus Christ our Lord. Amen.

But if not an Abbot :

℣. Under the shadow of Thy wings shall be my refuge.
℟. Until this tyranny be overpast.

Ant. to Mag. Thou hast left thy father and thy mother, and the land of thy nativity : the Lord recompense thy work, and a full reward be given thee of the Lord God of Israel, under Whose wings thou art come to trust.

COLLECT. *(Paris.)*

ALMIGHTY, everlasting God, bestowing exceeding great rewards on those who for Thy sake trample on earthly things; grant us, by the example and intercession of blessed *N.*, whose departure we this day celebrate, to despise all temporal things, and with our whole heart to hasten unto things eternal; through Jesus Christ our Lord. Amen.

Lauds.

℣. O ye holy and humble men of heart, bless ye the Lord.

℟. Praise Him, and magnify Him for ever.

Psalms of Sunday.

Ant. 1. I will make with them a covenant of peace, and they shall dwell safely in the wilderness, and sleep in the woods : and I will make them and the places round about My hill a blessing.

Ant. 2. We wept when we remembered thee, O Sion : how shall we sing the Lord's song in a strange land?

Ant. 3. I have put off the clothing of prosperity, and put upon me the sackcloth of my prayer : I will cry unto the Everlasting in my days. And joy is come unto me from the Holy One.

Ant. 4. Then judgment shall dwell in the wilderness : and the work of righteousness shall be peace, and the effect of righteousness, quietness, and assurance for ever.

Ant. 5. Let us go forth therefore unto Him without the camp, bearing His reproach : for here we have no continuing city, but we seek one to come.

Chapter as at First Vespers.

HYMN. *Jesu Redemptor*, p. 223.

If an Abbot :

℣. Come, ye children, and hearken unto me.

℟. I will teach you the fear of the Lord.

Ant. to Ben. Behold, I and the children whom the Lord hath given me are for signs and for wonders in Israel : from the Lord of hosts, which dwelleth in Mount Sion.

Collect as at First Vespers.

If not an Abbot :

℣. I cried to Thee, O Lord, and said, Thou art my hope.

℟. And my stronghold.

Ant. to Ben. The Lord is my portion, saith my soul : therefore will I hope in Him.

Collect as at First Vespers.

Prime.

Ant. I will make with them a covenant of peace, and they shall dwell safely in the wilderness, and sleep in the woods : and I will make them and the places round about My hill a blessing.

Tierce.

Ant. We wept when we remembered thee, O Sion : how shall we sing the Lord's song in a strange land?

Chapter as at First Vespers.

℟. Come, My people, enter thou into thy chambers, hide thyself as it were for a little moment : until the indignation be overpast. ℣. Come ye apart into a desert place, and rest awhile. ℟. Until the indignation be overpast. ℣. Glory be to the Father, and to the Son : and to the Holy Ghost. ℟. Come, My people, enter thou into thy chambers, hide thyself as it were for a little moment : until the indignation be overpast.

℣. I had rather be a door-keeper in the house of my God.

℟. Than to dwell in the tents of ungodliness.

Sexts.

Ant. I have put off the clothing of prosperity, and put upon me the sackcloth of my prayer : I will cry unto the Everlasting in my days. And joy is come unto me from the Holy One.

CHAPTER. Heb. XII.

NOW no chastening for the present seemeth to be joyous, but grievous : nevertheless, afterward it yieldeth the peaceable fruit of righteousness unto them which are exercised thereby.

℟. I had rather be : a door-keeper in the house of my God. ℣. Than to dwell in the tents of ungodliness. ℟. A door-keeper in the house of my God. ℣. Glory be to the Father, and to the Son : and to the Holy Ghost. ℟. I had rather be a door-keeper in the house of my God.

℣. Thy statutes have been my songs.

℟. In the house of my pilgrimage.

Nones.

Ant. Let us go forth therefore unto Him without the camp, bearing His reproach : for here we have no continuing city, but we seek one to come.

CHAPTER. Ecclus. LI.

BEHOLD with your eyes, how that I have had but little labour, and have gotten unto me much rest.

℟. Thy statutes have been : my songs. ℣. In the house of my pilgrimage. ℟. My songs. ℣. Glory be to the Father, and to the Son :

and to the Holy Ghost. ℟. Thy statutes have been my songs.

℣. Seven times a day do I praise Thee.

℟. Because of Thy righteous judgments.

Second Vespers.

Ants. of Lauds.

Psalms of the Feria.

CHAPTER. Deut. VII.

THE Lord thy God, He is God, the faithful God, Which keepeth covenant and mercy with them that love Him and keep His commandments, to a thousand generations.

℟. Thanks be to God.

HYMN. *Jesu Redemptor omnium,* p. 223.

If an Abbot :

℣. The righteous shall flourish like a palm-tree.

℟. And shall spread abroad like a cedar in Libanus.

Ant. to Mag. Ye that follow after righteousness, ye that seek the Lord : look unto your father, for I called him alone, and blessed him, and increased him.

If not an Abbot :

℣. They shall flourish in the courts of the house of our God.

℟. That they may shew how true the Lord my strength is.

Ant. to Mag. as at First Vespers, p. 224.

OF A VIRGIN AND MARTYR.

First Vespers.

Ant. This is a wise virgin, who when the Bridegroom came had trimmed her lamp : and went in with the Lord to the marriage.

Psalms of the Feria.

OF A VIRGIN AND MARTYR.

Chapter. Ecclus. LI.

THEN lifted I up my supplication from the earth, O Lord my God, and prayed for deliverance from death. ℟. The kingdoms of the earth and all the glory of the world I despised for the love of my Lord Jesus Christ: Whom I have seen, Whom I have loved, in Whom I have believed, Whom I have desired. ℣. My heart is inditing of a good matter. I speak of the things which I have made unto the King. ℟. Whom I have seen, Whom I have loved, in Whom I have believed, Whom I have desired. ℣. Glory be to the Father, and to the Son : and to the Holy Ghost. ℟. In Whom I have believed, Whom I have desired.

HYMN.
Virginis proles opifexque matris.

OFFSPRING, yet Maker of Thy Virgin-Mother,
Maiden conceived Thee, Ever-maiden bare Thee,
Now as we sing a Virgin's blissful triumph
    Hear our petitions.

Lo! this Thy Virgin double glory winneth,
Proudly subduing woman's feeble nature,
O'er the fell torments of the world she gaineth
    Glorious conquest.

Calmly she greeteth death's approaching terrors,
Tortures unnumbered dauntless she confronteth,
Meetly, her life-blood shed, she straight ascendeth
    Joyous to Heaven.

God of all mercy, as for us she pleadeth,
Loosen sin's fetters, speed to us forgiveness,
So from pure spirits may our glad devotion
    Rise to thine honour.

Glory we give Thee, Sire and Son eternal,
Equal Thy glory, ever-quickening Spirit,
Godhead Triune, to Thee be adoration
    Now and for ever. Amen.

℣. Full of grace are thy lips.
℟. Because God hath blessed thee for ever.

Ant. to Mag. The kingdom of heaven is like unto a net, that was cast into the sea, and gathered of every kind : which, when it was full, they drew to shore, and gathered the good into vessels, but cast the bad away.

Collect. *(Sarum.)*

HEAR us, O God of our salvation, that as we rejoice in the feast of blessed *N.*, Thy Virgin [and Martyr]; so of Thy mercy we may be taught the spirit of devotion. Through.

Lauds.

℣. In thy grace and in thy beauty.
℟. Go forth, ride prosperously and reign.

Psalms of Sunday.

Ant. 1. This is a wise virgin : whom the Lord found watching.
Ant. 2. This is a wise virgin : and one of the number of the prudent.
Ant. 3. This is a virgin holy and glorious : for the Lord of all things hath chosen her.
Ant. 4. I bless Thee, O Father of my Lord Jesus Christ : because, through Thy Son, the fire of temptation is extinguished.
Ant. 5. Come, thou bride of Christ, receive the crown : which the Lord hath prepared for thee for ever.

Chapter as at First Vespers.

HYMN. *Jesu, corona Virginum.*

JESU, the Virgins' Crown, do Thou
  Accept us, as in prayer we bow ;
Born of that Virgin, whom alone
The mother and the maid we own.

Amongst the lilies Thou dost feed,
With virgin choirs accompanied ;
With glory decked, the spotless brides
Whose bridal gifts Thy love provides.

They, wheresoe'er Thy footsteps bend,
With hymns and praises still attend ;
In blessed troops they follow Thee,
With dance, and song, and melody.

We pray Thee therefore to bestow
Upon our senses here below,
Thy grace, that so we may endure,
From taint of all corruption pure.

All laud to God the Father be :
All laud, Eternal Son, to Thee :
All laud, as is for ever meet,
To God the Holy Paraclete. Amen.

℣. The virgins that be her fellows shall bear her company.
℟. And shall be brought unto Thee.
Ant. to Ben. When the Bridegroom came, the wise virgin : being ready, went in with Him to the marriage.
Collect as at First Vespers.

Prime.

Ant. This is a wise virgin : whom the Lord found watching.

Tierce.

Ant. This is a wise virgin : and one of the number of the prudent.
Chapter as at First Vespers.
℟. Full of grace : are thy lips. ℣. Because God hath blessed thee for ever. ℟. Are thy lips. ℣. Glory be to the Father, and to the Son : and to the Holy Ghost. ℟. Full of grace are thy lips.
℣. In thy grace and in thy beauty.
℟. Go forth, ride prosperously and reign.

Sexts.

Ant. This is a virgin, holy and glorious : for the Lord of all things hath chosen her.
CHAPTER. Ecclus. LI.

I WILL praise Thy Name continually, and will sing praise with thanksgiving; because my prayer was heard.
℟. In thy grace : and in thy beauty.
℣. Go forth, ride prosperously and reign. ℟. In thy beauty. ℣. Glory be to the Father, and to the Son : and to the Holy Ghost. ℟. In thy grace and in thy beauty.
℣. God hath given her the help of His countenance.
℟. God is in the midst of her, therefore shall she not be removed.

Nones.

Ant. Come, thou bride of Christ, receive the crown : which the Lord hath prepared for thee for ever.
CHAPTER. Ecclus. LI.

THOU savedst me from destruction and deliveredst me from the evil time : therefore will I give thanks, and praise Thee, and bless Thy Name, O Lord.
℟. God hath given her : the help of His countenance. ℣. God is in the midst of her, therefore shall she not be removed. ℟. The help of His countenance. ℣. Glory be to the Father, and to the Son : and to the Holy Ghost. ℟. God hath given her the help of His countenance.
℣. The virgins that be her fellows shall bear her company.
℟. And shall be y brought unto Thee.

Second Vespers.

Ant. to Psalms. This is a wise virgin : whom the Lord found watching.
Psalms of the Feria.
Chapter as at First Vespers.
HYMN. *Jesu, corona Virginum*, ℣. and ℟., p. 227.
Ant. to Mag. The kingdom of heaven is like unto a merchant man, seeking goodly pearls : who, when he had found one pearl of great price, went and sold all that he had, and bought it.

OF A VIRGIN NOT MARTYR.
The Office is the same, except the Chapters, the second and third verses of the Hymn at First Vespers being omitted.

Both Vespers, Lauds, and Tierce.

CHAPTER. 2 Cor. x.

HE that glorieth, let him glory in the Lord. For not he that com-

Sexts.

CHAPTER. 2 Cor. XI.

I AM jealous over you with godly jealousy : for I have espoused you to one husband, that I may present you as a chaste virgin to Christ.

Nones.

CHAPTER. Wisdom VII. VIII.

VICE shall not prevail against wisdom. Wisdom reacheth from one end to another mightily : and sweetly doth she order all things.

OF A MATRON.

First Vespers.

Ant. to Psalms. The kingdom of heaven is like unto a net, that was cast into the sea, and gathered of every kind : which, when it was full, they drew to shore, and gathered the good into vessels, but cast the bad away.

Psalms of the Feria.

CHAPTER. Prov. XXXI.

WHO can find a virtuous woman? for her price is far above rubies. The heart of her husband doth safely trust in her, so that he shall have no need of spoil.

HYMN. *Hujus obtentu.*

GOD of all mercy, as for us she pleadeth,
Loosen sin's fetters, speed to us forgiveness,
So from pure spirits may our glad devotion
    Rise to Thine honour.

Glory we give Thee, Sire and Son eternal,
Equal Thy glory, ever-quickening Spirit,
Godhead Triune, to Thee be adoration
    Now and for ever.

℣. Full of grace are thy lips.

℟. Because God hath blessed thee for ever.

Ant. to Mag. My soul failed when my Beloved spake : I sought Him, but I could not find Him; I called Him, but He gave me no answer. The watchmen that went about the city found me, they smote me, they wounded me : the keepers of the walls took away my veil from me. I charge you, O daughters of Jerusalem, if ye find my Beloved, that ye tell Him, that I am sick of love.

COLLECT.

O GOD, the Creator and Ruler of all things, Who on this day hast made us glad by the festival of blessed *N.* : grant, we beseech Thee, that, while she pleads before Thee, we may be released from the chain of our sins. Through.

Lauds.

℣. God is in the midst of her, therefore shall she not be removed.

℟. God shall help her, and that right early.

Psalms of Sunday.

Ant. 1. Thy name is as ointment poured forth : therefore do the virgins love thee.

Ant. 2. His left hand is under my head : and His right hand doth embrace me.

Ant. 3. While the King sitteth at His table : my spikenard sendeth forth the smell thereof.

Ant. 4. Lo, the winter is past : the rain is over and gone.

Ant. 5. As the apple tree among the trees of the wood : so is my Beloved among the sons.

Chapter as at First Vespers.

HYMN. *Hæc rite mundi gaudia.*

THE world and all its boasted good
As vain and passing she eschewed;
And therefore with angelic bands,
In endless joys for ever stands.

Grant then that we, O gracious God,
May follow in the steps she trod;

And, freed from every stain of sin,
As she hath won, may also win.
To Thee, O Christ, our loving King,
All glory, praise, and thanks, we bring;
All glory, as is ever meet,
To Father and to Paraclete. Amen.

℣. God hath elected and pre-elected her.

℟. And made her to dwell in His tabernacle.

Ant. to Ben. The kingdom of heaven is like unto a merchant man seeking goodly pearls : who when he had found one pearl of great price, went and sold all that he had, and bought it.

Ant. to Mag. as at First Vespers.

Prime.

Ant. Thy name is as ointment poured forth : therefore do the virgins love thee.

Tierce.

Ant. His left hand is under my head : and His right hand doth embrace me.

Chapter as at First Vespers.

℟℟. and ℣℣. *at the Hours as of a Virgin.*

Sexts.

Ant. While the King sitteth at His table : my spikenard sendeth forth the smell thereof.

CHAPTER. Prov. xxxi.

SHE girdeth her loins with strength, and strengtheneth her arms. She perceiveth that her merchandise is good : her candle goeth not out by night.

Nones.

Ant. As the apple tree among the trees of the wood, so is my Beloved among the sons.

CHAPTER. Prov. xxxi.

A WOMAN that feareth the Lord, she shall be praised. Give her of the fruit of her hands : and let her own works praise her in the gates.

Second Vespers.

Ant. Thy name is as ointment poured forth : therefore do the virgins love thee.

Psalms of the Feria.
Chapter as at First Vespers.

HYMN. *Hæc rite mundi gaudia,*
℣. *and* ℟. *as at Lauds.*

Ant. to Mag. I went down into the garden of nuts to see the fruits of the valley, and to see whether the vine flourished, and the pomegranates budded. Return, return, O Shulamite ; return, return, that we may look upon thee.

ANNIVERSARY OF THE DEDICATION
OF A CHURCH.

First Vespers.

Ant. to Psalms. O how dreadful is this place! : truly this is none other but the house of God, and the gate of heaven. *In Easter-tide is added :* Alleluia.

Psalms of the Feria.

In Christmas-tide the Ants. and Psalms are as at Second Vespers of Christmas-Day. p. 96.

CHAPTER. Rev. xxi.

I SAW the holy city, new Jerusalem, coming down from God out of heaven, prepared as a bride adorned for her husband.

℟. How dreadful is this place! this is none other but the house of God, and the gate of heaven : Surely the Lord is in this place : and I knew it not. (*In Easter-tide :* Alleluia.)
℣. And when Jacob awaked out of his sleep, he said. ℟. Surely the Lord is in this place, and I knew it not. (Alleluia.) ℣. Glory be to the Father, and to the Son: and to the Holy Ghost.
℟. Surely the Lord is in this place : and I knew it not. (*But in Easter-tide :* ℟. Alleluia.)

ANNIVERSARY OF THE DEDICATION OF A CHURCH.

HYMN. *Urbs beata Hierusalem.*

BLESSED city, heavenly Salem,
  Vision dear of peace and love,
Who, of living stones upbuilded,
  Art the joy of heaven above,
And, with angel cohorts circled,
  As a bride to earth dost move!

From celestial realms descending,
  Ready for the nuptial bed,
To His presence, decked with jewels,
  By her Lord shall she be led;
All her streets, and all her bulwarks,
  Of pure gold are fashioned.

Bright with pearls her portal glitters!
  It is open evermore;
And, by virtue of His merits,
  Thither faithful souls may soar,
Who for Christ's dear Name, in this world
  Pain and tribulation bore.

Many a blow and biting sculpture
  Polished well those stones elect,
In their places now compacted
  By the heavenly Architect,
Who therewith hath willed for ever
  That His palace should be decked.

Laud and honour to the Father;
  Laud and honour to the Son;
Laud and honour to the Spirit;
  Ever Three, and ever One:
Consubstantial, Co-eternal,
  While unending ages run. Amen.

℣. Holiness becometh Thy house, O Lord.

℟. For ever.

Ant. to Mag. The Lord hath sanctified His tabernacle; this is the house of the Lord, wherein men shall call upon His Name : whereof it is written, My Name shall be there, saith the Lord. (Alleluia.)

COLLECT.

O GOD, Who year by year renewest the consecration day of this Thy holy temple, and bringest us again in safety to Thy holy mysteries; hear the prayers of Thy people, and grant that whosoever entereth this temple to ask for blessings, may rejoice in their fulfilment. Through.

Lauds.

℣. My house.

℟. Shall be called the house of prayer. (Alleluia.)

Psalms of Sunday.

Ant. 1. Holiness becometh Thy house, O Lord : for ever. (Alleluia.)

Ant. 2. My house shall be called : the house of prayer. (Alleluia.)

Ant. 3. This is the house of the Lord, firmly builded : it is well grounded on a firm rock. (Alleluia.)

Ant. 4. The house of the Lord is well grounded : on a firm rock. (Alleluia.)

Ant. 5. All thy walls shall be built up with precious stones : and the towers of Jerusalem with jewels. (Alleluia.)

CHAPTER. 1 Cor. III.

BUT let every man take heed how he buildeth thereupon. For other foundation can no man lay than that is laid, which is Jesus Christ.

℟. Thanks be to God.

HYMN. *Angulare fundamentum.*

CHRIST is made the sure Foundation,
  And the precious Corner-stone,
Who, the two-fold walls surmounting,
  Binds them closely into one;
Holy Sion's help for ever,
  And her confidence alone.

All that dedicated city,
  Dearly loved by God on high,
In exultant jubilation
  Pours perpetual melody;
God the One, and God the Trinal,
  Singing everlastingly.

To this Temple, where we call Thee,
  Come, O Lord of Hosts, to-day!
With Thy wonted loving kindness
  Hear Thy people as they pray;
And Thy fullest benediction
  Shed within its walls for aye.

Here vouchsafe to all Thy servants
  That they supplicate to gain :
Here to have and hold for ever
  Those good things their prayers obtain :
And hereafter in Thy glory
  With Thy blessed ones to reign.

Laud and honour to the Father;
  Laud and honour to the Son;
Laud and honour to the Spirit;
  Ever Three, and ever One:
Consubstantial, co-eternal,
  While unending ages run. Amen.

℣. Blessed are they that dwell in Thy house, O Lord.

℟. They will be alway praising Thee.

Ant. to Ben. Zaccheus, make haste, and come down, for to-day I must abide at thy house; and he made haste, and came down, and received Him joyfully into his house : To-day is salvation come to this house from God. (Alleluia.)

Collect.

O GOD, Who hast vouchsafed to call the Church Thy Bride, that she who had grace through devotion of faith, might also receive dignity from her name : grant that all this Thy people, the servants of Thy Name, may be found worthy to share that title of Thy Church. Who liveth.

This Collect is said at every Hour except Second Vespers.

Prime.

Ant. Holiness becometh Thy house, O Lord : for ever. (Alleluia.)

℟. *With* Alleluia. ℣. Who sitteth.

Tierce.

Ant. My house shall be called : the house of prayer. (Alleluia.)

Chapter as at Lauds.

℟. Holiness becometh Thy house, O Lord. Alleluia. Alleluia. ℣. For ever. ℟. Alleluia. Alleluia. ℣. Glory be to the Father, and to the Son : and to the Holy Ghost. ℟. Holiness becometh Thy house, O Lord. Alleluia. Alleluia.

From Septuagesima to Easter this ℟. is thus said:

℟. Holiness becometh : Thy house, O Lord. ℣. For ever. ℟. Thy house, O Lord. ℣. Glory be to the Father, and to the Son : and to the Holy Ghost. ℟. Holiness becometh Thy house, O Lord.

℣. My house.
℟. Shall be called the house of prayer. (Alleluia.)

Sexts.

Ant. This is the house of the Lord, firmly builded : it is well grounded on a firm rock. (Alleluia.)

Chapter. Rev. xxi.

BEHOLD, the tabernacle of God is with men, and He will dwell with them, and they shall be His people, and God Himself shall be with them, and be their God.

℟. My house : Alleluia. Alleluia. ℣. Shall be called the house of prayer. ℟. Alleluia. Alleluia. ℣. Glory be to the Father, and to the Son : and to the Holy Ghost. ℟. My house. Alleluia. Alleluia.

From Septuagesima to Easter this ℟. is thus said:

℟. My house : saith the Lord. ℣. Shall be called the house of prayer. ℟. Saith the Lord. ℣. Glory be to the Father, and to the Son : and to the Holy Ghost. ℟. My house, saith the Lord.

℣. Blessed are they that dwell in Thy house.
℟. They will be always praising Thee.

Nones.

Ant. All thy walls shall be built up with precious stones : and the towers of Jerusalem with jewels. (Alleluia.)

Chapter. 1 Cor. iii.

AND every man shall receive his own reward according to his own labour. For we are labourers together with God : ye are God's husbandry, ye are God's building.

℟. Blessed are they that dwell in Thy house, O Lord. Alleluia. Alleluia. ℣. They will be alway praising Thee. ℞. Alleluia. Alleluia. ℣. Glory be to the Father, and to the Son : and to the Holy Ghost. ℞. Blessed are they that dwell in Thy house, O Lord. Alleluia. Alleluia.

From Septuagesima to Easter this ℞. is thus said:

℞. Blessed are they that dwell : in Thy house, O Lord. ℣. They will be alway praising Thee. ℞. In Thy house, O Lord. ℣. Glory be to the Father, and to the Son : and to the Holy Ghost. ℞. Blessed are they that dwell in Thy house, O Lord.

℣. This is the house of the Lord firmly builded.

℞. It is well grounded on a firm rock.

Second Vespers.

Ant. Holiness becometh Thy house, O Lord : for ever. (Alleluia.)

Credidi propter. Ps. cxvi. 10, p. 52.
Lætatus sum. Ps. cxxii., p. 54.
Nisi Dominus. Ps. cxxvii., p. 56.
Laudate Dominum, quia. Ps. cxlvi., p. 65.
Lauda Hierusalem. Ps. cxlvii. 12, p. 65.

Chapter as at First Vespers.

℞. My house shall be called the house of prayer, saith the Lord. For therein every one that asketh receiveth; and he that seeketh findeth; and to him that knocketh it shall be opened. (*In Easter-tide:* Alleluia.) ℣. Holiness becometh Thine house, O Lord, for ever. ℞. For therein every one that asketh receiveth; and he that seeketh findeth; and to him that knocketh it shall be opened. (*In Easter-tide:* Alleluia.) ℣. Glory be to the Father, and to the Son : and to the Holy Ghost. ℞. For therein every one that asketh receiveth; and he that seeketh findeth; and to him that knocketh it shall be opened. (*But in Easter-tide.* ℞. Alleluia.)

HYMN. *Urbs beata,*
℣. *and ℞. as at First Vespers.*

Ant. to Mag. Behold, the tabernacle of God is with men, and the spirit of God dwelleth in you : for the temple of God is holy, which temple ye are, for Whose sake ye celebrate this day the joys of the temple with a season of festivity. (Alleluia.)

Collect as at First Vespers.

The office is thus said on every day throughout the Octave, except a feast of nine lessons occur : the Lauds Collect is said at every hour.

The following Antiphons are said through the Octave to Ben. and Mag. or in the memorial of the Dedication on any occurrent double feast.

1. Bless, O Lord, this house which I have builded for Thy Name : and the prayers of them that shall come hither hear Thou in heaven Thy dwelling place. (Alleluia.)

2. And Jacob rose up early in the morning, and set up the stone for a pillar, and poured oil on the top of it, and vowed a vow to the Lord : Surely this place is holy, and I knew it not. (Alleluia.)

3. Blessed art Thou in the holy temple of Thy glory : which is builded to the praise and glory of Thy Name, O Lord. (Alleluia.)

4. Other foundation can no man lay : than that is laid, which is Jesus Christ. (Alleluia.)

5. May this shrine receive from God the grace of blessing : and mercy from Christ the Lord. (Alleluia.)

6. In the dedication of this temple, praise God all ye hosts of heaven : and let all the earth praise the Name of the Lord; for His Name only is excellent. (Alleluia.)

7. In His wisdom hath God laid the foundations of this temple, wherein the Angels praise the Lord of heaven : lét the floods come, and the winds blow; it shall not fall, for it is founded upon a rock. (Alleluia.)

8. Look upon this house, O Thou Shepherd of Israel, Thou that leadest Joseph like a sheep : multiply Thy blessing upon it, Thou that sittest upon the cherubim ; hearken unto the prayers and supplications of them that confess Thy Name therein. (Alleluia.)

9. Bless, O Lord, this house, which I have builded for Thy Name : that Thine eyes may be open upon it day and night. (Alleluia.)

10. They decked the forefront of the temple with crowns of gold : and dedicated the altar to the Lord. (Alleluia.)

The ordinary memorials are not said during this Octave; except, if between Christmas and Candlemas, memorial of S. Mary : or, if between Low Sunday and Ascension Day, of the Resurrection.

On Sunday in the Octave, all as on the festival: First and Second Vespers being said as Second of the feast, omitting ℟. At First Vespers, memorials of Sunday, the Holy Trinity, the Cross, and S. Mary. The Psalms at Lauds are said under one Ant.

On the Octave, all as on the first day, except that the ℟. is omitted at Second Vespers.

☩

✠

COMMON MEMORIALS OF SAINTS.

Said at Vespers and at Lauds.

OF A MARTYR.

IN EASTER-TIDE.

Every Memorial is said both at Vespers and Lauds with this

Ant. Daughters of Jerusalem, come and behold the Martyr with the crown : wherewith the Lord crowned Him in the day of solemnity and gladness. Alleluia. Alleluia.

At Vespers :

℣. Your sorrow.

℟. Shall be turned into joy. Alleluia.

At Lauds :

℣. Rejoice in the Lord, ye righteous.

℟. For it becometh well the just to be thankful. Alleluia. Alleluia.

Collect of the Proper, if any : otherwise of the Common through the year.

THROUGH THE YEAR.

Vespers.

Ant. He made him like to the glorious saints, and shewed him part of His glory : He made him to hear His voice, and gave him commandments before His face.

℣. Thou hast crowned him, O Lord, with glory and worship.

℟. Thou makest him to have dominion of the works of Thine hands.

COLLECT.

WE beseech Thee, O Lord, (blessed *N.*, Thy Martyr interceding,) grant us constancy in Thy faith and truth, that being grounded in divine love, we may be moved from its perfection by no temptations. Through.

If a Bishop.
COLLECT.

O GOD, Whose grace elected blessed *N.* Thy Bishop to the Priesthood, Whose learning instructed him in preaching, Whose power strengthened him in perseverance; grant us, after his pattern, to instruct Thy people by our lives, and to strengthen them by our patience. Through.

If a Priest, not a Bishop.
COLLECT.

O GOD, from Whom cometh constant faith, and Whose strength is made perfect in weakness; grant, we beseech Thee, that (by the pattern and the prayers of blessed *N.*, Thy Priest and Martyr,) the horrors of persecution and terrors of death may be overcome through the confession of Thy Name. Through.

Lauds.

Ant. Verily, verily, I say unto you, Except a corn of wheat fall into the ground and die, it abideth alone: but if it die, it bringeth forth much fruit.

℣. The righteous shall blossom as a lily.

℟. He shall flourish for ever before the Lord.

Collect as at Vespers.

Of Many Martyrs.
Vespers.

Ant. In heaven rejoice the souls of the Saints, who followed the footsteps of Christ : and because for His love they shed their blood, therefore with Christ they shall reign for ever.

℣. Wonderful art Thou in Thy Saints, O God.

℟. And glorious in Thy majesty.

Collect.

ALMIGHTY, everlasting God, Who didst kindle the fire of Thy love in the hearts of Thy holy Martyrs (and Bishops *or* Priests) *M.* and *N.*: give to our hearts the strength of the same faith and charity, that we may profit by the example of those in whose triumphs we rejoice. Through.

Lauds.

Ant. Theirs is the kingdom of heaven who despised the life of this world : and have gained a reward in the kingdom, and have washed their robes in the Blood of the Lamb.

℣. Wonderful art Thou in Thy Saints, O God.

℟. And glorious in Thy majesty.

Collect as at Vespers.

Of a Confessor.
Vespers.

Ant. I will liken him to a wise man : which built his house upon a rock.

℣. The Lord loved him and beautified him with comely ornaments.

℟. He clothed him with a robe of glory.

Collect.

GRANT, we beseech Thee, Almighty God, that as we venerate the solemnity of blessed *N.*, Thy Confessor [and Bishop] so it may avail to increase in us true devotion, and strengthen us in the way that leadeth to everlasting life. Through.

Lauds.

Ant. Well done, good and faithful servant; thou hast been faithful over a few things, I will make thee ruler over many things : enter thou into the joy of thy Lord.

℣. The righteous shall blossom as a lily.

℟. He shall flourish for ever before the Lord.

Collect as at Vespers.

Of an Abbot.
Vespers.

Ant. Get thee out of thy country, and from thy kindred : and come into the land which I shall shew thee.

℣. His seed shall be mighty upon earth.

℟. The generation of the faithful shall be blessed.

Collect.

O GOD, Who didst grant to blessed *N.*, the Abbot, to imitate Christ in his poverty, and with humble heart to follow Him to the end : grant to all who have entered on the path of Thy commandments, neither to look back, nor err in the way, but, hasting to Thee without stumbling, to attain eternal life. Through the same.

Lauds.

Ant. Behold, I and the children whom the Lord hath given me : are for signs and for wonders in Israel from the Lord of hosts, Which dwelleth in Mount Sion.

℣. Come, ye children, and hearken unto me.

℟. I will teach you the fear of the Lord.

Collect as at Vespers.

Of a Virgin.
Vespers.

Ant. The kingdom of heaven is like unto a net, that was cast into the sea, and gathered of every kind : which, when it was full, they drew to shore, and gathered the good into vessels, but cast the bad away.

℣. Full of grace are thy lips.

℟. Because God hath blessed thee for ever.

Collect.

HEAR us, O God of our salvation, that as we rejoice in the feast of blessed N., Thy Virgin [and Martyr]; so of Thy mercy we may be taught the spirit of devotion. Through.

Lauds.

Ant. When the Bridegroom came, the wise virgin, being ready : went in with Him to the marriage.

℣. The virgins that be her fellows shall bear her company.

℟. And shall be brought unto Thee.

Collect as at Vespers.

Of a Matron.
Vespers.

Ant. My heart rejoiceth in the Lord : my mouth is enlarged, because I rejoice in Thy salvation.

℣. O turn away mine eyes, lest they behold vanity.

℟. And quicken Thou me in Thy way.

Collect.

O GOD of mercy, enlighten the hearts of Thy faithful people, and blessed N. [Thy Martyr] interceding, make us to despise things earthly, and love things heavenly. Through.

Lauds.

Ant. The prayer of the humble pierceth the clouds : he will not depart till the Most High shall behold.

℣. I humbled my soul with fasting.

℟. And my prayer shall turn into mine own bosom.

In places where any feast, here simply commemorated, is to be kept with full Office, the Common will be used of a Martyr, Confessor, &c., according as the case may be : and if the memorial have proper Ants., ℣., ℟., and Collect, such Collect will be the proper Collect of the Office, and the ℣., ℟., and Ant. will be used at Magnificat *in First Vespers.*

Where a feast of which the Office is here given, is to be simply commemorated, the memorial at Vespers and Lauds will be made by taking the Ants. to Mag. *and* Ben., *the ℣℣. and ℟℟. of the hymns, and the proper Collect.*

PROPER OF SAINTS.

November 30.
S. ANDREW, APOSTLE AND MARTYR.

First Vespers.

Ant. to Psalms. One of the two which followed the Lord : was Andrew, Simon Peter's brother. Alleluia.

Psalms of the Feria.

CHAPTER. Rom. x.

FOR with the heart man believeth unto righteousness, and with the mouth confession is made unto salvation. For the Scripture saith, Whosoever believeth on Him shall not be ashamed.

℟. The man of God was being led to crucifixion, but the people cried with a loud voice, saying : his innocent blood is condemned without cause. ℣. And as the executioners were leading him to be crucified, the people ran together, crying and saying. ℟. His innocent blood is condemned without cause. ℣. Glory be to the Father, and to the Son : and to the Holy Ghost. ℟. His innocent blood is condemned without cause.

HYMN. *Annue Christe*, p. 215.

℣. The Lord loved Andrew.
℟. In the odour of sweetness.

Ant. to Mag. Jesus, walking by the sea of Galilee, saw Peter and Andrew his brother : and saith unto them, Follow Me, and I will make you fishers of men ; and they straightway left their nets and the ship, and followed Him.

COLLECT.

ALMIGHTY God, Who didst give such grace unto Thy holy Apostle Saint Andrew, that he readily obeyed the calling of Thy Son Jesus Christ, and followed Him without delay ; grant unto us all, that we, being called by Thy holy word, may forthwith give up ourselves obediently to fulfil Thy holy commandments ; through the same Jesus Christ our Lord. Amen.

If in Advent, Memorial of the Feria.

Lauds.

℣. The Lord loved Andrew.
℟. In the odour of sweetness.

Psalms of Sunday.

Ant. 1. Hail, precious Cross : receive the disciple of Him Who hung on thee, my Master Christ.

Ant. 2. Blessed Andrew prayed, saying : O Lord, King of eternal glory, receive me who hang in torture.

Ant. 3. Lord, suffer not me Thy servant to be parted from Thee : it is time that Thou commend my body to the earth.

Ant. 4. Andrew was the companion of Christ, a worthy Apostle of God : brother of Peter, and his fellow in passion.

Ant. 5. Lord, Thou didst cast into hell him who persecuted the righteous man : and on the tree of the Cross Thou wast the leader of the righteous.

Chapter as at First Vespers.

℟. Thanks be to God.

HYMN. *Exultet cælum laudibus,* p. 215.

Ant. to Ben. Grant us the just man : restore us the holy man, slay not the man dear to God, just, meek, and pious.

If in Advent, Memorial of the Feria.

Prime.

Ant. Hail, precious Cross : receive the disciple of Him Who hung on thee, my Master Christ.

Tierce.

Ant. Blessed Andrew prayed, saying : O Lord, King of eternal glory, receive me who hang in torture.

Chapter as at First Vespers.

℟℟. *of the Common of Apostles,* p. 216.

Sexts.

Ant. Lord, suffer not me Thy servant to be parted from Thee : it is time that Thou commend my body to the earth.

CHAPTER. Rom. x.

FOR there is no difference between the Jew and the Greek : for the same Lord over all is rich unto all that call upon Him.

℟℟. *of the Common of Apostles,* p. 216.

Nones.

Ant. Lord, Thou didst cast into hell him who persecuted the righteous man : and on the tree of the Cross Thou wast the leader of the righteous.

CHAPTER. Rom. x.

FOR whosoever shall call upon the Name of the Lord shall be saved.

℟℟. *of the Common of Apostles,* p. 216.

Second Vespers.

Psalms of the Common of Apostles, p. 216, *said under first Ant. of Lauds.*

Chapter as at First Vespers.

℟. I have stretched forth my hands all day long upon the Cross unto a disobedient and gainsaying people : who walk in no good way, but do after their own lusts. ℣. The God to Whom vengeance belongeth hath lifted up Himself. He hath arisen to judge the earth, and to reward the proud after their own deserving. ℟. Who walk in no good way, but do after their own lusts. ℣. Glory be to the Father, and to the Son : and to the Holy Ghost. ℟. Who walk in no good way, but do after their own lusts.

HYMN. *Exultet cælum,* p. 215.

Ant. to Mag. O Lord Jesus Christ, good Master, receive my spirit in peace : for it is now time that I come ; and I long to behold Thee.

If in Advent, Memorial of the Feria.

FEASTS OF DECEMBER.

[*On the first day unhindered is said the Office of the Dead.*]

December 3.

S. FRANCIS XAVIER, CONFESSOR.*

All of the Common of a Confessor not a Bishop, p. 224, *except the*

COLLECT.

GOD, Who didst will to gather to Thy Church the nations of India, by the preaching and miracles of blessed Francis ; mercifully grant that as we venerate his glorious merits, so we may imitate the pattern of his virtue. Through.

Memorial of the Feria at both Vespers and at Lauds.

December 4.

S. Drostane, Abbot and Confessor.*

All of the Common of an Abbot, p. 224, except the

Collect.

O GOD, Who didst adorn blessed Drostane, Thy Confessor and Abbot, by glorious miracles; grant, we beseech Thee, that we may attain to those eternal rewards which Thou hast bestowed on him in heaven; through Jesus Christ our Lord, Who liveth and reigneth with Thee and the Holy Ghost, without end. Amen.

December 6.

S. Nicolas, Bishop.*

All of the Common of a Bishop and Confessor, p. 222.

Memorial of the Feria at both Vespers aud at Lauds.

December 8.

The Conception of the Blessed Virgin Mary.

First Vespers.

Psalms as at First Vespers of Christmas Day, p. 94.

Ant. 1. Of the woman came the beginning of sin : and through her we all die.

Ant. 2. The Lord God said unto the woman, What is this that thou hast done? : And the woman said, The serpent beguiled me.

Ant. 3. The Lord God said unto the serpent, Because thou hast done this : I will put enmity between thee and the woman, and between thy seed and her seed.

Ant. 4. It shall bruise thy head : and thou shalt bruise his heel.

Ant. 5. The help that is done upon earth He doeth it Himself : Thou smotest the heads of Leviathan in pieces.

Chapter. Zeph. iii.

BE ye glad and rejoice with all thy heart, O daughter of Jerusalem. The Lord hath taken away thy judgments, He hath cast out thine enemy : the King of Israel, even the Lord, is in the midst of thee.

℞. Thou art our sister : be thou the mother of thousands of millions. ℣. And let thy Seed possess the gate of them that hate thee. ℞. Be thou the mother of thousands of millions. ℣. Glory be to the Father, and to the Son : and to the Holy Ghost. ℞. Be thou the mother of thousands of millions.

Hymn. *Ave! maris Stella, p. 210.*

℣. To the brightness of thy rising all shall come.

℞. And they shall shew forth the praises of the Lord. Alleluia.

Ant. to Mag. Behold, darkness shall come over the earth, and thick darkness the nation : but the Lord shall arise upon thee.

Collect.

HEAR, we beseech Thee, O merciful God, the prayers of Thy servants, that we who are gathered together to celebrate the Conception of the Virgin Mother of God, may, assisted by her prayers, be delivered by Thee from the perils that oppress us. Through.

Memorial of the Feria.

Lauds.

Psalms of Sunday.

Ant. 1. O' daughter, blessed art thou of the most high God : above all the women upon the earth.

Ant. 2. The Lord that made thee and formed thee from the womb : will help thee.

Ant. 3. Out of thee shall He come forth unto me that is to be ruler in Israel : Whose goings forth have been from of old, from everlasting.

Ant. 4. Thou art our sister; be thou the mother of thousands of millions : and let thy Seed possess the gate of those which hate them.

Ant. 5. In thee : shall all families of the earth be blessed.

CHAPTER. Rom. xv.

THERE shall be a root of Jesse, and He that shall rise to reign over the Gentiles; in Him shall the Gentiles trust.

HYMN. *O gloriosa fœmina*, ℣. and ℟. p. 211.

Ant. to Ben. He hath not taken away His mercy from the house of Israel : but hath destroyed our enemies by mine hand.

Memorial of the Feria.

Prime.

Ant. O daughter, blessed art thou of the most high God : above all the women upon the earth.

Tierce.

Ant. The Lord that made thee and formed thee from the womb : will help thee.

Chapter as at Lauds.

℟. His salvation is nigh them that fear Him : Alleluia. Alleluia. ℣. That glory may dwell in our land. ℟. Alleluia. Alleluia. ℣. Glory be to the Father, and to the Son : and to the Holy Ghost. ℟. Alleluia. Alleluia.

℣. The Lord shall shew loving-kindness.

℟. And our land shall give her increase.

Sexts.

Ant. Out of thee shall He come forth unto me that is to be ruler in Israel : Whose goings forth have been from of old, from everlasting.

CHAPTER. Micah v.

THEREFORE will He give them up, until the time that she which travaileth hath brought forth : then the remnant of His brethren shall return unto the children of Israel.

℟. The Lord shall shew loving-kindness : Alleluia. Alleluia. ℣. And our land shall give her increase. ℟. Alleluia. Alleluia. ℣. Glory be to the Father, and to the Son : and to the Holy Ghost. ℟. Alleluia. Alleluia.

℣. He is thy God, worship thou Him.

℟. The rich also among the people shall make their supplications before thee.

Nones.

Ant. In thee : shall all families of the earth be blessed.

CHAPTER. Judith xiii.

THIS thy confidence shall not depart from the heart of men, which remember the power of God for ever.

℟. He is thy Lord God, and worship thou Him. Alleluia. Alleluia. ℣. The rich also among the people shall make their supplications before thee. ℟. Alleluia. Alleluia. ℣. Glory be to the Father, and to the Son : and to the Holy Ghost. ℟. Alleluia. Alleluia.

℣. I will remember Thy Name from one generation to another.

℟. Therefore shall the people give thanks unto Thee, world without end.

Second Vespers.

Psalms as at Second Vespers of Christmas Day, p. 96, *said under first Ant. of Lauds.*

CHAPTER. Is. LXII.

THOU shalt be called by a new name, which the mouth of the Lord shall name. Thou shalt also be a crown of glory in the hand of the Lord, and a royal diadem in the hand of thy God.

HYMN. *Ave maris Stella,* ℣. and ℟. p. 210.

Ant. to Mag. My dove, my undefiled is but one : the daughters saw her, and blessed her.

Memorial of the Feria.

December 13.

S. LUCY, VIRGIN AND MARTYR.*

All of the Common of a Virgin and Martyr, p. 226, *except*

16

Both Vespers.

Ant. to Mag. In thy patience thou hast possessed thy soul, Lucy, bride of Christ: thou hast hated the things that are in the world, and dost glow among the angels; resisting unto blood thou hast overcome the enemy.

Lauds.

Ant. to Ben. I bless Thee, Father of my Lord Jesus Christ: because by Thy Son the fire around me is extinguished.

Memorial of the Feria at both Vespers and at Lauds.

December 21.
S. THOMAS, APOSTLE AND MARTYR.

All of the Common of Apostles, p. 214, *except as follows:*

First Vespers.

Ant. to Mag. O Christ, Who didst vouchsafe to be touched by Thomas Didymus, hear our prayers: and help us in our sorrows, nor condemn us with the wicked, when Thou shalt come to judge.

COLLECT.

ALMIGHTY and everliving God, Who for the more confirmation of the faith didst suffer Thy holy Apostle Thomas to be doubtful in Thy Son's Resurrection; grant us so perfectly, and without all doubt, to believe in Thy Son Jesus Christ, that our faith in Thy sight may never be reproved. Hear us, O Lord, through the same Jesus Christ, to Whom, with Thee and the Holy Ghost, be all honour and glory, now and for evermore. Amen.

MEMORIAL OF ADVENT.

Ant. O Orient, Brightness of the Eternal Light, and Sun of Righteousness: come, and lighten them that sit in darkness, and in the shadow of death.

℣. Drop down, ye heavens, from above.

℟. And let the skies pour down righteousness: let the earth open, and let them bring forth salvation.

Collect of the week.

Lauds.

MEMORIAL OF ADVENT.

Ant. Fear not: for on the fifth day our Lord shall come to you.

℣. A voice crying in the wilderness.

℟. Prepare ye the way of the Lord: make straight a highway for our God.

Collect of the week, or of the Ember Day, if it so fall.

Second Vespers.

Ant. to Magnificat *as at First Vespers.*

MEMORIAL OF ADVENT.

Ant. O King of the Gentiles, and their Desire, the Corner-stone, Who madest both one: come, and save man, whom Thou hast made out of the dust of the earth.

℣. Drop down, ye heavens, from above.

℟. And let the skies pour down righteousness: let the earth open, and let them bring forth salvation.

Collect of the week, or of the Ember Day.

FEASTS OF JANUARY.

[*On the first day unhindered is said the Office of the Dead.*]

January 3.
S. GENOVEVA, VIRGIN.

Memorial of a Virgin, p. 237.

January 8.
S. LUCIAN, PRIEST AND MARTYR, AND HIS COMPANIONS.

Memorial of many Martyrs, p. 236.

January 13.
S. Hilary, Bishop and Confessor.
Memorial of a Bishop and Confessor, p. 236, except the
Collect. *(Paris.)*

GRANT, O Lord, that the festival of the blessed Bishop Hilary may be profitable to us: that, as he preserved throughout Gaul the pure faith in Thy Consubstantial Son, so, by the help of his prayers, we may be enabled to continue steadfast in the same faith. Through.

On the same day:

S. Kentigern, Bishop and Confessor.
Memorial of a Bishop and Confessor, p. 236.

January 15.
S. Maur, Deacon and Abbot.*
All of the Common of an Abbot, p. 224, except the
Collect.

O GOD, Who didst bestow on blessed Maur the grace not only of wisdom in governing, but also of humility in obeying: grant, we beseech Thee, that, after his example, we being subject one to another as the children of obedience, may serve Thee with the freedom of love. Through.

On the same day:

S. Paul, Hermit.
Memorial.
At Vespers.

Ant. Get thee hence, and hide thyself, for thou shalt drink of the brook: Have I not commanded the ravens to feed thee there?

℣. Cast thy burden on the Lord.

℟. And He shall nourish thee.

Collect. *(Brev. S. Maur.)*

WE beseech Thee, O Lord, that after the example of blessed Paul, we may be enabled to tame our bodies with such severity that, having conquered every evil desire, we may live a heavenly life on earth. Through.

At Lauds.

Ant. ℣. and ℟. of the Common of a Monk, p. 225.

Collect as at Vespers.

January 17.
S. Antony, Abbot.*
All of the Common of an Abbot, p. 224, except the
Collect. *Paris.*

O GOD, Who outwardly by the hearing of Thy word, and inwardly by Thy grace, didst move Antony to forsake all things that he might be made perfect: grant that all who have entered on the course of evangelical perfection may so run as to attain the goal of everlasting happiness. Through.

At Second Vespers, Memorial of the following.

January 18.
S. Prisca, Virgin and Martyr.*
All of the Common of a Virgin and Martyr, p. 226.

Vespers of the following.

January 19.
S. Wulstan, Bishop and Confessor.*
All of the Common of a Confessor and Bishop, p. 222, except the
Collect.

POUR upon us, O Lord, the Spirit of Thy love, that aided by the intercession of blessed Wulstan, Thy Confessor and Bishop, we may be counted worthy to taste of Thy sweetness in eternal bliss. Through. In the unity of the same.

Vespers of the following.

January 20.
SS. Fabian and Sebastian, Martyrs.*
All of the Common of many Martyrs, p. 219, except:

Vespers.

Ant. to Mag. The Lord chose a man out of the people and gave him the glory of the Eternal Vision : Let us celebrate the solemnity of Sebastian the Martyr. Joy be in heaven, and on earth peace to men of good will. Alleluia. Alleluia.

Collect.

GOD, Who didst strengthen Thy blessed Martyrs, Fabian and Sebastian, with the power of constancy in suffering : grant us by their example, for love of Thee, to despise the wealth of this world, and fear none of its adversity. Through.

Lauds.

Ant. to Ben. Blessed art thou, and happy shalt thou be, O noble Martyr Sebastian : for with the Saints thou shalt rejoice, and with the Angels shalt exult for ever.

Collect as at Vespers.

January 21.
S. Agnes, Virgin and Martyr.*

All of the Common of a Virgin and Martyr, p. 226, except that which follows :

First Vespers.

Chapter. Ecclus. LI.

I WILL thank Thee, O Lord and King, and praise Thee, O God my Saviour : I do give praise unto Thy Name. For Thou art my defender and helper, and hast preserved my body from destruction.

Ant. to Mag. Blessed Agnes standing in the midst of the flames, with outstretched hands prayed : I call upon Thee, O Father most worshipful, Father most awful : because by Thy holy Son I have escaped the threats of the wicked tyrant, and passed with unspotted foot through the foulness of the flesh : and lo! I come to Thee, Whom I have loved, Whom I have sought, Whom I have always desired.

Collect.

ALMIGHTY and eternal God, Who hast chosen the weak things of the world to confound the things which are mighty; grant, we beseech Thee, that by the commemoration of Thy holy Virgin and Martyr Agnes we may glory in Thy power; through Jesus Christ our Lord, Who liveth and reigneth with Thee and the Holy Ghost, ever one God, world without end. Amen.

Memorial of SS. Fabian and Sebastian.

To be used only if their full Office have been said on the previous day.

Ant. Behold, thy name is written in the book of life : and thy memorial shall endure for ever.

℣. Wonderful art Thou in Thy Saints, O God.

℟. And glorious in Thy Majesty.

Collect as at First Vespers.

Lauds.

Psalms of Sunday.

Ant. 1. Jesus my Lord hath betrothed me with His ring : and adorned me as a bride with a crown.

Ant. 2. He hath circled my right arm and neck with precious stones : He hath set in mine ears priceless pearls.

Ant. 3. To Him alone I keep faith : to Him with full devotion I commit myself.

Ant. 4. I bless Thee, Father of my Lord Jesus Christ : because by Thy Son the fire around me is extinguished.

Ant. 5. Rejoice with me, and rejoice for me : amidst all these I have received a shining throne.

Chapter as at First Vespers.

Ant. to Ben. Blessed Agnes, standing in the midst of the flames, prayed to the Lord : Almighty, worshipful, awful, I bless Thee, and glorify Thy Name for ever.

Prime.

Ant. Jesus my Lord hath betrothed me with His ring : and adorned me as a bride with a crown.

Tierce.

Ant. He hath circled my right arm and neck with precious stones : He hath set in mine ears priceless pearls.

Chapter as at First Vespers.

Sexts.

Ant. To Him alone I keep faith : to Him with full devotion I commit myself.

CHAPTER. Ecclus. L. 1.

My soul praised the Lord, even unto death, and my life was near to hell.

Nones.

Ant. Rejoice with me, and rejoice for me : amidst all these I have received a shining throne.

Chapter of the Common, p. 228.

Second Vespers.

Ants. of Lauds with Psalms of the Feria.
Chapter as at First Vespers.

Ant. to Mag. Lo, that which I longed for, I now behold, that which I hoped for, I now possess : to Him I am joined in heaven, Whom with entire devotion I loved on earth.

January 22.

S. VINCENT, DEACON AND MARTYR.*

All of the Common of a Martyr, p. 217, except

Both Vespers.

Ant. to Mag. Let us humbly commemorate this day, on which Vincent, the unvanquished Martyr of Christ : having vanquished the tyrant, gained the palm of victory, and joyfully entered heaven.

Lauds.

Ant. to Ben. Behold, O unvanquished Vincent, He for Whose Name thou didst faithfully strive : hath laid up a crown for thee in heavenly places.

January 24.

S. TIMOTHY, BISHOP AND CONFESSOR.*

All of the Common of a Bishop and Confessor, p. 222, except the

COLLECT.

O GOD, Who didst choose blessed Timothy to be a workman that needeth not to be ashamed, and a good minister of Jesus Christ: grant us, by the help of his prayers, so to follow in his footsteps, that, keeping the commandments without spot, we may lay hold on eternal life. Through the same.

On the same day :

S. CADOC, ABBOT.

Memorial of an Abbot, p. 236.

January 25.

THE CONVERSION OF S. PAUL.

First Vespers.

Ant. to Psalms. A light from heaven shined round about Saul ; and he fell to the earth, and heard a voice saying unto him, Saul, Saul, why persecutest thou Me? : and he said, Who art Thou, Lord? And the Lord said, I am Jesus of Nazareth, Whom thou persecutest; it is hard for thee to kick against the pricks.

Psalms of the Feria.

CHAPTER. Acts IX.

AND Saul, yet breathing out threatenings and slaughter against the disciples of the Lord, came near Damascus, and suddenly there shined round about him a light from heaven.

℟. Holy Paul the Apostle, preacher of the truth, and teacher of the Gentiles thou pleadest for us to the Lord Who chose thee. ℣. That we may be found worthy of the grace of God. ℟. Thou pleadest for us to the Lord Who chose thee. ℣. Glory be to the Father, and to the Son : and to the Holy Ghost. ℟. Who chose thee.

Hymn. *Annue Christe*, p. 215.

Ant. to Mag. The Lord chose a man out of the people, and gave him the glory of the Eternal Vision : let us celebrate the conversion of Saint Paul the Apostle.

Collect.

O GOD, Who, through the preaching of the blessed Apostle Saint Paul, hast caused the light of the gospel to shine throughout the world; grant, we beseech Thee, that we, having his wonderful conversion in remembrance, may shew forth our thankfulness unto Thee for the same, by following the holy doctrine which he taught; Through.

Lauds.

℣. Thou hast given an heritage.
℟. Unto those that fear Thy Name, O Lord.

Psalms of Sunday.

Immediately on the conclusion of each Psalm, the ℣. is begun by the leader, and continued by the choir, before the resuming of the antiphon.

Ant. 1. Saul, which is also called Paul, the great preacher, being strengthened by God : mightily convinced the Jews.
℣. Shewing that this is the Christ, the Son of the Living God.
Ant. 2. Brother Saul, the Lord, even Jesus that appeared unto thee in the way as thou camest, hath sent me, that thou mightest receive thy sight, and be filled with the Holy Ghost.
℣. And Ananias went his way and entered into the house, and putting his hands on him, said :
Ant. 3. And Ananias put his hands on him, and straightway there fell from his eyes as it had been scales : and he received sight forthwith and was baptized. And when he had received meat he was strengthened;
℣. Then was he certain days with the disciples that were at Damascus.
Ant. 4. He fell down a most furious persecutor, and arose a most faithful preacher : O Lord, as his words teach us of Thee, so let him avail to bring us to Thee.
℣. Among the Apostles in calling last, in preaching first.
Ant. 5. Paul, entering into the synagogues : preached Jesus to the Jews, proving that this is very Christ.
℣. But all that heard him were amazed.

Chapter as at First Vespers.

Hymn. *Exultet cœlum laudibus*,
℣. and ℟., p. 215.

Ant. to Ben. Let us celebrate the conversion of Saint Paul the Apostle; for he, on this day, instead of a persecutor was made a chosen vessel : let Angels rejoice and Archangels exult, and praise in heaven the Son of God.

Prime.

Ant. Saul, which is also called Paul, the great preacher, being strengthened by God : mightily convinced the Jews.

The ℣℣. *are omitted after the Ants. at the Hours, except at Vespers.*

Ant. to Quicunque. Thee duly praise, p. 31.

Tierce.

Ant. Brother Saul, the Lord, even Jesus that appeared unto thee in the way as thou camest, hath sent me, that thou mightest receive thy sight, and be filled with the Holy Ghost.

Chapter as at First Vespers.
℟℟. *of the Common of Apostles*, p. 216.

Sexts.

Ant. And Ananias put his hands on him, and straightway there fell from his eyes as it had been scales : and he received sight forthwith and was baptized.

And when he had received meat he was strengthened.

℟℣. *of the Common of Apostles*, p. 216.

Nones.

Ant. Paul, entering into the synagogues : preached Jesus to the Jews, proving that this is very Christ.

CHAPTER. Acts IX.

AND Ananias went his way, and entered into the house, and putting his hands on him, said, Brother Saul, the Lord, even Jesus, that appeared unto thee in the way as thou camest, hath sent me that thou mightest receive thy sight, and be filled with the Holy Ghost.

℟℣. *of the Common of Apostles*, p. 216.

Second Vespers.

Antiphons and ℣℣. of Lauds.
Psalms of the Common of Apostles, p. 216.
Chapter as at First Vespers.
HYMN. *Exultet cœlum laudibus,*
℣. *and* ℟., p. 215.

Ant. to Mag. But when it pleased God, Who separated me from my mother's womb, and called me by His grace, to reveal His Son to me, that I might preach Him among the heathen : immediately I conferred not with flesh and blood, neither went I to them which were Apostles before me.

January 26.
S. POLYCARP, BISHOP AND MARTYR.*

All of the Common of a Martyr Bishop, p. 217, *except the*

COLLECT. *(Brev. S. Maur.)*

FULFIL, O Lord, our petitions, and receive us as whole burnt offerings unto Thee, together with blessed Polycarp, Thy Martyr and Bishop, in whose sufferings we this day rejoice. Through.

Vespers from Chapter of the following.

January 27.
S. JOHN CHRYSOSTOM, ARCHBISHOP.*

All of the Common of a Bishop and Confessor, p. 222, *except the*

COLLECT. *(Paris.)*

GRANT to Thy servants, O Lord, in their sacred ministry, the same spirit of wisdom and courage with which blessed John Chrysostom ceased not to warn sinners and overcome manifold persecutions for the love of Thy Name. Through.

January 29.
S. FRANCIS DE SALES, BISHOP AND CONFESSOR.*

All of the Common of a Bishop and Confessor, p. 222, *except the*

COLLECT. *(Paris.)*

O GOD, Who for the salvation of souls didst will that the blessed Bishop, Francis de Sales, should be made all things to all men : mercifully grant, we beseech Thee, that we, filled with the sweetness of Thy love, may, by the teaching of his counsels, and the assistance of his prayers attain everlasting joy. Through.

On the same day :

S. GILDAS, ABBOT.

Memorial of an Abbot, p. 236.

FEASTS OF FEBRUARY.
[*On the first day unhindered is said the Office of the Dead.*]

February 1.
S. BRIDGET, VIRGIN.*

All of the Common of a Virgin not a Martyr, p. 228.

On the same day :

S. IGNATIUS, BISHOP AND MARTYR.

Memorial of a Martyr Bishop, p. 235, *except the*

COLLECT. *(Leonine.)*

ALMIGHTY, Everlasting God, Who shewest Thine infinite power in the strength of all Thy Saints: grant that we, who keep the festival of blessed Ignatius, may duly reverence and diligently follow his example, who, as the Martyr and Bishop of Thy Son, sealed by his testimony the teaching of his ministry, and confirmed by his example the doctrine of his words. Through.

No Memorial of S. Bridget or of S. Ignatius shall be made at First Vespers of the Purification.

February 2.

The Purification of the Blessed Virgin Mary.

First Vespers.

Psalms as at Second Vespers of Christmas Day, p. 96.

Ants. as at Lauds of the Circumcision, p. 109, except

Ant. 5. O marvellous mystery! The womb of a Virgin who knew not man is become the unspotted temple of God: of her He taketh flesh, and to Him shall all nations come, saying, Glory be to Thee, O Lord.

Chapter. Mal. III.

BEHOLD, I will send My messenger, and he shall prepare the way before Me: and the Lord, whom ye seek, shall suddenly come to His temple, even the Messenger of the Covenant, whom ye delight in.

℞. Behold the miracle of the Mother of the Lord; a Virgin hath conceived who knew no man: upon Mary was laid a noble burden: and she knew herself to be a joyful mother who knew not herself to be a wife. ℣. Him fairer than the children of men she conceived in her chaste womb: and, blessed for ever, brought forth for us God and Man. ℞. Upon Mary was laid a noble burden: and she knew herself to be a joyful mother who knew not herself to be a wife. ℣. Glory be to the Father, and to the Son: and to the Holy Ghost. ℞. And she knew herself to be a joyful mother who knew not herself to be a wife.

Hymn. *Quod chorus vatum.*

THAT which of old the reverend choir of prophets
Sang, by the Holy Spirit's inspiration,
Now is fulfilled in Mary, Virgin Mother
 Of our Salvation.

Him, Lord of earth, and God of highest heaven,
She both conceived and bare, a Maid unstained,
And after Childbirth still a stainless Virgin
 Ever remained.

Him now the aged Simeon, the righteous,
In the Lord's temple in his arms enfoldeth,
Christ the Salvation, longed for and expected,
 Glad he beholdeth.

Thee, then, we laud in canticles of triumph,
Mary, thou Mother of the King eternal.
Who now art glowing in the heavenly kingdom
 With light supernal.

Now unto God be majesty and worship,
Glory and might, and praise all praise excelling,
Who on the throne of heaven's eternal glory
 Ever is dwelling. Amen.

℣. It was revealed unto Simeon by the Holy Ghost.
℞. That he should not see death, until he had seen the Lord's Christ.

Ant. to Mag. There was a man in Jerusalem, whose name was Simeon: and the same man was just and devout, waiting for the consolation of Israel: and the Holy Ghost was upon him.

Collect.

ALMIGHTY and everliving God, we humbly beseech Thy Majesty: that as Thy Only-begotten Son was this day presented in the temple in substance of our flesh, so we may be presented unto Thee, with pure and clean hearts, by the same Thy Son Jesus Christ our Lord. Amen.

Compline.

Ant. to Psalms. A Virgin, she conceived the Word; a Virgin, she abode: a Virgin she brought forth the King of kings.

Ant. to Nunc Dim. We glorify thee, Mother of God: for of thee Christ was born.

This Ant. is said to Nunc Dim. on all Feasts and Octaves of the Blessed Virgin and in her commemoration, throughout the year, except in Advent and Eastertide, and on the Annunciation, when Compline of the Season is retained.

Lauds.

℣. It was revealed unto Simeon by the Holy Ghost.
℟. That he should not see death, until he had seen the Lord's Christ.

Psalms of Sunday.

Ant. 1. Simeon was just and devout, waiting for the consolation of Israel : and the Holy Ghost was upon him.
Ant. 2. It was revealed unto Simeon by the Holy Ghost : that he should not see death, until he had seen the Lord.
Ant. 3. Simeon taking up the Child in his arms, and giving thanks : blessed the Lord.
Ant. 4. Lord, now lettest Thou Thy servant depart in peace : for mine eyes have seen Thy salvation.
Ant. 5. Mine eyes have seen Thy salvation : which Thou hast prepared before the face of all people.

Chapter as at First Vespers.

HYMN. *O gloriosa fæmina,* p. 211.

℣. We wait for Thy loving-kindness, O Lord.
℟. In the midst of Thy temple.

Ant. to Ben. The old man carried the Child, but the old man was ruled by the Child whom the Virgin bare : and after child-bearing she remained a Virgin, and worshipped Him Whom she bare.

Prime.

Ant. Simeon was just and devout, waiting for the consolation of Israel : and the Holy Ghost was upon him.

Tierce.

Ant. It was revealed unto Simeon by the Holy Ghost : that he should not see death, until he had seen the Lord.

Chapter as at First Vespers.

℟. Holy Mother of God : Ever-Virgin Mary. ℣. Thou pleadest for us to the Lord our God. ℟. Ever-Virgin Mary. ℣. Glory be to the Father, and to the Son : and to the Holy Ghost. ℟. Holy Mother of God : Ever-Virgin Mary.
℣. After child-bearing thou remainedst a Virgin.
℟. O Mother of God.

Sexts.

Ant. Simeon taking up the Child in his arms, and giving thanks : blessed the Lord.

CHAPTER. Malachi III.

HE is like a refiner's fire, and like fuller's sope : and He shall sit as a refiner and purifier of silver : and He shall purify the sons of Levi.
℟. After child-bearing : thou remainedst a Virgin. ℣. O Mother of God. ℟. Thou remainedst a Virgin. ℣. Glory be to the Father, and to the Son : and to the Holy Ghost. ℣. After child-bearing thou remainedst a Virgin.
℣. Thou art become fair and pleasant.
℟. In thy delights, O holy Mother of God.

Nones.

Ant. Mine eyes have seen Thy salvation : which Thou hast prepared before the face of all people.

CHAPTER. Malachi III.

AND He shall purge them as gold and silver, that they may offer unto the Lord an offering in righteousness.
℟. Thou art become fair : and pleasant. ℣. In thy delights, O holy Mother of God. ℟. And pleasant. ℣. Glory be to the Father, and to the Son : and to the Holy Ghost. ℟. Thou art become fair and pleasant.
℣. God hath elected her and pre-elected her.
℟. He hath made her to dwell in His tabernacle.

Second Vespers.

Psalms as at Second Vespers of Christmas Day, p. 96, said under the first Ant. of Lauds.

Chapter as at First Vespers.

℟. Rejoice, rejoice, rejoice, O Mary, who believedst that which was spoken of Gabriel the Archangel : being a Virgin, thou broughtest forth God and Man : and after child-bearing remainedst a spotless Virgin. ℣. We know that the Archangel Gabriel brought thee a heavenly message, and that the Holy Ghost overshadowed thee. ℟. Being a Virgin, thou broughtest forth God and Man : and after childbearing remainedst a spotless Virgin. ℣. Glory be to the Father, and to the Son : and to the Holy Ghost. ℟. And after child-bearing remainedst a spotless Virgin.

SEQUENCE. *Lætabundus.*

FULL of gladness,
  Let our faithful Choir be singing
    Alleluia.
Monarch's Monarch.
From unspotted Maiden springing :
    Alleluia.
Him the Holy Virgin bore,
Wonderful and Counsellor,
  Sun from star had spring :
Sun, that never knoweth night :
Star, for ever shining bright,
  Ever glittering.
As a star a ray most fair,
Thus the Virgin also bare,
  Like in form, the Child ;
Nor the star by that its ray,
Nor the Virgin any way
  By the Birth defiled.
Now conforms the cedar tall
To the hyssop of the wall
  In our vale of tears :
He, God's Word and Essence, came
To assume our mortal frame,
  And with man appears.
Though Isaiah had foreshewn,
Though the Synagogue had known,
  Yet the truth she will not own,
    Still remaining blind :
If she do her prophets wrong,
If she will not hear their throng,
Still she may, in Gentile song,
    Seek the deed, and find.
Turn, Judæa, and repent,
Credit thine Old Testament :
Why upon destruction bent,
    Miserable race !

Whom its oracles foretold,
Born to save the world, behold ;
Him a Virgin's arms enfold,
    Full of truth and grace. Amen.

In Septuagesima. HYMN, *Quod Chorus vatum,* p. 248.

℣. We wait for Thy loving-kindness, O God.

℟. In the midst of Thy temple.

Ant. to Mag. When the parents brought in the child Jesus, Simeon took Him up in his arms, and blessed God, and said : Lord, now lettest Thou Thy servant depart in peace.

No Memorial of S. Blaise is made at these Vespers, but only, if it so occur, of Septuagesima, Sexagesima, or Quinquagesima Sunday. If this Feast fall on Saturday before Septuagesima, the Second Vespers are of the Feast without Alleluia, with Memorial of Sunday: if on Septuagesima, the Office is wholly of the Feast, with Memorial of Sunday.

February 3.

S. BLAISE, BISHOP AND MARTYR.*

All of the Common of a Martyr Bishop, p. 217.

February 5.

S. AGATHA, VIRGIN AND MARTYR.*

All of the Common of a Virgin and Martyr, p. 226, except that which follows :

First Vespers.

Ant. to Mag. Agatha, holy virgin of noble race : suffered a glorious passion for the sake of Christ.

COLLECT.

O GOD, Who among the other miracles of Thy power hast bestowed the crown of martyrdom even on the weaker sex ; mercifully grant, that as we celebrate the birthday of Thy blessed Martyr Agatha, so by her example we may come to Thee. Through.

Lauds.

Ant. to Ben. But I, being helped of the Lord, will constantly confess Him : for He hath saved me, and comforted me.

Second Vespers.

Ant. to Mag. Agatha most joyfully and gloriously went to prison as it were to a banquet : and commended her sufferings to her Lord.

On all Festivals throughout Lent, Memorials of the Feria are to be said at both Vespers and Lauds.

February 7.

S. ROMUALD, ABBOT.*

All of the Common of an Abbot, p. 224.

February 10.

S. SCHOLASTICA, VIRGIN.*

All of the Common of a Virgin not a Martyr, p. 228.

February 14.

S. VALENTINE, PRIEST AND MARTYR.*

All of the Common of a Martyr, p. 217.

February 18.

S. COLMAN, BISHOP AND CONFESSOR.*

All of the Common of a Bishop and Confessor, p. 222.

On the same day :

S. SIMEON, BISHOP AND MARTYR.

Memorial of a Martyr Bishop, p. 217.

February 24.

S. MATTHIAS, APOSTLE AND MARTYR.

All of the Common of Apostles, p. 214, except the

COLLECT.

O ALMIGHTY God, Who into the place of the traitor Judas didst choose Thy faithful servant Matthias to be of the number of the twelve Apostles; grant that Thy Church, being always preserved from false Apostles, may be ordered and guided by faithful and true pastors; through Jesus Christ our Lord. Amen.

FEASTS OF MARCH.

[*On the first day unhindered is said the Office of the Dead.*]

March 1.

S. DAVID, BISHOP AND CONFESSOR.*

All of the Common of a Bishop and Confessor, p. 222, except the

COLLECT. *(Brev. Hereford.)*

O GOD, Who didst raise up the blessed Bishop David to be a teacher of Thy Church : mercifully grant that in Thy presence he may ever help us by his prayers as our loving Bishop. Through.

Vespers, from Chapter of the following.

March 2.

S. CHAD, BISHOP AND CONFESSOR.*

All of the Common of a Bishop and Confessor, p. 222, except the

COLLECT. *(Brev. Hereford.)*

O GOD, the Crown of Thy chosen Bishops, and the glorious victory of them them that strive : Who didst bestow on blessed Chad, Thy Confessor and Bishop, the highest gifts of the priesthood : Grant, we beseech Thee, that we, assisted by his prayers in Thy sight, may be united to him in everlasting blessedness. Through.

March 8.

SS. PERPETUA AND FELICITAS, MARTYRS.*

All of the Common of many Martyrs, p. 219, except the

COLLECT. *(Brev. Sarum.)*

GRANT us, we beseech Thee, O Lord God, to honour with unceasing devotion the victorious palms of Thy holy martyrs Perpetua and Felicitas; that we, who are not worthy to keep their festival, may yet do them reverence with humble service. Through.

On the same day:

S. THOMAS AQUINAS, CONFESSOR AND DOCTOR.

Memorial of a Confessor not a Bishop, p. 236, except the

COLLECT. *(Brev. Rom.)*

O GOD, Who hast enlightened Thy Church by the wonderful learning of blessed Thomas Thy Confessor, and enriched it by the holiness of his life: grant to us, we beseech thee, both to understand his teaching, and to follow the example of his life. Through.

March 10.

THE FORTY MARTYRS OF SEBASTE.*

All of the Common of many Martyrs, p. 219, except the

COLLECT.

WE entreat Thee, O Lord, that through the remembrance of Thy Martyrs being rooted and grounded in Thy love, we may with willing and unconquered minds endure the sufferings of this present life, for the desire of the glory that is to be revealed in us. Through.

March 12.

S. GREGORY THE GREAT, BISHOP, CONFESSOR AND DOCTOR.*

All of the Common of a Bishop and Confessor, p. 222, except the

COLLECT.

O GOD, Who hast bestowed on the soul of Thy servant Gregory the rewards of eternal blessedness: grant that aided by his prayers in Thy presence, we who are weighed down by the burden of our sins may mercifully be lifted up. Through.

March 17.

S. PATRICK, BISHOP AND CONFESSOR.*

All of the Common of a Bishop and Confessor, p. 222, except the

COLLECT.

GOD, Who didst vouchsafe to send Thy Confessor and Bishop Patrick, to preach Thy glory to the nations, grant to his intercessions, that those things which Thou teachest us to do, of Thy mercy we may have power to perform. Through.

At Second Vespers, Memorial of the following.

March 18.

S. EDWARD, KING AND MARTYR.*

All of the Common of a Martyr, p. 217, except the

COLLECT.

O GOD, Ruler of an eternal kingdom, mercifully look upon Thy family; and as Thou didst vouchsafe to glorify Thy Martyr Edward with heavenly gifts, so grant us likewise to attain eternal felicity. Through.

On the same day:

S. CYRIL, BISHOP AND CONFESSOR.

Memorial of a Confessor, p. 236. Vespers of the following.

March 19.

S. JOSEPH, FOSTER-FATHER OF OUR LORD.*

All of the Common of a Confessor not a Bishop, p. 224, except as follows:

Both Vespers.

Ant. to Mag. Take this Child: and nurse It for me.

COLLECT.

O LORD, Who didst appoint blessed Joseph to be the foster-father of Thine only-begotten Son, and the guardian of His Virgin Mother: keep us, we beseech Thee, under Thy perpetual care. Through the same.

Lauds.

Ant. to Ben. And He went down with them, and came to Nazareth : and was subject unto them.

At Second Vespers Memorial of the following.

March 20.

S. Cuthbert, Bishop and Confessor.*

All of the Common of a Bishop and Confessor, p. 222.
Vespers from Chapter of the following.

March 21.

S. Benedict, Abbot.*

All of the Common of an Abbot, p. 224, *except the*

Collect.

ALMIGHTY and Everlasting God, Who on this day didst deliver Thy most blessed Confessor Benedict from the prison-house of the flesh, and didst exalt him to heaven: grant, we beseech Thee, to us Thy servants who keep this festival, forgiveness of all our sins; that we, who with glad hearts rejoice in his glory, may, at his prayer, be partakers of his blessedness. Through.

The Antiphons are said throughout with Alleluia *on all Feasts occurring in Easter-tide.*

March 25.

The Annunciation of the Blessed Virgin Mary.

If this Feast be kept in Easter-tide, the office is said as below, with solemn memorial of the Resurrection at both Vespers and at Lauds, and Alleluia *after every Ant. and* ℟. *Easter Compline does not change, except in the doxology, which is,* All honour, laud, and glory be, &c., *after the verse,* We pray Thee, King with glory decked: *and so end all hymns of the Blessed Virgin in this metre during Easter-tide.*

First Vespers.

Ant. to Psalms. The Saviour of the world shall arise as the sun : and come down into the Virgin's womb as the showers upon the grass. [Alleluia.]

Psalms of the Feria.

Chapter. Isaiah VII.

BEHOLD, a virgin shall conceive, and bear a son, and shall call his name Immanuel. Butter and honey shall he eat, that he may know to refuse the evil, and choose the good.

℟. And Mary said unto the Angel, Behold the handmaid of the Lord : be it unto me according to thy word. [Alleluia.] ℣. The Holy Ghost shall come upon thee, and when the Angel thus made answer, Mary said. ℟. Be it unto me according to thy word. [Alleluia.] ℣. Glory be to the Father, and to the Son: and to the Holy Ghost. ℟. Be it unto me according to thy word. [Alleluia.]

Hymn. *Ave maris Stella,* p. 210.

℣. Drop down, ye heavens, from above, and let the skies pour down righteousness.

℟. Let the earth open, and let them bring forth salvation. [Alleluia.]

Ant. to Mag. The Angel came in unto Mary, and said : Hail, Mary, full of grace, the Lord is with thee. [Alleluia.]

Collect.

WE beseech Thee, O Lord, pour Thy grace into our hearts; that as we have known the Incarnation of Thy Son Jesus Christ by the message of an Angel, so by His Cross and Passion we may be brought unto the glory of His Resurrection; through the same Jesus Christ our Lord. Amen.

[*Or this:*

O GOD, Who didst will that at the word of an Angel Thy Word should take flesh in the womb of Blessed Mary, ever-Virgin: grant to us, Thy suppliants, that we who believe her to be truly the Mother of God, may be aided by her pleading before Thee. Through the same.]

Compline.

As in Lent or Easter, according to the season: no change being made except in the doxology to the hymn.

Lauds.

℣. Send, O Lord, the Lamb, the Ruler of the land.
℞. From the rock of the wilderness unto the mountain of the daughter of Sion. [Alleluia.]

Psalms of Sunday.

Ant. 1. The Angel of the Lord brought tidings unto Mary: and she conceived of the Holy Ghost. [Alleluia.]
Ant. 2. Fear not, Mary, for thou hast found favour with God: behold, thou shalt conceive, and bring forth a Son. [Alleluia.]
Ant. 3. How shall this be, O Angel of God, seeing I know not a man?: Hearken, Mary, Virgin of Christ, the Holy Ghost shall come upon thee, and the power of the Highest shall overshadow thee. [Alleluia.]
Ant. 4. The Holy Ghost shall come upon thee: fear not, Mary, thou that hast in thy womb the Son of God. [Alleluia.]
Ant. 5. Behold the handmaid of the Lord: be it unto me according to thy word. [Alleluia.]

Chapter as at First Vespers.

Hymn. *O gloriosa fæmina,*
℣. *and* ℞., p. 211.

Ant. to Ben. The Angel Gabriel was sent to Mary: a Virgin espoused to Joseph. [Alleluia.]

Prime.

Ant. The Angel of the Lord brought tidings unto Mary: and she conceived of the Holy Ghost. [Alleluia.]

℞.℞. *as on Christmas Day*, p. 90.

Tierce.

Ant. Fear not, Mary, for thou hast found favour with God: behold, thou shalt conceive and bring forth a Son. [Alleluia.]

Chapter as at First Vespers.

℞. Full of grace: are thy lips. ℣. Because God hath blessed thee for ever. ℞. Are thy lips. ℣. Glory be to the Father, and to the Son: and to the Holy Ghost. ℞. Full of grace: are thy lips.
℣. In thy grace, and in thy beauty.
℞. Go forth, ride prosperously, and reign.

Sexts.

Ant. How shall this be, O Angel of God, seeing I know not a man?: Hearken, Mary, Virgin of Christ, the Holy Ghost shall come upon thee, and the power of the Highest shall overshadow thee. [Alleluia.]

Chapter. Isaiah xi.

THERE shall come forth a rod out of the stem of Jesse, and a Branch shall grow out of his roots; and the spirit of the Lord shall rest upon Him.

℞. In thy grace: and in thy beauty. ℣. Go forth, ride prosperously, and reign. ℞. In thy beauty. ℣. Glory be to the Father, and to the Son: and to the Holy Ghost. ℞. In thy grace: and in thy beauty.
℣. God hath given her the help of His countenance.
℞. God shall help her, and that right early.

Nones.

Ant. Behold the handmaid of the Lord: be it unto me according to thy word. [Alleluia.]

Chapter. Is. xxvi.

FOR behold the Lord cometh out of His place.
℞. God hath given her: the help of His countenance. ℣. God shall help her, and that right early. ℞. The help of His countenance. ℣. Glory be to the Father, and to the Son: and to the Holy Ghost. ℞. God hath

given her: the help of His countenance.

℣. God is in the midst of her.
℟. Therefore shall she not be removed.

Second Vespers.

Psalms of Second Vespers of Christmas Day, p. 96, *said under first Ant. of Lauds.*

Chapter as at First Vespers.

℟. Then said Mary, How shall this be, seeing I know not a man? And the Angel said unto her: The Holy Ghost shall come upon thee, and the power of the Highest shall overshadow thee. [Alleluia.] ℣. Therefore also that Holy Thing which shall be born of thee shall be called the Son of God. ℟. The Holy Ghost shall come upon thee, and the power of the Highest shall overshadow thee. [Alleluia.] ℣. Glory be to the Father, and to the Son: and to the Holy Ghost. ℟. The Holy Ghost shall come upon thee, and the power of the Highest shall overshadow thee. [Alleluia.]

HYMN. *Ave maris Stella*, p. 210.

℣. *and* ℟. *as at Lauds.*

Ant. to Mag. O Virgin Mother of God: through thee, Eternal Light hath vouchsafed to dawn on us. [Alleluia.]

FEASTS OF APRIL.

[*On the first day unhindered is said the Office of the Dead.*]

April 1.
S. GILBERT, BISHOP AND CONFESSOR.*

All of the Common of a Bishop and Confessor, p. 222.
Vespers from Chapter of the following.

April 2.
S. FRANCIS DE PAULA, CONFESSOR.*

All of the Common of a Confessor not a Bishop, p. 224.
Vespers from Chapter of the following.

April 3.
S. RICHARD, BISHOP AND CONFESSOR.*

All of the Common of a Bishop and Confessor, p. 222.
Vespers from Chapter of the following.

April 4.
S. AMBROSE, BISHOP AND CONFESSOR.*

All of the Common of a Bishop and Confessor, p. 222, *except the*

COLLECT. *(Hereford.)*

GOD, Who didst bestow on blessed Ambrose, Thy Bishop and Confessor, the clear light of faith, and the power of holiness: grant us at his intercession the same firmness of faith in the truths which he taught, and a fellowship with him in Thine eternal glory. Through.

Vespers from Chapter of the following.

April 5.
S. VINCENT FERRER, PRIEST AND CONFESSOR.*

All of the Common of a Confessor not a Bishop, p. 224.

April 11.
S. LEO, BISHOP AND CONFESSOR.*

All of the Common of a Bishop and Confessor, p. 222, *except the*

COLLECT.

O GOD, Who by the words and acts of Thy holy Bishop Leo didst oppose the enemies of Thy Sacred Humanity and of Thy Church: we beseech Thee to grant that, taught by the light of his writings, we may attain to walk in the path of his virtues. Who livest.

On the same day:

S. GUTHLAC, CONFESSOR.

Memorial of a Monk, p. 224.

April 16.
S. Magnus, King and Martyr.*
All of the Common of a Martyr, p. 217, except the

Collect. *(Aberdeen.)*

O GOD, Who by the operation of Thy majesty hast bestowed on blessed Magnus the rich treasures of Thy grace: grant that we who magnify Thee by proclaiming his merits, may both obtain present help, and be partakers of future glory. Through.

April 19.
S. Alphege, Bishop and Martyr.*
All of the Common of a Martyr Bishop, p. 217.

April 21.
S. Anselm, Bishop and Confessor.*
All of the Common of a Bishop and Confessor, p. 222.

April 23.
S. George, Martyr.*
All of the Common of a Martyr, p. 217.

April 25.
S. Mark, Evangelist and Martyr.
All of the Common of an Apostle in Easter-tide, p. 212, except the Chapters and Collect.

First Vespers.
Chapter. Eph. iv.

UNTO every one of us is given grace, according to the measure of the gift of Christ. Wherefore He saith, When He ascended up on high, He led captivity captive, and gave gifts unto men.

Collect.

O ALMIGHTY God, Who hast instructed Thy holy Church with the heavenly doctrine of Thy Evangelist Saint Mark; give us grace, that, being not like children, carried away with every blast of vain doctrine, we may be established in the truth of Thy holy Gospel. Through.

Lauds, Tierce, and Second Vespers.
Chapter as at First Vespers.

Sexts.
Chapter. Eph. iv.

HE that descended is the same that ascended up far above all heavens, that He might fill all things.

Nones.
Chapter. Eph. iv.

AND He gave some Apostles, and some Prophets, and some Evangelists, and some pastors and teachers; for the perfecting of the saints.

FEASTS OF MAY.
[On the first day unhindered is said the Office of the Dead.]

May 1.
SS. Philip and James, Apostles and Martyrs.

First Vespers.
Ant. I go to prepare a place for you; but I will see you again. Alleluia: and your heart shall rejoice. Alleluia. Alleluia.

Psalms of the Feria.

Chapter. Wisd. v.

THEN shall the righteous man stand in great boldness before the face of such as have afflicted him, and made no account of his labours.

R℟., Hymn, *Tristes erant*, ℣. and R℟., *as in the Common*, p. 212.

Ant. to Mag. Have I been so long time with you, and yet hast thou not known Me, Philip? : He that hath seen Me hath seen the Father. Alleluia.

SS. PHILIP AND JAMES.

Collect.

O ALMIGHTY God, Whom truly to know is everlasting life; grant us perfectly to know Thy Son Jesus Christ to be the Way, the Truth, and the Life; that, following the steps of Thy holy Apostles Saint Philip and Saint James, we may steadfastly walk in the way that leadeth to eternal life; through the same Thy Son Jesus Christ our Lord.

Memorial of the Resurrection, p. 173.

Lauds.

℣. He was known of them.
℞. In breaking of bread. Alleluia.

Psalms of Sunday.

Ant. 1. Lord, shew us the Father: and it sufficeth us. Alleluia.
Ant. 2. Philip, he that hath seen Me: hath seen the Father. Alleluia.
Ant. 3. I am the Way, the Truth, and the Life : no man cometh to the Father, but by Me. Alleluia.
Ant. 4. O ye spirits and souls of the righteous : bless ye the Lord. Alleluia.
Ant. 5. If ye abide in Me, and My words abide in you : ye shall ask what ye will, and it shall be done unto you. Alleluia.

Chapter as at First Vespers.

Hymn. *Claro Paschali gaudio*, ℣. *and* ℞. *as in the Common of Apostles in Eastertide*, p. 213.

Ant. to Ben. Let not your heart be troubled, ye believe in God, believe also in Me : in My Father's house are many mansions. Alleluia. Alleluia.

Memorial of the Resurrection, p. 173.

Prime.

Ant. Lord, shew us the Father : and it sufficeth us. Alleluia.

Tierce.

Ant. Philip, he that hath seen Me : hath seen the Father. Alleluia.

Chapter as at First Vespers.

℞. Then were the disciples glad : Alleluia. Alleluia. ℣. When they saw the Lord. ℞. Alleluia. Alleluia. ℣. Glory be to the Father, and to the Son : and to the Holy Ghost. ℞. Then were the disciples glad : Alleluia. Alleluia.
℣. Lord, shew us the Father.
℞. And it sufficeth us. Alleluia.

Sexts.

Ant. I am the Way, the Truth, and the Life : no man cometh to the Father, but by Me. Alleluia.

Chapter. Acts iv.

AND with great power gave the Apostles witness of the resurrection of the Lord Jesus : and great grace was upon them all.

℞. Lord, shew us the Father : Alleluia. Alleluia. ℣. And it sufficeth us. ℞. Alleluia. Alleluia. ℣. Glory be to the Father, and to the Son : and to the Holy Ghost. ℞. Lord, shew us the Father : Alleluia. Alleluia.
℣. Let not your heart be troubled.
℞. Neither let it be afraid. Alleluia.

Nones.

Ant. If ye abide in Me, and My words abide in you : ye shall ask what ye will, and it shall be done unto you. Alleluia.

Chapter. Acts iv.

AND they departed from the council, rejoicing that they were counted worthy to suffer shame for His Name.

℞. Let not your heart be troubled : Alleluia. Alleluia. ℣. Neither let it be afraid. ℞. Alleluia. Alleluia. ℣. Glory be to the Father, and to the Son : and to the Holy Ghost. ℞. Let not your heart be troubled : Alleluia. Alleluia.
℣. He was known of them.
℞. In breaking of bread. Alleluia.

Second Vespers.

Psalms of the Common of Apostles, p. 216, *said under first Ant. of Lauds.*

Chapter and ℞.℞. *as at First Vespers.*

Hymn. *Claro Paschali gaudio,* ℣. *and* ℞., p. 213.

Ant. to Mag. If ye had known Me, ye should have known My Father also: and from henceforth ye know Him, and have seen Him. Alleluia.

May 2.

S. Athanasius, Bishop and Confessor.*

All of the Common of a Bishop and Confessor, p. 222, except the

Collect. *(Brev. S. Maur.)*

GRANT, we beseech Thee, Almighty God, that we be enabled to believe in our hearts, and to confess with our mouths the truth of Thy Consubstantial Word, which blessed Athanasius maintained with marvellous constancy amidst innumerable labours. Through the same.

On the same day :-

S. Asaph, Bishop and Confessor.

Memorial of a Bishop and Confessor, p. 236.

May 3.

The Invention of the Holy Cross.

First Vespers.

Ant. to Psalms of the Feria.
Sweetest wood and sweetest iron,
Sweetest weight was hung on thee:
Thou alone wast counted worthy
This world's ransom to uphold.
Alleluia.

Chapter. Gal. vi.

BUT God forbid that I should glory, save in the cross of our Lord Jesus Christ, by Whom the world is crucified unto me, and I unto the world.

R̷. O Cross, thou tree of life, wheron hung the Saviour, the King of Israel; how sweet thy wood, how sweet thy nails, how sweet the burden thou bearest; O most precious wood, O most precious nails : honoured by supporting the Body of Christ. Alleluia. V̷. Guard, O Lord, Thy flock which Thou hast redeemed by the wood of the Holy Cross. R̷. Honoured by supporting the Body of Christ. V̷. Glory be to the Father, and to the Son : and to the Holy Ghost. R̷. Alleluia.

Hymn. *Impleta sunt quæ concinit.*

FULFILLED is all that David told
In true prophetic song of old;
Amidst the nations God, saith he,
Hath reigned and triumphed from the Tree.
O Tree of beauty, Tree of light;
O Tree with royal purple bright!
Elect on whose triumphal breast
Those holy Limbs should find their rest:
On whose dear Arms, so widely flung,
The weight of this world's Ransom hung:
The price of human kind to pay,
And spoil the spoiler of his prey.
O Cross, our one reliance, hail!
This holy festal-tide avail
To give fresh merit to the saint,
And pardon to the penitent.
To Thee, eternal Three in One,
Let homage meet by all be done:
Whom by the Cross Thou dost restore,
Preserve and govern evermore! Amen.

V̷. This sign of the Cross shall be in heaven.
R̷. When the Lord shall come to judge.

Ant. to Mag. O blessed Cross: which alone wast counted worthy to bear the King and Lord of the heavens. Alleluia.

Collect.

O GOD, Who in the glorious discovery of the saving Cross didst set forth the marvels of Thy Passion; grant that by the ransom paid on the tree of life, we may attain to the rewards of eternal life. Who livest.

No memorial of the Resurrection is said on this day : but if it occur on Sunday, memorial of the Sunday is made at both Vespers and at Lauds. If on Saturday, memorial of Sunday at Second Vespers. But if it fall between the Ascension and Whitsun-Day, the memorial of the Ascension is said.

Lauds.

V̷. Tell it out among the nations.
R̷. That the Lord reigneth from the tree.

Psalms of Sunday.

THE INVENTION OF THE HOLY CROSS.

Ant. 1. O mighty work of love : death died, when Life died on the wood. Alleluia.

Ant. 2. Behold the Cross of the Lord; flee away, ye adversaries : the Lion of the tribe of Judah, the Root of David, hath conquered. Alleluia.

Ant. 3. O admirable Cross! : healer of wounds, restorer of health! Alleluia.

Ant. 4. Above all cedar trees art thou alone exalted : whereon hung the Life of the world, whereon Christ triumphed, and death for ever vanquished death. Alleluia.

Ant. 5. The blessed Cross shines forth : whereon the Lord hung in our flesh, and with His Blood cleansed our wounds. Alleluia.

Chapter as at First Vespers.

HYMN. *Crux fidelis.*

FAITHFUL Cross! above all other,
  One and only noble Tree;
None in foliage, none in blossom,
  None in fruit thy peers may be;
Sweetest wood and sweetest iron!
  Sweetest weight is hung on thee.

Bend thy boughs, O Tree of glory!
  Thy relaxing sinews bend;
For awhile the ancient rigour,
  That thy birth bestow'd, suspend;
And the King of Heavenly Beauty
  On thy bosom gently tend.

Thou alone wast counted worthy
  This world's ransom to uphold;
For a shipwreck'd race preparing
  Harbour, like the ark of old :
With the sacred Blood anointed
  From the smitten Lamb that roll'd.

To the Trinity be glory
  Everlasting, as is meet;
Equal to the Father, equal
  To the Son and Paraclete;
Trinal Unity, Whose praises
  All created things repeat. Amen.

℣. All the world shall worship Thee, O Christ.

℟. And bless Thy Name.

Ant. to Ben. Blessed art thou, O Cross : for on thee hung the Saviour of the world, and on thee triumphed the King of Angels. Alleluia.

Prime.

Ant. O mighty work of love : death died, when Life died on the wood. Alleluia.

Tierce.

Ant. Behold the Cross of the Lord; flee away, ye adversaries : the Lion of the tribe of Judah, the Root of David, hath conquered. Alleluia.

Chapter as at First Vespers.

℟. This sign of the Cross shall be in heaven. Alleluia. Alleluia. ℣. When the Lord shall come to judge. ℟. Alleluia. Alleluia. ℣. Glory be to the Father, and to the Son : and to the Holy Ghost. ℟. This sign of the Cross shall be in heaven. Alleluia. Alleluia.

℣. Tell it out among the heathen.

℟. That the Lord hath reigned from the tree.

Sexts.

Ant. O admirable Cross! : healer of wounds, restorer of health! Alleluia.

CHAPTER. 1 Cor. i.

THE preaching of the Cross is to them that perish foolishness; but unto us which are saved it is the power of God.

℟. Tell it out among the heathen : Alleluia. Alleluia. ℣. That the Lord hath reigned from the tree. ℟. Alleluia. Alleluia. ℣. Glory be to the Father, and to the Son : and to the Holy Ghost. ℟. Tell it out among the heathen : Alleluia. Alleluia.

℣. We worship Thee, O Christ, and bless Thee.

℟. For by Thy Cross Thou hast redeemed the world. Alleluia. Alleluia.

Nones.

Ant. The blessed Cross shines forth : whereon the Lord hung in our flesh, and with His Blood cleansed our wounds. Alleluia.

CHAPTER. 1 Cor. i.

BUT we preach Christ crucified, unto the Jews a stumbling-block, and unto the Greeks foolishness; but unto them which are called, both Jews and Greeks, Christ the power of God, and the wisdom of God.

℟. We worship Thee, O Christ, and bless Thee : Alleluia. Alleluia. ℣. For by Thy Cross Thou hast redeemed the world. ℟. Alleluia. Alleluia. ℣. Glory be to the Father, and to the Son: and to the Holy Ghost. ℟. We worship Thee, O Christ, and bless Thee. Alleluia. Alleluia.

℣. All the earth shall worship Thee, O Christ.

℟. And praise Thy Name. Alleluia.

Second Vespers.

Psalms of the Feria said under First Ant. of Lauds.

Chapter as at First Vespers.

℟. By Thy Cross, save us, O Christ our Redeemer, Who by dying hast destroyed our death : and by rising again hast restored our life. Alleluia. ℣. Have mercy on us, O gentle Jesu, Who of Thy great goodness hast suffered for us. ℟. And by rising again hast restored our life. Alleluia. ℣. Glory be to the Father, and to the Son: and to the Holy Ghost. ℟. Alleluia.

Hymn. *Crux fidelis*, ℣. *and* ℟. *as at Lauds.*

Ant. to Mag. He endured the Holy Cross Who burst the bars of hell : He is girded with power. He rose on the third day. Alleluia.

May 4.

S. Monica, Matron.*

All of the Common of a Matron, p. 229. except the

Collect. *(Paris.)*

O GOD, Comforter of mourners, and Salvation of them that hope in Thee; Who didst graciously regard the godly tears shed by Saint Monica for the conversion of Augustine her son; grant us, aided by their intercession, truly to lament our sins, and to obtain Thy gracious pardon. Through.

May 6.

S. John before the Latin Gate.

All of the Common of an Apostle in Eastertide, p. 212, except as follows :

First Vespers.

Chapter. Ecclus. xv.

HE that feareth the Lord will do good: and he that hath the knowledge of the law shall obtain wisdom. And as a mother shall she meet him.

Ant. to Mag. Into a vessel of boiling oil the Apostle John was cast : but by the power of protecting grace, he issued forth unhurt. Alleluia.

Collect. *(S. Maur.)*

O GOD, Who with the oil of holy gladness didst anoint blessed John a companion in the tribulation and patience of the Lord Jesus : grant us, according to his pattern, so to rejoice in the fellowship of Christ's Passion, that we may rejoice abundantly in the revelation of His glory. Who liveth.

Lauds.

Chapter as at First Vespers.

Ant. to Ben. Cast into exile for constancy in preaching : divine visions and words brought him exceeding comfort. Alleluia.

Tierce.

Chapter as at First Vespers.

Sexts.

Chapter. Ecclus. xv.

WITH the bread of understanding shall she feed him, and give him the water of wisdom to drink. He shall be stayed upon her, and shall not be moved : and shall rely upon her, and shall not be confounded. She shall exalt him above his neighbours.

Nones.

Chapter. Ecclus. xv.

IN the midst of the congregation shall she open his mouth. He shall find joy and a crown of gladness, and she shall cause him to inherit an everlasting name.

Second Vespers.

Chapter as at First Vespers.

Ant. to Mag. A multitude both of men and women went out to meet blessed John returning from exile : crying out and saying, Blessed is he that cometh in the Name of the Lord. Alleluia.

May 7.

S. JOHN OF BEVERLEY, BISHOP AND CONFESSOR.*

All of the Common of a Bishop and Confessor, p. 222.

May 9.

S. GREGORY NAZIANZEN, BISHOP, CONFESSOR AND DOCTOR.*

All of the Common of a Bishop and Confessor, p. 222.

May 12.

S. COMGALL, ABBOT.*

All of the Common of an Abbot, p. 224.

On the same day :

S. PANCRAS, MARTYR, AND HIS COMPANIONS.

Memorial of many Martyrs, p. 236.

May 14.

S. PACHOMIUS, ABBOT.*

All of the Common of an Abbot, p. 224.

May 19.

S. DUNSTAN, BISHOP AND CONFESSOR.*

All of the Common of a Bishop and Confessor, p. 222.

May 20.

S. BERNARDINE OF SIENNA, CONFESSOR.*

All of the Common of a Confessor not a Bishop, p. 224.

May 25.

S. ALDHELM, BISHOP AND CONFESSOR.*

All of the Common of a Bishop and Confessor, p. 222, *except the*

COLLECT. *(Brev. Hereford.)*

O GOD, Who among the apostolic teachers of Thy Church didst cause blessed Aldhelm Thy Bishop and Confessor to shine with heavenly light : grant that as from him we have learned the form of faith, so we may be enabled to tread in his footsteps. Through.

May 26.

S. AUGUSTINE OF CANTERBURY, BISHOP AND CONFESSOR.*

All of the Common of a Bishop and Confessor, p. 222, *except the*

COLLECT.

GOD, Who didst give blessed Augustine, the Bishop, to be the first teacher of the English people : by his help grant that our sins may be forgiven, and that with him we may come to the fruition of heavenly joys. Through.

On the same day :

S. PHILIP NERI, PRIEST AND CONFESSOR.

Memorial of a Confessor not a Bishop, p. 236.

May 27.

VENERABLE BEDE, PRIEST AND CONFESSOR.*

All of the Common of a Confessor not a Bishop, p. 224, *except the*

COLLECT. *(Roman.)*

O GOD, Who dost glorify Thy Church by the learning of blessed Bede, Thy Confessor and Doctor : mercifully grant to Thy servants that they may be ever enlightened by his wisdom, and assisted by his prayers. Through.

FEASTS OF JUNE.

(On the first day unhindered is said the Office of the Dead.)

June 1.

S. NICOMEDE, PRIEST AND MARTYR.*

All of the Common of a Martyr, p. 217.

June 2.

SS. POTHINUS AND BLANDINA, MARTYRS.*

All of the Common of Many Martyrs, p. 219, except the

COLLECT. *(S. Maur.)*

O GOD, the invincible strength of Thy faithful, Who amidst the adversities of our earthly life dost comfort us with the glory of Thy Saints: mercifully pour into our hearts the fortitude of that love which was mighty in Thy blessed Martyrs Pothinus the Bishop and Blandina the Virgin. Through.

June 5.

S. BONIFACE, BISHOP AND MARTYR, AND HIS COMPANIONS.*

All of the Common of Many Martyrs, p. 219, except the

COLLECT.

ALMIGHTY, everlasting God, who didst bestow on blessed Boniface and his companions the Martyr's palm: grant us mercy, we beseech Thee, with them to whom Thou didst vouchsafe the crown. Through.

June 6.

S. NORBERT, BISHOP AND CONFESSOR.*

All of the Common of a Bishop and Confessor, p. 222, except the

COLLECT. *(Cistercian.)*

O GOD, who madest blessed Norbert, Thy Confessor and Bishop, a chosen preacher of Thy word, and by him didst enrich Thy Church with new offspring: grant to us, we beseech Thee, that what he taught by word and deed, we, by Thy divine assistance, and aided by his prayers, may fulfil in our lives. Through.

June 9.

S. COLUMBA, ABBOT.*

All of the Common of an Abbot, p. 224, except as follows:

Vespers.

℣. *and* ℟. *after Hymn,*

℣. Thy name went far into the islands.
℟. And for thy peace thou wast beloved.

Ant. to Mag. Blessed Columba, God raised thee up to be a most strong tower: for those whom sin had stained, and biting care consumed.

COLLECT.

WE pray Thee, O Lord, inspire our hearts with the desire of heavenly glory; and grant that we, bringing our sheaves with us, may enter that place where Thy holy Abbot Columba shineth like a star before Thee. Through.

Lauds.

℣. *and* ℟. *after Hymn,*

℣. The righteous shall blossom as a lily.
℟. He shall flourish for ever before the Lord.

Ant. to Ben. Hail, loving Columba, ruler in thine island home: hail, faithful servant of thy Lord: may He incline our ears to His praise, and draw us from our sins to the joys of life eternal.

Collect as above.

June 11.

S. BARNABAS, APOSTLE AND MARTYR.

All of the Common of an Apostle in or out of Eastertide, as the case may be, except the

THE NATIVITY OF S. JOHN BAPTIST. 263

Collect.

O LORD GOD Almighty, Who didst endue Thy holy Apostle Barnabas with singular gifts of the Holy Ghost; leave us not, we beseech Thee, destitute of Thy manifold gifts, nor yet of grace to use them alway to Thy honour and glory. Through.

June 12.

S. Ternan, Bishop and Confessor.*

All of the Common of a Bishop and Confessor, p. 222.

June 14.

S. Basil the Great, Bishop, Confessor, and Doctor.*

All of the Common of a Bishop and Confessor, p. 222, except the

Collect. *(S. Maur.)*

STIR up, we beseech Thee, O Lord, in Thy Church, that spirit wherewith the blessed Bishop and Doctor Basil served Thee: that we, being filled with the same, may endeavour to love what he loved, and to fulfil in our lives what he taught. Through.

June 17.

S. Alban, Protomartyr of England.*

All of the Common of a Martyr, p. 217, except the -

Collect.

O GOD, Who hast hallowed this day by the martyrdom of blessed Alban: grant, we beseech Thee, that he in whose yearly festival we rejoice, may ever guard us by his assistance. Through.

On the same day:

S. Botolph, Abbot.

Memorial of an Abbot, p. 236.

June 19.

Translation of S. Margaret, Queen of Scotland.*

All of the Common of a Matron, p. 229, except the

Collect. *(Aberdeen.)*

GRANT to us, Lord, we beseech Thee, that as we celebrate with loving remembrance the translation of Margaret our Queen, and the many gifts of grace wherewith Thou didst adorn her, we too, assisted by her prayers, may pass from labour to rest, and from the land of exile to our heavenly country. Through.

June 20.

S. Edward, King and Martyr.*

All of the Common of a Martyr, p. 217, except the

Collect.

O GOD, Ruler of an eternal kingdom, mercifully look upon Thy family who celebrate the translation of King Edward; and grant that, as Thou didst vouchsafe to glorify him with celestial gifts, so his intercession may assist us to obtain eternal happiness. Through.

June 24.

Nativity of S. John Baptist.

First Vespers.

Ant. The Angel of the Lord came down to Zacharias, saying: Receive a son in thine old age; and thou shalt call his name John Baptist.

Psalms of the Feria.

Chapter. Jer. i.

BEFORE I formed thee in the belly I knew thee: and before thou camest forth out of the womb I sanctified thee, and ordained thee a prophet unto the nations.

℟. Among them that are born of women there hath not risen a greater prophet than John the Baptist. Who prepared the way of the Lord in the wilderness. ℣. There was a man sent from God whose name was John. ℟. Who prepared the way of the Lord in the wilderness. ℣. Glory be to the Father, and to the Son : and to the Holy Ghost. ℟. Who prepared the way of the Lord in the wilderness.

HYMN. *Ut queant laxis.*

OH that once more, to sinful men descending,
    Thou from polluted lips their chains wert rending,
So, holy John, might worthy hymns ascending,
    Tell of thy wonders.

Lo! from the hill of heaven's eternal glory,
Comes a bright herald to thy father hoary,
Gives thee thy name, thy birth and wondrous story,
    Truly foretelling.

But, while the heav'nly word he disbelieveth,
Lo! all his power of ready utt'rance leaveth,
Till by thy birth his tongue again receiveth
    Power of speaking.

Thou, while thy mother's womb was thee containing,
Knewest thy King, in secret still remaining,
Thus was each parent through her child obtaining
    Knowledge of mysteries.

Father and Son, to Thee be adoration,
Spirit of Both, to Thee like veneration,
Praise to the One true God of our salvation,
    Ever and ever. Amen.

℣. There was a man sent from God.
℟. Whose name was John.

Ant. to Mag. When Zacharias went into the temple of the Lord : there appeared unto him an angel standing on the right side of the altar of incense.

COLLECT.

GRANT, we beseech Thee, Almighty God, that Thy family may walk in the way of salvation, and, following the counsels of blessed John the Forerunner, may safely come to Him Whom he foretold, Thy Son Jesus Christ our Lord. Amen.

Lauds.

℣. There was a man sent from God.
℟. Whose name was John.

Psalms of Sunday.

Ant. 1. Elizabeth brought forth a son : John Baptist, the forerunner of the Lord.

Ant. 2. They made signs to his father, how he would have him called : and he wrote, saying, His name is John.

Ant. 3. Thou shalt call his name John : and many shall rejoice at his birth.

Ant. 4. His name is John; he shall drink neither wine nor strong drink : and many shall rejoice at his birth.

Ant. 5. This child shall be great in the sight of the Lord : for His hand is with him.

CHAPTER. Is. XLIX.

LISTEN, O isles, unto me ; and hearken, ye people from far : the Lord hath called me from the womb; from the bowels of my mother hath He made mention of my name.

℟. Thanks be to God.

HYMN. *O nimis felix.*

O SAINT thrice happy, merit high attaining,
    Whose snowy pureness no foul spot is staining,
Mightiest Martyr, home in deserts gaining,
    Greatest of Prophets.

He who bare thirty-fold bright garlands weareth,
He who bare sixty double glory shareth,
His triple chaplet who an hundred beareth,
    Holy one, decks thee.

Come then, thou mighty Saint, of worth past telling,
All stony hardness from each breast expelling,
And in each rugged, crooked pathway quelling,
    Roughness and windings.

So this world's gracious Author and Salvation,
In each pure spirit, free from degradation,
Shall, when He cometh, find a fitting station,
    For His dear footsteps.

Now let celestial choirs, glad anthems pouring,
God, One and Trinal, praise Thee, while adoring,
We too, all prostrate, pardon are imploring :
    Spare Thy redeemed ones. Amen.

℣. The righteous shall blossom as a lily.
℟. They shall flourish for ever before the Lord.

Ant. to Ben. And the mouth of Zacharias was opened, and he prophesied, saying : Blessed be the Lord God of Israel.

The first words of the Canticle are not repeated, but it begins, For He hath visited.

THE NATIVITY OF S. JOHN BAPTIST.

Collect.

ALMIGHTY God, by Whose providence Thy servant John Baptist was wonderfully born, and sent to prepare the way of Thy Son our Saviour, by preaching of repentance; make us so to follow his doctrine and holy life, that we may truly repent according to his preaching: and after his example constantly speak the truth, boldly rebuke vice, and patiently suffer for the truth's sake. Through.

[*Or this:*

GOD, Who hast made this day honourable to us by the birth of blessed John: grant to Thy people the grace of spiritual joys: and vouchsafe to guide the hearts of all Thy faithful in the way that leadeth to everlasting salvation. Through.]

Prime.

Ant. Elizabeth brought forth a son: John Baptist, the forerunner of the Lord.

Tierce.

Ant. They made signs to his father, how he would have him called: and he wrote, saying, His name is John.

Chapter as at Lauds, ℟℣. at Tierce, Sexts, and Nones of the Common of a Martyr, p. 218.

Sexts.

Ant. Thou shalt call his name John: and many shall rejoice at his birth.

Chapter. Is. xlix.

AND now, saith the Lord that formed me from the womb to be His servant, I will also give thee for a light to the Gentiles, that thou mayest be My salvation unto the end of the earth.

Nones.

Ant. This child shall be great in the sight of the Lord: for His hand is with him.

Chapter. Is. xlix.

KINGS shall see and arise, princes also shall worship, because of the Lord that is faithful, and the Holy One of Israel, and He shall choose thee.

Second Vespers.

Psalms of the Feria said under First Ant. of Lauds.

Chapter, ℟℣., Hymn, Ut queant laxis, ℣. and ℟., as at First Vespers.

Ant. to Mag. And it came to pass, that on the eighth day they came to circumcise the child: and they called him Zacharias, after the name of his father. And his mother answered and said, Not so; but he shall be called John.

Collect as at Lauds.

The Feast of S. John Baptist is kept through the Octave; except as hereafter noted, and on Sunday, when the Office is of the Sunday, with Memorial of the Octave.

Vespers are said on each day with Psalms of the occurrent Feria.

The following Ants. are said to Mag. and Ben. throughout the Octave, when the Office is of S. John Baptist, and for the Memorial, when the Office is not of this Saint, with

℣. There was a man sent from God.
℟. Whose name was John.

Collect as at Lauds on the Feast.

1. Among them that are born of women: there hath not risen a greater prophet than John the Baptist.
2. Thou, child, shalt be called the prophet of the Highest: for thou shalt go before the face of the Lord to prepare His ways.
3. Because thou hast not believed, thou shalt be dumb and not able to speak: till the day of his birth.

On the Days of this Octave are said Memorials of the Holy Cross, S. Mary, and All Saints.

June 28.

S. Irenæus, Bishop and Martyr.

Memorial of a Martyr Bishop, p. 235.

June 29.
SS. Peter and Paul, Apostles and Martyrs.

First Vespers.

Ant. Whom say men that I the Son of man am? said Jesus to His disciples; and Peter answered and said, Thou art the Christ, the Son of the living God: And I say also unto thee, that thou art Peter; and upon this rock I will build My Church.

Psalms of the Feria.

Chapter. Acts XII.

PETER therefore was kept in prison; but prayer was made without ceasing of the church to God for him.
℟. Cornelius the centurion, a devout man, and one that feared God, saw evidently an Angel of God, saying to him: Cornelius, send and call for Simon, whose surname is Peter: he shall tell thee what thou oughtest to do. ℣. While Cornelius was praying, as yet unregenerate in Christ, an Angel appeared unto him, saying. ℟. Cornelius, send and call for Simon, whose surname is Peter: he shall tell thee what thou oughtest to do. ℣. Glory be to the Father, and to the Son: and to the Holy Ghost. ℟. He shall tell thee what thou oughtest to do.

Hymn. *Aureâ luce et decore roseô.*

WITH golden light of morn,
With rosy hues of day,
O Light of Light thou shed'st
Thine all-pervading ray:
Thou deck'st the sky with joy,
For now the day is come—
The day of glorious strife,
Of holy martyrdom.

Two saints have shed their blood;
To one Thou gav'st command,
"Behold! of heav'n the keys,—
I give them to thine hand:"
In faith the other came,
The Gentile world to win;
By cross, by sword, they both
To their reward went in.

Thy Lord hath marked thy love,
Good shepherd of the sheep;
Well, Peter, hast thou kept
The charge His flock to keep:
Complete is now thy work,
The wage is thine for aye,
The crown of endless life
That fadeth not away.

Thy sound, O Paul, hath gone
From land to land abroad;
From thee the world hath known
The tidings of the Lord:
May we with thee behold
With full and grateful heart,
What now we darkly see
What now we know in part.

Twin olive-boughs of peace,
Strong hope and earnest faith
Your hearts in life impelled,
Sustained your souls in death:
In life, in death, we know
Whate'er our lot befall
The strength which aided you
Is still the strength for all.

To God the Three in One
Eternal glory be;
All honour, praise, and might,
Blest Trinity to Thee:
To Father, and to Son,
And Holy Ghost on high,
While endless ages run,
To all eternity.

℣. Thou art Peter.
℟. And upon this rock I will build My Church.

Ant. to Mag. Blessed Peter the Apostle saw Christ coming to meet him: he worshipped Him, and said, Lord, whither goest Thou? I come to Rome, to be crucified afresh.

Collect.

O ALMIGHTY God, Who by Thy Son Jesus Christ didst give to Thy Apostle Saint Peter many excellent gifts, and commandedst him earnestly to feed Thy flock; make, we beseech Thee, all bishops and pastors diligently to preach Thy holy word, and the people obediently to follow the same, that they may receive the crown of everlasting glory. Through.

No Memorial of S. John Baptist at any Office of this day.

Lauds.

℣. Thou art Peter.
℟. And upon this rock I will build My Church.

Psalms of Sunday.

Ant. 1. Now Peter and John went up together into the temple at the hour of prayer : being the ninth hour.

Ant. 2. Silver and gold have I none : but such as I have give I thee.

Ant. 3. The angel said unto Peter : cast thy garment about thee, and follow me.

Ant. 4. Peter, lovest thou Me? Feed My sheep : Lord, Thou knowest that I love Thee.

Ant. 5. Thou art Peter : and upon this rock I will build My Church.

Chapter as at First Vespers.

HYMN. *Exultet cœlum laudibus,*
V̄. *and* R̄., p. 215.

Ant. to Ben. Whatsoever thou shalt bind on earth, shall be bound in heaven : and whatsoever thou shalt loose on earth, shall be loosed in heaven, said the Lord to Simon Peter.

COLLECT.

O GOD, Who hast consecrated this day by the Martyrdom of Thine Apostles Peter and Paul; grant that Thy Church may in all things follow their precepts, from whom it received the first principles of the faith. Through.

Prime.

Ant. Now Peter and John went up together into the temple at the hour of prayer : being the ninth hour.

Tierce.

Ant. Silver and gold have I none : but such as I have give I thee.

Chapter as at First Vespers.

R̄R̄. *of the Common,* p. 216, *at Tierce, Sexts, and Nones.*

Sexts.

Ant. The angel said unto Peter : cast thy garment about thee, and follow me.

CHAPTER. Acts XII.

AND behold, the angel of the Lord came upon him, and a light shined in the prison; and he smote Peter on the side, and raised him up, saying, Arise up quickly. And his chains fell off from his hands.

Nones.

Ant. Thou art Peter : and upon this rock I will build My Church.

CHAPTER. Acts XII.

AND he went out and followed him; and wist not that it was true which was done by the Angel; but thought he saw a vision.

Second Vespers.

All as in the Common, p. 216, *except the* R̄R̄., *Who are these, &c.,* p. 215.

HYMN. *Aurea luce, as at First Vespers.*

V̄. Their sound is gone out into all lands.

R̄. And their words into the ends of the world.

Ant. to Mag. These glorious princes of the earth, as in life they loved each other : so in death they were not divided.

Collect as at Lauds.

June 30.

COMMEMORATION OF S. PAUL, APOSTLE AND MARTYR.

(*If the Church be dedicated to S. Paul, this festival is kept as follows : at First Vespers, instead of the Office of S. Peter, as above, Psalms of Sunday, Ants, and Chapter as set down below at Lauds, Hymn, V̄. and R̄., and Ant. to Magnificat, of the Common of Apostles,* p. 215; *Collect as at Lauds; Memorial of S. Peter, as follows :*

Ant. Blessed Peter the Apostle saw Christ coming to meet him : he worshipped Him, and said, Lord, whither goest Thou? I come to Rome, to be crucified afresh.

V̄. Thou art Peter.

R̄. And upon this rock I will build My Church.

Collect as in Memorial of S. Peter at Lauds.

No Memorial of S. John Baptist at these Vespers, nor at Lauds. Lauds and the other Hours till Second Vespers, as below. At Second Vespers, Ants. and Chapter as at Lauds; Hymn, ℣. and ℟. and Ant. to Mag. as at Second Vespers of the Common of Apostles, p. 217, *with these two Memorials :*

MEMORIAL OF S. PETER

As at First Vespers, p. 266.

MEMORIAL OF S. JOHN BAPTIST

As at Second Vespers, p. 265.)

Lauds.

℣. Thou hast given an heritage.
℟. Unto those that fear Thy Name, O Lord.
℣℣. *to be said according to direction,* p. 246.

Psalms of Sunday.

Ant. 1. I planted, Apollos watered: but God gave the increase. Alleluia.
℣. Every man shall receive his own reward : according to his labour.
Ant. 2. Most gladly therefore will I rather glory in my infirmities : that the power of Christ may rest upon me.
℣. When I am weak : then am I strong.
Ant. 3. His grace which was bestowed upon me was not in vain : but His grace is with me alway.
℣. By the grace of God I am what I am.
Ant. 4. At Damascus the governor under Aretas the king was desirous to apprehend me : and through a window in a basket was I let down by the wall, and escaped his hands in the name of the Lord.
℣. The God and Father of our Lord Jesus Christ knoweth that I lie not.
Ant. 5. Holy Paul the Apostle, preacher of the truth and teacher of the Gentiles : thou pleadest for us to God Who chose thee.
℣. That we may be found worthy of the grace of God.

CHAPTER. Gal. I.

I CERTIFY you, brethren, that the gospel which was preached of me is not after man, neither received I it of man, neither was I taught it, but by the revelation of Jesus Christ.
℟. Thanks be to God.

HYMN. *Exultet cœlum laudibus,* ℣. *and* ℟., p. 216.

Ant. to Ben. I am now ready to be offered, and the time of my departure is at hand. I have fought a good fight, I have finished my course, I have kept the faith : henceforth there is laid up for me a crown of righteousness, which the Lord, the righteous Judge, shall give me at that day.

COLLECT.

O GOD, Who didst teach the multitude of the Gentiles by the preaching of blessed Paul Thine Apostle; grant that we, who celebrate his nativity, may profit by his prayers. Through.

MEMORIAL OF S. PETER.

Ant. Peter, lovest thou Me? Feed My sheep : Lord, Thou knowest that I love Thee.
℣. Thou art Peter.
℟. And upon this rock I will build My Church.

COLLECT.

O GOD, Who didst give to blessed Peter Thine Apostle the office of binding and loosing souls, conferring on him the keys of the heavenly kingdom; grant, we pray Thee, that his intercession may assist to deliver us from the chains of our sins. Who livest.

MEMORIAL OF S. JOHN BAPTIST.

Ant. Among them that are born of women : there hath not risen a greater prophet than John the Baptist.
℣. There was a man sent from God.
℟. Whose name was John.

COLLECT.

O GOD, Who hast made this day honourable to us by the nativity of blessed John; grant to Thy people the gift of spiritual joys, and direct the minds of all the faithful in the way of everlasting salvation. Through.

Prime.

Ant. I planted, Apollos watered : but God gave the increase. Alleluia.

Tierce.

Ant. Most gladly therefore will I rather glory in my infirmities : that the power of Christ may rest upon me.

Chapter as at Lauds.

R̸/R̸. of the Common, p. 216, at Tierce, Sexts and Nones.

Sexts.

Ant. His grace which was bestowed upon me was not in vain : but His grace is with me alway.

CHAPTER. Phil. I. and Gal. VI.

TO me to live is Christ, and to die is gain. But God forbid that I should glory, save in the cross of our Lord Jesus Christ, by whom the world is crucified unto me, and I unto the world.

Nones.

Ant. Holy Paul the Apostle, preacher of the truth and teacher of the Gentiles : thou pleadest for us to God who chose thee.

CHAPTER. 2 Tim. IV.

I HAVE fought a good fight, I have finished my course, I have kept the faith. Henceforth there is laid up for me a crown of righteousness, which the Lord, the righteous Judge, shall give me at that day.

Vespers.

All as in the Common, p. 216, except the HYMN, *Aurea luce,* p. 266.
V̸. *and* R̸., p. 215.

COLLECT.

O GOD, Who hast consecrated this day by the Martyrdom of Thine Apostles Peter and Paul : grant that Thy Church may in all things follow their precepts, from whom it received the first principles of the faith. Through.

And thus Vespers are said of both Apostles together.

MEMORIAL OF S. JOHN BAPTIST.

Ant. When Zacharias went into the temple of the Lord : there appeared unto him an angel of the Lord, standing on the right side of the altar of incense.
V̸. There was a man sent from God.
R̸. Whose name was John.

Collect for S. John Baptist.

If the Commemoration of S. Paul fall on Saturday, the Second Vespers are of the ensuing Sunday, with Memorial of the Apostles, of S. John Baptist, and of S. Servan, Abbot, p. 236 : and then of the Trinity and the Holy Cross as usual.

FEASTS OF JULY.
(*On the first day unhindered is said the Office of the Dead.*)

July 1.

OCTAVE OF S. JOHN BAPTIST.

Lauds and all the Offices till Vespers are said as on the Feast of S. John Baptist, p. 264, except that the Psalms at Lauds are all said under the First Ant. and the Ant. to Ben. is as at Second Vespers on the Festival. At Lauds is said this

MEMORIAL OF SS. PETER AND PAUL.

Ant. Peter the Apostle and Paul, teacher of the Gentiles : these have taught us Thy law, O Lord.
V̸. And all men that see it shall say, this hath God done.
R̸. For they shall perceive that it is His work.

Collect as on Feast of SS. Peter and Paul.

If the Octave of S. John Baptist fall on Sunday, the Office is wholly of Sunday, with Memorials of the Octave of S. John Baptist, of the Apostles, and of S. Servan.

On the same day :

S. SERVAN, ABBOT.

Memorial of an Abbot, p. 236.

July 2.

THE VISITATION OF THE BLESSED VIRGIN MARY.

First Vespers.

Ant. 1. The Son of the Eternal Father delighted in Mary : from the splendour of the Saints He entered into His Mother.
Dixit Dominus. Ps. cx. p. 47.

Ant. 2. The Lily of the valleys shedding forth fragrance and bearing the Heavenly Flower : adorns the pathway of the mountains.
Laudate pueri. Ps. cxiii. p. 48.

Ant. 3. When the Heavenly Fruit of Paradise was brought nigh : the unborn babe was filled with joy.
Lætatus sum. Ps. cxxii. p. 54.

Ant. 4. The Lord kindled the lamp of the True Light : whereby He found and delivered our lost piece of silver.
Nisi Dominus. Ps. cxxvii. p. 56.

Ant. 5. Comfort thy sons, O Mother : making true peace in the borders of Jerusalem.
Lauda Hierusalem. Ps. cxlvii. 12. p. 65.

CHAPTER. Ecclus. xxiv.

I AM the Mother of fair love, and fear, and knowledge, and holy hope.

℞. In the spirit of Elias the babe leaped for joy : his mother partaking in a wonderful prophecy. At the visitation of Mary the heavens flow down with delight. ℣. The Lord blessed the house of Zacharias because of the Ark of God. ℞. At the visitation of Mary the heavens flow down with delight. ℣. Glory be to the Father, and to the Son : and to the Holy Ghost. ℞. At the visitation of Mary the heavens flow down with delight.

HYMN. *Festum matris gloriosæ.*

OF the glorious Virgin Mother, now the festal day is come ;
Grace we seek by her who won it through the travail of the womb,
Grace and honour, which the Matron bade her on this day assume.

To the wife of Zacharias came the Mother of fair love,
To the aged came the maiden with her burden from above,
Hears the salutation telling what for either shall behove.

In the silence of the morning was the Word Eternal known ;
Fell a veil of awful reverence on the Truth divinely shewn ;
To the Virgin bowed the Matron, Mother of her God to own.

"Whence is this to me," she murmurs, "comes the mother of my Lord ?
Doth the Queen of all creation deign to greet me with a word ?
Doth my bosom's fruit salute Him, ere mine eyes His Form record ?"

From the lips of Virgin sweetness then the tones eternal fell,
Fell and rose and filled the portals of the heavenly citadel,
God's great love and man's obeisance in one hymn of joy to tell.

Sang she of her Lord Almighty, of His love to men below,
How the lowly and meek-hearted may alone that presence know,
How on her all generations should the Blessed name bestow.

Triune God, Who reign'st for ever, look upon Thy children here,
At the prayer of our sweet Mother drive away all forms of fear,
Till in light of day supernal from all eyes Thou wipe the tear.

℣. Full of grace are thy lips.
℞. Because God hath blessed thee for ever.

Ant. to Mag. Upon a ten-stringed psaltery the royal Virgin sings praise to the Lord : magnifying the Lord Who hath done great things ; in divine justice putting down the mighty from their seat; in mercy exalting the humble.

COLLECT.

O GOD, Who didst cause the most holy Virgin Mary, Mother of Thy Only-begotten Son, to visit blessed Elizabeth for the grace of mutual encouragement ; mercifully grant to us, Thy servants, that we may be strengthened continually by His visitations, and protected by Thy power against all adversities ; through the same Jesus Christ our Lord. Who.

Memorial of the Apostles to be made at

both Vespers and at Lauds : and so till the day of their Octave.

At Vespers.

Ant. These glorious princes of the earth, as in life they loved each other: so in death they were not divided.

℣. Their sound is gone out into all lands.

℟. And their words unto the ends of the world.

Collect.

O GOD, Who hast consecrated this day by the martyrdom of Thine Apostles Peter and Paul : grant that Thy Church may in all things follow their precepts, from whom it received the first principles of the faith; through Jesus Christ our Lord. Who.

At Lauds.

Ant. Peter the Apostle, and Paul, Teacher of the Gentiles : these have taught us Thy law, O Lord.

℣. And all they that see it shall say, This hath God done.

℟. For they shall perceive that it is His work.

Collect as at Vespers.

Lauds.

℣. Thou art the holy Mother of God.
℟. O Mary, ever Virgin.

Psalms of Sunday.

Ant. 1. The Daybreak of grace climbs the mountains, shining with the light of heavenly glory : bringing to the just, the Sun of Justice, and a new day of gladness.

Ant. 2. At the joyful meeting of the mothers, the unborn babe, rejoicing as infant with Infant : silently heralds his unborn King.

Ant. 3. Elizabeth, filled with heavenly gifts, seeing the Dew poured upon the fleece, and that the Bush burning with fire is not consumed : cries aloud, that the Rod of Jesse flowers.

Ant. 4. The conception of the Saviour is made manifest, a pure Virgin becomes a mother : most worthily is she called Blessed, from whom the Fruit of Life springs forth.

Ant. 5. The holy Mother full of grace praises God with joyful voice : because He hath regarded His handmaiden.

Chapter as at First Vespers.

Hymn. *O Salutaris fulgens stella maris.*

STAR with thy bright beams shining o'er
   the ocean,
Kindling with light the sun of truth and glory,
Thee do we hail the Queen of all creation,
   Virgin and Mother.

Thee would we praise with hymn of gratulation,
Thee whose pure soul with God in joy consenteth,
Theme which no tongue of mortal man may venture,
   None may attain it.

Rose of the morning, filling with thy fragrance
Tracts of the mountain desert, sweetest Mother,
Flow'rets shall deck thy feet : of all the flow'rets
   Thou art the fairest.

Voices of Rachel weeping for her children,
Plead through the ages, how she prays with anguish ;
Thou through whose soul the sword of grief hath stricken,
   Travailest with her.

Hope of the lost world, praise of all the angels,
Stay of the fainting soul in tribulation,
Lily that bloomest in the vale of shadow,
   Mother of mercy.

Praise to the Father, Son, and Holy Spirit,
Through Whom alone she found the Crown of blessing—
Crown which shall ring her Virgin brow with glory
   Now and for ever.

℣. God hath chosen her.
℟. And made her to dwell in His tabernacle.

Ant. to Ben. The Redeemer, the king of Israel cometh in a virgin shrine ; Elizabeth is filled with the Holy Ghost: the child prophesies, a new and marvellous thing is wrought; praise be to Thee, O Lord.

Prime.

Ant. The Daybreak of grace climbs the mountains, shining with the light of heavenly glory : bringing to the just, the Sun of Justice, and a new day of gladness.

℟. *as at Christmas,* p. 94.

Tierce.

Ant. At the joyful meeting of the mothers, the unborn babe, rejoicing as infant with Infant : silently heralds his unborn King.

Chapter as at Lauds.

R̲/R̲. *at Tierce, Sexts, and Nones, as on the Annunciation,* p. 254.

Sexts.

Ant. Elizabeth, filled with heavenly gifts, seeing the Dew poured upon the fleece, and that the Bush burning with fire is not consumed : cries aloud, that the Rod of Jesse flowers.

CHAPTER. Cant. II.

RISE up, my love, my fair one, and come away, for lo, the winter is past, the rain is over and gone, the flowers appear on the earth ; the time of the singing of birds is come.

Nones.

Ant. The holy Mother full of grace praises God with joyful voice : because He hath regarded His handmaiden.

CHAPTER. Cant. II.

O MY dove, that art in the clefts of the rock, in the secret places of the stairs, let me see thy countenance, let me hear thy voice; for sweet is thy voice, and thy countenance is comely.

Second Vespers.

Psalms of Second Vespers of Christmas Day, p. 96, *said under First Ant. of Lauds.*

Chapter as at First Vespers.

R̲. Happy mother, and birth at which is present the Queen of Virgins : there can be no danger where is the Saviour of the world. V̄. According to the prophecy of Gabriel, many shall rejoice at his birth. R̲. There can be no danger where is the Saviour of the world. V̄. Glory be to the Father, and to the Son : and to the Holy Ghost. R̲. There can be no danger where is the Saviour of the world.

Hymn as at First Vespers.

V̄. *and* R̲. *as at Lauds.*

Ant. to Mag. The Virgin of virgins rejoices in God her Saviour : Who hath holpen His servant Israel, as He promised Abraham and his seed, and hath sent the Word of God from heaven.

Throughout the Octave of the Visitation, the Office, when of the Festival, is as on the first day, except that at Lauds the Psalms are said under the first Antiphon, and, except on the Octave day, the Ants. to Ben. and Mag. are taken from the Ants. to Psalms at First Vespers of the feast. Memorials of SS. Peter and Paul are said at Lauds and Vespers, p. 271. *On Sunday the Office is of the Festival, with memorial of the Sunday, and at First Vespers, of the Holy Trinity and the Cross.*

But if precedence be given to the Octave of SS. Peter and Paul, the Office is of the Apostles, with memorials of the Visitation at Vespers and Lauds ; and so till the day of their Octave.

If the Feast of the Visitation fall on Saturday, memorial is made of Sunday and of the Holy Trinity.

July 4.

TRANSLATION OF S. MARTIN, BISHOP AND CONFESSOR.

Memorial of a Confessor, p. 236, *except* COLLECT.

O GOD, Who didst make blessed Martin to be a minister of eternal salvation on earth ; grant, we beseech Thee, that as he fulfilled Thy commandments upon earth, so he may alway intercede for us in heaven. Through.

OCTAVE OF SS. PETER AND PAUL.

All as in the Common of Apostles, p. 215, *except that which follows :*

First Vespers.

CHAPTER. Ecclus. XLIV.

THESE were merciful men, whose righteousness hath not been forgotten. With their seed shall continually remain a good inheritance, and their children are within the covenant.

HYMN. *Aurea luce*, p. 266.

Ant. to Mag. Glorious Apostles, pillars of the Church, declarers of the truth, lamps burning with the fire of the Holy Ghost : ye have lightened the world, put to flight the darkness of error, and now ye plead for us to God Who chose you.

COLLECT.

O GOD, Whose right hand upheld blessed Peter, walking upon the waves, that he might not sink, and delivered his fellow-Apostle Paul, thrice shipwrecked, from the depths of the sea; mercifully hear us, and grant that their help may avail to bring us to eternal glory. Who livest.

This Collect is said throughout the day.

Memorial of the Visitation.

Lauds.

All of the Common, except Chapter as at First Vespers, and

Ant. to Ben. These are the two olive trees, and the two candlesticks standing before the Lord of the whole earth : these have power to shut the clouds of heaven, and to open the gates thereof, for their tongues are made to be the keys of heaven. Alleluia.

Memorial of the Visitation.

Tierce.

Chapter as at First Vespers.

Sexts.

CHAPTER. Ecclus. xliv.

THEIR bodies are buried in peace; but their name liveth for evermore.

Nones.

CHAPTER. Ecclus. XLIV.

THE people tell of their wisdom, and the congregation will shew forth their praise.

Second Vespers.

All of the Common of Apostles, except Chapter, Hymn and Collect as at First Vespers of this day.

On the same day:

S. PALLADIUS, BISHOP AND CONFESSOR.

Memorial of a Bishop and Confessor, p. 236.

July 7.

TRANSLATION OF S. THOMAS OF CANTERBURY.

Memorial of a Bishop and Confessor, p. 236, *except the*

COLLECT.

O GOD, Who grantest us to celebrate the translation of blessed Thomas, Thy Martyr and Bishop; we humbly beseech Thee to hear the prayers of Thy Church, and bring us from vice to virtue, and from prison to the kingdom. Through.

July 9.

OCTAVE OF THE VISITATION.

First Vespers.

All as at First Vespers of the Feast, except that the Psalms are all said under the First Ant. The R/. R/. are said. All the other hours as on the Feast-day, except that at Second Vespers the R/. R/. are omitted.

July 12.

JOHN GUAIBERT, ABBOT.*

All of the Common of an Abbot, p. 224.

July 14.

S. BONAVENTURA, BISHOP AND CONFESSOR.*

All of the Common of a Bishop and Confessor, p. 222.

July 15.

Translation of S. Swithun, Bishop and Confessor.*

All of the Common of a Bishop and Confessor, p. 222.

July 16.

Translation of S. Osmund, Bishop and Confessor.*

All of the Common of a Bishop and Confessor, p. 222, except the

Collect.

O GOD, Who didst call blessed Osmund Thy Bishop from earthly to heavenly warfare: grant to us, that having cast away earthly desires, we may attain to the good things of heaven. Through.

July 19.

S. Vincent de Paul, Priest and Confessor.*

All of the Common of a Confessor, p. 224, except the

Collect. *(Roman.)*

GOD, Who didst strengthen Blessed Vincent with Apostolic virtue, for preaching the Gospel to the poor, and promoting the honour of ecclesiastical order; grant, we beseech Thee, that we, venerating his holy merits, may also be instructed by the example of his virtues. Through.

July 20.

S. Margaret, Virgin and Martyr.

All of the Common of a Virgin Martyr, p. 226, except the

Collect.

O GOD, Who on this day didst cause the blessed Virgin Margaret to enter heaven by the palm of martyrdom; grant us, we beseech Thee, that following her example, we may attain unto Thee. Through.

July 22.

S. Mary Magdalene.

First Vespers.

Ant. to Psalms. When Jesus sat at meat in the house of Simon the Pharisee: Mary Magdalene came unto Him, bringing a box of precious ointment.

Psalms of the Feria.

Chapter. Prov. xxxi.

WHO can find a virtuous woman? for her price is far above rubies. The heart of her husband doth safely trust in her, so that he shall have no need of spoil.

R̷. O surely, great was the love of Mary Magdalene: she outstayed the disciples at the tomb of the Lord. V̷. Glowing with the fervour of love, and believing Him to be taken away, whom she had seen laid in the sepulchre. R̷. She outstayed the disciples at the tomb of the Lord. V̷. Glory be to the Father, and to the Son: and to the Holy Ghost. R̷. She outstayed the disciples at the tomb of the Lord.

Hymn. *Collaudemus Magdalene.*

SING we now of Mary's trial;
  Joy and sorrow let us tell,
Both uniting in one rapture,
  Heavenward in one note to swell,
When the dove's glad note was mingled
  With the dirge of Philomel.

Nought the number of the feasters,
  Seeking Jesus, did she fear;
She her Master's feet anointed,
  Washed them with the falling tear;
With her flowing hair she wiped them,
  Made them ready for the bier.

Lo! the cleansed doth wash the Cleanser;
  On the Fount doth fall the rain;
Lo! the flower the raindrop sheddeth,
  Which returns to wash her stain;
Heaven to earth in dew descendeth,
  Earth gives back her dew again.

Spikenard in the alabaster,
  Offers she as tribute there;
In the pouring of the unguent,
  She a mystic sign doth bear:
Sick, anointeth her Physician,
  Her own healing to prepare.

Gazed the Lord in deep compassion
  Down on Mary bending low :
Much she loves : her sins are many ;
  They are all forgiven now :
On the Resurrection morning,
  Mary first her Lord shall know.

Glory to the Paschal Victim,
  To our God all praise and might :
For the Lamb by death hath conquered,
  Lion, Victor in the fight ;
Rose He on the morn of triumph,
  With the spoils of death bedight. Amen.

℣. Mary hath chosen that good part.
℟. Which shall not be taken away from her.

Ant. to Mag. In those days a woman in the city, which was a sinner, when she knew that Jesus sat at meat in the house of Simon the leper, brought an alabaster box of ointment, and stood at His feet behind Him weeping : and began to wash His feet with tears, and did wipe them with the hairs of her head, and kissed His feet, and anointed them with the ointment.

COLLECT.

WE humbly entreat Thy mercy, O Lord, on this holy festival of blessed Mary Magdalene, that as we venerate her great devotion, so we may be partakers of her glory. Through.

[*Or this :*

GRANT to us, we pray Thee, most merciful Father, that as blessed Mary Magdalene, loving Thy Only-begotten Son above all things, obtained forgiveness of her sins, so she may ask for us from Thy mercy, everlasting blessedness. Through the same.]

Lauds.

℣. Mary hath chosen that good part.
℟. Which shall not be taken away from her.

Psalms of Sunday.

Ant. 1. Mary saw Jesus standing, and knew not that it was Jesus : Jesus saith unto her, Woman, why weepest thou? whom seekest thou?

Ant. 2. She, supposing Him to be the gardener, saith unto Him : Sir, if thou have borne Him hence, tell me where thou hast laid Him, and I will take Him away.

Ant. 3. Jesus saith unto her, Mary : she turned herself, and saith unto Him, Rabboni ; which is to say, Master.

Ant. 4. Jesus saith unto her, Touch Me not : for I am not yet ascended to My Father.

Ant. 5. Go to My brethren, and say unto them : I ascend to My Father and to your Father, and to My God and your God.

Chapter as at First Vespers.

HYMN. *O Maria, noli flere.*

WEEP not, Mary, weep no longer,
  Nor another seek to find :
Here indeed the Gardener standeth,
  Gardener of the thirsty mind :
In the spirit's inner garden
  Seek that Gardener ever kind.

Whence thy grief and lamentation?
  Lift, faint soul, thy heart on high,
Seek not memory's consolation :
  Jesus, Whom thou lov'st is nigh :
Dost thou seek thy Lord? thou hast Him,
  Though unseen by human eye.

Whence thy sorrow, whence thy weeping?
  True the joy thou hast within ;
Lives within thee what thou know'st not,
  Balm to heal the wounds of sin :
'Tis within, why wander vainly,
  Seeking languor's medicine?

Now I wonder not, thy Master
  If thou know'st not while He sows ;
For His seed, the word eternal,
  Unto fulness in thee grows ;
"Mary," saith He—thou, "Rabboni"—
  And the soul her Saviour knows.

Glory be to God the Giver,
  That His grace is given free,
To the humble sigh of Mary
  Summoned by the Pharisee ;
Grace's foretaste to the sinner,
  Then life's full feast giveth He. Amen.

℣. Her sins, which are many, are forgiven.
℟. For she loved much.

Ant. to Ben. Jesus appeared first to Mary Magdalene, out of whom He had cast seven devils : And she went and told them that had been with Him, as they mourned and wept.

Prime.

Ant. Mary saw Jesus standing, and knew not that it was Jesus : Jesus saith unto her, Woman, why weepest thou? whom seekest thou?

Tierce.

Ant. She, supposing Him to be the gardener, saith unto Him: Sir, if thou have borne Him hence, tell me where thou hast laid Him, and I will take Him away.

Chapter as at First Vespers.

℟/℣. at Tierce, Sexts, and Nones of the Common of a Virgin, p. 228.

Sexts.

Ant. Jesus saith unto her, Mary: she turned herself, and saith unto Him, Rabboni; which is to say, Master.

CHAPTER. Prov. xxxi.

SHE girdeth her loins with strength, and strengtheneth her arms. She perceiveth that her merchandize is good: her candle goeth not out by night.

Nones.

Ant. Go to My brethren, and say unto them: I ascend to My Father and to your Father, and to My God and your God.

CHAPTER. Prov. xxxi.

A WOMAN that feareth the Lord, she shall be praised. Give her of the fruit of her hands; and let her own works praise her in the gates.

Second Vespers.

Psalms of the Feria said under first Ant. of Lauds.

Chapter as at First Vespers.

HYMN. O Maria, noli flere, ℣. and ℟., as at Lauds, p. 275.

Ant. to Mag. My heart is joyful in Thy salvation: I will sing of the Lord, because He hath dealt so lovingly with me.

July 23.

S. APOLLINARIS, BISHOP AND MARTYR.*

All of the Common of a Martyr, p. 217.

July 25.

S. JAMES, APOSTLE AND MARTYR.

All of the Common of Apostles, p. 214, except the

COLLECT.

GRANT, O merciful God, that as Thine holy Apostle Saint James, leaving his father and all that he had, without delay was obedient unto the calling of Thy Son Jesus Christ, and followed Him; so we, forsaking all worldly and carnal affections, may be evermore ready to follow Thy holy commandments. Through.

July 26.

S. ANNE, MOTHER OF THE BLESSED VIRGIN MARY.

All of the Common of a Matron, p. 229, except the

COLLECT.

O GOD, Who on this day didst lift to the joys of heavenly life blessed Anne, parent of Thy most dear Mother; grant us to attain to everlasting blessedness in union with her through whose blessed childbearing Thou didst vouchsafe to assume human flesh for the salvation of the world. Who livest.

July 28.

S. SAMPSON, BISHOP AND CONFESSOR.*

All of the Common of a Bishop and Confessor, p. 222.

July 31.

S. GERMANUS, BISHOP AND CONFESSOR.*

All of the Common of a Bishop and Confessor, p. 222.

FEASTS OF AUGUST.

[*On the first day unhindered is said the Office of the Dead.*]

August 1.
S. Peter's Chains.

First Vespers.

Psalms of the Feria.

Ant. May chains of earth be riven at God's command : and opened wide the gates of heaven stand.

Chapter. Acts xii.

PETER therefore was kept in prison: but prayer was made without ceasing of the Church unto God for him.

Hymn. *Jam bone pastor.*

THY Lord hath marked thy love,
Good shepherd of the sheep;
Well, Peter, hast thou kept
The charge His flock to keep:
Complete is now thy work,
The wage is thine for aye,
The crown of endless life
That fadeth not away.

Annue Christe, ℣. *and* ℟., p. 215.

Ant. to Mag. Thou art shepherd of the sheep, and chief of the Apostles : to thee are committed the keys of the kingdom of heaven.

Collect.

O GOD, Who didst cause blessed Peter the Apostle to be loosed from his chains, and to depart unhurt; break, we beseech Thee, the bonds of our sins, and mercifully put away all evil things from us. Through.

Memorial of the Holy Maccabees.

Ant. The King of the world shall give to them that have died for His laws : the resurrection of eternal life.

℣. The Lord will avenge His people.

℟. And be gracious unto His servants.

Collect.

GRANT, O Lord, that the crown which Thou didst bestow on the martyr brothers may bring joy to our hearts; that we, being comforted by the prayers of many Saints on our behalf, may be strengthened in faith and in the performance of such things as are pleasing in Thy sight. Through.

Lauds.

℣. Thou art Peter.

℟. And on this rock I will build My Church.

Ant. 1. The Angel of the Lord came upon him, and a light shined in the prison : and he smote Peter on the side, and raised him up, saying, Arise up quickly.

Ant. 2. The Angel said unto Peter : Cast thy garment about thee, and follow me.

Ant. 3. And Peter went out, and followed him : and wist not that it was true which was done by the Angel.

Ant. 4. The Lord hath sent His Angel : and hath delivered me out of the hand of Herod. Alleluia.

Ant. 5. May chains of earth be riven at God's command : and opened wide the gates of heaven stand.

Chapter as at First Vespers.

Hymn. *Exultet cœlum laudibus,*
℣. *and* ℟., p. 215.

Ant. to Ben. Whatsoever thou shalt bind on earth shall be bound in heaven : and whatsoever thou shalt loose on earth shall be loosed in heaven, said the Lord to Simon Peter.

Memorial of the Maccabees, as at First Vespers.

Prime.

Ant. The Angel of the Lord came upon him, and a light shined in the prison : and he smote Peter on the side, and raised him up, saying, Arise up quickly.

Tierce.

Ant. The Angel said unto Peter : Cast thy garment about thee, and follow me.

Chapter as at First Vespers.

℣℟. *at Tierce, Sexts, and Nones, as in the Common of Apostles,* p. 216.

Sexts.

Ant. And Peter went out, and followed him : and wist not that it was true which was done by the Angel.

CHAPTER. Acts XII.

AND behold, the Angel of the Lord came upon him, and a light shined in the prison; and he smote Peter on the side, and raised him up, saying, Arise up quickly. And his chains fell off from his hands.

Nones.

Ant. May chains of earth be riven at God's command : and opened wide the gates of heaven stand.

CHAPTER. Acts XII.

PETER went out, and followed him; and wist not that it was true which was done by the Angel.

Second Vespers.

Psalms of the Common of Apostles, p. 216, *said under first Antiphon of Lauds.*

Chapter as at First Vespers.

℟/℣. *of the Common.*

HYMN. *Exultet cœlum laudibus,*
℣. *and* ℟., p. 215.

Ant. to Mag. And when Peter was come to himself, he said ; Now I know of a surety that the Lord hath sent His Angel : and hath delivered me out of the hand of Herod, and from all the expectation of the people of the Jews.

August 4.

S. DOMINIC, CONFESSOR.*

All of the Common of a Confessor not a Bishop, p. 224.

August 5.

S. OSWALD, KING AND MARTYR.

All of the Common of a Martyr, p. 217, *except the*

COLLECT.

O GOD, Who hast made this day glorious with joyful and holy gladness by the passion of Thy blessed servant Oswald : grant to our hearts an increase of love and charity ; that as we celebrate the shedding of his blood on earth, so we may perceive the blessing of his love in heaven. Through.

August 6.

THE TRANSFIGURATION OF OUR LORD JESUS CHRIST.

First Vespers.

Psalms of First Vespers of Christmas Day, p. 91.

Ant. 1. Jesus took His disciples and bringeth them up into an high mountain : and was transfigured before them.

Ant. 2. And when Jesus was transfigured : Moses and Elias appeared unto the disciples talking with the Lord.

Ant. 3. Then answered Peter, and said unto Jesus, Lord, if Thou wilt, let us make here three tabernacles : one for Thee, and one for Moses, and one for Elias.

Ant. 4. While he yet spake : behold, a bright cloud overshadowed them.

Ant. 5. And behold a voice out of the cloud, which said : This is My beloved Son, in Whom I am well pleased; hear ye Him.

CHAPTER. Phil. III.

WE look for the Saviour, the Lord Jesus Christ : Who shall change our vile body, that it may be fashioned like unto His glorious body, according to the working whereby He is able even to subdue all things unto Himself.

℟. Jesus, taking Peter and James, and John his brother : He went up with them into a high mountain apart, where, transfiguring Himself, He shewed them the excellence of His glory. ℣. That seeing His Passion they should not be troubled, but might be more firmly established. ℣. He went up with them into a high mountain apart, where, transfiguring Himself, He shewed them the excellence of His glory. ℟. Glory be to the Father, and to the Son : and to the Holy Ghost. ℟. He went up with them into a high mountain apart, where, transfiguring Himself, He shewed them the excellence of His glory.

Hymn. *Cælestis formam gloriæ.*

A TYPE of those bright rays on high
For which the Church hopes longingly,
Christ on the holy mountain shews,
Where brighter than the sun He glows :

Tale for all ages to declare :
For with the three disciples there,
Where Moses and Elias meet,
The Lord holds converse, high and sweet.

The chosen witnesses stand nigh,
Of grace, the law, and prophecy :
And from the cloud the Holy One
Bears record to the Only Son.

With face more bright than noontide ray,
Christ deigns to manifest to-day
What glory shall be theirs above,
Who joy in God with perfect love.

And faithful hearts are raised on high
By this great vision's mystery ;
For which, in yearly course, we raise
The voice of prayer, and hymn of praise.

Thou, Father, Thou, Eternal Son,
Thou, Holy Spirit, Three in One,
To this same glory bring us nigh,
That we may see Thee eye to eye.   Amen.

℣. Let us worship the Father, the Son, and the Holy Ghost.
℟. Reigning in His Majesty.

Ant. to Mag. Tell the vision to no man : until the Son of Man be risen again from the dead.

Collect.

O GOD, Who by the testimony of the Fathers didst confirm the sacraments of faith in the transfiguration of Thine Only-begotten Son, and didst wonderfully prefigure by the voice from the bright cloud, the perfect adoption of sons ; grant, we beseech Thee, that we may be co-heirs of the King of glory, and partakers of the same glory. Through the same.

Compline.

As on Festivals, p. 67, *except the doxology to the Hymn*, Salvator mundi, *which is that of Christmas, and so at the ensuing Hours of this Festival.*

Lauds.

℣. Let us worship the Father, the Son, and the Holy Ghost.
℟. Reigning in His Majesty.

Psalms of Sunday.

Ant. 1. Jesus came and touched His disciples, fallen for fear of the heavenly voice : and said, Arise, and be not afraid.

Ant. 2. And when they had lifted up their eyes : they saw no man, save Jesus only.

Ant. 3. That He might receive witness from the law and from the prophets : Jesus appeared transfigured between Moses and Elias.

Ant. 4. The law was signified by Moses and prophecy by Elias : who were beheld talking with the Lord in the mount, and shining with glory.

Ant. 5. And as they came down from the mountain, Jesus charged them, saying : Tell the vision to no man, until the Son of man be risen again from the dead.

Chapter as at First Vespers.

Hymn. *O nata Lux de lumine.*

O LIGHT which from the Light hast birth !
Jesu, Redeemer of the earth ;
Thy suppliant flock vouchsafe to spare,
Receive our gift of praise and prayer.

Thou, Who for man's salvation's sake
Thyself hast deigned our flesh to take ;
O make us members true and sure
Of that Thy Body blest and pure.

Beyond the sun Thine aspect bright,
Thy garments as the snowdrift white ;
Creator, on the mountain shown,
Thou wast to chosen few made known.

The Prophets, wondrous Seer, with Thine
Thou didst as meet disciples join,
On both with matchless power bestow
Thee as eternal God to know.

The Father from His heavenly throne
Proclaims aloud the Only Son ;
And we with faithful hearts no less,
Thee, glorious King of Saints, confess.

O may Thy servants day by day
Thy virtues in their lives display,
So unto joys beyond the skies,
In holy converse heavenward rise.

We speak Thy glorious praise abroad,
Eternal King of kings, O God:
Who Threefold Deity, alone,
Dost reign through endless ages, One. Amen.

℣. Blessed be the Name of the Lord.
℟. From this time forth for evermore.

Ant. to Ben. To the three disciples, troubled by the thought of His death: lest they should doubt the resurrection He foretold, the Lord in His transfiguration shewed the glory He had predicted.

Prime.

Ant. Jesus came and touched His disciples, fallen for fear of the heavenly voice: and said, Arise, and be not afraid.

℟. *as Christmas*, p. 95.

Tierce.

Ant. And when they had lifted up their eyes: they saw no man, save Jesus only.

Chapter as at First Vespers.

℟. Let us worship the Father, the Son, and the Holy Ghost: Alleluia, Alleluia. ℣. Reigning in glory. ℟. Alleluia. Alleluia. ℣. Glory be to the Father, and to the Son: and to the Holy Ghost. ℟. Alleluia. Alleluia.

℣. A hallowed day hath shone upon us.
℟. Come, ye nations, and worship the Lord.

Sexts.

Ant. That He might receive witness from the law and from the prophets: Jesus appeared transfigured between Moses and Elias.

CHAPTER. 2 S. Peter i.

WE made known unto you the power and coming of our Lord Jesus Christ, but were eyewitnesses of His majesty.

℟. A hallowed day hath shone upon us: Alleluia. Alleluia. ℣. Come, ye nations, and worship the Lord. ℟. Alleluia. Alleluia. ℣. Glory be to the Father, and to the Son: and to the Holy Ghost. ℟. Alleluia. Alleluia.

℣. Worship the Lord.
℟. In His holy temple.

Nones.

Ant. And as they came down from the mountain, Jesus charged them, saying: Tell the vision to no man, until the Son of Man be risen again from the dead.

CHAPTER. 2 S. Peter i.

FOR He received from God the Father honour and glory, when there came such a voice to Him from the excellent glory, This is My beloved Son, in Whom I am well pleased.

℟. Worship the Lord: Alleluia. Alleluia. ℣. In His holy temple. ℟. Alleluia. Alleluia. ℣. Glory be to the Father, and to the Son: and to the Holy Ghost. ℟. Alleluia. Alleluia.
℣. Worship the Lord.
℣. All ye angels of His.

The Second Vespers are superseded by First Vespers of the Holy Name, unless the Transfiguration be the feast of the place.

Second Vespers.

Psalms of Sunday said under first Ant. of Lauds.

Chapter as at First Vespers.

℟. For the confirmation of the disciples, and their instruction in the true faith: Moses and Elias appeared talking with the Lord. ℣. For it was fitting that the Gospel of Christ should receive witness from the law and the prophets. ℟. Moses and Elias appeared talking with the Lord. ℣. Glory be to the Father, and to the Son: and to the Ghost. ℟. Moses and Elias appeared talking with the Lord.

HYMN. *O nata Lux de lumine,*
℣. *and* ℟., *as at Lauds.*

Ant. to Mag. To-day, when the Father spake, Moses and Elias were present in glory with the transfigured Lord: and spake of His death which He should accomplish.

MEMORIAL OF THE HOLY NAME OF
JESUS.

Ant. But I will rejoice in the Lord, and I will exult in Jesus my God : for He that is mighty hath done to me great things, and holy is His Name. Alleluia.
℣. All the world shall worship Thee, and sing of Thee.
℟. And praise Thy Name.

Collect of the Holy Name.

August 7.

THE MOST SWEET NAME OF JESUS.

*If this Office be used as a commemoration through the year, it may be said on any day unhindered by a Vigil or Double Feast (see Rubric on Commemorations), except in Advent and Lent. Alleluia is not said, except during the Octave of the Feast and in Eastertide. At all other times, in the ℣/℟. the repetition is from the *.*

First Vespers.

Ant. 1. From the rising up of the sun unto the going down of the same : the Lord's blessed Name of Jesus be praised. [Alleluia.]

Laudate pueri. Psalm cxiii., p. 48.

Ant. 2. Whosoever shall call on the Name of the Lord : shall be saved. [Alleluia.]

Dilexi. Psalm cxvi., p. 51.

Ant. 3. O Lord, Thou hast broken my bonds in sunder : I will offer unto Thee the sacrifice of thanksgiving, and will call upon the Name of the Lord. [Alleluia.]

Credidi. Psalm cxvi. 10, p. 52.

Ant. 4. For thither the tribes go up, even the tribes of the Lord : to testify unto Israel, to give thanks unto the Name of the Lord. [Alleluia.]

Lætatus sum. Psalm cxxii., p. 54.

Ant. 5. In the presence of the Angels will I sing praise unto Thee : I will worship toward Thy holy temple, and praise Thy Name, O Lord. [Alleluia.]

Confitebor tibi. Psalm cxxxviii., p. 60.

CHAPTER. Phil. ii.

HE humbled Himself, and became obedient unto death, even the death of the Cross. Wherefore God also hath highly exalted Him, and given Him a Name which is above every name : that at the Name of Jesus every knee should bow, of things in heaven, and things in earth, and things under the earth.

℟. O praise the Lord with me, and let us magnify His Name together : for our heart shall rejoice in Him, because we have hoped in His holy Name. ℣. Tell of all His marvellous works, sing praise to His holy Name. ℟. For our heart shall rejoice in Him, because we have hoped in His holy Name. ℣. Glory be to the Father, and to the Son and to the Holy Ghost. ℟. Because we have hoped in His holy Name.

HYMN. *Exultet cor precordiis.*

O LET the heart exulting beat,
  When Jesus' holy Name resounds ;
Above all other it is sweet,
And in all gladness it abounds.

Jesus, Who comforteth in woe,
Jesus, Who heals the wounds of sin,
Jesus, Who curbs the fiends below,
Jesus, Who routs Death's arms within.

Jesus ! it soundeth sweetest, best,
In every measure, hymn, and song ;
And with its comfort soothes the breast,
And lifts us up, and makes us strong.

Let that great Name of Him the Lord,
Jesus, from tongues of all men peal ;
And let the voice and heart accord,
That every ill its sound may heal.

Jesu, Who savest sinners lost,
Be present as we kneel in prayer ;
Guide Thou the erring, tempest-tost,
And us, Thy guilty servants, spare.

O let Thy Name be our defence,
In every peril guard and stay,
And purging us from sin's offence,
Perfect us in the better way.

O Christ, all glory be to Thee,
Who shinest with this Name above,
Honour, and worship, majesty,
Be Thine, O Jesu, Lord of love.

O Jesu, from the Virgin sprung,
All glory be ascribed to Thee,
Like praise be to the Father sung,
And Holy Ghost eternally. Amen.

℣. All the world shall worship Thee, and sing of Thee.

℞. And praise Thy Name.

Ant. to Mag. But I will rejoice in the Lord, and I will exult in Jesus my God : for He that is mighty hath done to me great things, and holy is His Name. [Alleluia.]

COLLECT.

GOD, Which hast made the glorious Name of Jesus Christ Thy Son our Lord most dear to Thy faithful people, and most terrible to evil spirits; grant, we beseech Thee, that all we, who worship this Name on earth, may receive in this life the sweetness of Thy holy consolations, and in the world to come, the joy of exultation, and of eternal blessedness in heaven. Through the same.

MEMORIAL OF THE TRANSFIGURATION.

Ant. To-day, when the Father spoke, Moses and Elias were present in glory with the transfigured Lord : and spake of His death which He should accomplish.

℣. Let us worship the Father, the Son, and the Holy Ghost.

℞. Reigning in His Majesty.

Collect of the Transfiguration.

Compline.

Ant. to Psalms. Have mercy upon me, O Lord : as Thou usest to do unto those that love Thy Name.

HYMN. *Alma chorus,* p. 185, *or*
Jesus in pace imperat.

JESUS now reigns in Heaven, and thence
Sheds peace which passeth every sense;
To this my eager spirit turns,
For this it longs, and pants, and yearns.

Where'er I go, where'er I stay,
I seek for Jesus every way;
How happy when I find at last,
How joyous when I hold Him fast.

Thine own dear love, O Jesu! this
Is very rapture, very bliss;
A thousand, thousand times more sweet
Than heart can think or words repeat.

Good Jesu! grant us to possess
Thy love's unfading loveliness;
Give me by penitence to see
The glory of Thy Majesty.

All honour, laud, and glory be,
O Jesu, Virgin-born, to Thee;
All glory, as is ever meet,
To Father and to Paraclete. Amen.

The Office Hymns, except Alma chorus *and* Exultet cor, *all take the Christmas Doxology, as at Lauds.*

Ant. to Nunc Dim. O King, glorious among Thy Saints, Who art ever to be praised, and yet art ineffable : Thou, Lord, art in the midst of us, and we are called by Thy Name : leave us not, O our God; and in the day of judgment vouchsafe to number us amongst Thy Saints, O blessed King.

Lauds.

℣. Our help is in the Name of the Lord.

℞. Who hath made heaven and earth.

Psalms of Sunday.

Ant. 1. His Name was called Jesus, which was so named of the Angel : before He was conceived in the womb. [Alleluia.]

Ant. 2. O praise the Name of our Lord Jesus Christ : because it is lovely, and His mercy endureth for ever. [Alleluia.]

Ant. 3. As long as I live will I magnify Thee, O Lord Jesus : and lift up my hands in Thy Name. [Alleluia.]

Ant. 4. The righteous spoiled the ungodly, and praised Thy holy Name, O Lord : and magnified with one accord Thine hand, that fought for them. [Alleluia.]

Ant. 5. Young men and maidens, old men and children, praise the Name of the Lord : for His Name only is excellent. [Alleluia.]

CHAPTER. 1 Cor. I.

TO all that in every place call upon the Name of Jesus Christ our Lord, both theirs and ours : grace unto you, and peace, from God our Father, and the Lord Jesus Christ.

℞. Thanks be to God.

THE MOST SWEET NAME OF JESUS.

HYMN. *Jesu auctor clementiæ.*

JESU, Thou source of pity blest,
   Thou hope and gladness of the breast,
O stream of beauty, source of grace,
Delight of every heart and place!

Jesu, the Beauty Angels see,
The ears' ecstatic minstrelsy,
The nectar of the Heavenly Home,
The lips' delicious honey comb.

Flower of Virgin Mother blest,
Jesu, true sweetness, purest, best,
Of man the honour and the head,
Thy light of lights upon us shed.

More glorious than the sun to see,
More fragrant than the balsam-tree,
My heart's desire, and boast, and mirth,
Jesu, Salvation of the earth.

Jesu, Who highest bounty art,
And wondrous joyaunce of the heart,
Of goodness the infinity,
Constrain us with Thy charity.

O King of Virtues, King renowned,
With glory and with victory crowned,
Jesu, by Whom all grace is given,
Thou honour of the courts of heaven!

Let choirs of Angels sing Thy Name,
And echo all Thy matchless fame,
Jesus on joyful earth hath smiled,
And us with God hath reconciled.

All honour, laud, and glory be,
O Jesu, Virgin-born to Thee;
All glory, as is ever meet,
To Father and to Paraclete. Amen.

℣. Blessed be the Name of the Lord Jesus.

℟. From this time forth for evermore.

Ant. to Ben. Joseph, thou son of David, fear not to take unto thee Mary thy wife; for that which is conceived in her is of the Holy Ghost : and she shall bring forth a Son, and thou shalt call His Name Jesus; for He shall save His people from their sins.

Prime.

Ant. His Name was called Jesus, which was so named of the Angel : before He was conceived in the womb. [Alleluia.]

℟. *as on Christmas Day,* p. 95.

Tierce.

Ant. O praise the Name of our Lord Jesus Christ : because it is lovely, and His mercy endureth for ever. [Alleluia.]

Chapter as at Lauds.

℟. I will praise the Name of the Lord * with a song. [Alleluia, Alleluia.] ℣. And magnify it with thanksgiving. ℟. [Alleluia, Alleluia.] ℣. Glory be to the Father, and to the Son : and to the Holy Ghost. ℟. I will praise the Name of the Lord with a song. [Alleluia, Alleluia.]

℣. Praise the Lord, O my soul.

℟. And all that is within me praise His holy Name.

Sexts.

Ant. As long as I live will I magnify Thee, O Lord Jesus : and lift up my hands in Thy Name. [Alleluia.]

CHAPTER. Col. III.

WHATSOEVER ye do in word or deed, do all in the Name of the Lord Jesus, giving thanks to God and the Father by Him.

℟. Praise the Lord * O my soul [Alleluia. Alleluia.] ℣. And all that is within me, praise His holy Name. ℟. [Alleluia, Alleluia.] ℣. Glory be to the Father, and to the Son : and to the Holy Ghost. ℟. Praise the Lord, O my soul. [Alleluia. Alleluia.]

℣. Not unto us, O Lord, not unto us.

℟. But unto Thy Name give the praise.

Nones.

Ant. Young men and maidens, old men and children, praise the Name of the Lord : for His Name only is excellent. [Alleluia.]

CHAPTER. 2 Thess. III.

NOW we command you, brethren, in the Name of our Lord Jesus Christ, that ye withdraw yourselves from every brother that walketh disorderly, and not after the tradition which he received of us.

℟. Not unto us, O Lord; * not unto us : [Alleluia, Alleluia]. ℣. But unto Thy Name give the praise. ℟. [Alleluia, Alleluia]. ℣. Glory be to the Father, and to the Son : and to the Holy

PROPER OF SAINTS.

Ghost. ℟. Not unto us, O Lord, not unto us : [Alleluia, Alleluia].

℣. Blessed be the Name of the Lord Jesus.

℟. From this time forth for evermore.

Second Vespers.

Psalms of First Vespers, said under First Ant. of Lauds.

Chapter as at Lauds.

℟. But these are written, that ye might believe that Jesus is the Christ, the Son of God : and that believing ye might have life through His Name. ℣. O give thanks unto the Lord, and call upon His Name; tell the people what things He hath done. ℟. That believing ye might have life through His Name. ℣. Glory be to the Father, and to the Son : and to the Holy Ghost. ℟. Through His Name.

HYMN. *Exultet cor precordiis,* ℣. *and* ℟., *as at Lauds.*

Ant. to Mag. Then Joseph being raised from sleep, did as the Angel of the Lord had bidden him, and took unto him his wife : and knew her not till she had brought forth her firstborn Son : and he called His Name Jesus. [Alleluia.]

No memorials are said on this day, unless the feast fall on Saturday, in which case memorial is made of Sunday and the Holy Trinity; or on Sunday, when memorial is made of the Sunday.

For observance of the Octave, see rubric for Octave of the Visitation, p. 272: but when any Saint's Day be kept, its Compline is as on Festivals in Trinity season.

August 10.

S. LAWRENCE, DEACON AND MARTYR.

First Vespers.

Ant. to Psalms. My servant, fear not, for I am with thee : if thou passest through the fire, it shall not hurt thee.

Psalms of the Feria.

CHAPTER. 2 Cor. IX.

HE which soweth sparingly shall reap also sparingly; and he which soweth bountifully shall reap also bountifully.

℟. Blessed Lawrence, cried and said, I worship my God, and serve Him only : and therefore I fear not thy torments. ℣. My night has no darkness ; but all glows in light. ℟. And therefore I fear not thy torments. ℣. Glory be to the Father, and to the Son : and to the Holy Ghost. ℟. And therefore I fear not thy torments.

HYMN. *Martyr Dei,* p. 289.

℣. He hath dispersed abroad and given to the poor.

℟. His righteousness remaineth for ever.

Ant. to Mag. Blessed Lawrence laid and burning upon the grating, said to the tyrant : The riches of the Church which thou dost seek have been carried to the heavenly treasuries by the hands of the poor.

COLLECT.

GRANT, we beseech Thee, Almighty God, that in the unchanging light of heaven we may worthily honour with fervent faith the triumph achieved on earth, in despite of the flames, by Thy blessed martyr Lawrence. Through.

MEMORIAL OF THE HOLY NAME.

Ant. Whosoever shall call on the Name of the Lord : shall be saved. Alleluia.

℣. All the world shall worship Thee, and sing of Thee.

℟. And praise Thy Name.

Collect of the Holy Name.

Lauds.

℣. He hath dispersed abroad and given to the poor.

℟. His righteousness remaineth for ever.

Psalms of Sunday.

Ant. 1. The martyr Lawrence entered into the fire : and confessed the Name of the Lord Jesus Christ.

S. LAWRENCE.

Ant. 2. The deacon Lawrence wrought a good work : who by the sign of the Cross enlightened the blind.

Ant. 3. My soul hangeth on Thee : because my flesh is burnt in the fire for Thee, my God.

Ant. 4. The Lord sent His Angel, and delivered me from the midst of the fire : and I was not burned.

Ant. 5. Blessed Lawrence prayed, saying, I give Thee thanks, O Lord : for Thou hast counted me worthy to enter Thy gates.

Chapter as at First Vespers.

HYMN. *Deus tuorum militum,* ℣. and ℟., p. 218.

Ant. to Ben. On the iron grating I have not denied Thee to be God : and lying over the fire I have confessed Thee to be Christ : Thou hast tried me with fire, and hast found no wickedness in me ; Thou hast proved my heart, O Lord, and visited me in the night season.

MEMORIAL OF THE HOLY NAME.

Ant. From the rising up of the sun unto the going down of the same : the Lord's blessed Name of Jesus be praised.

℣. Blessed be the Name of the Lord Jesus.

℟. From this time forth for evermore.

Collect of the Holy Name.

Prime.

Ant. The martyr Lawrence entered into the fire : and confessed the Name of the Lord Jesus Christ.

Tierce.

Ant. The deacon Lawrence wrought a good work : who by the sign of the Cross enlightened the blind.

Chapter as at First Vespers.

℟.℟. *at Tierce, Sexts and Nones of Common of a Martyr,* p. 218.

Sexts.

Ant. My soul hangeth on Thee : because my flesh is burnt in the fire for Thee, my God.

CHAPTER. 2 Cor. IX. 8, 9.

AND God is able to make all grace abound toward you ; that ye, always having all sufficiency in all things, may abound to every good work : as it is written, He hath dispersed abroad ; he hath given to the poor ; his righteousness remaineth for ever.

Nones.

Ant. Blessed Lawrence prayed, saying, I give Thee thanks, O Lord : for Thou hast counted me worthy to enter Thy gates.

CHAPTER. 2 Cor. IX. 10.

NOW He that ministereth seed to the sower both minister bread for your food, and multiply your seed sown, and increase the fruits of your righteousness.

Second Vespers.

Psalms of the Feria, said under first Ant. of Lauds.

Chapter as at Lauds.

HYMN. *Deus tuorum militum,* ℣. and ℟., p. 218.

Ant. to Mag. Come, thou good and faithful servant, come ; My Angels shall receive thee : for when burnt thou didst not deny Me, when tried thou didst confess Me.

Memorial of the Holy Name, p. 284.

August 12.

S. CLARE, VIRGIN.

Memorial of a Virgin, p. 237.

August 14.

OCTAVE OF THE HOLY NAME.

All as on the Festival, except that at First Vespers the Psalms are all said under the first Ant.

[*At Lauds.*

MEMORIAL OF THE VIGIL.

Ant. Thy loving kindness is better than the life itself : my lips shall praise Thee.

℣. My soul is athirst for the living God.
℞. When shall I come to appear before the presence of God?

COLLECT.

O GOD, Who didst vouchsafe to choose the Virgin shrine of blessed Mary wherein to rest: grant, we beseech Thee, that, guarded by that defence, we may joyfully assist at her festival. Who livest.]

August 15.

THE REPOSE OF THE BLESSED VIRGIN MARY.

First Vespers.

Psalms of the First Vespers of Christmas Day, p. 91.

Ant. 1. Thou art all fair, my love, there is no spot in thee: thy lips drop as the honey-comb, honey and milk are under thy tongue: the smell of thine ointments is better than all spices. The winter is past, the rain is over and gone, the flowers appear on the earth, the vines give a good smell, and the voice of the turtle is heard in our land. Arise, my love, my fair one, and come from Lebanon.

Ant. 2. My soul failed when my Beloved spake: I sought Him, but I could not find Him; I called Him, but he gave me no answer: the watchmen that went about the city found me, they smote me, they wounded me; the keepers of the walls took away my veil from me. Daughters of Jerusalem, tell my Beloved that I am sick of love.

Ant. 3. What is thy Beloved more than another beloved, O thou fairest among women? My Beloved is white and ruddy, the chiefest among ten thousand: His left Hand is under my head, and His right Hand doth embrace me.

Ant. 4. This is my Beloved, and this is my Friend: O daughters of Jerusalem.

Ant. 5. I went down into the garden of nuts to see the fruits of the valley, and to see whether the vines flourished, and the pomegranates budded: return, return, O Shulamite; return, return, that we may look upon thee.

CHAPTER. Ecclus. xxiv.

WITH all these I sought rest: and in whose inheritance shall I abide? So the Creator of all things gave me a commandment, and he that made me caused my tabernacle to rest.

℞. All generations shall call me blessed: for He that is mighty hath magnified me, and holy is His Name.
℣. My soul doth magnify the Lord, and my spirit hath rejoiced in God my Saviour. ℞. For He that is mighty hath magnified me. ℣. Glory be to the Father, and to the Son: and to the Holy Ghost. ℞. And holy is His Name.

HYMN. *O quam glorifica luce coruscas.*

O WITH what glorious lustre resplendent
   Shinest Thou, David's own royal descendant,
Mary, the Virgin who loftily dwellest,
And in God's favour all women excellest.

Mother, yet all honour virginal bearing,
For the Lord of all angels a chamber preparing,
Him in thy bosom thou chastely enshrinest,
And from thy womb cometh Christ the Divinest,

Whom the whole earth venerating adoreth,
Every knee bowing for ever imploreth,
From Whom we seek, with thee thy prayer lending,
Light in our darkness, and joy never ending.

Father of lights, Thou these blessings bestowing,
Grant for Thy Son, from the Holy Ghost flowing,
Who, as with Thee He in glory abideth,
All things for ever disposeth and guideth.
                     Amen.

℣. Thou art the holy Mother of God.
℞. O Mary, ever virgin.

Ant. to Mag. Christ ascending above the heavens prepared a place for His most pure Mother: where she abideth, ever mindful of us in her pity.

COLLECT. *(S. Maur.)*

O GOD, Who, regarding the humility of the Blessed Virgin Mary, didst exalt her to such excellent grace that of her, according to the flesh, thine Only-

Begotten Son should be born; and, as on this day, didst crown her with superabundant glory; grant, we beseech Thee, that we, humbling ourselves in all things after her example, may attain to be exalted. Through the same.

MEMORIAL OF THE HOLY NAME.

Compline.

Ant. to Psalms. Of thee was born the King of the whole earth : O holy Virgin Mary.

Ant. to Nunc Dim. as on the *Purification*, p. 248.

Lauds.

℣. Thou art the holy Mother of God.
℞. O Mary, ever virgin.

Psalms of Sunday.

Ant. 1. Mary is exalted : let Angels rejoice, and bless the Lord with praise.

Ant. 2. The gates of Paradise were closed to all by Eve : and again through thee set open.

Ant. 3. Because of the savour of thy good ointments thy name is as ointment poured forth : therefore do the virgins love thee.

Ant. 4. Thou art blessed of thy Son, O Mother : for through thee we have received the Fruit of Life.

Ant. 5. Thou art beautiful and comely, O daughter of Jerusalem : terrible as an army with banners.

Chapter as at First Vespers.

HYMN. *O gloriosa fœmina,* p. 211.

℣. God hath elected her and pre-elected her.

℞. And made her to dwell in His tabernacle.

Ant. to Ben. Who is this that looketh forth as the morning, fair as the moon, clear as the sun, and terrible as an army with banners?

Collect as at First Vespers.

Prime.

Ant. to Psalms. Mary is exalted : let Angels rejoice, and bless the Lord with praise.

Tierce.

Ant. The gates of Paradise were closed to all by Eve : and again through thee set open.

Chapter as at First Vespers.

℞/℞. at Tierce, Sexts, and Nones, as on the *Purification*, p. 249.

Sexts.

Ant. Because of the savour of thy good ointments thy name is as ointment poured forth : therefore do the virgins love thee.

CHAPTER. Ecclus. XXIV.

AND so was I established in Sion. Likewise in the beloved city He gave me rest, and in Jerusalem was my power.

Nones.

Ant. Thou art beautiful and comely, O daughter of Jerusalem : terrible as an army with banners.

CHAPTER. Ecclus. XXIV.

AND I took root in an honourable people, even in the portion of the Lord's inheritance.

Second Vespers.

Psalms as on Second Vespers of Christmas Day, p. 96, *said under First Antiphon of Lauds.*

Chapter as at First Vespers.

℞. Fair Virgin of Paradise, dear to the companions, garden enclosed, ever blossoming in perpetual spring : whom the whole world rightly praises. ℣. She was found worthy to bring forth her Lord. ℞. Whom the whole world rightly praises. ℣. Glory be to the Father, and to the Son : and to the Holy Ghost. ℞. Rightly praises.

HYMN. *Lætabundus,* p. 250.

℣. Thou art the holy Mother of God.
℞. O Mary, ever Virgin.

Ant. to Mag. The Virgin Mary is

exalted with joy: and dwells with Christ for evermore.

Collect as at First Vespers.
For observance of the Octave see rubric for Octave of the Visitation, p. 272.

August 20.
S. BERNARD, CONFESSOR AND ABBOT.*

All of the Common of an Abbot, p. 224, except the

COLLECT. *(Paris.)*

O GOD, Who didst cause blessed Bernard the Abbot, kindled with the fire of Thy love, to be a burning and a shining light in Thy Church; grant that, assisted by his prayers, we may burn with the spirit of love, and walk before Thee as children of light. Through.

August 21.
S. JANE FRANCES DE CHANTAL, MATRON.*

All of the Common of a Matron, p. 229, except the

COLLECT.

ALMIGHTY and merciful God, Who didst kindle in blessed Jane Frances the fire of Thy love, endowing her with marvellous fortitude in all the ways of life on the path of perfection, and didst will by her to enrich Thy Church with new offspring: vouchsafe to hear her prayers, that we, acknowledging our weakness, and leaning on the help of Thy heavenly grace, may overcome all adversities. Through.

August 22.
OCTAVE OF THE REPOSE OF THE BLESSED VIRGIN MARY.

All as on the Festival except that at First Vespers the Pss. are all said under the first Ant. and that at Second Vespers the ℟/℟. are not said.

August 24.
S. BARTHOLOMEW, APOSTLE AND MARTYR.

All of the Common of Apostles, p. 214, except the

COLLECT.

O ALMIGHTY and everlasting God, Who didst give to Thine Apostle Bartholomew grace truly to believe and to preach Thy Word; grant, we beseech Thee, unto Thy Church, to love that Word which he believed, and both to preach and receive the same. Through.

August 25.
S. LOUIS, KING AND CONFESSOR.*

All of the Common of a Confessor, p. 224, except the

COLLECT. *(S. Maur.)*

O GOD, Who amidst the deceits of an earthly kingdom didst fill blessed King Louis Thy servant with the spirit of truth and soberness; make us by his example, lovers of the heavenly city for which he yearned; so that, despising all transitory joys, we may hasten earnestly to those that only shall abide. Through.

On the same day:
S. HILDA, VIRGIN AND ABBESS.
Memorial of a Virgin, p. 237.

August 28.
S. AUGUSTINE OF HIPPO, BISHOP, CONFESSOR AND DOCTOR.*

All of the Common of a Bishop Confessor, p. 222, except the

COLLECT. *(Paris.)*

ALMIGHTY and merciful God, Who by Thy grace didst raise up blessed Augustine to be a witness and defender of the gospel in the Church: we beseech Thee shew forth in us the same grace; that by Thy teaching we may know Thy will, and by Thine operation we may also attain to perform the same with a free heart. Through.

August 29.
Beheading of S. John Baptist.

First Vespers.

Of the Common of a Martyr, p. 217, till

CHAPTER. Prov. x.

THE hope of the righteous shall be gladness: but the expectation of the wicked shall perish. The way of the Lord is strength to the upright: but destruction shall be to the workers of iniquity.

℟. The holy man, now about to receive rest for labour, constant in confession of the Christian faith : like a meek lamb bent his neck to the sword. ℣. Rejoicing to be dissolved and to be with Christ. ℟. Like a meek lamb he bent his neck to the sword. ℣. Glory be to the Father, and to the Son : and to the Holy Ghost. ℟. Like a meek lamb he bent his neck to the sword.

HYMN. *Martyr Dei qui Unicum.*

THOU followest, Martyr of thy God,
The path the Only Son hath trod,
Thy conquered foes thou treadest down,
And gloriest in a victor's crown.

Thy prayers for us may yet obtain
The cleansing of each sinful stain,
May aid sin's sickness in its flight,
And make life's weary load more light.

The cruel chains are now unwound
That once thy sacred body bound;
So may God's Son earth's fetters break
From us, for His own love's dear sake.

All praise to God the Father be;
All praise, eternal Son, to Thee;
All praise, as is for ever meet,
To God the Holy Paraclete. Amen.

℣. Thou hast crowned him, O Lord, with glory and worship.

℟. Thou makest him to have dominion of the works of Thy hands.

Ant. to Mag. Herod the king sent forth and laid hold on John, and bound him in prison : for he said unto him, It is not lawful for thee to have thy brother's wife.

COLLECT. *(Paris.)*

O GOD, Who didst vouchsafe to blessed John Baptist to be in birth and death the forerunner of Thy Son; grant that as he was slain for truth and righteousness' sake, so we may fight unto death for truth and righteousness. Through.

Lauds.

All of the Common of a Martyr, p. 218, except

Chapter as at First Vespers, and

Ant. to Ben. The king commanded an executioner to behead John in the prison : and when his disciples heard of it, they came and took up his corpse, and laid it in a tomb.

Collect as at First Vespers.

At Prime, Tierce, Sexts, Nones, all of the Common, except these Chapters.

Tierce.

Chapter as at First Vespers.

Sexts.

CHAPTER. Prov. x.

THE righteous shall never be removed; but the wicked shall not inhabit the earth.

Nones.

CHAPTER. Prov. xi.

THE righteous is delivered out of trouble, and the wicked cometh in his stead.

Second Vespers.

All of the Common, except

Chapter as at First Vespers, and

Ant. to Mag. The disciples of blessed John came : and took up his body, and buried it.

Collect as at First Vespers.

August 31.
S. Aydan, Bishop and Confessor.*

All of the Common of a Bishop and Confessor, p. 222, except the

Collect.

O GOD, Who hast exalted blessed Aydan Thy Confessor and Bishop to the glory of eternal blessedness; mercifully grant, we beseech Thee, that we Thy servants may obtain in heaven the blessings which he proclaimed by his life of unwearied warfare upon earth. Through.

FEASTS OF SEPTEMBER.

[*On the first day unhindered is said the Office of the Dead.*]

September 7.

S. Evurtius, Bishop and Confessor.*

All of the Common of a Bishop and Confessor, p. 222.

September 8.

The Nativity of the Blessed Virgin Mary.

First Vespers.

Psalms as at First Vespers of Christmas Day, p. 91.

Ant. 1. There shall come a Star out of Jacob : and a Sceptre shall rise out of Israel.

Ant. 2. The ark went upon the face of the waters : and the waters prevailed exceedingly upon the earth.

Ant. 3. The Lord Himself shall give you a sign : Behold, a Virgin shall conceive, and bear a Son.

Ant. 4. When she which travaileth hath brought forth : then the remnant of his brethren shall return unto the children of Israel.

Ant. 5. The same is the woman : whom the Lord hath pointed out for my Master's Son.

Chapter. Ecclus. xxiv.

AS the vine brought I forth pleasant savour, and my flowers are the fruit of honour and riches.

℟. The stem of Jesse hath brought forth a branch and the branch a Flower : and on that Flower the Holy Ghost doth rest. ℣. The Virgin Mother of God is the branch, the Flower is her Son. ℟. And upon that Flower the Holy Ghost doth rest. ℣. Glory be to the Father, and to the Son : and to the Holy Ghost. ℟. The Holy Ghost doth rest.

Hymn. *Ave, maris Stella*, p. 210.

℣. Holy Mother of God, ever Virgin Mary.

℟. Thou pleadest for us to the Lord our God.

Ant. to Mag. The work is great, for the palace is not for men : but for the Lord God.

Collect. *(Brev. Paris.)*

GOD, Who in Thy good pleasure didst will to reconcile the world unto Thyself; grant, we beseech Thee, that we who joyfully celebrate the Nativity of the Virgin Mary, Mother of our Saviour Christ, may, assisted by her prayers, attain the salvation wrought out for us by her Son. Who liveth.

Compline.

Ant. to Psalms. Blessed art thou, O Mother : spotless and glorious Virgin.

Ant. to Nunc Dim. as on the Purification, p. 248.

Lauds.

℣. The Lord shall come down like the rain into a fleece of wool.

℟. Even as the drops that water the earth.

Psalms of Sunday.

Ant. 1. Who is she that looketh forth as the morning : fair as the moon, clear as the sun?

Ant. 2. My dove, my undefiled is but one : she is the only one of her mother, she is the choice one of her that bare her.

Ant. 3. The daughters saw her and blessed her : yea, the queens, and they praised her.

Ant. 4. Arise, and come away, O my dove : let me see thy countenance.

THE NATIVITY OF THE BLESSED VIRGIN MARY.

Ant. 5. How fair and how pleasant art thou : O love, for delights.

Chapter as at First Vespers.

HYMN. *O gloriosa fœmina,* ℣. *and* ℟., p. 211.

Ant. to Ben. For behold, darkness shall cover the earth, and gross darkness the people : but the Lord shall arise upon thee.

Prime.

Ant. Who is she that looketh forth as the morning : fair as the moon, clear as the sun?

The ℟℟. *are said with this*

℣. Thou Who wast born of the Virgin Mary.

Tierce.

Ant. My dove, my undefiled is but one : she is the only one of her mother, she is the choice one of her that bare her.

Chapter as at First Vespers.

℟℟. at Tierce, Sexts, and Nones as on the Purification, p. 249.

Sexts.

Ant. The daughters saw her and blessed her : yea, the queens, and they praised her.

CHAPTER. Ecclus. xxiv. 19, 20.

COME unto me, all ye that be desirous of me, and fill yourselves with my fruit. For my memorial is sweeter than honey, and mine inheritance than the honey-comb.

Nones.

Ant. How fair and how pleasant art thou : O love, for delights.

CHAPTER. Ecclus. xxiv. 22.

HE that obeyeth me shall never be confounded; and they that work by me shall not do amiss.

Second Vespers.

Psalms as at Second Vespers of Christmas Day, p. 96, said under first Ant. of Lauds.

Chapter as at First Vespers.

℟. Mary, star of the sea, she who was to give birth to the Son of Righteousness, the Most High King : upon this day was born. ℣. In the heavenly light, rejoice ye faithful. ℟. She who was to give birth to the Son of Righteousness, the Most High King : upon this day was born. ℣. Glory be to the Father, and to the Son : and to the Holy Ghost. ℟. She who was to give birth to the Son of Righteousness, the Most High King : upon this day was born.

HYMN. *Lætabundus,* p. 250.

℣. God hath elected her and pre-elected her.

℟. And made her to dwell in His tabernacle.

Ant. to Mag. Out of thee shall He come forth unto Me that is to be Ruler in Israel : Whose goings forth have been from of old, from everlasting. And this Man shall be the peace.

September 14.

THE EXALTATION OF THE HOLY CROSS.

All, but the Collect, of the Invention of the Holy Cross, p. 258, except that Alleluia *is only said in the* ℟℟. *at Prime.*

COLLECT.

O GOD, Who hast vouchsafed to redeem the human race by the precious Blood of Thine Only-Begotten Son Jesus Christ; mercifully grant that all who venerate His life-giving Cross may be delivered from the bonds of their sins. Through the same.

September 16.

S. NINIAN, BISHOP AND CONFESSOR.*

All of the Common of a Bishop and Confessor, p. 222, except the

COLLECT.

O GOD, Who hast made this day honourable to us by the feast of

...sed Ninian, Thy Confessor and ..shop; mercifully grant, that they who have received the light of Thy truth from his teaching, may, assisted by his intercession, come to the joys of eternal life. Through.

September 17.
S. Lambert, Bishop and Confessor.*

All of the Common of a Bishop and Confessor, p. 222.

September 21.
S. Matthew, Apostle, Evangelist and Martyr.

First Vespers.

Ant. to Psalms. He pleased God, and was beloved of Him : for grace and mercy is to His Saints, and He hath a care for His elect.

Psalms of the Feria.
Chapter. Ezek. i.

AS for the likeness of their faces, they four had the face of a man, and the face of a lion, on the right side: and they four had the face of an ox on the left side; they four also had the face of an eagle.

℟. The living creatures ran and returned as the appearance of a flash of lightning : their appearance was like burning coals of fire; and out of the fire went forth lightning. ℣. It went up and down among the living creatures. ℟. Their appearance was like burning coals of fire; and out of the fire went forth lightning. ℣. Glory be to the Father, and to the Son and to the Holy Ghost. ℟. And out of the fire went forth lightning.

Hymn. *Annue Christe,* ℣. *and* ℟. *of the Common of Apostles and Evangelists,* p. 215.

Ant. to Mag. I John looked, and behold a door was opened in heaven; and behold a throne was set in heaven, and One sat on the throne : and in the midst of the throne, and round about the throne were four living creatures full of eyes before and behind, giving glory and honour and thanks to Him that sat on the throne, Who liveth for ever and ever.

Collect.

O ALMIGHTY God, Who by Thy blessed Son didst call Matthew from the receipt of custom to be an Apostle and Evangelist; grant us grace to forsake all covetous desires, and inordinate love of riches, and to follow the Same. Who liveth.

Lauds.

℣. Thou hast given an heritage.
℟. Unto those that fear Thy Name, O Lord.

Psalms of Sunday.

Ant. 1. Beloved of God and men are the holy Evangelists : who adorned the times of Christ with good odour to the end of their lives.

Ant. 2. The Saints shewed the glory of their works in the congregation : therefore their memory is blessed for ever.

Ant. 3. Out of all men these praised the holy Name of the Lord : that they might magnify the name of His holiness.

Ant. 4. The Lord filled them with the spirit of wisdom and understanding : joy and exultation He laid in store for them.

Ant. 5. Their work was wrought in truth; therefore in their land they shall have double : and everlasting joy shall be theirs in Christ.

Chapter as at First Vespers.

Hymn. *Exultet cœlum laudibus,* ℣. *and* ℟., *as in the Common,* p. 215.

Ant. to Ben. In the midst of the throne, and round about the throne, were four living creatures, having each of them six wings, and full of eyes within : and they rest not day and night, saying, Holy, holy, holy, Lord God Almighty, which was, and is, and is to come.

In Embertide the Feria is commemorated at Lauds.

Prime.

Ant. Beloved of God and men are the holy Evangelists : who adorned the times of Christ with good odour to the end of their lives.

Tierce.

Ant. The Saints shewed the glory of their works in the congregation : therefore their memory is blessed for ever.

Chapter as at First Vespers.

The R̅/R̅/. *at Tierce, Sexts, and Nones of the Common,* p. 216.

Sexts.

Ant. Out of all men these praised the holy Name of the Lord : that they might magnify the name of His holiness.

CHAPTER. Ezek. I.

AS for the likeness of the living creatures, their appearance was like burning coals of fire, and like the appearance of lamps.

Nones.

Ant. Their work was wrought in truth ; therefore in their land they shall have double : and everlasting joy shall be theirs in Christ.

CHAPTER. Ezek. I.

IT went up and down among the living creatures ; and the fire was bright, and out of the fire went forth lightning. And the living creatures ran and returned as the appearance of a flash of lightning.

Second Vespers.

Antiphons and Psalms of the Common, p. 216.

Chapter as at First Vespers.

R̅/. When the living creatures went, the wheels went by them : whithersoever the Spirit was to go, they went : and the wheels were lifted up over against them. V̅. When those were lifted up from the earth, the wheels were lifted up over against them. R̅/. Whithersoever the Spirit was to go, they went : and the wheels were lifted up over against them. V̅. Glory be to the Father, and to the Son : and to the Holy Ghost. R̅/. And the wheels were lifted up over against them.

HYMN. *Exultet cœlum,*
V̅. *and* R̅/. *of the Common,* p. 215.

Ant. to Mag. The holy Evangelists sought out the wisdom of the elders : and by their words confirmed the sayings of the prophets.

September 22.

S. MAURICE AND HIS COMPANIONS, MARTYRS.*

All of the Common of Many Martyrs, p. 219, *except the*

COLLECT. *(Paris.)*

O GOD, Who art the strength of them that fight for Thee, and the crown of them that conquer through Thee : grant, we beseech Thee, that we who proclaim Thy power in the sufferings of the blessed martyrs, Maurice and his companions, may by the same power be strengthened in steadfastness of faith against the enemies of our salvation. Through.

On the same day :

S. THOMAS OF VILLANOVA, BISHOP AND CONFESSOR.

Memorial of a Bishop and Confessor, p. 236.

COLLECT. *(Roman.)*

O GOD, Who didst bestow on the blessed Bishop Thomas the grace of wonderful pity for the poor : vouchsafe, we beseech Thee, while he pleads for us, to pour the riches of Thy mercy upon those who pray to Thee. Through.

September 23.

S. ADAMNAN, CONFESSOR AND ABBOT.*

All of the Common of an Abbot, p. 224.

September 26.

S. Cyprian, Bishop and Martyr.*

All of the Common of a Martyr, p. 217, except the

COLLECT. *(Paris.)*

GRANT, we beseech Thee, O Lord, that the holy prayers of blessed Cyprian may commend us unto Thee; for he shone resplendent both in the vigour of his priesthood, and in the triumph of his glorious passion. Through.

September 27.

SS. Cosmas and Damian, Martyrs.*

All of the Common of Many Martyrs, p. 219.

September 29.

S. Michael and all Angels.

First Vespers.

Ant. to Psalms. The heavenly host adore the Son of the great King: Cherubin and Seraphin proclaim Him holy.

Psalms of the Feria.

CHAPTER. Rev. i.

GOD signified things which must shortly come to pass; by His Angel unto His servant John: who bare record of the word of God, and of the testimony of Jesus Christ, and of all things that he saw.

℟. Thee, Holy Lord, all Angels praise in the highest, saying: Thou art worthy, O Lord, to receive: glory and honour. ℣. Cherubin also and Seraphin proclaim Thee holy, with all the ranks of heaven, saying. ℟. Thou art worthy, O Lord, to receive glory and honour. ℣. Glory be to the Father, and to the Son: and to the Holy Ghost. ℣. Glory and honour.

HYMN. *Tibi Christe Splendor Patris.*

THEE, O Christ, the Father's Splendour,
  Life and virtue of the heart,
In the presence of the Angels
  Sing we now with tuneful art:
Meetly in alternate chorus
  Bearing our responsive part.

Thus we praise with veneration
  All the armies of the sky;
Chiefly him, the warrior Primate
  Of celestial chivalry:
Michael, who in princely virtue
  Cast Abaddon from on high.

By whose watchful care, repelling,
  King of Everlasting grace!
Every ghostly adversary,
  All things evil, all things base;
Grant us of Thine only goodness
  In Thy paradise a place.

Laud and honour to the Father;
  Laud and honour to the Son;
Laud and honour to the Spirit;
  Ever Three and ever One:
Consubstantial, Co-eternal,
  While unending ages run. Amen.

℣. In the presence of the Angels will I sing praise unto Thee.

℟. I will worship toward Thy holy temple, and praise Thy Name, O Lord.

Ant. to Mag. When John discerned the sacred mystery, Michael the Archangel sounded his trumpet: pardon us, O Lord our God, that openest the book, and breakest the seals thereof. Alleluia.

COLLECT.

O EVERLASTING God, Who hast ordained and constituted the services of Angels and men in a wonderful order; mercifully grant, that as Thy holy Angels alway do Thee service in heaven, so by Thy appointment they may succour and defend us on earth. Through.

Lauds.

℣. The smoke of the incense ascended up.

℟. Before God out of the Angel's hand.

Psalms of Sunday.

Ant. 1. When Michael the Archangel had fought with the dragon, I heard a voice, saying: Salvation unto our God. Alleluia.

Ant. 2. When the dragon had joined battle with Michael the Archangel: there was heard a voice of thousands of thousands, saying, Salvation unto our God.

Ant. 3. The accuser of our brethren is cast down, and they overcame him: therefore rejoice, ye heavens, and ye that dwell in them.

Ant. 4. O ye Angels of the Lord : bless ye the Lord for ever.

Ant. 5. Angels, archangels, thrones, and dominions, principalities and powers, virtues of heaven : praise the Lord of heaven. Alleluia.

Chapter as at First Vespers.

HYMN.
Christe sanctorum decus Angelorum.

CHRIST, of the holy Angels light and gladness,
Maker and Saviour of the human race,
O may we reach the world unknown to sadness,
  And see Thy face.

Angel of peace, may Michael to our dwelling
Down from high heaven in mighty calmness come,
Breathing all peace, and hideous war dispelling
  To hell's dark gloom.

Angel of might, may Gabriel swift descending
Far from our gates our ancient foes repel,
And, as of old o'er Zacharias bending,
  In temples dwell.

Angel of health, may Raphael lighten o'er us,
To every sick bed speed his healing flight,
In deeds of doubt direct the way before us,
  Guide us aright.

Mary, the harbinger of peace supernal,
Mother of God, with all the Angel train,
All Saints be with us, till the bliss eternal
  In Christ we gain.

Be this by Thy thrice holy Godhead granted,
Father and Son, and Spirit ever blest;
Whose glory by the Angel host is chanted,
  By all confest. Amen.

℣. Praise the Lord, all ye Angels of His.

℟. Praise Him, all His host. Alleluia.

Ant. to Ben. There was silence in heaven when the dragon joined battle : and Michael fought with him, and won the victory. Alleluia.

Prime.

Ant. When Michael the Archangel had fought with the dragon, I heard a voice, saying : Salvation unto our God. Alleluia.

℟℟. *with* Alleluia.

Tierce.

Ant. When the dragon had joined battle with Michael the Archangel : there was heard a voice of thousands of thousands, saying, Salvation unto our God.

Chapter as at First Vespers.

℟. An Angel stood at the altar : Alleluia, Alleluia. ℣. Having a golden censer in his hand. ℟. Alleluia, Alleluia. ℣. Glory be the Father, and to the Son : and to the Holy Ghost. ℟. An Angel stood at the Altar : Alleluia, Alleluia.

℣. The smoke of the incense ascended up.

℟. Before God out of the Angel's hand.

Sexts.

Ant. The accuser of our brethren is cast down, and they overcame him : therefore rejoice, ye heavens, and ye that dwell in them.

CHAPTER. Rev. XII.

AND there was war in heaven: Michael and his Angels fought against the dragon; and the dragon fought and his angels, and prevailed not; neither was their place found any more in heaven.

℟. The smoke of the incense ascended up : Alleluia. Alleluia. ℣. Before God out of the Angel's hand. ℟. Alleluia. Alleluia. ℣. Glory be to the Father, and to the Son : and to the Holy Ghost. ℟. The smoke of the incense ascended up : Alleluia. Alleluia.

℣. In the presence of the Angels will I sing praise unto Thee.

℟. I will worship toward Thy holy temple, and praise Thy Name, O Lord.

Nones.

Ant. Angels, archangels, thrones and dominions, principalities and powers, virtues of heaven : praise the Lord of heaven. Alleluia.

CHAPTER. Rev. VIII.

THERE was silence in heaven about the space of half an hour. And I saw the seven angels which stood before God; and to them were given seven trumpets.

℟. In the presence of the Angels will

I sing praise unto Thee : Alleluia. Alleluia. ℣. I will worship toward Thy holy temple, and praise Thy Name, O Lord. ℟. Alleluia. Alleluia. ℣. Glory be to the Father, and to the Son : and to the Holy Ghost. ℟. In the presence of the Angels will I sing praise unto Thee : Alleluia. Alleluia.
℣. Praise the Lord, all ye Angels of His.
℟. Praise Him, all His host. Alleluia.

Second Vespers.

Psalms of the Feria said under first Ant. of Lauds.

Hymn. *Christe Sanctorum,*
℣. *and* ℟., *as at Lauds.*

The rest as at First Vespers, except the

Ant. to Mag. Michael, Gabriel, Cherubin and Seraphin, continually do cry : Thou art worthy, O Lord, to receive glory. Alleluia.

September 30.

S. Jerome, Priest, Confessor and Doctor.*

All of the Common of a Confessor, p. 222, except the

Collect.

O GOD, Who through blessed Jerome Thy Priest and Confessor hast vouchsafed to make known to us the truth of Holy Scripture, and its hidden meanings; grant, we beseech Thee, that we who keep his festival may receive teaching from his doctrine, and help from his prayers. Through.

FEASTS OF OCTOBER.

[*On the first day unhindered is said the Office of the Dead.*]

October 1.

S. Remigius, Bishop and Confessor.*

All of the Common of a Bishop and Confessor, p. 222.

October 2.

The Holy Guardian Angels.

First Vespers.

Psalms of the Feria.

Ant. 1. Behold, I send an Angel before thee : to keep thee in the way, and to bring thee into the place which I have prepared.
Ant. 2. If thou shalt indeed obey his voice, and do all that I speak : then I will be an enemy unto thine enemies. For Mine Angel shall go before thee.
Ant. 3. I will bring you away peaceably, saith the Lord : for Mine Angel is with you, and I myself caring for your souls.
Ant. 4. He had power over the Angel and prevailed : he found him in Bethel.
Ant. 5. The Lord heard our voice, and sent an Angel : and brought us forth out of Egypt.

Chapter. Is. lxiii.

IN all their affliction He was afflicted, and the Angel of His presence saved them : in His love and in His pity He redeemed them; and He bare them, and carried them all the days of old.
℟. There shall no evil happen unto thee; for He shall give His Angels charge over thee to keep thee in all thy ways : they shall bear thee in their hands, that thou hurt not thy foot against a stone. ℣. The Angel said unto me, I am thy fellow-servant, and of thy brethren the prophets; worship God. ℟. They shall bear thee in their hands, that thou hurt not thy foot against a stone. ℣. Glory be to the Father, and to the Son : and to the Holy Ghost. ℟. There shall no evil happen unto thee; for He shall give His Angels charge over thee to keep thee in all thy ways : they shall bear thee in their hands, that thou hurt not thy foot against a stone.

Hymn.

Custodes hominum psaltimus Angelos.

WATCHFUL guardians of men,
  Sing we the Angel host,
Whom God sends from His throne,
  Aids to be unto us,

When our foes lie in wait,
  Crafty and rancorous,
  Seeking whom they may spoliate.
That fierce Angel of pride
  Roameth about the fold ;
  Lost for him is the joy—
  Joy of his heritage.
Now he burns to ensnare
  Souls of the chosen ones,
  Whom God calls to His Paradise.

Guardian, come to our help,
  Keep and watch over us;
Thou hast charge to avert
  Ills of the weary soul.
Come, then, drive from our heart ·
  All that disquiets us,
All that mars our tranquillity.

Now be glory and praise
  Unto the Trinity,
By Whom all things are ruled,
  Earthly and heavenly ;
Whose great honour and might
  Through all eternity
Now and ever be glorified. Amen.

℣. The Angel of the Lord tarrieth round about them that fear Him.

℟. And delivereth them.

Ant. to Mag. O Lord of heaven, send a good Angel before us : and through the might of Thine arm let those be stricken with terror that come against Thy holy people to blaspheme.

COLLECT.

O GOD, Who by an ineffable Providence hast vouchsafed to send Thy holy Angels to guard us; grant to Thy suppliants, that we may be defended by their protection in this life, and in the next, be gladdened by their companionship. Through.

Lauds.

℣. O praise the Lord, ye Angels of His.

℟. Ye that excel in strength, and hearken unto the voice of His words.

Psalms of Sunday.

Ant. 1. God, Which dwelleth in heaven, prosper your journey : and the Angel of God keep you company.

Ant. 2. The Lord, before Whom I walk, will send His Angel with thee : and prosper thy way.

Ant. 3. Blessed be God that hath sent His Angel : and delivered His servants that trusted in Him.

Ant. 4. The Angel of the Lord answered and said, O Lord of hosts : how long wilt Thou not have mercy on Jerusalem and on the cities of Judah, against which Thou hast had indignation ?

Ant. 5. I have set watchmen upon thy walls, O Jerusalem : which shall never hold their peace day nor night.

CHAPTER. 2 Kings VI.

AND when the servant of the man of God was risen early and gone forth, behold, an host compassed the city both with horses and chariots. And his servant said unto him, Alas, my master! how shall we do ? And he answered, Fear not : for they that be with us are more than they that be with them.

HYMN. *Eterne Rector siderum.*

ETERNAL Ruler of the sky,
  Whose might hath made and governs all ;
Beneath Thy care and loving eye,
  All things Thou hast created fall.

Hear Thou the cry of sinful man,
  As spread the gloomy shades of night ;
Our souls enlighten Thou anew
  Who gav'st the word, "Let there be light."

Send Thou the Angel Thou didst set
  To be our guardian and our friend ;
May He from taint of sin and death
  Our soul and all its powers defend.

The wily serpent's envious craft
  May his angelic might destroy,
Lest Satan's net and snares unseen,
  Our heedless souls with guile annoy.

Far from our land may he repel
  Alarm of war and bloody fray,
Give tranquil peace to Christian homes,
  Drive plague and pestilence away.

Glory to God the Father be,
  Whose mercy sends the Angel host
To guard the souls by Christ set free,
  And hallowed by the Holy Ghost. Amen.

℣. He bowed the heavens also, and came down.

℟. He rode upon the Cherubim.

Ant. to Ben. Their Angels do alway behold the face of My Father : Which is in heaven.

Prime.

Ant. God, Which dwelleth in heaven,

prosper your journey : and the Angel of God keep you company.

Tierce.

Ant. The Lord, before Whom I walk, will send His Angel with thee : and prosper thy way.

Chapter as at Lauds.

R₇. Rise up, O Lord : and let Thine enemies be scattered. V̄. And let them that hate Thee flee before Thee. R₇. And let Thine enemies be scattered. V̄. Glory be to the Father, and to the Son : and to the Holy Ghost. R₇. Rise up, O Lord : and let Thine enemies be scattered.

V̄. Let their way be dark and slippery.

R₇. And let the Angel of the Lord persecute them.

Sexts.

Ant. Blessed be God that hath sent His Angel : and delivered His servants that trusted in Him.

CHAPTER. Zech. IX.

I WILL encamp about Mine house because of the army, because of him that passeth by, and because of him that returneth : and no oppressor shall pass through them any more : for now have I seen with Mine eyes.

R₇. Let their way be : dark and slippery. V̄. And let the Angel of the Lord persecute them. R₇. Dark and slippery. V̄. Glory be to the Father, and to the Son : and to the Holy Ghost. R₇. Let their way be : dark and slippery.

V̄. O Lord my God, Thou art become exceeding glorious.

R₇. He maketh His Angels spirits, and His ministers a flaming fire.

Nones.

Ant. I have set watchmen upon thy walls, O Jerusalem : which shall never hold their peace day nor night.

CHAPTER. Eccles. v.

SUFFER not thy mouth to cause thy flesh to sin ; neither say thou before the Angel that it was an error : wherefore should God be angry at thy voice, and destroy the work of thine hands?

R₇. O Lord my God : Thou art become exceeding glorious. V̄. He maketh His Angels spirits, and His ministers a flaming fire. R₇. Thou art become exceeding glorious. V̄. Glory be to the Father, and to the Son : and to the Holy Ghost. R₇. O Lord my God : Thou art become exceeding glorious.

V̄. The chariots of God are twenty thousand, even thousands of Angels.

R₇. And the Lord is among them.

Second Vespers.

Psalms of the Feria.

Ant. 1. Take heed that ye despise not one of these little ones, for I say unto you : That in heaven their Angels do alway behold the face of my Father Which is in heaven.

Ant. 2. I say unto you, There is joy in the presence of the Angels of God : over one sinner that repenteth.

Ant. 3. And He shall send His Angels : and they shall gather together His elect.

Ant. 4. Are they not all ministering spirits : sent forth to minister for them who shall be heirs of salvation?

Ant. 5. They fell down before the Lamb, having every one of them harps : and golden vials full of odours, which are the prayers of Saints.

CHAPTER. Gen. XXXII.

AND Jacob went on his way, and the Angels of God met him. And when Jacob saw them, he said, This is God's host.

Hymn, V̄. and R₇., as at Lauds.

Ant. to Mag. One of the Angels shewed me the great city, heavenly Jerusalem : and it had twelve gates, and at the gates twelve Angels.

On the same day :

S. THOMAS OF HEREFORD, BISHOP AND CONFESSOR.

Memorial of a Bishop and Confessor, p. 236.

October 4.
S. Francis of Assisi.

All of the Common of a Confessor not a Bishop, p. 224, *except the*

Collect. *(Paris.)*

O GOD Who hast not disdained to reveal Thyself to the childlike and lowly of heart: grant, we beseech Thee, that after the example of blessed Francis we may learn to count the wisdom of this world as foolishness, and only to know Jesus Christ crucified. Who liveth.

October 6.
S. Faith, Virgin and Martyr.*

All of the Common of a Virgin and Martyr, p. 226.

October 7.
S. Bruno, Confessor and Abbot.*

All of the Common of an Abbot, p. 224, *except the*

Collect. *(S. Maur.)*

ALMIGHTY and everlasting God, Who for them that forsake the world hast prepared mansions in heaven: we humbly entreat Thy boundless mercy that, blessed Bruno interceding, we may faithfully fulfil our vows, and attain in peace to the promises Thou hast bestowed on them that persevere to the end. Through.

October 9.
S. Denys and his Companions, Martyrs.*

All of the Common of Many Martyrs, p. 219, *except the*

Collect. *(Aberdeen.)*

O GOD, Who on this day didst strengthen blessed Denys with the grace of constancy in suffering, and Who didst cause Rusticus and Eleutherius to be joined with him in setting forth Thy glory to the Gentiles: grant, we beseech Thee, that after their example we may despise the pleasures of this world, and fear none of its adversities. Through.

October 10.
S. Paulinus of York, Bishop and Confessor.*

All of the Common of a Bishop and Confessor, p. 222.

October 12.
S. Wilfrid, Bishop and Confessor.*

All of the Common of a Bishop and Confessor, p. 222.

October 13.
Translation of S. Edward, King and Confessor.*

All of the Common of a Confessor not a Bishop, p. 224.

October 15.
S. Theresa, Virgin.*

All of the Common of a Virgin not a Martyr, p. 228, *except at*

Vespers.

℣. *and* ℟. *after Hymn.*

℣. Forget also thine own people and thy Father's house.
℟. So shall the King have pleasure in thy beauty.

Ant. to Mag. The people shall tell of her wisdom: and the Church shall shew forth her praise.

Lauds.

℣. *and* ℟. *after Hymn.*

℣. The Lord shall help her.
℟. And that right early.

Ant. to Ben. The Lord gave her wisdom, and prudence exceeding great: and largeness of heart, like as the sand which is on the sea shore.

Collect. *(Roman.)*

O GOD, Who by the teaching and example of blessed Theresa, hast raised up to Thyself servants and handmaidens, to fill them with Thy spirit : grant that we, aided by her prayers, and following in her steps, may receive the food of heavenly doctrine, and glow with the desire of true perfection. Through.

October 17.

Translation of S. Etheldred, Virgin, Queen and Abbess.

All of the Common of a Virgin not a Martyr, p. 228.

October 18.

S. Luke, Evangelist.

All as on the Festival of S. Matthew, p. 292, except the

Collect.

ALMIGHTY God, Who calledst Luke the Physician, whose praise is in the Gospel, to be an Evangelist, and Physician of the soul; may it please Thee, that, by the wholesome medicines of the doctrine delivered by him, all the diseases of our souls may be healed. Through the merits.

October 19.

S. Peter of Alcantara, Priest and Confessor.*

All of the Common of a Confessor not a Bishop, p. 224, except the

Collect. *(Roman.)*

O GOD, Who didst bestow on blessed Peter Thy Confessor, the gift of marvellous penitence and high contemplation : grant, we beseech Thee, that by the mortification of our flesh we may the more readily attain to heavenly joys. Through.

On the same day :

S. Frideswide, Virgin.

Memorial of a Virgin not a Martyr, p. 237.

October 21.

S. Hilarion, Abbot.*

All of the Common of an Abbot, p. 224, except the

Collect. *(S. Maur.)*

O GOD, the Author and Rewarder of all good works, Who, in blessed Hilarion, hast given us a pattern of humility and penitence; grant that we may be counted worthy to tread the narrow way he trod before us, and to attain the heavenly kingdom. Through.

October 23.

S. Justin and his Companions, Martyrs.*

All of the Common of Many Martyrs, p. 219.

October 25.

SS. Crispin and Crispinian, Martyrs.*

All of the Common of Many Martyrs, p. 219.

October 28.

SS. Simon and Jude, Apostles and Martyrs.

All as in the Common of Apostles, p. 214, except that at First Vespers, Lauds, Tierce, and Second Vespers, is said the following :

Chapter. Rom. viii.

WE know that all things work together for good to them that love God, to them who are the called according to His purpose.

Collect.

O ALMIGHTY God, Who hast built Thy Church upon the foundation of the Apostles and Prophets, Jesus Christ Himself being the head corner-stone; grant us so to be joined together in unity of spirit by their doctrine, that we may be made an holy temple acceptable unto Thee. Through.

October 31.
S. BEGHA, VIRGIN.*
All of the Common of a Virgin not a Martyr, p. 228.

FEASTS OF NOVEMBER.

[*On the first day unhindered is said the Office of the Dead.*]

November 1.
ALL SAINTS.
First Vespers.
Psalms as at First Vespers of Christmas Day, p. 91.

Ant. 1. May all Saints of God in the company of the heavenly citizens : plead for us.

Ant. 2. O how glorious is the kingdom where all the Saints rejoice with Christ : they are clothed in white robes, and follow the Lamb whithersoever He goeth.

Ant. 3. The righteous shall shine, and run to and fro like sparks among the stubble : they shall judge the nations, and have dominion over the people.

Ant. 4. A holy and very and marvellous light, shedding brightness on those who endured in the strife of the battle, they shall receive from Christ : everlasting splendour wherein they shall be glad and rejoice.

Ant. 5. All the elect of God remember us before God : that, aided by their prayers, we may be united to them.

CHAPTER. Rev. VII.

AND I saw another Angel ascending from the east, having the seal of the living God : and he cried with a loud voice to the four Angels, to whom it was given to hurt the earth and the sea, saying, Hurt not the earth, neither the sea, nor the trees, till we have sealed the servants of our God in their foreheads.

℟. Praise our God, all ye His Saints, and ye that fear Him, both small and great : for the Lord God Omnipotent reigneth : let us be glad and rejoice, and give glory to Him. ℣. Chosen generation, royal priesthood, peculiar people, shew forth the praises of God. ℟. For the Lord God Omnipotent reigneth : let us be glad and rejoice, and give glory to Him. ℣. Glory be to the Father, and to the Son : and to the Holy Ghost. ℟. Let us be glad, and rejoice, and give glory to Him.

HYMN. *Jesu Salvator seculi.*

O JESU, Saviour of the earth,
  Help Thy redeemed ones in their need,
And let the Maid who gave Thee birth
For hapless sinners ever plead.

Let Angel armies kneel to Thee,
And Patriarchs in shining train,
And Seers in goodly company,
That we may full remission gain.

The Baptist, herald of Thy face,
The bearer of the mystic keys,
With all Apostles, ask Thy grace
To grant us prisoners release.

The Martyr-choir in heavenly seat,
The Priests who made confession bold,
The stainless Virgin ranks, intreat
That we be loosed from evil's hold.

The prayers of all Thy ministry,
Of all the dwellers in the skies,
Join with the vows we make to Thee,
To win us life's eternal prize.

All laud to God the Father be,
All laud, eternal Son, to Thee,
All laud for ever, as is meet,
To God the Holy Paraclete. Amen.

℣. Be glad, O ye righteous, and rejoice in the Lord.

℟. And be joyful, all ye that are true of heart.

Ant. to Mag. Blessed are ye, all ye Saints of God : who have been counted worthy to become coheirs with heavenly powers, and enjoy the brightness of glory.

Collect as at Lauds.

[*Or, at this Office only,*
(Sarum.)

O LORD our God, multiply Thy grace upon us; and, as we hasten to keep the festival of all Thy Saints, grant us to attain those joys whereunto their holy lives have led them. Through.]

No Memorial is said on this day at First Vespers, Lauds, or Second Vespers, unless it falls on Sunday, in which case Memorial is made of Sunday. If it falls on Saturday, Memorial is made of Sunday and of the Holy Trinity at Second Vespers.

Compline.

Ant. to Psalms. Hearkening to the prayers of all Saints, O Christ : restore health of body and soul to Thy servants.

The rest as in the Psalter, p. 67.

Lauds.

℣. The righteous live for evermore.
℟. But their reward is with the Lord.

Psalms of Sunday.

Ant. 1. I beheld, and lo, a great multitude, which no man could number : of all nations, and kindreds, and people, and tongues, stood before the throne.

Ant. 2. And all the Angels stood round about the throne : and fell before the throne on their faces, and worshipped God.

Ant. 3. Thou hast redeemed us to God by Thy blood out of every kindred, and tongue, and people, and nation : and hast made us unto our God kings.

Ant. 4. Bless the Lord, all ye His Angels : make the day joyful and give thanks unto Him.

Ant. 5. All His Saints shall praise Him, even the children of Israel, even the people that serveth Him : such honour have all His Saints.

Chapter as at First Vespers.

HYMN. *Christe redemptor omnium.*

O CHRIST, Redeemer of mankind,
Thy servants here protect and spare,
Who hearest, with a loving mind,
The blessed Virgin's holy prayer.

May those glad hosts which see Thy face,
The spirits of the heavenly home,
Away from us all evils chase,
Both past, and present, and to come.

The Prophets of the Judge most high,
The twelve Apostles of the Lord,
For us, with interceding cry,
Pray that Thou keep us in Thy ward.

God's Martyrs, who have won renown,
His Confessors, in bright array,
Ask that we too may win the crown
Which shines in everlasting day.

The choir of Virgins lily-white,
Thy Priests, and all Thy ministry,
With every Saint in prayer unite,
Till we be joined, O Christ, to Thee.

Then purge away all unbelief
From every land where Christians dwell,
That unto Thee, our Victor Chief,
All thanks and praises we may tell.

All laud to God the Father be,
All laud, eternal Son, to Thee,
All laud for ever, as is meet,
To God the Holy Paraclete. Amen.

℣. Wonderful art Thou in Thy Saints, O God.
℟. And glorious in Thy majesty.

Ant. to Ben. Thee, the glorious company of the Apostles; Thee, the goodly fellowship of the Prophets; Thee, the white-robed army of Martyrs : Thee all the elect with one voice acknowledge, O Blessed Trinity, One God.

COLLECT.

O ALMIGHTY God, Who hast knit together Thine elect in one communion and fellowship, in the mystical body of Thy Son Christ our Lord; grant us grace so to follow Thy blessed Saints in all virtuous and godly living, that we may come to those unspeakable joys, which Thou hast prepared for them that unfeignedly love Thee. Through.

Prime.

Ant. I beheld, and lo, a great multitude, which no man could number : of all nations, and kindreds, and people, and tongues, stood before the throne.

Tierce.

Ant. And all the Angels stood round about the throne : and fell before the throne on their faces, and worshipped God.

Chapter as at First Vespers.

℟℟. *at Tierce, Sexts, and Nones, as of the Common of Many Martyrs*, p. 221.

Sexts.

Ant. Thou hast redeemed us to God by Thy blood out of every kindred, and tongue, and people, and nation : and hast made us unto our God kings.

CHAPTER. Rev. vii.

I HEARD the number of them which were sealed; and there were sealed an hundred and forty and four thousand of all the tribes of the children of Israel.

Nones.

Ant. All His Saints shall praise Him, even the children of Israel, even the people that serveth Him : such honour have all His Saints.

CHAPTER. Rev. vii.

I BEHELD, and lo, a great multitude which no man could number, of all nations, and kindreds, and people, and tongues, stood before the throne, and before the Lamb, clothed with white robes, and palms in their hands.

Second Vespers.

Psalms as follow to be said under first Ant. of Lauds.

Psalm cxi. *Confitebor tibi,* p. 47.
Psalm cxvi. 10. *Credidi,* p. 52.
Psalm cxxvi. *In convertendo,* p. 55.
Psalm cxl. *Eripe me,* p. 62.
Psalm cxlvii. 12. *Lauda Hierusalem,* p. 65.

Chapter as at First Vespers.

℟. The righteous live for evermore : their reward also is with the Lord : and the care of them is with the most High. ℣. Therefore shall they receive a glorious kingdom, and a beautiful crown from the Lord's hand. ℟. Their reward also is with the Lord, and the care of them is with the most High. ℣. Glory, praise, honour, majesty, might, and jubilation be to the Father, and to the Only Begotten One, and to the Holy Ghost. ℟. The care of them is with the most High.

HYMN. *Christe redemptor omnium,*
℣. *and* ℟., *as at Lauds.*

Ant. to Mag. O Saviour of the world, save us all, and let Thy holy Virgin-mother pray for us, with the holy Apostles, Martyrs, Confessors, and Virgins : that being delivered from all evil, we may be counted worthy now and ever to be filled with good things.

The Vespers of All Saints being ended, forthwith are begun Festival Vespers of the Dead. See Occasional Offices.

Compline.

As on the previous day.

(*In the Sarum use, this feast has no Octave. If kept, see rubric for Octave of Visitation,* p. 272).

November 2.

COMMEMORATION OF ALL SOULS.

Lauds.

On this day is said before Lauds,

℣. May they rest in peace.
℟. Amen.

At Prime, and the other hours, is not to be said, O God, make speed to save us, *nor any Hymn, but the Antiphon is begun immediately after the usual introductory Prayers which are always said in silence. (In the Roman use the office of the Octave is resumed at Prime.)*

Prime.

Ant. Eternal rest grant unto them, O Lord : and light perpetual shine upon them.

Psalm liv. *Deus in nomine.*
Psalm cxix. *Beati immaculati,* and *Retribue servo tuo.*

The Psalms end without Gloria, *and the Antiphon is repeated. Then follows :*

Lord, have mercy.
Christ, have mercy.
Lord, have mercy.

Our Father.

℣. And lead us not into temptation. ℟. But deliver us from evil. ℣. Eternal rest grant unto them, O Lord. ℟. And light perpetual shine upon them. ℣. From the gates of hell. ℟. Deliver their souls, O Lord. ℣. I believe verily to see the goodness of the Lord. ℟. In the land of the living. ℣. The Lord be with you. ℟. And with thy spirit.

Let us pray.

Collect.

O GOD, the Creator and Redeemer of all the faithful, grant to the souls of Thy servants and handmaidens remission of all their sins; that the pardon they have always desired, by pious supplications may be obtained; Who livest and reignest with God the Father, in the unity of the Holy Spirit, God, throughout all ages. Amen.

After the Collect is not said, The Lord be with you.

℣. May they rest in peace.

℟. Amen.

Thus are said Prime, Tierce, Sexts, and Nones, on this day. After Prime, the Martyrology is read as usual, followed by Right dear, &c., *the Blessing,* ℣. The Lord be with you. ℟. And with thy spirit. ℣. Bless we the Lord. ℟. Thanks be to God. *(Vespers are of the Octave.) If the day falls on Sunday, the commemoration of All Souls is deferred till the morrow.*

November 3.

S. Winifred, Virgin and Martyr.*

All of the Common of a Virgin and Martyr, p. 226, *except the*

Collect. *(Paris.)*

ALMIGHTY and everlasting God, Who hast adorned blessed Winifred with the reward of virginity; grant, we pray Thee, that we, assisted by her intercession, may despise the allurements of this world, and with her attain a throne of everlasting glory. Through.

November 4.

S. Charles Borromeo, Bishop and Confessor.*

All of the Common of a Bishop and Confessor, p. 222, *except the*

Collect. *(S. Maur.)*

MULTIPLY, we beseech Thee, O Lord, on Thy Church, the grace wherewith Thou didst inspire blessed Charles, Thy Bishop: that Thy flock throughout the world may draw nigh unto Thee, and that the shepherds ruling in Thy Name may find grace in Thy sight. Through.

November 6.

S. Leonard, Abbot.*

All of the Common of an Abbot, p. 224.

(November 8.

Octave of All Saints.)

November 11.

S. Martin, Bishop and Confessor.*

All of the Common of a Bishop and Confessor, p. 222, *except at*

Vespers.

Ant. to Mag. Lord, if I am yet needful to Thy people, I refuse not to labour: Thy will be done.

Lauds.

Ant. to Ben. Let my soul be fixed on the Lord, that the enemy may find nothing in me: but that Abraham's bosom may receive me.

November 13.

S. Britius, Bishop and Confessor.*

All of the Common of a Bishop and Confessor, p. 222.

November 14.

S. Dubritius, Bishop and Confessor.*

All of the Common of a Bishop and Confessor, p. 222.

November 15.

S. Machutus, Bishop and Confessor.*

All of the Common of a Bishop and Confessor, p. 222.

November 16.
S. Edmund, Bishop and Confessor.*
All of the Common of a Bishop and Confessor, p. 222.

November 17.
S. Hugh, Bishop and Confessor.*
All of the Common of a Bishop and Confessor, p. 222.

November 19.
S. Elizabeth, Queen and Matron.*
All of the Common of a Matron, p. 229.

November 20.
S. Edmund, King and Martyr.*
All of the Common of a Martyr, p. 217, except the

Collect. *(Paris.)*
O GOD of unspeakable mercy, through Whose gifts the most blessed King Edmund overcame his foe by dying for Thy Name; mercifully grant to us Thy family that, assisted by his prayers, we may attain victoriously to ward off the darts of the old enemy. Through.

November 21.
S. Columbanus, Abbot.*
All of the Common of an Abbot, p. 224, except the

Collect. *(S. Maur.)*
O GOD, Who gavest grace to blessed Columbanus the Abbot to walk in the way of evangelical perfection, and also to lead others unto Thee; mercifully order our steps in Thy Word, that we may run the way of Thy commandments when Thou hast set our heart at liberty. Through.

November 22.
S. Cecilia, Virgin and Martyr.*
All of the Common of a Virgin and Martyr, p. 226, except the

Collect.
O GOD, Who dost gladden us with the feast of blessed Cecilia, Thy Virgin and Martyr; grant that while we venerate her birthday, we may also imitate her constancy in suffering. Through.

November 23.
S. Clement, Bishop and Martyr.*
All of the Common of a Martyr, p. 217.

November 24.
S. John of the Cross, Priest and Confessor.*
All of the Common of a Confessor, p. 224.

November 25.
S. Katharine, Virgin and Martyr.*
All of the Common of a Virgin and Martyr, p. 226, except as follows:

First and Second Vespers, Lauds, and Tierce.
Chapter. Ecclus. li.

I WILL thank Thee, O Lord and King, and praise Thee, O God, my Saviour: I do give praise unto Thy Name. For Thou art my defender and helper, and hast preserved my body from destruction.

Sexts.
Chapter. Ecclus. li.

MY soul praised the Lord, even unto death, and my life was near to hell.

Collect. *(Paris.)*
O GOD, Who hast made pure hearts Thy dwelling-place; grant, that as we venerate with humble reverence the purity of Thy bride Katharine the Virgin, so we may follow the pattern of her holy life. Through.

November 27.
S. Ode, Virgin and Martyr.*
All of the Common of a Virgin and Martyr, p. 226.

OCCASIONAL OFFICES.

PREPARATION FOR HOLY COMMUNION.

Ant. Remember not, Lord, our offences.

Quam dilecta! Psalm LXXXIV.

O HOW amiable are Thy dwellings: Thou Lord of hosts!
2 My soul hath a desire and longing to enter into the courts of the Lord : my heart and my flesh rejoice in the living God.
3 Yea, the sparrow hath found her an house, and the swallow a nest where she may lay her young : even Thy altars, O Lord of hosts, my King and my God.
4 Blessed are they that dwell in Thy house : they will be alway praising Thee.
5 Blessed is the man whose strength is in Thee : in whose heart are Thy ways.
6 Who going through the vale of misery use it for a well : and the pools are filled with water.
7 They will go from strength to strength : and unto the God of gods appeareth every one of them in Sion.
8 O Lord God of hosts, hear my prayer : hearken, O God of Jacob.
9 Behold, O God our defender : and look upon the face of thine Anointed.
10 For one day in Thy courts : is better than a thousand.
11 I had rather be a doorkeeper in the house of my God : than to dwell in the tents of ungodliness.
12 For the Lord God is a light and defence : the Lord will give grace and worship, and no good thing shall He withold from them that live a godly life.
13 O Lord God of hosts : blessed is the man that putteth his trust in Thee.
Glory be, etc.

Benedixisti, Domine. Psalm LXXXV.

LORD, Thou art become gracious unto Thy land : Thou hast turned away the captivity of Jacob.
2 Thou hast forgiven the offence of Thy people : and covered all their sins.
3 Thou hast taken away all Thy displeasure : and turned Thyself from Thy wrathful indignation.
4 Turn us then, O God our Saviour : and let Thine anger cease from us.
5 Wilt Thou be displeased at us for ever : and wilt Thou stretch out Thy wrath from one generation to another?
6 Wilt Thou not turn again, and quicken us : that Thy people may rejoice in Thee?
7 Shew us Thy mercy, O Lord : and grant us Thy salvation.

8 I will hearken what the Lord God will say concerning me : for He shall speak peace unto His people, and to His saints, that they turn not again.

9 For His salvation is nigh them that fear Him : that glory may dwell in our land.

10 Mercy and truth are met together : righteousness and peace have kissed each other.

11 Truth shall flourish out of the earth : and righteousness hath looked down from heaven.

12 Yea, the Lord shall shew lovingkindness : and our land shall give her increase.

13 Righteousness shall go before Him : and He shall direct His going in the way.

Glory be, etc.

Inclina, Domine. Psalm LXXXVI.

BOW down Thine ear, O Lord, and hear me : for I am poor, and in misery.

2 Preserve Thou my soul, for I am holy : my God, save Thy servant that putteth his trust in Thee.

3 Be merciful unto me, O Lord : for I will call daily upon Thee.

4 Comfort the soul of Thy servant : for unto Thee, O Lord, do I lift up my soul.

5 For Thou, Lord, art good and gracious : and of great mercy unto all them that call upon Thee.

6 Give ear, Lord, unto my prayer : and ponder the voice of my humble desires.

7 In the time of my trouble I will call upon Thee : for Thou hearest me.

8 Among the gods there is none like unto Thee, O Lord : there is not one that can do as Thou doest.

9 All nations whom Thou hast made shall come and worship Thee, O Lord : and shall glorify Thy Name.

10 For Thou art great, and doest wondrous things : Thou art God alone.

11 Teach me Thy way, O Lord, and I will walk in Thy truth : O knit my heart unto Thee, that I may fear Thy Name.

12 I will thank Thee, O Lord my God, with all my heart : and will praise Thy Name for evermore.

13 For great is Thy mercy toward me : and Thou hast delivered my soul from the nethermost hell.

14 O God, the proud are risen against me : and the congregations of naughty men have sought after my soul, and have not set Thee before their eyes.

15 But Thou, O Lord God, art full of compassion and mercy : longsuffering, plenteous in goodness and truth.

16 O turn Thee then unto me, and have mercy upon me : give Thy strength unto Thy servant, and help the son of Thine handmaid.

17 Shew some token upon me for good, that they who hate me may see it, and be ashamed : because Thou, Lord, hast holpen me, and comforted me.

Glory be, etc.

Credidi. Psalm CXVI. 10.

I BELIEVED, and therefore will I speak ; but I was sore troubled : I said in my haste, All men are liars.

11 What reward shall I give unto the Lord : for all the benefits that He hath done unto me?

12 I will receive the cup of salvation : and call upon the Name of the Lord.

13 I will pay my vows now in the presence of all His people : right dear in the sight of the Lord is the death of His saints.

14 Behold, O Lord, how that I am

Thy servant : I am Thy servant, and the son of Thine handmaid; Thou hast broken my bonds in sunder.

15 I will offer to Thee the sacrifice of thanksgiving : and will call upon the Name of the Lord.

16 I will pay my vows unto the Lord, in the sight of all His people : in the courts of the Lord's house, even in the midst of thee, O Jerusalem. Praise the Lord.

Glory be, etc.

De profundis. Psalm cxxx.

OUT of the deep have I called unto Thee, O Lord : Lord, hear my voice.

2 O let Thine ears consider well : the voice of my complaint.

3 If Thou, Lord, wilt be extreme to mark what is done amiss : O Lord, who may abide it?

4 For there is mercy with Thee : therefore shalt Thou be feared.

5 I look for the Lord; my soul doth wait for Him : in His word is my trust.

6 My soul fleeth unto the Lord : before the morning watch, I say, before the morning watch.

7 O Israel, trust in the Lord, for with the Lord there is mercy : and with Him is plenteous redemption.

8 And He shall redeem Israel : from all his sins.

Glory be, etc.

Ant. Remember not, Lord, our offences, nor the offences of our forefathers, neither take Thou vengeance of our sins : Spare us, good Lord, spare Thy people whom Thou hast redeemed with Thy most Precious Blood, and be not angry with us for ever.

  Lord, have mercy.
   Christ, have mercy.
  Lord, have mercy.
   Our Father.

℣. And lead us not into temptation.

℟. But deliver us from evil.

℣. I said, Lord, be merciful unto me.

℟. Heal my soul, for I have sinned against Thee.

℣. Turn Thee again, O Lord, at the last.

℟. And be gracious unto Thy servants.

℣. O Lord, let Thy mercy be shewed upon us.

℟. As we do put our trust in Thee.

℣. Let Thy priests be clothed with righteousness.

℟. And let Thy saints sing with joyfulness.

℣. Cleanse me, O Lord, from my secret faults.

℟. Keep Thy servant also from presumptuous sins.

℣. O Lord, hear my prayer.

℟. And let my cry come unto Thee.

Let us pray.

O MERCIFUL Lord, incline Thine ears to our prayers, and enlighten our hearts by the grace of Thy Holy Spirit : that we may worthily celebrate Thy holy Mysteries, and love Thee with an everlasting love.

WE pray Thee, O Lord, that the Comforter Who proceedeth from Thee may illuminate our minds, and lead us, as Thy Son hath promised, into all truth.

MAY the power of Thy Holy Spirit, O Lord, be present with us to cleanse us from all evil, and defend us from all adversities.

VISIT, O Lord, we beseech Thee, and cleanse our consciences, that Thy Son, our Lord Jesus Christ, when He cometh, may find in us a mansion prepared for Himself.

Through the same. Who liveth. In the Unity of the same.

To be said daily.

ALMIGHTY Everlasting God, lo, we draw near to the Sacrament of Thy Only-begotten Son, our Lord Jesus Christ. As sick, we approach to the Physician of Life; unclean, to the Fountain of Mercy; blind, to the Light of Eternal Brightness: poor and needy, to the Lord of heaven and earth; sinful creatures, to the Creator; wandering sheep, to the Good Shepherd; desolate, to the Comforter. We implore Thee, therefore, out of the abundance of Thy boundless bounty, that Thou wouldst vouchsafe to heal our sickness, to wash our defilements, to enrich our poverty, and to clothe our nakedness, that we may receive the Bread of Angels, the King of kings, the Lord of lords, with such reverence and devotion, such contrition and humility, such faith and purity, such purpose and intention as is expedient for the health of our souls. Grant, we beseech Thee, that we may receive not only the Sacrament of the Body and Blood of the Lord, but the substance also and virtue of that Sacrament. O most merciful God, grant us so to receive the Body of Thy Only-begotten Son, our Lord Jesus Christ, Which He took of the Virgin Mary, that we may be incorporated in His mystical Body, and accounted among His members. And, O most loving Father, grant that Whom now we purpose to receive under a veil, we may at length behold, with unveiled Face, even Thy beloved Son, Who with Thee and the Holy Ghost.

SUNDAY.

O SUPREME High Priest and true chief Bishop, Jesus Christ, Who didst offer Thyself to God the Father a pure and spotless Victim upon the Altar of the Cross for us miserable sinners, and Who didst give us Thy Flesh to eat and Thy Blood to drink, and didst ordain that Mystery in the power of the Holy Spirit, saying, "This do, in remembrance of Me;" I pray Thee, by the same Blood, the great price of our salvation; I pray Thee, by that wonderful and unspeakable love wherewith Thou didst vouchsafe so to love us miserable and unworthy, as to wash us from our sins in Thy Blood, teach me, Thy unworthy servant, by Thy Holy Spirit, to approach so great a mystery with such reverence and honour, with such devotion and fear, as I ought and as it becometh me. Make me through Thy grace always so to believe and understand, to conceive and firmly to hold, to think and to speak of this wondrous Mystery as shall please Thee and benefit my soul. Let Thy good Spirit enter my heart, there to be heard without utterance, and without the sound of words speak all truth. For these things are exceeding deep and covered with a sacred veil. Of Thy great mercy grant me to assist at this Solemnity with a clean heart and pure mind. Free my heart from all defiling and unholy, from all vain and hurtful thoughts. Fence me with the holy and faithful guard and powerful protection of Thy blessed Angels, that the enemies of all good may go away ashamed. By the virtue of this great Mystery, and by the hand of Thy holy Angels, drive away from me and all Thy servants the hard spirit of pride and vain glory, of impurity and uncleanness, of doubting and mistrust. Let them be confounded that seek after my soul to destroy it: let them perish that seek my hurt.

Monday.

KING of virgins and Lover of chastity and innocence, extinguish in my frame, by the dew of Thy heavenly blessing, the fuel of evil concupiscence, that so one even purity of soul and body may abide in me. Mortify in my members the lusts of the flesh, and all harmful emotions, and give me true and persevering chastity with Thine other gifts which please Thee in truth, so that I may with chaste body and pure heart offer unto Thee the sacrifice of praise. For with what mighty contrition of heart and fountain of tears, with what reverence and awe, with what chastity of body and purity of soul, should that divine and heavenly Sacrifice be celebrated, wherein Thy Flesh is indeed eaten, where Thy Blood is indeed drunk, wherein things lowest and highest, earthly and divine, are united, where is the presence of the holy Angels, where Thou art in a marvellous and unspeakable manner both Sacrifice and Priest.

Tuesday.

WHO can worthily celebrate this Sacrifice unless Thou, O God, makest him worthy? I know, O Lord, yea, truly do I know, and this do confess to Thy loving-kindness, that I am unworthy to approach so great a Mystery, by reason of my numberless sins and negligences; but I know, and truly with my own heart do I believe, and with my mouth confess, that Thou canst make me worthy, Who alone canst make that clean which proceedeth from that which is unclean, and sinners to be righteous and holy. By this Thine Almighty power I beseech Thee, O my God, to grant that I, a sinner, may assist at this Sacrifice with fear and trembling, with purity of heart and streams of tears, with spiritual gladness and heavenly joy; may my mind feel the sweetness of Thy most blessed Presence, and the guardianship of Thy holy Angels round about me.

Wednesday.

FOR now, O Lord, mindful of Thy venerable Passion, I draw near to Thine Altar, to offer Thee that Sacrifice which Thou hast instituted, and commanded to be offered in remembrance of Thee for our well-being. Receive it, we beseech Thee, O God Most High, for Thy holy Church, and for the people whom Thou hast redeemed with Thy Blood. We bring before Thee, O Lord, if Thou wilt graciously vouchsafe to behold, the tribulations of the poor, the perils of the people, the groans of prisoners, the miseries of orphans, the necessities of strangers, the helplessness of the weak, the depression of the weary, the infirmities of the aged, the aspirations of the young, the vows of virgins, the lamentations of widows.

Thursday.

FOR Thou, O Lord, art merciful unto all, and hatest nothing that Thou hast made. Remember what is our substance, because Thou art our Father and our God. Be not angry with us for ever, nor restrain the multitude of Thy mercies upon us, for it is not in our righteousness that we pour forth our prayers before Thy face, but of Thy great compassion. Take from us our iniquities, and graciously kindle the fire of Thy Holy Spirit within us. Take away the heart of stone from our flesh, and give us a heart of flesh, to love Thee, choose Thee, please Thee, follow Thee, enjoy Thee. We pray Thy mercy, O Lord, that Thou wouldst vouchsafe graciously to look upon Thy family attending on the ministry of Thy holy Name, and that the prayers of none may be in vain, the petitions of none unfruitful, do Thou put into our minds those prayers which Thou art graciously pleased to hear and fulfil.

Friday.

WE beseech Thee also, O Lord, Holy Father, for the souls of the faithful departed . . . . that this great Sacrament of Thy love may be unto them salvation and health, joy and refreshment. O Lord my God, grant them this day a great and abundant feast of Thee, the living God, Who didst come down from heaven, and gavest life unto the world, even of Thy holy and blessed Flesh, the Lamb without spot, Who takest away the sins of the world; even of that Flesh, which was taken of the holy and glorious Virgin Mary, and conceived of the Holy Ghost, and of that Fountain of mercy which the soldier's spear caused to flow from Thy most sacred Side, that therewith enlarged and satiated, refreshed and comforted, they may rejoice in Thy praise and glory.

I pray Thy mercy, O Lord, that on the bread to be offered unto Thee may descend the fulness of Thy benediction, and the sanctification of Thy Divinity. May there descend also the invisible and incomprehensible Majesty of Thy Holy Spirit, as it came down of old on the sacrifices of the fathers, Which may make our oblations Thy Body and Blood. And teach us, Thy unworthy servants, to approach so great a Mystery with purity of heart and the devotion of tears, with reverence and trembling, so that Thou mayest graciously and favourably receive this sacrifice for the good of all, living and departed.

Saturday.

I INTREAT Thee also, O Lord, by this most holy mystery of Thy Body and Blood, wherewith we are daily fed, washed, and sanctified in Thy Church, and are made partakers of the One Supreme Divinity, grant unto me Thy holy virtues, that fulfilled therewith I may draw near with a good conscience unto Thy holy Altar, so that these Sacraments may be made unto me salvation and life; for Thou hast said with Thy holy and blessed mouth, "The Bread which I will give is My Flesh, which I will give for the life of the world. I am the Living Bread Which came down from heaven. If any man eat of this Bread, he shall live for ever."

O most sweet Bread, heal the palate of my heart, that I may taste the sweetness of Thy love. Heal it of all infirmities, that I may find sweetness in nothing out of Thee. O most pure Bread, having all delight and all savour, which ever refreshest us, and never failest, let my heart feed on Thee, and may my inmost soul be fulfilled with the sweetness of Thy savour. The Angels feed on Thee fully. Let pilgrim man feed on Thee after his measure, refreshed by this nourishment on his way. Holy Bread! Living Bread! Pure Bread! Who didst come down from heaven, and givest life unto the world; enter my heart, and cleanse me from all impurity of flesh and spirit. Come into my soul; heal and cleanse me within and without; be the protection and continual health of my soul and body, so that I may by a straight way arrive at Thy kingdom, where, not as now in mysteries, but face to face, we shall behold Thee; when Thou shalt have delivered up the kingdom to God Thy Father, and shalt be God All in all, then shalt Thou satisfy me with Thyself by a wondrous fulness, so that I shall never hunger nor thirst any more. Who with the same God the Father and the Holy Ghost, livest.

Daily.

JOY with peace, amendment of life, space for true repentance, the grace and comfort of the Holy Spirit, perseverance in good works, a contrite and humble heart, and a happy consummation of my life, grant unto me, O Almighty and merciful Lord; for Thy mercy's sake. Amen.

THANKSGIVING AFTER HOLY COMMUNION.

Ant. Let us sing the Song of the Three Children.

Benedicite, omnia opera.

O ALL ye works of the Lord, bless ye the Lord : praise Him, and magnify Him for ever.

O ye Angels of the Lord, bless ye the Lord : O ye Heavens, bless ye the Lord.

O ye Waters that be above the Firmament, bless ye the Lord : O all ye Powers of the Lord, bless ye the Lord.

O ye Sun and Moon, bless ye the Lord : O ye Stars of Heaven, bless ye the Lord.

O ye Showers and Dew, bless ye the Lord : O ye Winds of God, bless ye the Lord.

O ye Fire and Heat, bless ye the Lord : O ye Winter and Summer, bless ye the Lord.

O ye Dews and Frosts, bless ye the Lord : O ye Frost and Cold, bless ye the Lord.

O ye Ice and Snow, bless ye the Lord : O ye Nights and Days, bless ye the Lord.

O ye Light and Darkness, bless ye the Lord : O ye Lightnings and Clouds, bless ye the Lord.

O let the Earth bless the Lord : yea, let it praise Him, and magnify Him for ever.

O ye Mountains and Hills, bless ye the Lord : O all ye Green Things upon the Earth, bless ye the Lord.

O ye Wells, bless ye the Lord : O ye Seas and Floods, bless ye the Lord.

O ye Whales and all that move in the Waters, bless ye the Lord : O all ye Fowls of the Air, bless ye the Lord.

O all ye Beasts and Cattle, bless ye the Lord : O ye Children of Men, bless ye the Lord.

O let Israel bless the Lord : praise Him, and magnify Him for ever.

O ye Priests of the Lord, bless ye the Lord : O ye Servants of the Lord, bless ye the Lord.

O ye Spirits and Souls of the Righteous, bless ye the Lord : O ye holy and humble Men of heart, bless ye the Lord.

O Ananias, Azarias, and Misael, bless ye the Lord : praise Him, and magnify Him for ever.

Instead of Glory be, etc.

Let us bless the Father, the Son,

and the Holy Ghost : let us praise and exalt Him above all for ever.

Blessed art Thou, O Lord, in the firmament of heaven : and above all to be praised and glorified for ever.

Laudate Dominum. Psalm CL.

O PRAISE God in His holiness : praise Him in the firmament of His power.

2 Praise Him in His noble acts : praise Him according to His excellent greatness.

3 Praise Him in the sound of the trumpet : praise Him upon the lute and harp.

4 Praise Him in the cymbals and dances : praise Him upon the strings and pipe.

5 Praise Him upon the well-tuned cymbals : praise Him upon the loud cymbals.

6 Let every thing that hath breath : praise the Lord.

Glory be to the Father, and to the Son : and to the Holy Ghost.

As it was in the beginning, is now, and ever shall be : world without end. Amen.

Nunc dimittis. S. Luke II. 29.

LORD, now lettest Thou Thy servant depart in peace : according to Thy word.

2 For mine eyes have seen : Thy salvation.

3 Which Thou hast prepared : before the face of all people ;

4 To be a light to lighten the Gentiles : and to be the glory of Thy people Israel.

Glory be to the Father, and to the Son : and to the Holy Ghost.

As it was in the beginning, is now, and ever shall be : world without end. Amen.

Ant. Let us sing the Song of the Three Children : which they sang as they blessed the Lord in the furnace of fire.

Lord, have mercy.
Christ, have mercy.
Lord, have mercy.

Our Father.

℣. And lead us not into temptation.

℟. But deliver us from evil.

℣. Let us bless the Father, the Son, and the Holy Ghost.

℟. Let us praise and exalt Him above all for ever.

℣. Blessed art Thou, O Lord, in the firmament of heaven.

℟. And above all to be praised and glorified for ever.

℣. May the Holy Trinity bless us and keep us.

℟. Amen.

℣. Enter not into judgment with Thy servant, O Lord.

℟. For in Thy sight shall no man living be justified.

℣. Turn us again, O Lord God o Hosts.

℟. Shew the light of Thy countenance, and we shall be whole.

℣. Hear my prayer, O Lord.

℟. And let my crying come unto Thee.

℣. The Lord be with you.

℟. And with thy spirit.

Let us pray.

O GOD, Who for the three children didst assuage the flames of fire : mercifully grant that the flames of sin may not kindle upon us Thy servants.

INFLAME our hearts, O Lord, we beseech Thee, with the fire of Thy Holy Spirit; that we may serve Thee in chastity of body, and please Thee in purity of heart.

PREVENT us, O Lord, in all our doings with Thy most gracious favour, and further us with Thy continual help; that in all our works begun, continued, and ended in Thee, we may glorify Thy holy Name, and finally by Thy mercy obtain everlasting life.

And these three Prayers end thus:

Through Jesus Christ our Lord. Amen.

Daily.

ALMIGHTY and everlasting God, the Preserver of souls and the Redeemer of the world, look favourably upon us, Thy servants, prostrate before Thy Majesty, and most graciously accept this Sacrifice at which, in honour of Thy Name, we have assisted, for the saving health of the faithful, living as well as departed, as also for all our sins and offences. Take away Thine anger from us, stretch out Thine hand unto us; open unto us the gates of Paradise; deliver us by Thy power from all evils; and whatever guilt we have of our own sinfulness incurred, do Thou forgive; and make us so to persevere in Thy precepts in this world, that we may be rendered worthy to be joined to the company of Thine elect; of Thine only gift, O my God, Whose blessed Name, honour and dominion, endureth for ever and ever. Amen.

I RENDER thanks to Thee, O Lord, Holy Father, Everlasting God, Who hast vouchsafed, not for any merits of ours, but of Thy great mercy only, to feed us sinners, Thine unworthy servants, with the Body and Blood of Thy Son, our Lord Jesus Christ; and we pray that this Holy Communion may not be for our judgment or condemnation, but for our pardon and salvation. Let it be unto us an armour of faith and a shield of good purpose, a riddance of all vices, and a rooting out of all evil desires; an increase of love and patience, of humility and obedience, and of all virtues, a firm defence against the wiles of all our enemies, visible and invisible; a perfect quieting of all our impulses, fleshly and spiritual, a cleaving unto Thee, the one true God, and a blessed consummation of our end, when Thou dost call. And I pray that Thou wouldest vouchsafe to bring us sinners to that unspeakable Feast, where Thou, with Thy Son, and Thy Holy Spirit, art to Thy holy ones true light, fulness of blessedness, everlasting joy, and perfect happiness. Through the same.

As time may allow:

O MOST sweet Lord Jesu Christ, transfix the affections of my inmost soul with that most joyous and healthful wound of Thy love, with true, serene, holiest Apostolic charity, that my soul may ever languish and melt with entire love and longing for Thee, that it may desire Thee, and faint for Thy courts, long to be dissolved and to be with Thee. Grant that my soul may hunger after Thee, the Bread of Angels, the Refreshment of holy souls, our daily and supersubstantial Bread, Who hast all sweetness and savour, and every possible delight. Let my heart ever hunger after and feed upon Thee, Whom the Angels desire to look into, and my inmost soul be filled with the sweetness of Thy savour. May it ever thirst for Thee, the Fountain of life, the Source of wisdom and knowledge, the Fountain of eternal light, the Torrent of pleasure, the Richness of the House of God. May it ever compass Thee, seek Thee, find Thee, stretch towards Thee, attain to Thee, meditate upon Thee, speak of Thee, and do all things to the praise and glory of Thy holy

Name, with humility and discretion, with love and delight, with readiness and affection, with perseverance even unto the end. And be Thou ever my Hope and my whole Confidence; my Riches; my Delight, my Pleasure, and my Joy; my Rest and Tranquility; my Peace, my Sweetness, and my Fragrance; my sweet Savour, my Food and Refreshment; my Refuge and my Help; my Wisdom; my Portion, my Possession, and my Treasure, in Whom my mind and my heart may ever remain fixed and firm, and rooted immoveably, henceforth and for evermore. Amen.

GRADUAL PSALMS AND LITANY.

[*Here is set down, in case it be preferred :*

THE ROMAN USE.

The Gradual Psalms are said on every Wednesday in Lent before Matins in Choir, except on the concurrence of a Double Festival; out of Choir they are to be said as occasion serves.

The first five Psalms, Psalm cxx. Ad Dominum, Psalm cxxi. Levavi oculos, Psalm cxxii. Lætatus sum, Psalm cxxiii. Ad te levavi oculos meos, *and* Psalm cxxiv. Nisi quia Dominus, *are said without Antiphon, and without* Glory be, etc. *At the end of the last is said:*

℣. Eternal rest : grant unto them, O Lord. ℟. And light perpetual : shine on them.

Then is said kneeling :

Our Father :

Silently to the end. The reader repeats :

℣. And lead us not into temptation. ℟. But deliver us from evil. ℣. From the gates of hell. ℟. Deliver their souls, O Lord. ℣. May they rest in peace. ℟. Amen. ℣. Hear my prayer, O Lord. ℟. And let my crying come unto Thee. ℣. The Lord be with you. ℟. And with thy spirit.

Let us pray.

COLLECT.

HAVE mercy, O Lord, upon the souls of Thy servants, and of Thine handmaidens, and of all the faithful departed : and loose them from all bonds of sin; that they may obtain an inheritance among Thy Saints in the glory of the First Resurrection. Through.

Then follow Psalm cxxv. Qui confidunt, Psalm cxxvi. In convertendo, Psalm cxxvii. Nisi Dominus, Psalm cxxviii. Beati omnes, *and* Psalm cxxix. Sæpe expugnaverunt; *each with* Glory be, etc.

Then is said kneeling :

Lord, have mercy.
Christ, have mercy.
Lord, have mercy.

Our Father

Silently to the end. The reader repeats :

℣. And lead us not into temptation. ℟. But deliver us from evil. ℣. O think upon Thy congregation. ℟. Whom Thou hast purchased and redeemed of old. ℣. Hear my prayer, O Lord. ℟. And let my crying come unto Thee. ℣. The Lord be with you. ℟. And with thy spirit.

Let us pray.

COLLECT.

O GOD, Whose nature and property is ever to have mercy and to forgive, receive our humble petitions; and though we be tied and bound with the chain of our sins, yet let the pitifulness of Thy great mercy loose us; for the honour of

Jesus Christ, our Mediator and Advocate. Amen.

Then follow Psalm cxxx. De profundis, Psalm cxxxi. Domine non est, Psalm cxxxii. Memento Domine, Psalm cxxxiii. Ecce quam bonum, *and* Psalm cxxxiv. Ecce nunc; *each with* Glory be, etc.

Then is said kneeling :
Lord, have mercy.
Christ, have mercy.
Lord, have mercy.
Our Father :

Silently to the end. The reader repeats :

℣. And lead us not into temptation. ℟. But deliver us from evil. ℣. O Lord, save Thy servants. ℟. That put their trust in Thee. ℣. Hear my prayer, O Lord. ℟. And let my crying come unto Thee. ℣. The Lord be with you. ℟. And with thy spirit.

Let us pray.

COLLECT.

STRETCH forth, O Lord, to Thy servants and to thine handmaidens the arm of Thy heavenly help: that they may both seek Thee with their whole heart, and also may obtain of Thee such things as they ask. Through.]

SARUM USE.

Ad Dominum. Psalm cxx.

WHEN I was in trouble I called upon the Lord : and He heard me.

2 Deliver my soul, O Lord, from lying lips : and from a deceitful tongue.

3 What reward shall be given or done unto thee, thou false tongue : even mighty and sharp arrows, with hot burning coals.

4 Wo is me that I am constrained to dwell with Mesech : and to have my habitation among the tents of Kedar.

5 My soul hath long dwelt among them : that are enemies unto peace.

6 I labour for peace, but when I speak unto them thereof : they make them ready to battle.

Glory be, etc.

Levavi oculos. Psalm cxxi.

I WILL lift up mine eyes unto the hills : from whence cometh my help.

2 My help cometh even from the Lord : Who hath made heaven and earth.

3 He will not suffer thy foot to be moved : and He that keepeth thee will not sleep.

4 Behold, He that keepeth Israel : shall neither slumber nor sleep.

5 The Lord Himself is thy keeper : the Lord is thy defence upon thy right hand;

6 So that the sun shall not burn thee by day : neither the moon by night.

7 The Lord shall preserve thee from all evil : yea, it is even He that shall keep thy soul.

8 The Lord shall preserve thy going out, and thy coming in : from this time forth for evermore.

Glory be, etc.

Lætatus sum. Psalm cxxii.

I WAS glad when they said unto me : We will go into the house of the Lord.

2 Our feet shall stand in thy gates : O Jerusalem.

3 Jerusalem is built as a city : that is at unity in itself.

4 For thither the tribes go up, even the tribes of the Lord : to testify unto Israel, to give thanks unto the Name of the Lord.

5 For there is the seat of judgment : even the seat of the house of David.

6 O pray for the peace of Jerusalem : they shall prosper that love thee.

7 Peace be within thy walls : and plenteousness within thy palaces.
8 For my brethren and companions' sakes : I will wish thee prosperity.
9 Yea, because of the house of the Lord our God : I will seek to do thee good.
Glory be, etc.

Ad te levavi oculos meos. Ps. CXXIII.

UNTO Thee lift I up mine eyes : O Thou that dwellest in the heavens.
2 Behold, even as the eyes of servants look unto the hand of their masters, and as the eyes of a maiden unto the hand of her mistress : even so our eyes wait upon the Lord our God, until He have mercy upon us.
3 Have mercy upon us, O Lord, have mercy upon us : for we are utterly despised.
4 Our soul is filled with the scornful reproof of the wealthy : and with the despitefulness of the proud.
Glory be, etc.

Nisi quia Dominus. Psalm CXXIV.

IF the Lord Himself had not been on our side, now may Israel say : if the Lord Himself had not been on our side, when men rose up against us ;
2 They had swallowed us up quick : when they were so wrathfully displeased at us.
3 Yea, the waters had drowned us : and the stream had gone over our soul.
4 The deep waters of the proud : had gone even over our soul.
5 But praised be the Lord : Who hath not given us over for a prey unto their teeth.
6 Our soul is escaped even as a bird out of the snare of the fowler : the snare is broken, and we are delivered.

7 Our help standeth in the Name of the Lord : Who hath made heaven and earth.
Glory be, etc.

Qui confidunt. Psalm CXXV.

THEY that put their trust in the Lord shall be even as the mount Sion : which may not be removed, but standeth fast for ever.
2 The hills stand about Jerusalem : even so standeth the Lord round about His people, from this time forth for evermore.
3 For the rod of the ungodly cometh not into the lot of the righteous : lest the righteous put their hand unto wickedness.
4 Do well, O Lord : unto those that are good and true of heart.
5 As for such as turn back unto their own wickedness : the Lord shall lead them forth with the evil doers, but peace shall be upon Israel.
Glory be, etc.

In convertendo. Psalm CXXVI.

WHEN the Lord turned again the captivity of Sion : then were we like unto them that dream.
2 Then was our mouth filled with laughter : and our tongue with joy.
3 Then said they among the heathen : The Lord hath done great things for them.
4 Yea, the Lord hath done great things for us already : whereof we rejoice.
5 Turn our captivity, O Lord : as the rivers in the south.
6 They that sow in tears : shall reap in joy.
7 He that now goeth on his way weeping, and beareth forth good seed : shall doubtless come again with joy, and bring his sheaves with him.
Glory be, etc.

Nisi Dominus. Psalm cxxvii.

EXCEPT the Lord build the house: their labour is but lost that build it.

2 Except the Lord keep the city: the watchman waketh but in vain.

3 It is but lost labour that ye haste to rise up early, and so late take rest, and eat the bread of carefulness: for so He giveth His beloved sleep.

4 Lo, children and the fruit of the womb: are an heritage and gift that cometh of the Lord.

5 Like as the arrows in the hand of the giant: even so are the young children.

6 Happy is the man that hath his quiver full of them: they shall not be ashamed when they speak with their enemies in the gate.

Glory be, etc.

Beati omnes. Psalm cxxviii.

BLESSED are all they that fear the Lord: and walk in His ways.

2 For thou shalt eat the labours of thine hands: O well is thee, and happy shalt thou be.

3 Thy wife shall be as the fruitful vine: upon the walls of thine house.

4 Thy children like the olive-branches: round about thy table.

5 Lo, thus shall the man be blessed: that feareth the Lord.

6 The Lord from out of Sion shall so bless thee: that thou shalt see Jerusalem in prosperity all thy life long.

7 Yea, that thou shalt see thy children's children: and peace upon Israel.

Glory be, etc.

Sæpe expugnaverunt. Psalm cxxix.

MANY a time have they fought against me from my youth up: may Israel now say.

2 Yea, many a time have they vexed me from my youth up: but they have not prevailed against me.

3 The plowers plowed upon my back: and made long furrows.

4 But the righteous Lord: hath hewn the snares of the ungodly in pieces.

5 Let them be confounded and turned backward: as many as have evil will at Sion.

6 Let them be even as the grass growing upon the house-tops: which withereth afore it be plucked up.

7 Whereof the mower filleth not his hand: neither he that bindeth up the sheaves his bosom.

8 So that they who go by say not so much as, The Lord prosper you: we wish you good luck in the Name of the Lord.

Glory be, etc.

De profundis. Psalm cxxx.

OUT of the deep have I called unto Thee, O Lord: Lord, hear my voice.

2 O let Thine ears consider well: the voice of my complaint.

3 If Thou, Lord, wilt be extreme to mark what is done amiss: O Lord, who may abide it?

4 For there is mercy with Thee: therefore shalt Thou be feared.

5 I look for the Lord, my soul doth wait for Him: in His word is my trust.

6 My soul fleeth unto the Lord: before the morning watch, I say, before the morning watch.

7 O Israel, trust in the Lord, for with the Lord there is mercy: and with Him is plenteous redemption.

8 And He shall redeem Israel: from all his sins.

Glory be, etc.

Domine, non est. Psalm cxxxi.

LORD, I am not high-minded: I have no proud looks.

2 I do not exercise myself in great matters : which are too high for me.
3 But I refrain my soul, and keep it low, like as a child that is weaned from his mother : yea, my soul is even as a weaned child.
4 O Israel, trust in the Lord : from this time forth for evermore.
Glory be, etc.

Memento, Domine. Psalm cxxxii.

LORD, remember David : and all his trouble.
2 How he sware unto the Lord ; and vowed a vow unto the Almighty God of Jacob.
3 I will not come within the tabernacle of mine house : nor climb up into my bed ;
4 I will not suffer mine eyes to sleep, nor mine eye-lids to slumber : neither the temples of my head to take any rest,
5 Until I find out a place for the temple of the Lord : an habitation for the mighty God of Jacob.
6 Lo, we heard of the same at Ephrata : and found it in the wood.
7 We will go into His tabernacle : and fall low on our knees before His footstool.
8 Arise, O Lord, into Thy resting-place : Thou, and the ark of Thy strength.
9 Let Thy priests be clothed with righteousness : and let Thy saints sing with joyfulness.
10 For Thy servant David's sake : turn not away the presence of Thine Anointed.
11 The Lord hath made a faithful oath unto David : and He shall not shrink from it ;
12 Of the fruit of thy body : shall I set upon thy seat.
13 If thy children will keep My covenant, and My testimonies that I shall learn them : their children also shall sit upon thy seat for evermore.
14 For the Lord hath chosen Sion to be an habitation for Himself : He hath longed for her.
15 This shall be My rest for ever : here will I dwell, for I have a delight therein.
16 I will bless her victuals with increase : and will satisfy her poor with bread.
17 I will deck her priests with health : and her saints shall rejoice and sing.
18 There shall I make the horn of David to flourish : I have ordained a lantern for Mine anointed.
19 As for his enemies, I shall clothe them with shame : but upon himself shall his crown flourish.
Glory be, etc.

Ecce, quam bonum. Psalm cxxxiii.

BEHOLD, how good and joyful a thing it is : brethren, to dwell together in unity.
2 It is like the precious ointment upon the head, that ran down unto the beard : even unto Aaron's beard, and went down to the skirts of his clothing.
3 Like as the dew of Hermon : which fell upon the hill of Sion.
5 For there the Lord promised His blessing : and life for evermore.
Glory be, etc.

Ecce nunc. Psalm cxxxiv.

BEHOLD now, praise the Lord : all ye servants of the Lord ;
2 Ye that by night stand in the house of the Lord : even in the courts of the house of our God.
3 Lift up your hands in the sanctuary : and praise the Lord.
4 The Lord that made heaven and earth : give thee blessing out of Sion.
Glory be, etc.

LITANY,
Which follows the Gradual Psalms according to the use of Sarum.

LORD, have mercy.
  Christ, have mercy.
  Lord, have mercy.
O Christ, hear us.
  O Christ, graciously hear us.
O God the Father, of heaven,
O God the Son, Redeemer of the world,
O God, the Holy Ghost,
O holy Trinity, One God,   *Have mercy upon us.*

Be merciful : spare us, good Lord.

From all evil,
From the snares of the devil,
From eternal damnation,
From the dangers threatening our sins,
From the assaults of evil spirits,
From the spirit of fornication,
From the desire of vain glory,
From all impurity of soul and body,
From anger and hatred and all ill-will,
From impure thoughts,
From blindness of heart,
From lightning and tempest,
From sudden and unprepared death,
By the mystery of Thy holy Incarnation,
By Thy Nativity,
By Thy holy Circumcision,
By Thy Baptism,
By Thy Fasting,
By Thy Cross and Passion,
By Thy precious Death,
By Thy glorious Resurrection,
By Thy wonderful Ascension,
By the grace of the Holy Ghost, the Comforter,   *Good Lord, deliver us.*

In the hour of death : help us, good Lord.
In the day of judgment : deliver us, good Lord.

We sinners : beseech Thee to hear us.
That Thou wouldest give us peace,
That Thy mercy and pity may keep us,
That Thou wouldest rule and defend Thy Church,
That Thou wouldest keep the Bishops and all Orders of the Church in holy religion,
That Thou wouldest give peace, true concord and victory to our kings and princes.
That Thou wouldest keep the congregations of all the faithful in Thy holy service,
That Thou wouldest keep all Christian people redeemed with Thy precious Blood,
That Thou wouldest reward all our benefactors with eternal blessings,
That Thou wouldest deliver our souls and the souls of our kinsfolk from eternal damnation,
That Thou wouldest give and preserve the fruits of the earth,
That Thou wouldest again cast the eyes of Thy mercy upon us,
That Thou wouldest make the obedience of our service reasonable,
That Thou wouldest raise our minds to heavenly desires,
That Thou wouldest look upon and lighten the miseries of the poor and of captives,
That Thou wouldest give eternal rest to all the faithful departed,
That Thou wouldest hear us,   *We beseech Thee to hear us.*

Son of God : we beseech Thee to hear us.
O Lamb of God, that takest away the sins of the world,
  Hear us, good Lord.

O Lamb of God, that takest away the sins of the world,
> Spare us, good Lord.

O Lamb of God, that takest away the sins of the world,
> Have mercy upon us.

> Lord, have mercy.
> Christ, have mercy.
> Lord, have mercy.
> Our Father.

℣. And lead us not into temptation. ℟. But deliver us from evil. ℣. Shew us Thy mercy, O Lord. ℟. And grant us Thy salvation. ℣. Let Thy loving mercy come also unto us, O Lord. ℟. Even Thy salvation according unto Thy word. ℣. We have sinned with our fathers. ℟. We have done amiss, and dealt wickedly. ℣. O Lord, deal not with us after our sins. ℟. Neither reward us after our iniquities. ℣. Let us pray for all orders of the Church. ℟. Let Thy priests be clothed with righteousness, and Thy saints sing with joyfulness. ℣. For our brethren and sisters. ℟. My God save Thy servants and handmaidens, which put their trust in Thee. ℣. For all Christian people. ℟. Save Thy people, O Lord, and give Thy blessing unto Thine inheritance; feed them, and set them up for ever. ℣. Peace be within Thy walls. ℟. And plenteousness within Thy palaces. ℣. May the souls of Thy servants and handmaidens rest in peace. ℟. Amen. ℣. Hear my prayer, O Lord. ℟. And let my crying come unto Thee. ℣. The Lord be with you. ℟. And with thy spirit.

> Let us pray.
> COLLECTS.

O GOD, Whose nature and property is ever to have mercy and to forgive, receive our humble petitions; and though we be tied and bound with the chain of our sins, yet let the pitifulness of Thy great mercy loose us.

ALMIGHTY and everlasting God, Who alone workest great marvels: send down upon our Bishops, and Curates, and all congregations committed to their charge, the healthful Spirit of Thy grace; and that they may truly please Thee, pour upon them the continual dew of Thy blessing.

WE beseech Thee, Almighty God, that Thy servant, our Sovereign, *N.*, who has received from Thy mercy the government of this realm, may also receive the increase of all virtues, and being adorned therewith, may both shun the depths of sin, and overcome *his* enemies; and, being filled with grace, may be found worthy to come to Thee, the Truth and the Life, and be acceptable in Thy sight.

O GOD, Who by the grace of the Holy Ghost hast poured the gifts of charity into the hearts of Thy faithful people: grant unto Thy servants and Thy handmaidens for whom we entreat Thy mercy, health both of soul and body; that they may love Thee with all their strength, and may work out with unreserved affection the things that are well-pleasing unto Thee.

O GOD, from Whom all holy desires, all good counsels, and all just works do proceed; give unto Thy servants that peace which the world cannot give; that both our hearts may be set to obey Thy commandments, and also that by Thee we, being defended from the fear of our enemies, may pass our time in rest and quietness.

WE beseech Thee, O Lord, graciously to shew us Thine ineffable mercy, that Thou mayest both deliver us from all our sins, and set us free from the punishments which they deserve.

O GOD, the Creator and Redeemer of all the faithful, grant to the souls of Thy servants and handmaidens remission of all their sins; that the pardon they have always desired, by pious supplications may be obtained.

WE beseech Thee, O Lord, in Thy compassion to unloose the chains of our sins, and by the intercession of Mary, the blessed and glorious and ever Virgin Mother of God, and of all Saints, keep us Thy servants, and the whole Catholic Church, in all sanctity; and purge from their vices those joined to us by kindred or friendship, or in the confession of the faith, and adorn them with virtues; grant us peace and safety; drive away from our friends all enemies visible and invisible, and keep them from sickness; grant charity to our enemies, and to all Thy faithful, living and departed, life in the land of the living, and eternal rest; through Jesus Christ our Lord, who liveth and reigneth with Thee and the Holy Ghost, ever one God, world without end. Amen.

THE PENITENTIAL PSALMS.

According to the Sarum use, the seven Penitential Psalms are said daily in Lent, one at each Office with Psalm li., Miserere. But before a Festival in Lent, at Nones of the Vigil, the three last Psalms are said, namely, Psalm cii., Domine exaudi; Psalm cxxx., De profundis; and Psalm cxliii., Domine exaudi: that they may be completed before the First Vespers of the Festival. They are appointed to be said consecutively, after Sexts on Ash-Wednesday, before the blessing of ashes, and the ejection of penitents; after Nones on Maundy Thursday, at the reconciliation of penitents; and on Rogation Monday after Nones.

[According to the Roman use, which some may prefer, the seven Psalms are not said daily, but only on Fridays in Lent, with Litany, after Lauds. (The Sarum Litany, p. 320,' may thus be used.)

The earlier part of the Sarum Ash-Wednesday Office is here subjoined, in order to form a Penitential Office for use when occasion shall serve.]

Ant. Remember not.

[*Against Anger.*]
Domine, ne in furore. Psalm VI.

O LORD, rebuke me not in Thine indignation : neither chasten me in Thy displeasure.

2 Have mercy upon me, O Lord, for I am weak : O Lord, heal me, for my bones are vexed.

3 My soul also is sore troubled : but, Lord, how long wilt Thou punish me?

4 Turn Thee, O Lord, and deliver my soul : O save me for Thy mercy's sake.

5 For in death no man remembereth Thee : and who will give Thee thanks in the pit?

6 I am weary of my groaning; every night wash I my bed : and water my couch with my tears.

7 My beauty is gone for very trouble : and worn away because of all mine enemies.

8 Away from me, all ye that work vanity : for the Lord hath heard the voice of my weeping.

9 The Lord hath heard my petition : the Lord will receive my prayer.

10 All mine enemies shall be confounded, and sore vexed : they shall be turned back, and put to shame suddenly.

Glory be, etc.

[*Against Pride.*]

Beati, quorum. Psalm xxxii.

BLESSED is he whose unrighteousness is forgiven : and whose sin is covered.

2 Blessed is the man unto whom the Lord imputeth no sin : and in whose spirit there is no guile.

3 For while I held my tongue : my bones consumed away through my daily complaining.

4 For Thy hand is heavy upon me day and night : and my moisture is like the drought in summer.

5 I will acknowledge my sin unto Thee : and mine unrighteousness have I not hid.

6 I said, I will confess my sin unto the Lord : and so Thou forgavest the wickedness of my sin.

7 For this shall every one that is godly make his prayer unto Thee, in a time when Thou mayest be found : but in the great water-floods they shall not come nigh him.

8 Thou art a place to hide me in, Thou shalt preserve me from trouble : Thou shalt compass me about with songs of deliverance.

9 I will inform thee, and teach thee in the way wherein thou shalt go : and I will guide thee with mine eye.

10 Be ye not like to horse and mule, which have no understanding : whose mouths must be held with bit and bridle, lest they fall upon thee.

11 Great plagues remain for the ungodly : but whoso putteth his trust in the Lord, mercy embraceth him on every side.

12 Be glad, O ye righteous, and rejoice in the Lord : and be joyful, all ye that are true of heart.

Glory be, etc.

[*Against Gluttony.*]

Domine, ne in furore. Psalm xxxviii.

PUT me not to rebuke, O Lord, in Thine anger : neither chasten me in Thy heavy displeasure.

2 For Thine arrows stick fast in me : and Thy hand presseth me sore.

3 There is no health in my flesh, because of Thy displeasure : neither is there any rest in my bones, by reason of my sin.

4 For my wickednesses are gone over my head : and are like a sore burden, too heavy for me to bear.

5 My wounds stink and are corrupt : through my foolishness.

6 I am brought into so great trouble and misery : that I go mourning all the day long.

7 For my loins are filled with a sore disease : and there is no whole part in my body.

8 I am feeble, and sore smitten : I have roared for the very disquietness of my heart.

9 Lord, Thou knowest all my desire : and my groaning is not hid from Thee.

10 My heart panteth, my strength hath failed me : and the sight of mine eyes is gone from me.

11 My lovers and my neighbours

did stand looking upon my trouble : and my kinsmen stood afar off.

12 They also that sought after my life laid snares for me : and they that went about to do me evil talked of wickedness, and imagined deceit all the day long.

13 As for me, I was like a deaf man, and heard not : and as one that is dumb, who doth not open his mouth.

14 I became even as a man that heareth not : and in whose mouth are no reproofs.

15 For in Thee, O Lord, have I put my trust : Thou shalt answer for me, O Lord, my God.

16 I have yrequired that they, even mine enemies, should not triumph over me : for when my foot slipped, they rejoiced greatly against me.

17 And I, truly, am set in the plague : and my heaviness is ever in my sight.

18 For I will confess my wickedness : and be sorry for my sin.

19 But mine enemies live, and are mighty : and they that hate me wrongfully are many in number.

20 They also that reward evil for good are against me : because I follow the thing that good is.

21 Forsake me not, O Lord my God : be not Thou far from me.

22 Haste Thee to help me : O Lord God of my salvation.

Glory be, etc.

[*Against Lust.*]

Miserere mei, Deus. Psalm LI.

HAVE mercy upon me, O God, after Thy great goodness : according to the multitude of Thy mercies do away mine offences.

2 Wash me throughly from my wickedness : and cleanse me from my sin.

3 For I acknowledge my faults : and my sin is ever before me.

4 Against Thee only have I sinned, and done this evil in Thy sight : that Thou mightest be justified in Thy saying, and clear when Thou art judged.

5 Behold, I was shapen in wickedness : and in sin hath my mother conceived me.

6 But lo, Thou requirest truth in the inward parts : and shalt make me to understand wisdom secretly.

7 Thou shalt purge me with hyssop, and I shall be clean : Thou shalt wash me, and I shall be whiter than snow.

8 Thou shalt make me hear of joy and gladness : that the bones which Thou hast broken may rejoice.

9 Turn Thy face from my sins : and put out all my misdeeds.

10 Make me a clean heart, O God : and renew a right spirit within me.

11 Cast me not away from Thy presence : and take not Thy Holy Spirit from me.

12 O give me the comfort of Thy help again : and stablish me with Thy free Spirit.

13 Then shall I teach Thy ways unto the wicked : and sinners shall be converted unto Thee.

14 Deliver me from blood-guiltiness, O God, Thou that art the God of my health : and my tongue shall sing of Thy righteousness.

15 Thou shalt open my lips, O Lord : and my mouth shall shew Thy praise.

16 For Thou desirest no sacrifice, else would I give it Thee : but Thou delightest not in burnt offerings.

17 The sacrifice of God is a troubled spirit : a broken and contrite heart, O God, shalt Thou not despise.

18 O be favourable and gracious

unto Sion : build Thou the walls of Jerusalem.

19 Then shalt Thou be pleased with the sacrifice of righteousness, with the burnt offerings and oblations : then shall they offer young bullocks upon Thine altar.

Glory be, etc.

[*Against Avarice.*]
Domine, exaudi. Psalm CII.

HEAR my prayer, O Lord : and let my crying come unto Thee.

2 Hide not Thy face from me in the time of my trouble : incline Thine ear unto me when I call; O hear me, and that right soon.

3 For my days are consumed away like smoke : and my bones are burnt up as it were a fire-brand.

4 My heart is smitten down, and withered like grass : so that I forget to eat my bread.

5 For the voice of my groaning : my bones will scarce cleave to my flesh.

6 I am become like a pelican in the wilderness : and like an owl that is in the desert.

7 I have watched, and am even as it were a sparrow : that sitteth alone upon the house-top.

8 Mine enemies revile me all the day long : and they that are mad upon me are sworn together against me.

9 For I have eaten ashes as it were bread : and mingled my drink with weeping;

10 And that because of Thine indignation and wrath : for Thou hast taken me up and cast me down.

11 My days are gone like a shadow: and I am withered like grass.

12 But Thou, O Lord, shalt endure for ever : and Thy remembrance throughout all generations.

13 Thou shalt arise, and have mercy upon Sion : for it is time that Thou have mercy upon her, yea, the time is come.

14 And why? Thy servants think upon her stones : and it pitieth them to see her in the dust.

15 The heathen shall fear Thy Name, O Lord : and all the kings of the earth Thy majesty;

16 When the Lord shall build up Sion : and when His glory shall appear;

17 When He turneth Him unto the prayer of the poor destitute : and despiseth not their desire.

18 This shall be written for those that come after : and the people which shall be born shall praise the Lord.

19 For He hath looked down from His sanctuary : out of the heaven did the Lord behold the earth;

20 That He might hear the mournings of such as are in captivity : and deliver the children appointed unto death;

21 That they may declare the Name of the Lord in Sion : and His worship at Jerusalem;

22 When the people are gathered together : and the kingdoms also, to serve the Lord.

23 He brought down my strength in my journey : and shortened my days.

24 But I said, O my God, take me not away in the midst of mine age : as for Thy years, they endure throughout all generations.

25 Thou, Lord, in the beginning hast laid the foundation of the earth : and the heavens are the work of Thy hands.

26 They shall perish, but Thou shalt endure : they all shall wax old as doth a garment;

27 And as a vesture shalt Thou change them, and they shall be changed : but Thou art the same, and Thy years shall not fail.

28 The children of Thy servants shall continue : and their seed shall stand fast in Thy sight.
Glory be, etc.

[*Against Envy.*]
De profundis. Psalm cxxx.

OUT of the deep have I called unto Thee, O Lord : Lord, hear my voice.

2 O let Thine ears consider well : the voice of my complaint.

3 If Thou, Lord, wilt be extreme to mark what is done amiss : O Lord, who may abide it?

4 For there is mercy with Thee : therefore shalt Thou be feared.

5 I look for the Lord; my soul doth wait for Him : in His word is my trust.

6 My soul fleeth unto the Lord : before the morning watch, I say, before the morning watch.

7 O Israel, trust in the Lord, for with the Lord there is mercy : and with Him is plenteous redemption.

8 And He shall redeem Israel from all his sins.
Glory be, etc.

[*Against Sloth.*]
Domine, exaudi. Psalm cxliii.

HEAR my prayer, O Lord, and consider my desire : hearken unto me for Thy truth and righteousness' sake.

2 And enter not into judgment with Thy servant : for in Thy sight shall no man living be justified.

3 For the enemy hath persecuted my soul; he hath smitten my life down to the ground : he hath laid me in the darkness, as the men that have been long dead.

4 Therefore is my spirit vexed within me : and my heart within me is desolate.

5 Yet do I remember the time past; I muse upon all Thy works : yea, I exercise myself in the works of Thy hands.

6 I stretch forth my hands unto Thee : my soul gaspeth unto Thee as a thirsty land.

7 Hear me, O Lord, and that soon, for my spirit waxeth faint : hide not Thy face from me, lest I be like unto them that go down into the pit.

8 O let me hear Thy loving-kindness betimes in the morning, for in Thee is my trust : shew Thou me the way that I should walk in, for I lift up my soul unto Thee.

9 Deliver me, O Lord, from mine enemies : for I flee unto Thee to hide me.

10 Teach me to do the thing that pleaseth Thee, for Thou art my God : let Thy loving Spirit lead me forth into the land of righteousness.

11 Quicken me, O Lord, for Thy Name's sake : and for Thy righteousness' sake bring my soul out of trouble.

12 And of Thy goodness slay mine enemies : and destroy all them that vex my soul; for I am Thy servant.
Glory be, etc.

Ant. Remember not, Lord, our offences, nor the offences of our forefathers; neither take Thou vengeance of our sins : spare us, good Lord, spare Thy people, whom Thou hast redeemed with Thy most precious blood, and be not angry with us for ever.

Lord, have mercy.
Christ, have mercy.
Lord, have mercy.
Our Father :

Silently to the end. The Priest repeats aloud :

℣. And lead us not into temptation.
℟. But deliver us from evil. ℣. O God, save Thy servants and hand-

maidens. ℟. Who put their trust in Thee. ℣. Send them help, O Lord, from the sanctuary. ℟. And strengthen them out of Sion. ℣. Help us, O God of our salvation. ℟. And for the glory of Thy Name deliver us; and be merciful unto our sins, for Thy Name's sake. ℣. Hear my prayer, O Lord. ℟. And let my crying come unto Thee. ℣. The Lord be with you. ℟. And with thy spirit.

Let us pray.

Collects.

O LORD, we beseech Thee, mercifully hear our prayers, and spare all those that confess their sins unto Thee; that they whose consciences by sin are accused, by Thy merciful pardon may be absolved.

WE beseech Thee, O Lord, inspire Thy servants with saving grace, that their hearts may be melted by true contrition, and Thine anger turned away by due repentance.

GRANT, we beseech Thee, O Lord, our God, that these Thy penitent servants may be continually mindful of their purification; and that they may bring the same to good effect, let the grace of Thy presence ever prevent and follow them.

LET Thy compassion, O Lord, we beseech Thee, prevent these Thy servants, that all their iniquities may be blotted out by Thy ready forgiveness.

O LORD, hear our supplications, and shew forth Thy loving mercy to Thy servants; heal their wounds, and forgive their sins, that they, being separated from Thee by no iniquities, may ever hold fast unto Thee their Lord.

O LORD, Who in Thy mercy art not wearied by our sin, but dost accept our penitence; look, we beseech Thee, upon Thy servants who confess that they have grievously sinned against Thee; for to Thee it pertaineth to absolve offences, and pardon sinners, and Thou hast said that Thou wouldest not the death of a sinner, but his repentance. Grant therefore, O Lord, that these Thy servants may keep unto Thee the vigil of penitence here, and amending their ways, may hereafter give Thee thanks for eternal joys.

O GOD, Whose pardon all men need, remember Thy servants and handmaidens: and because through the deceitfulness and frailty of their mortal bodies they are despoiled of virtue, and have done amiss in many things, we beseech Thee, pardon them who confess, spare them who entreat: that they who by their deserts are accused, by Thy mercy may be saved; through Jesus Christ our Lord, Who liveth and reigneth with Thee and the Holy Ghost, ever one God, world without end. Amen.

ORDER FOR THE COMMENDATION OF A SOUL BEFORE DEATH.

First is said a short Litany as follows:

Lord, have mercy.
    Christ, have mercy.
Lord, have mercy.
Be merciful : spare *him*, good Lord.
Be merciful : help *him*, good Lord.
Be merciful : deliver *him*, good Lord.

From Thy wrath,
From an evil death,
From the power of the devil,
From the pains of hell,
By Thy Nativity,
By Thy Cross and Passion,
By Thy Death and Burial,
By Thy glorious Resurrection,
By Thy wonderful Ascension,
By the grace of the Holy Ghost, the Comforter,
In the Day of Judgment,
                    Good Lord, deliver him.

We sinners, beseech Thee to hear us.

That Thou wouldest spare *him* : we beseech Thee to hear us, good Lord.

Lord, have mercy.
    Christ, have mercy.
Lord, have mercy.
    Our Father.

℣. And lead us not into temptation.
℟. But deliver from evil.

While the soul is in its agony is said :

(1)

DEPART, Christian soul, out of this world; in the Name of God the Father Almighty, Who created thee; in the Name of Jesus Christ, the Son of the Living God, Who suffered for thee; in the Name of the Holy Ghost, Who regenerated thee. Thus, when thou shalt have departed from the body, mayest thou have an entrance to Mount Sion, the city of the living God, the heavenly Jerusalem, and to an innumerable company of Angels, and to the general assembly of the Church of the firstborn which are written in heaven. Let God arise, and let His enemies be scattered; let the powers of darkness flee before Him; nor let them dare to assault a lamb, redeemed by the precious blood of Christ. Christ, Who suffered His agony for thee, preserve thee now in this agony of death. Christ, Who died on the Cross for thee, preserve thee from everlasting death. He, the good Shepherd, acknowledge His own lamb and set thee in the fold of His elect. He give thee to see thy Redeemer face to face, and, being present with Him, to behold with happy eyes the full manifestation of the truth for ever and ever. Amen.

(2)

O MERCIFUL God, O Gracious God, O God Who according to the multitude of Thy mercies dost blot out the sins of the penitent, and by the grace of remission dost remove the guilt of past transgressions, mercifully look upon this Thy *servant*, *N.*, and hear *him*, who with entire and hearty confession hath implored the pardon of all *his* sins. Renew in *him*, O most tender Father, whatsoever has been corrupted through earthly frailty, or injured by the fraud of the devil; and bring *him*, a member of the body of the Church, into the unity of the Redeemed. Have compassion on *his* groaning, O Lord, have compassion on *his* tears; and since *he* trusteth only in Thy mercy, admit *him* to the sacrament of Thy reconciliation. Through.

[*Instead of Prayers* (1) *and* (2), *may be said the following*:

I COMMEND thee, dearest *brother*, to Almighty God, and commit thee to Him, Whose creature thou art; that when thou shalt have paid the debt of mankind by death, thou mayest return to thy Maker, Who formed thee from the dust of the earth. When, therefore, thy soul shall depart from the body, may the resplendent host of Angels hasten to thee; may the judicial council of Apostles come to thee; may the triumphant army of white-robed Martyrs meet thee; may the white and ruddy band of Confessors encompass thee; may the choir of joyful Virgins receive thee; and may the love of the Blessed who rest in the bosom of the Patriarchs enfold thee. May Christ Jesus appear to thee with a mild and gracious countenance, and may He assign thee to be one of those who ever stand before Him. Mayest thou know nothing of the horror of darkness, of the flames of hell, of racking torments. May the most hateful adversary and his spirits give way before thee; may he tremble at thine approach with accompanying Angels, and flee away into the vast chaos of eternal night. Let God arise, and let His enemies be scattered, and let them also that hate Him flee before Him; as the smoke vanisheth, let them vanish, and as wax melteth before the fire, so let the sinners perish before God. And let the righteous be glad and rejoice before God. Let then the legions of hell be confounded and brought to shame, and let not the ministers of Satan dare to hinder thy way. May Christ, Who was crucified for thee, deliver thee from torment; may Christ, Who vouchsafed to die for thee, deliver thee from death; may Christ, the Son of the living God, place thee in the ever verdant pastures of His Paradise, and may He, the true Shepherd, number thee amongst His sheep. May He absolve thee from all thy sins, and may He assign thee a portion at His right hand among His elect. Mayest thou see thy Redeemer face to face, and standing before Him for ever, behold with happy eyes the open vision of the truth. And placed thus among the hosts of the blessed, mayest thou enjoy the sweetness of divine contemplation for ever and ever. Amen.]

Let us pray.

RECEIVE Thy *servant*, O Lord, into the place of salvation, hoped for from Thy mercy. R). Amen.

Deliver *his* soul, O Lord, from all the perils of hell, from the dangers of suffering, and from all tribulation. R). Amen.

Deliver *his* soul, O Lord, as Thou didst deliver Enoch and Elias from the common death of the world. R). Amen.

Deliver *his* soul, O Lord, as Thou didst deliver Noah from the flood. R). Amen.

Deliver *his* soul, O Lord, as Thou didst deliver Abraham from Ur of the Chaldees. R). Amen.

Deliver *his* soul, O Lord, as Thou didst deliver Job out of his sufferings. R). Amen.

Deliver *his* soul, O Lord, as Thou didst deliver Isaac from being sacrificed by the hand of his father Abraham. R). Amen.

Deliver *his* soul, O Lord, as Thou

didst deliver Lot from Sodom and the flames of fire. ℟. Amen.

Deliver *his* soul, O Lord, as Thou didst deliver Moses from the hand of Pharaoh, king of Egypt. ℟. Amen.

Deliver *his* soul, O Lord, as Thou didst deliver Daniel from the lions' den. ℟. Amen.

Deliver *his* soul, O Lord, as Thou didst deliver the three children from the fiery furnace, and from the hand of an unrighteous king. ℟. Amen.

Deliver *his* soul, O Lord, as Thou didst deliver Susanna from false witness. ℟. Amen.

Deliver *his* soul, O Lord, as Thou didst deliver David from the hand of king Saul, and from the hand of Goliath. ℟. Amen.

Deliver *his* soul, O Lord, as Thou didst deliver Peter and Paul from prison. ℟. Amen.

And, as Thou didst deliver Thy most blessed Virgin and Martyr Thecla from three most horrible torments, so deign to deliver the soul of this Thy *servant*, and make *him* to enjoy with Thee the blessedness of heaven. ℟. Amen.

Let us pray.

TO Thee, O Lord, we commend the soul of Thy *servant*; and we pray Thee, O Lord Jesus Christ, Saviour of the world, that Thou wouldest not delay to place *him* in the bosom of the Patriarchs, for whom Thou didst mercifully descend into this earth. Acknowledge, O Lord, Thy creature, not created by strange gods, but by Thee, the only true and living God; for there is none other God beside Thee, O Lord, and none that can do as Thou doest. Make the soul of Thy *servant*, O Lord, joyful in Thy presence, and remember not *his* former sins and excesses, which the violence or heat of evil desires excited; for although *he* hath sinned, yet *he* hath not denied the Father, the Son, and the Holy Spirit, but hath believed, and had a zeal for God within *him*, and hath worshipped God Who made all things. ℟. Amen.

Let us pray.

REMEMBER not, O Lord, we pray Thee, the sins and ignorances of *his* youth, but according to Thy great mercy remember *him* in the brightness of Thy glory. May the heavens be opened unto *him*, may the Angels be gathered unto *him*; receive, O Lord, Thy *servant* into Thy kingdom. May holy Michael the Archangel receive *him*, who attained to be the prince of the heavenly warfare. May the holy Angels of God meet *him* on the way, and lead *him* into the city of the heavenly Jerusalem. May blessed Peter the Apostle receive *him*, to whom the keys of the heavenly kingdom were given by God. May holy Paul assist *him*, who was counted worthy to be a vessel of election. May holy John, the chosen Apostle of God, intercede for *him*, to whom heavenly secrets were revealed. May all the holy Apostles pray for *him*, to whom the power of binding and loosing was given by the Lord. May all the Saints of God intercede for *him*, who for the Name of Christ bore pain in this world; that *he*, delivered from the bands of the flesh, may be counted worthy to come to the glory of the heavenly kingdom, being presented by the same Thy Son our Lord Jesus Christ, Who liveth.

If the soul continue in its agony, that which follows, or any part of it, may be said.

Domine, quid multiplicati? Psalm III.

LORD, how are they increased that trouble me : many are they that rise against me.

2 Many one there be that say of my soul : There is no help for him in his God.

3 But Thou, O Lord, art my defender : Thou art my worship, and the lifter up of my head.

4 I did call upon the Lord with my voice : and He heard me out of His holy hill.

5 I laid me down and slept, and rose up again : for the Lord sustained me.

6 I will not be afraid for ten thousands of the people : that have set themselves against me round about.

7 Up, Lord, and help me, O my God : for Thou smitest all mine enemies upon the cheek-bone; Thou hast broken the teeth of the ungodly.

8 Salvation belongeth unto the Lord : and Thy blessing is upon Thy people.

Glory be, etc.

 Lord, have mercy.
 Christ, have mercy.
 Lord, have mercy.
 Our Father.

℣. And lead us not into temptation. ℟. But deliver us from evil. ℣. Save me, O God. ℟. For the waters are come in, even unto my soul. ℣. Take me out of the mire that I sink not. ℟. O let me be delivered from them that hate me, and out of the deep waters. ℣. Let not the water-flood drown me, neither let the deep swallow me up. ℟. And let not the pit shut her mouth upon me. ℣. Awake, and stand up to judge my quarrel. ℟. Avenge Thou my cause, my God and my Lord. ℣. Shew some token upon me for good, that they who hate me may see it and be ashamed. ℟. Because Thou, Lord, hast holpen me, and comforted me. ℣. The Lord be with you. ℟. And with thy spirit.

 Let us pray.

ONLY-BEGOTTEN and Beloved Son of the Living God, Who for the redemption of the world didst vouchsafe to be born in a manger, to be set at nought of the Jews, to be betrayed by Judas with a kiss, to be bound with fetters, to be led as a lamb to the slaughter, to be torn with scourges, to be defiled with spitting, to be crowned with thorns, to be fastened to the Cross, to be reckoned among the transgressors, to die in agony: we beseech Thee that by these Thy most holy sufferings, and by Thy Cross and Death, Thou wouldest vouchsafe to deliver Thy *servant* from the pains of hell, and to bring *him* into that place whither Thou didst bring the thief that was crucified with Thee; Who livest and reignest with the Father and the Holy Ghost, ever one God, world without end. Amen.

The Passion of our Lord Jesus Christ according to the Four Evangelists.

JESUS taketh with Him Peter and James and John, and began to be sore amazed and very heavy: and saith unto them, My soul is exceeding sorrowful unto death, tarry ye here and watch with Me. And He went a little farther and fell on His face and prayed, saying, O My Father, if it be possible, let this cup pass from Me; nevertheless, not as I will, but as Thou wilt. And there appeared an Angel unto Him from heaven, strengthening Him. He went away again the second time and prayed, saying, Abba, Father, all things are possible unto Thee, take away this cup from Me: nevertheless, not what I will, but what Thou wilt. And being in an agony, He prayed more earnestly, and His sweat was as it were great drops of blood, falling down to the ground.

Deus in adjutorium. Psalm LXX.

Haste Thee, O God, to deliver me: make haste to help me, O Lord.

2 Let them be ashamed and confounded that seek after my soul : let them be turned backward and put to confusion that wish me evil.

3 Let them for their reward be soon brought to shame : that cry over me, There, there.

4 But let all those that seek Thee be joyful and glad in Thee : and let all such as delight in Thy salvation say alway, The Lord be praised.

5 As for me, I am poor and in misery : haste Thee unto me, O God.

6 Thou art my helper, and my redeemer : O Lord, make no long tarrying.

Glory be, etc.

℣. Hear my prayer, O God, and hide not Thyself from my petition. ℟. Take heed unto me, and hear me. ℣. My heart is disquieted within me. ℟. And the fear of death is fallen upon me. ℣. Fearfulness and trembling are come upon me. ℟. And an horrible dread hath overwhelmed me. ℣. But my hope hath been in Thee, O Lord. ℟. I have said, Thou art my God, my time is in Thy hand. ℣. Lighten mine eyes, that I sleep not in death. ℟. Lest mine enemy say, I have prevailed against him. ℣. O keep my soul and deliver me. ℟. Let me not be confounded, for I have put my trust in Thee. ℣. The Lord be with you. ℟. And with thy spirit.

Let us pray.

Lord Jesu Christ, we humbly beseech Thy mercy, by that Thy sorrow of soul, even unto death, and by the agony which, when Thy Passion was at hand, Thou didst endure, when Thy sweat was, as it were, great drops of blood falling down to the ground, deliver this Thy *servant*, now surrounded by the agony of death: guard *him* in this hour against all assaults of the devil: deliver *him* from the terrors of approaching death: and because *he* fears through the remembrance of *his* sin, bid *him* be of good courage, through the abundance of Thy mercy. Who livest.

℣. Look upon my adversity and misery. ℟. And forgive me all my sin. ℟. Thou, O Lord God, art full of compassion and mercy, longsuffering, plenteous in goodness and truth. ℟. Turn Thee then unto me, and have mercy upon me. ℣. Forsake me not, O Lord my God. ℟. Be not Thou far from me. ℣. O that I had wings like a dove. ℟. Then would I flee away and be at rest. ℣. Let me die the death of the righteous. ℟. And let my last end be like his.

Let us pray.

Lord Jesu Christ, Who by the mouth of Thy prophet didst say, I have loved thee with an everlasting love, therefore with loving-kindness have I drawn thee: we beseech Thee by the love wherewith Thou hast loved us, that Thou wouldest vouchsafe to offer and to shew forth to God the Father for the soul of this Thy *servant*, all the bitterness of the Passion which Thou didst endure upon the Cross, and deal with *him* at this hour, not as *his* sins have deserved, but as Thy Death hath merited. Who livest.

These Psalms and Prayers having been finished (or before they are finished, if the moment of the soul's departure be at hand), let there be read over the

ORDER FOR THE COMMENDATION OF A SOUL BEFORE DEATH. 333

dying person that which follows of the Passion of our Lord Jesus Christ:

AND one of the malefactors which were hanged railed on Him, saying, If Thou be Christ, save Thyself and us. But the other answering, rebuked him, saying, Dost not thou fear God, seeing thou art in the same condemnation? and we indeed justly: for we receive the due reward of our deeds: but this Man hath done nothing amiss. And he said unto Jesus, Lord, remember me when Thou comest into Thy kingdom. And Jesus said unto him, Verily I say unto thee, To-day shalt thou be with Me in paradise. And it was about the sixth hour, and there was a darkness over all the earth until the ninth hour. And about the ninth hour Jesus cried with a loud voice, saying, Eli, Eli, lama sabachthani? that is to say, My God, My God, why hast Thou forsaken Me? After this, Jesus knowing that all things were now accomplished, that the scripture might be fulfilled saith, I thirst. Now there was set a vessel full of vinegar: and they filled a sponge with vinegar, and put it upon hyssop, and put it to His mouth. When Jesus therefore had received the vinegar, He said, It is finished. And when He had cried with a loud voice, He said, Father, into Thy hands I commend My Spirit: and having said thus, He gave up the ghost.

Let us pray.

BE mindful, O most loving Jesu, of that hour, in which, hanging on the Cross Thou didst cry, My God, My God, why hast Thou forsaken Me? And again, Father, into Thy hands I commend My Spirit: and having said this, didst give up the ghost. By that Thy most precious Death, which was our life, we pray Thee not to forsake this Thy *servant*, who hath none other helper beside Thee; but vouchsafe to receive *his* spirit and to cause *him* to enter into Thy kingdom, where *he* may love Thee and the Father and the Holy Ghost, with perpetual love, and together with Thy Saints and elect, may tell of Thy loving-kindness for ever and ever. Amen.

[*If the agony of death still continues, these Psalms, or any of them, may be said:*

Psalm xxii. *Deus, Deus meus*, p. 26.
Psalm liv. *Deus, in nomine tuo*, p. 29.
Psalm xci. *Qui habitat*, p. 68.
Psalm cxxxix. *Domine, probasti me*, p. 61.]

As soon as the soul has departed, is said:

℟. In Thee, O Lord, have I put my trust, let me never be put to confusion; make haste to deliver me. Into Thy hands I commend my spirit: Thou hast redeemed me, O Lord, Thou God of truth; cause the light of Thy countenance to shine upon Thy *servant*. ℣. Lord Jesus: receive my spirit. ℟. Thou hast redeemed me, O Lord, Thou God of Truth; cause the light of Thy countenance to shine upon Thy *servant*.

Lord, have mercy.
Christ, have mercy.
Lord, have mercy.

Our Father.

℣. Enter not into judgment with Thy servant, O Lord. ℟. For in Thy sight shall no man living be justified. ℣. O deliver not the soul of Thy turtle dove into the hand of the enemy. ℟. And forget not the congregation of the poor for ever. ℣. Hear my prayer, O Lord. ℟. And let my crying come unto Thee.

Let us pray.

TO Thee, O Lord, we commend Thy *servant* whom Thou hast taken from the world; and as Thou hast delivered *him* from the contagion of mortality, so be Thou pleased to give *him* a portion and an inheritance among Thy Saints. Who livest.

[*Or, instead of the above Versicles and Prayers:*

℟. Come, holy ones, hasten, angels of the Lord: receiving *his* soul: and presenting it before the face of the Most High. ℣. May Christ, Who called thee, receive thee; and may angels lead thee into Abraham's bosom. ℟. Receiving *his* soul. ℣. Eternal rest grant unto *him*, O Lord: and light perpetual shine on *him*. ℟. Presenting it before the face of the Most High.

Lord, have mercy.
Christ, have mercy.
Lord, have mercy.
Our Father.

℣. And lead us not into temptation. ℟. But deliver us from evil. ℣. Eternal rest grant unto *him*, O Lord. ℟. And light perpetual shine upon *him*. ℣. From the gates of hell. ℟. Deliver *his* soul, O Lord. ℣. May *he* rest in peace. ℟. Amen. ℣. Hear my prayer, O Lord. ℟. And let my crying come unto Thee. ℣. The Lord be with you. ℟. And with thy spirit.

Let us pray.

TO Thee, O Lord, we commend the soul of Thy *servant, N.*, that dead unto the world, it may live unto Thee; and the sins which *he* has committed through the frailty of this earthly life, do Thou mercifully blot out by Thy pitying forgiveness. Through.]

OFFICE OF THE DEAD.

The Office of the Dead is said on every feria through Advent till Christmas Eve, from the morrow of the Octave of Epiphany till Tuesday in Holy Week inclusive, and from the morrow of Trinity Sunday till Advent, but never on Double Feasts, or through their Octaves.

On these days are said usually, only Vespers, one Nocturn, and Lauds: Noct. 1 on Monday and Thursday, Noct. 2 on Tuesday and Friday, Noct. 3 on Wednesday and Saturday: but, if festivals intervene, so arranging as, if possible, to say the 3 Nocts. once in the course of the week.

The three Nocturns are said on special occasions, on the first vacant feria in Holy Week, and on All Soul's Day.

[*In Roman use this is said, except in Easter-tide, on the first day of every month, not hindered by a Double Feast, in which case it is said on the first day not so hindered. But in Advent and Lent, on every Monday not so hindered, except in Holy Week. In Choirs it is said after the Office of the day, i.e. Vespers after Vespers, and Matins after Lauds of the day, unless the use of the place be different: out of Choir it is said as occasion serves.*]

Some Roman variations are bracketed.

Vespers

begin at once with the

Ant. I will walk before the Lord.

This Ant. is sung after v. 8, at the close of the psalm, v. 9 being omitted.

Dilexi, quoniam. Psalm cxvi.

I AM well pleased : that the Lord hath heard the voice of my prayer;

2 That He hath inclined His ear unto me : therefore will I call upon Him as long as I live.

3 The snares of death compassed me round about : and the pains of hell gat hold upon me.

4 I shall find trouble and heaviness, and I will call upon the Name of the Lord : O Lord, I beseech Thee, deliver my soul.

5 Gracious is the Lord and righteous : yea, our God is merciful.

6 The Lord preserveth the simple : I was in misery, and He helped me.

7 Turn again then unto my rest, O my soul : for the Lord hath rewarded thee.

8 And why? Thou hast delivered my soul from death : mine eyes from tears, and my feet from falling.

[*At the end of every Psalm and Canticle is said in the Roman use :*

Eternal rest : grant unto them, O Lord.

And light perpetual : shine upon them.

But neither this nor Gloria *according to Sarum.*]

Ant. I will walk before the Lord : in the land of the living.

Ant. Wo is me.

Ad Dominum. Psalm cxx.

WHEN I was in trouble I called upon the Lord : and He heard me.

2 Deliver my soul, O Lord, from lying lips : and from a deceitful tongue.

3 What reward shall be given or done unto thee, thou false tongue : even mighty and sharp arrows, with hot burning coals.

4 Wo is me, that I am constrained to dwell with Mesech : and to have my habitation among the tents of Kedar.

5 My soul hath long dwelt among them : that are enemies unto peace.

6 I labour for peace, but when I speak unto them thereof : they make them ready to battle.

[Eternal rest, etc.]

Ant. Wo is me : that I am constrained to dwell with Mesech.

Ant. The Lord shall preserve thee.

Levavi oculos. Psalm cxxi.

I WILL lift up mine eyes unto the hills : from whence cometh my help.

2 My help cometh even from the Lord : Who hath made heaven and earth.

3 He will not suffer thy foot to be moved : and He that keepeth thee will not sleep.

4 Behold, He that keepeth Israel : shall neither slumber nor sleep.

5 The Lord Himself is thy keeper : the Lord is thy defence upon thy right hand.

6 So that the sun shall not burn thee by day : neither the moon by night.

7 The Lord shall preserve thee from all evil : yea, it is even He that shall keep thy soul.

8 The Lord shall preserve thy going out, and thy coming in : from this time forth for evermore.

[Eternal rest, etc.] .

Ant. The Lord shall preserve thee from all evil : yea, it is even He that shall keep thy soul.

Ant. If Thou, Lord.

De profundis. Psalm cxxx.

OUT of the deep have I called unto Thee, O Lord : Lord, hear my voice.

2 O let Thine ears consider well : the voice of my complaint.

3 If Thou, Lord, wilt be extreme to mark what is done amiss : O Lord, who may abide it?

4 For there is mercy with Thee : therefore shalt Thou be feared.

5 I look for the Lord; my soul doth wait for Him : in His word is my trust.

6 My soul fleeth unto the Lord : before the morning watch, I say, before the morning watch.

7 O Israel, trust in the Lord, for with the Lord there is mercy : and with Him is plenteous redemption.

8 And He shall redeem Israel : from all his sins.

[Eternal rest, etc.]

Ant. If Thou, Lord, wilt be extreme to mark what is done amiss : O Lord, who may abide it?

Ant. Despise not then.

Confitebor tibi. Psalm cxxxviii.

I WILL give thanks unto Thee, O Lord, with my whole heart : even before the gods will I sing praise unto Thee.

2 I will worship toward Thy holy temple, and praise Thy Name, because of Thy loving-kindness and truth : for Thou hast magnified Thy Name, and Thy word, above all things.

3 When I called upon Thee, Thou heardest me : and enduedst my soul with much strength.

4 All the kings of the earth shall praise Thee, O Lord : for they have heard the words of Thy mouth.

5 Yea, they shall sing in the ways of the Lord : that great is the glory of the Lord.

6 For though the Lord be high, yet hath he respect unto the lowly : as for the proud, He beholdeth them afar off.

7 Though I walk in the midst of trouble, yet shalt Thou refresh me : Thou shalt stretch forth Thy hand upon the furiousness of mine enemies, and Thy right hand shall save me.

8 The Lord shall make good His loving-kindness toward me : yea, Thy mercy, O Lord, endureth for ever; despise not then the works of Thine own hands.

[Eternal rest, etc.]

Ant. Despise not then, O Lord : the works of Thine own hands.

℣. From the gates of hell.
℟. Deliver their souls, O Lord.

Ant. to Mag. I heard a voice from heaven, saying : Blessed are the dead which die in the Lord.

[℣. I heard a voice from heaven, saying unto me. ℟. Blessed are the dead which die in the Lord.

Ant. to Mag. All that the Father giveth Me, shall come unto Me : and him that cometh unto Me I will in no wise cast out.]

The Prayers following are said kneeling, and so likewise at Lauds :

Our Father, *in silence.* ℣. And lead us not into temptation. ℟. But deliver us from evil.

Psalm cxlvi. Lauda, anima mea, *at Vespers, as also* Psalm cxlv. Exaltabo te, Deus, *at the end of Lauds, is not said on All Souls' Day, nor on the day of a death or burial. At other times it is always said.*

Lauda, anima mea. Psalm cxlvi.

PRAISE the Lord, O my soul; while I live will I praise the Lord : yea, as long as I have any being, I will sing praises unto my God.

2 O put not your trust in princes, nor in any child of man : for there is no help in them.

3 For when the breath of man goeth forth he shall turn again to his

earth : and then all his thoughts perish.

4 Blessed is he that hath the God of Jacob for his help : and whose hope is in the Lord his God.

5 Who made heaven and earth, the sea, and all that therein is : Who keepeth His promise for ever;

6 Who helpeth them to right that suffer wrong : Who feedeth the hungry.

7 The Lord looseth men out of prison : the Lord giveth sight to the blind.

8 The Lord helpeth them that are fallen : the Lord careth for the righteous.

9 The Lord careth for the strangers; He defendeth the fatherless and widow : as for the way of the ungodly, He turneth it upside down.

10 The Lord thy God, O Sion, shall be King for evermore : and throughout all generations.

[Eternal rest, etc.]

℣. From the gates of hell. ℟. Deliver their souls, O Lord. [℣. May they rest in peace. ℟. Amen. ℣. Hear my prayer, O Lord. ℟. And let my crying come unto Thee. ℣. The Lord be with you. ℟. And with thy spirit.] ℣. I believe verily to see the Lord. ℟. In the land of the living. ℣. The Lord be with you. ℟. And with thy spirit.

When the corpse is present, both at Vespers and Lauds, is said the greater Collect.

O GOD, Whose property is ever to have mercy and to spare: we suppliants intreat Thee for the soul of Thy *servant* [or *handmaid*] *N.*, which to-day Thou hast called to depart from this world : that Thou wouldest not deliver it into the hands of the enemy, nor forget it finally, but command it to be received by the holy Angels, and led into the land of the living; and whereas it hath hoped and believed in Thee, may it be found worthy to rejoice in the society of Thy Saints. Through.

On the Month's Mind is said this Collect:

O GOD, Whose property is ever to have mercy and to spare : look favourably on the soul of Thy *servant*, and put away all *his* sins; that, loosed from the bonds of death, *he* may merit to pass unto life.

On the Anniversary.
COLLECT.

GOD, Who art the Lord of mercies, grant to the souls of Thy servants and handmaidens, the anniversary of whose burial we commemorate, a place of refreshment, the quiet of blessedness, and the glory of light. Through.

If the Anniversary of one only, it is said in the singular number.

For Bishops [or Priests] deceased.

GOD, Who among apostolic Priests hast raised up Thy *servants* to the dignity of the Episcopate [or Priesthood], mercifully grant *them* a share in their blessed companionship in heaven, whose office *they* held on earth.

For Brethren and Sisters.

GOD, Who art the Giver of pardon, and the Author of human salvation; we pray Thy mercy, that, Blessed Mary, ever Virgin, and all Thy Saints interceding, Thou wouldest grant to all the brethren and sisters of our congregation who have passed out of this world, to attain the fellowship of everlasting blessedness.

General Prayer.

GOD, the Creator and Redeemer of all the faithful, grant to the souls of Thy servants and handmaidens remission of all their sins: that the favour they have always desired, by pious supplications may be obtained. Who livest and reignest with God the Father, in the unity of the Holy Spirit, God, throughout all ages.

[*On the Day of a Burial.*]

COLLECT.

WE beseech Thee, O Lord, deliver the soul of Thy *servant* [or *handmaid*] *N.*, that, dead to the world, it may live unto Thee: and that which *he* hath committed by frailty of the flesh in *his* human conversation, wipe away by the grace of Thy most merciful lovingkindness. Through Jesus Christ our Lord, Who liveth.

For Father and Mother.

COLLECT.

O GOD, Who didst command us to honour our father and mother: graciously have mercy on the souls of *my father and mother*, and cause *me* to see *them* in the joy of eternal glory. Through.

If for many, it is said: the souls of our parents; *and us is substituted for* me.

If for a father only: the soul of my, *or,* our father.

If for a mother only: the soul of my, *or,* our mother.

For a Man Departed.

INCLINE Thine ear, O Lord, to our prayers who humbly entreat Thy mercy: that Thou wouldest grant to Thy *servant N.*, whom Thou hast called from this world, a place in the land of peace and light, and wouldest call *him* to the companionship of Thy Saints. Through.

For a Woman Departed.

COLLECT.

WE beseech Thee, O Lord, of Thy pity, have mercy on the soul of Thy *handmaid, N.*, and as Thou hast freed *her* from the contagion of mortality, so be Thou pleased to give *her* a portion and an inheritance among Thine elect. Through.]

℣. The Lord be with you. ℞. And with thy spirit.

[℣. Eternal rest grant unto them, O Lord. ℞. And light perpetual shine upon them.] ℣. May they rest in peace. ℞. Amen.

These last ℣℣. are not said when Matins follow immediately.

Matins.

[*Inv.* The King, to Whom all things live: O come let us worship. (*Repeat.*)

Venite. Psalm xcv.

O COME, let us sing unto the Lord: let us heartily rejoice in the strength of our salvation.

2 Let us come before His presence with thanksgiving: and shew ourselves glad in Him with psalms.

The King, to Whom all things live:
O come, let us worship.

3 For the Lord is a great God: and a great King above all gods.

4 In His hand are all the corners of the earth: and the strength of the hills is His also.

O come, let us worship.

5 The sea is His, and He made it: and His hands prepared the dry land.

6 O come, let us worship and fall down: and kneel before the Lord our Maker.

7 For He is the Lord our God: and we are the people of His pasture, and the sheep of His hand.

The King, to Whom all things live:
O come, let us worship.

8 To-day if ye will hear His voice, harden not your hearts: as in the day of provocation, and as in the day of temptation in the wilderness;

9 When your fathers tempted Me: proved Me, and saw My works.

O come, let us worship.

10 Forty years long was I grieved

with this generation, and said : It is a people that do err in their hearts, for they have not known My ways;

11 Unto whom I sware in My wrath : that they should not enter into My rest.

> The King, to Whom all things live : O come, let us worship.

Eternal rest grant unto them, O Lord : and light perpetual shine upon them.

> O come, let us worship.
>
> The King, to Whom all things live : O come, let us worship.

This Invitatory is said only on All Souls' Day, and on the day of a burial; on which days are said the three Nocturns following, in Roman use, with doubled Antiphons. At other times is said only one Nocturn, with Lauds, in this order:—on Monday and Thursday, Nocturn 1; on Tuesday and Friday, Nocturn 2; on Wednesday and Saturday, Nocturn 3.]

FIRST NOCTURN.

For Monday and Thursday.

[*After every Psalm in the Office is said, instead of* Glory be, *etc.:*

Eternal rest grant unto them, O Lord : and light perpetual shine upon them.]

Ant. Make Thy way plain.

Verba mea auribus. Psalm v., p. 11.

Ant. Make Thy way plain : O Lord, before my face.

Ant. Turn Thee.

Domine, ne in furore. Ps. vi., p. 12.

Ant. Turn Thee, O Lord, and deliver my soul : for in death no man remembereth Thee.

Ant. Lest.

Domine, Deus meus. Psalm vii.

O LORD my God, in Thee have I put my trust : save me from all them that persecute me, and deliver me;

2 Lest he devour my soul like a lion, and tear it in pieces : while there is none to help.

3 O Lord my God, if I have done any such thing : or if there be any wickedness in my hands;

4 If I have rewarded evil unto him that dealt friendly with me : yea, I have delivered him that without any cause is mine enemy;

5 Then let mine enemy persecute my soul, and take me : yea, let him tread my life down upon the earth, and lay mine honour in the dust.

6 Stand up, O Lord, in Thy wrath, and lift up Thyself, because of the indignation of mine enemies; arise up for me in the judgment that Thou hast commanded.

7 And so shall the congregation of the people come about Thee : for their sakes therefore lift up Thyself again.

8 The Lord shall judge the people; give sentence with me, O Lord : according to my righteousness, and according to the innocency that is in me.

9 O let the wickedness of the ungodly come to an end : but guide Thou the just.

10 For the righteous God : trieth the very hearts and reins.

11 My help cometh of God : Who preserveth them that are true of heart.

12 God is a righteous Judge, strong, and patient : and God is provoked every day.

13 If a man will not turn, He will whet His sword : He hath bent His bow, and made it ready.

14 He hath prepared for him the instruments of death : He ordaineth His arrows against the persecutors.

15 Behold, he travaileth with mischief : he hath conceived sorrow, and brought forth ungodliness.

16 He hath graven and digged up

a pit : and is fallen himself into the destruction that he made for others.

17 For his travail shall come upon his own head : and his wickedness shall fall on his own pate.

18 I will give thanks unto the Lord, according to His righteousness : and I will praise the Name of the Lord most High.

Ant. Lest he devour my soul like a lion : while there is none to help.

℣. From the gates of hell. ℟. Deliver their souls, O Lord.

Our Father (*wholly in silence*).

The Lessons are read without Absolutions, Benedictions, or Titles.

Lesson I. Job vii.

LET me alone; for my days are vanity. What is man, that Thou shouldest magnify him? and that Thou shouldest set Thine heart upon him? and that Thou shouldest visit him every morning, and try him every moment? How long wilt Thou not depart from me, nor let me alone till I swallow down my spittle? I have sinned; what shall I do unto Thee, O Thou Preserver of men? why hast Thou set me as a mark against Thee, so that I am a burden to myself? And why dost Thou not pardon my transgressions, and take away mine iniquity? for now shall I sleep in the dust; and Thou shalt seek me in the morning, but I shall not be.

The Lessons are ended without But Thou, etc., *or other conclusion.*

℟. I know that my Redeemer liveth, and that He shall stand at the latter day upon the earth : and in my flesh shall I see God my Saviour. ℣. Whom I shall see for myself, and mine eyes shall behold, and not another. And.

Lesson II. Job. x.

MY SOUL is weary of my life; I will leave my complaint upon myself; I will speak in the bitterness of my soul. I will say unto God, Do not condemn me; shew me wherefore Thou contendest with me. Is it good unto Thee that Thou shouldest oppress, that Thou shouldest despise the work of Thine hands, and shine upon the counsel of the wicked? Hast Thou eyes of flesh? or seest Thou as man seeth? are Thy days as the days of man? are Thy years as man's days? that Thou inquirest after mine iniquity, and searchest after my sin? Thou knowest that I am not wicked; and there is none that can deliver out of Thine hand.

℟. Thou Who didst raise Lazarus from the grave of corruption : do Thou grant them, O Lord, rest, and a place of pardon. ℣. Thou Who shalt come to judge the quick and the dead, and the world by fire. Do.

Lesson III. Job x.

THINE hands have made me and fashioned me together round about; yet Thou dost destroy me. Remember, I beseech Thee, that Thou hast made me as the clay; and wilt Thou bring me into dust again? Hast Thou not poured me out as milk, and curdled me like cheese? Thou hast clothed me with skin and flesh, and hast fenced me with bones and sinews. Thou has granted me life and favour, and Thy visitation hath preserved my spirit.

℟. Lord, when Thou shalt come to judge the earth, where shall I hide myself from the face of Thy wrath? For I have grievously sinned in my life. ℣. I dread and am ashamed of that I have done; when Thou shalt come to judge, condemn me not. For.

[℣. Eternal rest grant unto them, O Lord : and light perpetual shine upon them. For.]

When the corpse is present the ℞. is repeated from the beginning, as in Passion-tide.

Then follow Lauds, p. 346, when only one Nocturn is said.

SECOND NOCTURN.

For Tuesday and Friday.

Ant. He shall feed me.

Dominus regit me. Ps. xxiii., p. 27.

Ant. He shall feed me : in a green pasture.

Ant. Remember not.

Ad te, Domine, levavi. Ps. xxv., p. 28.

Ant. Remember not : the sins and offences of my youth, O Lord.

Ant. I believe verily.

Dominus illuminatio. Psalm xxvii.

THE Lord is my light, and my salvation; whom then shall I fear : the Lord is the strength of my life; of whom then shall I be afraid?

2 When the wicked, even mine enemies and my foes, came upon me to eat up my flesh : they stumbled and fell.

3 Though an host of men were laid against me, yet shall not my heart be afraid : and though there rose up war against me, yet will I put my trust in Him.

4 One thing have I desired of the Lord, which I will require : even that I may dwell in the house of the Lord all the days of my life, to behold the fair beauty of the Lord, and to visit His temple.

5 For in the time of trouble He shall hide me in His tabernacle : yea, in the secret place of His dwelling shall He hide me, and set me up upon a rock of stone.

6 And now shall He lift up mine head : above mine enemies round about me.

7 Therefore will I offer in His dwelling an oblation with great gladness : I will sing, and speak praises unto the Lord.

8 Hearken unto my voice, O Lord, when I cry unto Thee : have mercy upon me, and hear me.

9 My heart hath talked of Thee, Seek ye My face : Thy face, Lord, will I seek.

10 O hide not Thou Thy face from me : nor cast Thy servant away in displeasure.

11 Thou hast been my succour : leave me not, neither forsake me, O God of my salvation.

12 When my father and my mother forsake me : the Lord taketh me up.

13 Teach me Thy way, O Lord : and lead me in the right way, because of mine enemies.

14 Deliver me not over into the will of mine adversaries : for there are false witnesses risen up against me, and such as speak wrong.

15 I should utterly have fainted : but that I believe verily to see the goodness of the Lord in the land of the living.

16 O tarry thou the Lord's leisure : be strong, and He shall comfort thine heart; and put thou thy trust in the Lord.

Ant. I believe verily : to see the goodness of the Lord in the land of the living.

℣. The righteous shall be had in everlasting remembrance.

℞. He will not be afraid of any evil tidings.

Our Father (*wholly in silence*).

Lesson IV. Job xiii.

ANSWER Thou me. How many are mine iniquities and sins?

make me to know my transgression and my sin. Wherefore hidest Thou Thy face, and holdest me for Thine enemy? Wilt Thou break a leaf driven to and fro? and wilt Thou pursue the dry stubble? For Thou writest bitter things against me, and makest me to possess the iniquities of my youth. Thou puttest my feet also in the stocks, and lookest narrowly unto all my paths; Thou settest a print upon the heels of my feet. And he, as a rotten thing, consumeth, as a garment that is motheaten.

℟. Woe is me, O Lord, for I have greatly sinned in my life; what shall I do, and whither shall I fly, save to Thee, my God? Have mercy upon me: when Thou comest in the last day. ℣. My soul also is sore troubled, but Lord, do Thou succour it. When.

LESSON V. Job xiv.

MAN that is born of a woman is of few days, and full of trouble. He cometh forth like a flower, and is cut down: he fleeth also as a shadow, and continueth not. And dost Thou open Thine eyes upon such an one, and bringest me into judgment with Thee. Who can bring a clean thing out of an unclean? not one. Seeing his days are determined, the number of his months are with Thee, Thou hast appointed his bounds that he cannot pass; turn from him, that he may rest, till he shall accomplish, as an hireling, his day.

℟. Remember not my sins, O Lord: when Thou shalt come to judge the world by fire. ℣. Make my way plain before Thy face, O Lord my God. When.

LESSON VI. Job xiv.

O THAT Thou wouldest hide me in the grave, that Thou wouldest keep me secret, until Thy wrath be past, that Thou wouldest appoint me a set time, and remember me! If a man die, shall he live again? all the days of my appointed time will I wait, till my change come. Thou shalt call, and I will answer Thee: Thou wilt have a desire to the work of Thine hands. For now Thou numberest my steps: dost Thou not watch over my sin?

℟. O Lord, judge me not according to my deeds; I have done nothing worthy in Thy sight: therefore, I beseech Thy majesty, that Thou, O God, wouldst do away mine offences. ℣. Wash me throughly from mine iniquity, and cleanse me from my sin, for before Thee only have I sinned. Therefore.

Here follow Lauds, p. 346, when one Nocturn only is said.

THIRD NOCTURN.

ON WEDNESDAY AND SATURDAY.

Ant. O Lord, let it be Thy pleasure.

Expectans expectavi. Ps. XL.

I WAITED patiently for the Lord: and He inclined unto me, and heard my calling.

2 He brought me also out of the horrible pit, out of the mire and clay: and set my feet upon the rock, and ordered my goings.

3 And He hath put a new song in my mouth: even a thanksgiving unto our God.

4 Many shall see it, and fear: and shall put their trust in the Lord.

5 Blessed is the man that hath set his hope in the Lord: and turned not unto the proud, and to such as go about with lies.

6 O Lord my God, great are the wondrous works which Thou hast done, like as be also Thy thoughts

which are to us-ward : and yet there is no man that ordereth them unto Thee.

7 If I should declare them, and speak of them : they should be more than I am able to express.

8 Sacrifice, and meat-offering, Thou wouldest not : but mine ears hast Thou opened.

9 Burnt offerings and sacrifice for sin hast Thou not required : then said I, Lo, I come.

10 In the volume of the book it is written of me, that I should fulfil Thy will, O my God : I am content to do it; yea, Thy law is within my heart.

11 I have declared Thy righteousness in the great congregation : lo, I will not refrain my lips, O Lord, and that Thou knowest.

12 I have not hid Thy righteousness within my heart : my talk hath been of Thy truth, and of Thy salvation.

13 I have not kept back Thy loving mercy and truth : from the great congregation.

14 Withdraw not Thou Thy mercy from me, O Lord : let Thy lovingkindness and Thy truth alway preserve me.

15 For innumerable troubles are come about me; my sins have taken such hold upon me that I am not able to look up : yea, they are more in number than the hairs of my head, and my heart hath failed me.

16 O Lord, let it be Thy pleasure to deliver me : make haste, O Lord, to help me.

17 Let them be ashamed, and confounded together, that seek after my soul to destroy it : let them be driven backward, and put to rebuke, that wish me evil.

18 Let them be desolate, and rewarded with shame : that say unto me, Fie upon thee, fie upon thee.

19 Let all those that seek Thee be joyful and glad in Thee : and let such as love Thy salvation say alway, The Lord be praised.

20 As for me, I am poor and needy : but the Lord careth for me.

21 Thou art my helper and redeemer : make no long tarrying, O my God.

Ant. O Lord, let it be Thy pleasure to deliver me : make haste, O Lord, to help me.

Ant. Heal my soul, O Lord.

Beatus qui intelligit. Ps. XLI.

BLESSED is he that considereth the poor and needy : the Lord shall deliver him in the time of trouble.

2 The Lord preserve him, and keep him alive, that he may be blessed upon earth : and deliver not Thou him into the will of his enemies.

3 The Lord comfort him, when he lieth sick upon his bed : make Thou all his bed in his sickness.

4 I said, Lord, be merciful unto me : heal my soul, for I have sinned against Thee.

5 Mine enemies speak evil of me : When shall he die, and his name perish?

6 And if he come to see me, he speaketh vanity : and his heart conceiveth falsehood within himself, and when he cometh forth he telleth it.

7 All mine enemies whisper together against me : even against me do they imagine this evil.

8 Let the sentence of guiltiness proceed against him : and now that he lieth, let him rise up no more.

9 Yea, even mine own familiar friend, whom I trusted : who did also eat of my bread, hath laid great wait for me.

10 But be Thou merciful unto me,

O Lord : raise Thou me up again, and I shall reward them.

11 By this I know Thou favourest me : that mine enemy doth not triumph against me.

12 And when I am in my health, Thou upholdest me : and shalt set me before Thy face for ever.

13 Blessed be the Lord God of Israel : world without end. Amen.

Ant. Heal my soul, O Lord : for I have sinned against Thee.

Ant. My soul is athirst.

Quemadmodum. Psalm XLII.

LIKE as the hart desireth the water-brooks : so longeth my soul after Thee, O God.

2 My soul is athirst for God, yea, even for the living God : when shall I come to appear before the presence of God?

3 My tears have been my meat day and night : while they daily say unto me, Where is now thy God?

4 Now when I think thereupon, I pour out my heart by myself : for I went with the multitude, and brought them forth into the house of God;

5 In the voice of praise and thanksgiving : among such as keep holy day.

6 Why art thou so full of heaviness, O my soul : and why art thou so disquieted within me?

7 Put thy trust in God : for I will yet give Him thanks for the help of His countenance.

8 My God, my soul is vexed within me : therefore will I remember Thee concerning the land of Jordan, and the little hill of Hermon.

9 One deep calleth another, because of the noise of the water-pipes : all Thy waves and storms are gone over me.

10 The Lord hath granted His loving-kindness in the day-time : and in the night-season did I sing of Him, and made my prayer unto the God of my life.

11 I will say unto the God of my strength, Why hast Thou forgotten me : why go I thus heavily, while the enemy oppresseth me?

12 My bones are smitten asunder as with a sword : while mine enemies that trouble me cast me in the teeth;

13 Namely, while they say daily unto me : Where is now thy God?

14 Why art thou so vexed, O my soul : and why art thou so disquieted within me?

15 O put thy trust in God : for I will yet thank Him, which is the help of my countenance, and my God.

Ant. My soul is athirst for the living God : when shall I come to appear before the presence of God?

℣. Eternal rest grant unto them, O Lord.

℟. And light perpetual shine upon them.

Our Father *(wholly in silence)*.

LESSON VII. Job XVII.

MY breath is corrupt, my days are extinct, the graves are ready for me. Are there not mockers with me? and doth not mine eye continue in their provocation? Lay down now, put me in a surety with thee; who is he that will strike hands with me? My days are past, my purposes are broken of, even the thoughts of my heart. They change the night into day : the light is short because of darkness. If I wait, the grave is mine house : I have made my bed in the darkness. I have said to corruption, Thou art my father : to the worm, Thou art my mother, and my sister. And where is now my hope? as for my hope, who shall see it?

℞. On me who sin every day, on me who never repent, hath the fear of death fallen: because in the grave there is no redemption, have mercy upon me, O God, and save me. ℣. Save me, O God, for Thy Name's sake, and avenge me in Thy strength. Because.

LESSON VIII. Job xix.

MY bone cleaveth to my skin and to my flesh, and I am escaped with the yskin of my teeth. Have pity upon me, have pity upon me, O ye my friends; for the hand of God hath touched me. Why do ye persecute me as God, and are not satisfied with my flesh? Oh, that my words were now written! oh, that they were printed in a book! that they were graven with an iron pen and lead in the rock for ever! For I know that my Redeemer liveth, and that He shall stand at the latter day upon the earth: and though after my skin worms destroy this body, yet in my flesh shall I see God: whom I shall see for myself, and mine eyes shall behold, and not another; though my reins be consumed within me.

℞. Eternal rest grant unto them, O Lord: and light perpetual shine upon them. ℣. Thou Who didst raise Lazarus from the grave of corruption, do Thou, Lord, grant them rest. And.

LESSON IX. Job x.

WHEREFORE then hast Thou brought me forth out of the womb? Oh, that I had given up the ghost, and no eye had seen me! I should have been as though I had not been: I should have been carried from the womb to the grave. Are not my days few? cease then, and let me alone, that I may take comfort a little, before I go whence I shall not return, even to the land of darkness and the shadow of death; a land of darkness, as darkness itself; and of the shadow of death, without any order, and where the light is as darkness.

℞. Deliver me, O Lord, from eternal death in that tremendous day: when the heavens and the earth shall be shaken: when Thou shalt come to judge the world by fire. ℣. That day, that day of wrath, of calamity and misery, that great and very bitter day. When the. ℣. What then, most miserable, what shall I say, or what shall I do, when I have done no good thing before so great a judgment? When Thou. ℣. Now, O Christ, we entreat Thee, have mercy, we beseech Thee: Thou Who camest to redeem the lost, condemn not the redeemed. When Thou. Deliver me (*down to 1st* ℣).

This is always said when three Nocturns are used: otherwise

℞. Deliver me, O Lord, from the paths of hell, Thou Who brakest in pieces the gates of brass: and visitedst hell, and gavest light to them, that they might see Thee: who dwelt in the pains of darkness. ℣. Crying, and saying, Thou art come, our Redeemer. Who. Eternal rest grant unto them, O Lord: and light perpetual shine upon them. Who.

[*The following* ℞. *is said on All Souls' Day, and when nine Lessons are read:*

℞. Deliver me, O Lord, from eternal death, in that tremendous day: when the heavens and the earth shall be shaken: when Thou shalt come to judge the world by fire. ℣. I tremble and am full of fear at the judgment and the coming wrath. When the. ℣. That day, that day of wrath, of calamity and misery, that great and too bitter day.

When Thou. Eternal rest grant unto them, O Lord: and light perpetual shine upon them. Deliver (*down to first* ℣).]

Lauds

are begun at once with

℣. May they rest in peace. ℟. Amen.

Ant. The bones which have been humbled.

Miserere mei Deus. Psalm LI.

HAVE mercy upon me, O God, after Thy great goodness : according to the multitude of Thy mercies do away mine offences.

2 Wash me throughly from my wickedness : and cleanse me from my sin.

3 For I acknowledge my faults : and my sin is ever before me.

4 Against Thee only have I sinned, and done this evil in Thy sight : that Thou mightest be justified in Thy saying, and clear when Thou art judged.

5 Behold, I was shapen in wickedness : and in sin hath my mother conceived me.

6 But lo, Thou requirest truth in the inward parts : and shalt make me to understand wisdom secretly.

7 Thou shalt purge me with hyssop, and I shall be clean : Thou shalt wash me, and I shall be whiter than snow.

8 Thou shalt make me hear of joy and gladness : that the bones which Thou hast broken may rejoice.

9 Turn Thy face from my sins : and put out all my misdeeds.

10 Make me a clean heart, O God : and renew a right spirit within me.

11 Cast me not away from Thy presence : and take not Thy Holy Spirit from me.

12 O give me the comfort of Thy help again : and stablish me with Thy free Spirit.

13 Then shall I teach Thy ways unto the wicked : and sinners shall be converted unto Thee.

14 Deliver me from blood-guiltiness, O God, Thou that art the God of my health : and my tongue shall sing of Thy righteousness.

15 Thou shalt open my lips, O Lord : and my mouth shall shew Thy praise.

16 For Thou desirest no sacrifice, else would I give it Thee : but Thou delightest not in burnt-offerings.

17 The sacrifice of God is a troubled spirit : a broken and contrite heart, O God, shalt Thou not despise.

18 O be favourable and gracious unto Sion : build Thou the walls of Jerusalem.

19 Then shalt Thou be pleased with the sacrifice of righteousness, with the burnt offerings, and oblations : then shall they offer young bullocks upon Thine altar.

Ant. The bones which have been humbled : shall rejoice unto the Lord.

Ant. Hear, Lord, my prayer.

Te decet hymnus. Psalm LXV.

THOU, O God, art praised in Sion : and unto Thee shall the vow be performed in Jerusalem.

2 Thou that hearest the prayer : unto Thee shall all flesh come.

3 My misdeeds prevail against me : O be Thou merciful unto our sins.

4 Blessed is the man whom Thou choosest, and receivest unto Thee : he shall dwell in Thy court, and shall be satisfied with the pleasures of Thy house, even of Thy holy temple.

5 Thou shalt shew us wonderful things in Thy righteousness, O God

of our salvation : Thou that art the hope of all the ends of the earth, and of them that remain in the broad sea.

6 Who in His strength setteth fast the mountains : and is girded about with power.

7 Who stilleth the raging of the sea : and the noise of his waves, and the madness of the people.

8 They also that dwell in the uttermost parts of the earth shall be afraid at Thy tokens : Thou that makest the out-goings of the morning and evening to praise Thee.

9 Thou visitest the earth, and blessest it : Thou makest it very plenteous.

10 The river of God is full of water : Thou preparest their corn, for so Thou providest for the earth.

11 Thou waterest her furrows, Thou sendest rain into the little valleys thereof : Thou makest it soft with the drops of rain, and blessest the increase of it.

12 Thou crownest the year with Thy goodness : and Thy clouds drop fatness.

13 They shall drop upon the dwellings of the wilderness : and the little hills shall rejoice on every side.

14 The folds shall be full of sheep : the valleys also shall stand so thick with corn, that they shall laugh and sing.

Ant. Hear, Lord, my prayer : unto Thee shall all flesh come.

Ant. Thy right hand.

Deus, Deus meus. Psalm LXIII.

O GOD, Thou art my God : early will I seek Thee.

2 My soul thirsteth for Thee, my flesh also longeth after Thee : in a barren and dry land where no water is.

3 Thus have I looked for Thee in holiness : that I might behold Thy power and glory.

4 For Thy loving kindness is better than the life itself : my lips shall praise Thee.

5 As long as I live will I magnify Thee on this manner : and lift up my hands in Thy Name.

6 My soul shall be satisfied even as it were with marrow and fatness : when my mouth praiseth Thee with joyful lips.

7 Have I not remembered Thee in my bed : and thought upon Thee when I was waking?

8 Because Thou hast been my helper : therefore under the shadow of Thy wings will I rejoice.

9 My soul hangeth upon Thee : Thy right hand hath upholden me.

10 These also that seek the hurt of my soul : they shall go under the earth.

11 Let them fall upon the edge of the sword : that they may be a portion for foxes.

12 But the King shall rejoice in God; all they also that swear by Him shall be commended : for the mouth of them that speak lies shall be stopped.

Deus misereatur. Psalm LXVII.

GOD be merciful unto us, and bless us : and shew us the light of His countenance, and be merciful unto us;

2 That Thy way may be known upon earth : Thy saving health among all nations.

3 Let the people praise Thee, O God : yea, let all the people praise Thee.

4 O let the nations rejoice and be glad : for Thou shalt judge the folk righteously, and govern the nations' upon earth.

5 Let the people praise Thee, O God : let all the people praise Thee.

6 Then shall the earth bring forth

her increase : and God, even our own God, shall give us His blessing.

7 God shall bless us : and all the ends of the world shall fear Him.

Ant. Thy right hand : hath upholden me, O Lord.

Ant. From the gates of hell.

SONG OF HEZEKIAH.

Ego dixi.   Isaiah XXXVIII.

I SAID, in the cutting off of my days : I shall go to the gates of the grave.

2 I am deprived of the residue of my years : I said, I shall not see the Lord, even the Lord, in the land of the living.

3 I shall behold man no more : with the inhabitants of the world.

4 Mine age is departed : and is removed from me as a shepherd's tent.

5 I have cut off like a weaver my life : He will cut me off with pining sickness.

6 From day even to night wilt Thou make an end of me : I reckoned till morning that, as a lion, so will He break all my bones.

7 From day even to night wilt Thou make an end of me : like a crane or a swallow so did I chatter; I did mourn as a dove.

8 Mine eyes fail : with looking upward.

9 O Lord, I am oppressed; undertake for me : what shall I say? He hath both spoken unto me, and Himself hath done it.

10 I shall go softly all my years : in the bitterness of my soul.

11 O Lord, by these things men live, and in all these things is the life of my spirit : so wilt Thou recover me, and make me to live; behold, for peace I had great bitterness.

12 But Thou hast in love to my soul delivered it from the pit of corruption : for Thou hast cast all my sins behind Thy back.

13 For the grave cannot praise Thee, death cannot celebrate Thee : they that go down into the pit cannot hope for Thy truth.

14 The living, the living, he shall praise Thee, as I do this day : the father to the children shall make known Thy truth.

15 The Lord was ready to save me : therefore we will sing my songs to the stringed instruments all the days of our life in the house of the Lord.

Ant. From the gates of hell : deliver my soul, O Lord.

Ant. Let every spirit.

Laudate Dominum.   Psalm CXLVIII.

O PRAISE the Lord of heaven : praise Him in the height.

2 Praise Him, all ye angels of His : praise Him, all His host.

3 Praise Him, sun and moon : praise Him, all ye stars and light.

4 Praise Him, all ye heavens : and ye waters that are above the heavens.

5 Let them praise the Name of the Lord : for He spake the word, and they were made; He commanded, and they were created.

6 He hath made them fast for ever and ever : He hath given them a law which shall not be broken.

7 Praise the Lord upon earth : ye dragons, and all deeps;

8 Fire and hail, snow and vapours : wind and storm, fulfilling His word;

9 Mountains and all hills : fruitful trees and all cedars;

10 Beasts and all cattle : worms and feathered fowls;

11 Kings of the earth and all people : princes and all judges of the world.

12 Young men and maidens, old men and children, praise the Name of the Lord : for His Name only is excellent, and His praise above heaven and earth.

13 He shall exalt the horn of His people; all His saints shall praise Him : even the children of Israel, even the people that serveth Him.

Cantate Domino. Psalm CXLIX.

O SING unto the Lord a new song : let the congregation of saints praise Him.

2 Let Israel rejoice in Him that made him : and let the children of Sion be joyful in their King.

3 Let them praise His Name in the dance : let them sing praises unto Him with tabret and harp.

4 For the Lord hath pleasure in His people : and helpeth the meek-hearted.

5 Let the saints be joyful with glory : let them rejoice in their beds.

6 Let the praises of God be in their mouth : and a two-edged sword in their hands :

7 To be avenged of the heathen : and to rebuke the people :

8 To bind their kings in chains : and their nobles with links of iron.

9 That they may be avenged of them, as it is written : Such honour have all His saints.

Laudate Dominum. Psalm CL.

O PRAISE God in His holiness : praise Him in the firmament of His power.

2 Praise Him in His noble acts : praise Him according to His excellent greatness.

3 Praise Him in the sound of the trumpet : praise Him upon the lute and harp.

4 Praise Him in the cymbals and dances : praise Him upon the strings and pipe.

5 Praise Him upon the well-tuned cymbals : praise Him upon the loud cymbals.

6 Let every thing that hath breath : praise the Lord.

Ant. Let every spirit : praise the Lord.

℣. Eternal rest grant unto them, O Lord.

℟. And light perpetual shine upon them.

Ant. to Ben. I am the Resurrection and the Life : he that believeth in Me, though he were dead, yet shall he live, and whosoever liveth and believeth in Me, shall never die.

Lord, have mercy.
Christ, have mercy.
Lord, have mercy.

Our Father.

Psalm CXLV., *Exaltabo te Deus*, p. 64.

Petitions and Collects as at Vespers, except

On the Month's Mind.

COLLECT.

ALMIGHTY, Everlasting God, Whose mercies are never entreated without hope : be propitious to the soul of Thy *servant*, that, as *he* departed out of this life in the confession of Thy Name, so *he* may be gathered into the company of Thy Saints.

For Bishops (*or Priests*).

COLLECT.

O GOD, Whose mercies are without number, receive our prayers for the souls of Thy servants the *bishops;* and grant them a dwelling-place in light and joy among the company of Thy Saints.

For Brethren and Sisters.

COLLECT.

INCLINE Thine ear (p. 338).

Let us pray.

Then are said prayers for friends, in silence, after which is said aloud the following general

COLLECT.

WE beseech Thee, O Lord, let our prayers and supplications avail for the souls of all the faithful departed: that Thou mayest both deliver them from all their sins, and make them partakers of Thy redemption. Who livest.

℣. May they rest in peace. ℟. Amen.

Here ends the Office of the Dead.

ITINERARY.

Ant. Into the way of peace : and prosperity, the Almighty and merciful Lord direct *our* steps: and the Angel Raphael go with *us* in the way, that with peace, safety, and joy, *we* may return home.

Benedictus, p. 8.

Lord, have mercy.
Christ, have mercy.
Lord, have mercy.

Our Father.

℣. And lead us not into temptation. ℟. But deliver us from evil. ℣. O God, save Thy *servants.* ℟. Which put *their* trust in Thee. ℣. Send *us* help from the Sanctuary. ℟. And strengthen *us* out of Sion. ℣. Be unto *us,* O Lord, a tower of strength. ℟. From the face of the enemy. ℣. Let the enemy have no advantage over *us.* ℟. Neither the son of wickedness approach to hurt *us.* ℣. Blessed be the Lord this day. ℟. The God of our salvation make *our* journey prosperous. ℣. Shew us Thy ways, O Lord. ℟. And teach us Thy paths. ℣. O that my ways were made so direct. ℟. That I might keep Thy statutes. ℣. The crooked shall be made straight. ℟. And the rough places plain. ℣. God shall give His Angels charge over thee. ℟. To keep thee in all thy ways. ℣. Hear my prayer, O Lord. ℟. And let my crying come unto Thee. ℣. The Lord be with you. ℟. And with thy spirit.

Let us pray.

COLLECTS.

O GOD, Who leddest the children of Israel on dry land through the midst of the sea, and by the leading of a star didst shew the three Magi the way to come to Thee; grant *us,* we beseech Thee, a prosperous journey and a tranquil time, that, Thy holy Angel accompanying *us,* we may safely reach the place whither *we* go, and finally attain the haven of everlasting salvation.

O GOD, Who didst bring Abraham Thy servant from Ur of the Chaldees, and didst keep him in safety through all the ways of his pilgrimage; we beseech Thee that Thou wouldest protect Thy *servants*. Be to *us*, O Lord, in setting forth a support, in the way a consolation, in heat a shadow, in rain and cold a covering, in weariness a chariot, in adversity a support, in slippery places a staff, in shipwreck a port; that, Thou being *our* Leader, *we* may prosperously reach the place whither *we go*, and at length return in safety to *our* home.

ASSIST us mercifully, O Lord, in these our supplications and prayers, and dispose the way of Thy servants towards the attainment of everlasting salvation; that among all the changes and chances of this mortal life, they may ever be defended by Thy most gracious and ready help.

GRANT, we beseech Thee, Almighty God, that Thy family may walk in the way of salvation, and, following the counsels of blessed John the forerunner, may safely come to Him Whom he foretold, Thy Son Jesus Christ our Lord, Who liveth and reigneth with Thee and the Holy Ghost, ever one God, world without end. Amen.

℣. Let *us* go forth in peace.

℞. In the Name of the Lord. Amen.

✠

A TABLE

OF THE MOVEABLE FEASTS FOR TWENTY-ONE YEARS.

Year of our Lord.	The Golden Number.	The Epact.	Sunday Letter.	Sundays after Epiphany.	Septuagesima Sunday.	The First Day of Lent.	Easter Day.	Ascension Day.	Whitsun Day.	Corpus Christi.	Sundays after Trinity.	Advent Sunday.
1880	19	18	DC	2	Jan. 25	Feb. 11	Mar. 28	May 6	May 16	May 27	26	Nov. 28
1881	1	0	B	5	Feb. 13	Mar. 2	April 17	—— 26	June 5	June 16	23	—— 27
1882	2	11	A	4	—— 5	Feb. 22	—— 9	—— 18	May 28	—— 8	25	Dec. 3
1883	3	22	G	2	Jan. 21	—— 7	Mar. 25	—— 3	—— 13	May 24	27	—— 2
1884	4	3	FE	4	Feb. 10	—— 27	April 13	—— 22	June 1	June 12	24	Nov. 30
1885	5	14	D	3	—— 1	—— 18	—— 5	—— 14	May 24	—— 4	25	—— 29
1886	6	25	C	6	—— 21	Mar. 10	—— 25	June 3	June 13	—— 24	22	—— 28
1887	7	6	B	4	—— 6	Feb. 23	—— 10	May 19	May 29	—— 9	24	—— 27
1888	8	17	AG	3	Jan. 29	—— 15	—— 1	—— 10	—— 20	May 31	26	Dec. 2
1889	9	28	F	5	Feb. 17	Mar. 6	—— 21	—— 30	June 9	June 20	23	—— 1
1890	10	9	E	3	—— 2	Feb. 19	—— 6	—— 15	May 25	—— 5	25	Nov. 30
1891	11	20	D	2	Jan. 25	—— 11	Mar. 29	—— 7	—— 17	May 28	26	—— 29
1892	12	1	CB	5	Feb. 14	Mar. 2	April 17	—— 26	June 5	June 16	23	—— 27
1893	13	12	A	3	Jan. 29	Feb. 15	—— 2	—— 11	May 21	—— 1	26	Dec. 3
1894	14	23	G	2	—— 21	—— 7	Mar. 25	—— 3	—— 13	May 24	27	—— 2
1895	15	4	F	4	Feb. 10	—— 27	April 14	—— 23	June 2	June 13	24	—— 1
1896	16	15	ED	3	—— 2	—— 19	—— 5	—— 14	May 24	—— 4	25	Nov. 29
1897	17	26	C	5	—— 14	Mar. 3	—— 18	—— 27	June 6	—— 17	23	—— 28
1898	18	7	B	4	—— 6	Feb. 23	—— 10	—— 19	May 29	—— 9	24	—— 27
1899	19	18	A	3	Jan. 29	—— 15	—— 2	—— 11	—— 21	—— 1	26	Dec. 3
1900	1	0	G	5	Feb. 11	—— 28	—— 15	—— 24	June 3	—— 14	24	—— 2

A TABLE

OF THE VIGILS, FASTS AND DAYS OF ABSTINENCE TO BE OBSERVED IN THE YEAR.

The Evens or Vigils before

The Nativity of our Lord,	Ascension Day,	S. Bartholomew,
The Purification of the Blessed Virgin Mary,	Pentecost,	S. Matthew,
	S. Matthias,	SS. Simon and Jude,
The Annunciation of the Blessed Virgin,	S. John Baptist,	S. Andrew,
	S. Peter,	S. Thomas,
Easter Day,	S. James,	All Saints.

Note, that if any of these Feast-days fall upon a Monday, then the Vigil or Fast-day shall be kept upon the Saturday, and not upon the Sunday, next before it.

Days of Fasting or Abstinence.

I.—The Forty Days of Lent.

II.—The Ember Days at the Four Seasons, being the Wednesday, Friday, and Saturday after the First Sunday in Lent, the Feast of Pentecost, September 14, and December 13.

III.—The Three Rogation Days, being the Monday, Tuesday, and Wednesday before Holy Thursday, or the Ascension of our Lord.

IV.—All the Fridays in the year, except Christmas Day.

INDEX OF PSALMS.

	Psalm	Page		Psalm	Page
Ad Dominum	cxx.	52	Ecce nunc benedicite	cxxxiv.	68
Ad Te, Domine, levavi	xxv.	28	Ecce quam bonum	cxxxiii.	58
Ad Te levavi oculos meos	cxxiii.	54	Eripe me, Domine	cxl.	62
			Exaltabo Te, Deus	cxlv.	64
Beati immaculati	cxix.	30	Expectans expectavi	xl.	342
Beati omnes	cxxviii.	56			
Beatus qui intelligit	xli.	343	Inclina, Domine	lxxxvi.	307
Beati quorum	xxxii.	36	In convertendo	cxxvi.	55
Beatus vir	cxii.	48	In exitu Israel	cxiv.	48
Benedictus Dominus	cxliv.	63	In te, Domine, speravi	xxxi. (to v. 6)	67
Benedixisti, Domine	lxxxv.	306			
Bonum est confiteri	xcii.	22	Jubilate Deo	c.	4
			Judica me, Deus	xliii.	14
Cantate Domino	cxlix.	7	Judica me, Domine	xxvi.	29
Confitebor tibi	cxi.	47			
Confitebor tibi, quoniam	cxxxviii.	60	Lætatus sum in his	cxxii.	54
Confitemini Domino, quoniam	cxviii.	29	Lauda anima mea	cxlvi.	65
Confitemini Domino, quoniam (2)	cxxxvi.	59	Lauda Hierusalem	cxlvii. (v. 12)	65
Credidi	cxvi. (v. 10)	52	Laudate Dominum de cœlis	cxlviii.	6
Cum invocarem	iv.	67	Laudate Dominum in sanctis	cl.	7
			Laudate Dominum omnes	cxvii.	52
De profundis	cxxx.	56	Laudate Dominum, quoniam	cxlvii.	65
Deus, Deus meus	xxii.	26	Laudate nomen Domini	cxxxv.	58
Deus, Deus meus (2)	lxiii.	5	Laudate, pueri	cxiii.	48
Deus, in adjutorium	lxx.	332	Levavi oculos meos	cxxi.	37
Deus in nomine	liv.	29			
Deus misereatur	lxvii.	5	Memento, Domine	cxxxii.	57
Dilexi quoniam	cxvi.	51	Miserere mei, Deus	li.	10
Dixit Dominus	cx.	47			
Domine, clamavi	cxli.	62	Nisi Dominus	cxxvii.	56
Domine, Deus meus	vii.	339	Nisi quia Dominus	cxxiv.	54
Domine exaudi	cii.	46	Non nobis Domine	cxv.	49
Domine exaudi (2)	cxliii.	19			
Domine, ne in furore	vi.	12	Quam dilecta	lxxxiv.	306
Domine, ne in furore (2)	xxxviii.	41	Quemadmodum	xlii.	344
Domine, non est	cxxxi.	57	Qui confidunt in Domino	cxxv.	55
Domine probasti	cxxxix.	61	Qui habitat	xci.	68
Domine, quid multiplicati?	iii.	330			
Domine refugium	xc.	17	Sæpe expugnaverunt me	cxxix.	56
Domini est terra	xxiv.	27	Super flumina	cxxxvii.	60
Dominus illuminatio	xxvii.	341	Te decet hymnus	lxv.	15
Dominus regit me	xxiii.	27	Verba mea auribus	v.	11
Dominus regnavit	xciii.	30	Voce mea ad Dominum	cxlii.	62

INDEX OF HYMNS.

	Page		Page
Ad Cœnam Agni providi	171	Jesus, in pace imperat	282
Adesto Sancta Trinitas	191	Jesu, nostra Redemptio	179
Æterne cœli gloria	121	Jesu, quadrigenariæ	142
Æterne rerum Conditor	119	Jesu, Redemptor omnium	223
Æterne Rector siderum	297	Jesu, Salvator seculi	169
Æterne Rex Altissime	179	Jesu, Salvator seculi (2)	301
Ales diei nuntius	120		
Alma chorus Domini	185	Lætabundus	250
Angulare fundamentum	231	Lucis Creator optime	49
Annue Christe	215	Lustra sex, qui jam peracta	151
A Patre unigenitus	114	Lux ecce surgit aurea	121
A solis ortus cardine	94		
Audi, Benigne Conditor	133	Magnæ Deus potentiæ	121
Aureâ luce et decore roseô	266	Martyr Dei	289
Aurora jam spargit polum	122	Nox et tenebræ et nubila	120
Ave maris stella	210	Nunc Sancte nobis Spiritus	38
Beata nobis gaudia	188	O gloriosa fœmina	211
		O lux beata Trinitas	66
Christe Redemptor omnium	302	O Maria, noli flere	275
Chorus novæ Hierusalem	168	O nata Lux de lumine	279
Christe, qui lux es et dies	132	O nimis felix	264
Christe sanctorum decus Angelorum	295	O Pater sancte, mitis atque pie	192
Claro paschali gaudio	213	O salutaris fulgens stella maris	271
Cœlestis formam gloriæ	279	O quam glorifica luce coruscas	286
Collaudemus Magdalene	274	Plasmator hominis Deus	121
Cœli Deus sanctissime	121		
Conditor alme siderum	75	Quod chorus vatum	248
Cultor Dei memento	150	Rector potens, verax Deus	41
Custodes hominum psallimus Angelos	296	Rerum Deus tenax vigor	44
Crux fidelis	259	Rex gloriose martyrum	104
Deus, Creator omnium	118	Sacris solemniis	194
Deus, tuorum militum	218	Salvator mundi Domine	69
Ecce jam noctis	7	Sancte Dei pretiose	99
Ecce tempus idoneum	141	Sanctorum meritis	220
Ex more docti mystico	131	Sermone blando Angelus	170
Exultet cœlum laudibus	215	Splendor Paternæ gloriæ	119
Exultet cor precordiis	281	Te lucis ante terminum	69
Festum matris gloriosæ	270	Telluris ingens Conditor	120
		Tibi Christe splendor Patris	294
Hæc rite mundi gaudia	229	Tristes erant Apostoli	212
Hostis Herodes impie	113	Tu Christe nostrum gaudium	180
Hujus obtentu	229		
		Urbs beata Hierusalem	231
Immense cœli Conditor	120	Ut queant laxis resonare fibris	264
Impleta gaudent viscera	186		
Impleta sunt qua concinit	258	Veni Creator Spiritus	187
Iste Confessor	222	Veni Redemptor gentium	93
		Veni Sancte Spiritus	186
Jam Christus astra ascenderat	185	Verbum supernum prodiens	195
Jam lucis orto sidere	25	Vexilla Regis prodeunt	149
Jesu, auctor clementiæ	283	Virginis proles opifexque matris	227
Jesu, corona Virginum	227	Vox clara ecce intonat	77

INDEX OF HYMNS.

	Page
All glorious King of Martyrs Thou	104
Almighty God, Who from the flood	121
A type of those bright rays on high	279
A thrilling voice by Jordan rings	77
Ave, Star of ocean	210
Before the ending of the day	69
Behold the golden dawn arise	121
Be present, Holy Trinity	191
Blest joys for mighty wonders wrought	188
Blessed city, heavenly Salem	231
Breathed on by God the Holy Ghost	186
Choir of the Lord our God	185
Christ is made the sure foundation	231
Christ, of the holy Angels light and gladness	295
Come Holy Ghost, our souls inspire	187
Come Holy Ghost, with God the Son	38
Come, Thou Holy Paraclete	186
Come, Thou Redeemer of the earth	93
Creator of the stars of night	75
Dawn sprinkles all the east with light	122
Dread Framer of the earth and sky	119
Earth's mighty Maker, Whose command	120
Eternal glory of the sky	121
Eternal ruler of the sky	297
Eternal monarch, King most high	179
Faithful Cross! above all other	259
From God the Father, Virgin-born	114
From lands that see the sun arise	94
Fulfilled is all that David told	258
Full of gladness	250
God of all mercy, as for us she pleadeth	229
He, the Confessor	222
Hence, night and clouds that night-time brings	120
In this our bright and Paschal day	213
Jesu, Redemption all divine	179
Jesu, the Law and Pattern, whence	142
Jesu, the Virgins' Crown, do Thou	227
Jesu, the world's Redeemer, hear	223
Jesu, Thou source of pity blest	283
Jesu, Who brought'st redemption nigh	169
Jesus now reigns in Heaven, and thence	282
Let the round world with songs rejoice	215
Let this our solemn feast	194
Lo, now is our accepted day	141
Lo, now the melting shades of night are ending	7
Maker of men, from Heaven Thy throne	121
Now Christ, ascending whence He came	185
Now that the daylight fills the sky	25
Offspring, yet Maker of Thy Virgin Mother	227
Of the glorious Virgin Mother, now the festal day is come	270
O blest Creator, God most high	118
O blest Creator of the light	49
O Christ, Thou Lord of worlds	215
O Christ, Redeemer of mankind	302
O Christ, Who art the Light and Day	132
O glorious Virgin, throned in rest	211
O God, creation's secret force	44
O God of truth, O Lord of might	41
O God, Thy soldiers' Crown and Guard	218
O God, Whose hand hath spread the sky	121
O great Creator of the sky	120
O Jesu, Saviour of the earth	301
O Maker of the world, give ear	133
O holy Father, merciful and loving	192
O let the heart exulting beat	281
O Light, which from the Light hath birth	279
O Saint thrice happy, merit high attaining	264
O that once more to sinful man descending	264
O Trinity of blessed light	66
O with what glorious lustre resplendent	286
Saviour of man and Lord alone	69
Saint of God, elect and precious	99
Servant of Christ, remember	150
Sing we now of Mary's trial	274
Star, with thy bright beams shining o'er the ocean	271
Th' Apostles' hearts were full of pain	212
That which of old the reverend choir of prophets	248
Thee, O Christ, the Father's splendour	294
The fast, as taught by holy lore	131
The Lamb's high banquet we await	171
The merits of the Saints	220
The royal banners forward go	149
The wingèd herald of the day	120
The Word of God proceeding forth	195
The world and all its boasted good	229
Thirty years among us dwelling	151
Thou, Christ, Who art our Joy alone	180
Thou Brightness of the Father's ray	119
Thou followest, martyr of thy God	289
Watchful guardians of men	296
Weep not, Mary, weep no longer	275
Why, impious Herod, vainly fear	113
With gentle voice the Angel gave	170
With golden light of morn	266
Ye choirs of new Jerusalem	168

J. PALMER, PRINTER, JESUS LANE, CAMBRIDGE.